Economic Analysis of the Rules and Regulations of the World Trade Organization

World Scientific Studies in International Economics
(ISSN: 1793-3641)

World Scientific Studies in International Economics includes works dealing with the theory, empirical analysis, and evaluation of international economic policies and institutions, with topics covering international macroeconomics and finance, international trade theory and policy, as well as international legal and political economy. Monographs and edited volumes will comprise the core of the publications.

Vol. 69 *Economic Analysis of the Rules and Regulations of the World Trade Organization*
edited by Kamal Saggi (Vanderbilt University, USA)

Vol. 68 *International Trade, Capital Flows and Economic Development*
edited by Francisco L. Rivera-Batiz (Columbia University, USA) &
Luis A. Rivera-Batiz (University of Puerto Rico, USA)

Vol. 67 *Megaregionalism 2.0: Trade and Innovation within Global Networks*
edited by Dieter Ernst (East-West Center, USA &
The Centre for International Governance Innovation/CIGI, Canada) &
Michael G. Plummer (The Johns Hopkins University, SAIS, Italy)

Vol. 66 *International and Interregional Migration: Theory and Evidence*
edited by Francisco L. Rivera-Batiz (Columbia University, USA)

Vol. 65 *International Trade Theory and Competitive Models: Features, Values, and Criticisms*
by Ronald W. Jones (University of Rochester, USA)

Vol. 64 *Information Spillovers and Market Integration in International Finance: Empirical Analyses*
by Suk-Joong Kim (University of Sydney, Australia)

Vol. 63 *Dimensions of Trade Policy*
by Martin Richardson (Australian National University, Australia)

Vol. 62 *International Trade and Labor Markets: Welfare, Inequality and Unemployment*
by Udo Kreickemeier (TU Dresden, Germany)

Vol. 61 *Achieving Financial Stability: Challenges to Prudential Regulation*
edited by Douglas D. Evanoff (Federal Reserve Bank of Chicago, USA),
George G. Kaufman (formerly Loyola University Chicago, USA),
Agnese Leonello (European Central Bank, Germany) &
Simone Manganelli (European Central Bank, Germany)

The complete list of the published volumes in the series can be found at
http://www.worldscientific.com/series/wssie

69 World Scientific Studies in International Economics

Economic Analysis of the Rules and Regulations of the World Trade Organization

Kamal Saggi
Vanderbilt University, USA

World Scientific
NEW JERSEY • LONDON • SINGAPORE • BEIJING • SHANGHAI • HONG KONG • TAIPEI • CHENNAI • TOKYO

Published by

World Scientific Publishing Co. Pte. Ltd.
5 Toh Tuck Link, Singapore 596224
USA office: 27 Warren Street, Suite 401-402, Hackensack, NJ 07601
UK office: 57 Shelton Street, Covent Garden, London WC2H 9HE

Library of Congress Cataloging-in-Publication Data
Names: Saggi, Kamal, author.
Title: Economic analysis of the rules and regulations of the World Trade Organization / Kamal Saggi, Vanderbilt University, USA.
Description: New Jersey : World Scientific, [2018] | Series: World scientific studies in international economics ; volume 69 | Includes bibliographical references.
Identifiers: LCCN 2018002040 | ISBN 9789813233041 (hardcover)
Subjects: LCSH: World Trade Organization. | International trade--Econometric models. | Commercial policy--Econometric models.
Classification: LCC HF1385 .S245 2018 | DDC 382/.92--dc23
LC record available at https://lccn.loc.gov/2018002040

British Library Cataloguing-in-Publication Data
A catalogue record for this book is available from the British Library.

For any available supplementary material, please visit
https://www.worldscientific.com/worldscibooks/10.1142/10790#t=suppl

Desk Editor: Sylvia Koh

Typeset by Stallion Press
Email: enquiries@stallionpress.com

Printed in Singapore

ACKNOWLEDGMENTS

The papers in this volume address questions and topics in which I became deeply interested after receiving tenure in 2001. Several of my Ph.D. students, especially H. Murat Yildiz, have played a major role in helping me develop the line of research that culminated in these papers. Murat has not just been a great collaborator but also a close personal friend. I thank him for his hard work and generosity of spirit. Nese Sara, Faruk Sengul, and Difei Geng have contributed significantly to my research agenda on a key underlying principle of the world trading system — i.e. the notion of non-discrimination. I thank them warmly.

Nuno Limão and I have written two related papers exploring the role of financial compensation in the enforcement of international trade disputes. Nuno's nuanced understanding of the multilateral trading system has contributed substantially to mine own. Mark Wu and I have collaborated on economic and legal analysis of several important WTO disputes. I look forward to continuing our intellectual dialogue.

Two co-authors deserve special mention: Bernard Hoekman and Petros C. Mavroidis. I first met Bernard as an Assistant Professor on sabbatical at the World Bank. Suffice it to say, my interest in policy issues has been tremendously enriched by our discussions, which have spanned more than twenty years and show no signs of slowing down. From Petros I have learnt not only that economists and lawyers can collaborate fruitfully, but also that disciplinary academic barriers can sometimes help propagate weak ideas by sheltering them from robust challenges from outside the discipline. Our conversations have taught me the true value of interdisciplinary scholarship, and for that I am grateful. His good humor is simply the icing on the cake.

Academic research is all consuming and it has required sacrifices not just on my part but also on the part of my family. My parents Yashpal and Chander Kanta Saggi have put up with me being far away from home (Chandigarh, India) almost continuously since the age of eighteen, pursuing an undergraduate degree, a doctorate, and then an academic career in the United States. They truly understand what it means to set someone free. As my own children — Neha and Kunaal — begin their high school journey, I strive to provide them with the same support and freedom that my parents have given me over the years. Their mother and the pillar of my life — Rupi — has answered my quirks and impatience with calmness and warmth. My life, both intellectual and otherwise, has been wonderfully enriched by our partnership. It is rare to be blessed, as I have been, in one's personal as well as professional life.

Finally, I would like to thank all my co-authors and the following publishers for granting the permissions necessary for re-producing the chapters in this book: American Economic Association, Cambridge University Press, Elsevier John Wiley, and Oxford University Press.

ABOUT THE AUTHOR

Kamal Saggi is the Dean of Social Sciences in the College of Arts and Science and the Frances and John Downing Family Professor of Economics at Vanderbilt University. Dr Saggi has published extensively in the areas of international trade and economic development. Two major themes underlying his research are: (i) the inter-relationships between intellectual property rights protection, trade, and technology transfer in the global economy and the (ii) economic underpinnings of the rules and regulations of the contemporary multilateral trading system as embodied in the major trade agreements of the World Trade Organization and its dispute settlement process.

CONTENTS

PART I

NON-DISCRIMINATION IN THE MULTILATERAL TRADING SYSTEM

CHAPTER 1

ELSEVIER

Journal of International Economics 63 (2004) 341–368

Journal of INTERNATIONAL ECONOMICS

www.elsevier.com/locate/econbase

Tariffs and the most favored nation clause

Kamal Saggi*

Department of Economics, Southern Methodist University, Dallas, TX 75275-0496, USA

Received 13 August 2001; received in revised form 25 February 2003; accepted 10 March 2003

Abstract

In an n country oligopoly model of intraindustry trade ($n \geq 3$), this paper explores the economics of the most-favored-nation (MFN) principle. Under the non-cooperative tariff equilibrium, each country imposes higher tariffs on low cost producers relative to high cost ones thereby causing socially harmful trade diversion. MFN adoption by each country improves world welfare by eliminating this trade diversion. Under linear demand, MFN adoption by the country with the average production cost is most desirable. High cost countries refuse *reciprocal* MFN adoption with other countries and also lose even if *others* engage in reciprocal MFN adoption amongst themselves.

Keywords: Tariffs; Most favored nation clause; Trade policy; Oligopoly; Intraindustry trade

JEL classification: F13; F12

1. Introduction

The most favored nation (MFN) clause is an integral part of all multilateral trade agreements. For example, this clause constitutes the very first article of the General Agreement on Tariffs and Trade (GATT). Similarly, all the other major multilateral agreements of the World Trade Organization (WTO) (such as the General Agreement on Trade in Services or the Agreement on Trade Related Aspects of Intellectual Property Rights) also contain an MFN clause. In fact, Horn and Mavroidis (2000) and Hoekman and Kostecki (2001) note that MFN constitutes one of the pillars of the WTO system. At the core of MFN is the idea of non-discrimination. Yet, as noted by several recent surveys (see Staiger, 1995; Horn and Mavroidis, 2000), there is no strong general case for non-

* Tel.: +1-214-768-3274; fax: +1-214-768-1821.
E-mail address: ksaggi@mail.smu.edu (K. Saggi).

0022-1996/$ - see front matter
doi:10.1016/S0022-1996(03)00057-6

discrimination in trade policy and the pervasiveness of MFN requires explanation. This paper develops a simple model to highlight the implications of MFN for equilibrium tariffs.[1] The model isolates the impact of MFN for tariff policies of individual countries when they cannot negotiate tariff levels directly.[2] The key motivating question is: Can countries achieve a mutually beneficial outcome by agreeing to constrain their choices via MFN given that they do not negotiate directly over tariff levels?

The model is partial equilibrium in nature and allows market size and production technology to differ across countries.[3] Imperfect competition is central to the model and the trade that occurs is intraindustry. Furthermore, unlike Bagwell and Staiger (1999) and other related works where countries impose tariffs to improve their terms of trade, here tariffs are used to extract rents from foreign firms some of which go to the government as revenue and the rest to the local firm as profits (as in Brander and Spencer, 1984). It is worth emphasizing why a model of intraindustry trade with imperfect competition is a useful one for exploring MFN. First, as is well known, the bulk of trade between industrialized countries is intraindustry in nature and analyses of MFN that do not capture such trade might omit some important considerations. Second, and perhaps more importantly, as Brander and Spencer (1984) note, tariffs can improve global welfare in models of imperfect competition if they result in production being allocated in favor of efficient producers. Thus, it is natural to ask whether a regime of MFN tariffs is better or worse than one of tariff discrimination. From the viewpoint of global welfare maximization, tariff discrimination dominates MFN since a social planner can always choose not to discriminate. But are non-cooperatively chosen MFN tariffs preferable to similarly chosen discriminatory tariffs? The simple model developed here shows that this indeed can be the case.

The model is a three-stage game involving n ($n \geq 3$) countries. Production in each country is carried out by a single firm and markets are assumed to be segmented (so that equilibrium prices generally differ across countries).[4] In the first stage, all countries simultaneously decide whether or not to commit to MFN (i.e., to non-discrimination). Next, given their MFN commitments, countries choose their trade policies (a vector of specific import tariffs) to maximize their own welfare defined as the sum of local firm's profits, consumer surplus, and tariff revenue. Finally, firms choose their output levels and consumption takes place. An important result of the model is that under tariff discrimination each country levies higher tariffs on low cost exporters relative to high cost ones (see also Gatsios, 1990; Hwang and Mai, 1991; Choi, 1995). By definition, when a country grants MFN to all exporters to its market, it imposes the same tariff on all of them.

[1] Like existing literature, the paper restricts attention to tariffs. Furthermore, it focuses on MFN and abstracts from several other crucial aspects of trade agreements. For example, in recent work, Ethier (2000a,b) has highlighted the inter-relationships between MFN, reciprocity, unilateralism, and multilateralism. Bagwell and Staiger (1997) provide an overview of theoretical work dealing with MFN and reciprocity.

[2] See Ludema (1991) Caplin and Krishna (1988) for models in which countries can negotiate over tariffs.

[3] For general equilibrium analyses of MFN, see Bagwell and Staiger (1999), and Takemori (1994).

[4] See Brander and Krugman (1983) for an early treatment of the effects of trade restrictions under segmented markets. More recently, in a model quite similar to ours, Krishna (1998) explores how regional trade agreements affect the incentives for multilateral liberalization.

It turns out that country *i*'s MFN tariff is lower than its discriminatory tariff on country *j* if and only if country *j*'s cost of production is lower than the average production cost of all exporters to country *i*.

The results show that welfare gains from MFN adoption can arise even when countries cannot (or do not) negotiate over tariff levels because the constraints implied by MFN lower the inefficiency associated with the equilibrium use of beggar-thy-neighbor discriminatory tariffs. It is worth noting that while GATT rules require member countries to adopt MFN, they do not require that countries adopt free trade. In fact, tariff liberalization under the GATT has been achieved over many years via a series of tariff negotiations. Such negotiations have frequently proved to be time-consuming and MFN tariffs of many GATT-member countries have typically stayed positive and unrestricted from their unilaterally chosen levels for substantial lengths of time. The present paper shows that MFN adoption by member-countries (which was a requirement for GATT membership) may have yielded welfare gains during early years of the GATT despite the fact that tariffs of member countries were otherwise unrestricted during these years.[5]

The model is also suitable for addressing the contribution that individual countries make to global welfare if they decide to adopt MFN. Which country's adoption of MFN contributes most to world welfare? Interestingly, the country whose adoption of MFN is most valuable is the one with the *average production cost*. Intuitively, the country with the average production cost introduces the strongest distortion in world trade since it diverts more trade from low to high cost sources relative to any other country. For example, when $n = 3$, MFN adoption by the country with the intermediate cost is most valuable but it is precisely the one that loses the most from adopting MFN. This conflict between individual country incentives and world welfare implies that coordination (or international transfers) among countries over MFN must recognize that, despite its flavor of non-discrimination, MFN generates *asymmetric* losses and benefits for adopting and recipient countries.

Since MFN treatment can be extended on a *selective basis* to countries that do not belong to the WTO—witness the annual ritual in the US Congress over China's MFN status prior to China's accession to the WTO—examining the consequences of MFN under the assumption that MFN implies symmetric treatment of *all* trading partners misses some important aspects of MFN.[6] In fact, existing literature has restricted attention to the case where MFN is either granted on a multilateral basis or not at all. By contrast, the present paper also examines a country's incentive to grant MFN to only a subset of its trading partners. How does the cost of granting MFN to a country depend upon its production cost? Does selective MFN adoption necessarily raise world welfare? This issue is especially interesting because the literature on preferential trade agreements has shown that selective trade liberalization can lower world welfare if it results in more trade diversion than creation. Finally, given that no country has a unilateral incentive to adopt MFN (of any kind: multilateral or selective), can *reciprocal* adoption of MFN (wherein

[5] I thank Robert Staiger for providing the above interpretation of my results. This interpretation helps demonstrate the practical relevance of this paper.

[6] Often, MFN is viewed as 'symmetric treatment for all'. In fact, if country *i* grants country *j* MFN status, it simply agrees to treat country *j no worse than any other country*. Under selective MFN, the distinction between 'symmetric treatment for all' and 'treatment no worse than that given to another country' becomes crucial.

country i and j agree to grant MFN only to each other) be sustained in equilibrium?[7] For the case of $n = 3$, the main result is that the country with the highest production cost has no incentive to engage in reciprocal adoption, whereas the other two countries do. Furthermore, all else equal, the country with the bigger market gains less from reciprocal adoption, whereas the country with the lower cost gains more. Thus, if the bigger country also has the lower cost of production, the gains from reciprocal adoption are somewhat evenly distributed between the two countries.

The rest of the paper is organized as follows. Section 2 presents the basic model and contrasts tariff discrimination with MFN. Section 3 assumes linear demand and studies selective and reciprocal MFN. Section 4 concludes followed by Appendix A.

2. Basic model

There are n countries indexed by $i = 1 \ldots n$. There are two goods: x and y and preferences in country i over these goods are quasi-linear:[8]

$$U_i(x, y) = u_i(x) + y$$

Good y is the numeraire good produced under perfect competition with constant returns to scale technology. Good x is produced by a monopolist in each country. We refer to country i's monopolist as firm i. The marginal cost of production for firm i is given by c_i, where $c_{i+1} \geq c_i$ for all $i = 1 \ldots n$. Firms compete in quantities (Cournot competition) and make independent decisions regarding how much to sell in each market (i.e., markets are segmented). Firm j faces a specific tariff t_{ji} when exporting to country i, where $t_{ii} = 0$ for all i. These tariffs are endogenously determined (see below). Country i's tariff schedule $\mathbf{t}_i \equiv (t_{1i} \ldots t_{ni})$ is a $1 \times (n-1)$ dimensional vector. Denote the tariff schedules of all countries other than i by $\mathbf{t}_{-i}$. And finally, denote the vector of all countries trade policies by $\mathbf{t}$ where $\mathbf{t} \equiv (\mathbf{t} \ldots \mathbf{t}_i \ldots \mathbf{t}_n)$.

To examine the implications of MFN, consider a three-stage game. In the first-stage, countries simultaneously decide whether or not to adopt MFN with respect to their tariff schedules. Each country has a binary decision: to commit to MFN or not. Next, countries simultaneously choose their tariff schedules. Finally, firms choose their output levels.

2.1. MFN versus tariff discrimination

To obtain a subgame perfect Nash equilibrium, we solve the model backwards. Due to market segmentation, there are n first-order conditions for profit maximization for each firm (one for each market $i = 1 \ldots n$). In market i, exporting firm j's first-order condition is given by

$$p_i + p_i' x_{ji} = t_{ji} + c_j \qquad (1)$$

[7] Note the distinction from *reciprocity* which applies to reciprocal *trade liberalization* (see Bagwell and Staiger, 1997, 1999).

[8] The utility function has a subscript since demand is allowed to differ across countries.

Let $X_i = \sum_j x_{ji}$, where $j = 1 \ldots n$, denote the total output of good x sold in country i and let $X_{-i} = X_i - x_{ii}$ denote country i's total imports of good x.

At the trade policy stage, countries simultaneously choose their tariff schedules to maximize their own welfare. Due to linear costs and market segmentation, a country's optimal tariff schedule turns out to be independent of the tariff schedules of other countries.[9] As a result, from here on, the dependence of country i's welfare on the tariffs of other countries is ignored. Country i solves:

$$W_i(\mathbf{t_i}) \equiv CS_i(\mathbf{t_i}) + \pi_{ii}(\mathbf{t_i}) + TR_i(\mathbf{t_i}) \tag{2}$$

where $CS_i = u(X_i) - p_i X_i$ denotes consumer surplus in country i; $\pi_{ii} = (p_i - c_i)x_{ii}$ denotes the profit function of firm i in its own market; and $TR_i = \sum_{j \neq i} t_{ji} x_{ji}$ denotes country i's total tariff revenue.

Let $\mathbf{t_i^*}$ country i's optimal discriminatory tariff schedule where $\mathbf{t_i^*} \equiv \arg\max W_i(\mathbf{t_i})$. To describe this optimal tariff schedule, we make two preliminary observations. First, from firm i's perspective, a small increase in the tariff on firm j is equivalent to a small increase in the tariff on firm k:

$$\frac{\partial \pi_{ii}}{\partial t_{ji}} = \frac{\partial \pi_{ii}}{\partial t_{ki}} \quad \text{and} \quad \frac{\partial x_{ii}}{\partial t_{ji}} = \frac{\partial x_{ii}}{\partial t_{ki}}.$$

These equalities follow from the fact that the total output sold in country i (X_i) depends upon the sum of the tariff-included marginal costs of foreign firms and that firm i's sales in its own market depend only on the level of total imports into its market and not on their distribution across exporters. Second,

$$\frac{\partial x_{zi}}{\partial t_{ji}} = \frac{\partial x_{zi}}{\partial t_{ki}} \quad \text{for all } z \neq j, k.$$

In other words, an increase in the tariff on firm j is equivalent to an increase in the tariff on firm k from the viewpoint of all firms other than j and k.

Using $u'(.) = p_i$, country i's first-order condition for tariff t_{ji} can be written as:

$$\frac{\partial W_i}{\partial t_{ji}} = -p_i' X_i \frac{\partial X_i}{\partial t_{ji}} + \frac{\partial \pi_{ii}}{\partial t_{ji}} + x_{ji} + t_{ji} \frac{\partial x_{ji}}{\partial t_{ji}} + \sum_{\substack{z \neq i \\ z \neq j}} t_{zi} \frac{\partial x_{zi}}{\partial t_{ji}} = 0, \; j \neq k, i \tag{3}$$

[9] A similar (strategic) independence of trade policies also arises in Staiger (1995) because demand is assumed to be independent across countries. Strategic independence is unlikely in the real world but, as Staiger (1995) notes, it is also not clear how a country's optimal tariff schedule *ought* to depend upon the tariff schedules of other countries.

Similarly, for $k \neq j, i$, we have:

$$\frac{\partial W_i}{\partial t_{ki}} = -p_i' X_i \frac{\partial X_i}{\partial t_{ki}} + \frac{\partial \pi_{ii}}{\partial t_{ki}} + x_{ki} + t_{ki}\frac{\partial x_{ki}}{\partial t_{ki}} + \sum_{\substack{z \neq i \\ z \neq k}} t_{zi}\frac{\partial x_{zi}}{\partial t_{ki}} = 0,\ k \neq j, i \tag{4}$$

Subtracting (4) from (3) gives:

$$\left[x_{ji} + t_{ji}\frac{\partial x_{ji}}{\partial t_{ji}} - x_{ki} - t_{ki}\frac{\partial x_{ki}}{\partial t_{ki}}\right] + \left[\sum_{\substack{z \neq i \\ z \neq j}} t_{zi}\frac{\partial x_{zi}}{\partial t_{ji}} - \sum_{\substack{z \neq i \\ z \neq k}} t_{zi}\frac{\partial x_{zi}}{\partial t_{ki}}\right] = 0 \tag{5}$$

But

$$\sum_{\substack{z \neq i \\ z \neq j}} t_{zi}\frac{\partial x_{zi}}{\partial t_{ji}} - \sum_{\substack{z \neq i \\ z \neq k}} t_{zi}\frac{\partial x_{zi}}{\partial t_{ki}} = t_{ki}\frac{\partial x_{ki}}{\partial t_{ji}} - t_{ji}\frac{\partial x_{ji}}{\partial t_{ki}}$$

Using this, we can rewrite Eq. (5) as:

$$\left[x_{ji} - x_{ki}\right] + t_{ji}\left[\frac{\partial x_{ji}}{\partial t_{ji}} - \frac{\partial x_{ji}}{\partial t_{ki}}\right] - t_{ki}\left[\frac{\partial x_{ki}}{\partial t_{ki}} - \frac{\partial x_{ki}}{\partial t_{ji}}\right] \tag{6}$$

Further note that since

$$\frac{\partial x_{zi}}{\partial t_{ji}} = \frac{\partial x_{zi}}{\partial t_{ki}} \quad \text{for all } z \neq j, k \quad \text{and} \quad \frac{\partial X_i}{\partial t_{ji}} = \frac{\partial X_i}{\partial t_{ki}}$$

we must have:

$$\frac{\partial x_{ji}}{\partial t_{ji}} + \frac{\partial x_{ki}}{\partial t_{ji}} = \frac{\partial x_{ji}}{\partial t_{ki}} + \frac{\partial x_{ki}}{\partial t_{ki}}$$

As a result Eq. (6) becomes:

$$\left[x_{ji} - x_{ki}\right] + (t_{ji} - t_{ki})\left[\frac{\partial x_{ji}}{\partial t_{ji}} - \frac{\partial x_{ji}}{\partial t_{ki}}\right] = 0 \tag{7}$$

The expression in the square brackets in the above equation is negative because

$$\frac{\partial x_{ji}}{\partial t_{ji}} < 0 < \frac{\partial x_{ji}}{\partial t_{ki}}.$$

Furthermore, we know that

$$x_{ji} - x_{ki} = \frac{(c_j + t_{ji}) - (c_k + t_{ki})}{p_i'(.)} \tag{8}$$

Substituting from Eq. (8) into (7) and simplifying gives:

$$(t_{ji} - t_{ki})\left[1 + \underbrace{\left(\frac{\partial x_{ji}}{\partial t_{ji}} - \frac{\partial x_{ji}}{\partial t_{ki}}\right)p_i'(.)}_{>0}\right] = c_k - c_j \tag{9}$$

which implies $t_{ji} > t_{ki}$ iff $c_k > c_j$. Note also that $c_k - c_j > t_{ji} - t_{ki}$ since the term in square brackets on the left hand side is bigger than 1.

Proposition 1. *Under tariff discrimination, country i's optimal tariff on country j is higher than its tariff on country k iff country j has a lower cost of production than country k:* $t_{ji}^* \geq t_{ki}^*$ *iff* $c_k \geq c_j$. *Furthermore, the true cost ranking of countries is preserved under optimal tariff discrimination:* $t_{ji}^* + c_j \leq t_{ki}^* + c_k$ *iff* $c_k \geq c_j$.[10]

To see the intuition for this result, suppose $n = 3$ and imagine country i treats both exporters symmetrically so that $t_{ji}^* = t_{ki}^*$. Now consider a small change in country i's tariff policy whereby it increases t_{ji}^* by a small amount ε and decreases t_{ki}^* by the same amount such that country j remains the low cost supplier *under the new tariff schedule*. Such a policy change does not alter country i's total imports since these depend only upon the sum of marginal cost of the two exporters.[11] In fact, it is shown below that this policy change *increases* country i's total tariff revenue without altering any other component of its welfare. We know

$$\mathrm{d}TR_i = \mathrm{d}t_{ji}^* x_{ji}^* + t_{ji}^* \mathrm{d}x_{ji}^* + \mathrm{d}t_{ki}^* x_{ki}^* + t_{ki}^* \mathrm{d}x_{ki}^*$$

Since $\mathrm{d}t_{ji}^* = \varepsilon$ and $\mathrm{d}t_{ki}^* = -\varepsilon$, we have

$$\mathrm{d}TR_i = \varepsilon(x_{ji}^* - x_{ki}^*) + (t_{ji}^* - t_{ki}^*)\mathrm{d}x_{ji}^* + t_{ki}^*(\mathrm{d}x_{ji}^* + \mathrm{d}x_{ki}^*)$$

Using $\mathrm{d}x_{ji}^* + \mathrm{d}x_{ki}^* = 0$ and $t_{ki}^* = t_{ji}^*$, we have

$$\mathrm{d}TR_i = \varepsilon(x_{ji}^* - x_{ki}^*) > 0 \tag{10}$$

Thus, beginning at $t_{ki}^* = t_{ji}^*$, country i's tariff revenue increases if it raises its tariff on the low cost exporter and lowers it on the high cost exporter. Note from (10) that the bigger the cost differential between the two exporters, the stronger will be tariff discrimination.

The last part of Proposition 1 states that the higher tariff on the low cost exporter does *not* reverse the true cost ranking of the two exporters. Why is it *not* the case that

[10] Incidentally, since countries have asymmetric production costs, it is possible that the social planner may employ discriminatory tariffs. See Section 2.2 for more details.

[11] See Bergstrom and Varian (1985) for a general result regarding the independence of Nash equilibria of the distribution of agents' characteristics and Varian (1992), Chapter 16) for an illustration of the Cournot case with constant costs.

$c_j + t_{ji}^* > c_k + t_{ki}^*$? Suppose it were. Since $c_j < c_k$, it must be that $t_{ji}^* > t_{ki}^*$. Now, consider a small change in country i's tariff policy whereby it reduces t_{ji}^* by a small amount ε and increases t_{ki}^* by the same amount such that country j remains the high cost supplier *under* the new tariff schedule. It is easy to show that country i's tariff revenue must increase due to this policy change:

$$\mathrm{d}TR_i = \varepsilon(x_{ki}^* - x_{ji}^*) + (t_{ji}^* - t_{ki}^*)\mathrm{d}x_{ji}^* + t_{ki}^*(\mathrm{d}x_{ji}^* + \mathrm{d}x_{ki}^*)$$

Since $\mathrm{d}x_{ji}^* + \mathrm{d}x_{ki}^* = 0$, we must have:

$$\mathrm{d}TR_i = \varepsilon(x_{ki}^* - x_{ji}^*)_+ + (t_{ji}^* - t_{ki}^*)_+\mathrm{d}x_{ji}^* > 0_+$$

where $\mathrm{d}x_{ji}^* > 0$ because country j's tariff has been reduced. In other words, if the cost ranking were reversed due to tariffs, country i would be able to increase its tariff revenue by lowering the tariff on the true low cost exporter and increasing it on the other exporter. This argument applies as long as country i's tariff schedule forces the true low cost source to actually become inefficient (i.e., $c_j + t_{ji}^* > c_k + t_{ki}^*$). Thus, if tariffs are optimally chosen, it must be that $c_j + t_{ji}^* \le c_k + t_{ki}^*$. Note also that when $t_{ji}^* = t_{ki}^*$, we will have $x_{ki}^* < x_{ji}^*$ so that it is optimal for country i to increase its tariff on country j and lower it on country k. Thus, it must be that $t_{ji}^* > t_{ki}^*$ and $c_j + t_{ji}^* \le c_k + t_{ki}^*$.[12]

Now consider country i's optimal MFN tariff. Under MFN, country i solves:

$$W_i^M(t_i) \equiv CS_i(t_i) + \pi_{ii}(t_i) + t_i X_{-i} \tag{11}$$

Let t_i^M denote country i's optimal MFN tariff. The problem under MFN differs from the problem in (2) in only respect: now country i imposes the same tariff t_i on all exporters. Country i's first-order condition under MFN is given by:

$$\frac{\partial \partial W_i}{\partial \partial t_i} = -p_i' \frac{\partial \partial X_i}{\partial \partial t_i} X_{-i} + (p_i - c_i)\frac{\partial \partial x_{ii}}{\partial \partial t_i} + X_{-i} + t_i \frac{\partial \partial X_{-i}}{\partial \partial t_i} = 0 \tag{12}$$

The above equation defines the optimal MFN tariff t_i^M

$$t_i^M = \frac{\left(p_i' \dfrac{\partial \partial X_i}{\partial \partial t_i} - 1\right)(X_{-i}) - (p_i - c_i)\dfrac{\partial \partial x_{ii}}{\partial \partial t_i}}{\dfrac{\partial \partial X_{-i}}{\partial \partial t_i}} \tag{13}$$

[12] The above analysis abstracts from the situation where a country chooses to impose prohibitive tariffs on inefficient producers. Such tariffs may very well be infeasible in the real world. Furthermore, for the case of linear demand, we later provide conditions under which it is never in a country's interest to impose prohibitive tariffs.

Note that when $t_{ji} = t_{ki} = t_i$ for all $j, k \neq i$, we must have:

$$\frac{\partial \partial X_i}{\partial \partial t_i} = (n-1)\frac{\partial \partial X_i}{\partial \partial t_{ji}} = (n-1)\frac{\partial \partial X_i}{\partial \partial t_{ki}},$$
$$\frac{\partial \partial p_i}{\partial \partial t_i} = (n-1)\frac{\partial \partial p_i}{\partial \partial t_{ji}} = (n-1)\frac{\partial \partial p_i}{\partial \partial t_{ki}}, \quad \text{and}$$
$$\frac{\partial x_{ii}}{\partial t_i} = (n-1)\frac{\partial x_{ii}}{\partial t_{ji}} = (n-1)\frac{\partial x_{ii}}{\partial t_{ki}}$$

Evaluating the first-order condition under discrimination in (3) at $t_{ji} = t_{ki} = t_i$ and using the above relationships gives:

$$\left.\frac{\partial W_i}{\partial t_{ji}}\right|_{t_{ji}=t_{ki}=t_i} = \frac{-p_i'}{n-1}\frac{\partial X_i}{\partial t_i}X_{-i} + \frac{p_i - c_i}{n-1}\frac{\partial x_{ii}}{\partial t_i} + x_{ji} + t_i\frac{\partial X_{-i}}{\partial t_i}$$

Evaluating this equation at the optimal MFN tariff t_i^M gives:

$$\left.\frac{\partial W_i}{\partial t_{ji}}\right|_{t_{ji}=t_{ki}=t_i^M} = \frac{(n-1)x_{ji} - X_{-i}}{n-1} > 0 \quad \text{iff } c_j < \bar{c}_{-i} \equiv \frac{\sum_{k \neq i} c_{ki}}{n-1}$$

Thus, starting at the optimal MFN tariff t_i^M, country i gains from increasing its tariffs on countries that are low cost relative to the average cost exporter and lowering them on the rest. Our second main result is as follows:

Proposition 2. *Country i's MFN tariff on country j is lower than its discriminatory tariff on country j iff country j's cost of production is lower than the average cost of all exporters to country i:*

$$t_{ji}^* \geq t_i^M \quad \text{iff } c_j \leq \frac{\sum_{k \neq i} c_k}{n-1}.$$

The above proposition informs us that MFN adoption by a country has distributional implications for its trading partners. When a country adopts MFN, its lowest cost trading partner necessarily gains while the highest cost one necessarily loses. In general, the *distribution* of production costs across countries determines *how many gain* and *how many lose* when any one country decides to grant MFN to all. Suppose $n = 4$ and $c_2 = c$, $c_3 = \delta + c$, and $c_4 = \lambda + c$ where $\lambda \geq \delta$. Then, country 3 gains from country 1's MFN adoption iff $2\delta \leq \lambda$. If this condition fails, the adoption of MFN by country 1 hurts countries 3 and 4 and benefits only one country 2. Thus, if one were to divide the world into a group of developed and lesser-developed countries, the above result implies that only if developed countries have relatively similar production costs would all of them benefit from MFN adoption by any one country.[13]

2.2. Welfare effects of MFN

Define world welfare as the sum of welfare in each country:

$$W(\mathbf{t_i}, \mathbf{t_{-i}}) \equiv \sum_{i=1}^{n} W_i(\mathbf{t_i}, \mathbf{t_{-i}})$$

Due to market segmentation, a country's trade policy has no affect on any other aspect of welfare in other countries except their exporting profits. As a result, to evaluate the effects of MFN adoption by a country on world welfare it is sufficient to consider the sum of welfare in country i and the total profits of exporters in the rest of the world. MFN adoption by country i improves world welfare iff

$$W_i(\mathbf{t_i^*}) + \sum_{j \neq i} \pi_{ji}(\mathbf{t_i^*}) \geq W_i(t_i^M) + \sum_{j \neq i} \pi_{ji}(t_i^M)$$

where

$$W_i(\mathbf{t_i^*}) = u(X_i(\mathbf{t_i^*})) - p_i X_i(\mathbf{t_i^*}) + (p_i - c_i)x_{ii}(\mathbf{t_i^*}) + \sum_{j \neq i} t_{ji} x_{ji}(\mathbf{t_i^*})$$

and

$$\sum_{j \neq i} \pi_{ji}(\mathbf{t_i^*}) = \sum_{j \neq i} (p_i - c_i - t_{ji}^*) x_{ji}(\mathbf{t_i^*}).$$

Of course, replacing the optimal discriminatory tariffs by the optimal MFN tariff yields the relevant welfare metric under MFN. After making the appropriate substitutions, we have that MFN adoption by country i improves world welfare iff

$$W^M - W^D = u(X_i(t_i^M)) - u(X_i(\mathbf{t_i^*})) + \sum_{j=i}^{n} c_j(x_{ji}(t_i^M) - x_{ji}(\mathbf{t_i^*})) > 0 \quad (14)$$

The above inequality implies that, in principle, there are two possible reasons why MFN might improve world welfare. First, if $X_i(t_i^M) > X_i((\mathbf{t_i^*})$, i.e., total world output sold in country i maybe higher under MFN than under discrimination (i.e., MFN can improve welfare if it leads to some degree of aggregate trade liberalization). Second, and more surprisingly, MFN can contribute to world welfare even if leads to no aggregate trade liberalization so long as *the change in outputs of all firms selling in country i (caused due to MFN) is negatively correlated with their marginal costs of production*. In other words, MFN adoption by country i improves world welfare if, *on average*, it leads to an increase

[13] Note, however, that the adoption of MFN by a country constrains its choice set without altering the choices of others. Thus, no country has a unilateral incentive to adopt MFN.

in the output of low cost producers relative to high cost ones.[14] This result delivers strong support for the MFN principle. By removing the bias against efficient production, MFN ensures that more of the world's output is produced at lower cost than is possible under tariff discrimination.

It is trivial to note that a social planner seeking to maximize global welfare would prefer a regime of discrimination to one of MFN since he/she can always choose not to discriminate. But how does the nature of socially optimal tariff discrimination compare with the equilibrium of non-cooperative tariff game? The solution to the following problem yields the socially optimal tariff schedule of country i:[15]

$$\max_{\mathbf{t_i}} WW(\mathbf{t_i}) = W_i(\mathbf{t_i}) + \sum_{j \neq i} \pi_{ji}(\mathbf{t_i})$$

The first-order condition for tariff t_{ji}, where $j \neq i$, is given by

$$\frac{\partial WW(\mathbf{t_i})}{\partial t_{ji}} = \frac{\partial W_i(\mathbf{t_i})}{\partial t_{ji}} + \sum_{j \neq i} \frac{\partial \pi_{ji}(\mathbf{t_i})}{\partial t_{ji}} = 0$$

Using Eqs. (1) and (3), the above first-order condition can be written as:

$$\frac{\partial WW}{\partial t_{ji}} = (p_i - c_j) \underbrace{\frac{\partial x_{ji}}{\partial t_{ji}}}_{<0} + \sum_{k \neq j} (p_i - c_k) \underbrace{\frac{\partial x_{ki}}{\partial t_{ji}}}_{<0}$$

The interpretation of the above equation is straightforward. Suppose $c_j = c_i = c$ for all j, then we have:

$$\frac{\partial WW}{\partial t_{ji}} = (p_i - c) \underbrace{\frac{\partial X_i}{\partial t_{ji}}}_{<0} < 0$$

In other words, when all countries have the same cost, a tariff on country j by country i lowers world welfare by lowering total output sold in country i. However, when countries have asymmetric costs, tariffs can potentially improve world welfare.[16] This is because a tariff on country j allocates market share in favor of all other producers and such a change improves world welfare when country j is *sufficiently high cost compared to the rest of the world* so that $p_i - c_j$ is small relative to $p_i - c_k$, $k \neq j$. Note, however, that under the non-cooperative tariff game, individual countries actually impose higher tariffs on low cost producers. Thus, MFN adoption reduces the distortion imposed by non-cooperative discriminatory tariffs.

[14] As will be shown below, under linear demand MFN improves welfare even though it does not result in any trade liberalization.

[15] Of course, one needs to solve the tariff problems of all countries to obtain the socially optimal structure of tariff protection in the world but due to market segmentation it is sufficient to consider only one country's problem.

[16] See Appendix A for further details for the case of linear demand.

3. Further analysis

Assume that $u_i(x)$ is quadratic so that the demand curve for good x is linear in each country:

$$p_i = A_i - \sum_j x_{ji}(\mathbf{t_i}) \tag{15}$$

where x_{ji} denotes the output sold by firm j in country i and $i, j = 1 \ldots n$. One advantage of the linear demand assumption is that we can capture market size of a country by the parameter A_i.

After appropriate substitutions, welfare in country i can be written as

$$W_i(\mathbf{t}_i) = \frac{X_i^2(\mathbf{t}_i)}{2} + x_{ii}^2(\mathbf{t}_i) + \sum_{j \neq i} t_{ji} x_{ji}(\mathbf{t}_i)$$

It is easy to show that total output sold in country i decreases with any of its tariffs

$$\frac{\partial X_i}{\partial t_{ji}} = -\frac{1}{n+1} < 0 \text{ for } j \neq i$$

whereas country i's output and country k's exports to country i increase with the tariff on country j:

$$\frac{\partial x_{ii}}{\partial t_{ji}} = \frac{\partial x_{ki}}{\partial t_{ji}} = \frac{1}{n+1} > 0 \quad \text{for } j \neq i \text{ and } j \neq k$$

Finally, as expected, country j's exports to country i decrease with the tariff t_{ji}:

$$\frac{\partial x_{ji}}{\partial t_{ji}} = -\frac{n}{n+1} \quad \text{for } j \neq i$$

Using the above equations, the first-order conditions for welfare maximization for country i, can be written as

$$\frac{\partial W_i}{\partial t_{ji}} = -\frac{X_i}{n+1} + \frac{2x_{ii}}{n+1} + x_{ji} + \sum_{\substack{k \neq j \\ k \neq i}} \frac{t_{ki}}{n+1} - \frac{nt_j}{n+1}, \quad \text{for } j \neq i \tag{16}$$

Using the output levels from Cournot competition, we have:

$$x_{ki}(\mathbf{t}_i) - x_{ji}(\mathbf{t}_i) = c_j + t_{ji} - (c_k + t_{ki}) \tag{17}$$

Furthermore, using the first-order conditions (16), we have

$$t_{ji} - t_{ki} = x_{ji}(\mathbf{t}_i) - x_{ki}(\mathbf{t}_i) \tag{18}$$

Using the last two equations, we get $2(t_{ji}^* - t_{ki}^*) = c_k - c_j$. This equation illustrates Proposition 1 for linear demand: each country imposes higher tariffs on low cost exporters and the cost ranking of countries is preserved under optimal discriminatory tariffs.

Summing country i's first-order conditions yields:

$$2X_i(T_i) + (n-3)x_{ii}(T_i) - 2T_i = 0 \tag{19}$$

where $T_i = \sum_{k \neq i} t_{ki}$ is the sum of country i's tariffs. An important feature of Eq. (19) is that the total output imported by country i as well as the output of its own firm is a function of *only the sum* of its tariff rates T_i and does *not* depend upon the distribution of country i's tariffs across countries. This result is a consequence of two assumptions: firms compete in quantities and marginal cost is constant. Under these assumptions, each firm's output (and profits) depends only the sum of the marginal costs of all of its competitors, and a change in the tariff schedule of country i which does not alter T_i has no effect on the total output sold in the country (of course, exports of individual countries do change). Thus, the sum T_i can be usefully thought of as the *total protection* implemented by country i. We can solve Eq. (19) for the equilibrium level of total protection in country i:

$$T_i^* = \frac{3(n-1)A_i + (n-5)C_{-i} - (n-1)(n-2)c_i}{n+7} \tag{20}$$

where $C_{-i} = \sum_{k \neq i} c_k$ is the sum of marginal costs of all firms other than firm i. It is easy to see that country i's equilibrium level of total protection T_i^* is increasing in its market size, decreasing in its marginal cost, and increasing in the sum of the marginal cost of all other countries (so long as $n > 5$).

Finally, the optimal tariff on country j is easily obtained from Eqs. (16) and (20):

$$t_{ji}^* = \frac{1}{n-1}\left[\frac{C_{-i} - (n-1)c_j}{2} + T_i^*\right] \quad \text{for } j \neq i \tag{21}$$

An interpretation of the above formula is provided after a discussion of country i's MFN tariffs.

3.1 Tariffs under MFN

Suppose country i were to grant MFN to *all* of its trading partners and let t_i denote its MFN tariff. Country i's optimal MFN tariff solves the following problem:

$$\underset{t_i}{\text{Max}}\ W_i(t_i) = \frac{X_i^2(t_i)}{2} + x_{ii}^2(t_i) + \sum_{j \neq i} t_{ji}x_{ji}(t_i)$$

The first-order condition for this problem is given by

$$\frac{\mathrm{d}W_i}{\mathrm{d}t_i} = -2X_i + 2x_{ii}(n-3) - 2(n-1)t_i = 0, \quad \text{for } j \neq i \tag{22}$$

Let country i's total protection under MFN be defined by $T_i^M \equiv (n-1)t_i^M$ so that

$$t_i^M = \frac{T_i^M}{n-1}$$

We can rewrite Eq. (22) as:

$$\frac{\mathrm{d}W_i}{\mathrm{d}t_i} = -2X_i + 2x_{ii}(n-3) - 2T_i^M = 0$$

Since total output sold in country i as well as the output of the local firm depend only upon the total protection in country i, this last equation along with Eq. (19) implies that $T_i^M = T_i^*$. In other words, total (or average) protection in country i does *not* change when it grants MFN to all other countries.[17] An immediate implication of this result is that MFN adoption by a country does *not* alter its market equilibrium price and total imports. Thus, under linear demand, the only cost of MFN adoption for a country is the loss in tariff revenue it experiences due to its inability to discriminate between exporting countries.

The optimal tariff formula in Eq. (21) immediately implies:

$$t_{ji}^* - t_i^M = \frac{-1}{n-1}\left[\frac{(n-1)c_j - C_{-i}}{2}\right] \quad \text{for } j \neq i.$$

The above equation illustrates Proposition 2 for linear demand.

3.2. Welfare under linear demand

Under linear demand, we have shown that $T_i^M = T_i^*$. As a result, we have $p(X_i(\mathbf{t}_i^*)) = p(X_i(t_i^M))$ and $\sum_{j\neq i} x_{ji}(\mathbf{t}_i^*) = \sum_{j\neq i} x_{ji}(t_i^M)$. Then, Eq. (14) immediately implies that country i's MFN adoption improves world welfare iff

$$\sum_{j\neq i} c_j(x_{ji}(\mathbf{t}_i^*) - x_{ji}(t_i^M)) > 0 \tag{23}$$

Thus, *if on average*, exports of low cost countries increase, whereas those of high cost ones decrease when country i adopts MFN, such a policy change improves world welfare. This result can also be stated in terms of exogenous parameters. Since the sum of all tariffs is the same under the two scenarios (MFN to all by country i versus no MFN), we have

$$x_{ji}(\mathbf{t}_i^*) - x_{ji}(t_i^M) = t_i^M - t_{ji}^* = \frac{1}{2}\left[c_j - \frac{C_{-i}}{n-1}\right]$$

[17] In fact, a stronger result is proved later in the paper (see Lemma 3).

Thus, inequality (23) can be written as

$$\sum_{j \neq i} c_j \frac{1}{2}\left[c_j - \frac{C_{-i}}{n-1}\right] > 0$$

which is the same as

$$(n-1)\sum_{j \neq i} c_j^2 > \left[\sum_{j \neq i} c_j\right]^2 \tag{24}$$

delivering inequality (23) in terms of exogenous parameters n and $c_j, j \neq i$. It is shown in Appendix A that inequality (24) always holds. Thus, under linear demand, MFN necessarily improves world welfare.

Note that MFN adoption by a country can easily create many losers and few winners and yet improve total world welfare. Suppose the global distribution of costs is as follows: $c_2 = c$ and $c_j = \phi c$, for $j = 3 \ldots n$, where $\phi > 1$ and consider MFN adoption by country 1. If ϕ is large enough, the adoption of MFN by country 1 implies that only the tariff on country 2 falls whereas tariffs on *all other* countries increase.

Since countries are asymmetric, its worth asking whether MFN adoption by any two countries is equally valuable for world welfare or not.

Proposition 3. *Adoption of MFN by country i is more beneficial for the world than adoption by country j iff* $(c_i-c_j)(2\overline{c}-c_i-c_j)>0$ *where* $\overline{c} \equiv C/n$ *denotes the average production cost. Furthermore, if only one country is to adopt MFN, it should be the country with the average production cost* $\overline{c}$.[18]

Several interesting things can be inferred from the above proposition. First, adoption of MFN by country i is as beneficial for the world as that by country j either when they have identical costs, or when their average cost $c_i + c_j/2$ is equal to the average over all countries $\overline{c}$. In other words, the adoption of MFN by any two countries is equally beneficial for world welfare so long as their technologies are *equi-distant* from the average production cost (i.e., $\overline{c} - c_i = c_j - \overline{c}$). The intuition is clear: tariff discrimination by the country with the average production cost diverts trade from the lowest cost countries to the highest cost ones. Furthermore, if no country has exactly the average cost (easily possible since the number of countries is finite), then the country *closest* to the average should be the one to adopt MFN first.

According to the definition of MFN, if country i grants MFN to country j, it simply agrees to treat it *no worse* than the other countries (i.e., the tariff on country j can be *no higher* than the tariffs on all other countries). But what is country i's optimal tariff schedule when it grants MFN to *only a subset of* countries? Is it possible that selective MFN adoption might have adverse *efficiency consequences*?

[18] For $n = 3$, country 2 (the one with the intermediate production cost) loses the most from MFN adoption. Thus, there is a direct conflict between individual country incentives and the social desirability of MFN adoption.

3.3. Selective MFN

The following result (proved in Appendix A) describes country i's optimal tariff schedule under selective MFN:

Proposition 4. *When country i grants MFN to country j, there exists some country s who has higher cost than country j such that all countries that are high cost relative to country s automatically receive MFN along with country j.*

If country j's cost declines, the set of countries that receive automatic MFN treatment (when country j is given MFN by country i) expands. Intuitively, the lower a recipient country's cost, the higher the tariff it faces under tariff discrimination and larger the number of constraints that the MFN granting country must contend with. Let M be the set (and the number) of countries that have MFN with country i and let N be the set (and the number) of countries that do not have MFN with country i, where $n = M + N + 1$. Let t_i be country i's MFN tariff and let x_{mi} be the exports of a typical MFN country m to country i. Similarly, let the exports of a typical non-MFN country be given by x_{ki} and the associated tariff by t_{ki}. Let X_{MI} and X_{NI} be the aggregate exports of MFN and non-MFN countries, respectively:

$$X_{MI} = \sum_{k \in M} x_{mi} \quad \text{and} \quad X_{NI} = \sum_{k \in N} x_{ki}$$

To address the welfare implications of selective MFN, we first need the following lemma:

Lemma 3. *Country i's average tariff is independent of the number of countries (M) it grants MFN.*

The logic of this result is given below (supporting calculations are in Appendix A). When choosing its tariffs, country i solves:

$$\underset{t_i, \mathbf{t}_{ki}}{\text{Max}} \; W_i(t_i, \mathbf{t}_{ki}) = \frac{X_i^2(t_i, \mathbf{t}_{ki})}{2} + x_{ii}^2(t_i, \mathbf{t}_{ki}) + \sum_{k \neq i} t_{ki} x_{ki}(t_i, \mathbf{t}_{ki})$$

subject to the MFN constraints: $t_i \leq \min\{t_{ki} : k \in N\}$. Let λ_k be the Lagrange multiplier associated with constraint $k : t_i - t_{ki} \leq 0$. The MFN tariff must satisfy the following condition:

$$\frac{\partial W_i}{\partial t_i} - \lambda = 0 \text{ where } \lambda \equiv \sum_k \lambda_k \text{ and } \lambda_k \geq 0 \text{ forall } k \in N \tag{25}$$

whereas the first-order conditions for discriminatory tariffs are given by:

$$\frac{\partial W_i}{\partial t_{ki}} - \lambda_k = 0 \text{ forall } k \in N \tag{26}$$

From calculations in Appendix A, the first-order condition for an MFN country is:

$$\frac{\partial W_i}{\partial t_i} = \frac{-MX_i}{n+1} + \frac{2x_{ii}M}{n+1} + X_{MI} - \frac{Mt_i(N+2)}{n+1} + \frac{M\sum_{k\in N} t_{ki}}{n+1}$$

and that for a typical non-MFN country is:

$$\frac{\partial W_i}{\partial t_{ki}} = \frac{-X_i}{n+1} + \frac{2x_{ii}}{n+1} + x_{ki} - \frac{nt_{ki}}{n+1} + \frac{\sum_{\substack{j\in N\\ j\neq k}} t_{ji}}{n+1} + \lambda_k = 0 \quad \text{for all } k\in N.$$

with the associated complementary slackness conditions

$$\lambda_k(t_i - t_{ki}) = 0 \text{ forall } k\in N. \tag{27}$$

Summing the N first-order conditions for non-MFN countries, we have

$$-NX_i + 2Nx_{ii} + (n+1)X_{NI} + NT_i^M - (M+2)T_i^N + \lambda(n+1) = 0 \tag{28}$$

where $T_i^M = Mt_i$ and $T_i^N = \sum_{j\in N} t_{ki}$. Eq. (25) can be written as

$$-MX_i + 2Mx_{ii} + (n+1)X_{MI} + MT_i^N - (N+2)T_i^M - \lambda(n+1) = 0 \tag{29}$$

Adding (28) and (29) and using $X_i = x_{ii} + X_{MI} + X_{NI}$ and $n = N + M + 1$, we have:

$$2X_i(T_i) + (n-3)x_{ii}(T_i) - 2T_i = 0 \text{ where } T_i = T_i^M + T_i^N.$$

Note that this equation is identical to Eq. (19). Thus, country i's total (or average) protection T_i *does not* depend upon M and it equals T_i^* reported in Eq. (20). Consider now the welfare implications of selective MFN:

Proposition 5. *If while granting MFN selectively to another country (on either a unilateral or a reciprocal basis) country i retains its optimal discriminatory tariff on even a single non-MFN country, world welfare increases relative to full tariff discrimination by country i.*

Suppose country i grants country j MFN and along with it finds it optimal to extend MFN to some other countries who all have *higher costs than country j* (this must be the case given Proposition 4).[19] Such a policy change necessarily improves world welfare because it allocates production in favor of country i at the expense of higher cost producers without altering total world production. The logic is as follows. Let q be any

[19] Of course if only the highest cost exporter receives MFN, all countries face optimal discriminatory tariffs.

arbitrary non-MFN country (that must be high cost relative to country j). We know that all non-MFN countries face strictly higher tariffs relative to country i's MFN tariff t_{ji} (i.e., $t_{qi} - t_{ji} > 0$). As a result, Eqs. (26) and (27) imply that $2(t_{qi} - t_{pi}) = c_p - c_q$, where p and q are any two non-MFN countries. This is exactly the same relationship that emerges when country i practices full tariff discrimination. Thus, if country i retains its optimal discriminatory tariff on *any* country to which it does not grant MFN, it will do so for all non-MFN countries. More generally, one of the following three statements must hold: (i) $2[(t_{qi} + \alpha) - (t_{pi} + \alpha)] = c_p - c_q$ where $\alpha > 0$, i.e., tariffs on all non-MFN countries are higher than their respective discriminatory tariffs by the same amount or (ii) they are all lower by the same amount, i.e., $\alpha < 0$, or (iii) they are exactly the same, i.e., $\alpha = 0$.[20]

If discriminatory tariffs are retained on non-MFN countries, there is no trade diversion or creation *among the non-MFN countries* relative to full tariff discrimination. For MFN recipients, the true cost ranking is trivially retained since they all face the same tariff. In fact, their total exports to country i are the same as under full tariff discrimination except that the bias against low cost exporters inherent to the tariff discrimination is removed. Thus, when country i grants MFN to country j on a selective basis, world welfare improves because exports of low cost suppliers *among the set* of MFN countries increase while those of high cost suppliers decrease while the total exports of non-MFN countries (and of all countries together) are unaffected relative to full tariff discrimination.

3.4. Reciprocal MFN

The logic of the GATT is *not* that each country unilaterally adopt MFN but rather that each member country adopt MFN on a multilateral basis. Thus, a natural question is: given that no country will adopt MFN unilaterally, are any two countries willing to adopt MFN on a *reciprocal* basis? If so, how does this willingness depend upon their market sizes and production costs?[21]

To answer these questions, consider the case of $n = 3$ where $c_1 \leq c_2 \leq c_3$. In the first stage of the game, any country can offer reciprocal MFN to any other country. Reciprocal MFN adoption between two countries simply implies that each country agrees to impose a tariff on the other that is no higher than its tariff on the third country. For any country, the cost of agreeing to reciprocal MFN is the loss in tariff revenue implied by MFN, whereas the benefit is the increase in profits enjoyed by its own firm due to a (potentially) lower tariff. Its clear that in the absence of side-payments and transfers between countries, the country with the highest cost will not only refuse an offer of reciprocal adoption by either of the other countries but also oppose a move toward the

[20] Statement (ii) can be ruled out by the definition of MFN (which requires MFN countries to face lower tariffs than non-MFN countries) and from Lemma 3 (constancy of average tariff). In other words, *all* non-MFN countries can face higher tariffs relative to the discriminatory tariffs scenario only if all MFN countries face still higher tariffs. Since T_i is constant, this possibility cannot arise. Statement (i) cannot be ruled out and that is why the proposition is a conditional statement.

[21] Since coordination may be costly, one should expect those countries that have the most to gain from such cooperation to be ones that initiate the process.

reciprocal MFN between the *other two* countries.[22] The logic is transparent: the MFN tariff of both countries 1 and 2 on country 3 is higher than their respective discriminatory tariffs. Thus, country 3 has nothing to gain from being granted MFN whereas countries 1 and 2 can pass over some of the cost of reciprocal MFN to country 3 while retaining any potential benefits for themselves.

Under what circumstances do countries 1 and 2 agree to reciprocal MFN? If so, how are the gains from this agreement split between the two? The following proposition is proved in Appendix A:

Proposition 6. *Assume $n=3$. If the markets of countries 1 and 2 are of equal size (i.e., $A_1=A_2$) then country 1 gains more from reciprocal MFN than country 2 (since $c_1 \leq c_2$). If the two countries have the same cost (i.e., $c_1 = c_2$) then the country with the smaller market gains more from reciprocal MFN.*

When markets of the two countries are of equal size, country 1 enjoys a greater reduction in the tariff it faces than is enjoyed by country 2 when both grant MFN to each other. When costs are symmetric across the two countries, any given tariff concession results in greater increase in profits for the country exporting to the bigger market since the concession applies to a larger volume of exports. Thus, if the smaller country also has the lower cost then the bigger country may not find reciprocal adoption to be in its interest. Clearly, the more symmetric they are with respect to each other (in terms of both market size and costs), the more likely it is that both gain. In fact, it is shown in Appendix A that if $A_1 = A_2$ and $c_1 = c_2$ then countries 1 and 2 *necessarily* gain from reciprocal adoption.[23] Of course, when countries 1 and 2 are symmetric, part of what each loses from granting MFN is offset by what the other gains. As noted earlier, the 'extra gains' come at the expense of country 3 who ends up facing higher tariffs from both countries.

Finally, we comment on the case where n is an arbitrary number. It is easy to see that the logic behind Proposition 6 still applies. Suppose countries i and j are have the same cost and that this cost is lower than the average cost over all countries. If they grant each other MFN, they lower tariffs on each other. As a result, each loses some tariff revenue but gains some exporting profits. Since they are symmetric, their gains and losses are equal. But why does the profit gain necessarily outweigh the tariff revenue loss? The logic for this is as follows. We know MFN adoption by any country increases world welfare and that *only* the country that receives MFN experiences an increase in exports, whereas exports of others either decline or stay the same (if their tariffs remain unchanged). Thus, only the MFN recipient gains while others lose or are unaffected. Since aggregate world welfare necessarily increases, the increase in profits of the MFN recipient must dominate the loss

[22] Reciprocal adoption of MFN between low cost countries is similar to the formation of a preferential trade agreement: they agree to mutual trade liberalization coupled with an increase in tariffs on the high cost country.

[23] Note also that even if countries 1 and 2 are asymmetric, the above proposition implies that symmetry along one dimension need not be inimical to reciprocal adoption so long as it is counterbalanced by asymmetry along the other direction.

in tariff revenue of the MFN granting country. Thus, when countries are fully symmetric, both enjoy a net gain from reciprocal MFN adoption.

4. Conclusion

This paper develops a simple model that sheds light on the economics of the MFN principle. The model compares a world with MFN to one without and asks whether MFN has value even when countries do not negotiate over tariff levels. The analysis clarifies the role MFN plays within multilateral trade agreements such as the GATT. Overall, the results deliver strong support for MFN from the viewpoint of world welfare. In particular, it is shown that in the non-cooperative equilibrium, countries end up pursuing beggar-thy-neighbor policies under which efficient exporters face higher tariffs than inefficient ones. MFN improves upon this outcome by reducing the inefficiency associated with the use of such discriminatory tariffs.

Since no country has a unilateral incentive to adopt MFN, the model is extended to allow countries to grant MFN to each other on a reciprocal basis. In a world of three countries, it is shown that countries with relatively low production costs may agree to reciprocal adoption. However, such reciprocal adoption harms the high cost country even as it improves aggregate world welfare.

The robustness of Proposition 2 (the relationship between the nature of tariff discrimination and production efficiency) to the assumption of cost-linearity deserves comment. As Hwang and Mai (1991) have shown, linearity of costs is not crucial for Proposition 2 but is needed for tractability. If one allows for local production and exports in a model with non-linear costs, there is strategic interdependence between trade policies of countries and the analysis becomes quite complicated. Finally, it is worth noting that MFN adoption is a decision that applies at the economy-wide level, whereas the model presented here is a partial equilibrium one. However, the model does have an interesting implication for a world of multiple industries. Suppose there are two industries in each country. Then, if a country is relatively low cost in only one industry with respect to other countries, MFN adoption by its trading partners will benefit one industry and hurt the other so that the net effect will be ambiguous. These issues deserve future research.[24]

Acknowledgements

I thank Amy Glass, Bernard Hoekman, Hideo Konishi, Ping Lin, Aaditya Mattoo, Marcelo Olarreaga, Saltuk Ozerturk, Michael Sandfort, Robert Staiger, Larry Qiu, Murat Yildiz, two anonymous referees, and seminar audiences at Emory University, the Far Eastern Summer Meeting of the Econometric Society, Georgia Tech, the Hong Kong University of Science and Technology, Midwest International Economics Fall 2000

---

[24] The model also assumes that each country is perfectly informed about cost conditions in other countries. See McCalman (2002) and Ozerturk and Saggi (2002) for analyses of MFN under incomplete information.

Meetings, Southern Methodist University, the University of Colorado-Boulder, the University of Illinois at Urbana-Champaign, and the World Bank for helpful comments. The usual disclaimer applies.

Appendix A

Proofs of those propositions that are not proven in the text and derivations for the n country case are given below.

Derivations for the n country case under linear demand

Solving for the product market equilibrium yields:

$$x_{ii} = \frac{A_i - nc_i + C_{-i} + T_i}{n+1} \quad \text{and} \quad x_{ji} = \frac{A_i - n(c_j + t_{ji}) + (C_{-j} + T_{-j})}{n+1}$$

where

$$T_{-j} = T_i - t_{ji} = \sum_{k \neq j} t_{ki} \quad \text{and} \quad C_{-i} = C - c_i = \sum_j c_j - c_i.$$

Thus,

$$x_{ki} - x_{ji} = \frac{n(c_j - c_k) + (C_{-k} + T_{-k}) - (C_{-j} + T_{-j})}{n+1} = c_j + t_{ji} - (c_k + t_{ki})$$

and

$$X_i = \frac{nA_i - C - T_i}{n+1} = \frac{nA_i - C - T_i^M - T_i^N}{n+1}$$

Social planner's problem under linear demand

Suppose that $n = 3$, and consider the social planner's choice of country 1's tariffs. It is easy to show that:

$$\frac{\partial WW}{\partial t_{31}} - \frac{\partial WW}{\partial t_{21}} = c_3 - c_2 > 0$$

As a result, the two first-order conditions will never admit an interior solution with positive (but non-prohibitive) tariffs on both countries at the same time. Imposing $t_{21} = 0$ gives

$$\left.\frac{\partial WW}{\partial t_{31}}\right|_{t_{21}=0} = \frac{-t_{31} + 11c_3 - 5(c_1 + c_2) - A_1}{16} \tag{A.1}$$

Starting at $t_{31} = 0$, world welfare declines with an increase in t_{31} if

$$11c_3 - 5(c_1 + c_2) < A_1 \tag{A.2}$$

This inequality is sufficient to ensure that the social planner imposes zero tariffs on both exporters and it holds when the market size in country 1 is big enough relative to the cost asymmetry between countries 2 and 3.

Ruling out prohibitive tariffs in the non-cooperative equilibrium:

Suppose $n = 3$ and consider the equilibrium in country 1. Prohibitive tariffs will not be used if

$$x_{31}\Big|_{t_1 = t_1^M} > 0 \Leftrightarrow A_1 > 7c_3 - 3(c_2 + c_1) \tag{A.3}$$

If condition (A.2) holds then (A.3) is automatically satisfied since $c_3 \geq c_2 \geq c_1$.

Proof of inequality (24)

We need to show that

$$(n-1)\sum_{j\neq i}^{n} c_j^2 > \left[\sum_{j\neq i}^{n} c_j\right]^2$$

We prove the above inequality by induction. For $n = 3$, let $i = 3$. Without loss of generality we have: $2c_1^2 + 2c_2^2 > (c_1 + c_2)^2 \Leftrightarrow (c_2 - c_1)^2 > 0$. Suppose the inequality holds for $n = m - 1$, so that

$$(m-2)\sum_{j\neq i}^{m-1} c_j^2 > \left[\sum_{j\neq i}^{m-1} c_j\right]^2. \tag{A.4}$$

Now if we can show that it holds for $n = m$, we are done. So we need to show that

$$(m-1)\sum_{j\neq i}^{m} c_j^2 > \left[\sum_{j\neq i}^{m} c_j\right]^2.$$

We know

$$(m-1)\sum_{j\neq i}^{m} c_j^2 = (m-1)\left[\sum_{j\neq i}^{m-1} c_j^2 + c_m^2\right]$$

$$= (m-2)\sum_{j\neq i}^{m-1} c_j^2 + \sum_{j\neq i}^{m-1} c_j^2 + (m-1)c_m^2.$$

Given (A.4), if we can show that

$$\left[\sum_{j\neq i}^{m-1} c_j\right]^2 + \sum_{j\neq i}^{m-1} c_j^2 + (m-1)c_m^2 \quad > \quad \left[\sum_{j\neq i}^{m} c_j\right]^2 = \left[\sum_{j\neq i}^{m-1} c_j + c_m\right]^2$$

$$= \quad \left[\sum_{j\neq i}^{m-1} c_j\right]^2 + c_m^2 - 2c_m \sum_{j\neq i}^{m-1} c_j$$

then we are done. Simplifying, the above inequality can be rewritten as

$$\sum_{j\neq i}^{m-1} c_j^2 + (m-2)c_m^2 - 2c_m \sum_{j\neq i}^{m-1} c_j > 0$$

which necessarily holds since it is the same as:

$$\sum_{\substack{j\neq i\\ j\neq m}}^{m-1} (c_j - c_m)^2 > 0.$$

Proof of Proposition 3

Let $\Delta W^i \equiv W_w(t_i^M, \mathrm{t}_{-i}^*) - W_w(\mathrm{t}^*)$. We know that

$$\Delta W^i = \frac{1}{2(n-1)}\left[(n-1)\sum_{j\neq i} c_j^2 - \left[\sum_{j\neq i} c_j\right]^2\right]$$

Thus,

$$2(n-1)(\Delta W^i - \Delta W^j) = (n-1)\left[\sum_{j\neq i} c_j^2 - \sum_{k\neq j} c_k^2\right] - \left[\sum_{j\neq i} c_j\right]^2 + \left[\sum_{k\neq j} c_k\right]^2$$

The right hand side of the above equation equals $(n-1)(c_j^2 - c_i^2) + (C - c_i)^2 - (C - c_j)^2$ which is the same as $(c_i - c_j)[2C - n(c_i + c_j)]$. Thus,

$$\Delta W^i \geq \Delta W^j \Leftrightarrow \frac{c_i - c_j}{2(n-1)}\left[2C - n(c_i + c_j)\right] > 0$$

Suppose $c_i = \bar{c}$. Then,

$$\Delta W^i - \Delta W^j = \frac{(\bar{c} - c_j)\left[2\bar{c} - \bar{c} - c_j\right]}{2n(n-1)} = \frac{\left[\bar{c} - c_j\right]^2}{2n(n-1)} > 0 \quad \text{for } j \neq i.$$

Supporting calculations for Proposition 4

Let $C_M \equiv \sum_{k \in M} c_k$ and $C_N \equiv \sum_{k \in N} c_k$ so that $C = C_M + C_N + c_i$. Standard calculations show that

$$\begin{aligned} x_{ki} &= \frac{A_i - n(c_k + t_{ki}) + (C_{-k} + T_{-k})}{n+1} \quad \text{where } T_{-k} = T_i - t_{ki} \\ &= Mt_i + \sum_{\substack{j \in N \\ j \neq k}} t_{ji}. \end{aligned} \tag{A.5}$$

Summing (A.5) over all non-MFN countries, we have:

$$\begin{aligned} X_{NI} &= \sum_{k \in N} x_{ki} = \frac{NA_i - n(C_N + \sum_{k \in N} t_{ki}) + (NC - C_N + MNt_i) + (N-1)\sum_{k \in N} t_{ki}}{n+1} \\ &= \frac{NA_i - (n+1)C_N + (N-n-1)T_i^N + N(C + T_i^M)}{n+1} \end{aligned}$$

which immediately gives:

$$\frac{\partial X_{NI}}{\partial t_{ki}} = -\frac{(M+2)}{N+1} < 0 \quad \text{and} \quad \frac{\partial X_{NI}}{\partial t_i} = \frac{MN}{n+1} > 0.$$

Also,

$$\frac{\partial x_{ki}}{\partial t_{ki}} = \frac{-n}{n+1} < 0; \quad \frac{\partial x_{ki}}{\partial t_i} = \frac{M}{n+1} > 0; \quad \text{and} \quad \frac{\partial x_{ki}}{\partial t_{ji}} = \frac{\partial x_{ii}}{\partial t_{ji}} = \frac{1}{n+1} > 0.$$

Further,

$$x_{mi} = \frac{A_i - n(c_m + t_i) + C_{-m} + T_{-m}}{n+1}$$

for all $m \in M$ where

$$T_{-m} = (M-1)t_i + \sum_{k \in N} t_{ki} = T_i - t_i \quad \text{and} \quad T_i = Mt_i + \sum_{k \in N} t_{ki}.$$

We have:

$$\frac{\partial x_{mi}}{\partial t_i} = -\frac{N+2}{n+1} < 0 \quad \text{and} \quad \frac{\partial x_{ki}}{\partial t_i} = \frac{\partial x_{ii}}{\partial t_i} = \frac{M}{n+1} > 0.$$

Summing over all M countries, we have:

$$X_{MI} = \sum_{k \in M} x_{mi} = \frac{MA_i - n(C_M + Mt_i) + MC - C_M + (M-1)Mt_i + M\sum_{k \in N} t_{ki}}{n+1}$$
$$= \frac{MA_i - (n+1)C_M + (M-n-1)T_i^M + M(C + T_i^N)}{n+1}$$

It immediately follows that

$$\frac{\partial X_{MI}}{\partial t_i} = -\frac{M(N+2)}{n+1} \quad \text{and} \quad \frac{\partial X_{MI}}{\partial t_{ki}} = \frac{M}{n+1} > 0.$$

Proof of Proposition 4

Proposition 4 follows from the following two lemmas (proved below):

Lemma 1. *Suppose country i wishes to grant country j MFN. If, in doing so, it finds it optimal to grant MFN to any country p who is high cost relative to country j (i.e., $c_p > c_j$) it must find it optimal to grant MFN to all countries who are high cost relative to country p.*

Suppose country i wishes to grant country j MFN. It solves:

$$\underset{\mathbf{t_i}}{\text{Max}}\ W_i(\mathbf{t_i}) = \frac{X_i^2(\mathbf{t_i})}{2} + x_{ii}^2(\mathbf{t_i}) + \sum_{k \neq i} t_{ki}\, x_{ki}(\mathbf{t_i}) + t_{ji}\, x_{ji}$$

such that $t_{ji} \leq t_{ki}$ for all $k \neq i, j$.

The first-order condition with respect to the MFN recipient's tariff (t_{ji}) is:

$$\frac{-X_i}{n+1}+\frac{2x_{ii}}{n+1}+x_{ji}-\frac{nt_{ji}}{n+1}+\frac{\sum_{\substack{k\neq i\\ k\neq j}} t_{ki}}{n+1}-\lambda=0, \quad \text{where } \lambda\equiv\sum_{\substack{k\neq i\\ k\neq j}}\lambda_k=0$$

and for any other country k, where $k\neq j, i$, we must have:

$$\frac{-X_i}{n+1}+\frac{2x_{ii}}{n+1}+x_{ki}-\frac{nt_{ki}}{n+1}+\frac{\sum_{\substack{m\neq i\\ m\neq j\\ m\neq k}} t_{ki}}{n+1}+\lambda_k=0$$

From the last two equations, we have $x_{ji}-x_{ki}+t_{ki}-t_{ji}=\lambda+\lambda_k$ and we know that, under Cournot competition $x_{ki}-x_{ji}=c_j+t_{ji}-c_k-t_{ki}$. The last two equations together imply

$$2(t_{ki}-t_{ji})=c_j-c_k+\lambda+\lambda_k \tag{A.6}$$

Consider two non-MFN countries p and q where $c_q>c_p$. From Eq. (A.6), we have

$$2(t_{pi}-t_{qi})=c_p-c_q+\lambda_q-\lambda_p \tag{A.7}$$

Now, first we will show that if p gets MFN, *when j is given MFN*, so must country q, where $c_q>c_p$. Note that if p gets MFN given that j has MFN, it must be that $t_{pi}=t_{ji}$. As a result, from Eq. (A.7), we must have

$$c_j-c_p+\lambda+\lambda_p=0 \text{ or } \lambda=c_p-c_j-\lambda_p. \tag{A.8}$$

From Eq. (A.6) it follows that $2(t_{qi}-t_{ji})=c_j-c_q+\lambda+\lambda_q$. Substituting from (A.7) into (A.8) gives $2(t_{qi}-t_{ji})=c_p-c_q+\lambda_q-\lambda_p$. Since $t_{qi}\geq t_{ji}$, it must be that $\lambda_q-\lambda_p>0$ (because $c_p-c_q<0$). But all multipliers are non-negative: $\lambda_q>\lambda_p\geq 0$. As a result, the MFN constraint applicable to country q (i.e., $t_{qi}\geq t_{ji}$) must bind or else the relevant complementary slackness condition ($\lambda_q(t_{qi}-t_{ji})=0$) will fail. Thus, it must be that $t_{qi}=t_{ji}$.

Lemma 2. *When wishing to grant MFN to only country j, if country i does not find it optimal to grant MFN to some country q who is low cost relative to country j (i.e., $c_q<c_j$), it will not grant MFN to any country who is low cost relative to country q.*

Suppose country j is to be granted MFN and country i finds it optimal to *not* grant MFN to country q. Then, we must have:

$$2(t_{qi}-t_{ji})=c_j-c_q+\lambda+\lambda_q>0 \tag{A.9}$$

Since $t_{qi}-t_{ji}>0$, the complementary slackness condition ($\lambda_q(t_{qi}-t_{ji})=0$) implies that $\lambda_q=0$. From (A9), we must have $\lambda>c_q-c_j-\lambda_q=c_q-c_j$. Let p be any country who is low cost relative to country q, i.e., $c_p<c_q$. To show that country *p does not get* MFN, it is sufficient to show that $t_{pi}-t_{ji}>0$. We know that $2(t_{pi}-t_{ji})=c_j-c_p+\lambda+\lambda_p$. But $\lambda>c_q-c_j$ so that $c_j-c_p+\lambda+\lambda_p>c_q-c_p+\lambda_p>0$. Thus, it must be that $t_{pi}>t_{ji}$.

Proof of Proposition 6

Let G_j^{jk} denote the gain to country *j* of reciprocal MFN adoption with country *k*. Simple calculations yield

$$G_1^{12} - \frac{2}{5}c_3c_2 - \frac{3}{80}c_3^2 - \frac{3}{8}c_3c_1 - \frac{1}{8}c_2^2 - \frac{3}{20}c_2c_1 + \frac{23}{80}c_1^2 - \frac{1}{20}A_2c_1 + \frac{1}{20}A_2c_3$$

Replacing c_2 by c_1 and A_2 by A_1 in the above formula yields G_2^{12}. Reciprocal MFN between 1 and 2 occurs iff $G_1^{12} \geq 0$ and $G_2^{12} \geq 0$. When $A_2 = A_1 = A$, we have

$$\left[G_1^{12} - G_2^{12}\right]_{A_2-A_1-A} = \frac{(c_2 - c_1)(4A + 62c_3 - 33(c_1 + c_2))}{80}$$

Note that since $A > c_3 \geq c_2 \geq c_1$, we must have $G_1^{12} - G_2^{12}|_{A_2=A_1=A} > 0$. Further, when $c_2 = c_1 = c$, we have

$$\left[G_1^{12} - G_2^{12}\right]_{c_2-c_1-c} = \frac{(c_3 - c)(A_2 - A_1)}{20} > 0 \text{ iff } A_2 > A_1.$$

Finally, if $c_1 = c_2 = c$ then $\left[G_1^{12} - G_2^{12}\right]_{A_2=A_1=A} = 0$. Denote this common gain by G^{12}. We have

$$G^{12} = \frac{(c_3 - c)(4A - 3c_3 - c)}{80} > 0.$$

References

Bagwell, K., Staiger, R.W., 1997. GATT-think, University of Wisonsin-Madison and Columbia university, mimeo.

Bagwell, K., Staiger, R.W., 1999. An economic theory of GATT. American Economic Review 89, 215–248.

Bergstrom, T.C., Varian, H.R., 1985. When are Nash Equilibria independent of the distribution of agents' characteristics? The Review of Economic Studies 52, 715–718.

Brander, J.A., Krugman, P.R., 1983. A 'reciprocal dumping' model of international trade. Journal of International Economics 15, 313–323.

Brander, J.A., Spencer, B.J., 1984. Tariff protection and imperfect competition. In: Kierzkowski, H. (Ed.), Monopolistic Competition and International Trade. Oxford University Press, New York, NY.

Caplin, A., Krishna, K., 1988. Tariffs and the most favored nation clause: a game theoretic approach. Seoul Journal of Economics 1, 267–289.

Choi, J.P., 1995. Optimal tariffs and the choice of technology: discriminatory tariffs vs. the most favored nation clause. Journal of International Economics 38, 143–160.

Ethier, W.J., 2000a. Unilateralism in a multilateral world, University of Pennsylvania, mimeo.

Ethier, W. J., 2000b. Reciprocity, non-discrimination, in a multilateral world, University of Pennsylvania, mimeo.

Gatsios, K., 1990. Preferential tariffs and the 'most favoured nation' principle: a note. Journal of International Economics 28, 365–373.

Hoekman, B.M., Kostecki, M.M., 2001. The Political Economy of the World Trading System. Oxford University Press, New York, NY.

Horn, H., Mavroidis, P.C., 2000. Economic and legal aspects of the most-favored nation clause, Institute of International Economic Studies, Stockholm and Universite de Neuchatel, mimeo.

Hwang, H., Mai, C.-C., 1991. Optimum discriminatory tariffs under oligopolistic competition. Canadian Journal of Economics XXIV, 693–702.

Krishna, P., 1998. Regionalism and multilateralism: a political economy approach. The Quarterly Journal of Economics 113, 227–251.
Ludema, R., 1991. International trade bargaining and the most-favored-nation clause. Economics and Politics 3, 1–20.
McCalman, P., 2002. Multi-lateral trade negotiations and the most favored nation clause. Journal of International Economics 27, 151–176.
Ozerturk, S., Saggi, K., 2002. Tariff discrimination versus MFN under incomplete information, Southern Methodist University, mimeo.
Staiger, R.W., 1995. International rules and institutions for trade policy. In: Grossman, G.M., Rogoff, K. (Eds.), The Handbook of International Economics, Vol. 3. Elsevier, Amsterdam.
Takemori, S., 1994. The most favored nation clause. Keio Economic Studies 31, 37–50.
Varian, H.R., 1992. Microeconomic Analysis. W.W. Norton, New York, NY.

ELSEVIER
Journal of International Economics 67 (2005) 513–514
Journal of INTERNATIONAL ECONOMICS
www.elsevier.com/locate/econbase

Erratum

Erratum to "Tariffs and the Most Favored Nation clause" [J. Int. Econ. 63 (2004) 341–368]

Kamal Saggi*

Department of Economics, Southern Methodist University, Dallas, TX 75275-0496, USA

Received 13 August 2001; received in revised form 25 February 2003; accepted 10 March 2003

The publisher regrets that a number of errors occurred in the original printing of this article. The corrected text follows below:

1. On page 348, the eighth line from the top is **incorrectly stated** as:

$$\mathrm{d}TR_i = \varepsilon\left(x_{ki}^* - x_{ji}^*\right)_+ + \left(t_{ji}^* - t_{ki}^*\right)_+ \mathrm{d}x_{ji}^* > 0_+.$$

The **correct** line is:

$$\mathrm{d}TR_i = \varepsilon\underbrace{\left(x_{ki}^* - x_{ji}^*\right)}_{+} + \underbrace{\left(t_{ji}^* - t_{ki}^*\right)}_{+}\underbrace{\mathrm{d}x_{ji}^*}_{+} > 0.$$

2. On page 348, Eq. (12) is **incorrectly stated** as:

$$\frac{\partial\partial W_i}{\partial\partial t_i} = -p_i'\frac{\partial\partial X_i}{\partial\partial t_i}X_{-i} + \left(p_i - c_i\right)\frac{\partial\partial x_{ii}}{\partial\partial t_i} + X_{-i} + t_i\frac{\partial\partial X_{-i}}{\partial\partial t_i} = 0.$$

The **correct** Eq. (12) is:

$$\frac{\partial W_i}{\partial t_i} = -p_i'\frac{\partial X_i}{\partial t_i}X_{-i} + (p_i - c_i)\frac{\partial x_{ii}}{\partial t_i} + X_{-i} + t_i\frac{\partial X_{-i}}{\partial t_i} = 0.$$

DOI of original article: 10.1016/S0022-1996(03)00057-6.

* Tel.: +1 214 768 3274.
E-mail address: ksaggi@mail.smu.edu.

0022-1996/$ - see front matter
doi:10.1016/j.jinteco.2005.01.001

3. On page 348, Eq. (13) is **incorrectly stated** as:

$$t_i^{\mathrm{M}} = \frac{\left(p' \dfrac{\partial \partial X_i}{\partial \partial t_i} - 1\right)(X_{-i}) - (p_i - c_i)\dfrac{\partial \partial x_{ii}}{\partial \partial t_i}}{\dfrac{\partial \partial X_{-i}}{\partial \partial t_i}}.$$

The **correct** Eq. (13) is:

$$t_i^{\mathrm{M}} = \frac{\left(p' \dfrac{\partial X_i}{\partial t_i} - 1\right)(X_{-i}) - (p_i - c_i)\dfrac{\partial x_{ii}}{\partial t_i}}{\dfrac{\partial X_{-i}}{\partial t_i}}$$

4. On page 349, lines 2 and 3 are **incorrectly stated** as:

$$\frac{\partial \partial X_i}{\partial \partial t_i} = (n-1)\frac{\partial \partial X_i}{\partial \partial t_{ji}} = (n-1)\frac{\partial \partial X_i}{\partial \partial t_{ki}},$$

$$\frac{\partial \partial p_i}{\partial \partial t_i} = (n-1)\frac{\partial \partial p_i}{\partial \partial t_{ji}} = (n-1)\frac{\partial \partial p_i}{\partial \partial_{ki}}, \text{ and}$$

The **corrected** lines 2 and 3 are as follows:

$$\frac{\partial X_i}{\partial t_i} = (n-1)\frac{\partial X_i}{\partial t_{ji}} = (n-1)\frac{\partial X_i}{\partial t_{ki}},$$

$$\frac{\partial p_i}{\partial t_i} = (n-1)\frac{\partial p_i}{\partial t_{ji}} = (n-1)\frac{\partial p_i}{\partial t_{ki}}, \text{ and}$$

5. On page 351, the equation in line 14 as **incorrectly stated** as

$$\frac{\partial WW}{\partial t_{ji}} = (p_i - c_j)\underbrace{\frac{\partial x_{ji}}{\partial t_{ji}}}_{<0} + \sum_{k \neq j}(p_i - c_k)\underbrace{\frac{\partial x_{ki}}{\partial t_{ji}}}_{<0}.$$

The **corrected** equation is

$$\frac{\partial WW}{\partial t_{ji}} = (p_i - c_j)\underbrace{\frac{\partial x_{ji}}{\partial t_{ji}}}_{<0} + \sum_{k \neq j}(p_i - c_k)\underbrace{\frac{\partial x_{ki}}{\partial t_{ji}}}_{>0}.$$

6. On page 355, the third line below Proposition 3, the expression $c_i+c_j/2$ **is incorrect**. The **correct** expression is $(c_i+c_j)/2$.

7. On pages 356 and 357, in Eqs. (25), (26), and (27) the word ‘forall’ is incorrect; the correct phrase is ‘for all’.

CHAPTER 2

An analysis of the MFN clause under asymmetries of cost and market structure

Kamal Saggi *Department of Economics, Southern Methodist University*
Halis Murat Yildiz *Department of Economics, Ryerson University*

Abstract. We conduct a welfare comparison of MFN and tariff discrimination in an oligopoly model of trade between two exporting countries and one importing country. While MFN dominates tariff discrimination from a world welfare perspective when exporting countries are asymmetric with respect to either cost or market structure, such need not be the case when both types of asymmetries co-exist. In particular, when high-cost exporters are merged and the cost disadvantage of the merged unit relative to competing firms is of intermediate magnitude, tariff discrimination can be welfare preferred to MFN (even when the average tariff is actually lower under MFN). JEL classification: F13, F12

Une analyse de la clause de la nation la plus favorisée (NPF) quand il y a asymétrie des coûts et de la structure de marché. Ce texte fait une comparaison de bien-être de la clause NPF et de la discrimination tarifaire dans un modèle oligopolistique de commerce international entre deux pays exportateurs et un pays importateur. Alors que la stratégie NPF est supérieure à celle de la discrimination tarifaire du point de vue du bien-être mondial quand les pays exportateurs sont asymétriques soit dans leurs coûts soit dans la structure du marché, tel n'est pas nécessairement le cas quand les deux types d'asymétrie coexistent. En particulier, quand des exportateurs dont les coûts sont élevés sont fusionnés et que le désavantage de coûts est d'une magnitude moyenne, la discrimination tarifaire peut être préférée à la stratégie NPF (et ce même quand le droit de douane moyen est en fait plus bas dans un régime NPF).

We thank three anonymous referees of this journal for very helpful comments. All errors are our own. Email: hyildiz@ryerson.ca

Canadian Journal of Economics / Revue canadienne d'Economique, Vol. 38, No. 1
February / février 2005. Printed in Canada / Imprimé au Canada

0008-4085 / 05 / 242–254 /

1. Introduction

The most favoured nation (MFN) clause is widely recognized as one of the central pillars of the multilateral trading system. As is well known, at the heart of MFN is the principle of *non-discrimination*. Despite the pervasiveness of MFN in multilateral trade agreements, the economic case for non-discrimination in trade policy is hardly obvious (see Caplin and Krishna 1988 and Horn and Mavroidis 2001). Our goal in this paper is to contrast MFN with tariff discrimination in an environment where firms possess market power in order to shed further light on the economics of MFN. In particular, we ask whether or not MFN is welfare preferred to tariff discrimination when countries are asymmetric with respect to cost and market structure.[1]

To address our motivating question, we develop a simple partial-equilibrium oligopoly model of trade between two exporting countries and one importing country. In the model, two firms in each exporting country produce differentiated goods and compete in prices in the importing country's market. Exporting countries can be asymmetric with respect to market structure as well as production cost. More specifically, cost asymmetry refers to marginal cost differences across exporters whereas market structure asymmetry refers to a situation where firms in only one of the exporting countries are merged into a single unit (or are allowed to collude). With respect to market structure asymmetry, we are basically interested in situations where variation in merger and/or antitrust policies across countries results in differences in pricing behaviour of firms.

To highlight the role played by each type of asymmetry we initially consider each in isolation. When exporters differ only with respect to cost and the importing country is free to tariff discriminate, it imposes higher tariffs on low-cost exporters relative to high-cost ones. Similarly, when only market structure is asymmetric across exporting countries, a higher tariff is levied on the merged firm relative to competing ones. The preceding results obtain because the importing country can extract more rents via its tariffs from firms that enjoy higher mark-ups. If the importing country were to abandon tariff discrimination in favour of MFN, its tariff on low-cost (or merged) firms is lowered while that on high-cost (or competing) ones is raised.

As might be expected, the importing country has no unilateral incentive to adopt MFN since MFN constrains its choice set without conferring any benefit in return. But is MFN adoption necessarily desirable from the perspective of aggregate world welfare? Here, the answer is subtle: MFN indeed

1 In our model we consider a rather well-defined question and ignore several important aspects of MFN. For example, Bagwell and Staiger (2004) investigate whether MFN helps prevent bilateral opportunism while McCalman (2002) analyses the impact of MFN on trade negotiations under private information. Bagwell and Staiger (1999) show how MFN and reciprocity help to achieve Pareto efficiency in trade agreements.

improves world welfare when exporters are asymmetric along only one dimension (i.e., either they differ only with respect to costs or their merger status). However, when exporters are asymmetric along both dimensions, MFN can actually yield *lower* world welfare relative to tariff discrimination. This happens when the merged unit is relatively high cost, but its cost disadvantage is neither too small nor too big. The logic of this surprising result is that the high-cost merged firm can end up facing a *higher* tariff under tariff discrimination relative to low-cost competing firms because of its greater market power and such tariff discrimination can be socially desirable, since it diverts output *towards* relatively low-cost producers. To the best of our knowledge, ours is the only model that provides a demonstration of the claim that MFN does not always welfare dominate tariff discrimination. Since market structure differences are pervasive across countries, this result is relevant for assessing the practical desirability of MFN.

Like Saggi (2004), the present paper uses an oligopoly model to examine the implications of MFN. However, we differ from Saggi (2004) in two significant ways. First, in addition to exploring the role played by cost differences across countries, we also allow market structure to differ across countries. Second, we examine price competition among firms rather than quantity competition and thereby contribute to the literature on MFN under oligopoly all of which focuses on quantity competition – see Gatsios (1990), Hwang and Mai (1991), Choi (1995), Saggi (2004), and Ozerturk and Saggi (forthcoming).

2. Model

We consider a world comprised of three countries: home country (H), foreign country (F), and importing country (I). In both countries H and F, local industry comprises two firms, each of which produces a symmetrically differentiated good that is exported to country I. Let firms be indexed by i, where $i = 1, 2, 3, 4$. Firms 1 and 2 are home firms, while 3 and 4 are foreign firms. Let c_i denote the marginal cost of firm i where $c_i = c_h$ for $i = 1, 2$ and $c_i = c_f$ for $i = 3, 4$. Following Shubik (1980), the demand function facing firm i is given by

$$q_i(p_1, \ldots, p_N) = \frac{1}{N}(\alpha - p_i - \gamma(p_i - \frac{1}{N}\sum_{j=1}^{N} p_j)), \tag{1}$$

where p_i is the price charged by firm i, q_i its sales, and N denotes the total number of firms in the market. The parameter $\gamma > 0$ measures the degree of substitutability between different goods. When $\gamma \simeq 0$, goods become unrelated, and as it approaches infinity they become perfect substitutes.

Firm i faces a specific tariff t_i when exporting to country I where $t_i = t_h$ for $i = 1, 2$ and $t_i = t_f$ for firms 3 and 4. We study the following two-stage game under tariff discrimination and MFN. In the first stage, the importing country chooses its tariffs to maximize its own welfare (these tariffs depend upon whether the underlying policy regime is one of tariff discrimination or MFN). Next, firms compete in the product market by choosing their prices.

We consider the above policy game under four different market structures: (i) international duopoly with one firm in each country (*D*) (ii) international triopoly with a single home firm and two foreign firms (*HM*); (iii) international triopoly with a single foreign firm and two home firms (*FM*); and (iv) international oligopoly with two firms in each country (*O*). Implicitly, we view asymmetries in market structure across countries to be a consequence of differences in national merger and/or antitrust policies. For example, under market structure *HM*, home firms act as a single merged unit while those in the foreign country act as competitors. In fact, in our model, a merger of two firms is equivalent to perfect collusion between them. International market structure is denoted by *S*, where $S = D$, HM, FM, and O.

To obtain a subgame perfect Nash equilibrium, we solve the model backwards and begin with the product market stage. The maximization problem of firm i under international oligopoly is given by

$$\max_{\{p_i\}} \Pi_i(.) = \frac{1}{4}(p_i - c_i - t_i)(\alpha - p_i - \gamma(p_i - \overline{P_j})), \tag{2}$$

where $\overline{P_j}$ denotes the average price in the market and it equals

$$\overline{P_j} \equiv \frac{\sum_{j=1}^{4} p_j}{4}.$$

The first-order condition for the above problem yields firm i's reaction function under international oligopoly:

$$p_i = \frac{4\alpha + (3\gamma + 4)(c_i + t_i) + \gamma P_{-i}}{2(4 + 3\gamma)}, \tag{3}$$

where P_{-i} denotes the sum of prices of firm i's competitors and it equals

$$P_{-i} = \sum_{j \neq i} p_j.$$

The equilibrium price charged by firm i under oligopoly is found by solving the reaction functions of all firms simultaneously (the relevant expressions are easy to derive).[2] Denote equilibrium price of firm i under market structure S by p_i^S.

As might be expected, when international market structure is asymmetric ($S = HM$ or FM), reaction functions of firms are also asymmetric. We discuss

2 For detailed analytical derivations as well as for proofs of our main results, the reader is referred to our working paper, Saggi and Yildiz (2003), which is available upon request.

only the market structure *HM*, since reaction functions under *FM* are completely analogous. If home firms are merged, they internalize price competition between themselves and solve:

$$\max_{\{p_1,p_2\}} \Pi_h(.) = \sum_{i=1}^{2} \frac{1}{4}(p_i - c_i - t_i)(\alpha - p_i - \gamma(p_i - \overline{P_j})), \tag{4}$$

whereas the problem facing a typical foreign firm is analogous to that under oligopoly. The merged home firm's (common) reaction function for both products at the price competition stage is as follows:

$$p_i = \frac{4\alpha + (2\gamma + 4)(c_i + t_i) + \gamma P_{-i}}{4(2 + \gamma)}, \tag{5}$$

whereas a typical foreign firm's reaction function is

$$p_j = \frac{4\alpha + (3\gamma + 4)(c_j + t_j) + 2\gamma p_i + \gamma p_{\sim j}}{2(4 + 3\gamma)}, \tag{6}$$

where $\sim j$ denotes the other foreign firm. Note from the above reaction function that a unit increase in the price of the merged home firm induces a greater price increase by a foreign firm than does a unit price increase by the other foreign firm:

$$\frac{\partial p_j}{\partial p_i} = 2\frac{\partial p_j}{\partial p_{\sim j}}.$$

In other words, the home merger makes competing foreign firms more sensitive to price increases by the home firm. The intuition is simple: an increase in the price of the (merged) home firm *applies to two goods*, whereas that of a competing foreign firm applies to only one good. Similarly, a comparison of the reaction function of the merged firm to that of a typical firm under oligopoly shows that the merged firm is more responsive to price increases by its rivals (due to internalization of competition). The equilibrium prices charged by the home firm and competing foreign firms under market structure *HM* are easily calculated and the following lemma follows from straightforward differentiation:

LEMMA 1. *Let h denote the merged home firm and f a competing foreign firm. The following hold: (i)* $\frac{\partial p_h^{HM}}{\partial t_h} < \frac{\partial p_f^{HM}}{\partial t_f}$ *and (ii)* $\frac{\partial p_h^{HM}}{\partial t_f} > \frac{\partial p_f^{HM}}{\partial t_h}$.

In other words, the merged firm's price increase in response to an increase in own tariff is weaker than the corresponding response of a typical competing firm. On the other hand, the cross-tariff effect is weaker for competing firms relative to the merged firm. These results are useful for explaining the effects of MFN when international market structure is asymmetric (see section 3.2).

Now consider market competition under international duopoly. The maximization problems and the reaction functions of home and foreign mergers under international duopoly (D) are the same as in (4) and (5), respectively. As expected, the equilibrium price under D is the highest among all possible market structures. In the next section, we contrast two scenarios: one where the importing country is free to tariff discriminate among exporters and another where it must treat them symmetrically (MFN treatment).

3. MFN versus tariff discrimination

There are two main issues that deserve examination. First, the linkages between tariffs, production costs, and market concentration levels are of interest. Second, the effects of MFN on equilibrium tariffs and welfare deserve investigation. For this purpose, we begin by separately considering the two types of asymmetries.

3.1. MFN under cost asymmetry

Let $\mathbf{t} = (t_h, t_f)$ denotes the importing country's tariff vector under tariff discrimination. Given international market structure S, the importing country chooses its tariff schedule to maximize its own welfare (defined as the sum of the consumer surplus and tariff revenue):

$$\max_{\mathbf{t}} \ W(\mathbf{t}) \equiv CS(\mathbf{t}) + t_h \sum_{i=1}^{2} q_i(\mathbf{t}) + t_f \sum_{i=3}^{4} q_i(\mathbf{t}). \tag{7}$$

where consumer surplus equals

$$CS(\mathbf{t}) \equiv \frac{\sum_{i=1}^{4} (\alpha - p_i(\mathbf{t}))q_i(\mathbf{t})}{2}. \tag{8}$$

Let t_i^S denote the importing country's optimal discriminatory tariff on firm i under market structure S and let $\Delta c \equiv c_h - c_f$ denote the cost differential between firms. The following result is easy to show:

PROPOSITION 1. *Under symmetric market structures ($S = O$ or D), the importing country's optimal discriminatory tariff schedule has the following features: (i) the tariff imposed on foreign firms is higher than that imposed on home firms iff the cost of foreign firms is lower than that of home firms: $t_f^S \geq t_h^S$ iff $\Delta c \geq 0$; (ii) the true efficiency ranking of firms is preserved: $t_f^S \leq t_h^S + \Delta c$ iff $\Delta c \geq 0$; and (iii) tariffs increase with market concentration: $t_i^O < t_i^D$.*

Under symmetric market structures, the tariff on low-cost producers is higher because they enjoy bigger mark-ups and the importing country can extract more rents from them. Furthermore, the bigger the cost differential between firms, the stronger is the degree of tariff discrimination.[3] The logic behind part (ii) is that if the tariff on relatively low-cost exporters were actually high enough to make them relatively high cost (i.e., their tariff included costs exceed those of 'truly' high-cost producers), the volume of their exports would be lower, as would be the per unit revenue raised from them relative to that raised from the 'truly' high-cost firms. In such a situation, the importing country would benefit by lowering its tariffs on the low-cost firms to levels where they would actually be exporting more (which happens when the true cost ranking of exporters holds).

Under MFN, the importing country solves:

$$\max_{t} \; W^I(t) \equiv CS(t) + t\sum_{i=1}^{4} q_i(t). \tag{9}$$

The problem in (9) differs from the problem in (7) in only one respect: under MFN the importing country imposes the same tariff on all exporters irrespective of their costs. Define the (optimal) MFN tariff under market structure S as $t^S = \text{Arg max } W^I(t)$. We have

PROPOSITION 2. *Under symmetric market structures* ($S = O$ *or* D)*, the importing country's MFN tariff* t^S *has the following features: (i) it is lower (higher) than the discriminatory tariff on low (high) cost exporters:* $t_f^S \geq t^S \geq t_h^S$ *iff* $\Delta c \geq 0$*; (ii) the average tariffs under MFN and tariff discrimination are equal:* $t_h^S + t_f^S = 2t^S$*; and (iii) the MFN tariff increases with market concentration:* $t^O < t^D$.

Part (i) of the above proposition informs us that MFN adoption by a country has distributional implications for its trading partners: the low cost exporters gain while high cost ones lose. Part (ii) of the proposition shows that, in and of itself, MFN adoption need not imply any trade liberalization. Finally, part (iii) shows that an increase in the degree of market concentration leads the importing country to raise its MFN tariff. As might be expected, the importing country has no unilateral incentive to adopt MFN. But is MFN adoption socially desirable? Since MFN does not result in trade liberalization, the answer to this question is not immediately obvious.[4]

Define world welfare as the sum of welfare in each country:

$$WW(\mathbf{t}) = W^H(\mathbf{t}) + W^F(\mathbf{t}) + W^I(\mathbf{t}). \tag{10}$$

3 Results (i) and (ii) also hold in linear oligopoly models of Cournot competition; see Gatsios (1990), Hwang and Mai (1991), Choi (1995), and Saggi (2004). However, under both price and quantity competition, these results require linearity of cost.

4 One thing is clear from part (i) of the above proposition: MFN is not Pareto improving over tariff discrimination.

Substituting $\mathbf{t} = (t_h^S, t_f^S)$ yields world welfare under tariff discrimination, while setting $\mathbf{t} = (t^S, t^S)$ yields world welfare under MFN. Owing to market segmentation, it is sufficient to consider the sum of the welfare of the importing country and the profit of home and foreign exporters in the importing country. Under market structure S, MFN adoption improves world welfare if and only if

$$W^I(t^S) + \sum_{i=1}^{4} \Pi_i(t^S) \geq W^I(t_h^S, t_f^S) + \sum_{i=1}^{4} \Pi_i(t_h^S, t_f^S). \tag{11}$$

PROPOSITION 3. *Under symmetric market structures ($S = O$ or D), MFN yields higher world welfare than tariff discrimination*: $WW(t^S) \geq WW(t_h^S, t_f^S)$.

The above result shows that in the absence of market structure asymmetry, MFN adoption contributes to world welfare even though it is *not* accompanied by any trade liberalization. The reason is that tariff discrimination is biased against low-cost exporters and it diverts trade towards high-cost ones, whereas no such inefficiency exists under MFN.

3.2. *MFN under market structure asymmetry*

To isolate the effect of market structure asymmetry on the tariff response of the importing country and world welfare, assume that costs are equal across firms ($\Delta c = 0$). As before, we discuss only market structure HM wherein home firms are merged into a single unit, whereas foreign firms compete (the results under market structure FM are completely analogous). Let t_h^{HM} and t_f^{HM} denote the optimal discriminatory tariffs on home and foreign firms under the market structure HM. Similarly, let t^{HM} denote the corresponding MFN tariff.

PROPOSITION 4. *Suppose all exporters have the same cost* ($\Delta c = 0$). *Then the following hold: (i) under tariff discrimination, the merged firm faces a higher tariff than competing ones: $t_h^{HM} \geq t_f^{HM}$; (ii) the MFN tariff is bound by discriminatory tariffs: $t_h^{HM} \geq t^{HM} \geq t_f^{HM}$; (iii) the average tariff level is higher under tariff discrimination relative to MFN: $t_h^{HM} + t_f^{HM} \geq 2t^{HM}$; and (iv) world welfare is higher under MFN relative to tariff discrimination.*

Part (i) of the above result can be explained as follows. First, note that when free to discriminate, the importing country has an incentive to impose a higher rent-extracting tariff on the merged firm, since its mark-up is higher than that of competing firms. Second, lemma 1 states that the harmful effect of a unit tariff increase on local consumer surplus is lower when the increase applies to the merged unit relative to when it applies to a competing firm. The weaker price response of the merged firm to a tariff increase gives the importing country an additional incentive (besides the higher mark-up charged by the merged firm) to impose a higher tariff on the merged unit.

One implication of part (ii) is that the incentives of firms to merge under MFN are higher relative to tariff discrimination since the merged firm faces a lower tariff under MFN. Part (iii) of the above proposition shows that when international market structure is asymmetric, MFN adoption by the importing country results in some trade liberalization, since its average tariff is lower under MFN relative to tariff discrimination. This result can be understood as follows. By definition, under MFN, the importing country cannot treat the merged firm any worse than a typical competing firm. As a result, relative to tariff discrimination, the tariff imposed on the merged unit is lower under MFN, while that on a typical competing firm is higher. To compensate consumers for the relatively higher tariff on competing firms, the home country lowers its average tariff under MFN relative to discrimination (i.e., unilateral MFN adoption is accompanied by some degree of trade liberalization). Were the average level of tariff protection to remain the same under MFN and tariff discrimination, local consumers would be strictly worse off under MFN, owing to the relatively stronger price response of a competing firm to a tariff increase (lemma 1).

3.3. When both asymmetries coexist

When both types of asymmetries are present, two mutually exclusive scenarios need to be examined. In scenario (i) merging firms are low cost relative to competing firms (i.e., $\Delta c < 0$), whereas in scenario (ii) the opposite is true (i.e., $\Delta c > 0$).

Given proposition 1 and proposition 4, it is easy to see that under scenario (i), the importing country's optimal discriminatory tariff on the (low-cost) merging firms is higher than that on high-cost (competing) ones, and that the MFN tariff is bound by the two discriminatory tariffs. Furthermore, when we combine the world welfare ranking in proposition 3 and proposition 4, it is straightforward to argue that MFN adoption by the importing country necessarily improves world welfare under scenario (i). But what if merging firms are high cost? The following proposition addresses scenario (ii):

PROPOSITION 5. *Suppose merging firms are high cost (i.e., $\Delta c > 0$). Then, there exist two critical thresholds $\underline{\Delta c}$ and $\overline{\Delta c}$, where $\underline{\Delta c} < \overline{\Delta c}$ such that the following hold: (i) at both $\Delta c = \underline{\Delta c}$ and $\Delta c = \overline{\Delta c}$, global welfare under MFN and tariff discrimination is equal; (ii) over the intervals $0 < \Delta c < \underline{\Delta c}$ and $\Delta c > \overline{\Delta c}$, MFN yields higher global welfare than tariff discrimination, whereas (iii) over the interval $\underline{\Delta c} < \Delta c < \overline{\Delta c}$, tariff discrimination yields higher global welfare than MFN.*

The main message of proposition 5 is that when the merged unit's cost is rather similar to that of competing firms (i.e., $\Delta c < \underline{\Delta c}$), or when its cost is significantly higher than that of competing firms (i.e., $\Delta c > \overline{\Delta c}$), MFN welfare dominates tariff discrimination. However, when the merged unit is high cost but its cost disadvantage is moderate in nature, it is tariff discrimination that is preferable from a welfare perspective. We next explain the intuition behind this result.

When merging firms are high cost, two contradictory effects determine the comparison of tariffs chosen by the importing country under MFN and tariff discrimination. On the one hand, the fact that the high-cost merged firm has more market power calls for a higher discriminatory tariff on it. On the other hand, because the merged firm is high cost, the importing country has an incentive to impose higher tariffs on competing low-cost firms. These two effects cancel out at the critical cost differential $\overline{\Delta c}$, so that $t_h^{HM} \geq t_f^{HM}$ iff $\Delta c \leq \overline{\Delta c}$. At $\Delta c = \overline{\Delta c}$, even under tariff discrimination the importing country chooses *not* to discriminate between the merged high-cost unit and competing low-cost firms, implying that world welfare under the two regimes is equal. To understand why this is also the case at the lower threshold $\underline{\Delta c}$, consider how the importing country's tariffs under MFN and tariff discrimination compare when the merged unit is high cost. It is easy to show that

$$\Delta t = t^{HM} - \frac{t_h^{HM} + t_f^{HM}}{2} \leq 0 \text{ iff } \Delta c \leq \overline{\Delta c}, \tag{12}$$

where the equality holds when $\Delta c = \overline{\Delta c}$. In other words, the importing country's average MFN tariff is lower than that under tariff discrimination as long as the cost differential between firms falls below the upper threshold $\overline{\Delta c}$, so that in the range $\Delta c < \overline{\Delta c}$, MFN has a trade liberalization effect (whereas in the range $\Delta c > \overline{\Delta c}$, it is tariff discrimination that has a trade liberalization effect). Furthermore, as Δc increases, the trade liberalization impact of MFN gets smaller:

$$\frac{\partial|\Delta t|}{\partial \Delta c} \leq 0. \tag{13}$$

Given the above discussion, it is now clear exactly when and why MFN dominates tariff discrimination. In the range $0 < \Delta c < \underline{\Delta c}$, while tariff discrimination is socially useful because it penalizes the high-cost producer, the trade liberalization effect of MFN is strong enough for MFN to be welfare preferred to tariff discrimination.[5] When $\underline{\Delta c} < \Delta c < \overline{\Delta c}$, the trade liberalization effect of MFN is weak, and the fact that tariff discrimination is biased against the high-cost merged unit makes it more desirable from a welfare perspective than MFN. Finally, when $\Delta c > \overline{\Delta c}$, while it is tariff discrimination that has a trade liberalization effect, it is MFN that yields higher welfare because tariff

5 When $\Delta c = \underline{\Delta c}$, the trade liberalization benefit of MFN is exactly offset by the gain that results from tariff discrimination's being biased against the high-cost merged firm.

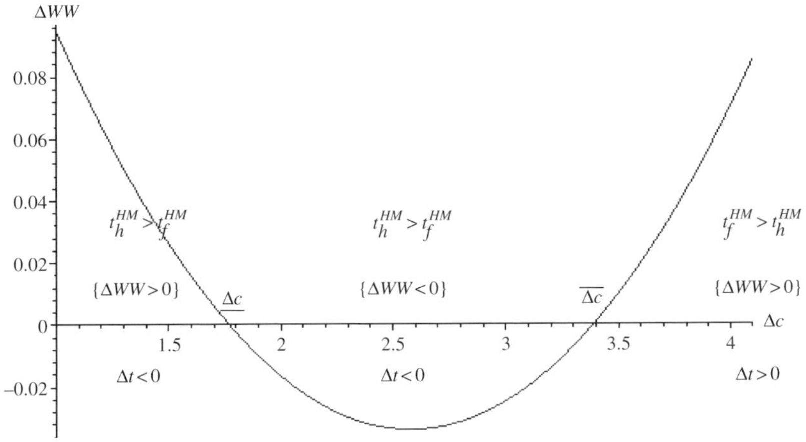

FIGURE 1 MFN vs tariff discrimination ($\alpha = 100$, $c_f = 0$, $\gamma = 1$)

discrimination is biased against low-cost competing firms and the large cost differential between firms implies that the trade liberalization effect of tariff discrimination is dominated by its trade diversion effect. Figure 1 summarizes this discussion by plotting $\Delta WW^{HM} = WW(t^{HM}) - WW(t_h^{HM}, t_f^{HM})$ against Δc (in this figure $c_f = 0$; $\gamma = 1$; and $\alpha = 100$).

A final point is worth noting. Either when the products become independent ($\gamma \to 0$) or when they become perfect substitutes ($\gamma \to \infty$), the critical thresholds $\overline{\Delta c}$ and $\underline{\Delta c}$ approach zero. Intuitively, at these extreme substitutability levels, a merger has no effect on world welfare, since market structure is either perfectly competitive (for $\gamma \to \infty$) or monopolistic (for $\gamma \to 0$) to begin with. Under either of these scenarios, only the cost differential between firms (i.e., Δc) matters, and we know from proposition 3 that MFN improves world welfare when countries are asymmetric only with respect to production costs. Thus, MFN adoption is more likely to lower world welfare more when the degree of product differentiation (as measured by γ) is neither too high nor too low.

4. Conclusion

In a simple three-country oligopoly model of trade, we contrast two scenarios: one where the importing country is free to tariff discriminate among exporters and another where it must treat them symmetrically (MFN treatment). The model allows for two types of asymmetries (production cost and market structure) that generate a rationale for tariff discrimination. When only market structure is symmetric across countries, the importing country's switch from a discriminatory tariff schedule to MFN benefits low-cost exporters and hurts high-cost ones. This result confirms a key insight provided by several quantity competition models: MFN improves world welfare by eliminating trade diversion that results from tariff discrimination. We also show that the desirable welfare effects of MFN continue to hold when countries are asymmetric only with respect to market structure.

The major result of the paper is that when both types of asymmetries coexist, MFN does not always yield higher welfare than tariff discrimination. In particular, if merging firms are high cost, MFN can deliver lower world welfare than tariff discrimination, even when the average tariff is relatively lower under MFN. Thus, asymmetries in the economic environment of countries (that may result from market forces and/or government policies) can be an important determinant of the desirability of MFN.

While our model delivers some new insights, it is somewhat special in nature, since it assumes that both demand and cost are linear. However, these assumptions would be more problematic if we sought to prove a general welfare result regarding MFN. Instead, we provide one possible scenario where MFN does not welfare dominate tariff discrimination, and our analysis is sufficient to argue that a general welfare ranking of the two policy regimes does not exist. Further research is needed to determine whether tariff discrimination might be preferable to MFN under alternative circumstances.

References

Bagwell, Kyle, and Robert W. Staiger (1999) 'An economic theory of GATT,' *American Economic Review* 89, 215–48

— (2004) 'Multilateral trade negotiations, bilateral opportunism and the rules of GATT/WTO.' *Journal of International Economics* 63, 1–29

Brander, James A., and Barbara J. Spencer (1985) 'Export subsidies and international market share rivalry,' *Journal of International Economics* 18, 83–100

Caplin, Andrew, and Kala Krishna (1988) 'Tariffs and the most favored nation clause: a game theoretic approach,' *Seoul Journal of Economics* 1, 267–89

Choi, Jay Pil (1995) 'Optimal tariffs and the choice of technology: discriminatory tariffs vs. the Most Favored Nation clause,' *Journal of International Economics* 38, 143–60

Gatsios, Konstantine (1990) 'Preferential tariffs and the "Most Favoured Nation" principle: a note,' *Journal of International Economics* 28, 365–73

Horn, Henrik, and Petros C. Mavroidis (2001) 'Economic and legal aspects of the Most-Favored Nation clause,' *European Journal of Political Economy* 17, 233–79

Hwang H., and C.-C Mai (1991) 'Optimum discriminatory tariffs under oligopolistic competition,' *Canadian Journal of Economics* 24, 693–702

Ludema, Rodney (1991) 'International trade bargaining and the Most Favored Nation clause,' *Economics and Politics* 3, 1–20

McCalman, Phillip (2002) 'Multi-lateral trade negotiations and the Most Favored Nation clause,' *Journal of International Economics* 27, 151–76

Ozerturk, Saltuk, and Kamal Saggi 'Tariff discrimination versus MFN under incomplete information,' *Journal of International Trade and Economic Development*, forthcoming

Saggi, Kamal (2004) 'Tariffs and the most favored nation clause,' *Journal of International Economics* 63, 341–68

Saggi, Kamal, and Halis M. Yildiz (2003). 'Notes on MFN under asymmetries of cost and market structure,' mimeo, Southern Methodist University and Ryerson University

Shubik, Martin (1980) *Market Structure and Behavior* (Cambridge, MA: Harvard University Press)

CHAPTER 3

INTERNATIONAL ECONOMIC REVIEW
Vol. 49, No. 4, November 2008

NATIONAL TREATMENT AT THE WTO: THE ROLES OF PRODUCT AND COUNTRY HETEROGENEITY*

BY KAMAL SAGGI AND NESE SARA[1]

Department of Economics, Southern Methodist University, U.S.A.

This paper analyzes the World Trade Organization's (WTO's) national treatment (NT) clause in a two-country model where quality of goods and/or market size are heterogenous across countries. When market size is symmetric across countries, a reciprocal NT agreement (i) benefits the high-quality country, (ii) hurts the low-quality country, and (iii) delivers higher aggregate world welfare. However, such an agreement can arise in equilibrium if the high-quality country's market is relatively bigger and the quality gap between goods is small (i.e., goods are sufficiently *alike*). The qualitative nature of these results does not change when quality is endogenously determined.

1. INTRODUCTION

Every multilateral agreement administered by the World Trade Organization (WTO) contains a national treatment (NT) clause that requires member countries to not discriminate between imported goods and like domestic goods with respect to their internal taxes and domestic regulations. For example, Article III of the General Agreement on Tariffs and Trade (GATT) states that "the products of the territory of any contracting party imported into the territory of any other contracting party shall be accorded treatment no less favorable than that accorded to like products of national origin in respect of all laws, regulations and requirements affecting their internal sale."

As is clear, the notion of *likeness* lies at the heart of NT as prescribed by GATT/WTO. However, the practical implementation of NT is beset with difficulties, the most fundamental of which is that competing products from different countries are often *differentiated* from one another. For example, although a Toyota Camry and a Ford Taurus are close substitutes (but yet not of identical quality), a high end Lexus is substantially superior to either car. It is not obvious whether the notion of like products should include all three cars in the same category. Furthermore, even for goods that are essentially homogenous, national origin itself can serve as a signal of quality and therefore a source of product differentiation. For

* Manuscript received September 2006; revised April 2007.

[1]For helpful comments and suggestions, we thank Bernard Hoekman, co-editor Charles Horioka, Petros Mavroidis, Saltuk Ozerturk, Santanu Roy, and four anonymous referees. The paper also benefitted from comments made by seminar audiences at the Fall 2007 Midwest International Economics Meetings held at the University of Michigan at Ann Arbor, 2007 Annual Meeting of the Southern Economics Association Meeting held at New Orleans, Hitotsubashi University, and Southern Methodist University. All errors are our own. Please address correspondence to: Kamal Saggi, Department of Economics, Southern Methodist University, Dallas, TX 75275, U.S.A. Phone: 214-768-3274. Fax: 214-768-3911. E-mail: *ksaggi@smu.edu*.

example, consumer perceptions of Japanese cars differ quite substantially from those of Eastern European ones. Similarly, consider French wine versus locally produced varieties in most countries. Or Italian shoes versus local ones, and so on. Motivated by this basic observation, we analyze NT under a scenario where countries produce similar but vertically differentiated goods. Our analysis is most relevant to situations where the quality differential between competing goods is not so large that the concept of NT itself loses meaning. The broader objective of this paper is to shed light on when and why do heterogenous countries producing differentiated goods find it in their mutual interest to subscribe to non-discrimination rules such as NT. Given the multitude of dimensions along which there is heterogeneity among actual WTO members, the relevance of this question seems self-evident.

Non-discrimination as captured by the most favored nation (MFN) clause has received substantial attention from economists—see, for example, Bagwell and Staiger (1999 and 2005). However, NT has only recently begun to receive formal scrutiny: In fact, Horn (2006) provides the first formal analysis of the role of NT in bilateral trade agreements.[2] The fact that NT levels the playing field between domestic and foreign firms whereas MFN does so between *only* foreign ones suggests that governments are likely to view the two rules rather differently, perhaps with NT being seen as a more binding constraint than MFN. And indeed it does not seem a stretch to say that the actual implementation of NT at the WTO has somewhat lagged behind that of MFN. This might partly help explain why NT has been neglected in the literature relative to MFN. As Horn (2006) notes, absent some discipline on internal taxes, international tariff agreements may be meaningless since countries can undo such agreements by imposing different internal taxes on imported and domestic goods. However, specifying constraints on *all* internal measures is virtually impossible given the myriad ways countries can intervene in domestic markets. Given this basic problem of "incompleteness" of trade agreements, Horn (2006) argues that NT serves as a device that blunts the use of internal instruments as tools of protectionism.[3] In fact, he shows that if tariff agreements account for subsequent tax setting incentives, NT can improve welfare even when it is socially optimal to discriminate against imports.

This paper builds on the two-country partial equilibrium framework of Horn (2006) by introducing heterogeneity along two important dimensions: quality and market size. These two types of heterogeneities are widely prevalent in the real world and are likely to be important determinants of the way in which WTO's non-discrimination rules affect its various members. Our basic model is a three-stage policy game where production is undertaken by a single firm in each country. In the first stage, the two countries decide whether or not to commit to a NT agreement under which each agrees to treat both firms in a non-discriminatory fashion with respect to its internal sales taxes (or subsidies). Next, given the policy regime,

[2] See Horn and Mavroidis (2001) for a survey of the literature on MFN from an economics and legal perspective and Horn and Mavroidis (2004) for a discussion of the lessons that can be learned from international disputes regarding violations of NT that have come before the WTO.

[3] In a paper of note, Horn et al. (2005) argue that an endogenous incomplete contracting approach (i.e., one wherein contracting parties make optimal decisions regarding what to contract over and what to leave out) can help explain some of the central features of GATT, one of which is the principle of non-discrimination as defined by MFN and NT.

each country chooses its taxes/subsidies to maximize its own welfare. Finally, firms compete in prices in both markets.

We ask whether and how a country's incentive to commit to a NT agreement depends upon the quality of its good relative to that of its trading partner as well as on the relative size of its market. In addition, we also examine the implications of a NT agreement for global welfare. Given the distortion created by each firm's market power, in the absence of international trade each country's optimal policy is a production subsidy that induces its local firm to produce the socially efficient level of output. However, under oligopolistic international trade each country has an incentive to extract rent from the other country's firm as well as to confer a strategic advantage on its own firm by treating it in a preferential manner. We show that each country finds it optimal to subsidize its firm while taxing its foreign rival—i.e., discrimination against the foreign product is in each country's interest. By definition, a NT agreement between the two countries rules out such "beggar-thy-neighbor" tax discrimination. However, we find that in the absence of international transfers, countries are not always willing to sign such an agreement. More specifically, if market size is equal across countries, while the high-quality country benefits from a NT agreement, the low-quality country *loses* from it and tax discrimination prevails even when NT yields higher aggregate global welfare.[4] On the other hand, when market size differs across countries, a NT agreement can make both countries better off relative to tax discrimination.[5] Intuitively, asymmetry in market size helps counterbalance the quality asymmetry between goods, thereby making NT acceptable to both parties.[6] Even so, a NT agreement arises only when the quality gap between goods is not too large. This result corresponds quite well with the emphasis placed on "likeness" in the context of non-discrimination at the WTO.

Our analysis suggests that countries that tend to produce goods of lower quality (perhaps because they lag behind the global technology frontier) may not necessarily benefit from a non-discrimination rule with respect to domestic taxation since they face lower taxes in export markets under tax discrimination.[7] Together with the findings of Gatsios (1990) and Saggi (2004)—where similar conclusions have been reached with respect to MFN in the absence of product differentiation—our results shed light on why so many developing countries appear to be dissatisfied with the rules and workings of the global multilateral trading system.

[4] Later in the paper, we show that this result holds even when quality is endogenously determined.

[5] We should note that if the high-quality country's market is sufficiently large, a NT agreement does not arise because the high-quality country rejects it—under such a scenario, from the perspective of the high-quality country, the gain in export profits conferred by a NT agreement is insufficient compensation for giving up the right to tax discriminate.

[6] It is noteworthy that Kanbur and Keen (1993) have shown that, in the context of tax harmonization, disparity in country size necessarily worsens the inefficiency that arises from non-cooperative behavior in a tax competition setting. Of course, whereas harmonization requires asymmetric countries to pursue the same tax policy, NT only requires that a country not discriminate between firms on the basis of national origin.

[7] NT as defined in GATT leaves a country free to treat foreign firms *more favorably* than domestic ones, but in our model this never happens in equilibrium. As a result, it is sufficient to view NT in a strict sense (i.e., as equal treatment of domestic and foreign firms).

A rather extensive literature explores the effects of trade policy when market structure is oligopolistic and firms produce differentiated goods. For example, Bond (1988) derives optimal tariff policy when products are vertically differentiated and the government's objective is to maximize welfare subject to providing a minimum level of profits to local producers. He shows that the presence of the profit constraint causes local consumers to choose lower-quality goods relative to free trade. While the importing country is a price taker in Bond's (1988) model, Das and Donnenfeld (1987) consider how various trade policies (such as tariffs and quotas) affect a foreign monopolist's choice regarding price/quantity and the quality of its product. In addition, they show that subjecting imports to a minimum quality requirement lowers the importing country's welfare.[8] Motta et al. (1997) examine a scenario where two countries producing different quality levels open up to trade and firms respond to international trade by adjusting their quality levels.[9] They show that by undertaking a sufficiently large investment in quality improvement, the low-quality country can leapfrog the high-quality country if the initial quality gap between countries is not too large. In a recent paper, Herguera et al. (2002) develop a two-country model in which a domestic and a foreign firm choose the qualities of their products and then compete in tariff-ridden product markets. They show that if governments choose tariffs after firms choose qualities, in equilibrium the domestic firm produces the high quality and the foreign firm the low quality.[10] The intuition for this interesting result is as follows. Since the domestic import tariff is increasing in the foreign firm's quality, the foreign firm has a weaker incentive to invest in quality improvement relative to its domestic competitor. Our analysis of endogenous quality follows the ex post timing structure of Herguera et al. (2002) but there are three important differences. First, in our paper, the policy instruments of governments are domestic taxes that apply to *both* firms, unlike a tariff that is imposed on only the foreign firm. Second, we focus on how market outcomes and welfare (of each country) under tax discrimination compare with that under NT. Third, our analysis of endogenous quality shows how differences in market size and tax policy regimes of governments jointly affect R&D incentives of firms. More specifically, we show that under tax discrimination each firm's R&D incentive is more responsive to the size of its domestic market whereas under NT it is equally responsive to both markets (i.e., an increase in size of the foreign market increases a firm's investment incentive just as much an increase in the size of its domestic market).[11]

Our analysis also overlaps to some degree with several key papers in the area of international tax competition. For example, using a two-country Cournot oligopoly model in which firms are free to relocate in order to exploit tax or

[8] In a related paper, Das and Donnenfeld (1989) examine the impact of quantity and quality restrictions on oligopolistic international trade.

[9] Their analysis builds on Motta (1993), who contrasts endogenous quality choices and market outcomes under Bertrand and Cournot competition.

[10] Moraga-González and Viaene (2004) analyze antidumping policies in a vertically differentiated international oligopoly and show that such policies can also lead to "quality reversals" between the domestic and the foreign firm.

[11] For this statement to hold precisely, the high quality's variable cost of production must be the same as that of the low quality.

subsidy differentials, Janeba (1998) shows that if governments cannot discriminate against foreign firms, laissez-faire prevails in equilibrium. He argues that a non-discrimination rule leads to a mutually beneficial outcome for both countries since it helps avoid a wasteful subsidy race. In our model, non-discrimination also has the potential to benefit both countries by curbing "beggar-thy-neighbor" behavior on their part. A related paper by Janeba and Peters (1999) demonstrates the value of non-discrimination in interest taxation when governments have to contend with the problem of tax evasion. More specifically, they examine a situation where governments collect taxes from two types of bases only one of which is mobile internationally. They show that if governments cannot discriminate between the two bases, tax revenue of at least one country increases whereas that of the other country remains unchanged. This result contrasts with Keen (2001), who argues that restrictions on discriminatory tax regimes can lower tax revenues of all countries that adopt such restrictions. As Janeba and Smart (2003) note, Keen's model differs from that of Janeba and Peters (1999) in two key respects.First, both tax bases are imperfectly mobile in his model. Second, the size of each tax base is perfectly inelastic with respect to changes in tax levels. Bucovetsky and Haufler (2007) showthat Keen's result is robust to differences in market size across countries whereas Haupt and Peters (2005) find that his result can be reversed if firms have a bias toward investing in their home markets.[12]

2. BASIC MODEL

We consider a world comprised of two countries. A single firm in each country produces good x that comes in two quality levels where s_h denotes the high quality and s_l the low quality.[13] Let $\Delta s \equiv s_h - s_l > 0$ measure the quality differential between firms. Let country H produce the high quality and country L the low quality. For now, we assume that both qualities are produced at zero cost (Section 5 relaxes this assumption).

Under autarky (i.e., the absence of trade), each country is served only by its local firm whereas under free trade both firms serve both markets. When both qualities are available, consumers choose among them as well as whether to make a purchase at all. If a consumer buys quality j at price p_j, his utility is given by

$$u = \theta s_j - p_j \quad \text{where} \quad j = h, l. \tag{1}$$

Utility under no purchase is normalized to zero and $\theta \geq 0$ is a taste parameter. As is clear from the above specification, all consumers prefer high quality for a

[12] Finally, we should note that this paper is also related to the literature on tax incidence under oligopoly—see, for example, Anderson et al. (2001a, 2001b). However, whereas we focus on the implications of NT, this literature examines the efficiency properties of ad valorem versus specific excise taxes and explores the extent to which both types of taxes are passed on to consumers under oligopoly.

[13] In a classic paper, Shaked and Sutton (1982) have shown that as long as there exists an arbitrarily small cost of entry and consumer incomes are uniformly distributed over $0 < a \leq b$, only two different quality levels are sold in equilibrium when $b < 4a$. Intuitively, entering firms choose to produce goods of different quality in order to soften price competition—hence the concept of a "natural oligopoly" (see Shaked and Sutton, 1984). Motta (1993) has shown that this result extends to the case of quantity competition.

given price but those with a higher θ value quality relatively more. In the following analysis we assume that θ is uniformly distributed over $[0, \mu^i]$ in country i with density 1 so that $\mu^i \geq 1$ measures country i's market size.

2.1. *Autarkic Equilibrium.* Under autarky, given the sales tax rate t^i (which may be negative) chosen by its government, the local firm in country i chooses its price p^i to maximize its profits. Given prices, consumers in the range $[\theta^i, \mu^i]$ buy the local good in country i where $\theta^i = \frac{p^i}{s_i}$. Let the demand curve facing firm i be given by $x^i(p^i)$. Firm i chooses p^i to maximize its profit π^i:

$$\max_{p^i} \pi^i = (p^i - t^i)x^i = (p^i - t^i)\left(\mu^i - \frac{p^i}{s_i}\right),$$

which gives the autarkic equilibrium price as

$$p^{ia} = \frac{\mu^i s_i + t^i}{2}. \tag{2}$$

Consumer surplus in country i equals

$$cs^i = \int_{\theta^i}^{\mu^i} (s_i\theta - p^{ia})\, d\theta = \left[s_i\frac{\theta^2}{2} - p^{ia}\theta\right]_{\theta^i}^{\mu^i} = (\mu^i - \theta^i)\left[\frac{s_i(\mu^i + \theta^i)}{2} - p^{ia}\right],$$

and the government's tax revenue is $t^i x^i$. Country i's government chooses its sales tax t^i to maximize local welfare, defined as the sum of consumer surplus, firm profits, and tax revenue:

$$\max_{t^i} w^i(t^i) = cs^i + \pi^i + t^i x^i, \tag{3}$$

which gives the optimal autarkic policy

$$t^{ia} = -\mu^i s_i, \tag{4}$$

i.e., achieving the first best outcome under autarky requires each country to subsidize its firm. This optimal autarkic subsidy t^{ia} eliminates the deadweight loss of the local monopoly. Under t^{ia}, we have $p^{ia} = 0$ and $x^i = \mu^i$. In other words, under the optimal subsidy all consumers purchase the good at marginal cost (which is zero). By contrast, in the absence of this subsidy we have $\theta^i|_{t^i=0} = \frac{p^i}{s_i}|_{t^i=0} = \frac{\mu^i s_i}{2s_i} = \frac{\mu^i}{2}$, so that only half the market is covered when $t^i = 0$.

2.2. *Benchmark Analysis: Free Trade and Laissez-Faire.* Now consider a situation where countries do not impose tariffs and/or other trade restrictions on one another but levy internal taxes on firms.[14] Let t_j^i denote country i's internal tax

[14] Like in Horn (2006), only a country's total tax burden on a product matters in our model—i.e., if import tariffs were not equal to zero, optimal internal taxes would have to be modified accordingly. Thus, allowing for positive tariffs would not affect our analysis.

(which may be negative) on good j, where $i = H, L$ and $j = h, l$. Country i's policy vector is denoted by $\mathbf{t}^i = (t_l^i, t_h^i)$. The global policy vector $(\mathbf{t}^L, \mathbf{t}^H)$ is determined by the following three-stage game. At the first stage, the two countries jointly decide whether or not to sign a binding NT agreement under which they both commit to practicing non-discrimination with respect to their internal taxes.[15] Next, given the policy regime in place, countries choose their respective tax policies. Finally, firms compete in prices and international trade takes place. Like much of related literature, we assume that each firm chooses a separate price for its domestic sales and for its exports (i.e., markets are segmented). To find the sub-game perfect Nash equilibrium of this policy game, we solve the model by backwards induction.

Given consumer preferences specified in (1), under free trade, country i's consumers can be partitioned into three groups on the basis of two threshold parameters θ_l^i and θ_h^i: those in the range $[0, \theta_l^i)$ buy neither high nor low quality, those in $[\theta_l^i, \theta_h^i)$ buy low quality, and those in $[\theta_h^i, \mu^i]$ buy high quality, where

$$\theta_l^i = \frac{p_l^i}{s_l} \quad \text{and} \quad \theta_h^i = \frac{p_h^i - p_l^i}{\Delta s}.$$

Using these threshold parameters, demand functions in country i for the two qualities are as follows:

$$x_j^i(p_l^i, p_h^i) = \begin{cases} \theta_h^i - \theta_l^i = \dfrac{p_h^i - p_l^i}{\Delta s} - \dfrac{p_l^i}{s_l} & \text{if } j = l \\[2ex] \mu^i - \theta_h^i = \mu^i - \dfrac{p_h^i - p_l^i}{\Delta s} & \text{if } j = h. \end{cases} \tag{5}$$

Given these demand functions and tax rates implemented by governments, firms choose prices to maximize their respective profits. In country i, firm l solves

$$\max_{p_l^i} \pi_l^i(p_l^i, p_h^i) = (p_l^i - t_l^i) x_l^i(p_l^i, p_h^i) = (p_l^i - t_l^i)\left(\frac{p_h^i - p_l^i}{\Delta s} - \frac{p_l^i}{s_l}\right),$$

whereas firm h solves

$$\max_{p_h^i} \pi_h^i(p_l^i, p_h^i) = (p_h^i - t_h^i) x_h^i(p_l^i, p_h^i) = (p_h^i - t_h^i)\left(\mu^i - \frac{p_h^i - p_l^i}{\Delta s}\right).$$

The first-order conditions for the above maximization problems yield the reaction functions of firms:

$$p_l^i = \frac{p_h^i s_l + t_l^i s_h}{2 s_h} \quad \text{and} \quad p_h^i = \frac{\mu^i \Delta s + p_l^i + t_h^i}{2} \tag{6}$$

[15] By assumption, countries have access to a mechanism via which they are able to commit to NT. In the real world, such commitment can be enforced via the WTO's dispute settlement system.

As expected, these reaction functions are upward sloping.[16] Equilibrium prices in country i in terms of tax levels and quality parameters are

$$(7)\qquad p_l^i = \frac{\mu^i s_l \Delta s + 2t_l^i s_h + s_l t_h^i}{3s_h + \Delta s} \quad \text{and} \quad p_h^i = \frac{s_h(2\mu^i \Delta s + 2t_h^i + t_l^i)}{3s_h + \Delta s}.$$

Inspection of (7) reveals that prices in country i are increasing in its taxes (t_h^i and t_l^i) as well as in its market size (μ^i).[17] Before deriving equilibrium policies, we briefly discuss market equilibrium in the absence of any government intervention. Let $\mathbf{0} \equiv (0, 0)$ denote the laissez-faire equilibrium (i.e., $t_l^i = t_h^i = 0$).

LEMMA 1. *Under laissez-faire (i) neither market is fully covered (i.e., $\sum_j x_j^i(\mathbf{0}) \leq \mu^i$), (ii) both firms produce positive quantities, and (iii) the high-quality firm charges a higher price and sells more than the low-quality firm in each market.*

The equilibrium under laissez-faire is inefficient due to two reasons. First, since the marginal cost of production is zero (while $\theta \geq 0$) efficiency requires that the market be fully covered—i.e., all consumers should be served. However, this does not occur in equilibrium since firms exploit their market power and restrict their output levels (i.e., there is an *underproduction* problem). Second, since both qualities are equally costly to produce, it is socially optimal to produce only the high quality. However, the laissez-faire equilibrium suffers from *allocative inefficiency* since both firms sell positive quantities. These are important points to which we return later.

3. EQUILIBRIUM POLICIES AND NATIONAL TREATMENT

If country i does not commit to a NT agreement it is free to discriminate between firms. Let profit of country i's firm in its domestic market be denoted by $\pi_d^i(t_l^i, t_h^i)$ and its export profit by $\pi_e^i(t_l^j, t_h^j)$.[18]

3.1. *Nash Equilibrium Without National Treatment.* In the absence of NT, country i chooses its tax vector to maximize its aggregate national welfare:

$$(8)\qquad \max_{t_l^i, t_h^i} w^i(\mathbf{t}^L, \mathbf{t}^H) = \sum_j cs_j^i(t_l^i, t_h^i) + \sum_j t_j^i x_j^i + \pi_d^i(t_l^i, t_h^i) + \pi_e^i(t_l^j, t_h^j).$$

The demand functions in (5) can be used to calculate consumer surplus in country i over the two qualities:

[16] Note that whereas the slope of the high-quality firm's reaction function equals 1/2, the slope of the low-quality firm's reaction function is $\frac{s_l}{2s_h} < \frac{1}{2}$—i.e., the high-quality firm is relatively more aggressive in increasing its price in response to an increase in its rival's price.

[17] If $\Delta s = 0$ the above price equilibrium reduces to the standard Bertrand equilibrium, where the firm facing the lower tax monopolizes the market by pricing at its rival's marginal cost (which is its tax rate).

[18] Since markets are segmented, a firm's profit in a given country depends only on the taxes of that country.

$$cs^i(t_l^i, t_h^i) = \sum_j cs_j^i(t_l^i, t_h^i) = \int_{\theta_l^i}^{\theta_h^i} (s_l\theta - p_l^i)\, d\theta + \int_{\theta_h^i}^{\mu^i} (s_h\theta - p_h^i)\, d\theta,$$

which simplifies to

$$cs_l^i(t_l^i, t_h^i) = (\theta_h^i - \theta_l^i)\left[\frac{s_l(\theta_h^i + \theta_l^i)}{2} - p_l^i\right] \quad \text{and}$$

$$cs_h^i(t_l^i, t_h^i) = (\mu^i - \theta_h^i)\left[\frac{s_h(\mu^i + \theta_h^i)}{2} - p_h^i\right].$$

Let $\sigma^i(t_l^i, t_h^i)$ denote country i's local surplus:

$$\sigma^i(t_l^i, t_h^i) = \sum_j cs_j^i(t_l^i, t_h^i) + \sum_j t_j^i x_j^i + \pi_d^i(t_l^i, t_h^i).$$

Country i's aggregate welfare can then be written as the sum of its local surplus and export profits

$$w^i(\mathbf{t}^L, \mathbf{t}^H) = \sigma^i(t_l^i, t_h^i) + \pi_e^i(t_l^j, t_h^j).$$

Let $\mathbf{t}^{i*} = (t_l^{i*}, t_h^{i*})$ denote country i's equilibrium tax vector in the absence of a NT agreement and let p_j^{i*} and x_j^{i*} denote the equilibrium price and quantity of good j in country i under $(\mathbf{t}^{L*}, \mathbf{t}^{H*})$. Solving the problems in (8) yields

$$\mathbf{t}^{L*} = (t_l^{L*}, t_h^{L*}) = \left(-\frac{2\mu^L s_l \Delta s}{3 s_h}, \frac{\mu^L \Delta s}{3}\right) \tag{9}$$

and

$$\mathbf{t}^{H*} = (t_l^{H*}, t_h^{H*}) = (0, -\mu^H \Delta s). \tag{10}$$

In what follows, unless otherwise noted, we normalize $\mu^L = 1$.

Proposition 1. *If countries do not sign a NT agreement, (i) they both subsidize their own firms ($t_i^{i*} < 0$), but their respective subsidies are smaller in magnitude than those under autarky (i.e., $|t_i^{i*}| < |t^{ia}|$); (ii) while country H imposes no tax on the low-quality foreign firm ($t_l^{H*} = 0$), country L taxes the high-quality foreign firm ($t_h^{L*} > 0$); (iii) the low-quality firm is shut out of country H's market ($x_l^{H*} = 0$) but has a larger market share of its own market ($0 < x_h^{L*} < x_l^{L*}$); and (iv) both markets are fully covered ($\sum_j x_j^{i*} = \mu^i$).*

To understand Proposition 1 first note that a country's optimal policy balances the following trade-off. On the one hand, each country has an incentive to subsidize its own firm to correct the underproduction problem. On the other hand, each

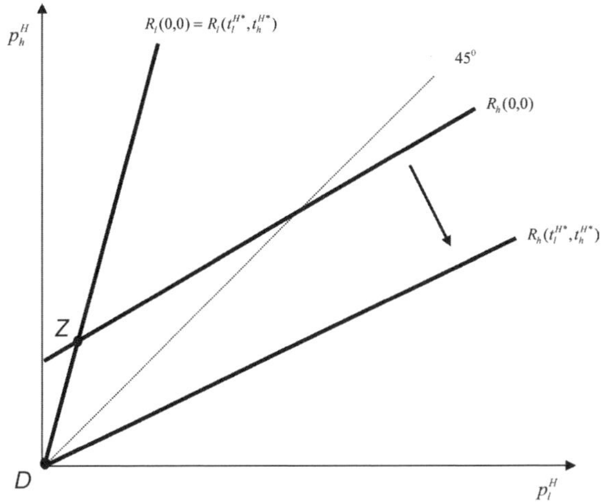

FIGURE 1

DISCRIMINATION VERSUS LAISSEZ-FAIRE IN COUNTRY *H*

would like to tax imports to extract rents from the foreign firm as well as to confer a strategic advantage on its own firm. A country's subsidy to its local firm is smaller under trade relative to autarky because the subsidy *softens* price competition and undermines the ability to extract rents from the foreign firm—all else equal, the subsidy shifts down the local firm's reaction function resulting in lower equilibrium prices for *both* firms. Figure 1 shows the effects of country *H*'s equilibrium policy on the product market: Prices of both qualities drop to marginal cost (i.e., the equilibrium moves from *Z* to *D*). In Figures 1 and 2, the reaction function of firm *j* is denoted by $R_j(.)$.

Even though country *H* does not tax the low-quality foreign firm, the subsidy it gives to its high-quality domestic firm is just enough to make the latter's price equal to that of the low-quality firm. Given equal prices, consumers prefer to buy only the high quality. On the other hand, country *L*'s optimal tax schedule results in a price differential in favor of the low quality and both qualities sell in its market. Figure 2 shows that country *L*'s equilibrium policy shifts the product market equilibrium from *Z* to *D*.

Part (*ii*) of Proposition 1 obtains because country *L*'s incentive to extract rents from the foreign firm is relatively stronger since the high-quality firm charges a higher price and sells more than the low-quality firm under laissez-faire (i.e., makes a much larger profit than the low-quality firm, part of which country *L* can extract via a tax).

Part (*iii*) is a straightforward consequence of the nature of equilibrium policies and it implies that in country *H*'s market, the allocative inefficiency that prevails under laissez-faire is eliminated since the low-quality firm is shut out of its market.

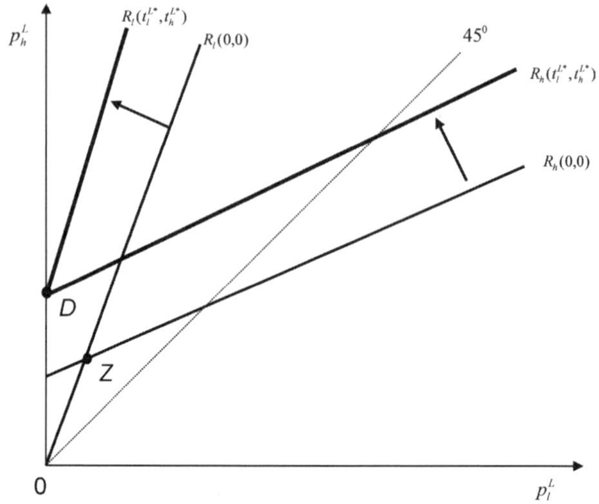

FIGURE 2

DISCRIMINATION VERSUS LAISSEZ-FAIRE IN COUNTRY *L*

However, such is not the case in country *L*'s market since it subsidizes its own firm and taxes the high-quality foreign firm. In fact, in equilibrium, the effective price collected by the high-quality firm in country *L*'s market is only half the equilibrium price (i.e., $t_h^{L*} = p_h^{L*}/2$)—i.e., half the burden of the tax t_h^{L*} falls on the shoulders of the high-quality firm, making it possible for country *L* to extract some rents in equilibrium. Thus, country *L* accepts a certain level of allocative inefficiency in order to shift some rents to its local firm. Part (*iv*) of Proposition 1 implies that, despite the presence of beggar-thy-neighbor motives, Nash equilibrium policies under tax discrimination *fully correct* the underproduction problem in each country. As a result, consumer surplus in country *i* is greater under discrimination relative to laissez-faire: $cs^i(t_l^{i*}, t_h^{i*}) > cs^i(0, 0)$. Furthermore, discriminatory policies increase profits of each firm in its local market while reducing them abroad: $\pi_d^i(t_l^{i*}, t_h^{i*}) > \pi_d^i(0, 0)$ and $\pi_e^i(t_l^{j*}, t_h^{j*}) < \pi_e^i(0, 0)$.

3.2. *A National Treatment Agreement.* Now suppose that countries do sign a reciprocal NT agreement in the first stage of the game. Under such an agreement, each country imposes the same internal tax on its domestic firm and its foreign rival. Let country *i*'s equilibrium NT tax be denoted by t^{iN}:

$$t^{iN} = \arg\max w^i\left(t_l^i, t_h^i\right) \text{ subject to } t_l^i = t_h^i. \tag{11}$$

Solving the problems in (11) yields:

Proposition 2. *Equilibrium policies under a NT agreement are* $t^{HN} = t^{LN} = 0$.

Thus, a NT agreement generates the laissez-faire equilibrium! The intuition for this surprising result is as follows. Without the constraint imposed by NT, each country subsidizes its local firm while taxing the foreign firm (Proposition 1). When forced to treat the two firms in a non-discriminatory fashion, each country finds it optimal to adopt the "middle ground" of zero taxes. The sharp nature of the result is partly an artifact of the assumptions underlying the model, particularly those of a uniform distribution of consumers and zero production costs. As we show later, when the higher quality is costly to produce, NT does not result in laissez-faire but rather in each country picking a tax rate that is bound by its two discriminatory tax rates.

Do the two countries ever find it in their mutual interest to commit to a NT agreement? If so, when? From each country's perspective, the benefit of a NT agreement is the gain in export profits that result from the elimination of tax discrimination in the foreign country ($\Delta\pi_e^i(\mathbf{t}^{j*}) \equiv \pi_e^i(\mathbf{0}) - \pi_e^i(\mathbf{t}^{j*}) > 0$) whereas the cost is the reduction in domestic surplus that results from forsaking tax discrimination itself ($\Delta\sigma^i(\mathbf{t}^{i*}) \equiv \sigma^i(\mathbf{0}) - \sigma^i(\mathbf{t}^{i*}) < 0$). Let country i's net gain from a NT agreement be defined by

$$\Delta w^i(\mathbf{t}^{L*}, \mathbf{t}^{H*}) \equiv w^i(\mathbf{0}, \mathbf{0}) - w^i(\mathbf{t}^{L*}, \mathbf{t}^{H*}) \tag{12}$$

$$= \Delta\sigma^i(\mathbf{t}^{i*}) + \Delta\pi_e^i(\mathbf{t}^{j*}). \tag{13}$$

As might be expected, the costs and benefits of a NT agreement are not uniform across countries since the agreement does not alter their discriminatory tax policies in the same fashion. From country H's perspective, a change from discrimination to NT by country L lowers its cost of selling abroad (country L eliminates the tax t_h^{L*}) while simultaneously increasing the cost of its foreign rival (country L eliminates the subsidy t_l^{L*}). Both these policy changes increase export profits of the high-quality firm. However, from country L's perspective a NT agreement *only* raises its rival's cost (country H eliminates the subsidy t_h^{H*}) *without* altering its *own* cost of exporting (since $t_l^{H*} = t^{HN} = 0$). Thus, the export profit gain from NT is relatively larger for country H. Furthermore, whereas country H's cost of agreeing to a NT agreement (i.e., $|\Delta\sigma^H|$) increases in μ^H making it less willing to sign such an agreement, country L's *benefit* of signing the agreement (i.e., $\Delta\pi_e^L$) increases in μ^H.[19]

In fact, it is straightforward to show that

$$\Delta w^L(\mathbf{t}^{L*}, \mathbf{t}^{H*}) > 0 \quad \text{iff } \mu^H > \underline{\mu}(s_l, s_h) \equiv \left[\frac{(3s_h + \Delta s)(s_h + 2s_l)}{6s_h s_l}\right]^{\frac{1}{2}}$$

[19] Two things are worth noting. First, recall that we have normalized $\mu^L = 1$. If μ^L were allowed to vary, it would obviously have analogous effects on $|\Delta\sigma^L|$ and $\Delta\pi_e^H$. Second, $\Delta\pi_e^i$ is independent of μ^i just as $|\Delta\sigma^i|$ is independent of μ^j: own market size does not affect a country's export profit (or changes in it) whereas foreign market size does not affect its domestic surplus (or changes in it).

whereas

$$\Delta w^H(\mathbf{t}^{L*}, \mathbf{t}^{H*}) > 0 \quad \text{iff } \mu^H < \bar{\mu}(s_l, s_h) \equiv \left[\frac{2(9s_h + \Delta s)(2s_h + s_l)}{9s_h(3s_h + \Delta s)}\right]^{\frac{1}{2}}.$$

PROPOSITION 3. *Country L gains from a NT agreement iff country H's market is bigger than the critical threshold* $\underline{\mu}(s_l, s_h)$ *whereas country H gains iff its market is smaller than the critical threshold* $\bar{\mu}(s_l, s_h)$.

Using $\Delta s > 0$, it is trivial to show that $\underline{\mu}(s_l, s_h) > 1$. Since μ^L has been normalized to 1, this implies that unless the underlying asymmetry in the quality of goods produced by the two countries is *counterbalanced* to some degree by asymmetry between their market sizes, a NT agreement may fail to materialize in equilibrium. More specifically, we can show the following:

COROLLARY 1. *If* $\mu^L \geq \mu^H$ *then country L loses from a NT agreement whereas country H gains:* $\Delta w^L(\mathbf{t}^{L*}, \mathbf{t}^{H*})|_{\mu^H \leq \mu^L} < 0 < \Delta w^H(\mathbf{t}^{L*}, \mathbf{t}^{H*})|_{\mu^H \leq \mu^L}$.

Thus, when $\mu^L \geq \mu^H$ a NT agreement does *not* arise in equilibrium. Note that this is true even when market size is symmetric across countries (i.e., $\mu^H = \mu^L = 1$). Given this, for the remainder of the paper, we restrict attention to the case where $\mu^L \leq \mu^H$.

Proposition 3 implies that a NT agreement arises in equilibrium iff $\Delta\mu^H(s_l, s_h) \equiv \bar{\mu}(s_l, s_h) - \underline{\mu}(s_l, s_h) > 0$. Differentiation yields

$$\frac{\partial \Delta\mu^H(s_l, s_h)}{\partial s_h} < 0 < \frac{\partial \Delta\mu^H(s_l, s_h)}{\partial s_l},$$

i.e., the higher the quality differential between firms, the *less* likely it is that a NT agreement can be sustained in equilibrium. Figure 3 illustrates the region over which a NT agreement benefits both countries and is therefore an equilibrium.

Since $\Delta s > 0$, in Figure 3 only the region above the 45 degree line (i.e., $\Delta s = 0$) is feasible (this is the lowest line). Along the $\Delta\mu^H = 0$ curve we have $\underline{\mu} = \bar{\mu}$ and both countries are indifferent to a NT agreement whereas below this curve, a NT agreement arises in equilibrium. Recall that NT in the WTO is required only for "like" products. In this context, it is reassuring to note that, in our model, a NT agreement emerges in equilibrium only when the quality differential between goods (Δs) is not too big.

4. GLOBAL WELFARE

Let world welfare (ww) be defined as the sum of the aggregate welfare of both countries:

$$ww(\mathbf{t}^L, \mathbf{t}^H) = \sum_i \sigma^i(t_l^i, t_h^i) + \sum_i \sum_j \pi_j^i(t_l^i, t_h^i). \tag{14}$$

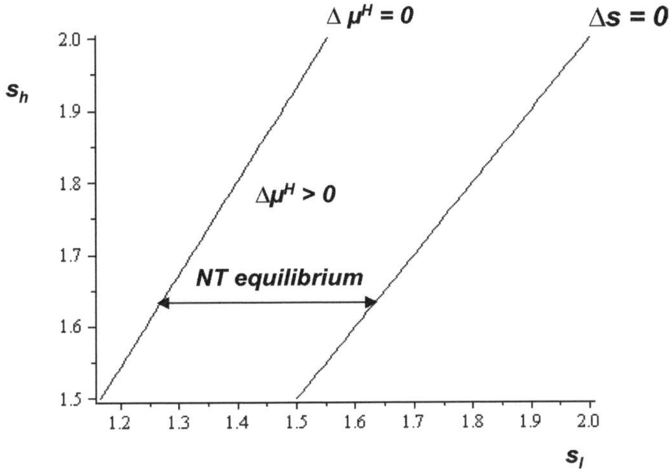

FIGURE 3

AN EQUILIBRIUM NT AGREEMENT

How does a NT agreement affect global welfare?[20] Let $\Delta ww \equiv \sum_i \Delta w^i$. Direct calculations show that:

PROPOSITION 4. *A NT agreement increases global welfare (i.e., $\Delta ww > 0$) iff $\mu^H < \mu_g^H$ where $\mu_g^H(s_l, s_h) \equiv [\frac{28s_h^2 - 5s_h s_l + 4s_l^2}{9s_h(s_h + 3\Delta s)}]^{\frac{1}{2}}$.*

The intuition for why NT does not increase global welfare when country H's market is bigger than μ_g^H is as follows. We already know from Lemma 1 that an equilibrium with zero taxes or subsidies (which is what NT generates) is not globally efficient since neither country's market is fully covered under laissez-faire. Of course, this does not imply that NT necessarily lowers world welfare relative to tax discrimination since we also need to consider how allocative efficiency fares under the two regimes. Here the news is mixed: While allocative efficiency in country L's market improves due to a NT agreement, the opposite is the case in country H. This is because, as shown below, the globally optimal discriminatory policy coincides with that of country H's individually optimal discriminatory policy. Thus, if country H's market is sufficiently big (i.e., $\mu^H > \mu_g^H$), the global welfare loss implied by the reduced allocative efficiency in its market under NT dominates the corresponding gain in country L's market leading to a decline in overall global

[20] Incidentally, due to market segmentation, globally optimal policies coincide with those that each country would adopt if both firms were domestic (i.e., the profits of the foreign firm were to count as part of a country's welfare function). Thus, the analysis of global welfare also allows us to understand the role national origin of firms plays in determining each country's optimal policy.

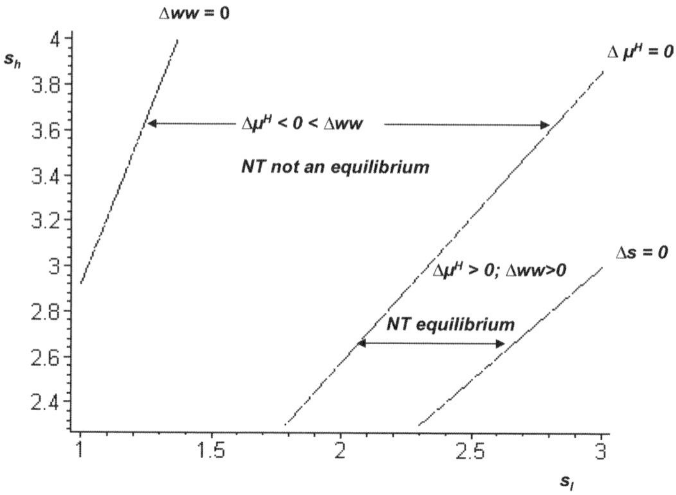

FIGURE 4

WELFARE EFFECTS OF A NT AGREEMENT

welfare. Furthermore, it is straightforward to show that NT increases global welfare when market size is symmetric across countries (i.e., $\mu^H = 1$).

By design, in our model a NT agreement emerges in equilibrium iff it makes both countries better off (and therefore increases aggregate world welfare). The above proposition implies that there potentially exist parameter values over which NT is welfare-improving but fails to emerge as an equilibrium. Figure 4 illustrates this possibility.

Figure 4 essentially superimposes the iso-welfare curve $\Delta ww = 0$ on Figure 3. Along $\Delta ww = 0$, world welfare is equal under NT and tax discrimination; below it NT improves welfare whereas the opposite is true above it. Recall from Figure 3 that a NT agreement is an equilibrium below the $\Delta\mu^H = 0$ curve and above the 45 degree line (which is $\Delta s = 0$). Thus, above the $\Delta\mu^H = 0$ curve and below the $\Delta ww = 0$ curve a NT agreement fails to emerge in equilibrium even though NT yields higher aggregate world welfare than tax discrimination. In this region, the loss that country L suffers from such an agreement is less than the gain that accrues to country H and if international transfers were feasible, a NT agreement could be sustained in equilibrium.

Our analysis assumes that under a NT agreement, countries choose taxes non-cooperatively to maximize their own welfare. Although this is a reasonable assumption for tax policies of sovereign nations, it is useful to briefly consider the case where countries choose taxes cooperatively to maximize aggregate global welfare. Let t_j^w denote the globally optimal tax imposed on firm j. We have:

PROPOSITION 5. *The globally optimal policy for country H coincides with its individually optimal policy* ($t_l^{Hw} = t_l^{H*} = 0$ *and* $t_h^{Hw} = t_h^{H*} = -\mu^H \Delta s$) *whereas the globally optimal policy for country L calls for a zero tax on the low-quality firm as opposed to a subsidy* ($t_l^{Lw} = 0 > t_l^{L*} = -\frac{2s_l \Delta s}{3s_h}$) *and a positive subsidy for the high-quality firm as opposed to a tax* ($t_h^{Lw} = -\Delta s < 0 < t_h^{L*} = \Delta s/3$). *Furthermore, both markets are fully covered by the high-quality good under globally optimal policies* ($x_h^{iw} = \mu^i$).

The result that only the high-quality good is sold in both markets under globally optimal tax policies follows from the assumption that the cost of production of both goods is the same (i.e., equals zero). As a result, it is socially optimal to provide the high-quality good to all consumers.[21] Note that even under tax discrimination, equilibrium price of the low quality drops to zero. However, the high quality sells for a strictly positive price under tax discrimination, whereas it sells at zero price under socially optimal policies. Note also that country L's discriminatory tax policy distorts the global equilibrium away from the first-best since the low-quality good continues to be sold in its market.

5. COSTLY PRODUCTION OF HIGH QUALITY

Our benchmark model assumes that both qualities can be produced at zero cost. It seems useful to examine a scenario where the high quality is costlier to produce. Let the marginal cost of production of high quality be given by $c > 0$.[22] Now, social optimality requires that a consumer with taste parameter θ should be provided the high quality only if

$$\theta s_h - c > \theta s_l \Leftrightarrow \theta > \theta_w \equiv \frac{c}{\Delta s}, \tag{15}$$

which implies that consumers in the interval $[\theta_w, \mu^i]$ should get the high quality whereas those in $[0, \theta_w)$ range should get the low quality. To rule out the uninteresting case where it is socially efficient to serve all consumers the low quality, we assume that $c \leq \Delta s$—i.e., the cost disadvantage of producing the high quality is outweighed by the quality differential.[23]

It is easy to show that country H's optimal subsidy under autarky equals $-\mu^H s_h + c$, which is strictly smaller than $-\mu^H s_h$ (because $c > 0$). As expected, when the high quality is costlier to produce it is optimal to subsidize it less. From (2) it follows that the autarkic equilibrium price under this subsidy equals c—i.e., it is

[21] Indeed, the only externality countries impose on each other is that their policies do not take into account the profits of foreign firms. But when $c = 0$, it is socially optimal for country H to ignore the profits of the low-quality firm. This is why the socially optimal policy under $c = 0$ is the same as that of country H's discriminatory policy vector. As is shown in Section 5, when $c > 0$, the two policies do not coincide.

[22] Section 6 considers the case where quality is endogenously determined as a result of fixed (sunk) investments by firms.

[23] From (15) it follows that it is socially optimal for sales of the high quality in country i to exceed those of the low quality iff $c < c^{iw}$ where $c^{iw} \equiv \frac{\mu^i \Delta s}{2}$.

optimal for country H to provide the high quality to only those consumers whose marginal valuation (θ) exceeds c.

Under free trade, allocative inefficiency under laissez-faire is less severe when $c > 0$ since it is optimal to supply the high quality to only consumers in the range $[\theta_w, \mu^i]$. Furthermore, Equation (15) implies that allocative efficiency under free trade requires that sales of the low quality should be equal in the two markets while more consumers should be supplied the high quality in the bigger market. This is because there are more high valuation consumers in the bigger market.

Calculations analogous to the case of $c = 0$ yield the following equilibrium under laissez-faire when $c > 0$:

$$\theta_l^i(0, 0; c) = \frac{\mu^i \Delta s + c}{3s_h + \Delta s} \quad \text{and} \quad \theta_h^i(0, 0; c) = \theta_l^i(0, 0; c)\left[1 + \frac{s_h}{\Delta s}\right].$$

Note that since $\theta_l^i(0, 0; c) > 0$, the market is once again incompletely covered in both countries. Furthermore, it is easy to show that the high quality firm's sales in country i exceed those of the low quality iff $c < c^{i*}$ where

$$c^{i*} \equiv \frac{\mu^i \Delta s}{2 + \frac{\Delta s}{s_h}}$$

and that Nash equilibrium policies under tax discrimination are as follows:

$$\mathbf{t}^{L*}(c) = (t_l^{L*}(c), t_h^{L*}(c)) = \left(-\frac{s_l(2\Delta s + c)}{3s_h}, \frac{\Delta s - c}{3}\right) \tag{16}$$

and

$$\mathbf{t}^{H*}(c) = (t_l^{H*}(c), t_h^{H*}(c)) = \left(\frac{cs_l}{3s_h}, -\frac{3s_h(\mu^H \Delta s - c) + 2cs_l}{3s_h}\right). \tag{17}$$

Note that individually optimal policies have the same qualitative nature as before (see Proposition 1): each country subsidizes its local firm while taxing the foreign one. As might be expected, the higher the cost of producing the high quality, the smaller the subsidy of country H while the larger the subsidy of country L (the opposite is true of their taxes). A larger c implies reduced profits for the high quality and larger profits for the low quality, and since taxes on foreign firms are motivated by rent extraction, it is intuitive that $t_h^{L*}(c)$ decreases in c while $t_l^{H*}(c)$ increases in it.

Now consider the effects of NT. If countries do sign a NT agreement, equilibrium policies are

$$t^{LN}(c) = -\frac{cs_l}{2s_l + s_h} \quad \text{while} \quad t^{HN}(c) = \frac{cs_l}{3s_h}. \tag{18}$$

Thus, under NT, country L subsidizes both firms while country H taxes both of them. This result is a simple generalization of Proposition 2 (which applies for $c = 0$). Under costly production of the high quality, individually optimal subsidy of country H to its own firm is low relative to the case of $c = 0$ whereas that of country L is high. Under a NT agreement, the middle ground policy now ends up being a subsidy for country L whereas its a tax for country H. Intuitively, costly production of the high quality reduces the rent extraction motive of country L while having the opposite effect on country H. At the same time, the allocative inefficiency under laissez-faire is less pronounced when production is costly. These altered underlying incentives then translate into equilibrium NT policies described in (18) above.

It is straightforward to show that the maximization of global welfare under $c > 0$ requires the following policies:

(19)
$$t_l^{Lw}(c) = t_l^{Hw}(c) = -\frac{cs_l}{s_h} \quad \text{and} \quad t_h^{Lw}(c) = -(\Delta s - c)$$
$$\text{and } t_h^{Hw}(c) = -(\mu^H \Delta s - c).$$

As before, under globally optimal policies, both firms are subsidized (since $\Delta s > c > 0$) and the higher quality firm gets a bigger subsidy so long as its cost is not too high. Furthermore, under these policies both markets are fully covered and the allocation of sales across firms is efficient—in both countries, the low quality is purchased by consumers in the $[0, \theta_w)$ range whereas the rest of the consumers buy the high quality. As might be expected, each country's subsidy to the low quality is increasing in c whereas that to the high quality is decreasing. Finally, it is straightforward to show that when $c > 0$ and $\mu^H = \mu^L = 1$, NT can now be an equilibrium. This result contrasts with Corollary 1, which says that NT is not an equilibrium when $c = 0$ and $\mu^H = \mu^L = 1$. Intuitively, when $c > 0$ the product market advantage enjoyed by country H is not as significant and market size asymmetry is no longer necessary to offset the quality disadvantage suffered by country L in order to induce it to sign a NT agreement.

Thus far, we have assumed that the quality of goods is exogenously given. We now endogenize quality.

6. NT UNDER ENDOGENOUS QUALITY

In this section, we analyze interaction between investments in quality improvement by firms and tax levels set by governments in the following four-stage game. In the first-stage, countries decide whether or not to sign a binding NT agreement. In the second stage, firms simultaneously choose their R&D investments that determine the quality of their respective goods. Next, given the tax regime and quality levels, each country chooses the level(s) of its respective taxes/subsidies to maximize its own welfare. Finally, given qualities and tax levels, firms compete in prices in both markets.[24]

[24] The timing of this game captures the idea that quality choices of firms are long-run decisions (and are harder to change) relative to the specific tax levels chosen by governments but are relatively easier to modify than the nature of the tax policy regime (NT or discrimination) that is in place. Intuitively, the underlying policy regime is based on a binding international agreement, and the successful negotiation of such agreements in the real world often requires substantial time and effort. Furthermore, this timing structure allows us to *isolate* the role regime choice plays in influencing quality decisions.

The subsequent analysis adopts the most widely used specification for quality choice: To obtain the quality level s, country H's firm has to incur the fixed cost $\frac{s^2}{2}$ whereas country L's firm incurs the cost $\frac{\gamma s^2}{2}$, where $\gamma \geq 1$. As in Herguera et al. (2002), Motta et al. (1997), and Motta (1993), R&D investment costs are sunk at the output stage. It is well known from existing literature that when firms are symmetric (i.e., $\gamma = 1$), this R&D game has two equilibria: one where country H's firm produces the high quality and country L's firm the low quality and another where their roles are reversed. However, when firms are asymmetric with respect to R&D costs (i.e., $\gamma > 1$), following Moraga-González and Viaene (2005) and Motta et al. (1997), it is straightforward to show that only the equilibrium under which the low cost firm produces the high quality satisfies the risk dominance criterion of Harsanyi and Selten (1988).[25] The intuition behind this argument is that the low cost R&D firm's incentive to become the high-quality firm is much stronger than that of the high cost R&D firm, and both firms take this into account when forming subjective probabilities of each other's behavior. It is also worth noting that Zhou et al. (2002) have shown that if one of the firms is sufficiently inefficient in R&D (i.e., if γ is big enough), there exists only one equilibrium and under it the high cost firm produces the low quality and the low cost firm the high quality.[26] In what follows, we maintain continuity with existing literature and focus on the equilibrium where the firm with the lower R&D cost (i.e., country H's firm) produces the high quality.

To determine how NT affects quality choice, we first derive endogenous qualities under tax discrimination. Note that our tax analysis in Section 3.1 remains relevant since it applies for arbitrarily given quality levels. To analytically highlight the role of market size asymmetry, we fix $c = 0$.

6.1. *R&D Competition.* Under tax discrimination, the formulas for equilibrium tax rates $\mathbf{t}^{L*}$ and $\mathbf{t}^{H*}$ are given by equations (9) and (10). While choosing their R&D investments, firms anticipate the effects of their investment choices on tax policies of governments. Let $s_h > s_l$ and consider the quality choice of the high quality firm

$$\max_{s_h} \Pi^h(s_l, s_h) \equiv \pi_d^h(s_l, s_h; \mathbf{t}^{H*}) + \pi_e^h(s_l, s_h; \mathbf{t}^{L*}) - \frac{s_h^2}{2} \tag{20}$$

where $\pi_d^h(s_l, s_h)$ is the high quality firm's domestic profit and $\pi_e^h(s_l, s_h)$ its export profit. To ease exposition define

$$\mu^w \equiv 1 + (\mu^H)^2 \quad \text{and} \quad \mu^m \equiv \mu^w + 8(\mu^H)^2 \tag{21}$$

[25] These calculations are omitted here to conserve space and are available from the authors upon request.

[26] Using the approach of Zhou et al. (2002), it is straightforward to show in our model that if $\gamma > 2.13$ then country L's firm necessarily produces the low quality in equilibrium since the configuration where it produces the high quality and country H the low quality is susceptible to leapfrogging.

where μ^w is simply the sum of the squares of the market size in each country and serves as a measure of the size of the world market. After substituting for the optimal tax rates from (9) and (10), this problem can be written as

$$\max_{s_h} \Pi^h(s_l, s_h) \equiv \frac{\mu^m \Delta s}{9} - \frac{s_h^2}{2}, \tag{22}$$

where $\mu^m \equiv \mu^w + 8(\mu^H)^2$. Similarly, the problem facing the low quality firm is given by

$$\max_{s_l} \Pi^l(s_l, s_h) = \frac{4s_l \Delta s}{9s_h} - \frac{\gamma s_l^2}{2}. \tag{23}$$

Taking the first-order conditions and solving them simultaneously yields the following quality levels under tax discrimination:

$$\mathbf{s}^* = \left(s_l^*, s_h^*\right) = \left(\frac{4\mu^m}{9(\gamma\mu^m + 8)}, \frac{\mu^m}{9}\right). \tag{24}$$

Denote the equilibrium profit of firm i under tax discrimination by $\Pi^i(s_l^*, s_h^*)$. As Motta (1993) has noted, for $\mathbf{s}^* = (s_l^*, s_h^*)$ to constitute a Nash equilibrium the following four inequalities must hold:

$$\Pi^l\left(s_l^*, s_h^*\right) \geq \Pi^l\left(s_l, s_h^*\right) \quad \text{for } s_l \leq s_h^* \tag{25}$$

$$\Pi^l\left(s_l^*, s_h^*\right) \geq \Pi^h\left(s_l, s_h^*\right) \quad \text{for } s_l \geq s_h^* \tag{26}$$

and

$$\Pi^h\left(s_l^*, s_h^*\right) \geq \Pi^h\left(s_l^*, s_h\right) \quad \text{for } s_l^* \leq s_h \tag{27}$$

$$\Pi^h\left(s_l^*, s_h^*\right) \geq \Pi^l\left(s_l^*, s_h\right) \quad \text{for } s_h \leq s_l^*. \tag{28}$$

The above inequalities are understood as follows. Given that the high-quality firm chooses s_h^*, inequality (25) checks that the optimal response of the low-quality firm is indeed s_l^*. Inequality (26) confirms that the low-quality firm has no incentive to *leapfrog* the quality chosen by the high-quality firm by choosing a quality level *above* s_h^* thereby reversing the identity of firms and becoming the high-quality firm. Similarly, given that the low-quality firm chooses s_l^*, inequality (27) confirms that the optimal response of the high-quality firm is indeed s_h^* whereas inequality (28) checks that the high-quality firm has no incentive to *undercut* the low-quality firm by choosing a quality level *below* s_l^* thereby itself becoming the low-quality firm. We show in the appendix that all four inequalities are satisfied and $\mathbf{s}^* = (s_l^*, s_h^*)$ is indeed the Nash equilibrium under tax discrimination.

Consider now the quality choice of the low-quality firm under NT. Using section 2.2, this problem can be written as

$$\text{(29)} \qquad \max_{s_l} \Pi^l(s_l, s_h) \equiv \frac{\mu^w \Delta s s_l s_h}{(3s_h + \Delta s)^2} - \frac{\gamma s_l^2}{2}.$$

Similarly, for the high-quality firm, we can write

$$\text{(30)} \qquad \max_{s_h} \Pi^h(s_l, s_h) \equiv \frac{4\mu^w \Delta s s_h^2}{(3s_h + \Delta s)^2} - \frac{s_h^2}{2}.$$

Let $\mathbf{s^N} = (s_l^N, s_h^N)$ denote the solution to the above first-order conditions under NT. Following the analysis under tax discrimination, we know that $\mathbf{s^N}$ constitutes an equilibrium pair of qualities under NT only if inequalities analogous to (25) through (28) are satisfied at $\mathbf{s^N} = (s_l^N, s_h^N)$. As before, in addition to confirming that s_l^N and s_h^N are best responses to each other, these inequalities rule out leapfrogging on the part of the low-quality firm and undercutting on the part of the high-quality firm.

As is clear from the maximization problems in (29) and (30), the aggregate profit of each firm under NT increases with μ^w—our measure of the size of the world market. Although analytical formulas for s_l^N and s_h^N for the general case are rather cumbersome, for $\gamma = 1$ we have

$$\text{(31)} \qquad \mathbf{s^N} = \left(s_l^N, s_h^N\right) = (0.048\mu^w, 0.253\mu^w).$$

As is clear from above, as long as μ^w is constant, changes in individual market sizes do not affect equilibrium quality levels. This is intuitive: Since firms have free access to both markets under NT (see Proposition 2), they care only about the aggregate size of the world market. By contrast, under tax discrimination, each firm gets preferential treatment in its own market and quality choices of firms are more sensitive to the sizes of their domestic markets.

We now compare equilibrium quality choices of firms and then derive conditions under which NT benefits both countries (and therefore emerges in equilibrium).

6.2. *A Comparison of Equilibrium Qualities.* To compare equilibrium qualities and to focus on the role of the underlying policy regime, suppose $\gamma = 1$. Then, from equations (24) and (31) note that both under tax discrimination and NT, equilibrium qualities of firms increase with an increase in μ^H—a larger market in country H implies a larger return from investing in quality improvement. Second, it is straightforward to show that the equilibrium quality differential between firms (Δs) increases with μ^H under both regimes. The underlying reason for this is follows. An increase in μ^H directly benefits the high-quality firm by increasing the number of consumers that value quality relatively more and this shifts its reaction function at the price competition stage outwards.[27] By contrast, an increase in μ^H has no direct effect on the low quality firm's reaction function at the price competition stage—from Equation (6) note that[28]

$$\frac{\partial p_h^H}{\partial \mu^H} = \Delta s/2 > 0 = \frac{\partial p_l^H}{\partial \mu^H}. \tag{32}$$

Under tax discrimination, an increase in μ^H also has a secondary effect on R&D incentives of firms that operates through the tax policies of countries.[29] In fact, recall from Proposition 1 that each government's subsidy to its local firm is proportional to local market size and the low-quality firm is shut out of country H's market. This implies that, under tax discrimination, an increase in μ^H has a direct impact on *only* the R&D incentive of the high-quality firm; the low-quality firm's R&D investment increases only as a strategic response to the high-quality firm's increase in investment. The general point is that each firm's R&D incentive is more responsive to the size of its domestic market since it receives preferential tax treatment there. As a result, as μ^H increases, s_h^* increases relatively more than s_l^*. In fact, from Equation (24), we have

$$\frac{\partial s_h^*}{\partial \mu^H} = 2\mu^H > \frac{\partial s_l^*}{\partial \mu^H} = \frac{64\mu^H}{(\gamma\mu^m + 8)^2}. \tag{33}$$

Recall from Proposition 1 that in the absence of NT, each country subsidizes only its own firm and while country L imposes a tax on the high-quality firm, country H does not do so. By contrast, under NT, both countries practise laissez-faire. Since the domestic subsidy it receives under tax discrimination is at least three times the magnitude of the tax it faces in the foreign market ($| - \mu^H \Delta s| \geq 3|\frac{\mu^L \Delta s}{3}|$), the high-quality firm's profitability under NT is lower relative to tax discrimination. From the low-quality firm's perspective, NT lowers its profits relative to discrimination iff μ^H is not too big: Under NT the low-quality firm loses the subsidy from its own government but it gains access to country H's market, something it loses completely under tax discrimination. When μ^H is big, from the low-quality firm's perspective, the higher export profits under NT more than offset its lower domestic profits: $|\Delta\pi_e^i(0,0)| > |\Delta\pi_d^i(t_l^{i*}, t_h^{i*})|$. For example, for $\gamma = 1$ we calculate that $s_l^N < s_l^*$ iff $\mu^H < 2.69$ whereas $s_h^N < s_h^*$ for all $\mu^H \geq 1$.

6.3. *An Equilibrium NT Agreement.* We are now ready to consider the first stage of the game where countries decide whether or not to sign a NT agreement. As was noted earlier, since $\gamma \geq 1$, we focus on the equilibrium where country L

[27] When $\mu^H > \mu^L$ *all* consumers in country H in the range $[\mu^H - \mu^L, \mu^H]$ value quality more than any consumer in country L.

[28] An increase in μ^H does confer an *indirect* benefit on the low-quality firm since it too ends up charging a higher price in equilibrium when the high-quality firm's reaction function shifts outwards.

[29] An equivalent effect does not arise under NT since $t^{HN} = t^{LN} = 0$.

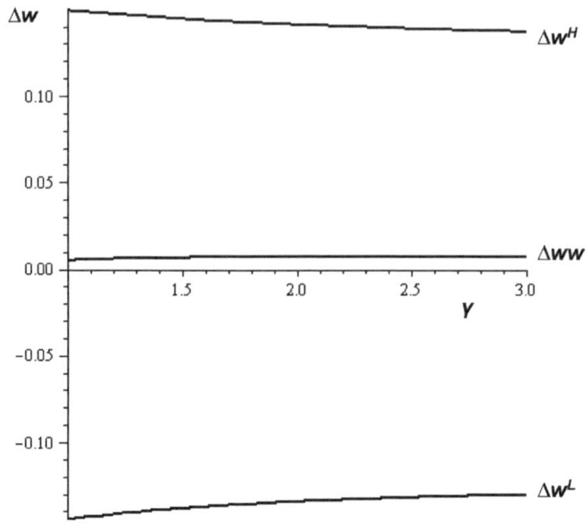

FIGURE 5

WELFARE EFFECTS OF NT—ROLE OF R&D COST ASYMMETRY

produces the low quality and country H the high quality. Let

$$\Delta w^i(\mathbf{s^N}, \mathbf{s}^*) \equiv w^i(\mathbf{s^N}) - w^i(\mathbf{s}^*) \tag{34}$$

measure the amount by which country i's welfare under a NT agreement exceeds that under tax discrimination when quality is endogenous. Similarly let the change in world welfare be measured by

$$\Delta ww(\mathbf{s^N}, \mathbf{s}^*) \equiv \sum_i \Delta w^i(\mathbf{s^N}, \mathbf{s}^*). \tag{35}$$

Straightforward calculations show that when market size is symmetric across countries (i.e., $\mu^H = \mu^L$), country H enjoys higher welfare under NT whereas country L prefers tax discrimination (i.e., $\Delta w^L < 0 < \Delta w^H$). Since analytical formulas for these changes in welfare levels are rather cumbersome, we illustrate our results graphically in Figure 5 (which is drawn for $\mu^H = \mu^L$).

Figure 5 shows that one of the major points of this paper—i.e., under market size symmetry, only the country that produces the high quality prefers NT to tax discrimination—holds even when quality is endogenously determined. Furthermore, as was true under exogenous quality, aggregate world welfare is higher under NT relative to tax discrimination when markets are symmetric (i.e., $\Delta ww > 0$).[30] The fact that aggregate world welfare improves with NT implies that when quality is endogenous and markets are symmetric, an ex post transfer from country H to

[30] Table A1 in the appendix shows that these results continue to hold when $c > 0$.

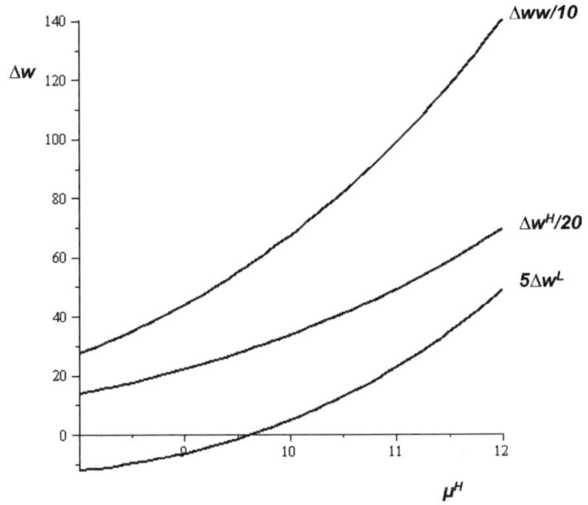

FIGURE 6

WELFARE EFFECTS OF NT—ROLE OF MARKET SIZE ASYMMETRY

country L can ensure that both countries gain from a NT agreement. If countries can commit to such a transfer up front while negotiating the agreement, a reciprocal NT would emerge in equilibrium even when $\mu^H = \mu^L$. Clearly, the minimum required transfer equals Δw^L. However, we show next that such a transfer is not always necessary when countries are asymmetric with respect to market size.

To highlight the role of market size asymmetry, in Figure 6, we fix $\gamma = 1.2$ and plot $\frac{\Delta w^H}{20}$, $5\Delta w^L$, and $\frac{\Delta ww}{10}$ as a function of μ^H. Note that re-scaling Δw^i and Δww improves exposition of Figure 6 without affecting our analysis, since what matters is whether changes in welfare levels are positive or negative.

Several observations can be made from Figure 6. First, it turns out that the high-quality country prefers NT to tax discrimination regardless of how large its market is relative to its trading partner. Thus, when quality is endogenous, the country whose firm is relatively efficient in R&D (i.e., country H) is always willing to sign a NT agreement ($\Delta w^H > 0$) whereas under exogenous quality country H benefits from a NT agreement only if its market size falls below the threshold $\bar{\mu}$ (see Proposition 3). This implies that country H's willingness to sign a NT agreement is higher when quality is endogenous. Second, and more importantly, Figure 6 shows that country L also benefits from a NT agreement if country H's market is sufficiently big ($\Delta w^L > 0$ if $\mu^H > 9.63$). This implies that when $\mu^H > 9.63$, a NT agreement is Pareto improving over tax discrimination. Finally, world welfare increases with NT regardless of μ^H (i.e. $\Delta ww > 0$), since country H's gain is large enough to dominate country L's loss even when $\mu^H < 9.63$.

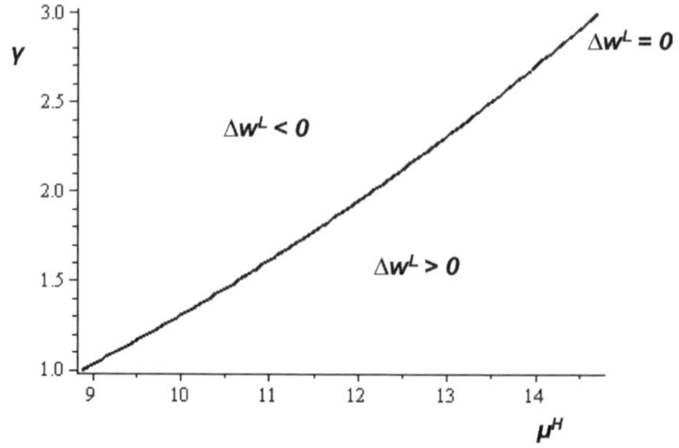

FIGURE 7

EFFECTS OF A NT AGREEMENT ON COUNTRY L

Since country L is the one that may lose from a NT agreement, it is useful to further consider how our two key parameters γ and μ^H affect Δw^L. Figure 7 plots the iso-welfare contour $\Delta w^L = 0$ in the (γ, μ^H) space. Above this contour, $\Delta w^L < 0$ whereas below it $\Delta w^L > 0$. As is clear from Figure 7, as γ increases, μ^H must increase for country L to remain indifferent between NT and tax discrimination—i.e., as country L's cost disadvantage in R&D increases, the market size of its trading partner must increase for it to remain indifferent between the two policy regimes.

7. CONCLUDING REMARKS

Though NT occupies a central place in all multilateral trade agreements administered by the WTO, analytical models that shed light on its effects are rather scarce. This paper analyzes NT in an environment where countries differ both with respect to the quality of goods that they produce as well as the size of their markets—two key dimensions along which there is substantial variation among countries. To the best of our knowledge, this is the first attempt to analyze NT in an environment where the costs and benefits of NT are asymmetric across countries. The analysis sheds light on the desirability of NT both from a global welfare perspective as well as a distributional one.

In our model, both countries have an incentive to impose discriminatory taxes that are biased against foreign firms. It seems self-evident that such an environment ought to be the natural starting point of any analysis of NT. Of course, tax discrimination can obtain even when countries are symmetric in every respect, since foreign profits typically would not enter a country's calculus of welfare-maximization. However, analyses of NT that ignore international differences in market size and technology cannot shed light on the very real possibility that

NT might not affect all countries in the same way, something that emerges quite sharply in our analysis and seems important for understanding the effects of NT in the real world. In our model, unless the high-quality country's market is relatively bigger, the low-quality country actually loses from a NT agreement. Furthermore, this result continues to hold when quality is determined endogenously as a result of strategic competition between firms. Thus, it appears that the notion of non-discrimination, which undoubtedly has much to commend it as the central principle of the WTO, may not always play to the advantage of countries with inferior technologies. Our results indicate that both in the short and the long run (i.e., a time horizon over which quality itself is endogenous), the lure of larger markets in countries that produce higher quality goods can induce smaller countries that produce lower quality goods to enter into non-discrimination agreements with them. Finally, since the long-run welfare gain from NT is always positive, there exist international transfers that can help offset any adverse effects of a NT agreement on countries that produce lower quality goods.

At the WTO, the idea of non-discrimination also manifests itself in the form of the MFN clause that requires each member country to treat like goods imported from two different sources in a non-discriminatory fashion with respect to its tariffs and other trade policies. By design, our model cannot analyze MFN, since it only contains one foreign producer. A more general model that could shed light on the role NT and MFN play together would be desirable and is worthy of future research. For analytical tractability and to focus on heterogeneity, we have chosen to analyze NT in isolation.

APPENDIX

Here, we report calculations not provided in the main text.

Lemma 1. Under laissez-faire, we have:

$$p_l^i(0,0) = \frac{\mu^i s_l \Delta s}{3s_h + \Delta s} < p_h^i(0,0) = \frac{2s_h}{s_l} p_l^i(0,0).$$

Using these prices, we can solve for the threshold taste parameters

$$\theta_l^i(0,0) = \frac{\mu^i \Delta s}{3s_h + \Delta s} < \theta_h^i(0,0) = \theta_l^i(0,0) + \frac{\mu^i s_h}{3s_h + \Delta s},$$

which yields the sales level of each firm

$$x_l^i(0,0) = \theta_h^i(0,0) - \theta_l^i(0,0) = \frac{\mu^i s_h}{3s_h + \Delta s} = \frac{x_h^i(0,0)}{2}.$$

Note that total sales in each country fall short of its market size:

$$\sum_j x_j^i(0,0) = \mu^i - \theta_l^i(0,0) \leq \mu^i \quad \text{since } \theta_l^i(0,0) \geq 0.$$

Proposition 1. Substituting $c = 0$ in the formula below delivers the proof of Proposition 1. We have

$$p_l^{L*}(c) = 0;\ p_h^{L*}(c) = \frac{2\Delta s - c}{3};\ p_h^{H*}(c) = c \quad \text{and} \quad p_l^{H*}(c) = \frac{2cs_l}{3s_h}$$

which implies

$$x_l^{L*}(c) = \frac{2\Delta s + c}{3\Delta s};\ x_h^{L*}(c) = \frac{\Delta s - c}{3\Delta s}, \quad \text{which gives } \sum_j x_j^{L*}(c) = 1$$

and

$$x_l^{H*} = \frac{c}{3\Delta s}; \quad \text{and} \quad x_h^{H*} = \mu^H - \frac{c}{3}\left[\frac{1}{\Delta s} + \frac{2}{s_h}\right]$$

which implies

$$\sum_j x_j^{H*}(c) = \mu^H - \frac{2c}{3s_h} < \mu^H \quad \text{for } c > 0.$$

Endogenous Quality. In order to show that $\mathbf{s}^* = (s_l^*, s_h^*) = (\frac{4\mu^m}{9(8+\gamma\mu^m)}, \frac{\mu^m}{9})$ constitutes a Nash equilibrium under tax discrimination, we confirm that (a) given that the high-quality firm chooses s_h^*, the optimal response of the low-quality firm is s_l^*; (b) the low-quality firm has no incentive to *leapfrog* its rival's quality level s_h^*; (c) given that the low-quality firm chooses s_l^*, the optimal response of the high-quality firm is s_h^*; and (d) the high-quality firm has no incentive to *undercut* its rival's quality level s_l^*.

(a) This is trivially satisfied since s_l^* solves the low-quality firm's first-order condition for quality choice given that its rival chooses s_h^*.

(b) If the low-quality firm chooses a quality level s higher than s_h^*, its profit function is given by

$$\Pi^h(s \mid s_h^*) = \frac{(s - s_h^*)\mu^m}{9} - \gamma\frac{s^2}{2}, \quad \text{for } s_h^* \leq s.$$

Let $s = ks_h^*$ where $k \geq 1$. Substituting for s and $s_h^* = \frac{\mu^m}{9}$ into $\Pi^h(s \mid s_h^*)$ gives

$$\Pi^h(k, \mu^m, \gamma) = -\frac{(\mu^m)^2(k^2(2\gamma - 1) - 2k + 2)}{162}.$$

Since $\Pi^h(k, \mu^m, \gamma)$ is negative for any value of $k \geq 1$, $\mu^m > 10$ and $\gamma \geq 1$, the low-quality firm has no incentive to leapfrog s_h^*:

$$\Pi^h(s, s_h^*) < 0 < \Pi^l(s_l^*, s_h^*), \quad \text{for } s_h^* \leq s.$$

TABLE A1

NT VERSUS TAX DISCRIMINATION UNDER COST HETEROGENEITY

$10c$	(s_h^*, s_l^*)	(s_h^N, s_l^N)	$\Delta w^L \times 10^{-3}$	$\Delta w^H \times 10^{-3}$	$\Delta ww \times 10^{-3}$
0	(1.1111, 0.2469)	(0.506620, 0.09648)	−144.46	149.88	5.44
0.100	(1.1083, 0.2489)	(0.506914, 0.10145)	−141.99	148.21	6.22
0.111	(1.1080, 0.2490)	(0.506921, 0.10201)	−141.71	148.02	6.31
0.125	(1.1076, 0.2494)	(0.506923, 0.10271)	−141.37	147.79	6.42
0.143	(1.1071, 0.2497)	(0.506914, 0.10362)	−140.92	147.48	6.56

(c) This is trivially satisfied since s_h^* solves the high-quality firm's first-order condition for quality choice given that its rival chooses s_l^*.

(d) If the high-quality firm chooses a quality level s lower than s_l^*, its profit function is given by

$$\Pi^l(s \mid s_l^*) = \frac{4s(s_l^* - s)}{9s_l^*} - \frac{s^2}{2}, \quad \text{for } s \leq s_l^*.$$

The function $\Pi^l(s \mid s_l^*)$ attains its maximum at $s = \frac{8+\gamma\mu^m}{18\mu^w+\gamma\mu^m} s_l^*$, where it equals $\frac{8\mu^m}{81(18\mu^w+\gamma\mu^m)}$. However, since $\Pi^h(s_l^*, s_h^*) = \frac{\gamma(\mu^m)^3}{162(8+\gamma\mu^m)} > \frac{8\mu^m}{81(18\mu^w+\gamma\mu^m)}$ for any value of $\mu^H \geq 1$ and $\gamma \geq 1$, the high-quality firm has no incentive to undercut s_l^*.

Effects of NT when $\mu^H = \mu^L$ *and* $c > 0$. Table A1 reports results for a typical case where the higher quality is costlier to produce (i.e., $c > 0$) and market size is symmetric across countries $\mu^H = \mu^L = 1$.

In addition to affirming the basic welfare results obtained for the case of $c = 0$, several other useful observations can be made from Table A1. First, as c increases, the equilibrium quality gap increases under both tax discrimination and NT. This is intuitive: As c increases, profitability of the high-quality firm shrinks while that of the low-quality firm increases and R&D investments of firms respond appropriately to these changes in profitability.

Second, the welfare loss suffered by the low-quality country from NT as well as the welfare gain enjoyed by high-quality country decrease with c. Intuitively, an increase in c partially nullifies the product market advantage of the high-quality firm and the overall welfare levels of the two countries (as well as changes in those welfare levels) converge closer to each other.

Third, the overall gain in world welfare from NT increases with c. The intuition for this is that the preferential treatment afforded under tax discrimination to the high-quality firm by its own government is socially less desirable when $c > 0$ (relative to the case where $c = 0$). As a result, the benefit of eliminating preferential treatment increases with c, making NT more attractive.

REFERENCES

ANDERSON, S., DE PALMA, A., AND B. KREIDER, "Tax Incidence in Differentiated Product Oligopoly," *Journal of Public Economics* 81 (2001a), 173–92.

——, ——, AND ——, "The Efficiency of Indirect Taxes under Imperfect Competition," *Journal of Public Economics* 81 (2001b), 231–51.

BAGWELL, K., AND R. W. STAIGER, "An Economic Theory of GATT," *American Economic Review* 89 (1999), 215–48.

——, AND ——, "Multilateral Trade Negotiations, Bilateral Opportunism and the Rules of GATT/WTO," *Journal of International Economics* 67 (2005), 268–94.

BOND, E. W., "Optimal Commercial Policy with Quality-Differentiated Products," *Journal of International Economics* 25 (1988), 271–90.

BUCOVETSKY, S., AND A. HAUFLER, "Preferential Tax Regimes with Asymmetric Countries," *National Tax Journal* 60 (2007), 789–95.

DAS, S., AND S. DONNENFELD, "Trade Policy and Its Impact on Quality of Imports: A Welfare Analysis," *Journal of International Economics* 23 (1987), 77–95.

——, AND ——, "Oligopolistic Competition and International Trade: Quantity and Quality Restrictions," *Journal of International Economics* 27 (1989), 299–318.

GATSIOS, K., "Preferential Tariffs and the 'Most Favoured Nation' Principle: A Note," *Journal of International Economics* 28 (1990), 365–73.

HARSANYI, J., AND R. SELTEN, *A General Theory of Equilibrium Selection in Games* (Cambridge, MA: The MIT Press, 1988).

HAUPT, A., AND W. PETERS, "Restricting Preferential Tax Regimes to Avoid Harmful Tax Competition," *Regional Science and Urban Economics* 35 (2005), 493–507.

HERGUERA, I., KUJAL, P., AND E. PETRAKIS, "Tariffs, Quality Reversals and Exit in Vertically Differentiated Industries," *Journal of International Economics* 58 (2002), 467–92.

HORN, H., "National Treatment in the GATT," *The American Economic Review* 96 (2006), 394–404.

——, AND P. C. MAVROIDIS, "Economic and Legal Aspects of the Most Favored Nation Clause," *European Journal of Political Economy* 17 (2001), 233–79.

——, AND ——, "Still Hazy after All These Years: The Interpretation of GATT/WTO Case Law on Tax Discrimination," *The European Journal of International Law* 15 (2004), 39–69.

——, MAGGI, G., AND R. W. STAIGER, "The GATT/WTO as an Incomplete Contract," Mimeo, 2005.

JANEBA, E., "Tax Competition in Imperfectly Competitive Markets," *Journal of International Economics* 44 (1998), 135–53.

——, AND W. PETERS, "Tax Evasion, Tax Competition and the Gains from Non-Discrimination: The Case of Interest Taxation in Europe," *Economic Journal* 109 (1999), 93–101.

——, AND M. SMART, "Is Targeted Tax Competition Less Harmful than Its Remedies?" *International Tax and Public Finance* 10 (2003), 259–80.

KANBUR, R., AND M. KEEN, "Jeux Sans Frontières: Tax Competition and Tax Coordination When Countries Differ in Size," *The American Economic Review* 83 (1993), 877–92.

KEEN, M., "Preferential Regimes Can Make Tax Competition Less Harmful," *National Tax Journal* 54 (2001), 757–62.

MORAGA-GONZÁLEZ, J. L., AND J.-M. VIAENE, "Anti-Dumping, Intra-Industry Trade and Quality Reversals," Discussion Paper No. 04-124/2, Tinbergen Institute Discussion Papers, 2004.

——, AND ——, "Trade Policy and Quality Leadership in Transition Economies," *European Economic Review* 49 (2005), 359–85.

MOTTA, M., "Endogenous Quality Choice: Price vs. Quantity Competition," *Journal of Industrial Economics* 41 (1993), 113–31.

——, THISSE, J., AND A. CABRALES, "On the Persistence of Leadership or Leapfrogging in International Trade," *International Economic Review* 38 (1997), 809–24.

SAGGI, K., "Tariffs and the Most Favored Nation Clause," *Journal of International Economics* 63 (2004), 341–68.

Shaked, A., and J. Sutton, "Relaxing Price Competition Through Product Differentiation," *Review of Economic Studies* 49 (1982), 3–13.
——, and ——, "Natural Oligopolies and International Trade," in H. Kierzkowski, ed., *Monopolistic Competition and International Trade* (Oxford: Oxford University Press, 1984).
Zhou, D., B. J. Spencer, and I. Vertinsky, "Strategic Trade Policy with Endogenous Choice of Quality and Asymmetric Costs," *Journal of International Economics* 56 (2002), 205–32.

CHAPTER 4

On the emergence of an MFN club: equal treatment in an unequal world

Kamal Saggi *Department of Economics, Southern Methodist University*
Faruk Sengul *Department of Mathematics, University of Texas at Arlington*

Abstract. Motivated by GATT, we endogenize the formation of a club whose members have to abide by the MFN principle of non-discrimination. The underlying model is that of oligopolistic intraindustry trade. While an MFN club does not alter average tariff levels across countries, it increases aggregate world welfare; makes non-members worse off; and can immiserize its high cost members. These results imply that (i) core WTO rules such as MFN are valuable even if multilateral negotiations deliver limited trade liberalization and (ii) the distributional effects of MFN maybe one reason why developing countries have been granted Special and Differential treatment at the WTO. JEL classification: F13, F10, F15

A propos de l'émergence d'un club des pays qui adhèrent au principe de la nation la plus favorisée (NPF): traitement égal dans un monde inégal. Inspiré par le GATT, les auteurs endogénisent la formation d'un club dont les membres adhèrent au principe de non-discrimination dit de la nation la plus favorisée. Le modèle sous-jacent est celui du commerce oligopolistique intra-industrie. Un tel club ne modifie pas le niveau de tarif douanier moyen entre pays, il tend à accroître le niveau mondial de bien-être; empire le sort des non-membres; et appauvrit ses membres qui opèrent à des coûts élevés. Ces résultats amènent à conclure que (i) les règles fondamentales de l'Office Mondial du Commerce (OMC) comme la NPF sont bénéfiques même si les négociations multilatérales engendrent un degré limité de libéralisation du commerce; et (ii) les effets de répartition de la NPF peuvent être une raison pour laquelle les pays en développement ont obtenu un traitement spécial et différentiel de la part de l'OMC.

We thank Keith Head, Bernard Hoekman, Saltuk Ozerturk, Santanu Roy, Bob Staiger, Halis M. Yildiz, two anonymous referees, and seminar audiences at Hitotsubashi University, McGill University, SMU, the Southern Economics Association meetings in Washington, DC, 2005, and the Indian Statistical Institute's 3rd Annual Conference on Economic Growth and Development in New Delhi, for helpful comments. This paper was written when Faruk Sengul was a doctoral student in economics at SMU. Kamal Saggi thanks the World Bank for financial support. The authors take responsibility for any errors. Email: ksaggi@smu.edu; fsengul@uta.edu

Canadian Journal of Economics / Revue canadienne d'Economique, Vol. 42, No. 1
February / février 2009. Printed in Canada / Imprimé au Canada

0008-4085 / 09 / 267–299 / © Canadian Economics Association

1. Introduction

The General Agreement on Tariffs and Trade (GATT) specifies several rules that each member country of the World Trade Organization (WTO) must abide by while choosing its trade policies towards other members. Furthermore, throughout the history of GATT, there have been rounds of trade negotiations during which its member countries have attempted to liberalize their trade policies towards one another. Thus, one can view the WTO as playing two important roles in international trade: (1) it establishes rules that all its members agree to follow by opting to join the organization, and (2) it provides a forum for global trade liberalization. This paper focuses on the first of these two roles of the WTO and argues that by requiring member countries to abide by the most favoured nation (MFN) principle, the WTO has had an important and beneficial effect on world trade.[1]

We show that useful insights regarding the role of GATT/WTO system in world trade can be achieved by analyzing GATT as a club whose only requirement for membership is that members grant MFN to each other.[2] More specifically, we endogenize the formation of an MFN club in an environment that abstracts from explicit tariff negotiations among its members.[3] Several interesting questions arise in this context. From an individual country's perspective, what are the costs and benefits of joining an MFN club? Are all countries willing to join? Does the formation of such a club raise aggregate world welfare? How does it affect members and non-members? To answer these and related questions, we examine two different games of club formation between four countries engaged in oligopolistic intra-industry trade of the type formulated in Brander and Krugman (1983). We use this model because it facilitates the analysis of endogenous tariffs in an environment of asymmetry.[4]

The existence of cost asymmetry in our oligopolistic trade model generates incentives for socially harmful tariff discrimination that is biased against low cost exporters (as in Gatsios 1990; Hwang and Mai 1991; Choi 1995; Saggi 2004; Saggi and Yildiz 2005).[5] It follows, then, that the desirability of an MFN club from

1 While multilateral trade agreements are quite complicated and contain a multitude of clauses, it is useful to focus on MFN, since it is widely acknowledged to be *the* fundamental idea underlying all such agreements (see Hoekman and Kostecki 2001).

2 Following Jackson (1997), we adopt the following definition of MFN: 'The MFN obligation calls for each contracting party (CP) to grant to every other, CP the most favorable treatment that it grants to any other country.'

3 It is worth emphasizing that tariffs are the only means of protection in our model and should be interpreted as a rough measure of market access.

4 Krishna (1998) uses a related model to investigate the effects of preferential trade agreements on incentives for multilateral trade liberalization.

5 Important contributions to the literature on MFN that are not based on the oligopoly trade model include Bagwell and Staiger (1999, 2004), Caplin and Krishna (1988), Ederington and McCalman (2003), Ludema (1991), Maggi (1999), McCalman (2002), and Takemori (1994). See Horn and Mavroidis (2001) for a survey.

a global welfare perspective depends upon how it alters the global distribution of tariffs relative to tariff discrimination. Taking this argument as a starting point, we derive the coalition proof Nash equilibria of two rather different games of club formation: (i) an open membership (OM) game and (ii) an exclusive membership (EM) game. Our approach is related to that of Aghion, Antràs, and Helpman (2007), Das and Ghosh (2006), Burbidge et al. (1997), and Yi (1996), all of whom analyze games of coalition formation with externalities. While Aghion et al. (2007), Das and Ghosh (2006), and Yi (1996) focus on endogenous free trade agreements, we consider a club whose members (only) exchange MFN status with one another.

We find that the formation of an MFN club enhances aggregate world welfare, and the larger the club, the more desirable it is from a welfare perspective. It is noteworthy that this result obtains, even though in our model the emergence of an MFN club does *not* affect average tariff levels across countries. This implies that adoption of the MFN rule by WTO members is of value, even when it is *not* accompanied by any trade liberalization among them. Furthermore, we show that among clubs that have the same number of members, those that include low-cost countries are socially more valuable because such countries face relatively higher tariffs under discrimination. Thus, the fact that most of the initial GATT members were advanced industrialized countries was probably a good thing.

Given that there exist myriad differences across countries, it is quite unlikely that a non-discrimination requirement such as MFN affects all countries in a similar fashion. We find that the desirability of an MFN club from a country's perspective depends upon how its production cost compares with others. In general, receiving MFN from others is of greater value to countries with relatively lower costs of production. In fact, we argue that the effect that an MFN club has on higher-cost countries in our model can shed some light on the actual experience of developing countries with the multilateral trading system. More specifically, it is noteworthy that developing-country members of the WTO have been granted Special and Differential (S&D) treatment ever since the Generalized System of Preferences (GSP) came into existence in the 1970s. Under S&D treatment, many developing countries receive preferential tariffs from major industrialized countries. As per Oyejide (2002): 'S&D provisions are meant to grant developing countries and least developed countries (LDCs) more favorable access to the markets of industrial countries,' and that the existence of such provisions in the GATT/WTO system reflects the idea that 'because of disparities in economic situation and capacities, there are *significant differences in the benefits* (italics added) that countries reap from the global trading system.' Thus, WTO's S&D provisions allow developing countries to receive *better-than-MFN* treatment from industrialized countries. Our results suggest that such exceptions to MFN might be necessary to undo some of the adverse distributional aspects of an MFN club.

An intriguing result of our model is that a high-cost country can voluntarily end up joining an MFN club, even though its welfare as a member is lower than that under tariff discrimination. Such a result obtains because the fate of a high-cost country as a non-member can be even worse than that as a member. In fact, we show that a three-country club can be an equilibrium, even when two of its (higher-cost) members are worse off relative to discrimination; both would be better off if neither were to join the club, but each has a unilateral incentive to join, given that the other does not. This immiserization result corresponds well with the widespread sense of ambivalence among developing-country members of the WTO regarding their status in the organization as well as the benefits that the multilateral trading system confers upon them (see Tussie and Lengyel 2002).

Recent empirical work regarding the effect of WTO membership on trade liberalization suggests that our analysis is not merely of theoretical interest. Rose (2004a) shows that membership in the GATT/WTO is *not* associated with enhanced trade, once one takes into account standard factors that help explain international trade flows (such as those captured in a typical gravity equation model). The question then becomes why this might be so. Using more than 60 measures of trade policy, Rose (2004b) argues that this is because trade policies of WTO members do *not* differ significantly from those of non-members. Furthermore, he finds that a country's trade liberalization significantly lags its entry into GATT and that many countries that were relatively closed at the time of their GATT entry remained so for long periods of time. Evidence regarding early GATT rounds supports this argument. For example, it is well known that, except for the Geneva round of 1947, initial GATT rounds failed to deliver any significant trade liberalization.[6] One response to Rose's findings is to examine their empirical robustness. For example, Subramanian and Wei (2006) argue that participation in the WTO has had a significantly positive impact on trade between developed countries, since up until the Uruguay Round most developing country members did not (and were not, in fact, required to) undertake much trade liberalization. In a somewhat different vein, Tomz, Goldstein, and Rivers (2007) argue that by mistakenly classifying many countries as non-members, Rose's empirical analysis underestimates the effects of WTO membership on world trade. In particular, they argue that GATT gave rights and obligations to three important categories of non-members (colonies, de facto members, and provisional members) and that this broader notion of GATT participation can be shown to substantially increase trade of its formal members as well as non-member participants (relative to those countries that were completely outside the system).[7]

6 As Irwin (2002) notes, 'after Geneva there was a long period in which relatively little was accomplished. Subsequent negotiating rounds were held at Annecy (1949), Torquay (1950–51), and Geneva (1955–56). These negotiations resulted in the accession of more countries to GATT, but further tariff reductions were negligible, about 2 percent in each round, on average. The Dillon Round (1960-61) also produced little in terms of tangible results.'

7 As Rose (2007) notes in his detailed response to these studies, the first line of criticism contends that his original analysis included too many countries as effective GATT members, while the second argues that it included too few. However, the fact remains that deviating from the original set of countries studied by Rose (2004a, 2004b) in either direction alters his results.

Given the ongoing empirical debate regarding the effects of GATT/WTO membership on trade liberalization, we think a useful way forward is to ask: *What, besides trade liberalization, can the GATT/WTO system do for world trade?* As Rose (2004a) himself suggests, the institutional features of the WTO – such as its core rules and the dispute settlement procedure – might provide significant benefits to its members and the world as a whole even if WTO membership itself has little effect on global trade liberalization. Along these lines, an important contribution of this paper is to show that the endogenous formation of a club based on the key principle underlying the WTO system (i.e., MFN) increases world welfare relative to tariff discrimination by reallocating output from high-cost to low-cost producers. However, such reallocation also implies that international transfers or some other indirect measures (such as the GSP) are needed to ensure that club membership benefits all members.

The rest of the paper is organized as follows. Section 2 presents our oligopoly model of international trade under tariff discrimination and MFN, and section 3 discusses the effects of different types of MFN clubs (taking their existence as a given). Sections 4 and 5 analyze the open membership game and the exclusive membership game, respectively. Section 6 extends our analysis in three different directions: subsection 6.1 integrates GSP into our core model; subsection 6.2 considers a two-sector model; and subsection 6.3 discusses how our model can be extended to shed light on the accession process of the WTO. Section 7 concludes, followed by an appendix. All proofs not provided in the text are in the appendix.

2. Tariffs in the oligopoly trade model

We begin with a brief description of the underlying trade model and then analyze two different games that endogenize the formation of an MFN club. There are four countries indexed by $i = a, b, c$, or d and two goods: x and y. Consumer preferences over the two goods are quasi-linear: $U(x, y) = u(x) + y$, where the numeraire good y is produced under perfect competition with constant returns-to-scale technology. Good x is produced by a monopolist in each country. We refer to country i's monopolist as firm i. The marginal cost of production of firm i is given by ζ_i, where $\zeta_d \geq \zeta_c \geq \zeta_b \geq \zeta_a = 0$.

Firms compete in quantities (Cournot competition) and make independent decisions regarding how much to sell in each market (i.e., markets are segmented). Firm j faces a specific tariff t_{ji} when exporting to country i, where $t_{ii} = 0$ for all i. Country i's tariff schedule $\mathbf{t_i} \equiv (t_{ai} \ldots t_{di})'$ is a 4×1 dimensional vector. Denote the tariff schedules of all countries other than i by $\mathbf{t_{-i}}$ and the matrix of all countries' trade policies by $\mathbf{t}$, where $\mathbf{t} \equiv (\mathbf{t_a} \ldots . \mathbf{t_d})$. Let $x_i = \sum_j x_{ji}$, where $j = a$, b, c, or d denotes the total output of good x sold in country i, and let $x_{-i} = x_i - x_{ii}$ denote country i's total imports of good x.

Whether or not an MFN club exists, all countries simultaneously choose their tariff schedules to maximize their own welfare. As is well known, under linear costs and market segmentation, a country's optimal tariff schedule is independent of the tariff schedules of other countries. Lack of interdependence of tariffs is clearly a limitation of our model but one that greatly simplifies the analysis. In the absence of linearity or market segmentation, the model would not have this feature. However, most related models make similar assumptions, and, as Staiger (1995) has noted, it is not clear whether tariffs ought to be treated as strategic substitutes or complements.

Hereafter, the dependence of country i's domestic surplus $S_i(\mathbf{t_i})$ (defined in equation (1), below, as the sum of consumer surplus and own firm's profits derived from the local market) on the tariffs of other countries is ignored. If country i practises tariff discrimination towards all other countries, it solves

$$\underset{\mathbf{t_i}}{\text{Max}}\ W_i(\mathbf{t}) \equiv S_i(\mathbf{t_i}) + \sum_{j \neq i} \pi_{ij}(\mathbf{t_j}), \text{ where } S_i(\mathbf{t_i}) \equiv CS_i(\mathbf{t_i}) + \pi_{ii}(\mathbf{t_i}) + TR_i(\mathbf{t_i}), \quad (1)$$

where CS_i denotes consumer surplus in country i and is given by

$$CS_i = u(x_i) - p_i x_i, \quad (2)$$

$\pi_{ii}(\mathbf{t_i})$ denotes the profit function of firm i in its own market, and $\sum_{j \neq i} \pi_{ij}(\mathbf{t_j})$ denotes its profit function for exports, where

$$\pi_{ii} = (p_i - \zeta_i)x_{ii} \text{ and } \pi_{ij} = (p_j - \zeta_i - t_{ij})x_{ij} \quad (3)$$

and $TR_i(\mathbf{t_i})$ denotes country i's total tariff revenue:

$$TR_i = \sum_{j \neq i} t_{ji} x_{ji}. \quad (4)$$

The welfare function in (1) includes export profits $\sum_{j \neq i} \pi_{ij}(\mathbf{t_j})$ because they contribute to domestic welfare (even though market segmentation implies that export profits are independent of a country's own tariffs).

Let $\mathbf{t_i^*}$ denote country i's optimal discriminatory tariff schedule:

$$\mathbf{t_i^*} \equiv \arg\max W_i(\mathbf{t}) = \arg\max S_i(\mathbf{t_i}) \quad (5)$$

If country i practises MFN towards all others, it imposes a non-discriminatory tariff (say t_i) on all foreign exporters and solves

$$\underset{t_i}{\text{Max}}\ W_i(t_i) \equiv S_i(t_i) + \sum_{j \neq i} \pi_{ij}(\mathbf{t_j}) \text{ where } S_i(t_i) \equiv CS_i(t_i) + \pi_{ii}(t_i) + t_i x_{-i}. \quad (6)$$

Let t_i^M denote country i's optimal MFN tariff. Before analyzing club formation, we quickly note two results that have been established in the existing literature on MFN (see Saggi 2004):

RESULT 1. $t^*_{ji} \geq t^*_{ki}$ *iff* $\zeta_k \geq \zeta_j$ and $t^*_{ji} \geq t^M_i$ iff $\zeta_j \leq \frac{\sum_{k \neq i} \zeta_k}{3}$.

RESULT 2. *Under linear demand,* $T_i \equiv \sum_{j \neq i} t^*_{ji} = 3t^M_i$.

An immediate corollary of result 1 in our context is that the highest-cost country (i.e., d) has nothing to gain from joining an MFN club, since it faces lower tariffs under discrimination. Result 2 says that the adoption of MFN by a country does *not* alter its total protection T_i (or its average tariff level). It is noteworthy that in our model the total volume of a country's imports of good x depends only upon its total protection T_i, not on the distribution of its tariffs.

We now describe the underlying trade-offs involved in joining an MFN club from the perspective of each country. Furthermore, to make analytical progress on the various questions of interest, we assume that $u(x)$ is quadratic, so that demand for good x is linear: $p = \alpha - q$.

3. How an MFN club affects global tariffs

In this section, we examine how different types of club affect the tariffs of members and non-member countries. As per the definition of MFN, we require that each member of an MFN club treat all other members in a non-discriminatory fashion and no worse than non-members. As noted above, since country d actually faces higher tariffs under MFN than it does under discrimination, including country d need not be examined.

3.1. Protection levels and tariff concessions

In this section, we report some preliminary results that are instrumental for our core analysis (contained in sections 4 and 5). While these results are quite closely linked to the existing literature on MFN under oligopoly, they have not been formally derived or discussed there.

The variation of total tariff protection across countries is as follows:

LEMMA 1. *The total tariff protection of country i (under tariff discrimination or any MFN club) is decreasing in its own cost:* $\partial T_i / \partial \zeta_i < 0$.

The intuition for this result has to do with the fact that tariffs are used to extract rents in the oligopoly model: since demand is symmetric across countries, any given reduction in imports does roughly equal harm to consumer welfare in all countries, whereas it results in a greater increase in local profits of domestic firms in lower-cost countries (because they enjoy higher mark-ups).

How does an MFN club alter tariffs relative to the status quo? Let $\Delta t_{ij}(m)$ denote the tariff concession received by country i from country j in the MFN club m:

$$\Delta t_{ij}(m) = t_{ij}(\phi) - t_{ij}(m), \tag{7}$$

where $\langle\{\phi\}\rangle$ denotes the status quo/tariff discrimination and $m = \langle\{abc\}\rangle, \langle\{ab\}\rangle, \langle\{ac\}\rangle$, or $\langle\{bc\}\rangle$. The first point to note is that whether or not a member actually receives tariff concessions (i.e., $\Delta t_{ij}(m) > 0$) from other members depends upon the distribution of production costs across countries. The following is shown in the appendix:

LEMMA 2. *In any MFN club m, the lowest-cost member receives tariff concessions from all other members. In general, the higher the cost of a member, the less likely it is that it receives tariff concessions from other members.*

Thus, the exchange of MFN among countries does *not* always result in all members granting tariff concessions to each other. The proof of lemma 2 provides conditions under which countries other than a also receive tariff concessions when they join an MFN club. To get some intuition for lemma 2, suppose $\langle\{abc\}\rangle$ is the MFN club and consider the tariffs faced by each country relative to $\langle\{\phi\}\rangle$. Recall from result 1 that country a faces the highest tariffs under $\langle\{\phi\}\rangle$. Under $\langle\{abc\}\rangle$, country a obtains MFN status from countries b and c and therefore receives tariff concessions from both of them. Similarly, from country a's perspective, country b is its most efficient partner, and so country b must receive a tariff concession from country a when $\langle\{abc\}\rangle$ obtains. But does country b necessarily receive a tariff concession from country c? The answer is no. From country c's perspective, country a is the most efficient exporter and it is the one that necessarily receives a tariff concession. Whether country b also receives a tariff concession from country c depends upon the distribution of production costs: when country b's cost is lower than the *average* of countries a and d, it receives a tariff concession from country c, or else it suffers a tariff increase in country c's market.

The second key point to establish is that the tariff concessions involved in an MFN club are asymmetric in nature:

LEMMA 3. *In any MFN club m, the tariff concession member i receives from member j is larger than the tariff concession it grants to member j iff its own production cost is relatively lower:* $\Delta t_{ij}(m) \geq \Delta t_{ji}(m)$ *iff* $\zeta_i \leq \zeta_j$.

Since the lowest-cost country faces the highest tariffs under $\langle\{\phi\}\rangle$, the formation of an MFN club forces other members to substantially reduce their tariffs on country a. Furthermore, recall that the total protection of a country decreases with own cost (lemma 1). Also, the least-cost and the highest-cost countries (i.e., a and d, respectively) do not have as strong an incentive to tariff discriminate as the intermediate countries (i.e., b and c), who are served by foreign exporters with bigger cost differentials. Therefore, country a's cost of joining the club is not as high as that of others for three reasons: (i) it is forced to lower its tariffs less than higher-cost countries; (ii) the tariff reductions it grants to the higher-cost countries apply to a smaller volume of imports, since exports of such countries are smaller; and (iii) it does not suffer as much as intermediate countries from not being able to tariff discriminate. We now investigate the costs and benefits of club membership in greater detail.

3.2. Costs and benefits of joining an MFN club

Owing to strategic independence of tariffs and segmentation of markets, the trade-off underlying a country's decision to join an MFN club is quite transparent: the cost of membership is the loss in domestic surplus that results from not being able to tariff discriminate, whereas the benefit is the (potential) increase in export profits generated by the tariff concessions received from other club members. Given result 2, MFN adoption only lowers the tariff revenue collected by a country without affecting its domestic surplus in other ways. Of course, the extent of revenue reduction depends upon who else joins the club.

Let $\Delta TR_i(m)$ measure the reduction in country i's tariff revenue when it joins the MFN club m, where $m = \langle\{abc\}\rangle, \langle\{ab\}\rangle, \langle\{ac\}\rangle$, or $\langle\{bc\}\rangle$. We have

$$\Delta TR_i(m) = TR_i(\phi) - TR_i(m). \tag{8}$$

The benefit to country i of joining club m is measured by the total increase in its export profits that results from any tariff concessions that accompany membership:

$$\Delta\pi_i(m) = \sum_{j\neq i} \pi_{ij}(m) - \sum_{j\neq i} \pi_{ij}(\phi). \tag{9}$$

Our first major result describes how the cost of membership depends upon the distribution of production costs across countries and the nature of the MFN club:

PROPOSITION 1. *For any two-member MFN club, the loss in tariff revenue relative to* $\langle\{\phi\}\rangle$ *is larger for the higher-cost member:* $\Delta TR_j(m) \geq \Delta TR_i(m)$ *iff* $\zeta_i \leq \zeta_j$, *where* $m = \langle\{ab\}\rangle, \langle\{ac\}\rangle$, *or* $\langle\{bc\}\rangle$. *In* $\langle\{abc\}\rangle$, *the loss in tariff revenue of the lowest-cost member is the smallest:* $\Delta TR_a(abc) \leq \min\{\Delta TR_b(abc), \Delta TR_c(abc)\}$.

The explanation for why the tariff revenue loss of countries b and c cannot be ranked unambiguously has to do with the conflict between the three effects described at the end of section 3.1. While country b loses relatively more from not being able to tariff discriminate (because the cost difference between countries a and c is larger than that between countries a and b), country c reduces its tariffs to a greater degree while also facing a larger volume of imports.

How does a country rank two potential partners from the perspective of loss in own tariff revenue?

LEMMA 4. *From member i's perspective, a two-country club with member j implies a larger loss in tariff revenue than a club with member k iff member j is relatively lower cost than member k:* $\Delta TR_i(ij) \geq \Delta TR_i(ik)$ *iff* $\zeta_j \leq \zeta_k$.

The reason for this result is twofold: not only does country i grant a larger tariff concession to country j under $\langle\{ij\}\rangle$ than it grants country k under $\langle\{ik\}\rangle$ (because $\zeta_j \leq \zeta_k$), the larger concession also applies to a larger volume of imports, since $x_{ji}(ij) > x_{ki}(ik)$.

Consider, now, the benefits received from different potential club partners from the perspective of a country:

LEMMA 5. *From member i's perspective, a club with member j yields a larger tariff concession from its partner than does a club with member k iff member j is relatively lower cost than member k:* $\Delta t_{ij}(ij) \geq \Delta t_{ik}(ik)$ *iff* $\zeta_j \leq \zeta_k$.[8]

However, a larger tariff concession from country j does *not* necessarily translate into a larger increase in total export profits for country i, since its volume of exports also varies across its trading partners. In fact, from lemma 1 and the second part of result 1, we know that $x_{ik}(ik) \geq x_{ij}(ij)$ iff $\zeta_j \leq \zeta_k$; that is, country i exports more to a relatively higher-cost club partner. Since the volume effect counteracts the tariff concession effect, country i's benefit of club $\langle\{ij\}\rangle$ can be either higher or lower than the benefit of club $\langle\{ik\}\rangle$. On the other hand, the asymmetric nature of tariff concessions involved in an MFN club gives us a clear result regarding the distribution of gains across its members:

PROPOSITION 2. *For any MFN club m, the increase in export profits enjoyed by member i is higher than the corresponding increase for member j iff member i is relatively lower cost than member j:* $\Delta\pi_i(m) > \Delta\pi_j(m)$ *iff* $\zeta_i \leq \zeta_j$.

An immediate implication of propositions 1 and 2 is that country a has the strongest incentive to join an MFN club: it suffers the lowest decline in tariff revenue and enjoys the highest increase in export profits. In fact, it would like to form an MFN club with whomever else is willing to do so. The following proposition compares various MFN clubs from each country's perspective:

PROPOSITION 3. *Let* $\succ_i$ *denote strict preference and* $\sim_i$ *indifference for country i. The following hold with respect to individual country rankings of the various MFN clubs: (i) country a:* $\langle\{abc\}\rangle \succ_a (\langle\{ac\}\rangle, \langle\{ab\}\rangle) \succ_a \langle\{\phi\}\rangle \sim_a \langle\{bc\}\rangle$ *; (ii) country b:* $\langle\{bc\}\rangle \succ_b \phi \succeq_b \langle\{ac\}\rangle$*; and (iii) country c:* $\langle\{bc\}\rangle \succ_c \langle\{ac\}\rangle$.

Part (i) of proposition 3 follows from lemmas 2 and 3: country a receives relatively large tariff concessions from all others that join and therefore likes the biggest MFN club the best. Perhaps more intriguing is the fact that country a

8 In fact, even under the club $\langle\{abc\}\rangle$ it is true that $\Delta t_{ij}(ij) \geq \Delta t_{ik}(ik)$ iff $\varsigma_j \leq \varsigma_k$.

does *not* have an unambiguous preference between the clubs $\langle\{ac\}\rangle$ and $\langle\{ab\}\rangle$. Why is this so? The answer is contained in lemmas 4 and 5: while country a receives a bigger tariff concession from country b under $\langle\{ab\}\rangle$ than it does from country c under $\langle\{ac\}\rangle$, it also has to grant country b a bigger concession relative to what it has to grant country c. Finally, why is country a indifferent between $\langle\{bc\}\rangle$ and $\langle\{\phi\}\rangle$? Result 2 says that the total protection of each member does not change relative to $\langle\{\phi\}\rangle$ when $\langle\{bc\}\rangle$ is formed. Since country a has the lowest production cost, country b imposes its optimal discriminatory tariff on it while imposing the average of its optimal discriminatory tariffs on the other two countries. An analogous argument applies to country c's tariff schedule under $\langle\{bc\}\rangle$. As a result, the sum total of tariff included marginal costs of rival exporters faced by country a under $\langle\{bc\}\rangle$ is the same as that under $\langle\{\phi\}\rangle$. Since its own domestic surplus does not change because of the formation of $\langle\{bc\}\rangle$, country a is strictly indifferent between $\langle\{\phi\}\rangle$ and $\langle\{bc\}\rangle$.

While a general ranking of country b's preferences among the various clubs is not possible, it turns out that for most parameter values country b prefers $\langle\{bc\}\rangle$ to $\langle\{ab\}\rangle$. Only when ζ_b is rather low does country b find $\langle\{ab\}\rangle$ more attractive than $\langle\{bc\}\rangle$. Country c, on the other hand, always prefers $\langle\{bc\}\rangle$ to $\langle\{ac\}\rangle$. As is clear from lemma 2, as the production cost of a country increases, its incentive to exchange MFN with the lowest-cost country declines.

How are non-members affected by the formation of an MFN club? The answer here is clear: non-members are (weakly) worse off relative to tariff discrimination, since member tariffs on non-members are never lower than those under discrimination, whereas their tariffs on other members are no higher than those on non-members. Note that under $\langle\{abc\}\rangle$ country c can face higher tariffs than under $\langle\{\phi\}\rangle$ and still remain in the club, since the tariffs it faces under $\langle\{ab\}\rangle$ would still be higher.

It is easy to show that the bigger the MFN club, the higher is aggregate world welfare (defined as the sum of the welfare of individual countries). This implies that the most desirable MFN club – that is, $\langle\{abcd\}\rangle$ – does not arise, because country d is always better off as a non-member. Of the remaining clubs, $\langle\{abc\}\rangle$ is clearly the next best option. But what about clubs $\langle\{ab\}\rangle$, $\langle\{ac\}\rangle$, and $\langle\{bc\}\rangle$? Here, the result is as follows:

PROPOSITION 4. *Among MFN clubs with only two members,* $\langle\{ab\}\rangle$ *yields the highest aggregate world welfare, while* $\langle\{bc\}\rangle$ *yields the lowest.*

The inclusion of country a in an MFN club is of vital importance for world welfare, because the large tariff reductions it receives in other markets help to allocate more of the world's production to the lowest-cost location. Similarly, since country b is lower cost than c, its inclusion in an MFN club is relatively more important. As a result, $\langle\{ab\}\rangle$ is welfare preferred to $\langle\{ac\}\rangle$. The club $\langle\{bc\}\rangle$ excludes the lowest-cost producer, who ends up facing the same tariffs as it does under $\langle\{\phi\}\rangle$ and is therefore of least value (although it is still preferable to $\langle\{\phi\}\rangle$

because it allocates output in favour of countries *b* and *c* at the expense of country *d*).

Having described how various types of MFN clubs affect tariffs and welfare, we are now ready to endogenize club formation.

4. An open-membership MFN club

In this section, we analyze an open-membership (OM) game that captures the following intuitive scenario that can be viewed as the 'beginning of GATT.' Imagine that there is a room (call it the MFN club) upon entering which a country has to grant MFN to all those that have entered as well. Each country is free to enter or leave the club. Countries that choose not to enter practise tariff discrimination and do not receive MFN status from those inside the club. An MFN club obtains in equilibrium if several countries enter the room and decide to stay. This club formation process can be formalized as the following game. In the first stage, countries simultaneously decide whether or not to adopt MFN with respect to their tariff schedules. Each country makes an announcement: it either commits to MFN or does not. After countries make their announcements, each country that commits to MFN grants MFN status to all others countries that make the same commitment. Next, given their policy regimes, all countries simultaneously choose their tariff schedules. Finally, firms choose their output levels.

It is easy to see that the OM game admits multiple (sub-game perfect) Nash equilibria; no country would stay in the MFN club as a singleton. As a result, status quo is a Nash equilibrium of the OM game, but it is not a very interesting one. Furthermore, it seems desirable to allow countries to form coalitions and deviate jointly from any outcome. When such deviations are possible, a more appropriate equilibrium concept is that of a coalition-proof Nash equilibrium. Intuitively, a Nash equilibrium is coalition proof if it is immune to credible or self-enforcing coalitional deviations (see Bernheim, Peleg, and Whinston 1987 for further details). However, in the OM game, under minor conditions all Nash equilibria turn out to be coalition proof (shown in the appendix). The reason for this is as follows. It is meaningful to examine coalitional deviations only when $\langle\{abc\}\rangle$ is the club. Furthermore, the only deviation to consider from $\langle\{abc\}\rangle$ is the joint deviation of countries *b* and *c* to $\langle\{\phi\}\rangle$.[9] However, under minor conditions, this deviation is not self-enforcing, since each deviating country wants to *further* deviate to form a club with country *a* alone. This argument is easy to see from figure 1, which illustrates equilibrium MFN clubs in the OM game in the (ζ_b, ζ_c) space.

9 Country *a* is free to enter the club and will always do so. Thus, when acting jointly, countries *b* and *c* can only leave the club together (i.e., by assumption, only one club can be formed, so that countries *b* and *c* cannot form a club by themselves). By contrast, under the exclusive membership game analyzed below, countries *b* and *c* have the ability to *exclude* country *a* from the club and coalitional deviations are more interesting there.

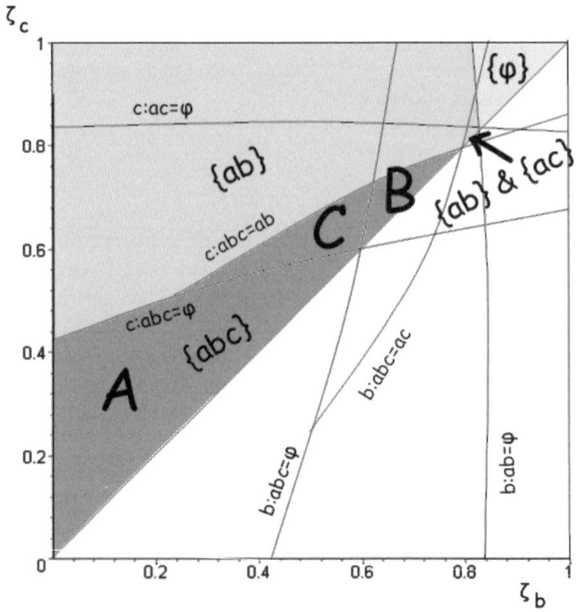

FIGURE 1 CPNE of the OM game

In figure 1, only the region above the 45 degree line is relevant, since $\zeta_c \geq \zeta_b$.[10] By using indifference conditions for all countries, the parameter space can be partitioned into regions over which various clubs obtain in equilibrium. For example, along the curve $c{:}ac = \phi$ country c is indifferent between clubs $\langle\{ac\}\rangle$ and $\langle\{\phi\}\rangle$; below the curve it prefers $\langle\{ac\}\rangle$ to $\langle\{\phi\}\rangle$, whereas the opposite is true above it. All other indifference curves are labelled similarly: the identity of a country is followed by the regimes among which it is indifferent along a particular indifference curve. The intuition for why indifference curves slope upwards is that granting MFN to an efficient country is costly in terms of forgone tariff revenue, whereas receiving MFN is attractive precisely when own cost is low. For example, for country c to remain indifferent between being part of a club versus being outside, an increase in its own cost has to be matched by an increase in the cost of country b.

Several important conclusions emerge from figure 1: (i) Over much of the parameter space, $\langle\{abc\}\rangle$ and $\langle\{ab\}\rangle$ emerge as MFN clubs. In other words, an equilibrium MFN club is more likely to have the lower-cost countries as its members; (ii) $\langle\{abc\}\rangle$ emerges when all countries have relatively similar (and

10 Parameter values are $\zeta_d = 1$ and $\alpha = 20$. Also recall that $\zeta_a = 0$ throughout the model.

low) costs of production; (iii) when both countries b and c have high costs, no one wants to join country a in an MFN club and $\langle\{\phi\}\rangle$ ends up as the equilibrium; (iv) there is a small region right above region B in which both $\langle\{ab\}\rangle$ and $\langle\{ac\}\rangle$ are equilibria. Note that this region is close to the 45 degree line – that is, when countries b and c have very similar costs, only one of them ends up as a member; and (v) the region over which $\langle\{abc\}\rangle$ obtains can be divided into three subregions: A, B, and C. In subregion A, all countries prefer $\langle\{abc\}\rangle$ to $\langle\{\phi\}\rangle$. However, this is *not* the case in the other two subregions. In subregion B, country b prefers $\langle\{\phi\}\rangle$ to $\langle\{abc\}\rangle$ but opts to join the club because it is worse off under $\langle\{ac\}\rangle$ than it is under $\langle\{abc\}\rangle$. Furthermore, in both subregions B and C, country c prefers $\langle\{\phi\}\rangle$ to $\langle\{abc\}\rangle$, but it ends up in the club because its welfare as member of $\langle\{abc\}\rangle$ is higher than that as a non-member outside $\langle\{ab\}\rangle$. The last result deserves emphasis:

PROPOSITION 5. *The MFN club $\langle\{abc\}\rangle$ can arise in equilibrium even though both its relatively high-cost members (i.e., countries b and c) are worse off relative to $\langle\{\phi\}\rangle$. Furthermore, if country b is worse off under $\langle\{abc\}\rangle$, then country c must also be worse off.*

Proposition 5 obtains because a country can end up joining an MFN club not because it prefers joining the club to $\langle\{\phi\}\rangle$ but rather because being a non-member is worse than being a member. But can not countries b and c prevent such an outcome by jointly deviating to $\langle\{\phi\}\rangle$ as a coalition? The answer to this question turns out to be no. If they were to deviate jointly to $\langle\{\phi\}\rangle$ together, then each would want to further deviate from that to form an MFN club with country a alone. As a result, the coalitional deviation of countries b and c to $\langle\{\phi\}\rangle$ is not credible.[11]

The cost asymmetry between countries is crucial in delivering proposition 5. This result can perhaps shed some light on the widespread sense of dissatisfaction among the WTO's developing country members, since it indicates that it is the higher-cost countries that can end up being reluctant members of an MFN club and that the higher a country's cost, the more likely it is that it loses as a member relative to $\langle\{\phi\}\rangle$.[12] Since it is a dominant strategy for country a to enter the MFN club, $\langle\{bc\}\rangle$ is not an equilibrium of the OM game. Thus, an attractive feature of the OM game is that the least desirable MFN club does not obtain as a stable equilibrium.

A natural question with respect to the above analysis is whether it extends to a scenario where there are more than four countries. To address this, suppose the

11 In fact, it is quite possible that a member actually suffers a decrease in export profits when it joins the club relative to $\langle\{\phi\}\rangle$ but ends up joining because its export profits as a non-member are still lower.

12 In equilibrium, there can be only two MFN clubs with two members: $\langle\{ab\}\rangle$ and $\langle\{ac\}\rangle$. As is clear, neither member of these clubs can be worse off relative to $\langle\{\phi\}\rangle$, since each is free to deviate unilaterally to $\langle\{\phi\}\rangle$.

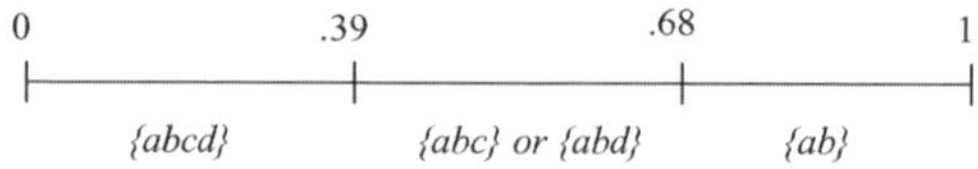

FIGURE 1a CPNE of the OM game ($n = 5$)

world comprises n countries and let t^*_{ji} denote country i's optimal discriminatory tariff on country j, and let t^M_i denote its optimal MFN tariff. In this context, we know from Saggi (2004) that $t^*_{ji} \geq t^M_i$ iff $\zeta_j \leq \sum_{k \neq i} \zeta_k/(n-1)$.[13] In other words, country i's MFN tariff on country j is smaller than its optimal discriminatory tariff on country j iff country j's cost is lower than the average production cost of all exporters to country i. This result tells us that the global *distribution* of production costs determines how many countries gain and how many lose when any one country decides to adopt MFN. Thus, if one were to divide the world into a group of developed and less-developed countries, only if all developing countries have relatively similar and high production costs would all of them lose from the MFN adoption of any country. Thus, the basic insight that guides our results regarding the effects of MFN remains in force for an arbitrary number of countries.

In accordance with the focus of this paper, consider, next, the endogenous formation of an MFN club when the number of countries exceeds four. Since analytical derivation of coalition-proof Nash equilibria of an OM game with n countries that have asymmetric production costs has not proved possible, it is useful to consider a special case that proves quite instructive.[14] Suppose $n = 5$, and for analytical convenience let $\zeta_a = \zeta_b = 0$, $\zeta_c = \zeta_d = \zeta$, where $0 < \zeta < 1$ and $\zeta_e = 1$. In figure 1a, the horizontal line shows coalition-proof Nash equilibria of the OM game as a function of ζ. Figure 1a illustrates that when $\zeta < 0.39$, $\langle\{abcd\}\rangle$ is the equilibrium; when $0.39 < \zeta < 0.68$, either $\langle\{abc\}\rangle$ or $\langle\{abd\}\rangle$ obtains; finally, when $\zeta > 0.68$, $\langle\{ab\}\rangle$ obtains. As is clear, these findings correlate quite well with the case of four countries. First, when $\zeta < 0.39$, production costs of countries c and d do not differ substantially from those of the two low-cost countries, so that all four countries opt to join the club. Second, when the production cost of countries c and d is moderately high (i.e., when $0.39 < \zeta < 0.68$), only one of them joins the club. Finally, when $\zeta > 0.68$, countries c and d both prefer to stay out of the club, as does country e. Recall that an interesting result under the four-country case was that a country with an intermediate production cost can

13 It is worth emphasizing that while this result does not require demand linearity, it does rely on cost linearity (which is essential for obtaining strategic independence of tariffs, in the absence of which the analysis becomes intractable).

14 Future research might consider a world of symmetric n countries in order to highlight the differences between our two games of club membership. However, in this paper, we have chosen to focus on cost heterogeneity among countries, something that has been under-explored in the literature. Given the multitude of dimensions along which WTO members differ from each other, our focused model is obviously just a first step and much further research is needed to fully understand when and why country heterogeneity matters.

end up joining the club, even though it is worse off as a member relative to tariff discrimination (proposition 5). This result continues to hold for the five-country case: it is easy to show that when $0.45 < \zeta < 0.68$, if $\langle\{abc\}\rangle$ emerges as the stable equilibrium, then member country c is worse off relative to discrimination, whereas if $\langle\{abd\}\rangle$ obtains, then country d suffers the same fate. Finally, we find that when the club comprises the three relatively efficient countries–that is, it is $\langle\{abc\}\rangle$–then all non-members are worse off relative to tariff discrimination. These findings for the $n = 5$ case suggest that our key results should continue to hold for an arbitrary number of countries.

In the OM game, if country j no longer wishes to be in a club if another (say country k) joins, the only option open to country j is to leave the club; it cannot unilaterally exclude any other country from joining the club. Given this, it seems reasonable to also consider a game where a subset of countries can indeed exclude others from the club if they benefit from doing so. In a simultaneous-move game, this idea can be captured by the following exclusive-membership game.

5. An exclusive-membership MFN club

In the first stage of the exclusive-membership (EM) game, each country makes an announcement regarding the list of potential MFN club members. For example, country a's strategy set is $S_a = \{\langle\{\phi\}\rangle, \langle\{ab\}\rangle, \langle\{ac\}\rangle, \langle\{abc\}\rangle\}$.[15] In the next stage, an MFN club is formed by those that make the same announcement. If no announcements match, status quo $\langle\{\phi\}\rangle$ prevails.

Before we proceed with the analysis of the EM game, two points are worth noting. First, in the EM game, whenever a country unilaterally deviates from a three-country MFN club, the other two countries remain within the club (as in the Γ game of Hart and Kurz 1983) and any unilateral deviation from a two-country club yields the status quo $\langle\{\phi\}\rangle$. Second, in both the OM game and the EM game we consider only the formation of a single club.[16] While this is not problematic in the OM game, in the EM game allowing countries to form more than a single club can have important effects on equilibrium outcomes. More specifically, the EM game can easily generate a situation where two different clubs co-exist in equilibrium. However, given that our paper is motivated by the GATT/WTO, to which there is no viable alternative in the real world, our focus on the formation of a single club is reasonable.[17]

As in the OM game, $\langle\{\phi\}\rangle$ is a Nash equilibrium of the EM game for all parameter values. However, in contrast to the OM game, Nash equilibria of the

15 The club $\langle\{abcd\}\rangle$ need not be considered, because country d never wants to join an MFN club.

16 We thank an anonymous referee for raising this issue.

17 We should note here that free trade agreements or customs unions are not really an alternative to the WTO, since WTO rules (in particular Article XXIV) permit countries to sign such preferential trade agreements (PTAs). As a result, countries do not have to choose between the WTO and PTAs.

TABLE 1
All clubs except $\langle\{abc\}\rangle$ are Nash but only $\langle\{bc\}\rangle$ is coalition-proof

Country $\Delta w_i(m)$	a	b	c	d
$\Delta w_i(ab)$	0.96	0.63	−0.11	−1.14
$\Delta w_i(ac)$	1.06	0.00	0.20	−0.98
$\Delta w_i(bc)$	0.00	0.79*	0.26*	−0.85
$\Delta w_i(abc)$	1.88	1.03	−0.25	−1.97

TABLE 2
All clubs are Nash but only $\{abc\}$ and $\{bc\}$ are coalition-proof

Country $\Delta w_i(m)$	a	b	c	d
$\Delta w_i(ab)$	0.95	0.63	0.12	−1.21
$\Delta w_i(ac)$	1.01	0.00	0.40	−1.07
$\Delta w_i(bc)$	0.00	0.75*	0.46*	−0.96
$\Delta w_i(abc)$	1.70*	0.88*	0.21*	−2.09

EM game are much less likely to be coalition proof. We illustrate this below with the help of two examples. Let $\Delta w_i(m)$ denote the difference between country i's welfare under club m and status quo $\langle\{\phi\}\rangle$: $\Delta w_i(m) \equiv w_i(m) - w_i(\phi)$.

EXAMPLE 1. *Suppose* $\zeta_a = 0, \zeta_b = 0.2, \zeta_c = 0.6, \zeta_d = 1,$ *and* $\alpha = 20$.

In table 1, row 1 shows that the formation of $\langle\{ab\}\rangle$ increases welfare of member countries and that of the world as a whole whereas it lowers the welfare of non-members. It is easy to verify, that in table 2, there are three Nash equilibria (in addition to $\langle\{\ \phi\}\rangle$): $\langle\{ab\}\rangle, \langle\{ac\}\rangle, \langle\{bc\}\rangle$. The club $\langle\{abc\}\rangle$ fails to be a Nash equilibrium because country c is better off under $\langle\{\phi\}\rangle$ and would unilaterally deviate from $\langle\{abc\}\rangle$ to leave the club. Of the three Nash equilibria, only $\langle\{bc\}\rangle$ is coalition proof; this is indicated in table 1 by the superscript * on the payoffs of club members. For example, $\langle\{ac\}\rangle$ is not coalition proof because countries b and c can raise their individual welfare levels by jointly deviating to $\langle\{bc\}\rangle$. Furthermore, this joint deviation is credible because neither country has a unilateral incentive to further deviate from $\langle\{bc\}\rangle$. Similar arguments can establish that $\langle\{ab\}\rangle$ and $\langle\{\phi\}\rangle$ are also not coalition proof.

EXAMPLE 2. *Now, suppose* $\zeta_a = 0, \zeta_b = 0.2, \zeta_c = 0.4, \zeta_d = 1,$ *and* $\alpha = 20$. *Here, all parameters are the same as that in example 1 except that* ζ_c *is lower.*

Now, $\langle\{ab\}\rangle, \langle\{ac\}\rangle, \langle\{bc\}\rangle, \langle\{abc\}\rangle$ all are Nash equilibria but only $\langle\{abc\}\rangle$ and $\langle\{bc\}\rangle$ are coalition proof, as is indicated in table 2 by the superscript * on the

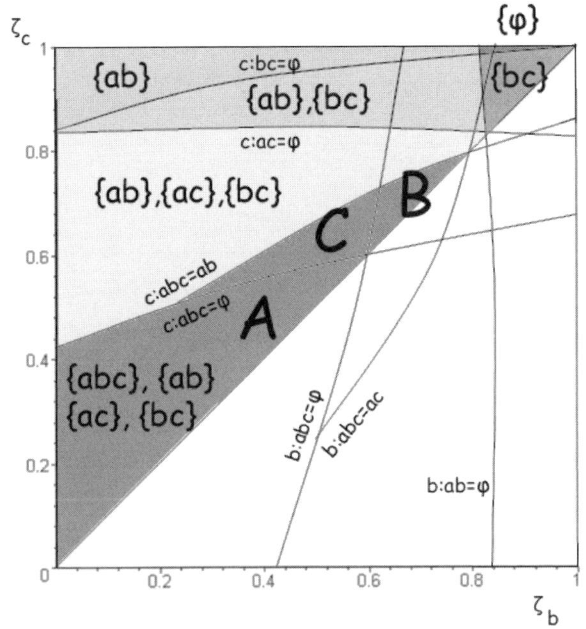

FIGURE 2 Nash Equilibrium of the EM game

payoffs of club members. Since country *c*'s cost is now relatively lower compared with that in example 1, it is a more willing participant in MFN clubs. To see, for example, why $\langle\{ab\}\rangle$ fails to be coalition proof, simply note that countries *b* and *c* can jointly deviate to $\langle\{bc\}\rangle$ and improve their welfare.

Figure 2 illustrates Nash equilibria of the EM game, while coalition-proof Nash equilibria are shown in figure 3. As is clear from figure 2, multiplicity of Nash equilibria obtains for almost all feasible parameter values. For example, in subregion A, $\langle\{abc\}\rangle$, $\langle\{ab\}\rangle$, $\langle\{ac\}\rangle$, and $\langle\{bc\}\rangle$ all are Nash equilibria. Such multiplicity makes it imperative to focus on coalition-proof Nash equilibria (see figure 3).

Consider a comparison of figures 1 through 3 in order to grasp the differences between the outcomes obtained under the two games of club formation. First, note that the parameter space over which $\langle\{abc\}\rangle$ is stable under the EM game is much smaller than the space over which it is a Nash equilibrium. Furthermore, $\langle\{bc\}\rangle$ is stable over a large parameter space in the EM game, whereas it is *never* so in the OM game. This finding is of particular interest because $\langle\{bc\}\rangle$ is the least desirable MFN club from the viewpoint of world welfare. Why is $\langle\{bc\}\rangle$ coalition proof for such a large range of parameter values in the EM game? It is

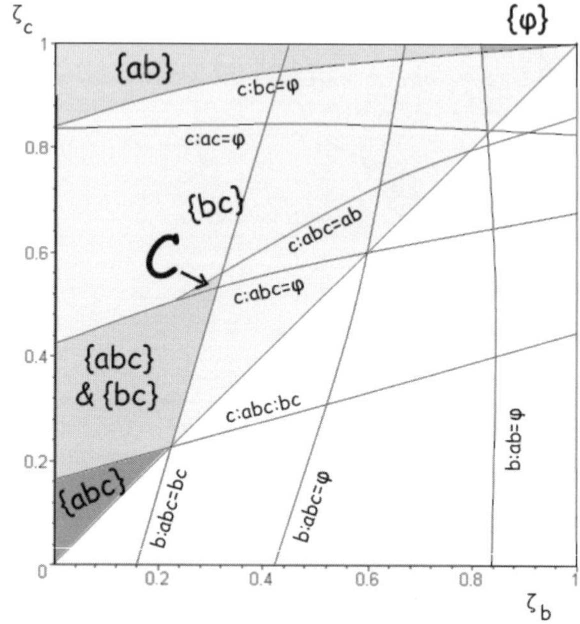

FIGURE 3 CPNE of the EM game

because countries b and c benefit substantially from the exclusion of country a, to whom they have to grant large tariff concessions as a member (see section 3). To gain more insight into this result, fix country b's cost at a low level (say, close to zero) and consider moving vertically in figure 3 plotted in the (ζ_b, ζ_c) space. Near the origin, where each country's cost is small, $\langle\{abc\}\rangle$ is the equilibrium. Here, no country has an incentive to exclude any other country from the club, since everyone is essentially low cost. As country c's cost increases, it has an incentive to exclude country a, whereas country b does not. Hence, both $\langle\{bc\}\rangle$ and $\langle\{abc\}\rangle$ are equilibrium MFN clubs. A further increase in country c's cost makes $\langle\{bc\}\rangle$ the only equilibrium; when country c's cost is really high, country b has a strong incentive to tariff discriminate between a and c (so that it wants to keep country a out of the club) and its tariff on country c is quite low (making $\langle\{bc\}\rangle$ attractive to country c). Finally, when country c's cost is almost equal to that of country d, the club $\langle\{ab\}\rangle$ emerges as the equilibrium, since country c does not gain much from being granted MFN by other countries (i.e., under $\langle\{\phi\}\rangle$ it faces fairly low tariffs).

As noted earlier, the most desirable MFN club (i.e., $\langle\{abc\}\rangle$) is coalition proof over a smaller region in the EM game relative to the OM game. In this respect, the EM game gives a worse outcome than the OM game. Furthermore, the club $\langle\{ac\}\rangle$ fails to be coalition proof under the EM game, since countries b and c have an incentive to jointly deviate to $\langle\{bc\}\rangle$ in order to exclude country a. All else equal, does the OM game yield outcomes that always dominate those yielded by the EM game? The answer to this question is in the affirmative, except when both country b and country c have relatively high costs (i.e., their costs are close to that of country d). Under such a world of one low-cost and several high-cost countries, no country wants to form a club with country a in the OM game, thereby yielding $\langle\{\phi\}\rangle$ as the equilibrium, whereas countries b and c want to form $\langle\{bc\}\rangle$ under the EM game, since they can exclude country a from the club. While $\langle\{bc\}\rangle$ is the least desirable MFN club, it still yields higher world welfare than $\langle\{\phi\}\rangle$. Furthermore, note also that, compared with the OM game, it is much less likely that an MFN club formed in the EM game immiserizes its higher-cost members relative to tariff discrimination. More specifically, in the EM game, country b is *never* worse off as a club member, whereas country c is worse off over a much smaller region relative to the OM game (compare region A in figures 1 and 3).

6. Extensions and discussion

In this section we discuss two important extensions of our model.[18] The first extension explicitly integrates GSP into our intra-industry trade model, while the second considers a two-sector trade model, where countries are free to utilize tariffs in both sectors. Both extensions help to establish the robustness of our analysis in certain respects while defining its limitations in others. Finally, we discuss how a modified version of our model can be applied to analyze accession to the WTO.

6.1. Integrating GSP into the model

Our model suggests that the preferential treatment granted to developing countries under GSP may help to undo the harmful effect that membership of an MFN club has on them. In other words, our model's interpretation of GSP is that it may serve as a form of *compensation* to developing countries in order to induce them to participate in an MFN-based system (i.e., the WTO). This interpretation naturally raises the question of whether explicitly introducing GSP into our model can actually induce membership on the part of the highest-cost country. To address this question, we now consider the following scenario under the OM game: suppose that, if the highest cost country (i.e., d) joins the MFN club it, receives better than MFN treatment from the lowest-cost country (i.e., a). For example, if the club comprises all four countries, then country d receives GSP

18 We thank two anonymous referees for suggestions that led to these extensions.

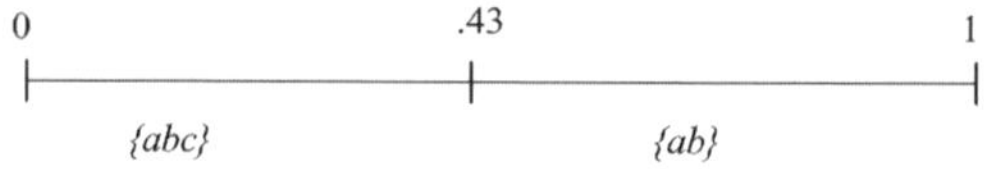

FIGURE 1b CPNE of the OM game without GSP ($n = 4$)

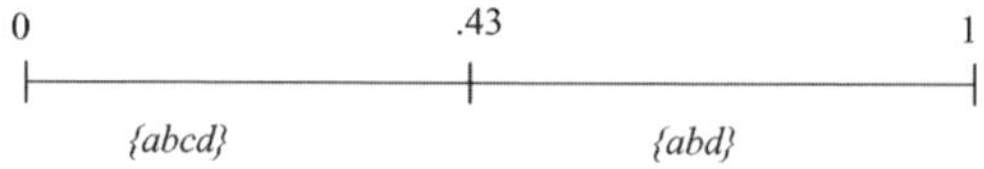

FIGURE 1c CPNE of the OM game with 10% GSP margin ($n = 4$)

treatment from country a, whereas all other countries impose MFN tariffs on each other.

The margin of preference accorded under GSP is obviously crucial in determining the extent to which GSP treatment can induce membership on the part of the highest-cost country. But existing empirical evidence makes it difficult to get a precise estimate of the actual margin of preference under GSP. For example, the GSP program of the EU does not extend preferential treatment under those sectors that are perceived to be 'sensitive.' Furthermore, while non-sensitive products enjoy duty free access to the EU market to exports of eligible countries, sensitive products (which account for 36% of tariff lines) receive only a 3.5% reduction in the MFN tariff rate (Hoekman and Ozden 2007). Similarly, under the GSP system of the US, only about 4,650 tariff lines qualify for GSP treatment from eligible countries. Furthermore, the list of eligible countries is subject to 'graduation' – that is, if a country reaches a sufficiently high level of exports or income level, it can be dropped from the GSP list, as has happened, for example, to countries such as Malaysia, Mexico, and South Korea. Since GSP treatment in our intra-industry one-good trade model essentially extends to all trade, it is reasonable to consider a margin of preference of around 10% to illustrate when and how GSP matters for club membership.[19]

To keep the analysis tractable, we focus on the case where $\zeta_a = \zeta_b = 0$, $\zeta_c = \zeta$, where $0 < \zeta < 1$ and $\zeta_d = 1$. To see how the introduction of GSP matters, first consider equilibrium outcomes in the OM game in the absence of GSP. In figure 1b, the horizontal line shows coalition proof equilibria as a function of ζ.

In other words, in line with the outcomes described in figure 1, we find that when $\zeta < .43$, $\langle\{abc\}\rangle$ is the coalition proof Nash equilibrium, whereas $\langle\{abc\}\rangle$ obtains when $\zeta > .43$. Now consider how the introduction of preferential treatment under GSP for the highest-cost country alters equilibrium outcomes. When the margin of GSP preference equals 10%, equilibrium outcomes in the OM game are as shown in figure 1c. Figure 1c indicates that the club $\langle\{abcd\}\rangle$ is coalition proof when $0 < \zeta < .43$. Thus, the preferential treatment given to the high-cost

19 In any case, it turns out that the qualitative nature of the results reported below is not particularly sensitive to small variations in this margin.

country can indeed result in every country joining the club, so long as the cost of country *c* (that does not receive GSP) is not too high. In this sense, the GSP margin provided to the highest-cost country (i.e., *d*) proves to be socially valuable, since, in its absence, the grand coalition does not emerge as a coalition proof Nash equilibrium. When $.43 < \zeta$, $\langle\{abd\}\rangle$ obtains as the coalition proof Nash equilibrium – here, the cost of country *c* is too high for it to be willing to join the club, but GSP treatment induces country *d* to join. Most interestingly, we find that while the 10% preference margin under GSP makes the highest-cost country better off relative to being an outsider and thereby induces it to join the club, it still does *not* make it better off relative to tariff discrimination. It would prefer that there be no club at all. This result suggests that, while helpful, GSP treatment in itself may not be sufficient to offset the impact that an MFN club has on countries with inferior production technologies relative to a world in which no such club exists. Furthermore, this result continues to hold, even when the margin of GSP preference is 15% or even 20% (which is surely a rather generous interpretation of the actual margin of preference accorded to developing countries under GSP, since, as noted above, such preferences do not cover a significant proportion of world trade).

6.2. A multi-sector model

The main reason we do not obtain the grand coalition as an MFN club in our basic model in the absence of GSP treatment is that the highest-cost country never gains from joining the club. In the real world, countries trade a variety of goods and a country that has a high cost of production in one good need not necessarily suffer a cost disadvantage in all other goods. Indeed, the classical theory of comparative advantage is built on the notion of relative cost differences across countries. Thus, it is useful to consider a scenario where countries produce multiple goods with varying degrees of efficiency to see whether we can have a coalition proof Nash equilibrium with all countries joining the MFN club.

To pursue this question, assume that, in addition to the numeraire good *y* and the oligopolistic good *x*, there exists a third good *z* that is produced under the same international market structure as good *x*. Let preferences be given by $U(x, y, z) = u(x) + u(z) + y$, so that demand for the two goods is symmetric. Let country *i*'s marginal cost of production of good *z* be given by ξ_i. To capture the underlying idea motivating our analysis of multiple sectors in the starkest possible fashion, let $\zeta_a = 0, \zeta_b = \zeta_c = \zeta$, where $0 < \zeta < 1$ and $\zeta_d = 1$ and $\xi_a = 1; \xi_b = \xi_c = \zeta$, where $0 < \xi < 1$ and $\xi_d = 0$. In other words, while country *a* is the lowest-cost producer of good *x*, its production cost of good *z* is the highest. Similarly, while country *d* is the highest-cost producer of good *z*, its production cost for good *x* is the lowest. Finally, the other two countries have intermediate costs for both goods. Under such a scenario, country *d*'s cost disadvantage in good *x* is offset by its cost advantage in good *z*. The question then becomes whether such a cost structure can induce all countries to join the club in equilibrium. Figure 1d shows that this indeed can be the case.

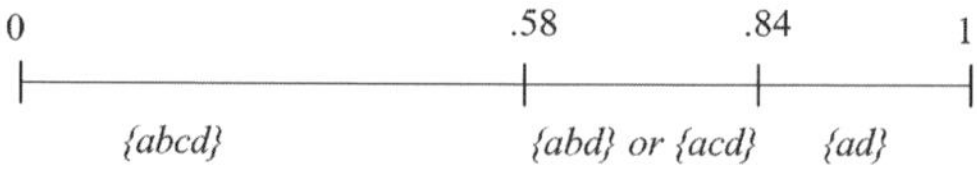

FIGURE 1d CPNE of the OM game with two sectors

As can be seen in figure 1d, the grand coalition $\langle\{abcd\}\rangle$ is the coalition-proof Nash equilibrium when $0 < \zeta < .58$; either $\langle\{abc\}\rangle$ or $\langle\{abd\}\rangle$ is coalition proof if $.58 < \zeta < .84$; and $\langle\{ad\}\rangle$ is coalition proof when $.84 < \zeta < 1$. Furthermore, the result that club members can be worse off relative to discrimination continues to hold: when $.29 < \zeta < .44$, all countries are better off as part of the grand club $\langle\{abcd\}\rangle$ relative to tariff discrimination, whereas only *b* and *c* are better off when $0 < \zeta < .29$. Under such a situation, countries *b* and *c* enjoy relatively low production costs in both goods and therefore gain substantially from receiving MFN status, whereas the other two countries have a substantial cost disadvantage in at least one of the two goods.

6.3. Accession to the club

In our static model, entry into the club takes place only once. As a result, by design, it cannot speak to the fact that membership of the WTO has grown over time; that is, the model is silent about issues of accession. It is worth discussing how our model might be applied to analyze accession at the WTO.[20] To do so, it is useful first to briefly discuss the actual accession process at the WTO. Accession by a country to the WTO requires the consent of all members of a Working Party, where any existing WTO member is free to join the Working Party. One would expect that those members that are most significantly affected by the accession of a new country would have an incentive to join the Working Party. In our model of intra-industry trade, the Working Party would comprise all existing members. As is clear, using our model to analyze accession properly would require that entry into the club be possible at two different stages at least. One possible approach is to consider a two-period world with the following structure. Entry into the club is possible at the beginning of each period. In the first period, since no club exists and anyone is free to join, suppose that all countries play the OM game. In the second period, any non-member country can apply to join the club with the understanding that such accession would occur only if all existing members of the club agree to it. Thus, the second-period game would be quite like our EM game, where any existing member has the ability to exclude the applicant.

From our existing results, we know that if the world were to last only one period, the highest-cost country would stay out of the club. Under such a scenario, we conjecture that if there are no underlying changes in production costs between the two periods, the equilibrium of the two-period model would coincide with that

20 We should note that our discussion of accession to the club is suggestive rather than definitive. Indeed, the issue is rich enough to make it worthy of future research.

of our static model. For the possibility of accession to arise, suppose, then, that at the end of period one the highest-cost country experiences a technology shock that lowers its production cost. If so, in the second period an actual application for accession on its part may arise if the positive technology shock experienced by it is significant enough. Interestingly, such accession could potentially be blocked by an existing member who may find that its own cost has become high relative to the applicant ex post's cost unless accession is accompanied by some sort of compensation on the part of the new entrant. Perhaps this is partly why WTO accession rules require negotiations between existing members and a potential entrant. Given this, one would expect that a high-cost country that stays out of the club in the first period would apply for and be granted membership if its technology improves sufficiently *and* if it grants adequate concessions to those existing members that might potentially lose from its accession (ensuring that they, too, become better off ex post). Since the biggest MFN club is the most beneficial one, we know that such a bargain can indeed be struck between existing members and a potential applicant for membership.

7. Conclusion

This paper analyzes two related games of club formation in order to gain insight into the emergence of various types of MFN clubs and to examine the welfare consequences of such clubs. The underlying trade model is one of oligopolistic intra-industry trade between four countries that are asymmetric with respect to production costs. This simple structure is sufficient to yield a basis for tariff discrimination on the part of individual countries whose tariff policies are constrained upon the adoption of an MFN clause.

We find that the formation of any MFN club increases world welfare, even though no such club has an effect on average tariff levels. This implies that WTO rules have value, even if rounds of negotiations between WTO members fail to deliver significant trade liberalization. This result is reassuring for those who think that the WTO has a useful role to play in the arena of international trade. However, one cannot immediately jump from this conclusion to the argument that membership in an MFN club necessarily makes all participating countries better off. In particular, high-cost members of the club can lose relative to the status quo, even though membership is entirely voluntary. The insight behind this result is that a country may be induced to join a club because being a nonmember is worse than being a member. Of course, if transfers (or issue linkages) are possible between countries, such an outcome can be avoided, since aggregate world welfare is necessarily increased from any type of MFN club.

Those that do not join the club are necessarily worse off relative to the status quo, and they remain outside either because membership further immiserizes them or because they are simply excluded by others (as in the exclusive-membership game). In the model, the country with the highest production cost never joins an MFN club, and it is always better off in a world where no such club exists. This result provides one possible rationale behind the Special and Differential (S&D) treatment accorded to developing-country members of the WTO under which they receive better than MFN treatment under GATT. The model suggests that absent such treatment, many developing countries may prefer to remain outside the GATT/WTO. Since aggregate world welfare is increasing in the size of the MFN club, S&D provisions might generate some indirect benefits for the world as a whole (the costs of such distortionary policies notwithstanding).

While our model provides some interesting insights, it does so under fairly specific assumptions. In our view, there are at least two directions in which future research is needed. First, a theory of an MFN club based on a partial equilibrium model such as ours can take us only so far. A general equilibrium approach such as Bagwell and Staiger (1999) to this issue would be welcome (but might prove intractable). Second, we adopt a welfare-maximizing framework and ignore political economy considerations. The introduction of such considerations into our model might modify some of our results.

Appendix

A.1. Derivation of optimal tariffs

Under tariff discrimination, country i solves

$$\operatorname*{Max}_{\mathbf{t_i}} \frac{x_i^2(\mathbf{t_i})}{2} + x_{ii}^2(\mathbf{t_i}) + \sum_{j \neq i} t_{ji} x_{ji}(\mathbf{t_i}), \tag{A1}$$

where

$$x_{ii} = \frac{\alpha - 4\zeta_i + Z_{-i} + T_i}{5} \text{ and } x_{ji} = \frac{\alpha - 4(\zeta_j + t_{ji}) + (Z_{-j} + T_{-j})}{5}, \tag{A2}$$

and

$$T_{-j} = T_i - t_{ji} = \sum_{k \neq j} t_{ki} \text{ and } Z_{-i} \equiv Z - \zeta_i \text{ and } Z \equiv \sum_{j=1}^{4} \zeta_j. \tag{A3}$$

Solving the above problem yields

$$t_{ji}(\phi) = \frac{1}{22}[6\alpha + 3Z - 7\zeta_i - 11\zeta_j]. \tag{A4}$$

Under MFN towards all countries, country i solves

$$\operatorname*{Max}_{t_i} S_i(t_i) \equiv CS_i(t_i) + \pi_{ii}(t_i) + TR_i(t_i), \tag{A5}$$

which gives

$$t_i^M = \frac{1}{33}[9\alpha - Z - 5\zeta_i]. \tag{A6}$$

Next, we show how optimal tariffs under various MFN clubs are derived. We divide the parameter space into four subregions:

(i) Region 1 (R1): $\zeta_b + \zeta_d \leq 2\zeta_c$.
(ii) Region 2 (R2): $2\zeta_b \leq \zeta_a + \zeta_d \leq 2\zeta_c \leq \zeta_b + \zeta_d$.
(iii) Region 3 (R3): $\zeta_a + \zeta_d \leq 2\zeta_b \leq 2\zeta_c \leq \zeta_b + \zeta_d$.
(iv) Region 4 (R4): $2\zeta_b \leq 2\zeta_c \leq \zeta_a + \zeta_d$.

As an example, consider country a's tariff problem under $\langle\{ab\}\rangle$:

$$\max_{\mathbf{t}_a} W_a(\mathbf{t}_a) \text{ subject to } t_{ba}(ab) \leq \min\{t_{da}(ab), t_{ca}(ab)\} \tag{A7}$$

Solving the above problem yields

$$t_{ba}(ab) = \begin{cases} t_a^M & \text{R1} \\ \frac{1}{44}(12\alpha - 5\zeta_b + 6\zeta_c - 5\zeta_d) & \text{elsewhere} \end{cases}, \tag{A8}$$

whereas

$$t_{ca}(ab) = \begin{cases} t_a^M & \text{R1} \\ \frac{1}{22}(6\alpha + 3\zeta_b - 8\zeta_c + 3\zeta_d) & \text{elsewhere} \end{cases}. \tag{A9}$$

Similarly, country b's tariffs are

$$t_{ab}(ab) = \begin{cases} \frac{1}{44}(12\alpha - 8\zeta_b + 6\zeta_c - 5\zeta_d) & \text{R4} \\ t_b^M & \text{elsewhere} \end{cases}, \tag{A10}$$

and

$$t_{cb}(ab) = \begin{cases} \frac{1}{22}(-8\zeta_c + 3\zeta_d + 6\alpha - 4\zeta_b) & \text{R4} \\ t_b^M & \text{elsewhere} \end{cases}. \tag{A11}$$

Tariffs under $\langle\{ac\}\rangle$ are calculated similarly.

A.2. Lemma 1
Total tariff protection by country i is

$$T_i \equiv \sum_{j \neq i} t_{ji} = \frac{9\alpha - Z - 5\zeta_i}{11}. \tag{A12}$$

From result 2, T_i under any MFN club is the same as that under $\langle\{\phi\}\rangle$. Direct computations show that $T_i \geq T_k$ iff $\zeta_i \leq \zeta_k$.

A.3. Lemma 2
It is straightforward that

$$t_{ba}(abc) - t_{ba}(\phi) = \frac{2\zeta_b - (\zeta_c + \zeta_d)}{6} < 0, \tag{A13}$$

whereas

$$t_{ca}(abc) - t_{ca}(\phi) = \frac{2\zeta_c - (\zeta_b + \zeta_d)}{6} < 0 \text{ iff } 2\zeta_c < \zeta_b + \zeta_d. \tag{A14}$$

Similar conclusions can be drawn about tariffs of countries b and c. We have

$$t_{ab}(abc) < t_{ab}(\phi) \text{ whereas } t_{cb}(abc) < t_{cb}(\phi) \text{ iff } 2\zeta_c < \zeta_d \tag{A15}$$

and

$$t_{ac}(abc) < t_{ac}(\phi) \text{ whereas } t_{bc}(abc) < t_{bc}(\phi) \text{ iff } 2\zeta_b < \zeta_d. \tag{A16}$$

Now, consider $\langle\{ab\}\rangle$. When $2\zeta_c < \zeta_d$, we can show that

$$t_{ba}(ab) - t_{ba}(\phi) = \frac{1}{4}(\zeta_b - \zeta_d) < 0 \text{ and } t_{ab}(ab) - t_{ba}(\phi) = -\frac{\zeta_d}{4} < 0, \tag{A17}$$

whereas $t_{ca}(ab) = t_{ba}(\phi)$ and $t_{cb}(ab) = t_{cb}(\phi)$. When $\zeta_d < 2\zeta_c < \zeta_b + \zeta_d$, we have

$$\begin{aligned} t_{ba}(ab) - t_{ba}(\phi) &= -\frac{1}{4}(\zeta_d - \zeta_b) < 0 \text{ and } t_{ab}(ab) - t_{ab}(\phi) \\ &= -\frac{1}{6}(\zeta_c + \zeta_d) < 0, \end{aligned} \tag{A18}$$

whereas

$$t_{ca}(ab) = t_{ca}(\phi) \text{ and } t_{cb}(ab) - t_{cb}(\phi) = \frac{1}{6}(2\zeta_c - \zeta_d) > 0. \tag{A19}$$

Finally, when $2\zeta_c > \zeta_b + \zeta_d$, we have

$$\begin{aligned} t_{ba}(ab) - t_{ba}(\phi) &= \frac{1}{6}(2\zeta_b - \zeta_c - \zeta_d) < 0 \text{ and } t_{ab}(ab) - t_{ab}(\phi) \\ &= -\frac{1}{6}(\zeta_c + \zeta_d) < 0, \end{aligned} \tag{A20}$$

whereas

$$\begin{aligned} t_{ca}(ab) - t_{ca}(\phi) &= \frac{1}{6}(2\zeta_c - \zeta_d - \zeta_b) > 0 \text{ and } t_{cb}(ab) - t_{cb}(\phi) \\ &= \frac{1}{6}(2\zeta_c - \zeta_d) > 0. \end{aligned} \tag{A21}$$

The analysis under $\langle\{ac\}\rangle$ is analogous to that of $\langle\{ab\}\rangle$, with the roles of countries b and c reversed. However, need to consider we only two cases: (i) $2\zeta_b < \zeta_d$ and (ii) $2\zeta_b > \zeta_d$. Under both cases, member countries receive concessions from each other. Under case (i), tariffs on country b are the same as that under $\langle\{\phi\}\rangle$ whereas under case (ii), it suffers a tariff increase in c's market, with the tariff in a's market staying the same as that under $\langle\{\phi\}\rangle$. Finally, under $\langle\{bc\}\rangle$ members receive concessions from each other, whereas non-members face the same tariffs as under $\langle\{\phi\}\rangle$.

A.4. Lemma 3

Consider $\langle\{ab\}\rangle$. We have

$$\Delta t_{ab}(ab) - \Delta t_{ba}(ab) = \begin{cases} \dfrac{\zeta_b}{3} \geq 0 & \text{R1} \\ \dfrac{2\zeta_c - \zeta_d + 3\zeta_b}{ab} \geq 0 & \text{R2-R3} \\ \dfrac{\zeta_b}{4} \geq 0 & \text{R4} \end{cases}. \tag{A22}$$

Under $\langle\{ac\}\rangle$ we have

$$\Delta t_{ac}(ac) - \Delta t_{ca}(ac) = \begin{cases} \dfrac{\zeta_c}{4} \geq 0 & \text{R1, R2, and R4} \\ \dfrac{2\zeta_b - \zeta_d + 3\zeta_c}{ab} \geq 0 & \text{R3} \end{cases}. \tag{A23}$$

and for $\langle\{bc\}\rangle$ we have

$$\Delta t_{bc}(bc) - \Delta t_{cb}(bc) = \frac{\zeta_c - \zeta_b}{4} \geq 0. \tag{A24}$$

Finally, under $\langle\{abc\}\rangle$ we have

$$\Delta t_{ab}(abc) - \Delta t_{ba}(abc) = \frac{\zeta_b}{3} \geq 0 \text{ and } \Delta t_{ac}(abc) - \Delta t_{ca}(abc) = \frac{\zeta_c}{3} \geq 0, \quad \text{(A25)}$$

and

$$\Delta t_{bc}(abc) - \Delta t_{cb}(abc) = \frac{\zeta_c - \zeta_b}{3} \geq 0. \quad \text{(A26)}$$

A.5. Proposition 1

For $\langle\{ab\}\rangle$ we have

$$\Delta TR_a(ab) - \Delta TR_b(ab) = \begin{cases} \frac{1}{6}\zeta_b(\zeta_b - \zeta_c - \zeta_d) \leq 0 & \text{R1} \\ \frac{1}{24}\left(4\zeta_c\zeta_d - 6\zeta_b\zeta_d - \zeta_d^2 - 4\zeta_c + 3\zeta_b\right) \leq 0 & \text{R2 and R3} \\ \frac{1}{8}\zeta_b(\zeta_b - 2\zeta_d) \leq 0 & \text{R4} \end{cases}. \quad \text{(A27)}$$

Under $\langle\{ac\}\rangle$ we have

$$\Delta TR_a(ac) - \Delta TR_c(ac) = \begin{cases} \frac{1}{8}\zeta_c(-2\zeta_d + \zeta_c) \leq 0 & \text{R1, R2, and R4} \\ \frac{1}{24}\left(4\zeta_b\zeta_d - \zeta_d^2 + 3\zeta_c - 6\zeta_c\zeta_d - 4\zeta_b\right) \leq 0 & \text{R3,} \end{cases} \quad \text{(A28)}$$

whereas under $\langle\{bc\}\rangle$ we have

$$\Delta TR_b(bc) - \Delta TR_c(bc) = \frac{1}{8}(\zeta_c - \zeta_b)(\zeta_b - 2\zeta_d + \zeta_c) \leq 0. \quad \text{(A29)}$$

Finally, under $\langle\{abc\}\rangle$ we have

$$\Delta TR_a(abc) - \Delta TR_b(abc) = \frac{1}{6}\zeta_b(\zeta_b - \zeta_c - \zeta_d) \leq 0 \quad \text{(A30)}$$

and

$$\Delta TR_a(abc) - \Delta TR_c(abc) = \frac{1}{6}\zeta_c(\zeta_c - \zeta_d - \zeta_b) \leq 0. \quad \text{(A31)}$$

A.6. Lemma 4

From country *a*'s perspective:

$$\Delta TR_a(ac) - \Delta TR_a(ab) = \begin{cases} -\frac{1}{24}(2\zeta_b - \zeta_c - \zeta_d)^2 \leq 0 & \text{R1} \\ -\frac{1}{8}(\zeta_b - \zeta_c)(-2\zeta_d + \zeta_b + \zeta_c) \leq 0 & \text{R2-R4} \end{cases}. \tag{A32}$$

For country *b* we have

$$\Delta TR_b(bc) - \Delta TR_b(ab) = \begin{cases} -\frac{1}{24}(\zeta_c + \zeta_d)^2 \leq 0 & \text{R1-R3} \\ -\frac{1}{8}\zeta_c(2\zeta_d - \zeta_c) \leq 0 & \text{R4} \end{cases}. \tag{A33}$$

Finally, for country *c* we have

$$\Delta TR_c(bc) - \Delta TR_c(ac) = \begin{cases} -\frac{1}{8}\zeta_b(2\zeta_d - \zeta_b) \leq 0 & \text{R1, R2, and R4} \\ -\frac{1}{24}(\zeta_b + \zeta_d)^2 \leq 0 & \text{R3} \end{cases}. \tag{A34}$$

Hence, $\Delta TR_i(ik) - \Delta TR_i(ij) \leq 0$ iff $\zeta_j \leq \zeta_k$ for all i, j, k.

A.7. Lemma 5

Note that

$$\Delta t_{ac} - \Delta t_{ab} = \begin{cases} \frac{\zeta_d - 2\zeta_c}{6} \leq 0 & \text{R1-R2} \\ \frac{\zeta_b - \zeta_c}{6} \leq 0 & \text{R3} \\ 0 & \text{R4} \end{cases}. \tag{A35}$$

Also,

$$\Delta t_{bc} - \Delta t_{ba} = \begin{cases} \frac{\zeta_b + \zeta_d - 2\zeta_c}{12} \leq 0 & \text{R1} \\ 0 & \text{R2-R4} \end{cases}. \tag{A36}$$

Finally, note that $\Delta t_{cb} - \Delta t_{ca} = 0$.

A.8. Equilibria of the OM game

First, note that the only Nash equilibrium from which coalitional deviations need to be examined is $\langle\{abc\}\rangle$. To see why, imagine any two-country club such as

$\langle\{ab\}\rangle$ that is a Nash equilibrium. If $\langle\{ab\}\rangle$ is a Nash equilibrium, by definition, no single country would deviate to $\langle\{\phi\}\rangle$. The deviation of both a and b to $\langle\{\phi\}\rangle$ would not occur, since country a loses from such a deviation. By similar arguments, any two-country club that is a Nash equilibrium is also coalition proof.

Now suppose $\langle\{abc\}\rangle$ is a Nash equilibrium. For $\langle\{abc\}\rangle$ to be coalition proof, we need only to ask whether a deviation by countries b and c to $\langle\{\phi\}\rangle$ is credible (since country a does not ever gain from leaving the club). It turns out that, under conditions specified below, if countries b and c deviate to $\langle\{\phi\}\rangle$, then at least one of them wants to further deviate to form a club with country a. As a result, their original deviation to $\langle\{\phi\}\rangle$ is not credible. More specifically, given that $\langle\{abc\}\rangle$ is Nash (which means that $w_b(abc) \geq w_b(ac)$ and $w_c(abc) \geq w_c(ab)$), then it is also coalition proof if either (i) $w_b(ab) \geq w_b(\phi)$ or (ii) $w_c(ac) \geq w_c(\phi)$ or both of these conditions hold. It turns out that these conditions are rather minor and are satisfied for the entire parameter space over which all our figures have been constructed.

A.9. Proposition 3

This result follows from direct calculations. As an example, consider country c's preferences. We have

$$w_c(bc) - w_c(ac)$$
$$= \begin{cases} F \equiv \frac{1}{88}(-\zeta_b)(11\zeta_b + 10\zeta_c - 32\zeta_d) \geq 0 & \text{R1, R2, and R4} \\ \quad = F + 1/24(\zeta_d - 2\zeta_b)^2 \geq 0 & \text{R3} \end{cases}. \tag{A37}$$

Similar calculations underlie the other rankings and we do not report the formulae in order to conserve space.

A.10. Proposition 4

Direct computations give

$$\Delta ww(bc) \equiv ww(bc) - ww(\phi) = \frac{1}{4}\left[(\zeta_d - \zeta_b)^2 + (\zeta_d - \zeta_c)^2\right] \geq 0. \tag{A38}$$

Similarly,

$$ww(ac) - ww(bc) = \begin{cases} \frac{1}{12}(-\zeta_d - \zeta_b)^2 \geq 0 & \text{R3} \\ \frac{1}{4}(-\zeta_b)(\zeta_b - 2\zeta_d) \geq 0 & \text{elsewhere} \end{cases} \tag{A39}$$

and

$$ww(ab) - ww(ac) = \begin{cases} K \equiv \frac{1}{4}(-\zeta_c + \zeta_b)(-2\zeta_d + \zeta_b + \zeta_c) \geq 0 & \text{R4} \\ K + \frac{1}{12}(-2\zeta_c + \zeta_d)^2 \geq 0 & \text{R1} \\ L \equiv \frac{1}{12}(-\zeta_c + \zeta_b)(-\zeta_b - 2\zeta_d - \zeta_c) \geq 0 & \text{R2} \\ L + \frac{1}{12}(\zeta_d - 2\zeta_b)^2 \geq 0 & \text{R3} \end{cases}. \tag{A40}$$

Finally,

$$ww(abc) - ww(ab) = \begin{cases} P \equiv \frac{1}{3}\left(\zeta_d - \frac{1}{2}\zeta_b\right)^2 + \frac{1}{4}(\zeta_b)^2 \geq 0 & \text{R1} \\ Q \equiv P + \frac{1}{12}(\zeta_d + \zeta_b - 2\zeta_c)^2 \geq 0 & \text{R2-R3} \\ Q + \frac{1}{12}(-2\zeta_c + \zeta_d)^2 \geq 0 & \text{R4} \end{cases}. \tag{A41}$$

Thus, we have shown that in every region

$$\Delta ww(abc) \geq \Delta ww(ab) \geq \Delta ww(ac) \geq \Delta ww(bc) \geq 0. \tag{A42}$$

References

Aghion, Philippe, Pol Antràs, and Elhanan Helpman (2004) 'Negotiating free trade,' *Journal of International Economics* 73, 1–30

Bagwell, Kyle, and Robert W. Staiger (1999) 'An economic theory of GATT,' *American Economic Review* 89, 215–48

Bagwell, Kyle, and Robert W. Staiger (2004) 'Multilateral trade negotiations, bilateral opportunism and the rules of GATT/WTO,' *Journal of International Economics* 63, 1–29

Bernheim, B. Douglas, Bezalel Peleg, and Michael D. Whinston (1987) 'Coalition-proof Nash equilibria: I concepts,' *Journal of Economic Theory* 42, 1–12

Brander, James A., and Paul R. Krugman (1983) 'A 'reciprocal dumping' model of international trade,' *Journal of International Economics* 15, 313–23

Brander, James A., and Barbara J. Spencer (1984) 'Tariff protection and imperfect competition,' in *Monopolistic Competition and International Trade*, ed. Henryk Kierzkowski (New York: Oxford University Press)

Burbidge, John B., James A. DePater, Gordon M. Myers, and Abhijit Sengupta (1997) 'A coalition-formation approach to equilibrium federations and trading blocs,' *American Economic Review* 87, 940–56

Caplin, Andrew, and Kala Krishna (1988) 'Tariffs and the most favored nation clause: a game theoretic approach,' *Seoul Journal of Economics* 1, 267–89

Choi, Jay Pil (1995) 'Optimal tariffs and the choice of technology: discriminatory tariffs vs. the most favored nation clause,' *Journal of International Economics* 38, 143–60

Das, S. and S. Ghosh (2006) 'Endogenous trading bloc formation in a North-South global economy,' *Canadian Journal of Economics* 39, 809–30

Dutta, Bhaskar, and Suresh Mutuswami (1997) 'Stable networks,' *Journal of Economic Theory* 76, 322–44

Ederington, Josh, and Phillip McCalman (2003) 'Discriminatory tariffs and international negotiations,' *Journal of International Economics* 61, 397–424

Gatsios, Konstantine (1990) 'Preferential tariffs and the 'most favoured nation' principle: a note,' *Journal of International Economics* 28, 365–73

Hart, Sergiu and Mordecai Kurz (1983) 'Endogenous formation of coalitions,' *Econometrica* 51, 1047–64

Hoekman, Bernard, and Caglar Ozden (2007) *Trade Preferences and Differential Treatment of Developing Countries* (Cheltenham, UK: Edward Elgar)

Horn, Henrik, and Petros C. Mavroidis (2001) 'Economic and legal aspects of the most-favored nation clause,' *European Journal of Political Economy* 17, 233–79

Hwang, Hong and Chao-Cheng Mai (1991) 'Optimum discriminatory tariffs under oligopolistic competition,' *Canadian Journal of Economics* 24, 693–702

Irwin, Douglas A. (2002) *Free Trade under Fire* (Princeton: Princeton University Press)

Jackson, John H. (1997) *The World Trading System* (Cambridge, MA: MIT Press)

Krishna, Pravin (1998) 'Regionalism and multilateralism: a political economy approach,' *Quarterly Journal of Economics* 113, 227–51

Ludema, Rodney D. (1991) 'International trade bargaining and the most favored nation clause,' *Economics and Politics* 3, 1–20

Maggi, Giovanni (1999) 'The role of multilateral institutions in international trade cooperation,' *American Economic Review* 89, 190–214

McCalman, Phillip (2002) 'Multi-lateral trade negotiations and the most favored nation clause,' *Journal of International Economics* 27, 151–76

Oyejide, T. Ademola (2002) 'Special and differential treatment,' in*Development, Trade, and the WTO: A Handbook* ed. A. Mattoo, B. Hoekman, and P. English (Washington, DC: World Bank)

Rose, Andrew (2004a) 'Do we really know that the WTO increases trade?' *American Economic Review* 94, 98–114

— (2004b) 'Do WTO members have a more liberal trade policy?' *Journal of International Economics* 63, 209–35

Rose, Andrew (2007) 'The GATT: it's everywhere you want it to be,' mimeo

Saggi, Kamal (2004) 'Tariffs and the most favored nation clause,' *Journal of International Economics* 63, 341–68

Saggi, Kamal, and Halis M. Yildiz (2005) 'An analysis of the MFN clause under asymmetries of cost and market structure,' *Canadian Journal of Economics* 38, 242–54

Staiger, Robert W. (1995) 'International rules and institutions for trade policy,' in *The Handbook of International Economics*, vol. 3, ed. Gene M. Grossman and Kenneth Rogoff (Amsterdam: Elsevier Science)

Subramanian, Arvind, and Shang-Jin Wei (2007) 'The WTO promotes trade, strongly but unevenly,' *Journal of International Economics* 72, 151–75

Takemori, Shumpei (1994) 'The most favored nation clause,' *Keio conomic Studies* 31, 37–50

Tomz, Michael, Judith Goldstein, and Douglas Rivers (2007) 'Do we really know that the WTO increases trade? Comment,' *American Economic Review* 97, 2005–18

Tussie, Diana, and Miguel F. Lengyel (2002) 'Developing countries: turning participation into influence,' in *Development, Trade, and the WTO: A Handbook*, ed. Aaditya Mattoo, Bernard Hoekman, and Philip English (Washington, DC: World Bank)

Yi, Sang-Seung (1996) 'Endogenous formation of customs unions under imperfect competition: open regionalism is good,' *Journal of International Economics* 41, 153–77

CHAPTER 5

Journal of International Economics 97 (2015) 14–28

Contents lists available at ScienceDirect

Journal of International Economics

journal homepage: www.elsevier.com/locate/jie

Is there a case for non-discrimination in the international protection of intellectual property?☆

Difei Geng, Kamal Saggi *

Department of Economics, Vanderbilt University, United States

ARTICLE INFO

Article history:
Received 25 July 2014
Received in revised form 6 April 2015
Accepted 24 May 2015
Available online 12 June 2015

JEL classification:
O31
O34
O38
F12
F13

Keywords:
International patent protection
National treatment
Discrimination
Welfare
Trade barriers

ABSTRACT

We evaluate the case for non-discrimination in international patent protection. When trade is not subject to any frictions/barriers, requiring national treatment (NT) does not affect the rate of innovation (and welfare) since unfavorable discrimination suffered abroad by innovators in the absence of NT is fully offset by favorable discrimination enjoyed by them at home. When trade barriers exist, however, such international offsetting in patent protection is incomplete and innovation incentives are actually lower under NT. By lumping domestic and foreign patent protection together, NT blunts the overall effectiveness of patent protection in incentivizing innovation in the presence of trade barriers.

1. Introduction

The Agreement on the Trade Related Aspects of Intellectual Property (TRIPS) was easily the most controversial outcome of the Uruguay Round of multilateral trade negotiations (1986–95). Due to this far-reaching agreement, all WTO members – regardless of their economic status and/or innovative capabilities – are obligated to adopt certain minimum standards of protection for all major types of intellectual property such as copyrights, patents, and trademarks.[1] For example, TRIPS mandates that the duration of patent protection granted by WTO members must be at least 20 years. In addition to such harmonization, an equally important aspect of TRIPS is that it requires intellectual property policies of WTO members to abide by certain fundamental principles, such as *non-discrimination*.[2] The non-discrimination requirement in TRIPS manifests itself in two forms: the principle of national treatment (NT) that forbids discrimination between domestic and foreign firms/nationals with regard to the protection of intellectual property and the most favored nation (MFN) clause that prohibits discrimination between foreign nationals originating from different countries.[3]

Our primary objective in this paper is to evaluate the case for NT in the protection of intellectual property. At first glance, the inclusion of NT in TRIPS seems hardly worthy of discussion; after all, NT is a central

☆ For their helpful comments, we thank two anonymous referees, editor Bob Staiger, and the seminar audiences at the following venues: Fifth Annual Conference of the International Economics and Finance Society of China (Shanghai; June 2013), Fall DISETTLE Workshop at ECARES, Université Libre de Bruxelles (Brussels; September 2013), Fall Midwest International Economics Meetings at the University of Michigan (Ann Arbor; October 2013), InsTED Conference at the University of Exeter Business School (Exeter; May 2013), and the University of International Business and Economics (Beijing; June 2013).

* Corresponding author at: Department of Economics Vanderbilt University VU Station B# 351828 2301 Vanderbilt Place Nashville, TN 37235-1828 USA.

E-mail addresses: difei.geng.1@vanderbilt.edu (D. Geng), kamal.saggi@vanderbilt.edu (K. Saggi).

[1] See Maskus (2000) for a comprehensive discussion of the economics of intellectual property rights protection in the global economy and the international externalities that a multilateral agreement such as TRIPS attempts to internalize.

[2] To be sure, the principle of non-discrimination predates TRIPS but historical international intellectual property treaties (such as the Paris and Berne Conventions) were not backed by a powerful dispute settlement procedure like the one that is available to WTO members today.

[3] The NT requirement is specified in Article 3 of TRIPS which says that "Each Member shall accord to the nationals of other Members treatment no less favorable than that it accords to its own nationals with regard to the protection of intellectual property." MFN is contained in Article 4 which says that "any advantage, favour, privilege or immunity granted by a Member to the nationals of any other country shall be accorded immediately and unconditionally to the nationals of all other Members." These twin principles of non-discrimination are found in some shape or form in every multilateral trade agreement of the WTO.

http://dx.doi.org/10.1016/j.jinteco.2015.05.003

principle of all other multilateral agreements of the WTO. So why should TRIPS be any different? Nevertheless, we show in this paper that the desirable properties of NT in the context of trade in goods and services do not automatically carry over to the domain of intellectual property. To investigate the economic effects of requiring countries to follow NT in the protection of intellectual property, we utilize an adapted version of the Grossman and Lai (2004) model of international patent protection and innovation.[4] Our conceptual approach is straightforward and informative: we simply compare equilibrium outcomes and welfare in the absence of NT with those obtained in its presence. While our model focuses on patent policy, the insights it yields should also be relevant for other instruments of intellectual property protection such as copyrights and trademarks.

In accordance with Article 3 of TRIPS, Grossman and Lai (2004) focus on non-discriminatory patent policies and show two major results. First, countries tend to offer too little patent protection in an open economy setting. Second, the harmonization of patent protection across countries is neither necessary nor sufficient for achieving efficiency since it does not address the underlying problem of under-protection. In the present paper, we build on their insights by examining the implications of the non-discrimination constraint on national patent policies imposed by NT thereby adding to our understanding of the economic consequences of TRIPS.[5]

Issues surrounding the international protection of intellectual property have often been examined in the literature through the lens of North-South models of international trade and endogenous innovation.[6] While these models provide important insights, they do not derive optimal patent policies: instead they either consider the effects of marginal changes in an exogenously given rate of Southern imitation or examine policies that, on the margin, lower incentives for (endogenous) imitation. Thus, by design, they do not address the implications of core TRIPS principles such as NT for equilibrium patent policies and welfare.

While little is known about how NT operates in the context of intellectual property, the effects of non-discrimination in the use of domestic tax instruments such as sales taxes are fairly well-understood in the literature. Horn (2006) makes the important point that while NT with respect to internal taxes and other such domestic instruments can prevent countries from pursuing legitimate objectives, trade agreements that do not contain such a clause can be easily subverted by national governments who have an incentive to favor domestic firms over foreign ones. Thus, according to this view, NT serves as a line of defense against beggar-thy-neighbor tendencies of individual nations.[7]

Horn's (2006) basic query is no less relevant in the realm of intellectual property: when and why does it make sense to constrain national policies in the manner specified by NT? To be sure, incentives to pursue beggar-thy-neighbor policies are pervasive in the context of intellectual property.[8] After all, a major reason the US and, to a lesser extent, the EU pushed hard for a multilateral agreement on intellectual property during the Uruguay round negotiations was that major developing economies such as Brazil, China, and India were offering little or no intellectual property protection to their firms, a policy environment that fostered widespread imitation and reverse-engineering of Western technologies by local firms in such countries. But does the presence of such beggar-thy-neighbor incentives necessarily generate a rationale for non-discrimination in the protection of intellectual property? Our analysis below shows that it *does not*.

Our baseline model considers a world of two countries and analyzes the effects of NT when trade between them is not subject to any frictions or barriers. Somewhat expectedly, we find that in the absence of a NT requirement, each country finds it optimal to grant weaker protection to foreign firms relative to domestic ones. This discrimination arises because governments do not care about the effects of their policies on the profits earned by foreign firms. However, we show that discrimination against foreign firms on the part of both countries does *not* have any welfare consequences. To understand the intuition for this surprising result, first note that a firm's incentive for innovation depends upon the level of *effective global protection* available to it under alternative policy regimes, where the level of effective global protection is defined as a weighted sum of the patent protection granted by each country, with a country's weight being equal to its market size. The reason NT fails to generate any welfare improvement under free trade in our model is that what each firm gains in terms of higher patent protection abroad if discrimination is replaced by NT is exactly offset by what it loses at home so that the effective global protection facing firms remains unchanged.

In Section 4, we show that this invariance of innovation incentives and welfare to NT does not obtain in the presence of trade frictions. When international trade is subject to frictions – such as transportation and/or communication costs – *NT lowers innovation incentives by reducing the effective global protection enjoyed by firms*. The intuition for this result is as follows. While trade frictions lower export profits and make foreign patent protection relatively less important for incentivizing innovation in each country, NT actually calls for each country to provide more of such protection rather than less. From the viewpoint of firms, in the presence of trade frictions favorable discrimination granted at home in the absence of NT more than offsets the negative incentive effects of unfavorable discrimination suffered abroad. Consumer welfare considerations reinforce the argument in favor of discrimination: due to trade frictions, the consumer surplus obtained by each country from foreign innovations is smaller than that obtained from domestic ones.[9] Indeed, we show that for any positive level of trade frictions, it is actually *jointly optimal* to have each country offer a lower level of patent protection to foreign firms relative to domestic ones, a policy configuration precluded by NT.

We also find that a reduction in trade frictions reduces each country's incentive to discriminate against foreigners since domestic consumers derive greater benefits from foreign innovations when trade is freer. This result points to a potential synergy between the acceptance of international disciplines on intellectual property and the degree of trade liberalization in the global economy. It is worth noting here that TRIPS agreement followed almost five decades of multilateral trade liberalization achieved over eight separate rounds of trade negotiations conducted under the auspices of the General Agreement on Tariffs and Trade (GATT). As is well known, pre-TRIPS rounds of GATT negotiations were successful in lowering the average global tariff on industrial goods from over 40% to under 4% (Bagwell and Staiger, 2002). Our analysis suggests that such multilateral trade liberalization during GATT years may have helped pave the way for TRIPS by making international disciplines on intellectual property more palatable to countries.

[4] Their work builds on Nordhaus (1969) who first addressed the question of optimal patent policy in a closed economy.

[5] In Grossman and Lai (2004) as well as in our model, all innovation is conducted by the private sector. See Scotchmer (2004) for an analysis of intellectual property treaties in a model where R&D is conducted by both the private and the public sector.

[6] Much of this literature follows Grossman and Helpman (1991) who provide a comprehensive and unified treatment of the two leading approaches – i.e. the variety expansion model and the quality ladders model. Further building on this work, Helpman (1993) analyzes how a decline in Southern imitation affects global welfare both in the steady state and during the transition path.

[7] Saggi and Sara (2008) take Horn's analysis further by studying the role of NT when countries are heterogeneous in market size and/or the quality of goods produced and the mutual agreement over NT is endogenously determined. Horn et al. (2010) examine the role of NT from the perspective of incomplete contracts.

[8] Lerner (2002) notes that prior to the emergence of major international agreements on intellectual property, discrimination against foreign patent applications was quite common during the mid-19th century across the world. Discriminatory measures used against foreigners included shorter duration of patents, higher fees, shorter extensions, and premature patent expirations. See also Goldstein (2001).

[9] The empirical link between the protection of intellectual property and the volume and pattern of international trade was first established by Maskus and Penubarti (1995). See Maskus and Yang (2013) for a more recent investigation of related issues.

Our analysis also shows that differences in market size across countries affects incentives for discrimination in somewhat surprising ways. An important result in this regard is that if the market size of a country increases relative to the other, its incentive to discriminate against foreign firms *declines* while its level of patent protection increases. Intuitively, as a country's market size increases, its weight in determining the level of effective global protection increases as does the benefit it enjoys from foreign innovations. Indeed, if one country becomes arbitrarily large relative to the other, its incentives for patent protection essentially converge to those of a closed economy since foreign consumers become a negligible part of the calculus determining optimal patent policies.

Our result that a larger market has a weaker incentive to discriminate against foreign nationals seems to accord quite well with the fact that, during the Uruguay round, multilateral disciplines on intellectual property were pushed strongly by the two largest economies in the world (i.e. the US and the EU). From the perspective of these economies, TRIPS was primarily a means for getting developing countries to accept disciplines such as NT and MFN along with an increase in the degree of intellectual property protection that they had to extend to innovators. Furthermore, the model also clarifies that small developing countries not only have a weaker incentive to protect intellectual property because their own markets are too small to affect global innovation, they also lose more from having to follow the non-discrimination principle of NT. In this regard, it is noteworthy that in accordance with the general principle of special and differential treatment at the WTO, when TRIPS was ratified in 1995, developing countries were given an additional five years to achieve TRIPS compliance while the least developed countries had until 2006 to do so, which was then further extended to 2013 in general, and to 2016 for the enforcement of pharmaceutical patents and laws applying to trade secrets.

Since an increase in market size asymmetry reduces the degree of discrimination in the larger market while it raises it in the smaller market, the average degree of discrimination declines in our model as markets become more unequal in size. For analogous reasons, the degree of effective global protection increases with market size asymmetry. Both of these factors imply that the global welfare loss generated by NT declines as markets become more asymmetric in size. This aspect of our model contrasts sharply with analyses of international trade agreements over conventional policy instruments such as tariffs and internal taxes since coordination over these traditional instruments as well as non-discrimination requirements with respect to their use generally become harder to implement as countries become less similar to each other – see, for example, Park (2000), Horn (2006), and Saggi and Sara (2008). In such models, as a country gets larger (i.e. has more market power) it tends to typically increase its tariff or tax but such a change immiserizes the other country. By contrast, in the present context, as the larger country increases its patent protection and lowers its discrimination against foreign firms, the smaller country's welfare increases as does its ability to *lower* its own protection since innovation incentives of firms depend only on the effective global protection that they receive, and not on its composition across countries. Thus, the type of international spillovers that an international agreement over intellectual property helps internalize is fundamentally different in character from those internalized by trade agreements over tariffs and other trade policies.[10] However, the different nature of spillovers in the context of patent protection is not the key driving force behind our surprising findings. Positive international spillovers created by patent protection only imply that there exists global under-protection of patents. The key reason discriminatory patent policies dominate NT in the presence of trade frictions is that such frictions make each country's innovation relatively less responsive to foreign patent protection and by forcing each country to offer the same level of protection to domestic and foreign firms, *NT reduces the overall effectiveness of patent protection as an instrument for encouraging innovation.*

Our paper echoes an emerging empirical literature that examines the extent to which countries practice non-discriminatory IPR policies during the post-TRIPS era. Rather surprisingly, existing evidence suggests that even WTO members tend to discriminate against foreign innovators in practice. For example, Webster et al. (2014) find that, all else equal, both European and Japanese patent offices are more likely to grant patents to domestic applicants relative to foreign ones. In similar vein, using data for Canada, Mai and Stoyanov (2014) find that Canadian firms are substantially more likely to win court cases when the dispute involves foreign firms as opposed to other Canadian firms. Consistent with these empirical findings, our paper shows that countries indeed have incentives to use discriminatory patent policies in the absence of NT. More importantly, our paper establishes that the use of such discriminatory patent policies can be welfare-enhancing relative to NT when international trade is subject to frictions.[11]

2. Baseline model

To study NT in the international protection of intellectual property, we utilize the two-sector model of ongoing innovation developed by Grossman and Lai (2004). Before describing policy choices, we summarize the underlying economic environment. The world consists of two countries: Home (H) and Foreign (F). In each country, a traditional sector produces a homogeneous good (which serves as the numeraire) while a modern sector produces a variety of differentiated goods. The representative consumer maximizes her lifetime utility

$$U(t) = \int_t^{\infty} e^{-\rho z} u(z) dz \tag{1}$$

where ρ is the subjective discount rate and $u(\cdot)$ is the instantaneous utility function given by

$$u(z) = y(z) + \int_0^{n(z)} h(x(k, z)) dk \tag{2}$$

where $y(z)$ and $x(k, z)$ represent respectively the consumptions of the homogeneous good and the kth differentiated good at time z and $n(z)$ denotes the measure of differentiated goods that are still alive at time z. As in Grossman and Lai (2004), the function $h(\cdot)$ is assumed to satisfy the following regularity conditions (*i*) $h' > 0$ and $h'' < 0$; (*ii*) every variety of differentiated goods is purchased in equilibrium (i.e. $h'(0) = \infty$); and (*iii*) optimal monopoly price of a typical differentiated good is finite (i.e. $-xh''/h' < 1$).

Given the preferences in Eqs. (1) and (2), the representative consumer first chooses the consumption of differentiated goods and then purchases the homogeneous good with the remainder of her income (which is assumed to be positive). There are M_i consumers in country i, where $i = H, F$, so that M_i measures country i's market size for differentiated goods.

There are two factors of production: capital (K) and labor (L). The amount of labor needed to produce one unit of the numeraire or that of a typical differentiated good in country i equals a_i. The total labor resource in country i, L_i, is assumed to be sufficiently large so that a positive amount of the numeraire good is produced in equilibrium in each country. Since the market for the numeraire good is assumed to be perfectly competitive, the wage rate in country i simply equals the marginal product of labor in the traditional sector: i.e. $w_i = 1/a_i$.

Prior to being produced, a differentiated good must be first invented by R&D which requires a combination of labor (L) and human capital

[10] Bagwell and Staiger (1999 and 2002) argue that the GATT/WTO principles of MFN and reciprocity help achieve efficiency when international trade agreements are motivated by the presence of terms of trade externalities between countries.

[11] Lai (2007) also examines incentives for discriminatory patent policies in the absence of NT. However, he only considers a world of free trade and does not analyze how innovation and welfare differ across the two types of patent regimes (i.e. discrimination and NT).

(K). For simplicity, the research technology in country i is assumed to take the Cobb–Douglas form:

$$\phi_i(z) = A[L_{Ii}(z)/a_i]^{\alpha}(K_i)^{1-\alpha} \tag{3}$$

where $\phi_i(z)$ is the flow of innovations at time z, $A > 0$ is a constant, $L_{Ii}(z)$ is the labor allocated to innovation, a_i represents labor productivity, and K_i represents the fixed stock of human capital.[12]

A differentiated good has a finite life span ($\overline{\tau}$) during which it generates positive utility for consumers. At the end of its life span, a differentiated good produces zero utility for consumers and is therefore no longer produced. Given the technology specified for innovation in Eq. (3), during each time period z, $\phi_i(z) + \phi_j(z)$ newly invented goods enter country i's market while a measure of $\phi_i(z-\overline{\tau}) + \phi_j(z-\overline{\tau})$ existing goods die and exit the market. As a result, the growth in the measure of differentiated good at a given point in time is $\dot{n}_i(z) = \phi_i(z)-\phi_i(z-\overline{\tau}) + \phi_j(z)-\phi_j(z-\overline{\tau})$. We focus on the steady state of the world economy where the measure of differentiated good in both markets remains constant over time, i.e. $\dot{n}_i(z) = 0$.

After it has been invented, a differentiated good can be targeted by imitators. To protect differentiated goods from imitation, the government in each country grants patent rights to inventing firms. While the patent is in effect, the patenting firm charges its optimal monopoly price. Let π be the instantaneous per capita profit of a monopolist producing a patented differentiated good so that $\pi = (p_m - a_iw_i)x_m$ where $a_iw_i = 1$. Let the index of patent protection be defined as

$$\Omega = (1-e^{-\rho\tau})/\rho \tag{4}$$

where ρ is the rate of time preference.[13] By design, the present value of expected per capita profits from patenting a newly invented good equals $\Omega\pi$. After the expiration of its patent, a differentiated good can be imitated free of cost. Imitation drives the price of the good to its competitive level so that the post-imitation profits of an innovator equal zero.

When analyzing optimal patent protection, Grossman and Lai (2004) focus on policies that abide by the non-discrimination principle of NT. As we noted earlier, Article 3 of TRIPS indeed requires countries to extend the same patent protection to all firms regardless of their national origin. One of our key objectives, however, is to examine the implications of the *constraint* that NT places on the patent policies of individual nations. To do so, we allow countries to *discriminate* between domestic and foreign firms by formulating and implementing patent protection policies that depend upon the national origin of firms. Accordingly, let country i extend patent protection Ω_{ii}^R to domestic firms and Ω_{ij}^R to foreign ones under regime R, where $R = D$ (discrimination) or NT and $\Omega_{ii} = \Omega_{ij}$ under NT.

Under regime R, a firm from country i that is successful in innovation earns total profit $\pi M_i\Omega_{ii}^R$ in the home market and $\pi M_j\Omega_{ji}^R$ overseas. The value of a typical innovating firm from country i therefore equals $v_i^R = (M_i\Omega_{ii}^R + M_j\Omega_{ji}^R)\pi$. Firms make decisions about their labor inputs for R&D based on their expected total profits in the global market. The first-order condition determining demand for labor in country i under regime R where $R = D$ or NT is

$$v_i^R\frac{\partial F_i(L_{Ii}, K_i)}{\partial L_{Ii}} = w_i.$$

Let C_m and C_c be the instantaneous (per capita) consumer surplus levels under monopoly and competition respectively, i.e. $C_m = h(x_m) - p_mx_m$ and $C_c = h(x_c) - p_cx_c$. Let $\overline{T} = \left(1-e^{-\rho\overline{\tau}}\right)/\rho$ be the present value of a 1 dollar flow over the entire useful life of a typical patented product. Then, the present value of surplus enjoyed by a typical consumer in country i over the entire life of a domestic differentiated product can be written as

$$C_m\Omega_{ii}^R + C_c\left(\overline{T}-\Omega_{ii}^R\right)$$

and that derived from a foreign differentiated good as

$$C_m\Omega_{ij}^R + C_c\left(\overline{T}-\Omega_{ij}^R\right)$$

Let Λ_0 denote the welfare derived from goods invented prior to the implementation of the patent policy. We may then write country i's national welfare under regime R where $R = D$ or NT, as

$$\begin{aligned} W_i^R = \Lambda_{i0} &+ \frac{w_i}{\rho}\left(L_i-L_{Ii}^R\right) + \frac{M_i\phi_i^R}{\rho}\left[C_m\Omega_{ii}^R + C_c\left(\overline{T}-\Omega_{ii}^R\right)\right] \\ &+ \frac{M_i\phi_j^R}{\rho}\left[C_m\Omega_{ij}^R + C_c\left(\overline{T}-\Omega_{ij}^R\right)\right] + \frac{\pi\phi_i^R}{\rho}\left(M_i\Omega_{ii}^R + M_j\Omega_{ji}^R\right). \end{aligned} \tag{5}$$

Similarly, let aggregate world welfare be defined simply as the sum of national welfare of each country:

$$WW^R = \sum_i W_i^R. \tag{6}$$

We proceed by deriving equilibrium policies under discrimination and then impose the NT constraint on each country to see how it affects equilibrium policies and welfare. It is obvious that, in our model, the unilateral imposition of NT on a country can only make it worse off since even in the absence of NT it can always choose not to discriminate if it is welfare-maximizing to do so. But the more subtle issue, and the one that we address below, is how the simultaneous adoption of NT by both countries affects market outcomes and welfare.

3. Effects of NT in the absence of trade frictions

We begin with the scenario where international trade is not subject to any frictions or barriers. An important implication of this assumption is that from a social welfare perspective, given equal market sizes, patent protection abroad is just as valuable to firms as patent protection in their domestic markets. In Section 4, we will show that the introduction of trade frictions breaks this equivalence which, in turn, has implications for equilibrium policies and welfare under the two types of patent regimes.

3.1. Discriminatory patent protection

In what follows, we derive the non-cooperative Nash equilibrium where each country simultaneously and independently determines its domestic and foreign patent protections, treating these protections in the other country as given. The objective of each government is to maximize national welfare. In particular, we assume *interior* solutions for both the NT and discrimination regimes, meaning that patent protections implemented by governments lie strictly between 0 and $\overline{T}$.

Let us first consider the case where countries are free to implement discriminatory patent policies. Following Grossman and Lai (2004), it

[12] Our major results continue to hold when the production function for research has a CES form of the type $\phi_i(z) = A[\alpha[L_{Ii}(z)/a_i]^{\beta} + (1-\alpha)K_i^{\beta}]^{1/\beta}$ with $\beta \le 0$. As is well-known, the Cobb–Douglas production function obtains when $\beta = 0$. In the more general CES case, the assumption that $\beta \le 0$ has two implications. First, the responsiveness of innovation to patent protection decreases as the latter rises. Second, patent protection policies of different countries are strategic substitutes for one another. We consider both these features to be quite realistic.

[13] In Grossman and Lai (2004) a patent is assumed to have two dimensions: length τ and the degree of enforcement ω where $\omega \in 0, 1]$. But since ω plays no role in our analysis that is separate from patent length, we normalize ω to 1.

turns out to be more intuitive to derive the best response curves of countries by equating each country's marginal benefit of patent protection to the associated marginal cost, taking the policies of the other country as given.

Consider the patent policies of country *i*. A marginal increase in its domestic protection Ω_{ii} raises the value of all domestic innovators by extending their monopoly tenures. This leads to more R&D investment and a greater variety of differentiated goods invented by such firms. Each new differentiated good generates a discounted per-consumer surplus of $C_m\Omega_{ii} + C_c(\overline{T}-\Omega_{ii})$ over its lifetime. It follows that country *i*'s marginal benefit of domestic protection Ω_{ii} is

$$\frac{M_i}{\rho}\frac{\partial \phi_i^D}{\partial \Omega_{ii}}\left[C_m\Omega_{ii} + C_c(\overline{T}-\Omega_{ii})\right] \tag{7}$$

where $\frac{\partial \phi_i^D}{\partial \Omega_{ii}}$ represents the response of local innovation to a small change in domestic patent protection.

In the Appendix A, we show that

$$\frac{\partial \phi_i^D}{\partial \Omega_{ii}} = \frac{\gamma \phi_i^D M_i}{M_i\Omega_{ii} + M_j\Omega_{ji}}$$

where $\gamma = \frac{\alpha}{1-\alpha}$ represents the responsiveness of innovation to the value of an innovation in elasticity form. Plugging this expression into Eq. (7), one obtains the following expression for country *i*'s marginal benefit of raising domestic protection

$$\frac{1}{\rho}\frac{\gamma \phi_i^D M_i^2}{M_i\Omega_{ii} + M_j\Omega_{ji}}\left[(C_m - C_c)\Omega_{ii} + C_c\overline{T}\right]. \tag{8}$$

On the other hand, a marginal increase in domestic patent protection allows all existing innovators to charge monopoly prices for a longer time period. This causes a loss of consumer surplus, which is partially offset by the greater monopoly profits accruing to domestic innovators. Since ϕ_i^D new goods are invented per unit of time, country *i*'s discounted marginal cost of domestic patent protection Ω_{ii} equals

$$\frac{M_i\phi_i^D(C_c - C_m - \pi)}{\rho}. \tag{9}$$

Equating the marginal benefit (8) of domestic patent protection Ω_{ii} to its marginal cost (9) and rearranging terms give the first order condition determining Ω_{ii}[14]:

$$C_c - C_m - \pi = \frac{\gamma M_i}{M_i\Omega_{ii} + M_j\Omega_{ji}}\left[(C_m - C_c)\Omega_{ii} + C_c\overline{T}\right]. \tag{10}$$

Eq. (10) describes country *i*'s best response Ω_{ii} to the degree of patent protection that country *j* extends to country *i* (Ω_{ji}). It is easy to see from Eq. (10) that since $C_m < C_c$, Ω_{ii} is a decreasing function of Ω_{ji}: country *i* finds it optimal to lower the patent protection that it grants to local innovating firms if they receive more protection from country *j*. The intuition behind this is straightforward. An increase in Ω_{ji} increases the value of innovation made by country *i*'s firms and thereby encourages them to invest more in R&D. However, due to diminishing returns in R&D, country *i*'s marginal benefit of extending patent protection to its own firms is lower when Ω_{ji} is larger. As a result, Ω_{ii} has to fall in order to bring the marginal benefit back to the level of the marginal cost, namely, $C_c - C_m - \pi$. This implies that Ω_{ii} and Ω_{ji} are *substitutable* patent policies.

Observe from Eq. (10) that in the absence of NT, changing country *j*'s domestic protection (Ω_{jj}) has *no direct effect* on country *i*'s decision regarding its domestic protection (Ω_{ii}). This is not the case under NT, since a country cannot choose its domestic and foreign patent policies separately.

Following the above logic, the best response curve for country *i*'s foreign protection, Ω_{ij}, can be obtained as

$$C_c - C_m = \frac{\gamma M_i}{M_i\Omega_{ij} + M_j\Omega_{jj}}\left[(C_m - C_c)\Omega_{ij} + C_c\overline{T}\right]. \tag{11}$$

It is important to note from this first order condition that country *i*'s marginal cost of strengthening its foreign protection Ω_{ij} is not mitigated by π, because the monopoly profits generated by extending such patent protection accrue to foreign firms. It follows that a country's marginal cost of foreign patent protection is necessarily larger than that of domestic protection, which is the sole reason for why it has an incentive to implement discriminatory patent policies (as shown below). It is also clear from Eq. (11) that Ω_{jj} and Ω_{ij} are substitutes for each other: if country *j* increases its domestic patent protection (Ω_{jj}) then country *i* will find it optimal to lower its foreign protection Ω_{ij}.

We can show the following[15]:

Proposition 1. *In the absence of NT, each country's patent policy discriminates in favor of domestic firms:* $\Delta\Omega_i^* \equiv \Omega_{ii}^* - \Omega_{ij}^* > 0$ *for* $i, j = H, F$.

Proposition 1 is similar in spirit to the findings of Horn (2006) and Saggi and Sara (2008) who focus on NT in the context of tax policies. In particular, they show that if NT is not binding then each country will tax foreign firms more severely because their profits do not count as part of national welfare. The logic here is the same: discriminatory patent policies arise naturally from the fact that countries care about profits accruing to domestic firms but not foreign ones. The key question that follows is whether eliminating such discrimination via NT brings about efficiency gains, which will be addressed in the analysis below.

Firms make R&D decisions based on the duration of patent protection in each country as well as its market size. The level of effective global protection received by firms from country *i* under discriminatory patent policies equals

$$P_i^* = M_i\Omega_{ii}^* + M_j\Omega_{ji}^*$$

where $i = H, F$. How does the level of effective global protection P_i^* vary with the national origin of firms? We can show the following:

Lemma 1. *When countries implement discriminatory patent policies, the effective patent protection available to firms is equal across countries:* $P_i^* = P^*, i = H, F$.

Lemma 1 implies that the incentives for innovation are the same for firms in either country. Intuitively, when country *i* protects its own firms more than country *j* protects its own firms – as would be true if the market size of country *i* is larger – then country *i* also protects foreign firms more than country *j*. Indeed, if country *i* is much larger than country *j*, it is possible for it to grant better protection to foreign firms than they receive from their own government even when country *i* discriminates against foreign firms. Such international offsetting of patent protection equalizes incentives for innovation across countries.

Since

$$M_i\Omega_{ii}^* + M_j\Omega_{ji}^* = M_j\Omega_{jj}^* + M_i\Omega_{ij}^*,$$

it follows that

$$M_i\Delta\Omega_i^* = M_j\Delta\Omega_j^* \Leftrightarrow \Delta\Omega_i^*/\Delta\Omega_j^* = M_j/M_i$$

which we state as:

[14] The second-order conditions can be shown to hold for both countries.

[15] Proofs of all propositions that are not in the text are provided in the appendix.

Proposition 2. *The relative degree of discrimination ($\Delta\Omega_i^*/\Delta\Omega_j^*$) practised by a country is inversely proportional to its relative market size (M_i/M_j), $i = H, F$.*

A country's weight in determining the level of effective global protection facing innovators increases with its own market size, as does the benefit it enjoys from foreign innovations. Therefore, the country with the larger market has a *weaker incentive to discriminate* against foreign nationals. As we noted in Section 1, in typical models of international trade agreements, as a country gets larger (i.e. has more market power) it tends to typically increase discrimination against foreign sellers. By contrast, the opposite happens here: if one country gets larger, the other country benefits from a reduction in patent discrimination faced by its firms abroad as well as from an increase in the degree of global patent protection (which leads to more innovation).

3.2. Patent protection under NT

Now suppose that each country must choose a non-discriminatory patent protection level that applies to all innovating firms, regardless of national origin. A detailed analysis of the NT regime is provided in Grossman and Lai (2004). Here, we focus on comparing outcomes under NT with those under discrimination. The best response curve for country i under NT can be written as follows

$$C_c - C_m - \mu_i \pi = \gamma \frac{M_i}{P_i(\Omega_i, \Omega_j)} \left[(C_m - C_c)\Omega_i + C_c \overline{T} \right] \tag{12}$$

where $P_i(\Omega_i, \Omega_j) = M_i\Omega_i + M_j\Omega_j$ and $\mu_i = \frac{\phi_i^{NT}}{\phi_i^{NT} + \phi_j^{NT}}$ is the proportion of innovation that occurs in country i. Since the R&D production function is Cobb–Douglas in nature, it turns out that

$$\mu_i = \frac{K_i}{K_i + K_j} < 1$$

i.e., μ_i is determined solely by the relative human capital stocks of countries and is unaffected by their patent policies.

Observe from Eqs. (10), (11), and (12) that country i's marginal cost of patent protection under NT is strictly in between the marginal costs of granting patent protection to domestic firms and foreign firms under discrimination:

$$C_c - C_m - \pi < C_c - C_m - \mu_i \pi < C_c - C_m.$$

This inequality follows from the fact that a country only cares about profits of local firms while NT forces it to treat all firms symmetrically. As a result, the profit of a typical innovating firm is discounted by μ_i, which increases in its home country's human capital (K_i). This means that when a large share of the global innovation is carried out by local firms, the marginal cost of patent protection facing a country is lower. In general, since NT forces countries into a scenario where the marginal cost of patent protection is a weighted average of the marginal costs associated with the discriminatory protection levels accorded to domestic and foreign firms, intuition suggests that NT might induce countries to select a level of protection that lies in the interval ($\Omega_{ii}^*, \Omega_{ij}^*$) – a conjecture we formally confirm below.

Proposition 3.

(i) *Under NT, each country selects a level of patent protection that exceeds the protection it grants to foreign firms under discrimination but falls short of that which it gives to its domestic firms: $\Omega_{ij}^* < \Omega_i^{NT} < \Omega_{ii}^*$ for $i, j = H, F$. If countries are symmetric then $2\Omega_i^{NT} = \Omega_{ii}^* + \Omega_{ij}^*$ for $i, j = H, F$.*

(ii) *The effective global protection available to firms as well as global welfare under NT is the same as that under discrimination: $P^{NT} = M_i\Omega_i^{NT} + M_j\Omega_j^{NT} = P^*$.*

To see more explicitly why welfare under NT is the same as that under discrimination, from Eq. (6) we can rewrite world welfare under regime R as

$$WW^R = \sum_i \Lambda_{i0} + \frac{1}{\rho} \sum_i w_i \left(L_i - L_{Ii}^R \right)$$

$$+ \frac{C_c \overline{T}}{\rho} \sum_i \phi_i^R M_i - \sum_i \phi_i^R P_i^R \left[\frac{C_c - C_m - \pi}{\rho} \right].$$

Observe from this that in the absence of NT, world welfare depends only upon the effective protection levels $P_i^R = M_i\Omega_{ii}^R + M_j\Omega_{ji}^R$ available to firms from both countries under regime R (where $R = NT$ or D) since P_i^R pins down all the other endogenous variables such as the allocation of resources to R&D (L_{Ii}^R) and the rates of innovation (ϕ_i^R). But from Proposition 3 we already know that $P_i^* = P^{NT}$. As a result, world welfare is invariant to whether or not the underlying patent regime abides by NT.[16] Therefore, mandating NT is neither necessary nor sufficient for achieving efficiency provided international trade is not subject to any frictions.

The welfare neutrality of NT in our model is a rather novel finding in the context of the literature on NT. As we noted earlier, models in which NT applies to taxation typically find results favorable to NT. Further, even in the context of patent protection, in a two period model Bond (2005) has shown that, holding constant the level of patent protection given to domestic firms, eliminating discrimination against foreign firms raises global welfare. The driving force behind this result is as follows: since each country offers less patent protection to foreign firms, the switch from discrimination to NT holding domestic protections constant increases overall patent protection thereby alleviating the inefficiency caused by the under-protection of patents in the non-cooperative Nash equilibrium. But our analysis shows that since it is optimal for both countries to lower their domestic patent protection when each of them increases its patent protection towards foreign firms, NT by itself does not raise welfare since it leaves the effective protection levels facing innovating firms unchanged.

Grossman and Lai (2004) showed that the Nash equilibrium under NT gives rise to under-protection of intellectual property due to the positive international externalities generated by national patent protection policies. From the above analysis, it is not hard to see that the free rider problem that plagues the Nash equilibrium under NT continues to exist even when countries institute discriminatory patent policies. While there is under-protection of patent protection in our model as well, our analysis highlights that a move towards increasing patent protection to foreigners driven by NT does not occur in isolation since each country simultaneously lowers the protection it grants to domestic firms. In fact, changes in patent protection granted to domestic firms as a result of NT exactly offset the increased protection granted to foreign firms so that NT does not alter the effective global protection available to firms. In this way, our model is able to separate the impact of NT on welfare from the increase in overall patent protection that results if NT is interpreted as a policy that brings up the patent protection granted to foreign nationals holding constant the protection granted to domestic firms.

[16] It is worth emphasizing that our model considers the simultaneous adoption of NT by both countries. One might also be interested in knowing the welfare consequences of a *unilateral violation* of NT by a single country, particularly since actual trade disputes among WTO members, particularly outside the realm of TRIPS, often involve a violation of the NT clause. We can show that given that country j abides by NT, a unilateral violation of NT by country i increases the effective global patent protection facing its firms while lowering that facing foreign firms, thereby increasing the rate of innovation in country i while lower it in country j.

4. NT in the presence of trade frictions

Since the welfare neutrality of NT in the benchmark model is driven by the *complete offsetting* of patent protection across countries when discriminatory policies are eliminated via NT, it is worth asking whether such international offsetting also obtains in the presence of trade barriers and/or frictions. We now address this issue and show that when trade frictions exist, NT induces incomplete offsetting of patent protection across countries and actually ends up *lowering* the effective level of global patent protection.

4.1. Trade frictions and discrimination

Before deriving the effect of trade frictions on the incentives for discrimination in patent protection, we make three simple observations. First, trade frictions reduce the surplus consumers derive from foreign goods. Second, by making it costlier for firms to export, trade frictions lower export profits of firms (while having no effect on their domestic profits).[17] Third, trade frictions do not affect the surplus consumers derive from goods whose patents have expired, regardless of where they were invented, since imitated goods are produced locally in each market so that there is no trade in such goods.

Denote the (inverse of) the degree of trade frictions between countries by θ, where $0 \le \theta \le 1$ and $\theta = 1$ represent free/costless trade while $\theta = 0$ indicates the complete absence of trade. In the presence of trade frictions, denote the consumer surplus derived from a patented imported good by θC_m while the export profits earned by a firm by $\theta\pi$. This parsimonious formulation of trade frictions (i.e. as being captured by a single parameter θ) is adopted purely for expositional simplicity.[18] Our results below hold as long as trade frictions lower the consumer surplus derived from foreign goods and the export profits of innovating firms, even if they do so in a non-linear fashion and/or at very different rates. All we require is that the due to the presence of trade frictions, the (per-capita) consumer surplus derived from imports be lower than that derived from locally produced goods and that the export profits (per-capita) of a firm be smaller than its domestic profits.

It is worth noting that in the context of patent protection, a world with prohibitive trade frictions ($\theta = 0$) is not the same as one in which the two economies are fully autarkic in the sense of being completely shut off from each other. In particular, if technology transfer does not depend on trade (i.e. if ideas can flow across national borders without trade in goods – see Rivera-Batiz and Romer (1991)), then a country can imitate foreign goods even in the complete absence of international trade (i.e. $\theta = 0$). As a result, one would expect a country to have less incentive to protect intellectual property when $\theta = 0$ relative to the autarky case. Indeed it is possible to show, for example, that patent protection under NT when $\theta = 0$ is lower in both countries relative to the autarkic level.

The key question we address below is: How do trade frictions affect incentives for discrimination? The overseas profit earned by a firm from country i equals $\theta M_j \Omega_{ji} \pi$ so that the corresponding firm value equals

$$v_i^D(\theta) = (M_i \Omega_{ii} + \theta M_j \Omega_{ji})\pi.$$

As is clear from above, due to the presence of trade frictions ($\theta < 1$) patent protection in export markets (i.e. Ω_{ji}) is relatively *less valuable* for firms than protection in their domestic markets (i.e. Ω_{ii}).

Now consider country i's decision regarding patent protection. The marginal cost of extending domestic protection remains unchanged relative to free trade since trade frictions do not affect the consumption of domestic goods and the profit firms make in their domestic markets. A country's marginal benefit of domestic protection, however, is different as trade frictions do affect the value of domestic firms by reducing their export profits and therefore the influence of foreign patent protection Ω_{ji} on their innovation incentives.

The marginal benefit of extending domestic protection Ω_{ii} equals

$$\frac{1}{\rho}\frac{\gamma\phi_i^D M_i^2}{M_i\Omega_{ii} + \theta M_j \Omega_{ji}}\left[(C_m - C_c)\Omega_{ii} + C_c\overline{T}\right].$$

Note that holding constant Ω_{ji} (i.e. the protection domestic firms get abroad), the marginal benefit of increasing Ω_{ii} (i.e. the protection to domestic firms) decreases with θ. All else equal, a reduction in trade frictions makes Ω_{ji} a more effective substitute for Ω_{ii} due to increased export profits of firms.

Country i's best response curve for domestic protection Ω_{ii} can be written as

$$C_c - C_m - \pi = \frac{\gamma M_i}{M_i\Omega_{ii} + \theta M_j \Omega_{ji}}\left[(C_m - C_c)\Omega_{ii} + C_c\overline{T}\right]. \tag{13}$$

Regarding the protection extended to foreign firms, note that consumers in country i only derive a surplus of θC_m units from buying a patented foreign good. Since consumers always buy the good from domestic imitators once the patent expires, the corresponding surplus post imitation equals C_c. Thus, the marginal cost of raising foreign protection equals

$$\frac{M_i\phi_j^D(C_c - \theta C_m)}{\rho}.$$

As is clear, holding constant the rate of innovation, the marginal cost of protecting foreign firms increases with trade frictions.

Country i's marginal benefit of protecting foreign firms can be written as

$$\frac{1}{\rho}\frac{\gamma\theta\phi_j^D M_i^2}{\theta M_i \Omega_{ij} + M_j \Omega_{jj}}\left[(\theta C_m - C_c)\Omega_{ij} + C_c\overline{T}\right].$$

Note that holding constant Ω_{jj} (i.e. the protection foreign firms get from their own government), the marginal benefit of increasing Ω_{ij} (i.e. the protection given by country i to foreign firms) increases as trade frictions fall.

The best response curve for Ω_{ij} is given by

$$C_c - \theta C_m = \frac{\gamma\theta M_i}{\theta M_i \Omega_{ij} + M_j \Omega_{jj}}\left[(\theta C_m - C_c)\Omega_{ij} + C_c\overline{T}\right]. \tag{14}$$

Using the above best response curves, we can show the following:

Proposition 4. *As trade frictions between countries fall (i.e. θ increases), each country increases the degree of patent protection granted to foreign firms $\Omega_{ij}^*(\theta)$ while decreasing that granted to domestic firms $\Omega_{ii}^*(\theta)$. Furthermore, a reduction in trade frictions increase the degree of effective global patent protection in both countries, i.e., $\frac{\partial P_i^*(\theta)}{\partial \theta} > 0$ where $P_i^*(\theta) = M_i\Omega_{ii}^*(\theta) + \theta M_j \Omega_{ji}^*(\theta)$.*

---

[17] Trade frictions do not affect domestic profits since each firm selling a patented product is a monopoly in its local market.

[18] If $h(x) = \zeta^{1/\varepsilon}\frac{\varepsilon}{\varepsilon - 1}x^{\frac{\varepsilon-1}{\varepsilon}}$ where $\varepsilon > 1$ and $\zeta > 0$ and trade barriers are of the ice-berg type, then it is straightforward to show that consumer surplus from imports and overseas profits earned by firms equal θC_m and $\theta\pi$ respectively, where $\theta = (1 + t)^{1-\varepsilon}$ is the inverse measure of trade frictions and $t > 0$ is the ice-berg type trade cost. Lai and Yan (2013) embed this formulation of trade costs in a model of patent protection with firm heterogeneity and FDI and show that trade liberalization helps alleviate the problem of under-protection in Nash equilibrium. Even in their model, trade frictions lower overseas profits and consumer surplus derived from imported goods. Thus, allowing for firm heterogeneity and FDI does not affect the main channel that renders foreign patent protection less effective than domestic protection in our model.

We now compare NT and discrimination in the presence of trade frictions. As before, a typical firm's value under the NT regime equals

$$v_i^{NT}(\theta) = (M_i\Omega_i + \theta M_j\Omega_j)\pi.$$

It is important to note that due to the existence of trade frictions, v_i will in general be different from v_j even under NT, which further implies that firms in different countries may face different levels of effective patent protection.[19]

Under NT, the cost and benefit of a marginal change in patent protection depend upon the level of trade frictions. As the derivation is similar to before, we simply report country i's best response curve for Ω_i without presenting the relevant details:

$$C_c-\left(\mu_i+\theta\mu_j\right)C_m-\mu_i\pi = \frac{\gamma M_i\mu_i}{M_i\Omega_i+\theta M_j\Omega_j}\left[(C_m-C_c)\Omega_i + C_c\overline{T}\right] + \frac{\gamma\theta M_i\mu_j}{\theta M_i\Omega_i+M_j\Omega_j}\left[(\theta C_m-C_c)\Omega_i + C_c\overline{T}\right]. \tag{15}$$

In Section 4.2, we investigate the efficiency impact of NT. To facilitate this analysis, we assume that countries are symmetric in all respects ($M_i = M_j = M$, $K_i = K_j = K$ and $a_i = a_j = a$). This is a useful simplification for three reasons. First, it helps isolate the effect of trade frictions on the international patent regimes. Second, the issue of non-discrimination is as relevant, if not more, in a North-North typesetting of relatively similar countries as it is in a North-South setting where there are significant differences across countries with respect to market size and human capital. Third, although analytical solutions under NT are difficult to calculate when countries are asymmetric in Section 4.3, we analyze the social planner's problem and show that the key argument in favor of discrimination does not rest on the assumption of symmetry. Finally, in Section 5.1, we use numerical examples to study Nash equilibrium outcomes under asymmetry and show that our result that the equilibrium under discrimination is more desirable does not require symmetry.

4.2. Effective patent protection

Denote the symmetric Nash equilibrium level of patent protection under NT by $\Omega^*(\theta)$. Under discrimination, let $\Omega_d^*(\theta)$ be the patent protection granted by each country to domestic firms and $\Omega_f^*(\theta)$ that given to foreign firms. We can then show the following:

Proposition 5. *Suppose countries are symmetric and there exist trade frictions between them* (i.e. $0 \le \theta < 1$). *Then the following hold:*

(i) *The degree of effective global protection received by firms under NT is lower than that under discrimination:*

$$P^{NT}(\theta) = M(1+\theta)\Omega^*(\theta) < P^*(\theta) = M\left(\Omega_d^*(\theta) + \theta\Omega_f^*(\theta)\right).$$

(ii) *The gap between the degree of effective patent protection under discrimination and NT decreases as trade frictions fall* (i.e. $P^*(\theta) - P^{NT}(\theta)$ *declines with* θ).[20]

When trade frictions exist, from the viewpoint of firms, protection abroad matters less for profitability than protection at home. As a result, trade frictions make foreign protection relatively less effective in inducing innovation in each country. However, NT forces each country to treat firms the same even though their innovation incentives respond more to domestic protection. As a result, *NT blunts the effectiveness of patent protection for incentivizing innovation* so that, in equilibrium, the effective degree of protection chosen by countries under NT ends up being lower. This result is important because it shows that while there is under-protection of intellectual property under both NT and discrimination in our model, this problem is *more* severe under NT. Thus, somewhat paradoxically, in the presence of trade frictions allowing countries to discriminate against foreign nationals with respect to patent protection actually leads to stronger innovation incentives in the global economy.

The intuition behind Proposition 5 can also be understood by examining the marginal benefit and cost of strengthening patent protection. Suppose that $P^{NT}(\theta) \ge P^*(\theta)$. Then from the right-hand sides of Eqs. (A6) and (A7) in the Appendix A, we can see that the marginal benefit of patent protection is larger under discrimination for both countries. Moreover, it exceeds the marginal cost of patent protection so that each country would want to increase its total patent protection. This implies that $P^{NT}(\theta) \ge P^*(\theta)$ cannot be sustained as a Nash equilibrium. As a result we must have $P^*(\theta) > P^{NT}(\theta)$.

We now consider the problem of choosing jointly (or socially) optimal domestic and foreign patent protection for country i's firms (i.e. Ω_{ii} and Ω_{ji}).

4.3. Social welfare

The jointly optimal policies solve

$$\underset{\Omega_{ii},\Omega_{ji}}{Max}\ WW^D(\theta) \text{ where } WW^D(\theta) = \sum_i W_i^D(\theta).$$

To derive the first order conditions for this problem, it is useful to separately consider the *social* marginal benefits and costs of patent protection in each country. Following our previous discussion, the social marginal cost of domestic patent protection in country i (i.e. Ω_{ii}) equals

$$\frac{1}{\rho}\phi_i^D M_i(C_c-C_m-\pi) \tag{16}$$

while the social marginal benefit is

$$\frac{\gamma}{\rho}\frac{\phi_i^D M_i}{P_i}\left[(C_m-C_c)(M_i\Omega_{ii}+M_j\Omega_{ji}) + (M_i+M_j)C_c\overline{T} - (1-\theta)C_m M_j\Omega_{ji}\right] \tag{17}$$

where $P_i = M_i\Omega_{ii} + \theta M_j\Omega_{ji}$.

Analogously, we can write the social marginal cost and benefit of Ω_{ji} as

$$\frac{1}{\rho}\phi_i^D M_j(C_c-\theta C_m-\theta\pi) \tag{18}$$

and

$$\frac{\gamma}{\rho}\frac{\phi_i^D M_j\theta}{P_i}\left[(C_m-C_c)(M_i\Omega_{ii}+M_j\Omega_{ji}) + (M_i+M_j)C_c\overline{T} - (1-\theta)C_m M_j\Omega_{ji}\right]. \tag{19}$$

respectively. Observe from Eq. (18) that when calculating the social cost of extending patent protection to foreign firms in country i, the social planner accounts for the export profits earned by these firms, which is why the term $\theta\pi$ appears in Eq. (18) but not in Eq. (14).

We can write the first order conditions for Ω_{ii} and Ω_{ji} by equating the respective marginal cost of each type of protection to its marginal benefit. For Ω_{ii} we have

[19] Recall that when trade is free, all firms receive the same effective level of global patent protection under NT.

[20] In Section 7.7 of the appendix we show that Propositions 5 and 6 also hold for the case of n countries, where $n > 2$.

$$C_c - C_m - \pi = \frac{\gamma}{P_i}\left[(C_m - C_c)(M_i\Omega_{ii} + M_j\Omega_{ji}) + (M_i + M_j)C_c\overline{T} - (1-\theta)C_m M_j\Omega_{ji}\right] \quad (20)$$

while for Ω_{ji} it is

$$C_c - C_m - \pi + \frac{1-\theta}{\theta}C_c = \frac{\gamma}{P_i}\left[(C_m - C_c)(M_i\Omega_{ii} + M_j\Omega_{ji}) + (M_i + M_j)C_c\overline{T} - (1-\theta)C_m M_j\Omega_{ji}\right]. \quad (21)$$

Note that for all $\theta < 1$ the right-hand sides of both FOCs are the same, but the left-hand side of Eq. (21) is larger. This implies that, except for the extreme case where each country is at a corner solution, both FOCs cannot hold simultaneously. In particular, if $\Omega_{ii} < \overline{T}$ (i.e. Eq. (20) holds), then it must be that Eq. (21) does not hold so that $\Omega_{ji} = 0$.[21] We can now state:

Proposition 6. *In the presence of trade frictions* (i.e. $\theta < 1$), *social optimality calls for each country to discriminate against foreign firms,* i.e. $\Omega_{ij}^{w} < \Omega_{ii}^{w}$ *for* $i, j = H, F$.[22] *Furthermore, if it is optimal to offer firms less protection in their domestic markets than the useful lifetime of products* (i.e. $\Omega_{ii}^{w} < \overline{T}$), *then it is optimal to give them no patent protection in their export markets* (i.e. $\Omega_{ji}^{w} = 0$).[23]

In fact, for the case where markets are symmetric ($M_i = M_j = M$), we can use the first order condition in Eqs. (20) and (21) to write

$$\frac{\partial WW^D(\theta)}{\partial\Omega_{ii}} - \frac{1}{\theta}\frac{\partial WW^D(\theta)}{\partial\Omega_{ji}} = \frac{\phi_i^D M(1-\theta)C_c}{\theta} > 0 \text{ for all } 0 < \theta < 1. \quad (22)$$

This equation explicitly shows that the net marginal social benefit of extending domestic patent protection to firms is strictly higher than the marginal benefit of foreign patent protection so long as their exist trade frictions between countries. Observe that this holds even when the human capital stocks of the two countries are unequal.

The central point of Proposition 6 is that trade frictions drive a wedge between the social value of domestic and foreign patent protections and social optimality calls for assigning a higher priority to domestic protection in each country. In other words, from the perspective of joint welfare, we care not only about the *level* of patent protection but also its *composition* across countries. In contrast, Grossman and Lai (2004) show that, under free trade, efficiency depends only on the level of total patent protection in the global economy and not on its composition across countries. In our model, this is easily verified by taking $\theta = 1$ in Eq. (22), so that domestic and foreign protections have equal net benefit. Proposition 6 shows that, in the realm of patent protection, the presence of trade costs makes it socially optimal to discriminate in favor of local innovators in each country. It is noteworthy that such discrimination is desirable even when beggar-thy-neighbor incentives are completely missing (as they are when countries maximize joint welfare).

[21] The case where $\Omega_{ii} = \overline{T}$ is discussed in the appendix.

[22] Since under this scheme of jointly optimal protection firms receive less protection abroad than they do at home, for any given innovation, foreign consumers begin to enjoy greater surplus (arising from local imitation) sooner than domestic ones. Indeed, if markets are unequal in size we can show that the degree of jointly optimal protection for firms in each country is increasing in the relative size of the other country's market: $\frac{\partial\Omega_{ii}^{w}}{\partial(M_j/M_i)} > 0$.

[23] A corner solution for foreign protection might not arise if there exist enforcement costs that are increasing in the level of patent protection. Under such costly enforcement, foreign protection may be utilized even if domestic protection does not reach the boundary $\overline{T}$. Even so, the rationale for discrimination would remain since such enforcement costs would presumably also apply to foreign protection, and might even be higher than those for domestic protection.

Bond (2005) has shown that it can be socially optimal to globally discriminate in favor of firms from one country provided the elasticity of innovation in that country with respect to patent protection is relatively higher. Note, however, that Bond's analysis provides conditions under which it is socially optimal to provide favorable treatment to firms from one country in *both* countries whereas we consider whether it can ever be optimal to have firms from both countries enjoy favorable treatment in their respective domestic markets, an inquiry that is more in line with the actual spirit behind the national treatment clause. Furthermore, our analysis shows that the mere existence of trade barriers is sufficient to make such type of discrimination socially desirable; one does not need the elasticity of innovation with respect to patent protection to be unequal across countries, although that could be an additional contributing factor in our framework as well if our model were extended to incorporate it.

An interesting implication of the presence of trade frictions is that it is socially desirable to discriminate more in favor of goods that are harder to trade. Specifically, in the extreme hypothetical case where all goods are non-tradable (i.e. $\theta = 0$), there would be no reason to protect foreign firms at all since their innovation incentives would be unresponsive to patent protection granted by countries other than their own. Indeed, if $\theta = 0$ protecting foreign innovations would only delay domestic consumption of newly invented foreign goods by the duration of the patent without affecting the foreign rate of innovation.

Comparing the first-order conditions determining the Nash equilibrium with those under joint welfare maximization, it is easy to see that the marginal cost of patent protection under the Nash equilibrium (as perceived by each country) is no less than the true social cost while the marginal benefit of such protection is smaller if effective protection under the two scenarios is the same (i.e. if $M_i\Omega_{ii}^{w} = M_i\Omega_{ii}^{*} + \theta M_j\Omega_{ji}^{*}$). Thus, in an interior solution we must have $M_i\Omega_{ii}^{*} + \theta M_j\Omega_{ji}^{*} < M_i\Omega_{ii}^{w}$, i.e. there is under-protection in Nash equilibrium even in the presence of trade frictions, although the magnitude of the externality from foreign protection is reduced. Another interesting observation about discriminatory patent policies is that while coordination always leads to weaker foreign protection, in an asymmetric Nash equilibrium a country's foreign protection can actually exceed the foreign country's domestic protection. This is because the larger country tends to discriminate less while the smaller country tends to free ride more. Notably, even though the smaller country may be "sheltered" by the policies of the larger one, Proposition 6 indicates that this is not justified from an efficiency point of view.

5. Further analysis

In this section, we extend our model in two directions. First, we examine the effects of NT in a North-South setting where countries are asymmetric with respect to market size and/or their human capital stocks. Second, to capture the effects of trade policy variables, we consider a setting where the degree of trade openness facing firms depends upon their national origin – i.e. the access enjoyed by firms from country i to country j's market is not necessarily the same as that enjoyed by firms from country j to country i's market. The analysis of this scenario allows us to address how the incentives for discrimination vary with domestic and foreign trade policies.

5.1. NT in a North-South setting

In this sub-section, we discuss how the relative performance of NT and discrimination depends upon the degree of asymmetry across countries. This issue is important because what made TRIPS negotiations especially difficult was the clash between the views of developing and developed countries regarding the desirability of multilateral disciplines in the area of intellectual property. Furthermore, since WTO members differ markedly in terms of their economic capabilities and factor endowments, it is important to know how NT operates in such an environment. Section 4.3 showed that, in the presence of trade frictions, if patent policies are chosen to maximize joint welfare then NT is less efficient than discrimination, regardless of the degree of asymmetry across countries. What is interesting to know is whether this is also true in a noncooperative Nash equilibrium when countries are asymmetric in terms of economic fundamentals and there is no policy coordination between them.

In particular, it seems useful to consider a North-South scenario where the North's market as well as the stock of its human capital is larger than that of the South: i.e. $M_i > M_j$ and $K_i > K_j$.[24] The non-linearity of first order conditions under NT (see Eq. (15)) makes it difficult to obtain analytical solutions under asymmetry. Nevertheless, we show below that the key driving forces behind NT being efficiency-reducing relative to discrimination continue to operate in a North-South setting. To this end, adding up FOCs for both countries under NT yields

$$\begin{aligned}2C_c-(1+\theta)C_m-\pi = \gamma\frac{\mu_i}{P_i^{NT}(\theta)}&[(C_m-C_c)P_i^{NT}(\theta)+(M_i+\theta M_j)C_c\overline{T}\\ &-(1-\theta)\theta M_j\Omega_j(\theta)]+\frac{\mu_j}{P_j^{NT}(\theta)}[(C_m-C_c)P_j^{NT}(\theta)\\ &+(M_j+\theta M_i)C_c\overline{T}-(1-\theta)\theta M_i\Omega_i(\theta)]].\end{aligned} \tag{23}$$

Similarly, adding the two FOCs under discrimination yields

$$\begin{aligned}2C_c-(1+\theta)C_m-\pi = \gamma\frac{1}{2P_i(\theta)}&(C_m-C_c)P_i(\theta)+(M_i+\theta M_j)C_c\overline{T}\\ &-(1-\theta)\theta M_j\Omega_{ji}(\theta)]+\frac{1}{2P_j(\theta)}[(C_m-C_c)P_j(\theta)\\ &+(M_j+\theta M_i)C_c\overline{T}-(1-\theta)\theta M_i\Omega_{ij}(\theta)]].\end{aligned} \tag{24}$$

Note that the left hand-side of both FOCs can be interpreted as the global marginal cost of patent protection, as it is the sum of marginal costs of patent protection across countries. Analogously, the right hand-side of both FOCs represents the global marginal benefit of patent protection. Observe that while the global marginal cost of patent protection under the two regimes is the same (since the left-hand sides of the two FOCs are identical), the global marginal benefit is not. Indeed, the global marginal benefit of patent protection under NT is lower than that under discrimination. This is because NT forces countries to overuse foreign protection when trade is subject to frictions, which other things being equal, tends to reduce the global marginal benefit of patent protection. Recall that this overuse of foreign protection under NT was the key driving force behind our analysis of the symmetric case so it is not surprising that this mechanism continues to exist under asymmetry. Indeed, observe that the incentive-reducing effects of trade frictions under NT, captured by the terms $(1-\theta)\theta M_i\Omega_i(\theta)$ and $(1-\theta)\theta M_j\Omega_j(\theta)$ in Eq. (23), are larger than those under discrimination, captured by the terms $(1-\theta)\theta M_i\Omega_{ij}(\theta)$ and $(1-\theta)\theta M_j\Omega_{ji}(\theta)$. This is because $\Omega_i(\theta) > \Omega_{ij}(\theta)$ and $\Omega_j(\theta) > \Omega_{ji}(\theta)$ in equilibrium.[25] Intuitively, when countries consider raising domestic patent protection under NT, they are more conscious of the negative incentive effects of trade frictions since the level of foreign protection has to raised by the same amount.

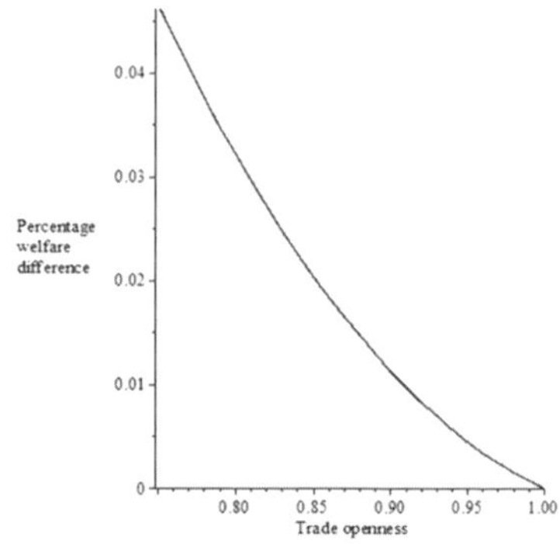

Fig. 1. Discrimination versus NT: how trade openness matters.

It is also worth noting that, as shown in Section 2, the above distortion generated by NT readily disappears when trade fractions vanish. When $\theta = 1$ domestic and foreign protections are equally effective so that the incentive-reducing terms in both Eqs. (23) and (24) drop out.

We conducted numerical simulations to further study NT under asymmetry. We now briefly discuss the results of this analysis. For simplicity, we consider a constant elasticity demand function ($x = p^{-\varepsilon}$ where $\varepsilon = 1.5$). With this specific demand function it can be shown that $C_m = \pi \approx 0.2Cc$. Also, we assigned the following values to the fundamental parameters of the model: $\alpha = 0.67$, $\gamma = 3$, $C_c = 5$ and $\overline{T} = 20$. Let $\rho \simeq 1$ without loss of generality. These parameter values ensure interior solutions under discrimination and NT and our results are robust to variations in them. To normalize away any level effects, we fix the total world market size ($M_i + M_j$) and the stock of human capital ($K_i + K_j$).

Fig. 1 shows how the welfare difference between discrimination and NT, i.e. $(WW^D - WW^{NT})/WW^{NT}$, varies with trade frictions θ, given $M_i = 10$, $M_j = 5$, $K_i = 2$ and $K_j = 1$. First note that so long as trade frictions exist ($\theta < 1$), discrimination generates strictly higher welfare than NT regardless of the level of such frictions. This is consistent with our results regarding the negative effects of NT under the presence of trade frictions. Moreover, as trade frictions fall (i.e. θ increases), the welfare differential between the two regimes converges to zero.

Table 1 compares the levels of total effective patent protection and national welfare across the two regimes for three different levels of trade frictions. First note that the level of patent protection under NT lies in between the two discriminatory protections regardless of the level of trade frictions (i.e. $\Omega_i^{NT}/\Omega_{ii}^* < 1 < \Omega_i^{NT}/\Omega_{ij}^*$). This verifies the distortion that NT causes by the excessive use of foreign protection. Using the first four columns of Table 1, it is easy to confirm that countries tend to discriminate less as trade frictions fall – i.e. $\Omega_{ij}^*/\Omega_{ii}^*$ and $\Omega_{jj}^*/\Omega_{ji}^*$ both decrease with θ – which is consistent with Proposition 4. Note also that the North (i.e. country i) is worse-off under NT even if it receives more total effective protection under NT relative to discrimination: i.e. $W_i^{NT}/W_i^D < 1$ even though $P_i^{NT}/P_i^D > 1$. The reason is that the South (i.e.

Table 1
Equilibrium patent protection and welfare in a North-South world.

θ	$\Omega_i^{NT}/\Omega_{ii}^*$	$\Omega_i^{NT}/\Omega_{ij}^*$	$\Omega_j^{NT}/\Omega_{jj}^*$	$\Omega_j^{NT}/\Omega_{ji}^*$	P_i^{NT}/P_i^D	P_j^{NT}/P_j^D	W_i^{NT}/W_i^D	W_j^{NT}/W_j^D
0.8	0.948	1.186	0.593	1.544	1.011	0.964	0.980	0.959
0.9	0.955	1.122	0.699	1.280	1.005	0.986	0.993	0.984
1.0	0.967	1.073	0.807	1.135	1.000	1.000	1.000	1.000

[24] One may also assume that the North has higher labor productivity (i.e. $a_i < a_j$), but this will not change our analysis in a substantive way.

[25] We have shown that this is true under free trade, that is, $\Omega_i^{NT}(\theta) > \Omega_{ij}^*(\theta)$ and $\Omega_j^{NT}(\theta) > \Omega_{ji}^*(\theta)$ when $\theta = 1$. As θ falls, both $\Omega_{ij}^*(\theta)$ and $\Omega_{ji}^*(\theta)$ decrease. Indeed, the marginal benefit of extending patent protection to foreigners becomes infinitesimally small as θ approaches zero (see the right hand-side of Eq. (14)). This is not true for $\Omega_i^{NT}(\theta)$ and $\Omega_j^{NT}(\theta)$ since the marginal benefit of patent protection under NT has a positive lower bound due to the fact that such protection also extends to domestic firms and part of their innovation incentive stems from domestic profits that remain unaffected by trade barriers (see the right hand-side of Eq. (15)). Therefore, $\Omega_i^{NT}(\theta)$ and $\Omega_j^{NT}(\theta)$ cannot be lower than $\Omega_{ij}^*(\theta)$ and $\Omega_{ji}^*(\theta)$.

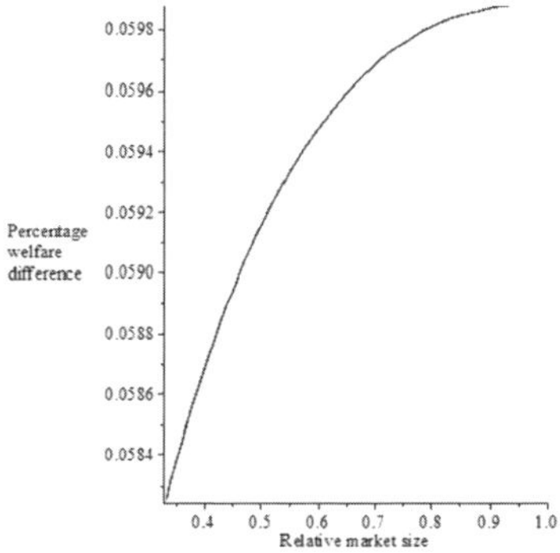

Fig. 2. Comparison when market size differs across countries.

country j) under-innovates due to it receiving lower effective protection under NT relative to discrimination, generating a large welfare loss for the North that ends up offsetting the benefit conferred by the higher degree of effective protection received by its firms under NT. Finally, the last two columns of Table 1 show that the welfare loss imposed on each country by NT increases with the level of trade frictions.

To see how the welfare gap between NT and discrimination is affected by the degree of asymmetry between the two countries, we studied the effects of changes in their relative market size and human capital stocks. We first set $K_i = K_j = 1$ and $\theta = 0.75$ and considered the effects of reducing the gap between M_i and M_j in the above experiment to 0, fixing their sum (at 15). Fig. 2 *shows that the welfare loss from NT is smaller when countries are more asymmetric in terms of market size.* To understand the intuition behind this result, recall from Proposition 2 that a country's incentive for discrimination is inversely related to its market size. Since an increase in market size asymmetry reduces discrimination in the larger market while it raises it in the smaller market, the average degree of discrimination *declines* in our model as markets become more unequal in size. For analogous reasons, the degree of effective global protection increases with market size asymmetry. Thus, *the global welfare loss generated by NT declines as markets become more unequal in size.* This finding suggests that the NT discipline may be a smaller concern in a North-South setting.

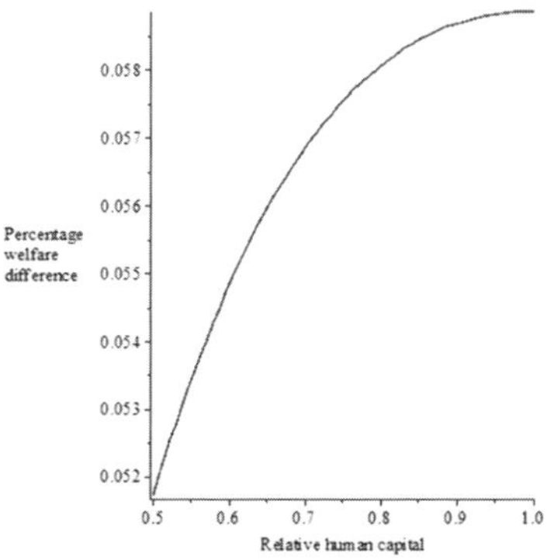

Fig. 3. Welfare difference with asymmetric human capital stocks.

Finally, we illustrate the effects of asymmetric human capital stocks. To this end, we equalize market size across countries by setting $M_i = M_j = 7.5$ and bring K_i and K_j closer to 1.5 from 2 and 1 respectively. Again, we see in Fig. 3 that NT generates a smaller welfare loss when human capital stocks are less equal across countries. The intuition is different from that in the case of market asymmetry, however, as we have shown that relative capital stock does not affect a country's tendency for discrimination. To see what drives our results, note that the North chooses stronger patent protection under NT as its human capital stock increases, since it is able to capture a larger share of global profits that result from innovation. In the meantime, Northern firms receive more total protection since the major component of their overall protection is Northern protection and the increase in such protection is not discounted by the level of trade frictions (θ). As a result, the North has a stronger incentive for innovation under NT, a pattern that promotes innovation and welfare. This helps explain why welfare under NT is higher when the distribution of human capital stock is more unequal across countries (although welfare under NT is still lower than that under discrimination).

To check the robustness of our findings, we also conducted further numerical analysis by varying relative market size and human capital stock simultaneously. Fig. 4 plots the relative welfare difference between discrimination and NT for one such simulation. We utilize the same parameter values as Fig. 1 and set $\theta = 0.75$. In the figure, the horizontal axes represent the two country characteristics of interest, each varying from 0.5 (very asymmetric) to 1 (symmetric). The first observation is that discrimination yields higher world welfare regardless of the degree of asymmetry, as illustrated by the welfare difference plane which lies above zero everywhere. Moreover, as can be seen from Fig. 4, the welfare difference between NT and discrimination becomes larger as countries become more alike in either characteristic (i.e. market size or human capital). In particular, the plane peaks at the upper-right hand corner where both market size and human capital stock are equal across countries.

5.2. Trade barriers and patent protection

Our analysis thus far assumes symmetric trade barriers in both directions since a single parameter θ captures the degree of trade openness of both countries. This approach is reasonable when trade frictions reflect underlying structural parameters such as transportation costs but is on weaker grounds if such frictions arise from tariffs and other trade policy barriers which can, and do, differ across countries. To understand how changes in national trade policies affect incentives for patent protection, we now extend our model to allow for the presence of asymmetric trade barriers. Let θ_i be the trade barriers facing imports flowing into country i, where an increase in θ_i implies unilateral trade liberalization on the part of country i. As before, such liberalization

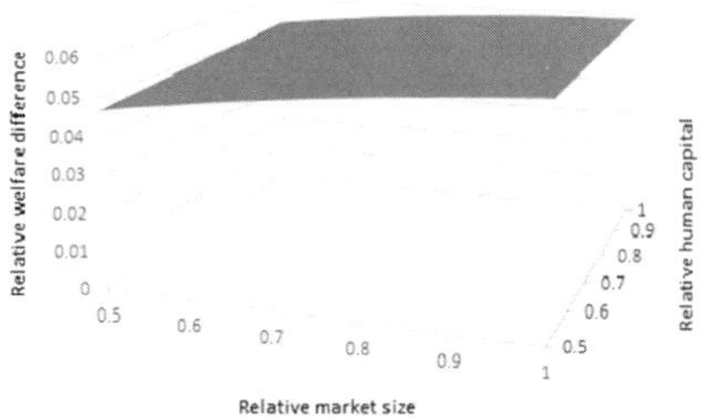

Fig. 4. Welfare difference with asymmetric market sizes and human capital stocks.

increases the export profits of country *i*'s firms as well as the surplus consumers in country *i* derived from imported goods.

In the absence of NT, country *i*'s FOCs for patent protection under asymmetric trade barriers can be written as

$$C_c - C_m - \pi = \frac{\gamma M_i}{M_i \Omega_{ii} + \theta_j M_j \Omega_{ji}} \left[(C_m - C_c)\Omega_{ii} + C_c \overline{T} \right], \tag{25}$$

and

$$C_c - \theta_i C_m = \frac{\gamma \theta_i M_i}{M_j \Omega_{jj} + \theta_i M_i \Omega_{ij}} \left[(\theta_i C_m - C_c)\Omega_{ij} + C_c \overline{T} \right] \tag{26}$$

Country *j*'s FOCs can be obtained by simply switching *i* and *j*.

To isolate the role of national trade barriers, we assume that countries are symmetric in terms of market size and human capital. Given this, it can then be shown that country *i*'s equilibrium levels of patent protections under discrimination are

$$\Omega_{ii}^*(\theta_i, \theta_j) = \frac{C_c \overline{T}[(1+\gamma-\theta_j)C_c - \gamma\theta_j C_m + \theta_j \pi]}{(C_c - \theta_j C_m)[(2+\gamma)(C_c - C_m) - \pi]} \tag{27}$$

and

$$\Omega_{ij}(\theta_i, \theta_j) = \frac{C_c \overline{T}[(\theta_i + \gamma\theta_i - 1)C_c - \gamma\theta_i C_m - \theta_i \pi]}{\theta_i (C_c - \theta_i C_m)[(2+\gamma)(C_c - C_m) - \pi]}. \tag{28}$$

Consider now the effects of unilateral trade liberalization by country *i* on its own patent policies when it is free to implement discriminatory patent policies. Using Eq. (27) we have

$$\frac{\partial \Omega_{ii}^*(\theta_i, \theta_j)}{\partial \theta_i} = 0 \tag{29}$$

and

$$\frac{\partial \Omega_{ij}^*(\theta_i, \theta_j)}{\partial \theta_i} = \frac{C_c \overline{T}\left[\theta_i^2 C_c C_m + \gamma\theta_i^2 C_c C_m - 2\theta_i C_c C_m - \pi\theta_i^2 C_m - \gamma\theta_i^2 C_m + C_c^2\right]}{\theta_i^2 (C_c - \theta_i C_m)^2 [(2+\gamma)(C_c - C_m) - \pi]} > 0 \tag{30}$$

i.e., a reduction in own trade barriers does not affect country *i*'s domestic protection but it increases the patent protection it grants to foreign innovators. Thus, own trade liberalization makes a country less willing to discriminate against foreign innovators with respect to its patent policies. The intuition is straightforward: since neither the profits of domestic innovators nor the surplus consumers enjoy from local goods depends upon local trade barriers, the value of patent protection granted to local firms is independent of local trade barriers.[26] On the other hand, the reduction of trade barriers by country *i* increases the profits foreign innovators derive from its market while also increasing the surplus consumers derive from foreign innovations. Both these factors increase the value of foreign innovations to country *i*, making it optimal to offer stronger patent protection to foreign innovators.

Note further that country *i*'s domestic protection falls with foreign trade liberalization:

$$\frac{\partial \Omega_{ii}^*(\theta_i, \theta_j)}{\partial \theta_j} = -\frac{C_c^2 \overline{T}(C_c - C_m - \pi)}{(C_c - \theta_j C_m)^2 [(2+\gamma)(C_c - C_m) - \pi]} < 0 \tag{31}$$

[26] This result is driven by the fact that there is no product market competition in our model since each new differentiated good is unrelated to existing goods (i.e. is produced by a true monopolist).

The intuition for this is that since $\frac{\partial \Omega_{ji}^*(\theta_i, \theta_j)}{\partial \theta_j} > 0$ (i.e. country *j*'s foreign protection increases with its trade liberalization) and patent protection policies are strategic substitutes across countries, it is optimal for country *i* to lower the protection it extends to domestic firms when they start receiving more protection abroad. Finally, since country *j*'s trade barriers affect neither consumers surplus in country *i* nor the profits of firms from country *j* in country *i*, we have:

$$\frac{\partial \Omega_{ij}^*(\theta_i, \theta_j)}{\partial \theta_j} = 0 \tag{32}$$

Let $\Delta\Omega_i^*(\theta_i, \theta_j) = \Omega_{ii}^*(\theta_i, \theta_j) - \Omega_{ij}^*(\theta_i, \theta_j)$ measure the degree of patent discrimination practised by *i*. It follows immediately from our results above that trade liberalization by either country reduces the degree of discrimination practised by both countries, i.e.

$$\frac{\partial \Delta\Omega_i^*(\theta_i, \theta_j)}{\partial \theta_i} < 0 \tag{33}$$

and

$$\frac{\partial \Delta\Omega_i^*(\theta_i, \theta_j)}{\partial \theta_j} < 0 \tag{34}$$

An important implication of Eqs. (33) and (34) is that global trade liberalization makes countries less resistant to accepting NT with respect to their patent policies.

6. Conclusion

The TRIPS agreement was controversial from the start. Developing countries fought hard against the inclusion of any multilateral agreement on intellectual property in the WTO, just as major developed countries put their considerable weight behind it. In addition to increasing the level of intellectual property protection in developing countries, TRIPS made it illegal for WTO members to discriminate against foreign nationals via the NT principle.

At first glance, the inclusion of a non-discrimination principle in TRIPS hardly seems worthy of comment. After all, the idea of non-discrimination is the very foundation of the multilateral trading system. Yet, our analysis has shown that the desirable properties of NT in the context of trade in goods do not extend automatically to the domain of intellectual property.

The key driving force behind our results is that incentives for innovation depend upon the overall patent protection firms receive in the global economy and the composition of such protection matters only when international market access is hampered by trade frictions. Absent such frictions, NT is inconsequential since what firms lose abroad is offset by what they gain at home. While we focus mostly on a two-country setting, we show that the key driving force behind our analysis carry over to a multi-country scenario.

When access to foreign markets is hampered by trade frictions (i.e. transportation costs and/or trade policy barriers), the case for non-discrimination in patent protection is even weaker. The intuition here is simple as it is undeniable: in the presence of trade frictions, substituting domestic patent protection for foreign protection affords innovating firms a higher level of effective patent protection because, all else equal, exports are less profitable than domestic sales. Furthermore, consumer welfare considerations reinforce this argument: trade frictions make foreign innovation relatively less valuable to domestic consumers in each country by making foreign goods costlier (or by reducing the volume of trade). As a result, in our model, imposing a NT constraint on national governments actually reduces global innovation and welfare in the presence of trade frictions.

Finally, it is important to recognize that our findings do not necessarily imply that NT should not have been included as a fundamental principle in TRIPS. Rather, we see our findings as highlighting one potential efficiency cost of NT that arises from the wedge that trade frictions create between the incentive effects of domestic and foreign patent protection. NT may yield other benefits that are not captured by our model, such as lower enforcement and implementation costs, greater consistency across international trade agreements, and potentially lower costs of international coordination across countries. Inclusion of these potential benefits of NT can make it more desirable than discrimination.

7. Appendix A

7.1. Supporting calculations

Here we show that

$$\frac{\partial \phi_i}{\partial \Omega_{ii}} = \frac{\gamma \phi_i M_i}{M_i \Omega_{ii} + M_j \Omega_{ji}}$$

Note that $\frac{\partial \phi_i}{\partial \Omega_i} = \frac{\partial \phi_i}{\partial v_i} \times \frac{\partial v_i}{\partial \Omega_i}$. Hence, $\frac{\partial \phi_i}{\partial v_i} = \frac{\partial \phi_i}{\partial L_{li}} \frac{\partial L_{li}}{\partial v_i} = F_L^i \times \frac{\partial L_{li}}{\partial v_i}$. Differentiating the firm's FOC $v_i F_L^i = w_i$ w.r.t. v_i we obtain $F_L^i + v_i F_{LL}^i \frac{\partial L_{li}}{\partial v_i} = 0$. This implies $\frac{\partial L_{li}}{\partial v_i} = -\frac{F_L^i}{v_i F_{LL}^i}$. Therefore, $\frac{\partial \phi_i}{\partial v_i} = -\frac{F_L^{i2}}{v_i F_{LL}^i} = -\frac{F_L^{i2}}{v_i F_{LL}^i \phi_i} \times \phi_i = \frac{\gamma}{v_i}\phi_i$ where $\gamma \equiv -\frac{F_L^{i2}}{F_{LL}^i \phi_i}$. Also note that $\frac{\partial v_i}{\partial \Omega_{ii}} = M_i \pi$. As a result, $\frac{\partial \phi_i}{\partial \Omega_{ii}} = \frac{\gamma}{v_i}\phi_i \times M_i \pi = \frac{\gamma \phi_i M_i}{M_i \Omega_{ii} + M_j \Omega_{ji}}$.

7.2. Proof of Proposition 1

Adding Eqs. (10) and (11) for countries i and j respectively yields:

$$2(C_c - C_m) - \pi = \frac{\gamma}{M_i \Omega_{ii} + M_j \Omega_{ji}} \left[(C_m - C_c)(M_i \Omega_{ii} + M_j \Omega_{ji}) + (M_i + M_j) C_c \overline{T} \right], \tag{A3}$$

and

$$2(C_c - C_m) - \pi = \frac{\gamma}{M_j \Omega_{jj} + M_i \Omega_{ij}} \left[C_m - C_c)(M_j \Omega_{jj} + M_i \Omega_{ij}) + (M_i + M_j) C_c \overline{T} \right]. \tag{A4}$$

It is easy to see that the right-hand sides of Eqs. (A3) and (A4) are monotonic functions of total protections $M_i \Omega_{ii} + M_j \Omega_{ji}$ and $M_j \Omega_{jj} + M_i \Omega_{ij}$ respectively. And they must also be equal to each other since the left hands sides of the two equations are the same. It follows that we must have $M_i \Omega_{ii}^* + M_j \Omega_{ji}^* = M_i \Omega_{ii}^* + M_j \Omega_{ji}^*$. Hence Eqs. (10) and (11) immediately imply that $\Omega_{ii}^* > \Omega_{ij}^*$ for $i, j = H, F$. ∎

7.3. Proof of Proposition 3

We first show part (*ii*). Adding up the first-order conditions for Ω_i and Ω_j under NT yields

$$2(C_c - C_m) - \pi = \frac{\gamma}{M_i \Omega_i + M_j \Omega_j} \left[(C_m - C_c)(M_i \Omega_i + M_j \Omega_j) + (M_i + M_j) C_c \overline{T} \right]. \tag{A5}$$

Comparing Eq. (A5) with either Eq. (A3) or Eq. (A4) and noting the monotonicity of the right-hand sides of these conditions regarding effective patent protection, we must have

$$P^{NT} = M_i \Omega_i^{NT} + M_j \Omega_j^{NT} = P^*, i, j = H, F$$

which establishes (*ii*).

Now notice that since $C_c - C_m - \pi < C_c - C_m - \mu_i \pi < C_c - C_m$, we must have $\frac{\gamma M_i}{P^*} \left[(C_m - C_c) \Omega_{ii}^* + C_c \overline{T} \right] < \frac{\gamma M_i}{P^{NT}} \left[(C_m - C_c) \Omega_i^{NT} + C_c \overline{T} \right] < \gamma \frac{M_i}{P^*} \left[(C_m - C_c) \Omega_{ij}^* + C_c \overline{T} \right]$ due to the first-order conditions for Ω_{ii}, Ω_i and Ω_{ij}. This implies

$$\Omega_{ii}^* > \Omega_i^{NT} > \Omega_{ij}^*, i, j = H, F$$

which is the desired result.

Finally, when countries are symmetric we may focus on the symmetric equilibria where $\Omega_{ii}^* = \Omega_{jj}^*$, $\Omega_{ij}^* = \Omega_{ji}^*$ under discrimination and $\Omega_i^{NT} = \Omega_j^{NT}$ under NT. Then Eqs. (A3) and (A5) together imply that

$$\frac{1}{\left(\Omega_{ii}^* + \Omega_{ij}^*\right)} \left[(C_m - C_c) \left(\Omega_{ii}^* + \Omega_{ij}^*\right) + 2 C_c \overline{T} \right] = \frac{1}{2 \Omega_i^{NT}} \left[(C_m - C_c) 2 \Omega_i^{NT} + 2 C_c \overline{T} \right], i, j = H, F.$$

Monotonicity of both sides ensures that we must have $\Omega_{ii}^* + \Omega_{ij}^* = 2\Omega_i^{NT}$. ∎

7.4. Proof of Proposition 4

One can obtain the first-order conditions for country j by reversing i and j in Eqs. (13) and (14). It is easy to show that

$$\Omega_{ii}^*(\theta) = \frac{C_c \overline{T}}{(2+\gamma)(C_c - C_m) - \pi} \left[(1+\gamma) - \frac{\eta \theta (C_c - C_m - \pi)}{(C_c - \theta C_m)} \right]$$

and

$$\Omega_{ij}^*(\theta) = \frac{C_c \overline{T}}{(2+\gamma)(C_c - C_m) - \pi} \left[\frac{(1+\gamma)(C_c - C_m) - \pi}{(C_c - \theta C_m)} - \frac{\eta}{\theta} \right]$$

where $\eta = M_j / M_i$. It follows that $\Omega_{ii}^*(\theta)$ decreases in θ since $\frac{\eta \theta (C_c - C_m - \pi)}{(C_c - y C_m)}$ is an increasing function of θ.

Similarly, $\Omega_{ij}^*(\theta)$ increases in θ since $\frac{(1+\gamma)(C_c - C_m) - \pi}{(C_c - \theta C_m)} - \frac{\eta}{\theta}$ is an increasing function of θ. Moreover, it can be shown that

$$P_i^*(\theta) = M_i \Omega_{ii}^*(\theta) + \theta M_j \Omega_{ji}^*(\theta) = \frac{\gamma C_c \overline{T}}{(2+\gamma)(C_c - C_m) - \pi} \left[M_i + M_j \frac{\theta (C_c - C_m)}{(C_c - \theta C_m)} \right].$$

Clearly, since $M_j \frac{\theta (C_c - C_m)}{(C_c - \theta C_m)}$ is an increasing function of θ, $P_i^*(\theta)$ is increasing in θ. ∎

7.5. Proof of Proposition 5

We know that $\Omega^*(\theta)$ satisfies the following first-order condition:

$$2C_c - (1+\theta) C_m - \pi = \frac{\gamma}{(1+\theta)\Omega^*(\theta)} \left[(C_m - C_c)(1+\theta)\Omega^*(\theta) + (1+\theta) C_c \overline{T} - (1-\theta)\theta C_m \Omega^*(\theta) \right]. \tag{A6}$$

Similarly, $\Omega_d^*(\theta)$ and $\Omega_f^*(\theta)$ respectively satisfy the following first order conditions:

$$C_c - C_m - \pi = \frac{\gamma}{\Omega_d^*(\theta) + \theta \Omega_f^*(\theta)} \left[(C_m - C_c) \Omega_d^*(\theta) + C_c \overline{T} \right]$$

and

$$C_c - \theta C_m = \frac{\gamma\theta}{\Omega_d^*(\theta) + \theta\Omega_f^*(\theta)}\left[(\theta C_m - C_c)\Omega_f^*(\theta) + C_c\overline{T}\right].$$

Adding up the last two equations we obtain

$$2C_c - (1+\theta)C_m - \pi = \frac{\gamma}{\Omega_d^*(\theta) + \theta\Omega_f^*(\theta)}\left[(C_m - C_c)\left(\Omega_d^*(\theta) + \theta\Omega_f^*(\theta)\right)\right. \quad \text{(A7)}$$
$$\left. + (1+\theta)C_c\overline{T} - (1-\theta)\theta C_m\Omega_f^*(\theta)\right].$$

Moreover, it can be shown that $\Omega^*(\theta) > \Omega_f^*(\theta)$, which further implies that $(1-\theta)\theta C_m\Omega^*(\theta) > (1-\theta)\theta C_m\Omega_f^*(\theta)$.[27] Since the right-hand sides of Eqs. (A6) and (A7) must be equal, and since both are decreasing functions of $\Omega_d(\theta) + \theta\Omega_f(\theta)$ and $(1+\theta)\Omega(\theta)$, we may conclude that

$$\Omega_d^*(\theta) + \theta\Omega_f^*(\theta) > (1+\theta)\Omega^*(\theta).$$

Multiplying both sides by the common market size M, we get

$$M\left(\Omega_d^*(\theta) + \theta\Omega_f^*(\theta)\right) > M(1+\theta)\Omega^*(\theta).$$

∎

7.6. Proof of Proposition 6

Here, we show that it is socially optimal to discriminate even when $\Omega_{ii} = \overline{T}$.[28] Suppose $\Omega_{ii} = \overline{T}$ and $\Omega_{jj} < \overline{T}$. Here we must have $\Omega_{ji} \geq 0$ and $\Omega_{ij} = 0$. It follows that country i discriminates (i.e. $\Omega_{ii} > \Omega_{ij}$). To show country j also discriminates (i.e. $\Omega_{jj} > \Omega_{ji}$), suppose $\Omega_{ji} > 0$ (otherwise we are done). Note that the social planner's FOC for Ω_{jj} is given by

$$C_c - C_m - \pi = \frac{\gamma}{P_j(\theta)}\left[(C_m - C_c)(M_j\Omega_{jj} + M_i\Omega_{ij})\right.$$
$$\left. + (M_i + M_j)C_c\overline{T} - (1-\theta)C_m M_j\Omega_{ij}\right]. \quad \text{(A8)}$$

Since $\Omega_{ij} = 0$, this simplifies Eq. (A8) as

$$C_c - C_m - \pi = \frac{\gamma}{M_j\Omega_{jj}}\left[(C_m - C_c)M_j\Omega_{jj} + (M_i + M_j)C_c\overline{T}\right]. \quad \text{(A9)}$$

Comparing Eq. (A9) with Eq. (21), we see that the left-hand side of Eq. (A9) is smaller than that of Eq. (21). This implies that the right-hand side of Eq. (A9) is also smaller than that of Eq. (21), i.e.

$$\frac{\gamma}{P_i}\left[(C_m - C_c)(M_i\Omega_{ii} + M_j\Omega_{ji}) + (M_i + M_j)C_c\overline{T} - (1-\theta)C_m M_j\Omega_{ji}\right]$$
$$> \frac{\gamma}{M_j\Omega_{jj}}\left[(C_m - C_c)M_j\Omega_{jj} + (M_i + M_j)C_c\overline{T}\right] \quad \text{(A10)}$$

We next show that

$$P_i = M_i\Omega_{ii} + \theta M_j\Omega_{ji} \leq M_j\Omega_{jj} \quad \text{(A11)}$$

Suppose not, i.e., suppose we have

$$M_i\Omega_{ii} + \theta M_j\Omega_{ji} > M_j\Omega_{jj}$$

Since $\theta \leq 1$, we have

$$M_j\Omega_{jj} < M_i\Omega_{ii} + \theta M_j\Omega_{ji} \leq M_i\Omega_{ii} + M_j\Omega_{ji}$$

Then it follows that we must have

$$\frac{\gamma}{M_j\Omega_{jj}}\left[(C_m - C_c)M_j\Omega_{jj} + (M_i + M_j)C_c\overline{T}\right]$$
$$> \frac{\gamma}{P_i}\left[(C_m - C_c)(M_i\Omega_{ii} + M_j\Omega_{ji}) + (M_i + M_j)C_c\overline{T} - (1-\theta)C_m M_j\Omega_{ji}\right]$$

which constitutes a contradiction of Eq. (A10). Therefore, it must be that

$$P_i = M_i\Omega_{ii} + \theta M_j\Omega_{ji} \leq M_j\Omega_{jj}.$$

Note that since Ω_{ji} is increasing in θ (so that it attains its maximum value at $\theta = 1$) while Ω_{jj} is independent of θ, if we can show that $\Omega_{jj} > \Omega_{ji}$ at $\theta = 1$ then it must be this inequality holds for all θ. When $\theta = 1$, Eq. (A11) binds so that $M_i\Omega_{ii} + M_j\Omega_{ji} = M_j\Omega_{jj}$. This immediately implies $M_j\Omega_{ji} < M_j\Omega_{jj}$ from which it follows that $\Omega_{ji} < \Omega_{jj}$, i.e. given that country i is discriminating, it is socially optimal to have country j discriminate under free trade. Moreover, Ω_{ji} falls while Ω_{jj} does not change as θ decreases, so $\Omega_{ji} < \Omega_{jj}$ continues to hold when $\theta < 1$. ∎

7.7. Multiple countries

For simplicity, our core model considers a two-country setting. We now show that the key driving forces behind our analysis carry over to a multi-country scenario. To shed light on the key mechanisms that operate in a multi-country setting, in the following analysis we assume that all countries are symmetric so that $\Omega_{ii} = \Omega_{jj} = \Omega_d$ and $\Omega_{ij} = \Omega_{ji} = \Omega_f$.

Consider a world composed of n symmetric countries with θ measuring the degree of trade openness between any two of them. Under discrimination we can write the equilibrium effective global patent protection received by a typical country as

$$P^*(\theta, n) = M\left[\Omega_d + \theta(n-1)\Omega_f\right]$$

Similarly, under NT the effective protection given to a country is

$$P^{NT}(\theta, n) = M\Omega[1 + \theta(n-1)]$$

Thus both $P^*(\theta, n)$ and $P^{NT}(\theta, n)$ are straightforward generalizations of the two-country case.

Under discrimination $P^*(\theta, n)$ satisfies the following FOCs for country i:

$$C_c - C_m - \pi = \frac{\gamma M}{P^*(\theta, n)}\left[(C_m - C_c)\Omega_d + C_c\overline{T}\right], \quad \text{(A12)}$$

and

$$C_c - \theta C_m = \frac{\gamma\theta M}{P^*(\theta, n)}\left[(\theta C_m - C_c)\Omega_f + C_c\overline{T}\right] \quad \text{for } j \neq i \quad \text{(A13)}$$

where Eq. (A12) is for domestic protection and Eq. (A13) is for the patent protection provided by country i to country j.

On the other hand, under NT each country simply chooses a uniform patent protection and the FOC for country i can be written as

$$C_c - \left[\frac{1 + (n-1)\theta}{n}\right]C_m - \frac{\pi}{n} = \frac{\gamma M}{nP^{NT}(\theta, n)}\left[(C_m - C_c)\Omega + C_c\overline{T}\right]$$
$$+ \frac{(n-1)\gamma\theta M}{nP^{NT}(\theta, n)}\left[(\theta C_m - C_c)\Omega + C_c\overline{T}\right]. \quad \text{(A14)}$$

[27] Note that $\Omega_d^*(\theta) > \Omega_f^*(\theta)$ in any interior equilibrium. Further, if $\Omega_f^*(\theta) \geq \Omega^*(\theta)$, then $\Omega_d^*(\theta) > \Omega_f^*(\theta) \geq \Omega^*(\theta)$ and this implies $\Omega_d^*(\theta) + \theta\Omega_f^*(\theta) > (1+\theta)\Omega^*(\theta)$. One can use the latter inequality to show that Eqs. (A6) and (A7) cannot hold simultaneously. As a result, we must have $\Omega^*(\theta) > \Omega_f^*(\theta)$ in equilibrium.

[28] We rule out the uninteresting case where both countries are at a corner solution in terms of domestic protection where $\Omega_{ii} = \Omega_{jj} = \overline{T}$.

Adding up the FOCs over all countries we obtain the following key equation in a symmetric equilibrium under discrimination:

$$\begin{aligned} &nC_c - [1+(n-1)\theta]C_m - \pi \\ &= \frac{\gamma}{P^*}\left[(C_m - C_c)P^* + [1+(n-1)\theta]C_c\overline{T} - (n-1)(1-\theta)\theta C_m \Omega_f(\theta)\right] \end{aligned} \quad (A15)$$

Similarly, under NT we can write

$$\begin{aligned} &nC_c - [1+(n-1)\theta]C_m - \pi \\ &= \frac{\gamma}{P^{NT}}\left[(C_m - C_c)P^{NT} + [1+(n-1)\theta]C_c\overline{T} - (n-1)(1-\theta)\theta C_m \Omega^*(\theta)\right]. \end{aligned} \quad (A16)$$

Since the left hand side of the two equations above are the same while $\Omega^*(\theta) > \Omega_f^*(\theta)$ (i.e. NT protection is greater than foreign protection under discrimination) it must be that, in equilibrium, we have $P^* > P^{NT}$ for every country. Therefore, in a n-country (symmetric) world, total patent protection and therefore innovation and aggregate welfare are higher under discrimination relative to NT.[29] The key mechanism is analogous as in the benchmark case: NT requires all countries to overuse foreign protection that, in the presence of trade frictions, is less effective than domestic protection for incentivizing innovation.

Consider now the perspective of the social planner. We have

$$\begin{aligned} \frac{\partial WW^D(\theta)}{\partial \Omega_d} = \frac{\phi M}{\rho}\Big[&\frac{\gamma}{P}[(C_m - C_c)(M\Omega_d + (n-1)M\Omega_f) + nMC_c\overline{T} \\ &- (1-\theta)(n-1)C_m M\Omega_f] - (C_c - C_m - \pi)\Big]. \end{aligned} \quad (A17)$$

Similarly, we have

$$\begin{aligned} \frac{1}{\theta}\frac{\partial WW^D(\theta)}{\partial \Omega_f} = \frac{\phi M}{\rho}\Big[&\frac{\gamma}{P}[(C_m - C_c)(M\Omega_d + (n-1)M\Omega_f) + nMC_c\overline{T} \\ &- (1-\theta)(n-1)C_m M\Omega_f] - (C_c - C_m - \pi) - \frac{(1-\theta)}{\theta}C_c\Big]. \end{aligned} \quad (A18)$$

From these two first equations it follows that

$$\frac{\partial WW^D(\theta)}{\partial \Omega_d} - \frac{1}{\theta}\frac{\partial WW^D(\theta)}{\partial \Omega_f} = \frac{\phi M(1-\theta)C_c}{\rho\theta} > 0,$$

where $M_i = M$ for $i \in 1, 2, \ldots, n$. Hence, the net social marginal benefit of domestic protection is higher than that of foreign protection even when there are more than two countries in the world.

[29] We also conduct numerical analysis for a 3-country asymmetric world. All the qualitative results under the 2-country world continue to hold.

References

Bagwell, Kyle, Staiger, Robert W., 1999. An economic theory of GATT. Am. Econ. Rev. 89 (1), 215–248.

Bagwell, Kyle, Staiger, Robert W., 2002. The Economics of the World Trading System. MIT Press, Cambridge, MA.

Bond, Eric, 2005. The Economics of International Trade Agreements and Dispute Settlement with Intellectual Property Rights. In: Maskus, Keith E., Reichman, Jerome H. (Eds.), International Public Goods and Transfer of Technology under a Globalized Intellectual Property Regime. Cambridge University Press, New York.

Goldstein, Paul A., 2001. International Copyright: Principles, Law, and Practice. Oxford University Press, New York.

Grossman, Gene M., Lai, Edwin L.C., 2004. International protection of intellectual property. Am. Econ. Rev. 94 (5), 1635–1653.

Grossman, Gene M., Helpman, Elhanan, 1991. Innovation and Growth in the Global Economy. MIT Press, Cambridge.

Helpman, Elhanan, 1993. Innovation, imitation, and intellectual property rights. Econometrica 61, 1247–1280.

Horn, Henrik, 2006. National treatment in the GATT. Am. Econ. Rev. 96 (1), 394–404.

Horn, Henrik, Maggi, Giovanni, Staiger, Robert, W., 2010. Trade agreements as endogenously incomplete contracts. Am. Econ. Rev. 100 (1), 394–419.

Lai, Edwin L.-C., 2007. Theory of International Policy Coordination in Protection of Ideas Chapter 11. In: Maskus, Keith E. (Ed.), Intellectual Property, Growth and Trade: Frontiers of Economics and Globalization volume 2, pp. 357–389.

Lai, Edwin L.-C., Yan, Isabel K.M., 2013. Would global patent protection be too weak without international coordination? J. Int. Econ. 89 (1), 42–54.

Lerner, Josh, 2002. 150 years of Patent Protection. Am. Econ. Rev. 92, 221–225.

Mai, Joseph and Stoyanov, Andrey. 2014. "Home Country Bias in the Legal System: Empirical Evidence from the Intellectual Property Rights Protection in Canada". Mimeo.

Maskus, Keith E., Penubarti, Mohan, 1995. How trade-related are intellectual property rights? J. Int. Econ. 39 (3-4), 227–248.

Maskus, Keith E., 2000. Intellectual Property Rights in the Global Economy. Institute for International Economics, Washington DC.

Maskus, Keith E., Yang, Le, 2013. The Impacts of Post-TRIPS Patent Reforms on the Structure of Exports. Discussion Paper 13030. Research Institute of Economy, Trade and Industry.

Nordhaus, William D., 1969. Invention, Growth and Welfare: A Theoretical Treatment of Technological Change. MIT Press, Cambridge, MA.

Park, Jee-Hyeong, 2000. International trade agreements between countries of asymmetric size. J. Int. Econ. 50, 473–495.

Rivera-Batiz, Luis A., Romer, Paul M., 1991. Economic integration and endogenous growth. Q. J. Econ. 106 (2), 531–555.

Scotchmer, Suzanne, 2004. The political economy of intellectual property treaties. J. Law Econ. Org. 20 (2), 415–437.

Saggi, Kamal, Sara, Nese, 2008. National treatment at the WTO: the roles of product and country heterogeneity. Int. Econ. Rev. 49 (4), 1365–1394.

Webster, Elizabeth, Jensen, Paul.H., Palangkaraya, Alfons, 2014. Patent examination outcomes and the national treatment principle. Rand J. Econ. 45 (2), 449–469.

PART II

PREFERENTIAL TRADE AGREEMENTS AND MULTILATERAL TRADE LIBERALIZATION

CHAPTER 6

INTERNATIONAL ECONOMIC REVIEW
Vol. 47, No. 1, February 2006

PREFERENTIAL TRADE AGREEMENTS AND MULTILATERAL TARIFF COOPERATION*

BY KAMAL SAGGI[1]

Department of Economics, Southern Methodist University, Dallas U.S.A.

Are preferential trade agreements (PTAs) *building* or *stumbling blocks* for multilateral trade liberalization? I address this question in an infinitely repeated tariff game between three countries engaged in intraindustry trade under oligopoly. The central result is that when countries are symmetric, a free trade agreement (FTA) undermines multilateral tariff cooperation by adversely affecting the cooperation incentive of the nonmember whereas a customs union (CU) does so via its effect on the cooperation incentives of members. However, when countries are asymmetric with respect to either market size or cost, there exist circumstances where PTAs facilitate multilateral tariff cooperation.

1. INTRODUCTION

Countries pursue trade liberalization regionally and/or preferentially, as well as multilaterally within the auspices of the World Trade Organization (WTO). In the last few decades, the preferential approach to trade liberalization has come to occupy an increasingly important role in world trade. As per the Web site of the WTO, by the year 2002 some 250 preferential trade agreements (PTAs) had been notified to the WTO with the number expected to reach 300 by the end of 2005.

Given their widespread prevalence, it is important to understand how PTAs affect incentives for multilateral trade liberalization of member and nonmember countries. In particular, under what circumstances are PTAs *stumbling blocks* for multilateral trade liberalization?[2] When, if ever, do they act as *building blocks*? I examine these questions in a three-country model of international trade by analyzing incentives for multilateral trade liberalization under two types of PTAs: (i) a free trade agreement (FTA) under which members impose zero tariffs on each other and individually optimal tariffs on the nonmember and (ii) a customs union (CU) under which members impose a jointly optimal tariff on the nonmember while practicing free trade toward one another. The two types of PTAs

* Manuscript received April 2003; revised September 2003.

[1] I thank three anonymous referees, Rod Falvey, Kishore Gawande, Amy Glass, Hideo Konishi, Mikhail Klimenko, Ping Lin, Saltuk Ozerturk, Santanu Roy, Halis M. Yildiz and seminar audiences at SMU and the 2003 summer meetings of the Econometric Society for helpful comments and discussions. All errors are my own. Please address correspondence to: Kamal Saggi, Department of Economics, Southern Methodist University, Dallas, TX 75295-0496. Phone: 214 768 3274. Fax: 214 768 1821. E-mail: *Ksaggi@emu.edu*.

[2] This terminology has been popularized by Jagdish Bhagwati. See Bhagwati (1991), Bhagwati and Panagariya (1999), and Winters (1998) for overviews of the main policy questions in the area.

are evaluated on the basis of whether they hamper or facilitate multilateral tariff cooperation relative to a scenario where all countries impose nondiscriminatory tariffs on one another. The principle of nondiscrimination, known as the most-favored-nation (MFN) clause, is specified in the very first Article of the General Agreement on Tariffs and Trade (GATT) and occupies a central place in *all* multilateral trade agreements of the WTO. Given the importance of MFN to the multilateral trading system, it is natural to use it as a benchmark for evaluating PTAs.

The basic model builds on the partial equilibrium oligopoly trade model of Brander and Krugman (1983). I first derive the Nash equilibrium of a one-shot noncooperative tariff game between three symmetric countries in which each country chooses its MFN tariff to maximize its national welfare (defined as the sum of the local firm's profits, consumer surplus, and tariff revenue). To determine whether multilateral cooperation under PTAs is easier or harder to sustain relative to that under MFN, I then analyze the infinite repetition of this one-shot tariff game. In this repeated game, countries attempt to cooperate multilaterally on a symmetric tariff that is lower than their static Nash tariffs. As in Riezman (1991), Bagwell and Staiger (1997a, 1997b, 1998a), and Bond et al. (2001), such cooperation is required to be *self-enforcing*: each country balances the current benefit of deviating from the cooperative tariff against the future losses it suffers under the permanent trade war that results from its defection.

The major result is that if countries are symmetric with respect to market size and production costs, PTAs hinder multilateral tariff cooperation. However, the mechanics underlying this result are rather subtle. Relative to MFN, an FTA makes members *more* willing to cooperate multilaterally whereas a CU has the opposite effect. However, the nonmember country has a stronger incentive to cooperate under a CU relative to MFN. Since the incentive constraint of the *least willing* participant determines the degree of equilibrium cooperation, an FTA undermines multilateral cooperation by reducing the nonmember's willingness to cooperate whereas a CU does so by having the same effect on members.[3] A comparison of the two types of PTAs shows that a CU is more detrimental to multilateral tariff cooperation than an FTA.

To gain some intuition for the above results, as an example consider the effect of an FTA on the nonmember's cooperation incentive. Defection from cooperation is equally attractive to the nonmember under an FTA and MFN whereas the punishment it faces under a trade war is relatively less severe under an FTA. This is because the static Nash tariffs of members are lower than their MFN tariffs (Bagwell and Staiger, 1997a, 1997b, call this the *tariff complementarity* effect). Desirable as it may seem, in the present model, tariff complementarity works *against* multilateral cooperation since such cooperation is sustained by punishment strategies whose efficacy depends upon the magnitude of static Nash tariffs. In

[3] A rather different view of PTAs is presented in Ethier (1998), who emphasizes that recent PTAs have typically resulted in modest trade liberalization and that the standard Vinerian perspective (of trade diversion vs. creation) is not that relevant for their evaluation. Instead, in his model small countries enter into PTAs in order to improve their access to foreign direct investment that is a source of technology transfer. See also Freund (2000a) for an alternative approach.

principle, there is no general reason why the formation of a PTA should always imply tariff complementarity. In the present model, the assumptions of cost and demand linearity as well as that of symmetry are important for delivering tariff complementarity. In the absence of these assumptions, tariff complementarity is not necessarily obtained (Section 4 sheds more light on the role of symmetry).

In a model similar to the one presented here, Krishna (1998) explores the relationship between PTAs and multilateral trade liberalization.[4] In his model, tariffs are exogenously given and PTAs are endogenous in the sense that only those PTAs that benefit producers in members are considered. Krishna (1998) finds that the formation of PTAs undermines support for multilateral trade liberalization.[5] The present article endogenizes tariffs but instead takes PTAs as given.[6] Most importantly, and unlike Krishna (1998), the relationship between PTAs and multilateralism is explored in a stationary repeated game. As noted above, when tariffs are endogenous PTAs can actually liberalize trade in the short run due to the tariff complementarity effect. However, analysis of the repeated game shows that when countries are symmetric, PTAs undermine multilateral trade liberalization (as is the case in Krishna, 1998).[7]

In Subsections 4.1 and 4.2, I consider scenarios where countries are asymmetric with respect to market size or cost. This analysis shows that such asymmetries matter in several important ways. First, the presence of either type of asymmetry reduces the scope for cooperation even under MFN—bigger and/or relatively higher cost countries find it less desirable to cooperate multilaterally since cooperation yields relatively minor benefits to them in foreign markets while inflicting relatively higher costs in their domestic markets (in terms of rents forgone to foreign sellers). Second, tariff complementarity survives a fair degree of asymmetry (even under a CU). Third, PTAs hamper cooperation incentives of the nonmember regardless of the degree of market size asymmetry. Finally, under either cost or demand asymmetry, certain types of PTAs can actually *facilitate* multilateral tariff cooperation relative to MFN. Intuitively, the following parallel can be drawn between this result and the classic theory of distortions: Since asymmetries of market size and/or cost weaken incentives for multilateral tariff cooperation under MFN, the *policy asymmetry* induced by PTAs can sometimes improve the scope for such cooperation. Several examples illustrating this possibility are provided in Section 4.

Most models of multilateral tariff cooperation generate international trade via endowment differences across countries (see Bagwell and Staiger, 1997a, 1997b,

[4] Also using the oligopoly trade model, Freund (2000b) shows that multilateral trade liberalization encourages preferential trade liberalization by making self-enforcing PTAs easier to sustain.

[5] Levy (1997) focuses on political economy considerations and finds that PTAs supplant multilateral free trade in the monopolistic competition model of *intraindustry* trade in differentiated goods. Unlike in the present article, tariffs do not play an important role in Levy's analysis since only the choice between free trade (bilateral as well as multilateral) and autarky is considered.

[6] See Saggi and Yildiz (2005) for a model that endogenizes both preferential and multilateral trade liberalization.

[7] Using data on U.S. tariff reductions, Limao (2003) finds that the U.S. PTAs were a stumbling block for its multilateral liberalization.

1998a, 1998b; Bond et al., 2001; Bond and Syropoulos, 1996).[8] In such models, trade is usually interindustry in nature and countries impose tariffs to improve their terms of trade. In contrast, in the oligopoly model presented here trade is intra-industry in nature, and countries use tariffs to extract rents from foreign firms (as in Brander and Spencer, 1984).[9] Of course, oligopoly is not the only route to obtain intraindustry trade: Such type of trade also arises in the monopolistic competition models of Ethier (1982) and Krugman (1980) due to the presence of economies of scale and product differentiation. However, these models do not permit as easy an examination of optimal tariffs under different trade regimes as does the oligopoly model of trade.

In traditional terms of trade models, a CU uses its market power to raise tariffs on nonmembers (see, for example, Kennan and Riezman, 1988, 1990). However, a recent report by the World Bank (2000) argues that there is little evidence in support of this result. Thus, it is useful to explore models in which members *voluntarily* find it optimal to *not* raise tariffs on nonmembers (as opposed to being prohibited from doing so by WTO rules). In one of the few micro level detailed studies available on the subject, Chang and Winters (2002) find that tariffs on nonmembers actually declined when members of MERCOSUR (the major Latin American CU) liberalized trade toward one another.[10] Similar evidence is also cited in Bohara et al. (2004) who argue that their results support Richardson's (1993) political economy model of endogenous protection.

The rest of the article is organized as follows. Section 2 presents the basic tariff game between three symmetric countries and compares tariff equilibria under three regimes: MFN, FTA, and CU. Section 3 analyzes the infinite repetition of this tariff game and evaluates incentives for tariff cooperation under the three regimes. Section 4 considers how the presence of asymmetries alters the main results of the article. Section 5 concludes.

2. BASIC TARIFF GAME

There are three symmetric countries (i, j, and k) and two homogenous goods: x and y. Preferences over the two goods are quasi-linear: $U(x, y) = u(x) + y$. Good y is freely traded and serves as the numeraire. It is produced under perfect competition with constant returns to scale technology whereas good x is produced by a single firm in each country.[11] The marginal cost of production of good x equals c, where $c \geq 0$.

[8] See Bhagwati et al. (1999) for a collection of many of the important papers in the area.

[9] The strategic trade policy argument (surveyed in Brander, 1995) serves as the underlying motive for tariffs here.

[10] Chang and Winters (2002) also show that the formation of MERCOSUR resulted in significant declines in prices of exports of nonmembers to MERCOSUR countries. Although they interpret their empirical results as evidence of terms of trade manipulation by members, the equation they estimate is derived from an *oligopoly model* of price competition. Thus, their approach captures revenue shifting effects and their empirical results show that PTAs can hurt nonmembers by reducing their export profits (like in the present model).

[11] The monopoly assumption is not crucial; all that is needed is that firms have market power.

Markets are segmented and each producer of good x (from hereon called a firm) makes independent decisions regarding how much to sell in each market.[12] Firm z faces a specific tariff t_{zi} when exporting to country i, where $t_{zz} = 0$ for all $z = i, j, k$. Denote the tariff schedule of country i by (t_{ji}, t_{ki}) and that of countries j and k by (t_{ij}, t_{kj}) and (t_{ik}, t_{jk}), respectively.

Furthermore, assume that $u(x)$ is quadratic so that the demand curve for good x is linear in each country. Specifically, the demand curve in country i is given by

$$p_i = a - x_i(t_{ji}, t_{ki}) \tag{1}$$

where $x_i = \Sigma_z x_{zi}(t_{ji}, t_{ki})$ and $x_{zi}(t_{ji}, t_{ki})$ denotes the output sold by firm z in country i. The demand functions for good x in countries j and k are analogous to Equation (1). In Section 4, the demand intercept (a) and the production cost (c) of good x are allowed to vary across countries. Till then, countries are assumed to be symmetric in both respects.

At the production stage, profit maximization in country i's market requires that the following first-order conditions must hold for each firm:

$$p_i + p_i' x_{zi} = t_{zi} + c \tag{2}$$

where $z = i, j, k$. Utilizing the demand function in (1), these first-order conditions can be easily solved for equilibrium outputs and profits of all firms.

2.1. *MFN Tariffs.* Under MFN, each country imposes a single nondiscriminatory tariff on its trading partners and all countries simultaneously choose their respective tariffs to maximize their own welfare. Since markets are segmented and marginal costs are constant, a country's MFN tariff does not depend upon the tariffs of other countries, and export profits are independent of own tariffs.[13] As a result, it is sufficient to focus on only one country (say i). Denote country i's MFN tariff by t_i. Country i solves

$$\max_{t_i} W_i(t_i) \equiv CS_i(t_i) + \pi_i(t_i) + t_i \sum_{z \neq i} x_{zi}(t_i) \tag{3}$$

where $CS_i \equiv u(x_i) - p_i x_i$ denotes consumer surplus in country i; $\pi_i = \sum_z (p_z - c - t_{iz}) x_{iz}$ denotes the total profits of firm i; and $TR_i = t_i \sum_{z \neq i} x_{zi}(t_i)$ denotes country i's tariff revenue.

[12] Empirical support for the segmented markets approach is found in the literature on exchange rate pass through and pricing to market behavior. This literature documents substantial international price discrimination even in industries with relatively homogenous products (see, for example, Knetter, 1989, 1993; Marston, 1990).

[13] Strategic independence of trade policies is a simplifying assumption that is common in the literature on PTAs. For example, such independence arises in Bagwell and Staiger (1997a, 1997b) because demand is assumed to be independent across countries. In fact, it is even a feature of the general equilibrium endowment model of Kennan and Riezman (1988).

Solving the welfare problem specified in (3) delivers country i's optimal MFN tariff: $t^M \equiv \arg\max W_i(t_i)$. This tariff is derived in the appendix (there is no subscript on t^M since countries are symmetric).

It is clear that countries find themselves in a undesirable Nash equilibrium under MFN: They would all be better off under free trade, but each has a unilateral incentive to impose a rent-extracting tariff on foreign exporters. Due to symmetry, all countries have the same equilibrium welfare level under MFN (denoted by $W^M(t^M)$).

2.2. *Free Trade Agreement.* Suppose countries i and j enter into an FTA under which they impose zero tariffs on each other. Under an FTA, member i solves

$$\max_{t_{ki}} W_i(0, t_{ki}) \equiv CS_i(0, t_{ki}) + \pi_{ii}(0, t_{ki}) + t_{ki}x_{ki}(0, t_{ki}) \tag{4}$$

Since members are symmetric, they impose the same tariff on the nonmember. Let t^F denote a member's optimal tariff on the nonmember: $t^F \equiv \arg\max W_i(0, t_{ki})$.

At a general level, it is *not* obvious how t^F and t^M compare with each other. As it turns out, much of importance hinges on this comparison. Under the assumption of the model, the following result is obtained:

Proposition 1. *An FTA member's Nash tariff on the nonmember is lower than the MFN tariff:* $t^F < t^M$.[14]

To understand this result, consider the costs and benefits to an FTA member i of a small increase in its tariff on the nonmember k. Relative to MFN, country i imports more from country j and less from the nonmember k. As a result, country i's incentive to tax country k declines: A given tariff on country k yields less tariff revenue under an FTA compared to MFN. Furthermore, under an FTA, a given increase in country i's tariff also confers less benefit to its local firm since it applies only to country k's exports. Thus, both tax revenue and local profit considerations argue in favor of a lower tariff on country k relative to that under MFN. However, consumer welfare considerations work in the opposite direction: A given tariff increase under MFN reduces consumer welfare more relative to that under an FTA since the FTA tariff increase applies only to the nonmember whereas the MFN tariff increase applies to both countries. However, under demand linearity, revenue and profit considerations dominate consumer welfare ones so that each FTA member's Nash tariff on the nonmember is lower than its MFN tariff.

Article XXIV of GATT permits the formation of PTAs, but it requires that members not raise tariffs on nonmembers (see Hoekman and Kosetcki, 2001, for an extended discussion of Article XXIV).[15] Proposition 1 implies this restriction

[14] Bagwell and Staiger (1998a) call this the *tariff complementarity* effect. In Richardson (1995), a similar result is obtained as FTA members attempt to secure greater tariff revenue for themselves.

[15] In addition, Article XXIV requires that members reduce internal tariffs to zero and that the PTA should cover almost all trade between them. It is clear that the PTAs examined here satisfy these two requirements trivially: Only one good is subject to tariffs in the absence of a PTA, and it is assumed that PTA members set zero tariffs on each other.

need *not* always bind—that is, FTA members may voluntarily reduce their tariffs on nonmembers. But what are the welfare effects of such liberalization? Denote the equilibrium welfare of an FTA member m (where $m = i, j$) by $W_m^F(t^F, t^M)$ whereas that of the nonmember k is denoted by $W_k^F(t^F, t^M)$. The following holds:

PROPOSITION 2. *All countries have higher welfare under an FTA than under MFN:* $W_m^F(t^F, t^M) > W_k^F(t^F, t^M) > W^M(t^M)$.

A general presumption underlying empirical work on the effects of PTAs is that such agreements hurt nonmembers iff they lower their exports to the integrating blocs. Chang and Winters (2002) and Winters (1998) note that this presumption is not fully satisfactory since the welfare of nonmembers need not be perfectly correlated with their exports. Although their general point is certainly correct, it is worth noting that in the present model, all else equal, an increase in a country's equilibrium exports necessarily implies an increase in its welfare. As a result, *a necessary and sufficient condition* for the nonmember to be better off under an FTA (relative to MFN) is that its total exports increase. This result holds due to market segmentation and the assumption that firms compete in quantities. Due to segmentation, an FTA does not alter the nonmember's domestic surplus and quantity competition implies that equilibrium profits of a firm are monotonically related to its equilibrium output.[16] In fact, since the nonmember's exports (and therefore its welfare) *increase* when the other two countries enter into an FTA, *world welfare also increases due to the formation of an FTA*.

2.3. *Nash Tariffs under a CU.* Under a CU, the two members impose a common external tariff on the nonmember while simultaneously eliminating tariffs on each other. Thus, members i and j solve

$$\max_t W_i(0, t) + W_j(0, t) \tag{5}$$

where $t_{ji} = t_{ij} = 0$ and $t_{ki} = t_{kj} = t$. Unlike an FTA, a CU takes into account the export profits that members derive from each other's markets. Due to market segmentation, the problem in (5) has the same solution as the following problem:

$$\max_t W_i(0, t) + \pi_{ji}(0, t) \tag{6}$$

Denote the optimal CU tariff by $t^U \equiv \arg\max W_i(0, t) + \pi_{ji}(0, t)$. Let the equilibrium welfare of a CU member be given by $W_m^U(t^U)$ and that of the nonmember by $W_k^U(t^U)$.

PROPOSITION 3. *The CU's common tariff on the nonmember is higher than the tariff of an FTA member but it is lower than the MFN tariff:* $t^F < t^U < t^M$.[17] *Although*

[16] Since the nonmember's tariff schedule under an FTA is the same as that under MFN, the formation of an FTA does not alter its domestic surplus.

[17] In the political economy model of Cadot et al. (1999), the CU tariff is also higher than the FTA tariff.

the welfare of a CU member is higher than that of an FTA member, the nonmember's welfare is lower under a CU than under both MFN and an FTA: $W_m^U(t^U) > W_m^F(t^F)$ *and* $W_k^F(t^F) > W^M(t^M) > W_k^U(t^U)$.

As expected, the tariff complementarity effect under a CU is weaker than that under an FTA and this weakened complementarity is enough to turn the welfare ranking from the nonmember's perspective in favor of MFN relative to a CU. It is worth noting that a CU harms the nonmember as well as world welfare even though it does *not* violate Article XXIV of the GATT since $t^U < t^M$. Thus, Proposition 3 exposes the *limits of Article XXIV*: Although this Article is generally a good idea, it does not go far enough in protecting the interests of nonmembers. Proposition 3 implies that the formation of a CU must be accompanied by *sufficient tariff reductions* for nonmembers if they are not to experience a decline in welfare relative to MFN.

In the one-shot tariff game considered above, countries do not attempt to achieve tariffs lower than the MFN level except bilaterally under a PTA. Thus, our main motivating question remains unaddressed: How does the formation of PTAs affect incentives for multilateral tariff cooperation? The following analysis answers this question by initially assuming countries to be symmetric and then examining how the main results depend upon this assumption.

3. TARIFF COOPERATION UNDER SYMMETRY

Following the paradigm in the literature, I model multilateral tariff cooperation as a stationary repeated game where cooperation can be sustained only if it is incentive compatible for all countries. Under this approach, each country weighs the benefit of defecting from the cooperative tariff against the future cost of such defection. By assumption, countries sustain cooperation via *trigger strategies*: Defection by any country results in a permanent trade war wherein all countries revert to their MFN tariffs.[18] After describing multilateral tariff cooperation under MFN, the effects of PTAs on incentives for cooperation are derived.

3.1. *Cooperation Incentives under MFN.* Suppose each country employs a multilaterally agreed upon tariff t until someone defects, in which case cooperation breaks down with all countries switching to their MFN tariffs forever. Let $W^M(t)$ denote the per period welfare of a country under the cooperative tariff t. It proves useful to write $W^M(t)$ as

$$W^M(t) = S^M(t) + 2\pi^M(t) \tag{7}$$

where $S^M(t)$ equals a country's domestic surplus (defined as the sum of consumer surplus and local profits) and $2\pi^M(t)$ its total export profits. Let $W^M(t^M, t)$ denote the welfare of a country that defects from the cooperative tariff t to its optimal MFN tariff t^M where

[18] In other words, all punishments are multilateral in this model. See Maggi (1999) for a comparison of bilateral versus multilateral punishments in the WTO.

$$W^M(t^M, t) = S^M(t^M) + 2\pi^M(t) \tag{8}$$

Note that in the above equation, defection from the cooperative tariff t to the MFN tariff t^M benefits the defecting country by increasing its domestic surplus from $S^M(t)$ to $S^M(t^M)$ without altering its export profits.

A country's one-time payoff of defecting from the cooperative tariff t to the MFN tariff t^M equals

$$B^M(t^M, t) = W^M(t^M, t) - W^M(t) = S^M(t^M) - S^M(t) \tag{9}$$

Note that, if $t = t^M$, then defection carries no benefit for a country. For tariff cooperation to be meaningful it must be that $t \le t^M$.

The per period cost to a country of the breakdown of cooperation is given by

$$C^M(t, t^M) = W^M(t) - W^M(t^M) = -B^M(t^M, t) + 2[\pi^M(t) - \pi^M(t^M)] \tag{10}$$

Note that since $\pi^M(t^M) \le \pi^M(t)$ for all $t \le t^M$, the per period cost of defection is always *lower* in absolute value than the current benefit of defection: $|C^M(t, t^M)| < |B^M(t^M, t)|$. Thus, multilateral tariff cooperation would be infeasible if countries were to completely discount the future. For tariff cooperation to be self-enforcing under MFN, the current benefit of defection must be less than the discounted lifetime cost of defection:

$$B^M(t^M, t) \le \frac{\delta}{1-\delta} C^M(t, t^M) \tag{11}$$

where δ denotes the discount factor so that $\frac{\delta}{1-\delta} C^M(t, t^M)$ measures the trade war's cost to each country under MFN. The incentive compatibility (IC) constraint in (11) can be written as

$$(t^M - t)[3\alpha - 5(t^M + t)] \le \frac{\delta}{1-\delta}(t^M - t)[\alpha + t^M + t]$$

where $\alpha \equiv a - c$. For $t^M > t$, the above IC becomes

$$\frac{3\alpha - 5(t^M + t)}{\alpha + t^M + t} \le \frac{\delta}{1-\delta}$$

The above constraint just binds at the smallest symmetric tariff (called t^*) for which cooperation is acceptable to all countries. Substituting for t^M and solving for t^* gives

$$t^* = \frac{(15 - 28\delta)\alpha}{10(5 - 4\delta)} \tag{12}$$

Note that

$$\frac{\partial t^*}{\partial \delta} = -\frac{8\alpha}{(5 - 4\delta)^2} < 0$$

that is, as countries become more patient, they are willing to cooperate on a lower tariff. It is easy to solve for the critical discount factor above cooperation over free trade is self-enforcing under MFN:

LEMMA 1. *Free trade ($t^* = 0$) can be sustained via multilateral cooperation under MFN iff all countries are patient enough (iff $\delta \geq \delta^M$ where $\delta^M = 0.54$).*

Now consider how an FTA alters incentives for multilateral tariff cooperation.

3.2. *Tariff Cooperation under an FTA.* Suppose two countries sign a binding FTA and eliminate tariffs on each other. By assumption, the FTA is permanent in nature—that is, members retain zero tariffs on each other even if cooperation with the nonmember breaks down. Recall that a member's statically optimal tariff on the nonmember is t^F, where $t^F < t^M$ due to the tariff complementarity effect emphasized in Proposition 1.

How does the formation of an FTA affect incentives for tariff cooperation between members and the nonmember? To answer this question, it is useful to discuss how the formation of an FTA changes the costs and benefits of multilateral cooperation for all countries. Furthermore, note that since $t^F < t^M$, the range of tariffs from t^F to t^M must be ruled out as candidates for cooperative tariffs: For cooperation to be even possible under an FTA, it must involve a greater degree of trade liberalization relative to MFN or else it would be unacceptable to the nonmember.

3.3. *How an FTA Alters Cooperation Incentives.* Under tariff cooperation, the per period welfare of an FTA member m (where $m = i, j$) equals

$$W_m^F(t) = S_m^F(t) + \pi_{mm}^F(t) + \pi_{mk}^F(t) \tag{13}$$

where $S_m^F(t)$ denotes its domestic surplus; $\pi_{mm}^F(t)$ its export profit in the *other member's market* (and *not* in its own market); and $\pi_{mk}^F(t)$ its export profit in the nonmember's market. Similarly, the welfare of nonmember k equals

$$W_k^F(t) = S_k^F(t) + 2\pi_{km}^F(t) \tag{14}$$

where $W_m^F(t) > W_k^F(t)$.

Since an FTA is permanent by assumption, under a trade war members raise their tariffs on only the nonmember (from t to t^F). If an FTA member defects from cooperation, its welfare in the period of defection equals

$$W_m^F(t^F, t) = S_m^F(t^F) + \pi_{mm}^F(t) + \pi_{mk}^F(t) \tag{15}$$

Similarly, a nonmember's welfare in the period of defection equals

$$W_k^F(t, t^M) = S_k^F(t^M) + 2\pi_{km}^F(t) \tag{16}$$

Denote the per period welfare of a member under a trade war by $W_m^F(t^F, t^M)$ and that of the nonmember by $W_k^F(t^F, t^M)$ where

(17) $$W_m^F(t^F, t^M) = S_m^F(t^F) + \pi_{mm}^F(t^F) + \pi_{mk}^F(t^M)$$

and

(18) $$W_k^F(t^F, t^M) = S_k^F(t^M) + 2\pi_{km}^F(t^F)$$

Thus, an FTA member's benefit from defection equals

(19) $$B_m^F(t^F, t) = W_m^F(t^F, t) - W_m^F(t) = S_m^F(t^F) - S_m^F(t)$$

that is an FTA member's benefit from defection equals the increase in its domestic surplus that results from raising the tariff on the nonmember from t to t^F. Recall that a country's benefit from defection under MFN equals $B^M(t^M, t) = S^M(t^M) - S^M(t)$. Thus,

(20) $$B_m^F(t^F, t) - B^M(t^M, t) = S_m^F(t^F) - S_m^F(t) - S^M(t^M) + S^M(t)$$

It is shown in the appendix that the above expression is negative: $B_m^F(t^F, t) < B^M(t^M, t)$. The reason behind this result is simple. The inability of an FTA member to increase its tariff on the other member reduces its current benefit of defection. By contrast, under MFN, a defecting country raises its tariff on both its trading partners.

What about a member's per period cost of defection? Suppose a member defects from the cooperative tariff t to the tariff t^F. Then, from next period on, the nonmember responds via its MFN tariff t^M and the other FTA member raises its tariff on the nonmember to t^F. By definition, a member's cost of defection $C_m^F(t^F, t^M, t)$ equals

$$C_m^F(t^F, t^M, t) = W_m^F(t) - W_m^F(t^F, t^M)$$

which can be rewritten as

(21) $$C_m^F(t^F, t^M, t) = -B_m^F(t^F) + [\pi_{mm}^F(t) - \pi_{mm}^F(t^F)] + [\pi_{mk}^F(t) - \pi_{mk}^F(t^M)]$$

As under MFN, an FTA member's per period benefit of defection exceeds the cost: $|C_m^F(t, t^F)| < |B_m^F(t, t^F)|$. The following is shown in the appendix:

LEMMA 2. *Relative to MFN, an FTA lowers both the benefit and the cost of defection for members:* $B_m^F(t^F, t^M) < B^M(t^M, t)$ *and* $C_m^F(t^F, t^M) < C^M(t, t^M)$. *However, the decline in cost is relatively smaller:*

$$\left|C_m^F(t^F, t^M) - C^M(t, t^M)\right| < \left|B_m^F(t^F, t^M) - B^M(t^M, t)\right|$$

The above lemma informs us that, relative to MFN, an FTA makes members *more* willing to cooperate multilaterally with the nonmember. Two opposing forces determine this surprising result. On the one hand, defection from cooperation is not as attractive to an FTA member as under MFN since it can act opportunistically only against the nonmember. On the other hand, the punishment a member faces under an FTA is also less severe than that under MFN because, in the event of a trade war, a member does not suffer any tariff increase in the other member's market whereas the nonmember does. It is worth emphasizing that whereas a trade war under MFN hurts all countries equally, under an FTA the tariff increase in a member's market *partially* benefits the other member since it applies only to the nonmember. Thus, for an FTA member the punishment phase carries a partial reward in the other member's market. Nevertheless, the reduction in the direct benefit of defection dominates the weakened punishment effect, making members more willing to cooperate. Does it imply that an FTA facilitates multilateral tariff cooperation? Not quite. To answer this question, the effect of an FTA on the IC constraint of the nonmember also needs to be considered.

If the nonmember defects from the cooperative tariff t, it imposes its optimal MFN tariff t^M on members. Thus, its welfare in the period of defection under an FTA equals $W_k^F(t, t^M)$ and its immediate benefit from defection under an FTA equals

$$B_k^F(t, t^M) = W_k^F(t, t^M) - W_k^F(t) = S_k^F(t^M) - S_k^F(t) \tag{22}$$

Recall that under MFN $B^M(t^M, t) = S^M(t^M) - S^M(t)$ where $S_k^F(t^M) = S^M(t^M)$ and $S_k^F(t) = S^M(t)$. As a result, the following lemma is immediate:

LEMMA 3. *The benefit of defection for an FTA nonmember is the same as that under MFN:* $B_k^F(t, t^M) = B^M(t, t^M)$.

The above lemma may seem counterintuitive since each FTA member enjoys a cost advantage over the nonmember in each other's markets. But relative to MFN, the gain from defection is no higher for the FTA nonmember because defection does nothing to change the level of its cost disadvantage.[19]

How is the nonmember's cost of defection affected by an FTA? By definition,

$$C_k^F(t^F, t, t^M) = W_k^F(t) - W_k^F(t^F, t^M, t)$$

As before, the above can be written as

$$C_k^F(t^F, t, t^M) = -B_k^F(t^F, t, t^M) + 2[\pi_{km}^F(t) - \pi_{km}^F(t^F)] \tag{23}$$

[19] One has to be careful here: The comparison is between the nonmember's export profits when it faces the same cooperative tariff t under MFN and an FTA (i.e. between $\pi^M(t)$) and $\pi_k^F(0, t)$) and *not* between its per period *equilibrium* profit under Nash tariffs under the two regimes (i.e., not between $\pi_k^F(0, t^F)$ and $\pi^M(0, t^M)$). So although $\pi^M(t) > \pi_k^F(0, t)$, it is also true that $\pi_k^F(0, t^F) > \pi^M(0, t^M)$ since $t^F < t^M$.

Since $\pi^F_{km}(t) > \pi^F_{km}(t^F)$, it must be that $|C^F_k(t, t^F)| < |B^F_k(t, t^F)|$. The following lemma is proved in the appendix:

LEMMA 4. *The nonmember's cost of defection is lower under an FTA relative to that under MFN:* $C^F_k(t^F, t, t^M) < C^M(t^M, t)$.

Since $t^F < t^M$, FTA members are not able to punish defections from cooperation by the nonmember as severely as they can under MFN. This reduction in the ability of members to punish the nonmember *lowers* the latter's cost of defection. Recall that the benefit of defection for a nonmember under an FTA is the same as that under MFN (Lemma 3). Since the cost of defection is lower for the nonmember under an FTA while the benefit is the same, the FTA nonmember has an *unambiguously stronger incentive to defect from multilateral tariff cooperation relative to MFN*. The first major result of this article can now be stated:

PROPOSITION 4. *For all cooperative tariffs t in the range* $0 \leq t < t^F$, *relative to MFN, the cooperation incentive of an FTA member is stronger whereas that of the nonmember is weaker.*

Due to symmetry, only one IC constraint is required to sustain cooperation under MFN. However, under an FTA there are two such constraints because members and the nonmember end up having differing incentives for cooperation. Let δ^F_m denote the critical discount factor above which an FTA member is willing to cooperate on free trade and let δ^F_k denote the corresponding discount factor for the nonmember. An important lemma to the above proposition is shown in the appendix:

LEMMA 5. *The range of discount factors for which an FTA member (nonmember) is willing to cooperate over multilateral free trade is larger (smaller) under FTA than that under MFN:* $\delta^F_m < \delta^M < \delta^F_k$.

The next section considers the case where the PTA takes the form of a CU rather than an FTA.

3.4. *Customs Union.* Recall that the tariff complementarity effect is weaker under a CU than under an FTA ($t^F < t^U < t^M$) and that nonmember is worse off under a CU than under MFN (from the viewpoint of static welfare). Following the logic above, suppose all countries agree to cooperate on some tariff t under a CU where $t < t^U$.

Under cooperation, let $W^U_m(t)$ denote the per period welfare of a member and $W^U_k(t)$ that of the nonmember

$$W^U_m(t) = S^U_m(t) + \pi^U_{mm}(t) + \pi^U_{mk}(t) \tag{24}$$

and

$$W^U_k(t) = S^U_k(t) + 2\pi^U_{km}(t) \tag{25}$$

where $W^U_m(t) > W^U_k(t)$.

Like an FTA, a CU is assumed to be a permanent agreement: Under a trade war, members impose zero tariffs on each other and the tariff t^U on the nonmember. Since $t^U > t^F$, tariff discrimination against the nonmember is stronger under a CU than under an FTA. Note also that, by the nature of the institution, *defection from cooperation by a CU involves defection by both members*. In the following discussion, *the welfare per CU member* is considered.

3.5. *Cooperation Incentives under a CU.* The CU's (per member) welfare in the period of defection equals

$$W_m^U(t^U, t) = S_m^U(t^U) + \pi_{mm}^U(t^U) + \pi_{mk}^U(t) \tag{26}$$

Similarly, if the nonmember defects, its welfare in the period of defection equals

$$W_k^U(t, t^M) = S_k^U(t^M) + 2\pi_{km}^U(t) \tag{27}$$

Denote the per period welfare of the CU under a trade war with the nonmember by $W_m^U(t^U, t^M)$ and that of the nonmember by $W_k^U(t^U, t^M)$ where

$$W_m^U(t^U, t^M) = S_m^U(t^U) + \pi_{mm}^U(t^U) + \pi_{mk}^U(t^M) \tag{28}$$

and

$$W_k^U(t^U, t^M) = S_k^U(t^M) + 2\pi_{km}^U(t^U) \tag{29}$$

Thus, a CU's benefit from defection from cooperation with the nonmember equals

$$B_m^U(t^U, t) = S_m^U(t^U) - S_m^U(t) + \pi_{mm}^U(t^U) - \pi_{mm}^U(t) \tag{30}$$

Note that defection by a CU leads to an increase in domestic surplus *as well as* export profits of its members since the tariff faced by the nonmember goes up in both markets. In contrast, under MFN and an FTA, defection only increases a defecting party's domestic surplus without increasing its export profit. Furthermore,

$$\begin{aligned} B_m^U(t^U, t) - B^M(t^M, t) = {} & S_m^U(t^U) - S_m^U(t) - S^M(t^M) + S^M(t) \\ & + \pi_{mm}^U(t^U) - \pi_{mm}^U(t) \end{aligned} \tag{31}$$

As in the case of an FTA, the above expression is negative (see the proof of Lemma 2A in the appendix). The reason is that a CU member can raise its tariff only against the nonmember. As a result, a CU member's gain from defection turns out to be lower than that under MFN. Of course, since $t^U > t^F$ and because defection by a CU also leads to an increase in export profits of members, the CU's incentive to defect is higher than that of an FTA (member):

$$B^M(t^M, t) > B_m^U(t^U, t) > B_m^F(t^F, t)$$

Consider next the CU's per period cost of defection. When a CU defects, it faces the tariff t^M in only the nonmember. Following the derivations under the FTA case gives

$$(32) \quad C_m^U(t^U, t^M) - C^M(t, t^M) = \left[B^M(t^M, t) - B_m^U(t^U, t)\right] - \left[\pi_{mk}^U(t^M) - \pi_{mk}^U(t)\right] - [2\pi^M(t) - 2\pi^M(t^M)]$$

We know that (i) $B_m^U(t^U, t) < B^M(t^M, t)$; (ii) $\pi_{mk}^U(t) < \pi_{mk}^U(t^M)$; and (iii) $\pi^M(t) > \pi^M(t^M)$. Thus, it follows immediately that

$$\left|C_m^U(t^U, t^M) - C^M(t, t^M)\right| < \left|B_m^U(t^U, t) - B^M(t^M, t)\right|$$

Furthermore, the appendix indicates that $C_m^U(t^U, t^M) < C^M(t, t^M)$.

LEMMA 2A. *Relative to MFN, (i) the cost and the benefit of defection are lower for members of a CU:* $C_m^U(t^U, t^M) < C^M(t, t^M)$ *and* $B_m^U(t^U, t) < B^M(t^M, t)$ *and (ii) the decline in the cost is smaller than the decline in benefit:* $|C_m^U(t^U, t^M) - C^M(t, t^M)| < |B_m^U(t^U, t) - B^M(t^M, t)|$. *Relative to an FTA, although a CU member's cost of defection is lower,* $C_m^U(t^U, t^M) < C^M(t, t^M)$, *its benefit of defection is higher,* $B_m^U(t^U, t) > B^F(t^F, t)$.

The major implication of Lemma 2A is that *members of a CU are less willing to cooperate multilaterally with the nonmember relative to both under MFN and an FTA*. First consider the comparison with MFN. On the one hand, the benefit from defection is not as high for a CU member as under MFN because the scope for opportunism is reduced: A CU can only raise its tariff on the nonmember. On the other hand, the punishment a CU faces is certainly less severe than that under MFN because its defection is punished by only the nonmember. Not only that, when a trade war results, the tariff increase in the other CU member benefits the defecting CU member (just as in the case of an FTA).

Relative to an FTA, defection is more beneficial to a CU because of the tariff coordination involved: The CU chooses a higher tariff on the nonmember than an FTA and secures more rents in the process. On the cost side, defection is not as severely punished either: Just like under an FTA its defection is punished only by the nonmember, and the fact that $t^U > t^F$ also works to the advantage of the defecting member.

Consider now the nonmember's incentive to defect from the cooperative tariff t. If the nonmember defects, it imposes its optimal MFN tariff t^M and its welfare in the period of defection equals $W_k^U(t, t^M)$. As a result, the benefit of defection for the nonmember equals

$$(33) \quad B_k^U(t, t^M) = W_k^U(t, t^M) - W_k^U(t) = S_k^U(t^M) - S_k^U(t)$$

Recall that

$$B_k^M(t, t^M) = S_k^M(t^M) - S_k^M(t) \quad \text{and} \quad B_k^F(t, t^M) = S_k^F(t^M) - S_k^F(t)$$

But

$$S_k^U(t^M) = S_k^F(t^M) = S_k^M(t^M) \quad \text{and} \quad S_k^U(t) = S_k^F(t) = S_k^M(t)$$

so that the nonmember's benefit of defection under a CU is the same as that under an FTA and MFN:

$$B_k^F(t, t^M) = B_k^M(t, t^M) = B_k^U(t, t^M)$$

The logic is the same as that under an FTA: Although a nonmember's export profits are lower under a CU than under an FTA (as well as under MFN), defection does *not* alter the level of those profits.

How is the nonmember's cost of defection affected by a CU? By definition

$$C_k^U(t^U, t, t^M) = W_k^U(t) - W_k^U(t^U, t^M) \tag{34}$$

First consider a comparison of this cost with that under MFN:

$$C_k^U(t^U, t, t^M) - C^M(t^M, t) = \pi^M(t^M) - \pi_{km}^U(t^U) + \pi_{km}^U(t) - \pi^M(t) \tag{35}$$

Note that $\pi_{km}^U(t^U) < \pi^M(t^M)$ because the tariff complementarity effect under a CU is weak and the degree of tariff discrimination suffered by the nonmember is relatively high under a CU (see Proposition 3). Furthermore, $\pi_{km}^U(t) < \pi^M(t)$ because the nonmember faces the same tariff under MFN and a CU whereas its rival exporter faces no tariff. However, given the assumptions of the model, the net result is as follows:

LEMMA 4B. *The nonmember's costs of defection under the three trade regimes can be ranked as follows:* $C_k^F(t^F, t, t^M) < C^M(t^M, t) < C_k^U(t^U, t, t^M)$.

The preceding two lemmas yield the second major result of this article:

PROPOSITION 5. *For all cooperative tariffs t in the range* $0 \leq t < t^F$, *relative to MFN, the nonmember has a stronger incentive to cooperate under a CU relative to both an FTA and MFN.*

Let δ_m^U denote the critical discount factor above which a CU member is willing to cooperate on free trade with the nonmember and let δ_k^U denote the corresponding discount factor for the nonmember. An important lemma to the above proposition is shown in the appendix:

LEMMA 6. *The range of discount factors for which a member is willing to cooperate over free trade under a CU is smaller relative to both MFN and an FTA* ($\delta_m^F <$

$\delta^M < \delta_m^U$) *whereas the corresponding range of discount factors for the nonmember is larger* ($\delta_k^U < \delta^M < \delta_k^F$).

If multilateral free trade cannot be supported under MFN because $\delta < \delta^M$, then the above lemma implies that although a CU would never be willing to cooperate over free trade, the nonmember would surely want to do so in the range $\delta_k^U \leq \delta \leq \delta^M$.[20]

4. ASYMMETRIES ACROSS COUNTRIES

Thus far the analysis assumes that countries are identical in all respects. It is worth investigating how the results derived in this article depend upon the assumption of symmetry.[21] Accordingly, in this section countries are allowed to be asymmetric with respect to market size and production costs. To keep the analysis tractable, I restrict attention to the most interesting case of $t = 0$ (i.e., where multilateral cooperation is over free trade).

4.1. *Asymmetric Market Sizes.* Let demand for good x vary across countries (indexed by $z = i, j, k$). In particular, let the intercept of the demand function for good x in country z be given by a_z. For example, in country i, we have $p_i = a_i - \Sigma_z x_{zi}(\mathbf{t_i})$. Suppose $c = 0$ for expositional ease so that $\alpha_z \equiv a_z - c = a_z$.

4.1.1. *MFN.* The first point to note is that since countries are asymmetric with respect to market size (as measured by $a_z = \alpha_z$), their *incentives for multilateral tariff cooperation differ under MFN*. Let δ_z^M denote the critical discount factor over which country z is willing to cooperate multilaterally over free trade. It turns out that $\delta_i^M < \delta_j^M$ iff $\alpha_i < \alpha_j$. The intuition for this result is straightforward—cooperation over free trade is relatively less attractive to bigger countries since they gain access to smaller foreign markets in exchange for granting access to relatively larger domestic markets.

Another useful way of seeing how asymmetry affects incentives for cooperation is to examine how the critical discount factor δ_z^M of country z changes with the distribution of market size across countries. It is easy to show that an increase in own market size makes a country less willing to cooperate whereas an increase in another country's market size makes it more willing to do so:

$$\frac{\partial \delta_z^M}{\partial \alpha_{\tilde{}z}} < 0 < \frac{\partial \delta_z^M}{\partial \alpha_z}, \quad z = i, j, k$$

and $\tilde{}z$ denotes any country other than z. However, since the crucial discount factor is the one for the least willing participant, it follows that incentives for multilateral cooperation under MFN are *weakened* due to asymmetry.

[20] Recall that under an FTA exactly the opposite conclusion holds.

[21] I thank two anonymous referees for raising this question.

4.1.2. *Free Trade Agreement.* Does asymmetry also weaken cooperation incentives under an FTA? To address this question, suppose two of the countries (say *i* and *j*) form an FTA. Let δ_m^F denote the critical discount factors above FTA member m (where $m = i, j$) willing to cooperate multilaterally over free trade and let δ_k^F denote the corresponding discount factor for the nonmember. It is easy to show that

$$\frac{\partial \delta_m^F}{\partial \alpha_k} < 0, \frac{\partial \delta_m^F}{\partial \alpha_m} > 0, \quad \text{and} \quad \frac{\partial \delta_m^F}{\partial \alpha_{\text{~}m}} > 0 \quad \text{for} \quad m = i, j$$

and ˜*m* denotes the FTA member country other than m. In other words, an increase in market size of *either* member makes both members less willing to cooperate whereas an increase in market size of the nonmember makes members more willing to do so. Similarly, with respect to the nonmember's critical discount factor δ_k^F we have

$$\frac{\partial \delta_k^F}{\partial \alpha_m} < 0 < \frac{\partial \delta_k^F}{\partial \alpha_k} \quad \text{for} \quad m = i, j$$

Thus, even under an FTA, market size asymmetry affects cooperation incentives much the same way as it does under MFN except that under an FTA, a member becomes less willing to cooperate even when the market size of the *other* member increases.

Of course, our main interest is in determining how cooperation incentives vary across trade regimes and how this variation depends upon the degree of underlying asymmetry. First consider the effect of the FTA between countries *i* and *j* on the nonmember *k*. Note that, due to market segmentation, the tariff complementarity effect of an FTA holds even when countries are asymmetric with respect to market size. We have

$$t_m^M - t_m^F = \frac{11\alpha_m}{70} > 0 \quad \text{for} \quad m = i, j$$

More importantly, simple calculations show that $\delta_k^F > \delta_k^M$—that is, *regardless of the degree of underlying market asymmetry between countries, the weaker punishment of an FTA makes the nonmember less willing to cooperate relative to MFN*. Thus, that part of Proposition 4 that refers to incentives of the nonmember holds under asymmetry without any qualifications.

How does the FTA between countries *i* and *j* alter their cooperation incentives? Here, the answer depends critically on the distribution of market sizes across countries. Let $\Delta\delta_m^{MF} \equiv \delta_m^M - \delta_m^F$. Figure 1 plots the zero-contours of the functions $\Delta\delta_i^{MF}$ and $\Delta\delta_j^{MF}$ in the (α_j, α_k) space.

In Figure 1, the horizontal line $\alpha_k = 0.89\alpha_i$ is the graph of $\Delta\,\delta_j^{MF} = 0$—above this line the FTA increases country *j*'s incentive to cooperate whereas the opposite is true below it. The upward sloping line $\alpha_k = 1.13\alpha_j$ is the graph of $\Delta\,\delta_i^{MF} = 0$—above (below) this line the FTA makes country *i* more (less) willing to cooperate. The

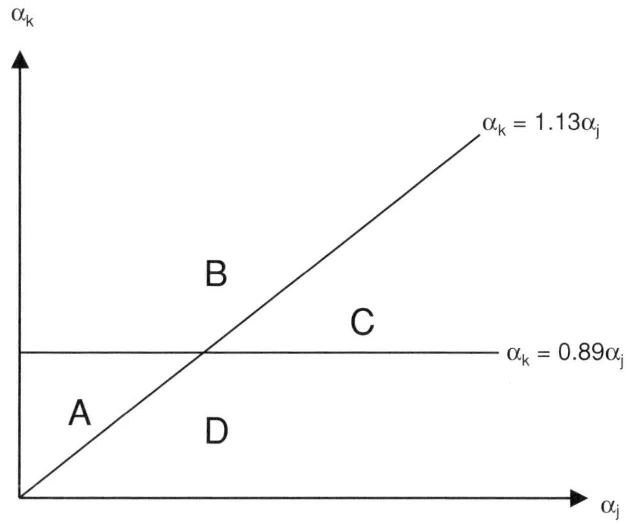

FIGURE 1

COOPERATION INCENTIVES OF FTA MEMBERS

two lines intersect at $\alpha_j = \alpha_i$ and $\alpha_k = 0.89\alpha_i$ and divide Figure 1 into four distinct regions: A, B, C, and D. In region B, the nonmember (country k) is comparable in size to (or bigger than) members (i and j) and, just as under symmetry, the FTA makes members more willing to cooperate multilaterally. In region A, country k is small relative to country i but not so with respect to country j, and the FTA makes country i more willing to cooperate and country j less willing to do so. In region C, the roles of the two FTA members are reversed relative to region A. And finally, in region D, country k is small relative to both members, and the FTA reduces cooperation incentives of both members. *Thus, even under market size asymmetry, cooperative incentives of FTA members are higher than that under MFN if the relative market size of the nonmember is not too small.* Furthermore, an increase in the market size of either member undermines their incentives for multilateral cooperation relative to MFN.

Although the presence of market size asymmetry can make members less willing to cooperate, to determine the impact of an FTA on overall multilateral cooperation, the pivotal country (i.e., the one that has the weakest incentive to cooperate) needs to be identified.[22] To do this, critical discount factors of member and nonmembers needs to be compared. To facilitate this comparison, suppose that $\alpha_i = \alpha_j = \alpha$ (i.e., members are symmetric). Then, it is easy to show that if the nonmember is not too small in size relative to members, then it is pivotal whereas when

[22] Recall that under symmetry the nonmember is always pivotal under an FTA (Lemma 5).

it is relatively small, it is the members that are pivotal. Since the nonmember's incentive to cooperate is lowered due to an FTA regardless of the degree of asymmetry between countries, we can conclude that if the nonmember is pivotal (which happens when it is bigger than or similar in size to members), an FTA necessarily undermines multilateral tariff cooperation.

What happens when members are pivotal? Recall that under symmetry, an FTA always makes members more willing to cooperate (see Lemma 5). This implies that if and when this result holds under market size asymmetry, it is possible that an FTA might *facilitate* multilateral tariff cooperation. The following example illustrates this case:

Example 1. Suppose $\alpha_i = \alpha_j = 1$ and $\alpha_k = 0.90$. Then, under MFN we have $\delta_k^M = 0.43 < \delta_i^M = \delta_j^M = 0.59$. Under an FTA, we have $\delta_k^F = 0.54 < \delta_j^F = \delta_i^F = 0.57$. In this example, (a) the bigger countries (i.e., *i* and *j*) are pivotal under both MFN and the FTA, and (b) the FTA *facilitates* multilateral cooperation since it makes the pivotal countries more willing to cooperate multilaterally (even though it reduces the cooperation incentive of the nonmember).

Now we are in a position to summarize the main result under market size asymmetry. If the nonmember is pivotal, then an FTA necessarily undermines incentives for multilateral tariff cooperation. However, if members are pivotal, then an FTA can increase the scope for multilateral cooperation.

4.1.3. *Customs Union.* Next consider the CU case under market asymmetry when countries *i* and *j* form a CU. The first point to note is that when countries are highly asymmetric, tariff complementarity does *not* necessarily hold under a CU. It is straightforward to show that

$$t^U = \frac{5(\alpha_i + \alpha_j)}{38} \quad \text{and that} \quad t_i^M - t^U = \frac{16\alpha_i}{95} - \frac{5\alpha_j}{38}$$

Switching the roles of α_i and α_j in the second formula gives the expression for $t_j^M - t^U$. These calculations imply that tariff complementarity holds for both members iff they are not significantly different in size (i.e., $0.78 \leq \frac{\alpha_i}{\alpha_j} \leq 1.28$). Outside this range, the formation of a CU implies that the tariff of one of the members (on the nonmember) declines relative to MFN whereas that of the other member increases.

Let δ_m^U denote the critical discount factor above which member m (where $m = i, j$) is willing to cooperate multilaterally over free trade. As before, to determine whether the CU increases or lowers a country's incentives for cooperation, we need to compare δ_m^U with δ_m^M. The expression for $\delta_m^M - \delta_m^U$ is rather complicated. However, numerical simulations show that $\delta_m^M > \delta_m^U$ for all reasonable parameter values, indicating that the CU reduces cooperation incentives of members. As in the case of an FTA, to determine the impact of a CU on overall cooperation, we first need to determine the pivotal country. Recall that under symmetry, CU members are always pivotal whereas under asymmetry the nonmember may be pivotal. The question then becomes whether there exist circumstances under which the nonmember is pivotal *and* it also has a stronger incentive to cooperate under a CU relative to MFN. The answer to this question turns out to be in the affirmative. An example is sufficient to make the point.

Example 2. Suppose $\alpha_i = \alpha_k = 1$ and $\alpha_j = 0.50$. Then $\delta_j^M = 0.14 < \delta_i^M = \delta_k^M = 0.86$ and $\delta_j^U = 0.38 < \delta_i^U = 0.50 < \delta_k^U = 0.84$. Here, (a) both countries i and k are pivotal under MFN whereas only the nonmember (i.e., k) is pivotal under the CU and (b) although the CU reduces the cooperation incentive of the smaller member, it *facilitates* overall multilateral cooperation since it makes the nonmember more willing to cooperate.[23]

4.2. *Cost Asymmetry.* This section presents a brief discussion of how the formation of PTAs between countries that differ with respect to production costs affects their incentives for multilateral cooperation. To focus on cost asymmetry, market size asymmetry is suppressed by assuming $a_z = a$ for all $z = i, j, k$ and let c_z denote country z's cost. Given the discussion in Subsection 4.2, it is clear that individual country incentives for cooperation under MFN will differ because of underlying differences in production costs. In fact, it is easy to show that, the higher the production cost of a country, the less willing it is to cooperate multilaterally over free trade: $\delta_i^M < \delta_j^M$ iff $c_i < c_j$. Intuitively, the higher the cost of a country, the greater the volume of imports it faces from low-cost foreign producers and the stronger its incentive to impose tariffs.

Suppose countries i and j form an FTA. A comparison of member i's external Nash tariff t_i^F on the nonmember with its optimal MFN tariff t_i^F indicates that tariff complementarity holds (i.e., $t_i^M > t_i^F$) for most reasonable parameter values. More specifically, we have $t_i^M > t_i^F$ iff $33a + 69c_k > 11c_i + 91c_j$. This condition is relatively minor and is satisfied if the (common) market size of countries is not too small or if the second member is not too high cost relative to the nonmember. As we know from previous analysis, tariff complementarity adversely affects cooperation incentives of the nonmember.

Regarding the impact of an FTA on members, the issue is whether members can end up being pivotal while also having higher incentives to cooperate under an FTA relative to MFN. Although the algebraic formulae for the critical discount factors are rather tedious, the following numerical examples show that the answer to this question depends upon the *nature* of the FTA under consideration. The following examples illustrate two different possibilities.

Example 3. Suppose $a = 10$, $c_i = c_j = 0$, and $c_k = 0.60$. Then $\delta_i^M = \delta_j^M = 0.48 < \delta_k^M = 0.70$ whereas $\delta_i^F = \delta_j^F = 0.23 < \delta_k^F = 0.85$. In other words, (a) the high-cost nonmember is pivotal under MFN as well as the FTA; (b) since $\delta_k^F > \delta_k^M$, the FTA undermines incentives for multilateral cooperation even though it makes

[23] For the parameter values utilized in Example 1, the CU hinders multilateral cooperation.

(nonpivotal) members more willing to cooperate relative to MFN ($\delta_i^F = \delta_j^F < \delta_i^M = \delta_j^M$).

What if the FTA is between a high-cost and a low-cost country? The next example considers such a case.

EXAMPLE 4. Suppose $a = 10$, $c_i = 0.60$, and $c_j = c_k = 0$. Then $\delta_j^M = \delta_k^M = 0.48 < \delta_i^M = 0.70$ whereas $\delta_j^F = 0.48 < \delta_k^F = 0.57 < \delta_i^F = 0.63$. In other words, (a) the high-cost member is pivotal under both MFN and the FTA; (b) since $\delta_i^F < \delta_i^M$, the FTA makes multilateral cooperation more likely relative to MFN even though it makes the (nonpivotal) nonmember less willing to cooperate ($\delta_k^M < \delta_k^F$).

Now suppose countries i and j form a CU. Rather than provide a repetitive analysis, it is useful to focus on the following question that arises naturally from the preceding discussion: Since the highest-cost country is pivotal under MFN and a CU makes the nonmember more willing to cooperate multilaterally, can the formation of a CU between two relatively low-cost countries make multilateral cooperation more likely relative to MFN? The following examples show that this is indeed possible.

EXAMPLE 5. Suppose $a = 10$, $c_i = c_j = 0$, and $c_k = 1$. Then $\delta_i^M = \delta_j^M = 0.45 < \delta_k^M = 0.88$ whereas $\delta_i^U = \delta_j^U = 0.52 < \delta_k^U = 0.86 < \delta_k^M = 0.88$. Here, the high-cost nonmember is pivotal under both regimes and it is more willing to cooperate under a CU relative to MFN.

To see how the distribution of production cost across countries matters, the following example considers the case where all parameters are same as that in Example 5 except that $c_j = 1$ so that the CU is between a high-cost and a low cost country.

EXAMPLE 6. Suppose $a = 10$, $c_i = 0$, and $c_j = c_k = 1$. Then $\delta_i^M = 0.38 < \delta_j^M = 0.67 = \delta_k^M$ whereas $\delta_j^U = 0.56 < \delta_k^U = 0.62 < \delta_i^U = 0.86$. Here, although the high-cost countries (i.e., j and k) are pivotal under MFN, it is the low-cost member that is pivotal under the CU. Furthermore, the CU between countries i and j hinders multilateral tariff cooperation.

5. CONCLUSION

This article evaluates the effect of PTAs on the degree of multilateral tariff cooperation in an oligopoly model of intraindustry trade. Although the existing literature provides many important insights, the question of whether these insights hold in a world of intraindustry trade remains relatively underinvestigated. This question is of substantial interest because the majority of world trade is intra-industry in nature.

My main result is that, when countries are symmetric, the formation of PTAs hinders multilateral trade liberalization. But the reasons behind this result are subtle. Under an FTA, the incentives of the nonmember prove detrimental for multilateral tariff cooperation whereas under a CU, it is the incentives of members that thwart cooperation. Nonmembers are actually more willing to cooperate under a CU because a CU is in a strong position to punish defections from cooperation. However, under either kind of PTA, the increased willingness of some of the countries to cooperate turns out *not* to matter in equilibrium. Regardless of the type of the PTA under consideration, it is the incentive constraint of the country that is less willing to cooperate that ends up determining the symmetric equilibrium. Under either form of PTA, there is always one country that is less willing to cooperate multilaterally relative to MFN.

When the model is extended to allow for market size or cost asymmetries across countries, it is found that the formation of PTAs can sometimes encourage cooperation relative to MFN. This is because the presence of asymmetries hinders cooperation under MFN and the *policy asymmetry* induced by PTAs can, under certain circumstances, alleviate the difficulties that confront multilateral cooperation under MFN. In fact, the argument here has the flavor of a well-known result from the theory of distortions—in the presence of an existing distortion, the introduction of a second distortion can sometime improve welfare.

To keep the analysis tractable, the article has focused on the effects of a single PTA that is taken as exogenously given. As is known from Baldwin (1996), when PTAs are endogenous, nonmembers may form PTAs in response to other PTAs. Whether the insights of the present analysis extend to a world of endogenous PTAs is an area worthy of future research.

APPENDIX

I first derive the Nash tariffs under the different trade regimes and then provide short proofs of propositions not proven in the text.

MFN Tariffs. It is sufficient to focus on any one country, say i. Using Equation (11), country i's objective function under MFN can be written as

$$\max_t W_i(t) \equiv \frac{x_i^2(t)}{2} + x_{ii}^2(t) + tx_{ji}(t) + tx_{ki}(t)$$

where

$$x_{ii}(t) = \frac{\alpha + 2t}{4}; \qquad x_{ji}(t) = x_{ki}(t) = \frac{\alpha - 2t}{4}$$

and

$$x_i(t) = \sum_z x_{zi}(t) = \frac{3\alpha - 2t}{4}$$

Solving for t^M gives

$$t^M = \frac{3\alpha}{10} \tag{A.1}$$

Tariffs under PTAs. Suppose countries i and j form an FTA. Then, country i solves

$$\max_{t_{ki}} W_i(0, t_{ki}) \equiv \frac{x_i^2(0, t_{ki})}{2} + x_{ii}^2(0, t_{ki}) + t_{ki}x_{ki}(0, t_{ki})$$

where

$$x_{ii}(0, t_{ki}) = x_{ji}(0, t_{ki}) = \frac{\alpha + t_{ki}}{4}; \quad x_{ki}(0, t_{ki}) = \frac{\alpha - 3t_{ki}}{4}$$

and

$$x_i(0, t_{ki}) = \sum_z x_{zi}(0, t_{ki}) = \frac{3\alpha - t_{ki}}{4}, \ z = i, j, k$$

Solving for the optimal external tariff of an FTA (denoted by t^F) gives

$$t^F = \frac{\alpha}{7} \tag{A.2}$$

A CU between i and j solves

$$\max_{t_{ki}} \frac{x_i^2(0, t_{ki})}{2} + 2x_{ii}^2(0, t_{ki}) + t_{ki}x_{ki}(0, t_{ki})$$

Solving the above problem gives the optimal external tariff of a CU:

$$t^U = \frac{5\alpha}{19} \tag{A.3}$$

PROOF OF PROPOSITION 1. Follows immediately from (A.1) and (A.2). ■

PROOF OF PROPOSITION 2. The only question here is whether the nonmember k is better off under an FTA between i and j relative to MFN. As argued in the text, to show this, it is sufficient to show that the nonmember's exports increase due to the FTA. We have

$$x_{ki}(0, t^F) - x_{ji}(t^M) = \frac{3\alpha}{70} > 0$$ ■

PROOF OF PROPOSITION 3. The fact that $t^U > t^F$ follows immediately from (A.2) and (A.3). Also, it is obvious that the nonmember's static welfare is lower under a CU relative to that under an FTA. The only issue is the comparison with MFN. We have

$$x_{ki}(0, t^U) - x_{ki}(t^M) = -\frac{9\alpha}{190} < 0 \qquad \blacksquare$$

PROOF OF LEMMA 1. Proved in the text. ■

PROOF OF LEMMA 2. We know that

$$B^M(t^M, t) = \frac{(t^M - t)[3\alpha - 5(t^M + t)]}{8} \quad \text{and}$$
$$B^F_m(t^F, t) = \frac{3(t^F - t)(2\alpha - 7(t + t^F))}{32}$$

To show that $B^F_m(t^F, t) < B^M(t^M, t)$, substitute for t^M and t^F from Equations (A.1) and (A.2) and note that the function $\Delta B^{FM} \equiv B^F_m(t^F, t) - B^M(t^M, t)$ increases in t. Next, note that at the maximum feasible value of t (i.e., $t = t^F$), $\Delta B^{FM} < 0$. Thus, $B^F_m(t^F, t) < B^M(t^M, t)$ for all feasible tariffs (i.e., for $t < t^F$).

Now consider the costs of defection. Recall that

$$\begin{aligned} C^M(t, t^M) &= S^M(t) + 2\pi^M(t) - S^M(t^M) - 2\pi^M(t^M) \\ &= -B^M(t^M, t) + 2[\pi^M(t) - \pi^M(t^M)] \end{aligned}$$

Similarly,

$$C^F_m(t^F, t^M, t) = -B^F_m(t^F, t) + \Delta\pi^F_m(t^F, t^M, t)$$

where

$$\Delta\pi^F_m \equiv \pi^F_{mm}(t) + \pi^F_{mk}(t) - \pi^F_{mm}(t^F) - \pi^F_{mk}(t^M)$$

measures a member's loss in export profits caused by the increase in the nonmember's tariff (from t to t^M). Note that $\Delta\pi^F_m < 0$.

Using $\pi^M(t) = \pi^F_{mm}(t)$ and $\pi^M(t^M) = \pi^F_{mk}(t^M)$, we have

$$\begin{aligned} C^F_m(t^F, t^M) - C^M(t, t^M) = &\left[B^M(t^M, t) - B^F_m(t^F, t)\right] \\ &+ \left[\pi^F_{mk}(t) - \pi^F_{mm}(t) + \pi^F_{mk}(t^M) - \pi^F_{mm}(t^F)\right] \end{aligned}$$

where we know that $\pi^F_{mk}(t) < \pi^F_{mm}(t)$ and that $\pi^F_{mk}(t^M) < \pi^F_{mm}(t^F)$. It immediately follows that

$$\left|C^F_m(t^F, t^M) - C^M(t, t^M)\right| < \left|B^F_m(t^F, t^M) - B^M(t^M, t)\right|$$

The result $C^F_m(t^F, t^M) < C^M(t, t^M)$ can be obtained by utilizing the expressions for profits and domestic surplus. ■

Proof of Lemma 3. Proved in the text. ■

Proof of Lemma 4. Recall that

$$C^M(t, t^M) = S^M(t) + \pi^M(t) - S^M(t^M) - \pi^M(t^M)$$

where

$$S^F(t) = S^M(t) \quad \text{and} \quad S^F_k(t^M) = S^F(t^M)$$

Using Equation (23) gives

$$C^F_k(t^F, t, t^M) - C^M(t^M, t) = \left[-\pi^F_{km}(t^F) + \pi^M(t^M)\right] + \left[-\pi^M(t) + \pi^F_{km}(t)\right]$$

The first term in brackets is negative due to the tariff complementarity effect whereas the second is negative because export profits of the nonmember are higher under an FTA than under MFN. Thus, $C^F_k(t^F, t, t^M) < C^M(t^M, t)$.

Proof of Proposition 4. Follows immediately from Lemmas 3 and 4. ■

Proof of Lemma 5. We already know from Lemma 1 that $\delta^M = 0.54$. The nonmember's IC constraint under an FTA at $t = 0$ is

$$441(1 - \delta) \leq 219\delta$$

This constraint binds at $\delta^F_k = 0.67$. Similarly, an FTA member's IC constraint at $t = 0$ is

$$525(1 - \delta) \leq 783\delta$$

which binds at $\delta^F_m = 0.40$. Thus $\delta^F_k > \delta^M > \delta^F_m$. ■

Proof of Lemma 2A.

1. *MFN versus CU.* As in Lemma 2, first it is shown that $B^U_m(t^U, t) < B^M(t^M, t)$. We know that

$$B^M(t^M, t) = \frac{(t^M - t)[3\alpha - 5(t^M + t)]}{8} \quad \text{and}$$

$$B^U_m(t^U, t) = \frac{(t^U - t)(10\alpha - 19(t^U + t))}{32}$$

The fact that $B_m^U(t^U, t) < B^M(t^M, t)$ can be shown by following steps analogous to those described in Lemma 2 where it was shown that $B_m^F(t^F, t) < B^M(t^M, t)$. Of course, in this case, the range of feasible multilateral tariffs is $t < t^U$.

Now consider the costs of defection. Recall that

$$C^M(t, t^M) = -B^M(t^M, t) + 2\pi^M(t) - 2\pi^M(t^M)$$

Similarly,

$$C_m^U(t^U, t^M, t) = -B_m^U(t^U, t) + \pi_{mk}^U(t) - \pi_{mk}^U(t^M)$$

where $\pi_{mk}^U(t) > \pi_{mk}^U(t^M)$. Substituting the appropriate expressions for profits and domestic surplus in $C^M(t, t^M) - C_m^U(t^U, t^M, t)$ immediately yields $C^M(t, t^M) > C_m^U(t^U, t^M)$.

2. *FTA versus CU.* It has been shown in the text of the article that $B_m^U(t^U, t) > B_m^F(t^F, t)$. To see why $C_m^U(t, t^U, t^M) < C_m^F(t, t^F, t^M)$ first note that

$$C_m^F(t^F, t^M) - C_m^U(t, t^U, t^M) = \left[B_m^U(t^U, t) - B_m^F(t^F, t)\right] + \left[\pi_{mm}^F(t) - \pi_{mm}^F(t^F)\right]$$

which is the same as

$$\begin{aligned} C_m^F(t^F, t^M) - C_m^U(t, t^U, t^M) = &\left[S_m^U(t^U, t) + \pi_{mm}^U(t^U) - \pi_{mm}^U(t) - S_m^U(t)\right] \\ &- \left[S_m^F(t^F, t) + \pi_{mm}^F(t^F) - S_m^F(t) - \pi_{mm}^F(t)\right] \end{aligned}$$

Since (i) $S_m^U(t) = S_m^F(t)$ and (ii) $\pi_{mm}^U(t) = \pi_{mm}^F(t)$, it follows that

$$C_m^F(t^F, t^M) - C_m^U(t, t^U, t^M) = \left[S_m^U(t^U, t) - S_m^F(t^F, t)\right] + \left[\pi_{mm}^U(t^U) - \pi_{mm}^F(t^F)\right]$$

Finally, because $S_m^U(t^U, t) > S_m^F(t^F, t)$ and $\pi_{mm}^U(t^U) > \pi_{mm}^F(t^F)$, it is immediate that $C_m^F(t^F, t^M) > C_m^U(t, t^U, t^M)$. ■

Proof of Lemma 4B. The comparison between MFN and CU has already been stated in the text. Consider the comparison between an FTA and CU.

$$C_k^F(t^F, t, t^M) - C_k^U(t^U, t, t^M) = -\pi_{km}^F(t^F) + \pi_k^U(t^U) < 0. \quad ■$$

Proof of Proposition 5. Follows from Lemmas 2A and 4B. ■

Proof of Lemma 6. The member's IC constraint under a CU at $t = 0$ is

$$625(1 - \delta) \leq 173\delta$$

This constraint binds at $\delta_m^U = 0.78$. Similarly, the nonmember's IC constraint at $t = 0$ is

$$3249(1 - \delta) \leq 3651\delta$$

which binds at $\delta_k^U = 0.47$. Thus, $\delta_m^U > \delta^M > \delta^{U_k}$. Since $\delta_m^U > \delta^M$, the IC constraint of the member proves pivotal. ■

REFERENCES

Bagwell, K., and R. W. Staiger, "Multilateral Cooperation during the Formation of Customs Unions," *Journal of International Economics* 42 (1997a), 91–123.

——, and ——, "Multilateral Cooperation during the Formation of Free Trade Areas," *International Economic Review* 38 (1997b), 291–319.

——, and ——, "Regionalism and Multilateral Tariff Cooperation," in J. Pigott and A. Woodland, eds., *International Trade Policy and the Pacific Rim* (London: Macmillan, 1998a).

——, and ——, "Will Preferential Agreements Undermine the Multilateral Trading System?" *Economic Journal* 108 (1998b), 1162–82.

Baldwin, R., "A Domino Theory of Regionalism," in R. Baldwin, P. Haaparanta, and J. Kiander, eds., *Expanding Membership of the European Union* (Cambridge: Cambridge University Press, 1996).

Bhagwati, J., *The World Trading System at Risk* (Princeton: Princeton University Press, 1991).

——, and A. Panagariya, "Preferential Trading Areas and Multilateralism—Strangers, Friends, or Foes?" in J. Bhagwati, A. Panagariya, and P. Krishna, eds., *Trading Blocs* (Cambridge: MIT Press, 1999).

——, ——, and P. Krishna, eds., *Trading Blocs* (Cambridge: MIT Press, 1999).

Bohara, A. K., K. Gawande, and P. Sanguinetti, "Trade Diversion and Declining Tariffs: Evidence from MERCOSUR," *Journal of International Economics* 64 (2004), 65–88.

Bond, E. W., and C. Syropoulos, "The Size of Trading Blocs: Market Power and World Welfare Effects," *Journal of International Economics* 40 (1996), 411–37.

——, ——, and L. A. Winters, "Deepening of Regional Integration and Multilateral Trade Agreements," *Journal of International Economics* 53 (2001), 335–62.

Brander, J. A., "Strategic Trade Policy," in G. M. Grossman and K. Rogoff, eds., *The Handbook of International Economics* (Amsterdam: Elsevier Science, 1995).

——, and P. R. Krugman, "A 'Reciprocal Dumping' Model of International Trade," *Journal of International Economics* 15 (1983), 313–23.

——, and B. J. Spencer, "Tariff Protection and Imperfect Competition," in H. Kierzkowski, ed., *Monopolistic Competition and International Trade* (Oxford: Oxford University Press, 1984).

Cadot, O., J. de Melo, and M. Olarreaga, "Regional Integration and Lobbying for Tariffs against Nonmembers," *International Economic Review* 40 (1999), 635–58.

Chang, W., and L. A. Winters, "How Regional Blocs Affect Excluded Countries: The Price Effects of MERCOSUR," *American Economic Review* 92 (2002), 889–904.

Ethier, W. J., "National and International Returns to Scale in the Modern Theory of International Trade," *American Economic Review* 72 (1982), 389–405.

——, "Regionalism in a Multilateral World," *Journal of Political Economy* 106 (1998), 1214–45.

Freund, C., "Different Paths to Free Trade: The Gains from Regionalism," *Quarterly Journal of Economics* 115 (2000a), 1317–41.

——, "Multilateralism and the Endogenous Formation of Preferential Trade Agreements," *Journal of International Economics* 52 (2000b), 359–76.

Hoekman, B. M., and M. M. Kostecki, *The Political Economy of the World Trading System* (New York: Oxford University Press, 2001).
Kennan, J., and R. Riezman, "Do Big Countries Win Tariff Wars?" *International Economic Review* 29 (1988), 81–85.
——, and ——, "Optimal Tariff Equilibria with Customs Unions," *Canadian Journal of Economics* 90 (1990), 70–83.
Knetter, M. M., "Price Discrimination by U.S. and German Exporters," *American Economic Review* 79 (1989), 198–210.
—— "International Comparisons of Pricing to Market Behavior," *American Economic Review* 83 (1993), 473–86.
Krishna, P., "Regionalism and Multilateralism: A Political Economy Approach," *The Quarterly Journal of Economics* 113 (1998), 227–51.
Krugman, P. R., "Scale Economies, Product Differentiation, and the Pattern of Trade," *American Economic Review* 70 (1980), 950–59.
Levy, P. I., "A Political-Economic Analysis of Free Trade Agreements," *American Economic Review* 87 (1997), 506–19.
Limao, N., "Preferential Trade Agreements as Stumbling Blocks for Multilateral Trade Liberalization: Evidence from the U.S.," Mimeo, University of Maryland, 2003.
Maggi, G., "The Role of Multilateral Institutions in International Trade Cooperation," *American Economic Review* 89 (1999), 190–214.
Marston, R. C., "Pricing to Market in Japanese Manufacturing," *Journal of International Economics* 29 (1990), 217–36.
Richardson, M., "Endogenous Protection and Trade Diversion," *Journal of International Economics* 34 (1993), 309–24.
——, "Tariff Revenue Competition in a Free Trade Area," *European Economic Review* 39 (1995), 1427–37.
Riezman, R., "Dynamic Tariffs with Asymmetric Information," *Journal of International Economics* 30 (1991), 267–83.
Saggi, K., and H. M. Yildiz, "Bilateral Trade Agreements and the Feasibility of Multilateral Free Trade," Mimeo, Southern Methodist University and Ryerson University, 2005.
Winters, L. A., "Regionalism versus Multilateralism," in R. E. Baldwin, D. Cole, A. Sapir, and A. J. Venables, eds., *Market Integration, Regionalism, and the Global Economy* (London: Cambridge University Press, 1998).
World Bank, *Trade Blocs* (Oxford: Oxford University Press, 2000).

CHAPTER 7

Journal of International Economics 81 (2010) 26–37

Contents lists available at ScienceDirect

Journal of International Economics

journal homepage: www.elsevier.com/locate/jie

Bilateralism, multilateralism, and the quest for global free trade☆

Kamal Saggi [a,*,1], Halis Murat Yildiz [b,2,3]

[a] Department of Economics, Southern Methodist University, Dallas, TX 75275-0496, United States
[b] Department of Economics, Ryerson University, 350 Victoria Street, Toronto, ON, Canada M5B 2K3

ARTICLE INFO

Article history:
Received 23 January 2007
Received in revised form 18 January 2010
Accepted 19 January 2010

JEL classification:
F13
F12

Keywords:
Bilateral trade agreements
Multilateral trade liberalization
Free trade agreements
GATT

ABSTRACT

We develop an equilibrium theory of trade agreements in which both the *degree* and the *nature* (bilateral or multilateral) of trade liberalization are endogenously determined. To determine whether and how bilateralism matters, we also analyze a scenario where countries pursue trade liberalization on only a multilateral basis. We find that when countries have asymmetric endowments or when governments value producer interests more than tariff revenue and consumer surplus, there exist circumstances where global free trade is a stable equilibrium only if countries are free to pursue bilateral trade agreements. By contrast, under symmetry, both bilateralism and multilateralism yield global free trade.

1. Introduction

Global trade liberalization occurs through a variety of channels, not all of which appear to be in harmony with one another. While practically every major nation is now a member of the World Trade Organization (WTO) and a participant in its complex process of multilateral trade liberalization, an average WTO member also belongs to six preferential trade agreements (PTAs) (World Bank, 2005). The schizophrenic nature of today's multilateral trading system is reflected in the somewhat conflicting rules of the WTO's key multilateral trade agreement, i.e. the General Agreement for Tariffs and Trade (GATT): while Article I of GATT requires member countries to undertake trade liberalization on a most-favored-nation (MFN) or non-discriminatory basis, Article XXIV of the very same agreement permits WTO member countries to pursue PTAs under which participating countries grant tariff (and other trade policy) concessions to each other that they do *not* have to extend to all member countries of the WTO.[4] This raises the following question: would GATT serve the cause of global free trade more effectively if it did *not* include the exception to MFN provided by Article XXIV? In other words, would global free trade be easier to achieve if all WTO members were to pursue trade liberalization on *only* a multilateral basis? To address this issue, we develop an equilibrium theory of trade agreements and use it to compare the pros and cons of bilateral and multilateral approaches to trade liberalization.

We analyze the coalition proof (or stable) Nash equilibria of a game of trade liberalization between three countries that differ with respect to their endowment levels. The game (which we refer to as *bilateralism*) proceeds as follows. In the first stage, each country announces the names of its trading partner(s) with whom it wishes to sign a free trade agreement (FTA). An FTA between two countries requires them to abolish tariffs on each other and it arises iff they both announce each other's name. Next, given the world trade regime, countries choose their tariffs. Finally, international trade and consumption take place. After analyzing equilibrium trade agreements under bilateralism, we examine the stable equilibria of this game under the restriction that countries can liberalize trade on *only* a

☆ For helpful comments, we thank seminar audiences at the Asia-Pacific Seminar at the University of Sydney, Fourth Annual Development Conference of the Indian Statistical Institute, George Washington University, Graduate School of Economics at Hitotsubashi University, IEFS-China Inaugural Conference at the University of International Business and Economics, Louisiana State University, National University of Singapore, SMU, University of Guelph, University of Missouri, World Bank, and the WTO. We also thank Kyle Bagwell, Rick Bond, Theresa Carpenter, Caroline Freund, Bernard Hoekman, Giovanni Maggi, Aaditya Mattoo, Andres Rodriguez-Clare, Bob Staiger, Alan Woodland, and two anonymous referees for many constructive comments and suggestions. Any remaining errors are our own.

* Corresponding author. Tel.: +1 214 768 3274; fax: +1 214 768 1821.
E-mail addresses: ksaggi@smu.edu (K. Saggi), hyildiz@ryerson.ca (H.M. Yildiz).

1 The author thanks the World Bank for financial support.

2 Tel.: +1 416 979 5000x6689; fax: +1 416 979 5289.

3 The author gratefully acknowledges financial support from the Social Sciences and Humanities Research Council of Canada (SSHRC).

4 While Article XXIV tries to limit the damage on non-member countries by requiring PTA members to not raise tariffs on outsiders, the fact remains that it contradicts the principle of non-discrimination that underlies the entire WTO system.

0022-1996/$ – see front matter © 2010 Elsevier B.V. All rights reserved.
doi:10.1016/j.jinteco.2010.01.004

multilateral basis (we call this game *multilateralism*). By comparing equilibrium outcomes under bilateralism with those under multilateralism, we isolate the consequences of the exception to multilateral trade liberalization available to WTO members under GATT Article XXIV.[5] To the best of our knowledge, our paper is the first to provide such a comparison in a model in which both the *nature* and the *degree* of trade liberalization are endogenously determined.

Consistent with actual WTO experience, under our multilateralism game a pair of countries can engage in mutual trade liberalization so long as each of them extends their respective tariff reductions also to the third country — as mandated by the GATT's MFN clause.[6] We find that the degree of trade liberalization undertaken by two countries (say i and j) under such a multilateral trade agreement $\langle\{ij^m\}\rangle$ is lower relative to that under the bilateral free trade agreement $\langle\{ij\}\rangle$. As a result, the non-participating country (i.e. k) actually faces *lower* tariffs in export markets under the bilateral FTA $\langle\{ij\}\rangle$ relative to the multilateral trade agreement $\langle\{ij^m\}\rangle$. However, the non-member country faces discriminatory tariffs in export markets under $\langle\{ij\}\rangle$ whereas no such discrimination exists under $\langle\{ij^m\}\rangle$. Due to this crucial difference between the two types of trade agreements, in our model the non-member country is worse off under the bilateral FTA $\langle\{ij\}\rangle$ relative to the multilateral agreement $\langle\{ij^m\}\rangle$.

Equilibrium analysis reveals that when countries are symmetric with respect to their endowment levels, global free trade is the only stable equilibrium under both bilateralism and multilateralism. In other words, under symmetry, the freedom to pursue purely bilateral agreements has no consequences at all insofar as the obtainment of global free trade is concerned. This immediately raises the question whether this irrelevance result holds when the underlying economic environment is asymmetric in some respects. To this end, we then analyze a scenario where endowment levels are unequal across countries and find that global free trade is stable over a larger parameter space under bilateralism relative to multilateralism. This result has a powerful and surprising implication: there exist circumstances where global free trade is a stable equilibrium *only if* countries are free to form bilateral FTAs. Why? The logic is as follows. While considering whether or not to participate in multilateral trade liberalization, each country has to take into account its welfare under the trade regime that emerges in the *absence* of its participation. Since a non-participating country (say k) is worse off under the bilateral FTA $\langle\{ij\}\rangle$ relative to the multilateral agreement $\langle\{ij^m\}\rangle$, each country's incentive to participate in multilateral trade liberalization is stronger when its non-participation results in a discriminatory bilateral FTA between the other two countries as opposed to when it results in a non-discriminatory multilateral agreement between them.[7] In this way, the freedom to pursue bilateral agreements can act as a force in favor of multilateral trade liberalization.

Our results show that heterogeneity across countries may be an important determinant of the potential for success of multilateralism and that bilateralism has a useful role to play in the process of global trade liberalization.[8] An important implication of our analysis is that to properly account for the role of bilateralism, we need to better understand *why* countries choose to enter into bilateral agreements when multilateral trade liberalization is an option. In this context it is noteworthy that while both Krugman (1991) and Grossman and Helpman (1995) noted that asymmetries across countries can play a crucial role in determining incentives for bilateral and multilateral trade liberalization, existing literature has tended to pay little attention to this issue. Indeed, in our model bilateral FTAs even fail to arise when countries have symmetric endowments since, under such circumstances, countries find it in their mutual interest to go all the way to global free trade.

In a recent paper, Aghion et al. (2007) examine a leading country's choice between sequential and multilateral bargaining of free trade agreements and provide a comparison of these bargaining processes. While we consider similar issues, there are important differences between their approach and ours. First, in our model, *all* countries are free to negotiate FTAs and countries can form multiple bilateral FTAs. Second, under multilateralism, Aghion et al. (2007) assume that countries have only a binary choice between global free trade and no agreement whereas we permit two countries to undertake trade liberalization on an MFN basis. In Aghion et al. (2007), when bilateral FTAs are forbidden (i.e. under their multilateral bargaining protocol), any single country (say country k) can ensure that no agreement $\langle\{\Phi\}\rangle$ prevails by simply opting to not practise free trade itself while such a country ends up facing the multilateral agreement $\langle\{ij^m\}\rangle$ in our model. As a result, while the nature of coalition externalities (i.e. whether they are negative or positive) shapes the choice between sequential and multilateral bargaining and the circumstances under which global free trade obtains in their model, the *relative degree of the positive externality* under the bilateral FTA $\langle\{ij\}\rangle$ compared to that under the multilateral agreement $\langle\{ij^m\}\rangle$ is the driving force behind our analysis. More specifically, while both $\langle\{ij\}\rangle$ and $\langle\{ij^m\}\rangle$ generate a positive externality for the non-member by increasing its welfare relative to the status quo, the degree of the positive externality is stronger under the multilateral agreement $\langle\{ij^m\}\rangle$. Finally, unlike Aghion et al. (2007), we do not allow transfers between different coalitions. This is important because when transfers are possible and global free trade maximizes aggregate welfare, it necessarily emerges as the equilibrium under both sequential and multilateral bargaining. When free trade does not maximize aggregate welfare, Aghion et al. (2007) find that FTAs facilitate the achievement of global free trade iff they create negative externalities for non-members. In our model, FTAs can have this effect even when free trade maximizes global welfare and FTAs generate a positive externality for the non-member.

Our paper shares some key elements with Goyal and Joshi (2006) and Furusawa and Konishi (2007), both of which employ the network formation game developed by Jackson and Wolinsky (1996) in examining whether or not a given trade configuration is pair-wise stable.[9] Under symmetry, global free trade is also stable under their approach. Unlike us, however, they only examine whether the formation of bilateral FTAs results in global free trade as the stable outcome and do not analyze the consequences of adopting a strictly multilateral approach to trade liberalization. Like us, Riezman (1999) also asks whether bilateralism facilitates or hinders the achievement of global free trade. However, while we analytically derive the stable Nash equilibria of a non-cooperative game of FTA formation, Riezman (1999) uses the cooperative solution concept of the core and illustrates his results via numerical examples. Second, our model allows us to focus on asymmetries across countries in a way that cannot be done in Riezman's (1999) framework. The relationship between preferential and multilateral liberalization has frequently been analyzed in the literature in

[5] We do not consider unilateral trade liberalization since the presence of terms of trade considerations in our model implies that such liberalization is not in any country's interest.

[6] Note that in our model countries are free to sign a multilateral agreement even under bilateralism. By contrast, the multilateralism game rules out a discriminatory bilateral FTA.

[7] Since political economy considerations can potentially play an important role in determining incentives for bilateral and multilateral trade liberalization, later in the paper (Section 6) we consider a scenario where governments put greater weight on producer interests relative to consumer surplus and tariff revenue. We find that the presence of such political economy motives actually enlarges the parameter space over which the freedom to pursue bilateral trade agreements is necessary for achieving global free trade. See Levy (1997), Krishna (1998), and Ornelas (2005b) for analyses focusing more directly on political economy considerations.

[8] Saggi and Yildiz (2006) consider cost differences across countries in an oligopolistic model of intraindustry trade and uncover similar results.

[9] Relative to our approach, the concept of pair-wise stability implies two constraints. First, the deviating coalition can contain at most two countries. Second, the deviation can consist of severing just one existing link or forming one additional link. In order to eliminate these constraints, we follow Bernheim et al. (1987) and use the concept of coalition proof Nash equilibrium to isolate stable equilibria.

models of repeated interaction between countries — see Bagwell and Staiger (1997), Bond et al. (2001), Freund (2000), and Saggi (2006).[10] We add value to this literature by treating both bilateral and multilateral liberalization as endogenous.[11]

2. Underlying trade model

To endogenize the formation of trade agreements among asymmetric countries, we utilize an appropriately adapted version of the partial equilibrium 'competing exporters' framework developed by Bagwell and Staiger (1999). There are three countries: *a*, *b*, and *c* and three (non-numeraire) goods: *A*, *B*, and *C*. Each country's market is served by two competing exporters and *I* denotes the good that corresponds to the upper case value of *i*. For example, if $i=a$ then $I=A$. Country *i* is endowed with zero units of good *I* and e_i units of the other two goods where $e_a \leq e_b \leq e_c$.[12]

The demand for good *z* in country *i* is given by $d(p_i^z)=\alpha-p_i^z$ where $z=A,B$, or *C*. As is well known, the above demand functions can be derived from a utility function of the form $U(c^z)=u(c^z)+w$ where c^z denotes consumption of good *z*; *w* denotes the numeraire good; and $u(c^z)$ is quadratic and additively separable in each of the three goods. Since each country possesses only two goods while it demands all three, country *i* must import good *I* in order to consume it and it can import it from either trading partner. For example, country *a* imports good *A* from both countries *b* and *c* while it exports good *B* to country *b* and good *C* to country *c*.

Let t_{ij} be the tariff imposed by country *i* on its imports of good *I* from country *j*. Ruling out prohibitive tariffs yields the following no-arbitrage conditions for good *I*:

$$p_i^I = p_j^I + t_{ij} = p_k^I + t_{ik} \tag{1}$$

where $i, j, k=a, b, c$, and $i \neq j \neq k$. Let m_i^I be country *i*'s imports of good *I*. Since country *i* has no endowment of good *I*, we have

$$m_i^I = d\left(p_i^I\right) = \alpha - p_i^I. \tag{2}$$

Each country's exports of a good must equal its endowment of that good minus its local consumption:

$$x_j^I = e_j - \left[\alpha - p_j^I\right]. \tag{3}$$

Market clearing for good *I* requires that country *i*'s imports equal the total exports of the other two countries:

$$m_i^I = \sum_{j \neq i} x_j^I. \tag{4}$$

Eqs. (1) through (4) imply that the equilibrium price of good *I* in country *i* equals:

$$p_i^I = \frac{1}{3}\left(3\alpha - \sum_{j \neq i} e_j + \sum_{j \neq i} t_{ij}\right). \tag{5}$$

Using these prices, the volume of trade is easily calculated. As is clear from Eq. (5), the price of good *I* in country *i* increases in its tariffs and decreases in the endowment levels of the other two countries. The effect of a country's tariff on its terms of trade is evident from Eq. (5): only a third of a given increase in either of its tariffs is passed on to domestic consumers with exactly two third of the increase falling on the shoulders of foreign exporters.

By design the model examines country *i*'s trade protection towards only good *I* (i.e. the only non-numeraire good that it imports). Since countries have asymmetric endowments, under free trade country *a* faces the largest volume of imports of protected goods (it imports $(e_b+e_c)/3$ units of good *A*) whereas country *c* faces the lowest volume of imports of such goods (it imports $(e_a+e_b)/3$ units of good *C*).[13] Note also that country *i*'s imports of good *I* do not equal its exports of other non-numeraire goods. For example, under free trade, country *a* exports $(2e_a-e_b)/3$ units of good *C* to country *c* and $(2e_a-e_c)/3$ units of good *B* to country *b* and the sum of these exports is lower than its total imports of good *C*: $0<4e_a-e_b-e_c<e_b+e_c$. In order to balance trade, in addition to exporting goods *B* and *C*, country *a* exports the numeraire good to both countries *b* and *c*. Similarly, country *c* imports the numeraire good from both its trading partners.

From a welfare perspective, given the partial equilibrium nature of the model, it suffices to consider only protected goods. A country's welfare is defined as the sum of consumer surplus, producer surplus, and tariff revenue over all such goods:

$$w_i = \sum_z CS_i^z + \sum_z PS_i^z + TR_i. \tag{6}$$

Using Eqs. (1) through (5) one can easily obtain welfare of country *i* as a function of endowment levels and tariffs. Let aggregate world welfare be defined as the sum of each country's welfare: $ww=\sum_i w_i$.

We proceed as follows. First, we consider a three stage game of trade liberalization under which each country is free to pursue either (a) no trade liberalization or (b) bilateral trade liberalization or (c) multilateral trade liberalization.[14] This game is meant to capture the various options regarding trade liberalization available to WTO members, option (b) being made possible by GATT Article XXIV. After deriving Nash equilibria and isolating those equilibria that are *stable* (more on this below), we ask how equilibrium outcomes are affected if countries cannot pursue bilateral trade liberalization and must instead choose between multilateral trade liberalization or no liberalization at all. This exercise allows to isolate the consequences of the exception to MFN provided under GATT Article XXIV.

3. Endogenous trade agreements

We now describe our game of trade liberalization (which we refer to as *bilateralism*). In the first stage, each country simultaneously announces whether or not it wants to sign a free trade agreement (FTA) with each of its trading partners. Country *i*'s announcement is denoted by σ_i and its strategy set Ω_i consists of four possible announcements: $\Omega_i=\{\{\phi, \phi\}, \{j, \phi\}, \{\phi, k\}, \{j, k\}\}$, where $\{\phi, \phi\}$ denotes an announcement in favor of the status quo or no trade liberalization; $\{j, \phi\}$ in favor of an FTA with only country *j*; $\{\phi, k\}$ in favor of an FTA with only country *k*; and $\{j, k\}$ in favor of FTAs with both of them (which is equivalent to announcing in favor of multilateral free trade). This stage determines the underlying trade policy regime. Next, given the policy regime, countries impose their optimal tariffs. Finally, given trade agreements and tariffs, international trade and consumption take place.

The following trade policy regimes can emerge in the bilateralism game: (*i*) No agreement or the status quo $\langle\{\Phi\}\rangle$ prevails when no two announcements match or the only matching announcements are

[10] See Bhagwati et al. (1999) for a collection of many of the important papers in the area.

[11] Note that while the joint welfare of members is often considered in determining whether or not a trade agreement would arise (see, for example, Ornelas (2005a) and Krishna (1998)), much of the existing literature on free trade agreements does not derive the equilibria of a game that fully specifies the process by which such agreements arise.

[12] In addition, all countries have large enough endowments of the numeraire good *w* to ensure trade balance.

[13] The same ranking applies with respect to the value of imports so long as $3\alpha>e_a+e_b+2e_c$, which is a minor condition that is assumed to hold.

[14] Since all countries have market power in our model, allowing for unilateral liberalization is not necessary: no country will choose to pursue such liberalization in our model.

$\{\phi, \phi\}$; (*ii*) an FTA between countries i and j denoted by $\langle\{ij\}\rangle$ is formed iff countries i and j announce each other's name, i.e., $j\in\sigma_i$ and $i\in\sigma_j$; (*iii*) two independent FTAs in which i is the common member denoted by $\langle\{ij, ik\}\rangle$ are formed iff (1) $j\in\sigma_i$ and $i\in\sigma_j$ and (2) $k\in\sigma_i$ and $i\in\sigma_k$; and (*iv*) free trade, denoted by $\langle\{F\}\rangle$, obtains iff all countries announce each others' names: i.e. $\sigma_i=\{j, k\}$ for all $i, j, k=a, b, c$.[15]

Before proceeding further, we clarify two expositional points. First, the regime $\langle\{ij, ik\}\rangle$ is a 'hub and spoke' trading arrangement where the 'hub' country (i.e. i) has an independent FTA with each of the two 'spoke' countries who do not have an FTA with each other. To simplify notation, we denote $\langle\{ij, ik\}\rangle$ as $\langle\{ih\}\rangle$ (i.e. country i is hub). Second, while changes in the underlying trade regime result from announcement deviations by countries, it proves convenient to refer directly to regime changes rather than changes in announcements. For example, when the bilateral FTA $\langle\{ij\}\rangle$ is in place, the unilateral announcement deviation of country i from $\{j, \phi\}$ to $\{\phi, \phi\}$ alters the underlying trade regime from $\langle\{ij\}\rangle$ to no agreement $\langle\{\Phi\}\rangle$ and we refer to this announcement deviation of country i as simply a deviation from $\langle\{ij\}\rangle$ to $\langle\{\Phi\}\rangle$.

Throughout the remainder of this section as well as Section 4, we maintain the following assumption[16]:

Assumption 1.

$e_i = e$ for all $i = a, b, c$. (symmetry)

Let country i's welfare as a function of trade regime r be denoted by $w_i(r)$ where $r \in \{\langle\{\Phi\}\rangle, \langle\{ij\}\rangle, \langle\{jk\}\rangle, \langle\{ih\}\rangle, \langle\{jh\}\rangle \text{ or } \langle\{F\}\rangle\}$ and $i, j, k=a, b, c$. Also, let $\Delta w_i(r-v)$ denote the difference between country i's welfare under trade regimes r and v: $\Delta w_i(r-v)\equiv w_i(r)-w_i(v)$.

Since Article I of GATT forbids tariff discrimination, we assume that under the status quo, each country imposes a non-discriminatory tariff on its trading partners: $t_{ij}=t_{ik}=t_i^{\phi}$ for all $i, j, k=a, b, c$. Country i's optimal MFN tariff is easily calculated:

$$t_i^{\phi} \equiv Arg\max w_i(\Phi) = \frac{e}{4}. \tag{7}$$

If two countries form an FTA, they remove their tariffs on each other and impose their optimal external tariffs on the non-member country: under $\langle\{ij\}\rangle$ we have $t_{ij}=t_{ji}=0$, $t_{ik}=t_i^f$ and $t_{jk}=t_j^f$. The optimal external tariff of country i on the non-member country k is given by:

$$t_i^f \equiv \text{Arg}\max w_i(ij) = \frac{e}{11}. \tag{8}$$

Note that under symmetry, we have $t_i^{\phi}=t_j^{\phi}=t^{\phi}$ and $t_i^f=t_j^f=t^f$. As in Bagwell and Staiger (1997, 1999), we find that the formation of a bilateral FTA induces each member to lower its tariff on the non-member country relative to the status quo (i.e. the model exhibits tariff complementarity): $t^f<t^{\phi}$.[17]

Before deriving equilibrium agreements, we report a useful lemma that is easy to establish:

Lemma 1. *Under symmetry,* $\Delta w_j(ih-F)<0<\Delta w_i(ih-F)$.

In other words, the hub country (i) of the hub and spoke agreement $\langle\{ih\}\rangle$ is better off relative to free trade $\langle\{F\}\rangle$ while each spoke country is worse off. Note that the hub country i enjoys privileged access in both spoke countries under $\langle\{ih\}\rangle$ since neither spoke imposes a tariff on the hub whereas both impose the tariff t^f on each other. As a result of this favorable treatment, country i is strictly better off under $\langle\{ih\}\rangle$ relative to $\langle\{F\}\rangle$. To see why the spokes are worse off under $\langle\{ih\}\rangle$ relative to $\langle\{F\}\rangle$, first note that aggregate global welfare is strictly higher under $\langle\{F\}\rangle$ relative to $\langle\{ih\}\rangle$. Since the hub is strictly better off under $\langle\{ih\}\rangle$ relative to $\langle\{F\}\rangle$ and welfare of the two spoke countries is equal due to symmetry, both spokes must be worse off under $\langle\{ih\}\rangle$ relative to $\langle\{F\}\rangle$. In fact, each spoke country has an incentive to revoke its FTA with the hub and become an outsider facing an FTA between the other two countries: $\Delta w_j(ik-ih)>0$.

We are now ready to derive equilibrium trade agreements under bilateralism. To economize space, we provide a rather condensed discussion of Nash equilibria. It is straightforward to show that given Assumption 1, *the status quo* $\langle\{\Phi\}\rangle$, *a bilateral FTA* $\langle\{ij\}\rangle$, *and free trade* $\langle\{F\}\rangle$ *are all Nash equilibria under bilateralism.* The hub and spoke regime fails to be an equilibrium because $\Delta w_j(ik-ih)>0$. A bilateral FTA $\langle\{ij\}\rangle$ is a Nash equilibrium because

$$\Delta w_i(ij-\Phi) = \Delta w_j(ij-\Phi) > 0 \tag{9}$$

i.e. a member country of a bilateral FTA has no unilateral incentive to break the agreement.[18] Global free trade $\langle\{F\}\rangle$ is a Nash equilibrium because Lemma 1 implies that no country will deviate to become a spoke and the deviation to become a non-member facing an FTA is ruled out because

$$\Delta w_i(F-jk) > 0. \tag{10}$$

To deal with the multiplicity problem and to capture the process of FTA formation in a more realistic fashion, we now isolate Nash equilibria that are coalition proof or *stable* (as in Dutta and Mutuswami, 1997).[19] We begin by considering the potential stability of free trade $\langle\{F\}\rangle$. Given Lemma 1, we need to consider only two joint deviations from free trade:

(JF1): Deviation of i and j from $\langle\{F\}\rangle$ to $\langle\{ij\}\rangle$.
(JF2): Deviation of i and j from $\langle\{F\}\rangle$ to $\langle\{\Phi\}\rangle$.

Deviation JF1 can be ruled out because, under symmetry, no two countries have a joint incentive to exclude the third country from free trade:

$$\Delta w_i(F-ij) > 0. \tag{11}$$

Finally, it is immediate from Eqs. (9) and (10) that the three countries have no incentive to deviate jointly from $\langle\{F\}\rangle$ to $\langle\{\Phi\}\rangle$ so that JF2 is ruled out. In fact, this inequality also implies that $\langle\{\Phi\}\rangle$ is not a stable Nash equilibrium since the joint deviation of countries i and j from $\langle\{\Phi\}\rangle$ to $\langle\{ij\}\rangle$ is self-enforcing: both countries benefit from this joint deviation and it is immune to further unilateral deviations by virtue of the fact that $\langle\{ij\}\rangle$ is a Nash equilibrium. By similar logic, it is easy to see that $\langle\{ij\}\rangle$ also fails to be stable since the joint deviation of all three countries to $\langle\{F\}\rangle$ is self-enforcing. Thus, we have shown the following:

Proposition 1. *Given symmetry, free trade* $\langle\{F\}\rangle$ *is the only stable trade agreement under bilateralism.*

[15] In order to eliminate redundant announcements, we assume that each announcement costs ε (where $\varepsilon>0$ is arbitrarily small).

[16] Calculations supporting the results reported in this section as well as the rest of the paper are contained in the Appendix A.

[17] See Bagwell and Staiger (1997, 1999) and Saggi and Yildiz (2009) for a detailed discussion of the tariff complementarity effect and Estevadeordal et al. (2008) for empirical evidence in its support. It is worth noting that tariff complementarity also arises in simple general equilibrium models of trade agreements such as Bond et al. (2004).

[18] Due to the tariff complementarity effect, the formation of an FTA generates a positive externality for the non-member: $\Delta w_k(ij-\Phi)>0$.

[19] Following Bernheim et al. (1987), a coalitional deviation is self-enforcing if a proper subset of players in the deviating coalition have no incentive to undertake a *further* deviation. Note that an alternative approach would have been to use the notion of a strong Nash equilibrium (SNE). However, the use of CPNE is more appealing since a SNE must be immune to *any* joint deviations, even those that are not self-enforcing.

It is worth noting that the above result also obtains under the network formation game of Goyal and Joshi (2006) under which countries pursue only bilateral trade agreements. Interestingly, Goyal and Joshi (2006) interpret this result as establishing the compatibility of bilateralism and free trade. As we shall see below, by providing a comparison of bilateralism and multilateralism our model suggests an alternative interpretation of this result.

We now analyze a scenario where any trade liberalization undertaken by countries must be multilateral or non-discriminatory in nature. This analysis helps assess how the prospects of attaining global free trade are affected if countries cannot form bilateral FTAs that, by their very nature, discriminate against the non-member country.

4. Endogenous agreements under multilateralism

Under a multilateral approach to trade liberalization (or simply *multilateralism*), the strategy set of country i is $\Omega_i=\{\phi, M\}, j\neq k\neq i$. In other words, each country announces either in favor of or against multilateral trade liberalization. If all three countries announce in favor, they choose the jointly optimal set of tariffs which, in our model, are equal to zero. Thus, a multilateral agreement in which all countries participate necessarily leads to global free trade. If only two countries (say i and j) announce in favor of multilateralism, they jointly choose their optimal tariffs subject to the constraint that they must not discriminate against country k – i.e. in accordance with the MFN clause of the WTO, any tariff cut undertaken by either country i or j must apply to imports from both its trading partners. Formally, countries i and j sign the multilateral agreement $\langle\{ij^m\}\rangle$ when individual country announcements are as follows: $\sigma_i=M$, $\sigma_j=M$, $\sigma_k=\phi$. Finally, note that if two (or more) countries announce against multilateralism, the status quo $\langle\{\Phi\}\rangle$ prevails under which each country imposes its individually optimal MFN tariff on every other country.

If countries i and j agree to sign the multilateral agreement $\langle\{ij^m\}\rangle$ they choose the tariff pair (t_i^m, t_j^m) to solve

$$\left(t_i^m, t_j^m\right) \equiv \operatorname{Arg\,max}\left[w_i(ij^m) + w_j(ij^m)\right]. \tag{12}$$

Under symmetry, $t_i^m = t_j^m = t^m$ and this jointly optimal MFN tariff t^m is given by:

$$t^m = \frac{e}{7} \text{ where } t^m < t^\phi = \frac{e}{4}. \tag{13}$$

Since $t^m < t^\phi$, it is immediate that under the multilateral agreement $\langle\{ij^m\}\rangle$ countries i and j lower their tariffs on each other as well as on the non-participating country (i.e. k). This result implies that under $\langle\{ij^m\}\rangle$ country k benefits from the multilateral trade liberalization undertaken by the other two countries without having to offer any liberalization in return since it retains its individually optimal MFN tariff t^ϕ on countries i and j. Furthermore, it is worth emphasizing that country k faces lower tariffs in export markets when the other two countries implement the bilateral FTA $\langle\{ij\}\rangle$ relative to when they sign the multilateral agreement $\langle\{ij^m\}\rangle$, i.e., $t^f < t^m$. In other words, the *degree of trade liberalization* undertaken by two countries is lower when they sign the multilateral agreement $\langle\{ij^m\}\rangle$ than when they sign the bilateral agreement $\langle\{ij\}\rangle$: $t^\phi - t^m < t^\phi - t^f$. Despite this, the welfare of the non-member country (k) is higher under $\langle\{ij^m\}\rangle$ compared to $\langle\{ij\}\rangle$: $w_k(ij) < w_k(ij^m)$. This is because the non-member is subject to *discriminatory treatment* in each member's market under the bilateral FTA $\langle\{ij\}\rangle$: while countries i and j face zero tariffs in each other's market under $\langle\{ij\}\rangle$, country k faces the tariff t^f. By contrast, such discriminatory treatment is absent under $\langle\{ij^m\}\rangle$ since trade liberalization undertaken by countries i and j is extended to country k on an MFN basis. As we will show below, this fundamental difference between bilateral and multilateral trade liberalization plays a crucial role in our analysis.

As under bilateralism, it is straightforward that the status quo $\langle\{\Phi\}\rangle$ is also a Nash equilibrium under multilateralism. Furthermore, $\langle\{ij^m\}\rangle$ is not a Nash equilibrium because the outside country (k) actually benefits from joining the agreement $\langle\{ij^m\}\rangle$ thereby converting it to $\langle\{F\}\rangle$:

$$\Delta w_k(F - ij^m) > 0. \tag{14}$$

The above inequality also implies that no country has a unilateral incentive to deviate from free trade. Thus, under symmetry, free trade $\langle\{F\}\rangle$ is also a Nash equilibrium. Furthermore, since all three countries benefit from a joint deviation from the status quo to free trade (from which there are no further coalitional deviations), we have:

Proposition 2. *Given symmetry, free trade $\langle\{F\}\rangle$ is the only stable agreement under multilateralism.*[20]

A comparison of Propositions 1 and 2 shows that when countries are symmetric, multilateralism is sufficient to reach global free trade. One interpretation of this result is that if the move from the status quo to global free trade were to confer equal gains upon all countries (which is what happens when countries have symmetric endowments), nothing would be lost by forsaking the freedom to pursue bilateral FTAs since such agreements would *not* even arise in equilibrium. Does this imply that bilateralism is irrelevant for the ultimate objective of achieving global free trade? Or are there circumstances under which the quest for global free trade is affected in a material way by the freedom (or the lack of it) to pursue bilateral FTAs? We show next that when endowment levels are asymmetric across countries, bilateral FTAs can not only arise in equilibrium but also the freedom to sign such agreements can be necessary for achieving multilateral free trade.

5. Trade liberalization under asymmetry

From hereon, we drop the assumption that endowment levels are symmetric across countries. In what follows, the size of a country is measured by its endowment of non-numeraire/protected goods relative to others. In this context, it is worth recalling that each country's endowment of the (unique) good it imports is zero and that asymmetry in endowments translates directly into asymmetries of volume of exports. In other words, an increase in a country's endowment in this model increases its exports of non-numeraire/protected goods without increasing its imports of such goods (since the model is partial equilibrium in nature and lacks any income effects). Indeed, since the country with the largest endowment of non-numeraire goods faces relatively smaller suppliers, its imports of such goods are the smallest. It is worth emphasizing that in our model no country is a price taker on world markets – in fact each country is the unique importer of a single good and therefore has market power that it can exploit via a tariff.

We next derive optimal tariffs under each regime under asymmetry.

5.1. Optimal tariffs

Country i's optimal non-discriminatory (or MFN) tariff is given by:

$$t_i^\phi \equiv \operatorname{Arg\,max} w_i(\langle\Phi\rangle) = \frac{e_j + e_k}{8}. \tag{15}$$

[20] In fact, we can show that under symmetry global free trade is the unique strong Nash equilibrium under both bilateralism and multilateralism.

Note that a country's MFN tariff increases with the endowments of its trading partners. Similar to Eq. (8), when countries i and j form a bilateral FTA $\langle\{ij\}\rangle$, they abolish tariffs on each other and choose their external tariffs independently. We have

$$t_i^f \equiv \text{Arg}\max w_i(ij) = \frac{5e_k - 4e_j}{11} \text{ and } t_j^f \equiv \text{Arg}\max w_j(ij) = \frac{5e_k - 4e_i}{11}. \quad (16)$$

It is easy to see that the external tariff of an FTA member increases with the endowment of the non-member whereas it decreases with that of its FTA partner.[21] Similarly, a comparison of t_i^ϕ and t_i^f implies that the magnitude of the tariff complementarity effect increases with the size of partner country's endowment whereas it decreases with the endowment of the non-member country. To guarantee that all tariffs are positive and non-prohibitive, given Eq. (16) we assume that $\min\{e_i, e_j, e_k\} \geq \frac{4}{5}\max\{e_i, e_j, e_k\}$.

Finally, under the multilateral agreement $\langle\{ij^m\}\rangle$ countries i and j choose the tariff pair (t_i^m, t_j^m) to maximize $w_i(ij^m) + w_j(ij^m)$. We have

$$t_i^m = \frac{2e_k - e_j}{7} \text{ and } t_j^m = \frac{2e_k - e_i}{7}. \quad (17)$$

5.2. Incentives for bilateral trade liberalization

How does a country's incentive to form a bilateral FTA with another depend on the distribution of endowments across countries? We address this key question by breaking it up into parts and stating three related lemmas[22]:

Lemma 2a. *Let country j be an FTA partner of country i under regime r but not under regime v and let the status of country k be the same under both regimes (i.e. either it is a partner of country i under both regimes or not). Then, the following holds:* $\frac{\partial \Delta w_i(r-v)}{\partial e_j} \leq 0 \leq \frac{\partial \Delta w_i(r-v)}{\partial e_i}$.

The intuition underlying the $\frac{\partial \Delta w_i(r-v)}{\partial e_i} \geq 0$ is as follows. Due to the smaller volume of their exports, countries with smaller endowments benefit less from tariff reductions granted by others. Similarly, such countries have relatively more to lose from eliminating their own optimal tariffs since these tariffs apply to relatively larger import volumes (or to relatively inelastic export supply curves). Thus, a country's willingness to enter into a bilateral trade agreement with another depends positively on its own endowment.

A similar intuition underlies the other inequality (i.e. $\frac{\partial \Delta w_i(r-v)}{\partial e_j} \leq 0$). The smaller the endowment of a country's partner, the larger the increase in its export surplus from the elimination of its partner's optimal tariff and the smaller the loss due to its own trade liberalization since the tariff reduction applies to a smaller volume of imports (due to the smaller size of its partner). The two inequalities reported in Lemma 2a imply that a country prefers to form a bilateral FTA with the smaller of its two trading partners:

$$w_i(ij) \geq w_i(ik) \text{ iff } e_k \geq e_j. \quad (18)$$

How does the endowment level of a competing exporter, denoted by k, affect the incentive of country i to form a bilateral FTA with country j?

Lemma 2b. *Let country j be an FTA partner of country i under regime r but not under regime v and let the status of country k be the same under both regimes (i.e. either it is a partner of country i under both regimes or not). Then,*

(i) $\frac{\partial \Delta w_i(r-v)}{\partial e_k} \leq 0$ *if country k is an FTA partner of country j under regimes r and v; whereas*

(ii) $\frac{\partial \Delta w_i(r-v)}{\partial e_k} \geq 0$ *if country k is not an FTA partner of country j under regimes r and v.*

The first part of the above lemma captures the idea that when country k is already an FTA partner of country j, country i's welfare gain from a bilateral FTA with country j decreases with the endowment of country k. Why is this true? Recall that both countries i and k export the same good to country j (i.e. they are competing exporters). When country k already enjoys free access to country j's market, the larger is country k's endowment the smaller the increase in country i's export surplus that results from the trade liberalization undertaken by country j. The intuition behind part (*ii*) of the lemma is analogous — when its rival exporter (i.e. country k) is *not* an FTA partner of country j, the strategic advantage gained by country i in country j's market from signing the bilateral FTA $\langle\{ij\}\rangle$ increases in country k's size, making the FTA more valuable from its perspective.

The following lemma examines the welfare implications of being a hub country (say i under $\langle\{ih\}\rangle$) relative to other trade regimes:

Lemma 3. $w_i(ih) > \max\{w_i(ij), w_i(F), w_i(\Phi)\}$ *for all* $i, j = a, b, c$.

The fact that hub country prefers $\langle\{ih\}\rangle$ to $\langle\{F\}\rangle$ informs us that the first part of Lemma 1 generalizes to the case of asymmetric endowments. The intuition is the same as that under symmetry: relative to free trade, the hub country enjoys privileged access in both spoke countries. One implication of this lemma is worth stressing: a hub country has no incentive to unilaterally revoke either one or both of its FTAs.

5.3. Multilateral trade liberalization

How do the incentives of a country to form (or join to) a multilateral agreement depend on the underlying endowment structure?

Lemma 4. *Under multilateralism, the following hold:*

(i) $\frac{\partial \Delta w_i(ij^m - \phi)}{\partial e_i} > 0$, $\frac{\partial \Delta w_i(ij^m - \phi)}{\partial e_j} < 0$ *and* $\frac{\partial \Delta w_i(ij^m - \phi)}{\partial e_k} < 0$*; and*

(ii) $\frac{\partial \Delta w_i(F - ij^m)}{\partial e_i} > 0$, $\frac{\partial \Delta w_i(F - ij^m)}{\partial e_j} < 0$ *and* $\frac{\partial \Delta w_i(F - ij^m)}{\partial e_k} < 0$.

The intuition underlying all of the inequalities reported in Lemma 4 is quite analogous to that which underlies parallel results under bilateralism with only one exception — i.e. whereas $\frac{\partial \Delta w_i(ij - \phi)}{\partial e_k} > 0$ under bilateralism when country k is a non-member country, the opposite is true under multilateralism, i.e., $\frac{\partial \Delta w_i(ij^m - \phi)}{\partial e_k} < 0$. To see why this is the case recall that under the multilateral agreement $\langle\{ij\}\rangle^m$, countries i and j lower their tariffs on not only to each other but also on country k whereas under the bilateral agreement $\langle\{ij\}\rangle$ they only lower tariffs on each other. The larger is country k's endowment, the smaller the increase in the export surplus that countries i and j obtain due to the multilateral agreement $\langle\{ij^m\}\rangle$ since their rival exporter (i.e. country k) captures a larger share of their markets.

5.4. Equilibrium trade agreements under asymmetry

To highlight the crucial role played by asymmetry, it proves instructive to consider a scenario where two countries (denoted by l and l') have larger endowments than the third (denoted by s; referred to as the 'smaller' country).[23] Accordingly, let the pattern of endowment asymmetry be given by[24]:

[21] It is obvious that the same optimal tariff obtains for a spoke country under a hub and spoke trading regime. By contrast, since the hub has an FTA with both spokes, it practices free trade.

[22] Welfare levels under all possible regimes are reported in the Appendix A and these can be used to prove Lemma 2a through Lemma 4.

[23] As noted earlier, in our model no country is 'small' in the traditional sense since all three can influence their terms of trade. Hence we use the word 'smaller' as opposed to 'small'.

[24] An earlier version of the paper also analyzed the case where $e_s = e_{s'} = \frac{e}{\theta} < e_l = e$ and $\frac{5}{4} \geq \theta > 1$. To save space, we omit a detailed discussion here and simply note that analogous results hold under this alternative type of asymmetry.

Assumption 2a.

$$e_s = \frac{e}{\theta} < e_l = e_{l'} = e \text{ and } 1 \leq \theta \leq \frac{5}{4}. \quad (19)$$

To avoid redundancy, we focus directly on stable agreements under bilateralism. First consider the perspective of the two larger countries. We know from Lemma 1 that spoke countries are worse off relative to free trade under symmetry. Similarly, Lemma 2a and Lemma 2b imply that $\frac{\partial \Delta w_l(F-l'h)}{\partial e_s} \leq 0$ and $\frac{\partial \Delta w_l(F-sh)}{\partial e_s} \leq 0$. Thus, a larger country (say l) under free trade has no incentive to revoke one of its FTAs and become a spoke:

$$\Delta w_l(F-sh) > 0 \text{ and } \Delta w_l(F-l'h) > 0 \text{ for all } \theta. \quad (20)$$

Similarly, we know from Eq. (10) that under symmetry, starting from global free trade a country has no incentive to unilaterally revoke its two FTAs. Lemma 2a and Lemma 2b reinforce this result for the larger countries under asymmetry. We have:

$$\frac{\partial \Delta w_l(F-sl')}{\partial e_s} = \underbrace{\frac{\partial \Delta w_l(F-sh)}{\partial e_s}}_{\leq 0} + \underbrace{\frac{\partial \Delta w_l(sh-sl')}{\partial e_s}}_{\leq 0} \leq 0. \quad (21)$$

Therefore, a larger country (say l) prefers $\langle\{F\}\rangle$ to $\langle\{sl'\}\rangle$:

$$\Delta w_l(F-sl') > 0 \text{ for all } \theta. \quad (22)$$

Thus, inequalities (20) and (22) show that a larger country has no unilateral incentive to defect from free trade.

It is immediate from Eq. (20) that a joint defection from free trade to any hub and spoke regime does not occur. This implies we only need to consider three possible joint defections from free trade:

(JF1): Joint deviation of l and s from $\langle\{F\}\rangle$ to $\langle\{sl\}\rangle$.
(JF2): Joint deviation of l and l' from $\langle\{F\}\rangle$ to $\langle\{ll'\}\rangle$.
(JF3): Joint deviation of l and s or l and l' or all countries from $\langle\{F\}\rangle$ to $\langle\{\Phi\}\rangle$.

We know from inequality (11) that under symmetry ($\theta = 1$) no two countries benefit from excluding the third country from free trade. Furthermore, we show in Appendix A that $\Delta w_l(F-sl)$ is monotonically decreasing in θ and that $\Delta w_l(F-sl) > 0$ at the smallest possible endowment of country s (i.e. at $\theta = \frac{5}{4}$). This implies that joint deviation JF1 cannot occur: $\Delta w_l(F-sl) > 0$ for all θ. It is immediate from this and inequality (18) that the two larger countries have no incentive to jointly deviate from $\langle\{F\}\rangle$ to $\langle\{ll'\}\rangle$: $\Delta w_l(F-ll') > 0$ for all θ. Therefore, joint deviation JF2 is also ruled out. Finally, the fact that $\Delta w_l(F-sl) > 0$ together with inequalities (9) and Lemma 2a implies that joint deviation JF3 also does not occur: $\Delta w_l(F-\Phi) > 0$ for all θ. Thus, we have shown the following:

Lemma 5. *Suppose Assumption 2a holds. Then, there exist no unilateral or coalitional deviations of larger countries from free trade.*

Lemma 5 suggests that the stability of global free trade depends critically upon the preferences of the smaller country. Let $\theta_i(r-v)$ denote the critical threshold at which country i is indifferent between regimes r and v. Direct calculations yield

$$\Delta w_s(F-ll') \geq 0 \text{ iff } \theta \leq \theta_s(F-ll') \text{ and } \Delta w_s(F-lh) \geq 0 \text{ iff } \theta \leq \theta_s(F-lh) \quad (23)$$

where we show in the Appendix A that $\theta_s(F-ll') < \theta_s(F-lh)$. Together with Eq. (23), this implies that free trade is stable iff $\theta \leq \theta_s(F-ll')$. What happens when $\theta > \theta_s(F-ll')$? Parts (*ii*) and (*iii*) of the following proposition (proved in the Appendix A) addresses this question:

Proposition 3a. *Given Assumption 2a, the following hold under bilateralism:*

(*i*) *$\langle\{F\}\rangle$ is uniquely stable when $\theta \leq \theta_s(F-ll')$;*
(*ii*) *both $\langle\{sl\}\rangle$ and $\langle\{ll'\}\rangle$ are stable when $\theta_s(F-ll') < \theta \leq \theta_{l'}(lh-sl)$; and*
(*iii*) *$\langle\{ll'\}\rangle$ is uniquely stable when $\theta > \theta_{l'}(lh-sl)$.*

Proposition 3a relates the degree of underlying asymmetry to the nature of stable agreements and it is illustrated in Fig. 1. Part (*i*) simply says that if the degree of endowment asymmetry is sufficiently small (i.e. when $\theta \leq \theta_s(F-ll')$ in Fig. 1), free trade is uniquely stable. This implies that Proposition 1 does not require symmetry but rather that the degree of endowment asymmetry be sufficiently small. Part (*ii*) says that if the degree of endowment asymmetry is moderate (i.e. $\theta_s(F-ll') < \theta \leq \theta_{l'}(lh-sl)$ in Fig. 1), both a bilateral trade agreement between a smaller and a larger country and a bilateral FTA between the two larger countries are stable whereas part (*iii*) says that if the degree of endowment asymmetry is sufficiently large (i.e. $\theta > \theta_{l'}(lh-sl)$ in Fig. 1), only an FTA between the two larger countries is stable – in such a situation, the smaller country prefers being a non-member to participating in multilateral free trade.[25]

It is noteworthy that multiple stable equilibria obtain when the degree of endowment asymmetry is moderate – i.e. when $\theta_s(F-ll') < \theta_{l'}(lh-sl)$. Since theory offers no guidance about which of these equilibria might be observed, we examine both of these possibilities hereafter.

6. When, why, and how bilateralism matters

To see how the ability to form bilateral FTAs matters, suppose countries were to follow only a multilateral approach to trade liberalization. What are the stable agreements under such an approach? To address this question, first consider the stability of free trade $\langle\{F\}\rangle$ and note from Lemma 5 that there can be no coalitional deviations from free trade to the status quo. Furthermore, Lemma 4 implies that the larger country l' has no incentive to unilaterally deviate from $\langle\{F\}\rangle$ to $\langle\{sl^m\}\rangle$. This implies that $\langle\{sl^m\}\rangle$ is not stable. The only deviation from free trade that we need to consider is the unilateral deviation of the smaller country from $\langle\{F\}\rangle$ to $\langle\{ll'^m\}\rangle$. It turns out that this deviation does not occur if the degree of endowment asymmetry is small enough:

$$\Delta w_s(F-ll'^m) \geq 0 \text{ iff } \theta \leq \theta_s(F-ll'^m). \quad (24)$$

It immediately follows that free trade is stable under multilateralism when $\theta \leq \theta_s(F-ll'^m)$. What if $\theta > \theta_s(F-ll'^m)$? We know that $\Delta w_l(ll'^m - \Phi) > 0$ under symmetry ($\theta = 1$). Since $\frac{\partial \Delta w_l(ll'^m - \Phi)}{\partial e_s} < 0$ (Lemma 4) we have

$$\Delta w_l(ll'^m - \Phi) > 0 \text{ for all } \theta. \quad (25)$$

Inequalities (24) and (25) imply that the multilateral agreement $\langle\{ll'^m\}\rangle$ is stable when $\theta > \theta_s(F-ll'^m)$. We can now state the following result:

Proposition 3b. *Given Assumption 2a, $\langle\{F\}\rangle$ is stable under multilateralism when $\theta \leq \theta_s(F-ll'^m)$. Otherwise $\langle\{ll'^m\}\rangle$ is stable.*

Fig. 2 shows stable agreements under multilateralism.

Recall that under bilateralism, global free trade is stable only when $\theta \leq \theta_s(F-ll')$ whereas it is stable under multilateralism only when

[25] A similar result obtains in Ludema (2002) where asymmetry takes the form of transportation costs as opposed to endowments.

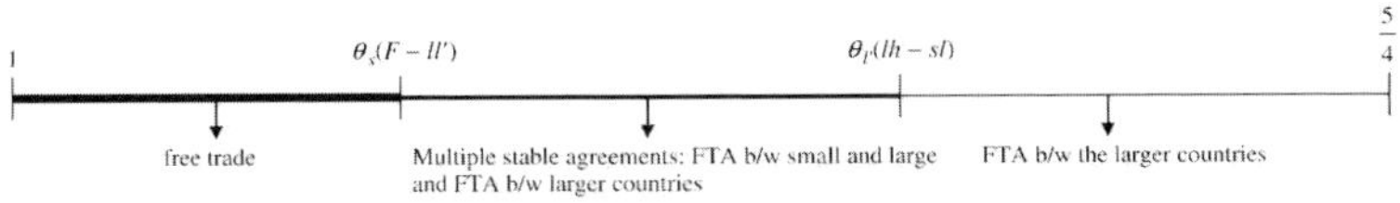

Fig. 1. Stable agreements under bilateralism.

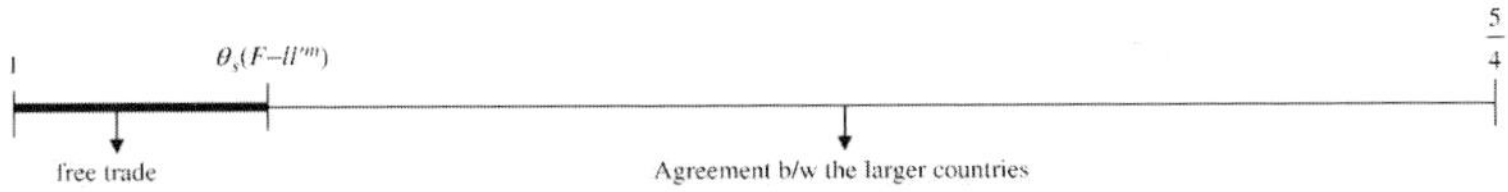

Fig. 2. Stable agreements under multilateralism.

$\theta \le \theta_s(F - ll'^m)$. A straightforward comparison of these critical thresholds delivers one of our major results and it is illustrated in Fig. 3:

Proposition 4. *Given* Assumption 2a, *the following hold:*

(*i*) *$\theta_s(F - ll'^m) < \theta_s(F - ll')$; and*
(*ii*) *over the parameter range $\theta_s(F - ll'^m) < \theta \le \theta_s(F - ll')$ the unique stable agreement under bilateralism is $\langle\{F\}\rangle$ whereas under multilateralism it is $\langle\{ll'^m\}\rangle$.*

Part (*i*) of Proposition 4 says that free trade is stable over a *larger* parameter space when countries are free to sign bilateral FTAs relative to when they cannot. Part (*ii*) demonstrates that there exist circumstances where the freedom to pursue bilateral FTAs is *necessary* for achieving global free trade because the smaller country has a greater incentive to choose global free trade under bilateralism relative to multilateralism. The precise parameter region over which this occurs is defined by the inequality $\theta_s(F - ll'^m) < \theta \le \theta_s(F - ll')$ and it is depicted as the thick dark line in Fig. 3. Such a region obtains because the smaller country is discriminated against its rival exporter in each larger member country's market under the bilateral FTA $\langle\{ll'\}\rangle$ whereas it suffers no such disadvantage under the multilateral agreement $\langle\{ll'^m\}\rangle$. This makes opting out of global free trade relatively costlier for the smaller country under bilateralism.[26] Thus, if the degree of endowment asymmetry is not too large, the threat of a bilateral FTA between the two larger countries and the discrimination that is inherent to such a trade agreement can be necessary to nudge the smaller country to announce in favor of global free trade. It is worth stressing that the very fact that the multilateral agreement is non-discriminatory in nature makes it *less* effective in altering the trade-off facing the smaller country since it does not lose as much from opting out of global free trade.[27]

When $\theta > \theta_s(F - ll')$, global free trade fails to obtain under both bilateralism and multilateralism. Intuitively, if the smaller country is sufficiently small, then even the possibility of a bilateral FTA between the two larger countries is not enough to induce it to opt for global free trade. When such is the case, one possible way forward is to ask how global welfare compares under the equilibrium agreements that obtain under bilateralism and multilateralism. From Proposition 3b we know that under bilateralism both $\langle\{ll'\}\rangle$ and $\langle\{sl\}\rangle$ are stable agreements when $\theta_s(F - ll') < \theta \le \theta_{l'}(lh - sl)$ whereas $\langle\{ll'\}\rangle$ is uniquely stable when $\theta > \theta_{l'}(lh - sl)$. Furthermore, Proposition 3b says that when global free trade does not obtain under multilateralism, $\langle\{ll'^m\}\rangle$ emerges as the unique stable equilibrium. Thus, when $\theta > \theta_s(F - ll')$, we need to consider two possible scenarios: (1) $\langle\{ll'\}\rangle$ is stable or (2) $\langle\{sl\}\rangle$ is stable. First, consider scenario (1) and note that *lower* internal and external tariffs (thus freer trade) obtain under $\langle\{ll'\}\rangle$ relative to $\langle\{ll'^m\}\rangle$: $t_l^m > t_l^f$. Thus, larger trade volumes and higher aggregate world welfare obtain under $\langle\{ll'\}\rangle$ relative to $\langle\{ll'^m\}\rangle$: $\Delta ww(ll' - ll'^m) > 0$.

Now consider scenario (2) where $\langle\{sl\}\rangle$ is the stable bilateral agreement. We show in the Appendix A that $\Delta ww(sl - ll'^m) > 0$ when $\theta_s(F - ll') < \theta \le \theta_{l'}(lh - sl)$. In other words, over the relevant parameter range, global welfare is higher under the bilateral agreement $\langle\{sl\}\rangle$ relative to the multilateral agreement $\langle\{ll'^m\}\rangle$. Thus, when free trade is out of reach, the option to pursue bilateral FTAs can yield welfare-improving trade liberalization that is foregone under a strictly multilateral approach.[28]

7. Political economy considerations

In order to determine whether and how the presence of political economy considerations affects our main results, suppose countries put greater weight on producer surplus relative to tariff revenue and consumer surplus:

$$w_i = \sum_z CS_i^z + TR_i + (1+\eta)\sum_z PS_i^z. \tag{26}$$

Since the model lacks an import competing industry, the additional weight (η) on producer surplus has no effect on the tariffs countries implement under no agreement and a bilateral FTA. As a result, domestic surplus stays unchanged under the bilateralism game. However, by increasing the importance of the export surplus gain that results from trade liberalization undertaken by partner countries, the additional weight on producer surplus makes participation in FTAs more desirable.

On the other hand, under the multilateral agreement $\langle\{ij^m\}\rangle$ countries *i* and *j* internalize each other's additional weights on export profits and their respective MFN tariffs fall with η:

$$t_i^m = \frac{2e_k - (1+3\eta)e_j}{7} \text{ and } t_j^m = \frac{2e_k - (1+3\eta)e_i}{7}. \tag{27}$$

As before, to guarantee that all tariffs are non-negative, we assume that (i) $\min\{e_i, e_j, e_k\} \ge \frac{4}{5}\max\{e_i, e_j, e_k\}$ and (ii) $\eta \le \frac{1}{5}$. For the case of symmetric endowments, we prove the following result in Appendix A:

[26] It is noteworthy that this result obtains even though the smaller country faces lower tariffs in its export markets under the bilateral FTA between the two larger countries $\langle\{ll'\}\rangle$ relative to the multilateral agreement $\langle\{ll'^m\}\rangle$.

[27] It is worth noting here that the result reported in part (*i*) of Proposition 4 depends crucially on the fact that, relative to the status quo, the degree of the positive externality enjoyed by the non-member is stronger under the multilateral agreement $\langle\{ll'^m\}\rangle$ relative to the bilateral FTA $\langle\{ll'\}\rangle$. In an alternative model, the relative strength of this positive externality under the two types of agreements might be reversed. And if so, the incentives for participating in global free trade could be stronger when discriminatory bilateral agreements are not permitted.

[28] Of course, aggregate world welfare does not necessarily speak to the fate of individual countries. It is immediate form (24) that, when the freedom to pursue bilateral FTAs is *necessary* for achieving global free trade, large countries are better off under bilateralism relative to multilateralism whereas the small country's fate is the opposite.

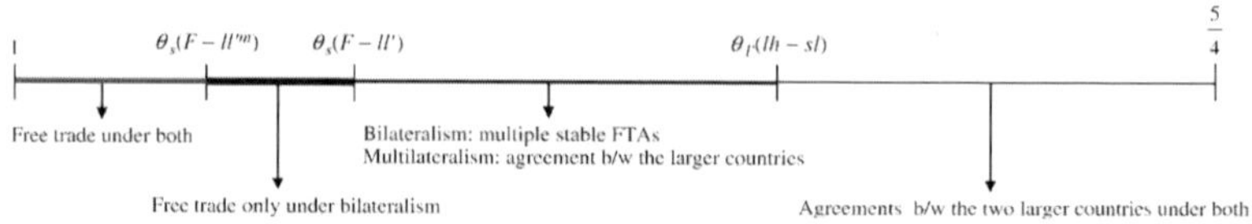

Fig. 3. Bilateralism versus multilateralism.

Proposition 5. *Given symmetric endowments ($e_i = e$ for all i), the following hold:*

(i) ⟨{F}⟩ is uniquely stable under bilateralism for all η whereas
(ii) ⟨{F}⟩ is uniquely stable under multilateralism only when $\eta \leq \frac{1}{10}$. Otherwise, ⟨{ij^m}⟩ is the stable equilibrium.

Thus, provided that the degree of political economy pressure is not too small (i.e. $\eta > \frac{1}{10}$), the freedom to pursue bilateral FTAs can be *necessary* for achieving global free trade *even when countries have symmetric endowments*. To understand the intuition behind this result, consider the perspective of the outside country (i.e. country k) under ⟨{ij^m}⟩: under multilateralism, the higher the weight on producer surplus, the lower the tariffs faced by the outside country in its export markets. As a result, the incentive to opt out of multilateral trade liberalization increases with the degree of political economy pressure η. By contrast, such a result does not obtain when the agreement involved is a bilateral FTA since the external tariffs of FTA members are independent of the degree of political economy pressure faced by them.

Now suppose that countries have asymmetric endowments. Let the pattern of endowment asymmetry be given by Assumption 2a and two countries (denoted by l and l') have larger endowments than the third (denoted by s). As before, let $\theta_i^p(r-v)$ denote the critical threshold at which country i is indifferent between regimes r and v, where $\theta_i^p(r-v)$ is now a function of η.

It is straightforward to show that Lemma 5 continues to hold under bilateralism – i.e. the two larger countries do not deviate either unilaterally or coalitionally from free trade. Thus, once again, the stability of free trade depends critically upon the preferences of the smaller country. Direct calculations establish that:

$$\Delta w_s(F-ll') \geq 0 \text{ iff } \theta \leq \theta_s^p(F-ll') \text{ and } \Delta w_s(F-lh) \geq 0 \text{ iff } \theta \leq \theta_s^p(F-lh) \quad (28)$$

where $\theta_s^p(F-ll') < \theta_s^p(F-lh)$ for all η. Therefore, free trade is stable under bilateralism iff $\theta \leq \theta_s^p(F-ll')$.

Similarly, under multilateralism, while the larger countries have no incentive to opt out of free trade, the smaller country benefits from deviating unilaterally from ⟨{F}⟩ to ⟨{ll'^m}⟩ if the degree of endowment asymmetry is large enough: $\Delta w_s(F-ll'^m) \geq 0$ iff $\theta \leq \theta_s^p(F-ll'^m)$. It follows that free trade is stable under multilateralism when $\theta \leq \theta_s^p(F-ll'^m)$. We prove the following result in the Appendix A:

Proposition 6. *Given* Assumption 2a, *the following hold:*

(i) $\theta_s^p(F-ll'^m) < \theta_s^p(F-ll')$ for all η;
(ii) over the parameter range $\theta_s^p(F-ll'^m) < \theta \leq \theta_s^p(F-ll')$, bilateralism yields ⟨{F}⟩ as the stable equilibrium whereas multilateralism yields ⟨{ll'^m}⟩;
(iii) when $\theta > \theta_s^p(F-ll')$, multilateralism yields ⟨{ll'^m}⟩ as the stable equilibrium whereas bilateralism yields ⟨{ll'}⟩ and also ⟨{sl}⟩ when in addition $\theta \leq \theta_{l'}^p(lh-sl)$ and
(iv) world welfare is higher under bilateralism relative to multilateralism for all η.

Proposition 6 provides a confirmation of our key insight that a country that is reluctant to liberalize has a greater incentive to opt out of global free trade under multilateralism relative to bilateralism. Moreover, this insight receives even stronger support as the additional weight on producer surplus increases since under multilateralism the smaller country does not suffer from discrimination (as it does under an FTA) and the tariff it faces as an outsider decreases with η.

Fig. 4 illustrates equilibrium agreements in the (η, θ) space to show how the degree of political economy pressure and endowment asymmetry jointly determine equilibrium outcomes under bilateralism and multilateralism.

Note from Fig. 4 that free trade is more likely to be stable under bilateralism as η increases. By contrast, free trade fails to be stable under multilateralism when η is sufficiently large ($\eta > \frac{1}{10}$). Finally, when $\theta > \theta_s^p(F-ll')$, free trade fails to obtain under both bilateralism and multilateralism. Under such a case, stable agreements under bilateralism (⟨{ll'}⟩ and ⟨{sl}⟩) lead to higher global welfare than the one under multilateralism (⟨{ll'^m}⟩).

8. Conclusion

One of the striking features of today's global policy landscape is the widespread prevalence of preferential trade agreements. Only a handful of countries are not involved in one and most simultaneously participate in several such agreements. Bhagwati (1991) famously raised concern about the potential adverse effects of the pursuit of preferential trade agreements on the prospects of multilateral trade liberalization. His work led to a rich body of research that has illuminated various aspects of the multi-faceted relationship between preferential and multilateral trade liberalization. However, this literature has often tended to treat bilateral trade agreements as exogenous or only considered an endogenous trade agreement between a pair of countries while treating the third country as a silent observer. By contrast, we present a model in which all countries are free to pursue both bilateral and multilateral agreements. To determine whether bilateralism hampers or facilitates the obtainment of global free trade, we also derive stable equilibria of a game that permits only a multilateral approach to trade agreements. This analysis helps shed light on the pros and cons of bilateralism and multilateralism.

A central result of this paper is that bilateralism can actually provide an impetus to multilateral trade liberalization. The point is that a country that is choosing whether or not to participate in global free trade must consider its fate under the agreement that would emerge in the *absence* of its participation. Due to the fact that a bilateral trade agreement discriminates against the outsider whereas a multilateral agreement does not, a non-participating country is worse off under the former relative to the latter. As a result, a country's incentive to opt for free trade is stronger when the alternative to free trade is a bilateral agreement between the other countries as opposed to a multilateral one.

An important implication of our analysis is that to properly account for the role of bilateralism, we need to better understand *why* countries choose to enter into bilateral agreements when multilateral trade liberalization is an option. To this end, the model suggests that the debate regarding preferential versus multilateral liberalization is moot in the absence of some type of asymmetry across countries. This is because, in our model, whether or not countries are free to pursue bilateral trade agreements, global free trade is the only stable equilibrium under symmetry. This result demonstrates that heterogeneity across countries with respect to the benefits that they enjoy from global free trade may be a critical determinant of the success of a

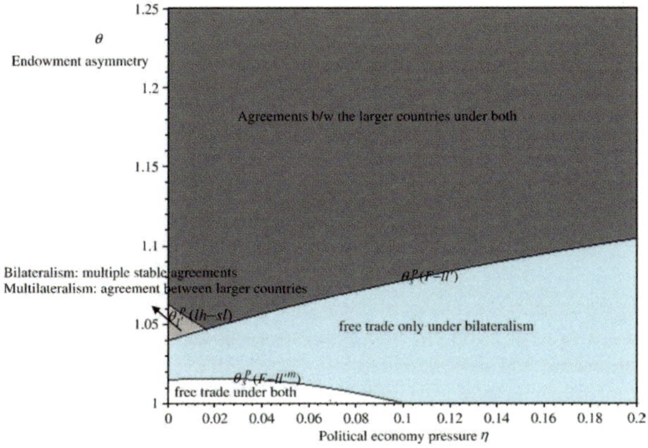

Fig. 4. Political economy considerations and bilateralism versus multilateralism.

purely multilateral approach to trade liberalization. In our view, such heterogeneity has received insufficient attention in the literature and its role merits further research.

Appendix A

This appendix contains supporting calculations and brief proofs of propositions stated in the paper.

A.1. Supporting calculations

We begin by reporting welfare levels under different policy regimes. Under bilateralism, we have:

$$w_i(F) = \frac{\left[\left(\sum_j \frac{e_j}{3}\right)^2 + \sum_j \left(\frac{e_j}{3}\right)^2\right]}{2} + e_i\left(2\alpha - \frac{2e_i + \sum_{j\neq i} e_j}{3}\right)$$

$$w_i(\Phi) = \frac{\sum_{j\neq i}\left[\frac{3(e_i+e_j)}{8}\right]^2}{2} + \left(\frac{e_j+e_k}{4}\right)^2 + e_i\left(2\alpha - \frac{6e_i + \sum_{j\neq i} 3e_j}{8}\right)$$

$$w_i(ij) = \frac{\left[\frac{3(e_i+e_j)}{8}\right]^2 + \left[\frac{(2e_k+5e_i)}{11}\right]^2}{2} + \frac{\left(4e_k^2 + 3e_j^2 - 2e_je_k\right)}{22} + e_i\left[2\alpha - \left(\frac{73e_i}{88} + \frac{3e_j}{8} + \frac{2e_k}{11}\right)\right]$$

$$w_i(jk) = \frac{\sum_{j\neq i}\left(\frac{7e_i+e_j}{11}\right)^2}{2} + \left(\frac{e_j+e_k}{4}\right)^2 + e_i\left(2\alpha - \frac{14e_i + \sum_{j\neq i} e_j}{11}\right)$$

$$w_i(ih) = \frac{1}{2}\left[\left[\frac{(e_j+e_k)}{3}\right]^2 + \sum_{j\neq i}\left[\frac{(2e_j+5e_i)}{11}\right]^2\right] + e_i\left(2\alpha - \frac{10e_i + \sum_{j\neq i} 2e_j}{11}\right)$$

and

$$w_i(jh) = \frac{\left(\frac{e_i+e_k}{3}\right)^2 + \left(\frac{7e_i+e_j}{11}\right)^2}{2} + \frac{\left(4e_k^2 + 3e_j^2 - 2e_je_k\right)}{22} + e_i\left(2\alpha - \frac{32e_i + 11e_k + 3e_j}{33}\right).$$

Under multilateralism, we have:

$$w_i(ij^m) = 2\alpha e_i + \frac{3(e_i+e_j)(3e_j - 13e_i)}{128} + \frac{(2e_i+3e_k)(3e_k-12e_i) + (3e_j+e_k)(e_j+5e_k)}{98}$$

$$w_i(jk^m) = 2\alpha e_i + \left(\frac{e_j+e_k}{4}\right)^2 + \frac{(3e_i+2e_j)(2e_j-11e_i) + (3e_i+2e_k)(2e_k-11e_i)}{98}.$$

Welfare levels under symmetry can be calculated by setting each country's endowment to e in the formulae above. The relevant comparisons under symmetry are as follows:

$$\Delta w_i(ij-\Phi) = \frac{47}{2}\left(\frac{e}{44}\right)^2 > 0;\ \Delta w_k(ij-\Phi) = 23\left(\frac{e}{44}\right)^2 > 0;$$
$$\Delta w_i(ih-F) = 23\left(\frac{e}{33}\right)^2 > 0;\ \Delta w_j(F-ih) = \frac{29}{2}\left(\frac{e}{33}\right)^2 > 0;$$
$$\Delta w_i(ih-ij) = \frac{1039}{2}\left(\frac{e}{132}\right)^2 > 0;\ \Delta w_j(ik-ih) = \frac{161}{2}\left(\frac{e}{132}\right)^2 > 0;$$
$$\Delta w_i(F-jk) = \frac{13}{3}\left(\frac{e}{22}\right)^2 > 0;\ \Delta w_i(F-ij) = \frac{101}{6}\left(\frac{e}{22}\right)^2 > 0$$

and

$$\Delta w_i(ij^m-\Phi) = \frac{1}{14}\left(\frac{e}{4}\right)^2 > 0;\ \Delta w_k(F-ij^m) = \frac{1}{3}\left(\frac{e}{14}\right)^2 > 0.$$

Proof of Lemma 3. First consider part (i). We know from Lemma 1 that $\Delta w_i(ih-F)>0$ under symmetry. Next, note that $\frac{\partial \Delta w_i(ih-F)}{\partial e_i} = \frac{134(e_j+e_k)-320e_i}{33^2} < 0$, $\frac{\partial \Delta w_i(ih-F)}{\partial e_j} = \frac{134e_i - 85e_j}{33^2} > 0$ and $\frac{\partial \Delta w_i(ih-F)}{\partial ek} =$

$\frac{134e_i - 85e_k}{33^2} > 0$. At $e_i = \frac{4e}{5}$ and $e_j = e_k = e$, we have $\Delta w_i(ih - F) = 3\left(\frac{e}{11}\right)^2 > 0$. Using analogous arguments, we can establish parts (*ii*) and (*iii*).

A.2. Critical thresholds

Since $e_l = e_{l'}$, we must have $\theta(F - lh) = \theta(F - l'h)$. Furthermore, $\theta(F - ll')_s \cong 1.0398$ and $\theta(F - lh)_s \cong 1.1487$.

A.3. Inequalities from the text

We have

$$\Delta w_l(F - sl)|_{\theta = \frac{5}{4}} = \frac{7}{2}\left(\frac{e}{12}\right)^2 > 0 \text{ and } \frac{\partial \Delta w_l(F - sl)}{\partial \theta} = -\frac{1357\theta - 1211}{6336\theta^3} < 0.$$

Proof of Proposition 3a. Note from Eq. (9) that under symmetry two countries always benefit from forming a bilateral FTA. Also, we know from Lemma 2b that $\frac{\partial \Delta w_l(ll' - \Phi)}{\partial e_s} > 0$. Next, note that $\Delta w_l(ll' - \Phi)|_{\theta = \frac{5}{4}} = \frac{3}{10}\left(\frac{e}{8}\right)^2 > 0$. This implies that $\langle\{\Phi\}\rangle$ is not stable:

$$\Delta w_l(ll' - \Phi) > 0 \text{ for all } \theta. \quad (29)$$

Furthermore, inequalities (18) and (29) together imply that

$$\Delta w_l(sl - \Phi) > 0 \text{ for all } \theta. \quad (30)$$

Consider now the smaller country's perspective under $\langle\{sl\}\rangle$. From Lemma 2a, we know that $\frac{\partial \Delta w_l(sl - \Phi)}{\partial e_s} > 0$. Further note that $\Delta w_s(sl - \Phi)|_{\theta = \frac{5}{4}} = \frac{719}{2}\left(\frac{e}{440}\right)^2 > 0$. This implies

$$\Delta w_s(sl - \Phi) > 0 \text{ for all } \theta. \quad (31)$$

It is immediate from Eq. (20) that the two larger countries jointly defect from $\langle\{sh\}\rangle$ to $\langle\{F\}\rangle$ and this defection is self-enforcing since neither has an incentive to further defect (Lemma 5). Thus, $\langle\{sh\}\rangle$ is not stable. Similarly, the smaller country defects unilaterally from $\langle\{lh\}\rangle$ to $\langle\{ll'\}\rangle$ so that $\langle\{lh\}\rangle$ is not stable.[29]

Next, we provide conditions under which $\langle\{sl\}\rangle$ and $\langle\{ll'\}\rangle$ are stable. There exist five possible coalitional deviations from $\langle\{sl\}\rangle$:

(JSL1): Deviation of l and l' from $\langle\{sl\}\rangle$ to $\langle\{ll'\}\rangle$.
(JSL2): Deviation of s and l' from $\langle\{sl\}\rangle$ to $\langle\{sh\}\rangle$.
(JSL3): Deviation of l and l' from $\langle\{sl\}\rangle$ to $\langle\{lh\}\rangle$.
(JSL4): Deviation of all countries from $\langle\{sl\}\rangle$ to $\langle\{l'h\}\rangle$.
(JSL5): Deviation of all countries from $\langle\{sl\}\rangle$ to $\langle\{F\}\rangle$.

Note from Eq. (18) that country l will not defect from $\langle\{sl\}\rangle$ to $\langle\{ll'\}\rangle$. Thus, JSL1 is ruled out. Next consider JSL2 and JSL3. We know from Lemma 3 that country s (l) has an incentive to defect from $\langle\{sl\}\rangle$ to $\langle\{sh\}\rangle$ ($\langle\{lh\}\rangle$). For these deviations to occur, the choice of country l' is pivotal. We have

$$\Delta w_{l'}(sh - sl) \geq 0 \textit{ iff } \theta \geq \theta_{l'}(sh - sl) = 1.0639 \quad (32)$$

and

$$\Delta w_{l'}(lh - sl) \geq 0 \textit{ iff } \theta \geq \theta_{l'}(lh - sl) = 1.0629. \quad (33)$$

Since $\theta \geq \theta_{l'}(lh - sl) > \theta_{l'}(sh - sl)$, JSL3 is the binding deviation.

Now consider JSL4. Since the smaller country has an incentive to unilaterally deviate from $\langle\{l'h\}\rangle$ to $\langle\{ll'\}\rangle$, even if JSL4 occurs, it is not self-enforcing. Finally, we know from Eq. (23) that JSL5 occurs when $\theta < \theta_s(F - lh)$ and it is self-enforcing only if $\theta < \theta_s(F - ll')$. Thus, $\langle\{sl\}\rangle$ is stable iff $\theta_{l'}(lh - sl) \geq \theta \geq \theta_s(F - ll')$.

We now derive conditions under which $\langle\{ll'\}\rangle$ is stable. Inequality (29) implies that there can be no deviations from $\langle\{ll'\}\rangle$ to $\langle\{\Phi\}\rangle$. Now consider the following coalitional deviations:

(JLL1): Deviation of s and l from $\langle\{ll'\}\rangle$ to $\langle\{sl\}\rangle$.
(JLL2): Deviation of s and l from $\langle\{ll'\}\rangle$ to $\langle\{lh\}\rangle$.
(JLL3): Deviation of all countries from $\langle\{ll'\}\rangle$ to $\langle\{sh\}\rangle$.
(JLL4): Deviation of all countries from $\langle\{ll'\}\rangle$ to $\langle\{F\}\rangle$.

From Lemma 3, it is immediate that JLL1 is not a self-enforcing deviation since country l has an incentive to further deviate to $\langle\{lh\}\rangle$. Moreover, JLL2 is ruled out since country s does not have an incentive to defect from $\langle\{ll'\}\rangle$ to $\langle\{lh\}\rangle$. We also know from Eq. (20) that even if JLL3 occurs, the two larger countries further deviate from $\langle\{sh\}\rangle$ to $\langle\{F\}\rangle$. Thus the initial deviation is not self-enforcing. Finally, Eq. (23) implies that all countries deviate from $\langle\{ll'\}\rangle$ to $\langle\{F\}\rangle$ when $\theta < \theta_s(F - ll')$ and this deviation is self-enforcing. Thus, $\langle\{ll'\}\rangle$ is stable iff $\theta \geq \theta_s(F - ll')$.

A.4. Other inequalities from the text

We have $\Delta w_s(F - ll'^m) \geq 0$ iff $\theta \leq \theta_s(F - ll'^m) = 1.0149$. Furthermore,

$$\frac{\partial \Delta ww(sl - ll'^{m})}{\partial \theta} = -\frac{8605\theta + 1949}{2\theta}\left(\frac{e}{308\theta}\right)^2 < 0.$$

Note that when $\theta = \theta_{l'}(lh - sl)$, $\Delta ww(sl - ll'^m) > 0$. Thus, $\Delta ww(sl - ll'^m) > 0$ when $\theta_s(F - ll') \leq \theta < \theta_{l'}(lh - sl)$.

Proof of Proposition 5.

$$\Delta w_i(F - \Phi) = \frac{e^2(8\eta + 1)}{48} > 0; \Delta w_i(F - jk) = \frac{176\eta + 13}{3}\left(\frac{e}{22}\right)^2 > 0;$$
$$\Delta w_i(F - ij) = \frac{616\eta + 101}{6}\left(\frac{e}{44}\right)^2 > 0; \Delta w_i(F - jh) = \frac{132\eta + 29}{2}\left(\frac{e}{33}\right)^2 > 0$$
$$\Delta w_i(F - jk) = \frac{(18\eta + 1)(1 - 10\eta)}{3}\left(\frac{e}{14}\right)^2 \geq 0 \textit{ iff } \eta \leq \frac{1}{10}.$$

Proof of Proposition 6. Part (i) is immediate from the fact that $\theta_s^p(F - ll') < \theta_s^p(F - ll'^m)$ for all feasible η.

Parts (ii) and (iii): The following is immediate from the proof of proposition 3a:

$$\Delta w_l(ll' - \Phi) > 0, \ \Delta w_l(sl - \Phi) > 0, \text{ and } \Delta w_s(sl - \Phi) > 0 \text{ for all } \theta, \eta \quad (34)$$

These inequalities imply that $\langle\{\Phi\}\rangle$ is not stable.

We know from Eq. (20) that two larger countries jointly defect from $\langle\{sh\}\rangle$ to $\langle\{F\}\rangle$ when $\eta = 0$. This defection also occurs for any $\eta > 0$ and is self-enforcing since neither country has an incentive to further defect. Therefore, $\langle\{sh\}\rangle$ is not stable.

Now consider $\langle\{lh\}\rangle$.[30] The smaller country defects from $\langle\{lh\}\rangle$ to $\langle\{ll'\}\rangle$ unless $\theta \leq \theta_s^p(lh - ll')$ where $\theta_s^p(lh - ll')$ is defined by $\Delta w_s(lh - ll') = 0$. However, when $\theta \leq \theta_s^p(lh - ll')$, the joint deviation of countries s and l' from $\langle\{lh\}\rangle$ to $\langle\{F\}\rangle$ is self-enforcing so that $\langle\{lh\}\rangle$ fails to be stable.

Next consider $\langle\{sl\}\rangle$ and $\langle\{ll'\}\rangle$. We know from Eq. (34) that unilateral defections from $\langle\{sl\}\rangle$ to $\langle\{\Phi\}\rangle$ and $\langle\{ll'\}\rangle$ to $\langle\{\Phi\}\rangle$ do not occur. There exist five possible coalitional deviations from $\langle\{sl\}\rangle$:

(JSL1-P): Deviation of l and l' from $\langle\{sl\}\rangle$ to $\langle\{ll'\}\rangle$.
(JSL2-P): Deviation of s and l' from $\langle\{sl\}\rangle$ to $\langle\{sh\}\rangle$.
(JSL3-P): Deviation of l and l' from $\langle\{sl\}\rangle$ to $\langle\{lh\}\rangle$.
(JSL4-P): Deviation of all countries from $\langle\{sl\}\rangle$ to $\langle\{l'h\}\rangle$.
(JSL5-P): Deviation of all countries from $\langle\{sl\}\rangle$ to $\langle\{F\}\rangle$.

[29] An analogous discussion applies to $\langle\{l'h\}\rangle$.

[30] See footnote 29.

JSL1-P is ruled out since country l does not defect from $\langle\{sl\}\rangle$ to $\langle\{ll'\}\rangle$. Next consider JSL2-P and JSL3-P. We know from Lemma 3 that country s (l) has an incentive to defect from $\langle\{sl\}\rangle$ to $\langle\{sh\}\rangle$ ($\langle\{lh\}\rangle$). For these deviations to occur, the choice of country l' is pivotal. We have $\Delta w_{l'}(sh-sl)\geq 0$ iff $\theta \geq \theta_{l'}^{p}(sh-sl)$ and $\Delta w_{l'}(lh-sl)\geq 0$ iff $\theta\geq\theta_{l'}^{p}(lh-sl)$. Since $\theta_{l'}(lh-sl)\geq\theta_{l'}(sh-sl)$ JSL3-P is the binding deviation.

Next note that since country l has no incentive to deviate from $\langle\{sl\}\rangle$ to $\langle\{l'h\}\rangle$, JSL4-P does not occur. Finally, note that the two larger countries have an incentive to jointly deviate from $\langle\{sl\}\rangle$ to $\langle\{F\}\rangle$ whereas the smaller country defects only when it has a relatively symmetric endowment $\Delta w_s(F-sl)\geq 0$ iff $\theta\leq\theta_s^p(F-sl)$ and this joint deviation is self-enforcing only if $\theta<\theta_s^p(F-ll')$. Thus, $\langle\{sl\}\rangle$ is stable iff $\theta_s^p(F-ll')\leq\theta\leq\theta_{l'}^p(lh-sl)$.

For $\langle\{ll'\}\rangle$ to be stable, we need to consider the following coalitional deviations:

(JLL1-P): Deviation of s and l from $\langle\{ll'\}\rangle$ to $\langle\{sl\}\rangle$.
(JLL2-P): Deviation of s and l from $\langle\{ll'\}\rangle$ to $\langle\{lh\}\rangle$.
(JLL3-P): Deviation of all countries from $\langle\{ll'\}\rangle$ to $\langle\{sh\}\rangle$.
(JLL4-P): Deviation of all countries from $\langle\{ll'\}\rangle$ to $\langle\{F\}\rangle$.

Note that JLL1-P is not a self-enforcing deviation since country l has an incentive to further deviate to $\langle\{lh\}\rangle$ and JLL2-P happens only when $\theta<\theta_s^p(lh-ll')$ and that it is a self-enforcing deviation. Even if JLL3-P occurs, the larger countries further deviate from $\langle\{sh\}\rangle$ to $\langle\{F\}\rangle$, making the initial deviation not self-enforcing. Finally, all countries deviate from $\langle\{ll'\}\rangle$ to $\langle\{F\}\rangle$ when $\theta<\theta_s^p(F-ll')$ and this deviation is self-enforcing. Since $\theta_s^p(lh-ll')<\theta_s^p(F-ll')$, $\langle\{ll'\}\rangle$ is stable iff $\theta\geq\theta_s^p(F-ll')$.

Under multilateralism, straightforward calculations show that (*i*) $\Delta w_{l'}(ll'^m-\Phi)$; (ii) $\Delta w_l(F-\Phi)>0$; (iii) $\Delta w_{l'}(F-sl^m)>0$; and (iv) $\Delta w_s(F-ll'^m)\geq 0$ iff $\theta\leq\theta_s^p(F-ll'^m)$.

References

Aghion, Philippe, Antràs, Pol, Helpman, Elhanan, 2007. Negotiating free trade. Journal of International Economics 73, 1–30.

Bagwell, Kyle, Staiger, Robert W., 1997. Multilateral tariff cooperation during the formation of free trade areas. International Economic Review 38, 291–319.

Bagwell, Kyle, Staiger, Robert W., 1999. Regionalism and multilateral tariff cooperation. In: Pigott, John, Woodland, Alan (Eds.), International Trade Policy and the Pacific Rim. Macmillan, London.

Bernheim, Douglas B., Peleg, Bezalel, Whinston, Michael, 1987. Coalition-proof Nash equilibria I. concepts. Journal of Economic Theory 42, 1–12.

Bhagwati, Jagdish, 1991. The World Trading System at Risk. Princeton University Press, Princeton, NJ.

Bhagwati, Jagdish, Panagariya, Arvind, Krishna, Pravin (Eds.), 1999. Trading Blocs. The MIT Press, Cambridge, MA.

Bond, Eric W., Constantinos, Syropoulos, Winters, L. Alan, 2001. Deepening of regional integration and multilateral trade agreements. Journal of International Economics 53, 335–362.

Bond, Eric W., Riezman, Raymond G., Syropoulos, Constantinos, 2004. A strategic and welfare theoretic analysis of free trade areas. Journal of International Economics 64, 1–27.

Dutta, Bhaskar, Mutuswami, Suresh, 1997. Stable networks. Journal of Economic Theory 76, 322–344.

Estevadeordal, Antoni, Freund, Caroline, Ornelas, Emanuel, 2008. Does regionalism affect trade liberalization toward non-members? Quarterly Journal of Economics 123, 1531–1575.

Freund, Caroline, 2000. Multilateralism and the endogenous formation of preferential trade agreements. Journal of International Economics 52, 359–376.

Furusawa, Taiji, Konishi, Hideo, 2007. Free trade networks. Journal of International Economics 72, 310–335.

Goyal, Sanjeev, Joshi, Sumit, 2006. Bilateralism and free trade. International Economic Review 47, 749–778.

Grossman, Gene M., Helpman, Elhanan, 1995. The politics of free-trade agreements. American Economic Review 85, 667–690.

Jackson, Matthew, Wolinsky, Asher, 1996. A strategic model of social and economic networks. Journal of Economic Theory 71, 44–74.

Krishna, Pravin, 1998. Regionalism and multilateralism: a political economy approach. Quarterly Journal of Economics 113, 227–251.

Krugman, Paul R., 1991. The move toward free trade zones. Policy Implications of Trade and Currency Zones: A Symposium Sponsored by the Federal Reserve Bank of Kansas City. Federal Reserve Bank of Kansas City, Kansas City, pp. 7–41.

Levy, Philip I., 1997. A political-economic analysis of free trade agreements. American Economic Review 87, 506–519.

Ludema, Rodney, 2002. Increasing returns, multinationals and geography of preferential trade agreements. Journal of International Economics 56, 329–358.

Ornelas, Emanuel, 2005a. Endogenous free trade agreements and the multilateral trading system. Journal of International Economics 67, 471–497.

Ornelas, Emanuel, 2005b. Rent destruction and the political viability of free trade agreements. Quarterly Journal of Economics 120, 1475–1506.

Riezman, Raymond, 1999. Can bilateral trade agreements help induce free trade? Canadian Journal of Economics 32, 751–766.

Saggi, Kamal, 2006. Preferential trade agreements and multilateral tariff cooperation. International Economic Review 47, 29–57.

Saggi, Kamal and Halis M. Yildiz, 2006. "Bilateral Trade Agreements and the Feasibility of Multilateral Free Trade". Mimeo.

Saggi, Kamal, Yildiz, Halis M., 2009. Optimal tariffs of preferential trade agreements and the tariff complementarity effect. Indian Growth and Development Review 2 (1), 5–17.

World Bank, 2005. Global Economic Prospects: Trade, Regionalism, and Development. The World Bank, Washington, D.C.

CHAPTER 8

Review of International Economics, 19(2), 356–373, 2011
DOI:10.1111/j.1467-9396.2011.00952.x

Bilateral Trade Agreements and the Feasibility of Multilateral Free Trade

*Kamal Saggi and Halis Murat Yildiz**

Abstract

We studied how the pursuit of bilateral free-trade agreements (FTAs) affects the likelihood of achieving multilateral free trade. We derive and compare the stable Nash equilibria of two games of trade liberalization: in the FTA game, each country can either form an FTA with one of its trading partners or both of them or none of them, whereas in the (restricted) No FTA game, purely bilateral FTAs are not permitted. The major result is that there exist circumstances under which the freedom to pursue (discriminatory) bilateral FTAs is *necessary* for achieving multilateral free trade.

1. Introduction

During recent years, there has been widespread concern that the ever-increasing prevalence of preferential trade agreements (PTAs) might have an adverse effect on the process of multilateral trade liberalization—the *raison d'être* of the World Trade Organization (WTO). Motivated by this concern, this paper focuses on free-trade agreements (FTAs), the most commonly occurring type of PTAs, and asks: how does the pursuit of FTAs interact with the process of multilateral trade liberalization? Would global free trade be harder or easier to achieve if countries were to pursue trade liberalization on only a multilateral basis? Or as Jagdish Bhagwati (1991) put it—are FTAs building or stumbling blocks for multilateral trade liberalization?

Existing literature has sometimes taken the view that FTAs are building blocks so long as their pursuit *does not prevent or eventually leads* to global free trade. We take this argument one step further and show that there exist circumstances where the freedom to pursue FTAs is *necessary* to attain global free trade. When such is the case, we say that FTAs act as *strong building blocks*. To the best of our knowledge, with the exception of Aghion et al. (2007) and Saggi and Yildiz (2010), this potential role of FTAs has been overlooked by the rather voluminous literature on the subject. The reason for this is easy to see: only a model in which both bilateral and multilateral negotiations are endogenous can lead to such an insight, whereas the existing literature has generally taken one type of trade liberalization (either bilateral or multilateral) to be exogenous.

---

* Saggi: Department of Economics, Vanderbilt University, VU Station PMB #351828, 2301 Vanderbilt Place, Nashville, TN 37235-1828, USA. Tel: 615 279 5415; Fax: 615-343-2391; E-mail: k.saggi@vanderbilt.edu. Yildiz: Department of Economics, Ryerson University, Toronto, Ontario M5B 2K3, Canada. Tel: 416-979-5000 ext. 6689; Fax: 416-979-5289; E-mail: hyildiz@ryerson.ca. For helpful comments, we thank seminar audiences at the following universities: Bilkent, Bologna, Guelph, Harvard, Manitoba, McGill, Princeton, Ryerson, Sabanci, SMU, Syracuse, Texas A&M, UC-Irvine, Vanderbilt, and York. We also thank Pol Antras, Rick Bond, Gene Grossman, Elhanan Helpman, Kyle Hyndman, Giovanni Maggi, Andres Rodriguez-Clare, and an anonymous referee for constructive comments and suggestions. We gratefully acknowledge financial support from the Social Sciences and Humanities Research Council of Canada (SSHRC). Any remaining errors are our own.

The general idea behind our strong building block result can be stated as follows. If bilateral FTAs are prohibited by multilateral rules (or infeasible due to some other reasons) and the choice is only between multilateral free trade or no agreement (i.e. the status quo), any single country can ensure that the status quo prevails by simply opting to not choose free trade itself. However, when the rest of the world is free to form bilateral FTAs, a country that makes such a choice can find itself worse-off relative to the status quo if some of the *other* countries choose to undertake preferential trade liberalization amongst themselves. Anticipating this outcome, it may then become quite willing to undertake multilateral trade liberalization. *Thus, the possibility of preferential trade liberalization amongst others can induce a country to participate in multilateral trade liberalization.* While we demonstrate this result in a variant of the Brander–Krugman (1983) oligopoly model of intraindustry trade, it is clear that the mechanism underlying it is likely to arise in any model of international trade in which adverse discriminatory treatment in foreign markets makes a country worse off.[1]

Formally, we analyze the coalition-proof Nash equilibria (or stable equilibria) of two games of trade liberalization between three countries.[2] Under the FTA game, countries can pursue bilateral, multilateral, or no trade liberalization, whereas under the No FTA game, they have only the latter two options. In the first stage of the FTA game, each country announces whether or not it wants to form an FTA with each of its trading partners. An FTA between two countries arises when they both announce each other's name. Similarly, free trade emerges when all countries call each other's names. Next, given trade agreements and tariffs, firms compete in the product market in a Cournot fashion. In the first stage of the No FTA game, each country can choose between only two alternatives: it can either announce in favor of free trade or no agreement (wherein they retain their existing tariffs on each other). The rest of the No FTA game proceeds just like the FTA game.

Since markets are assumed to be segmented, from each country's perspective, an FTA embodies the following tradeoff. On the one hand, forming a bilateral FTA lowers a country's domestic surplus relative to no agreement because of the tariff concession it grants to the other member. On the other hand, the reciprocal tariff reduction granted by the other member increases its export profits. Utilizing this tradeoff, we obtain several interesting results. First, we show that under symmetry, free trade is a stable equilibrium of both games. However, while free trade is the unique stable agreement of the No FTA game, a bilateral FTA can *also* be a stable equilibrium of the FTA game (i.e. FTAs have a *weak stumbling block effect* under symmetry). Second, when production costs are unequal across countries, there exist patterns of cost asymmetry for which multilateral free trade is an equilibrium *only if* countries have the option to form FTAs (i.e. FTAs act as *strong building blocks*). Third, despite the absence of any political economy considerations in our model, free trade can fail to be an equilibrium even when FTAs are *not* permissible provided the production cost of one of the countries is moderately high relative to others. Under such a scenario, FTAs act as *partial building blocks* by delivering welfare-improving bilateral trade liberalization. Fourth, a "hub-and-spoke" type arrangement—a regime where one country has a bilateral FTA with both its trading partners who in turn do *not* have an FTA with each other—fails to be a stable equilibrium under symmetry.

Given the importance of the topic, it is no surprise that there exists a large literature on PTAs. In what follows, we only discuss closely related papers and refer the reader to Bhagwati et al. (1999) for a collection of some of the important contributions in the area. Our conceptual approach is most closely related to that of Aghion et al. (2007) who examine a leading country's choice between sequential and multilateral bargaining of FTAs. Like us, Aghion et al. (2007) also identify building and stumbling block effects of an FTA. However, there are important differences between their approach and ours. First, in our model, a country can form a pair of bilateral FTAs, whereas in their model it has to either join a single grand coalition or stay out. Second, unlike them but like Grossman and Helpman (1995), we do not allow transfers between different coalitions.

This paper also shares some key elements with Krishna (1998), Goyal and Joshi (2006), Aghion et al. (2007), and Furusawa and Konishi (2007). Both Goyal and Joshi (2006) and Furusawa and Konishi (2007) apply the network formation game of Jackson and Wolinsky (1996) to examine whether or not a given trade configuration is pairwise stable. Under symmetry, they find that the continued formation of bilateral FTAs leads to global free trade. However, while they examine whether or not the formation of bilateral trade agreements leads to global free trade, they do not isolate the implications of restricting discriminatory (or purely bilateral) free trade agreements—something that is central to our paper.

Using a three-country version of the Brander–Krugman model (also utilized by us), Krishna (1998) has shown that the formation of an FTA between two countries reduces their incentives to liberalize trade with respect to the third country. However, in a model with endogenous tariffs, Ornelas (2005a) has shown that an FTA induces member countries to lower their tariffs on the nonmember country which in turn reduces its incentive to participate in multilateral trade liberalization. Unlike us, Krishna (1998) and Ornelas (2005a) do not build an equilibrium theory of FTAs and only consider the effects of a single FTA.[3]

2. The Model

There are three countries (a, b, c) and two goods: x and y. Preferences over the two goods are quasilinear: $U(x, y) = u(x) + y$. Good x is produced by a single profit-maximizing firm in each country at a constant marginal cost in terms of the numéraire good y. Firms compete in quantities and markets are segmented, as in Brander and Krugman (1983).

Production and Trade

Due to market segmentation, it is sufficient to focus on a single market. The status quo is a scenario where the WTO's core rule of nondiscrimination—i.e. the most favored nation (MFN) clause—is in place and each country imposes a nondiscriminatory tariff t on its trading partners.[4] Furthermore, in accordance with the major WTO rule governing the formation of PTAs (i.e. GATT Article XXIV), we assume that FTA member countries eliminate tariffs on each other and retain their respective status quo tariffs on the nonmember.[5]

Firm j's effective marginal cost of exporting equals $\zeta_j + t$, where $\zeta_j \geq 0$ equals its marginal cost of production for good x. By assumption, countries impose no taxes on local firms and the numéraire good is freely traded in order to balance trade.

Let x_{ji} denote country j's exports to country i; x_{ii} the sales of firm i in country i; and $x_i = x_{ii} + \sum_j x_{ji}$ denote total sales of good x in country i. Country j's profit function for exports to country i, denoted by Π_{ji}, can be written as:

$$\Pi_{ji} = [p_i(x_i) - \zeta_j - t]x_{ji}. \tag{1}$$

First-order conditions (FOCs) for profit maximization for exporters are

$$p_i + p_i' x_{ji} = \zeta_i + t. \tag{2}$$

The above FOCs together with an analogous condition for the local firm (i.e. $p_i + p_i' x_{ii} = \zeta_i$) determine the equilibrium output levels of all firms. Summing the FOCs for all firms in country i gives

$$3p_i + p_i' x_i = 2t + \sum_z \zeta_z, \quad \text{where } z = a, b, c. \tag{3}$$

If the left-hand side is decreasing in x_i (i.e. $4p_i' + p_i'' x_i < 0$) then total industry output sold in country i depends only on the sum of the (tariff included) marginal costs of production of all firms. Assume this property holds so that we have:

$$\frac{dx_i}{dt} < 0. \tag{4}$$

In addition, the following comparative statics are also assumed to hold:[6]

$$\frac{dx_{ji}}{dt} < 0 < \frac{dx_{ii}}{dt}. \tag{5}$$

In other words, an increase in the tariff rate (t) lowers country j's exports to country i (x_{ji}) while it increases the sales of its local firm (x_{ii}).

Welfare of country i is defined as the sum of its domestic surplus and total export profits:

$$W_i \equiv S_i + \sum_{j \neq i} \Pi_{ij}, \tag{6}$$

where domestic surplus S_i is defined as

$$S_i \equiv u(x_i) - p_i x_i + \Pi_{ii} + t \sum_j x_{ji}, \tag{7}$$

where $u(x_i) - p_i x_i$ is consumer surplus in country i; $\Pi_{ii} = (p_i - \zeta_i) x_{ii}$ equals firm i's profits in its own market; $t \sum_j x_{ji}$ equals country i's tariff revenue; and $\Pi_{ij} = (p_i - \zeta_i - t) x_{ij}$ its profits in foreign market j, where $j \neq i$. World welfare is defined as the sum of the welfare of individual countries:

$$WW = W_i + W_j + W_k. \tag{8}$$

Since the formation of FTAs results in the elimination of some of the tariffs, in what follows in functions $S(\cdot)$ and $W(\cdot)$ we list the tariffs faced by foreign countries in ascending alphabetical order. Also, in the export profit function $\Pi_{ij}(\cdot)$, the first argument is the tariff faced by country i while the second argument is the tariff faced by its rival exporter (i.e. country k).

As is well known from the work of Brander and Spencer (1984), under fairly general conditions, each country has a unilateral incentive to impose rent-extracting tariffs on its trading partners unless it commits not to do so via an FTA. Accordingly, we assume that the following holds:

Assumption 1. $S_i(t, t) > \max\{S_i(0, t), S_i(t, 0)\} > S_i(0, 0)$.

This assumption says that domestic surplus of each country is highest under the status quo and lowest when it practices free trade.

Let $\mathcal{T}$ be the set of all feasible trade policy regimes:

$$\mathcal{T} = \{\langle\Phi\rangle, \langle ab\rangle, \langle ac\rangle, \langle bc\rangle, \langle ab, ac\rangle, \langle ab, bc\rangle, \langle ac, bc\rangle, \text{or } \langle F\rangle\},$$

where $\langle\Phi\rangle$ denotes the status quo and $\langle F\rangle$ denotes global free trade. Let r and v be any two elements of $\mathcal{T}$. Further, let $w_i(r)$ denote country i's welfare and $ww(r)$ denote world welfare under regime r. Note that lower-case letters denote functions of trade regimes whereas upper-case letters denote functions of tariffs that prevail during those regimes. For example, country i's welfare under the FTA $\langle ij\rangle$ can be written either as $w_i(ij)$ or as $W_i(0, t)$. Similar notation applies to domestic surplus and export profit functions.

Define $\Delta w_i(r - v)$ as the difference between country i's welfare under regimes r and v:

$$\Delta w_i(r-v) \equiv w_i(r) - w_i(v). \tag{9}$$

As is well known, under Cournot competition, the higher a country's cost of producing good x, the smaller its volume of exports and the larger its volume of imports of good x. Given this, intuition suggests that an FTA is more likely to obtain when trade between potential partners is relatively balanced. This intuition motivates the following assumption:

ASSUMPTION 2.

$$\frac{\partial \Delta w_i(r-v)}{\partial \zeta_i} \leq 0 \leq \frac{\partial \Delta w_i(r-v)}{\partial \zeta_m}$$

where m is an FTA partner of country i under regime r (but not regime v).

To get further insight behind Assumption 2, consider regimes $\langle\Phi\rangle$ and $\langle ij\rangle$ from country i's perspective. The idea underlying $\partial \Delta w_i(ij - \Phi)/\partial \zeta_i \leq 0$ is as follows. Because of their larger volume of imports, higher-cost countries have relatively *more to gain* from using tariffs. Similarly, due to the smaller volume of their exports, higher-cost countries have *less to lose* from other countries' tariffs. As a result, a country's willingness to enter into a bilateral FTA with another ought to depend negatively on its own cost.

A similar intuition underlies $\partial \Delta w_i(ij - \Phi)/\partial \zeta_j \geq 0$. The higher the production cost of its trading partner, the larger the increase in export profits enjoyed by a country due to the trade liberalization undertaken by its partner and the smaller the loss in local profits suffered by the domestic firm due to its own trade liberalization.

3. Endogenous Free-Trade Agreements

Consider the following two-stage game of bilateral trade liberalization (called the FTA game). In the first stage, individual country announcements determine which FTAs, if any, are formed. Next, given trade agreements and tariffs, firms compete in product markets.

The formation of FTAs proceeds as follows. Each country announces whether or not it wants to form an FTA with each of its trading partners (country i's announcement is denoted by α_i). A country's strategy set consists of four possible announcements. Country i's strategy set Ω_i^F is:

$$\Omega_i^F = \{\{\phi, \phi\}, \{j, \phi\}, \{\phi, k\}, \{j, k\}\}, \tag{10}$$

where $\{\phi, \phi\}$ is an announcement in favor of the status quo. In order to conserve notation, each trade policy regime is denoted as follows: (i) the status quo $\langle\Phi\rangle$ is maintained when no two announcements match or when everyone announces $\{\phi, \phi\}$; (ii) an FTA between countries i and j denoted by $\langle ij \rangle$ is formed when they both announce each other's name $j \in \alpha_i$ and $i \in \alpha_j$; (iii) two independent bilateral FTAs $\langle ij, ik \rangle$ in which i is the common member are formed when (1) $j \in \alpha_i$ and $i \in \alpha_j$ and (2) $k \in \alpha_i$ and $i \in \alpha_k$; and (iv) free trade $\langle F \rangle$ obtains when all countries announce each others' names: i.e. $\alpha_a = \{b, c\}$, $\alpha_b = \{a, c\}$, and $\alpha_c = \{a, b\}$.[7]

Our method of analysis is to compare the FTA game with the following game of multilateral trade liberalization (called the No FTA game). In the first stage of the No FTA game, each country announces either in favor of or against multilateral free trade. If all countries announce in favor, free trade emerges. If not, the status quo prevails. Next, firms compete in the product market. Clearly, the No FTA game restricts the strategy set of country i to $\Omega_i = \{\{\phi, \phi\}, \{j, k\}\}$, $j \neq k \neq i$. We compare the equilibria of these two games of trade liberalization to determine how the freedom to pursue bilateral FTAs affects the likelihood of obtaining global free trade.

As might be expected, both games admit multiple Nash equilibria. To deal with this multiplicity and to capture the process of FTA formation in a more realistic fashion, we focus attention on Nash equilibria that are immune to *self-enforcing* coalitional deviations, i.e. are coalition proof (or *stable*).[8] It is useful to note that in the No FTA game, a unilateral deviation from free trade by any country restores the status quo whereas in the FTA game the same deviation results in the deviating country becoming either (i) a nonmember country under an FTA between the other two countries or (ii) a spoke under a pair of bilateral FTAs. Since the welfare of a country under these trade policy regimes can be lower/higher than its welfare under the status quo, it is *not* immediately obvious under which game the unilateral incentive to deviate from free trade is stronger. Thus, even though the set of possible deviations from free trade under the No FTA game is a strict subset of those under the FTA game, it does *not* follow that free trade is more likely to be a stable equilibrium of the No FTA game.

4. Equilibrium FTAs under symmetry

Throughout this section, we assume that the cost of producing good x is equal across countries: $\zeta_i = \zeta$ for all i. It proves convenient to begin with the effects of FTAs on global welfare.

Trade Liberalization and Welfare

Following Brander and Spencer (1984), it is straightforward to show that under symmetry a reduction in *any* tariff(s) (whether on a preferential or a nondiscriminatory basis) increases aggregate world welfare. This implies the following:

LEMMA 1. *Under symmetry, free trade yields higher world welfare than any other trade policy regime:* $ww(F) > ww(ij, ik) > ww(ij) > ww(\Phi)$.

The intuition behind this result is simple: when all countries have the same cost of production, the allocation of output across countries is immaterial and any trade restrictions (whether preferential or multilateral) simply lower aggregate world output and therefore welfare. Since any tariff creates a deadweight loss, rent extraction by an importing country is more than offset by the loss in profits of exporters.

Nash Equilibria

It is clear that $\langle\Phi\rangle$ is a Nash equilibrium of the No FTA game since no country has a unilateral incentive to announce another country's name if the latter does not announce its name in return. Furthermore, symmetry implies that the welfare of all countries is equal under $\langle\Phi\rangle$. Clearly, the same is true under $\langle F\rangle$. Since world welfare is higher under $\langle F\rangle$ than under $\langle\Phi\rangle$ (Lemma 1), it follows that each country is better off under $\langle F\rangle$ than under $\langle\Phi\rangle$. As a result, under symmetry, no country has a unilateral incentive to deviate from free trade since *any* other announcement on its part leads to the status quo where it (and everyone else) is worse off:

$$w_i(\Phi) < w_i(F) \quad \text{for all } i. \tag{11}$$

PROPOSITION 1. *Under symmetry, the status quo and free trade are both Nash equilibria of the No FTA game.*

The following two conditions prove useful in describing the Nash equilibria of the FTA game:

CONDITION 1. $w_k(ij, ik) < w_k(ij)$.

That is, if Condition 1 holds, each country prefers to be a nonmember under a bilateral FTA to being a spoke under a pair of bilateral FTAs. Condition 1 can be understood as follows. The tariff reduction that country k receives from country i under $\langle ij, ik\rangle$ removes the disadvantage it faces relative to country j while exporting to country i's market under $\langle ij\rangle$. However, to achieve equal footing with country j in country i's market, country k has to grant preferential access to country i in its hitherto fully protected market. Thus, country k's preference among regimes $\langle ij\rangle$ and $\langle ij, ik\rangle$ is ambiguous in general.

CONDITION 2. $w_i(F) < w_i(ij)$.

That is, if Condition 2 holds, each country is better off as a member of a bilateral FTA relative to free trade—i.e. two countries find it beneficial to exclude the third if Condition 2 holds.

It is clear that $\langle\Phi\rangle$ is a Nash equilibrium of the FTA game. Is $\langle ij\rangle$ a Nash equilibrium too? Comparing country k's welfare under $\langle ij\rangle$ and $\langle\Phi\rangle$, we note that export profits of country k are higher under $\langle\Phi\rangle$ relative to $\langle ij\rangle$ whereas its domestic surplus under the two regimes is the same. Therefore, we have:

LEMMA 2. *An FTA between two countries makes the third country worse off relative to the status quo:*

$$w_k(ij) < w_k(\Phi). \tag{12}$$

Since world welfare is higher under $\langle ij\rangle$ relative to $\langle\Phi\rangle$, the above inequality implies that the sum of countries i and j's welfare must surely be higher under $\langle ij\rangle$:

$$w_i(ij) + w_j(ij) > w_i(\Phi) + w_j(\Phi). \tag{13}$$

Since countries i and j are symmetric, we must have

$$w_i(ij) = w_j(ij) > w_i(\Phi) = w_j(\Phi). \tag{14}$$

Hence, a member country of an FTA has no incentive to deviate to $\langle\Phi\rangle$ and $\langle ij\rangle$ is indeed a Nash equilibrium of the FTA game.

Is $\langle ij, ik\rangle$ a Nash equilibrium? Before addressing this question we note that

$$w_i(ij, ik) > w_i(F). \tag{15}$$

The logic behind this inequality is as follows. Starting at free trade, if country k revokes its FTA with country j, export profits of country i increase in both markets because its rival exporters face tariffs whereas it itself does not: $\Pi_{ij}(0,t) > \Pi_{ij}(0,0)$ and $\Pi_{ik}(0,t) > \Pi_{ik}(0,0)$. Furthermore, the domestic surplus of country i does not change relative to free trade since its own tariff equals zero under both regimes: $s_i(ij, ik) = s_i(F) = S_i(0, 0)$. As a result, country i's welfare under $\langle ij, ik\rangle$ is *higher* than that under $\langle F\rangle$.

Next, we assert that $w_j(ij, ik) < w_j(ij)$: the move from $\langle ij\rangle$ to $\langle ij, ik\rangle$ makes country j worse off since it loses its preferential status in country i's market. Also note from Lemma 1 that $ww(ij, ik) > ww(ij)$. As a result, either country i or country k or both of them are better off under $\langle ij, ik\rangle$ relative to $\langle ij\rangle$. Given the fact that the hub country's welfare under $\langle ij, ik\rangle$ exceeds even that under free trade (see (15)), we make the following assumption:

Assumption 3. *The welfare of a hub country is higher than that of an FTA member country:*

$$w_i(ij, ik) > w_i(ij) = w_i(ik). \tag{16}$$

We are now ready to investigate whether $\langle ij, ik\rangle$ is a Nash equilibrium. Three possible unilateral deviations from $\langle ij, ik\rangle$ need to be considered: (UP1)—country i's deviation from $\langle ij, ik\rangle$ to $\langle\Phi\rangle$; (UP2)—country i's deviation from $\langle ij, ik\rangle$ to $\langle ij\rangle$ or $\langle ik\rangle$; and (UP3)—country k's deviation from $\langle ij, ik\rangle$ to $\langle ij\rangle$. Deviation (UP1) can be ruled out because $w_i(ij, ik) > w_i(\Phi)$, while deviation (UP2) can be ruled out on the basis of Assumption 3. Finally, note that deviation (UP3) cannot occur if Condition 1 fails: $w_k(ij, ik) > w_k(ij)$. As a result, a pair of bilateral FTAs $\langle ij, ik\rangle$ is a Nash equilibrium if Condition 1 fails.

Is free trade also a Nash equilibrium of the FTA game? To be able to answer this question in the affirmative, we need to rule out the following two deviations: (UF1)—country k's deviation from $\langle F\rangle$ to $\langle ij\rangle$; and (UF2)—country k's deviation from $\langle F\rangle$ to $\langle ij, ik\rangle$ or $\langle ij, jk\rangle$. Inequalities (11) and (12) imply that deviation (UF1) cannot occur:

$$w_k(F) > w_k(\Phi) > w_k(ij). \tag{17}$$

Furthermore, deviation (UF2) can be ruled out due to the following result:

Lemma 3. *Under a pair of independent bilateral FTAs, each spoke country is worse off relative to free trade.*

The logic behind this result is as follows. Since world welfare is lower under $\langle ij, ik\rangle$ relative to $\langle F\rangle$ whereas the welfare of the hub country is higher (see inequality (15)), the sum of the welfare of the two spoke countries (i.e. j and k) must be *lower* than that under free trade. Since both are symmetric, it follows that both must be worse off under $\langle ij, ik\rangle$ relative to $\langle F\rangle$:

$$w_j(ij, ik) = w_k(ij, ik) < w_j(F) = w_k(F). \tag{18}$$

The following proposition summarizes the Nash equilibria of the FTA game:

PROPOSITION 2. *The status quo, a bilateral FTA, and free trade are all Nash equilibria of the FTA game under symmetry. In addition, if Condition 1 fails then a pair of bilateral FTAs is also a Nash equilibrium.*

Propositions 1 and 2 show that both games admit multiple Nash equilibria. To resolve this multiplicity and to capture the process of FTA formation in a richer fashion, we now focus attention on Nash equilibria that are immune to self-enforcing coalitional deviations (i.e. are coalition proof or *stable*).

Stable Nash Equilibria

We begin with the No FTA game. It is easy to see that $\langle\Phi\rangle$ is not a stable equilibrium of this game since all three countries have a joint incentive to deviate from $\langle\Phi\rangle$ to $\langle F\rangle$. This joint deviation from $\langle\Phi\rangle$ to $\langle F\rangle$ is self-enforcing since no single country (or a pair of countries) has an incentive to *further deviate* from $\langle F\rangle$—any deviation from $\langle F\rangle$ reverts the world back to status quo under which everyone is worse off. We have:

PROPOSITION 3. *Free trade is the unique stable equilibrium of the No FTA game under symmetry.*

We now turn to the FTA game and begin with $\langle\Phi\rangle$. Consider a member country's welfare under the FTA $\langle ij\rangle$ relative to $\langle\Phi\rangle$. It is immediate from (14) that countries i and j have an incentive to jointly deviate from $\langle\Phi\rangle$ to $\langle ij\rangle$. Furthermore, since $\langle ij\rangle$ is a Nash equilibrium of the FTA game (Proposition 2), there can be no unilateral deviations from it. As a result, the initial joint deviation of countries i and j from $\langle\Phi\rangle$ to $\langle ij\rangle$ is self-enforcing and $\langle\Phi\rangle$ is *not* stable.

Now consider $\langle ij, ik\rangle$ as a candidate for a stable Nash equilibrium. We know from inequality (18) that countries j and k benefit from a joint deviation from $\langle ij, ik\rangle$ to $\langle F\rangle$. Once again, this joint deviation is self-enforcing since $\langle F\rangle$ is a Nash equilibrium. As a result, a pair of bilateral FTAs $\langle ij, ik\rangle$ is also *not* stable.

Two candidates for stable equilibria remain: $\langle F\rangle$ and $\langle ij\rangle$. Consider free trade first. For free trade to be stable, we need to rule out three types of coalitional deviations by a pair of countries: (JF1)—deviation of i and j from $\langle F\rangle$ to $\langle\Phi\rangle$; (JF2)—deviation of j and k from $\langle F\rangle$ to $\langle ij, ik\rangle$; and (JF3)—deviation of i and j from $\langle F\rangle$ to $\langle ij\rangle$.

Since $w_i(F) > w_i(\Phi)$ the joint deviation (JF1) cannot occur. Similarly, since $w_j(ij, ik) < w_j(F)$ we can rule out deviation (JF2). Can deviation (JF3) be ruled out? Clearly, if country i is worse off under a bilateral FTA relative to free trade (i.e. Condition 2 fails) then deviation (JF3) cannot occur. Under such a scenario, $\langle F\rangle$ is immune to all coalitional (as well as unilateral) deviations and is in fact the *unique* stable equilibrium of the FTA game.

But what if countries i and j have an incentive to jointly deviate from $\langle F\rangle$ to $\langle ij\rangle$ (i.e. Condition 2 holds)? To determine whether this deviation is self-enforcing or not, we need to consider two further deviations from $\langle ij\rangle$: (FD1)—deviation of country i from $\langle ij\rangle$ to $\langle\Phi\rangle$; and (FD2)—deviation of country i from $\langle ij\rangle$ to $\langle ij, ik\rangle$.

It is immediate from Lemma 1 and inequality (14) that deviation (FD1) cannot occur. What about deviation (FD2)? From Assumption 3 we know that, taking country k's announcement as given, country i has an incentive to further deviate from $\langle ij \rangle$ to $\langle ij, ik \rangle$—i.e. deviation (FD2) *will indeed occur*. As a result, the initial joint deviation (JF3) is *not* self-enforcing. Thus, $\langle F \rangle$ is stable even when Condition 2 holds.

Can $\langle ij \rangle$ also be stable when Condition 2 holds? It turns out that the answer to this question depends on whether Condition 1 holds or not. First consider the case where Condition 1 fails—i.e. countries i and k have a joint incentive to deviate from $\langle ij \rangle$ to $\langle ij, ik \rangle$. We know from Proposition 2 that $\langle ij, ik \rangle$ is a Nash equilibrium when Condition 1 fails. Therefore, when Condition 1 fails the initial deviation of countries i and k from $\langle ij \rangle$ to $\langle ij, ik \rangle$ is self-enforcing. As a result, if Condition 2 holds and Condition 1 fails, $\langle ij \rangle$ is *not* stable. Now consider the case where Condition 1 holds. First, since Condition 2 holds, there exists no incentive for all countries to multilaterally deviate from $\langle ij \rangle$ to $\langle F \rangle$. Second, since Condition 1 holds, countries i and k have no joint incentive to deviate from $\langle ij \rangle$ to $\langle ij, ik \rangle$. Finally, since Condition 2 holds, inequality (18) implies that country i has no incentive to jointly deviate with countries j and k from $\langle ij \rangle$ to $\langle ij, ik \rangle$ (or $\langle ik, jk \rangle$). As a result, $\langle ij \rangle$ is stable if both Condition 1 and Condition 2 hold. We summarize as follows:

Proposition 4. *Under symmetry, free trade is a stable Nash equilibrium of the FTA game and it is uniquely stable if either Condition 1 or Condition 2 fail. A bilateral FTA is a stable Nash if both Condition 1 and Condition 2 hold. Finally, the status quo and a pair of bilateral FTAs are not stable Nash equilibria.*

The above proposition clarifies that under symmetry FTAs end up acting as *weak stumbling blocks*: while free trade is uniquely stable under the No FTA game, there exist conditions under which a bilateral FTA is also stable under the FTA game. Yet, this is not a particularly strong indictment of FTAs—while free trade loses its uniqueness, it still continues to be a stable equilibrium.

Given these results, it is natural to ask whether a different role for FTAs might emerge when countries are not necessarily symmetric (say, with respect to their costs of production of good x). For example, is it possible that in the absence of symmetry, two countries are willing to enter into a bilateral FTA but unwilling to engage in multilateral free trade? Even more interestingly, can the option to form bilateral FTAs facilitate the obtainment of multilateral free trade? We now turn to these questions.

5. FTAs among Asymmetric Countries

From hereon, we drop the assumption that the production cost of good x is equal across countries. It proves instructive to focus on the case where two countries have symmetric and low costs relative to the third. Accordingly, throughout the analysis under asymmetry, let $\zeta_a = \zeta_b = 0$ and $\zeta_c = \zeta > 0$. Note also that Lemma 1 requires a slight modification: trade liberalization necessarily improves world welfare under asymmetry as long as it is not biased against low-cost producers. In other words, we know the following:[9]

$$ww(F) > ww(ab, ac) > ww(ab) > \max\{ww(\Phi), ww(ac)\}. \quad (19)$$

Intuitively, a bilateral FTA between a low-cost and a high-cost country has two conflicting effects on world welfare. On the one hand, it increases world welfare by raising the aggregate output of good x. On the other hand, it diverts production away from a low-cost source to a high-cost one, and this adverse allocation effect harms world welfare. It is easy to show that as long as the asymmetry between countries is not too high, an FTA between a high- and low-cost country also increases world welfare since the allocation distortion is mild in such circumstances.

We begin with the No FTA game and first show that under cost asymmetry global free trade may fail to obtain even when countries are not free to form bilateral FTAs.

Feasibility of Free Trade

Consider the perspective of the two low-cost countries (denoted by $i = a, b$). From Proposition 1 we know that under symmetry, the welfare of each low-cost country under $\langle F \rangle$ is higher than that under $\langle \Phi \rangle$:

$$\lim_{\zeta \to 0} \Delta w_i(F - \Phi) > 0 \quad \text{for } i = a, b. \tag{20}$$

Assumption 2 implies:

$$\frac{\partial \Delta w_i(F - \Phi)}{\partial \zeta} > 0 \quad \text{for } i = a, b, \tag{21}$$

i.e. the higher the cost of country k, the larger the gains of multilateral trade liberalization for the low-cost countries.

Inequalities (20) and (21) together imply that the two low-cost countries have no incentive (joint or unilateral) to deviate from free trade to the status quo:

$$w_i(F) > w_i(\Phi) \quad \text{for } i = a, b. \tag{22}$$

Next, consider the high-cost country's (i.e. c's) perspective. Define ζ^p to be the prohibitive cost level at which the export profits of country c under free trade equal zero in each foreign market:

$$\lim_{\zeta \to \zeta^P} \pi_{ca}(F) = \lim_{\zeta \to \zeta^P} \pi_{cb}(F) = 0. \tag{23}$$

Since domestic surplus of each country is higher under $\langle \Phi \rangle$ than under $\langle F \rangle$ the following is immediate:

$$\lim_{\zeta \to \zeta^P} \Delta w_c(\Phi - F) > 0 \quad \text{since } s_c(\Phi) > s_c(F). \tag{24}$$

Inequalities (20), (24), and Assumption 2 imply that there exists a critical threshold cost level (ζ^ϕ) such that:

$$w_c(\Phi) \geq w_c(F) \quad \text{iff } \zeta \geq \zeta^\phi. \tag{25}$$

Intuitively, opening up its market is unattractive to the high-cost country when it stands to gain very little (or nothing) from foreign trade liberalization. Thus, we have:

PROPOSITION 5. *Free trade is the unique stable equilibrium of the No FTA game whenever $\zeta < \zeta^\phi$.*[10]

When $\zeta > \zeta^\phi$, the status quo obtains as the unique stable equilibrium since country c is sufficiently high cost relative to the others. Recall from Proposition 3 that, under symmetry, free trade is uniquely stable under the No FTA game and when such is the case, FTAs can only act as stumbling blocks. Is this also true when countries are asymmetric? We now show that this is *not* so.

FTAs as Strong Building Blocks

In this subsection we show that the option to form bilateral FTAs can serve as *strong building blocks*—there exist circumstances where free trade is a stable equilibrium of the FTA game but not of the No FTA game. Intuitively, this result obtains since the high-cost country prefers the status quo to free trade which in turn it prefers to a bilateral FTA between the other two countries: $w_c(\Phi) > w_c(F) > w_c(ab)$. The key point is that under a purely multilateral approach, the high-cost country can preserve the status quo by voting against free trade, whereas it cannot do so when bilateral FTAs are permitted. As a result, in the FTA game it can end up calling in favor of free trade in order to avoid a situation where it is a nonmember facing an FTA between the other two countries. Before showing this, we state a preliminary result:[11]

PROPOSITION 6. *There exist no unilateral or self-enforcing joint deviations involving the two low-cost countries from free trade.*

Given this result, it is clear that the viability of free trade depends critically upon the preferences of the high-cost country. Following the definition of ζ^{ϕ} (in (25)) let ζ^{γ} define the critical threshold cost level below which the high-cost country prefers free trade to regime r:

$$w_c(F) \geq w_c(r) \quad \text{iff } \zeta \leq \zeta^{r}, \tag{26}$$

where $r = \{\langle\Phi\rangle, \langle ab\rangle, \langle ac\rangle, \langle bc\rangle, \langle ab, ac\rangle, \text{or } \langle ab, bc\rangle\}$. Arguments analogous to those that underlie the existence of ζ^{ϕ} ensure that these critical cost thresholds also exist for the other trade policy regimes.[12]

We know from (12) that the high-cost country always prefers $\langle\Phi\rangle$ to being a nonmember facing $\langle ab\rangle$: $w_c(\Phi) > w_c(ab)$. This is because its export profits are always higher under $\langle\Phi\rangle$ relative to $\langle ab\rangle$ while its domestic surplus under the two regimes is the same. As a result, we must have $\Delta w_c(\Phi - F) > \Delta w_c(ab - F)$ which implies that the critical cost threshold (ζ^{ϕ}) at which $\Delta w_c(\Phi - F) = 0$ is smaller than the one (ζ^{ab}) where $\Delta w_c(ab - F) = 0$:

LEMMA 4. $\zeta^{\phi} < \zeta^{ab}$.

Similarly, by definition, the high-cost country has an incentive to unilaterally deviate from $\langle F\rangle$ to $\langle ab, ac\rangle$ iff $\zeta > \zeta^{ab,ac}$. Before proceeding further, it is convenient to write down a condition analogous to Condition 1:

CONDITION 1A. $w_c(ab, ac) < w_c(ab)$.

Note that Condition 1A is equivalent to $\zeta^{ab} < \zeta^{ab,ac}$ and if it holds then $\langle ab, ac\rangle$ cannot be an equilibrium since country c prefers being a nonmember to being a spoke. We can now state:

PROPOSITION 7. *Suppose Condition 1A holds. If* $\zeta \leq \zeta^{ab}$ *then free trade is a stable equilibrium of the FTA game; otherwise the bilateral FTA* $\langle ab\rangle$ *is stable.*

Propositions 5 and 7 together imply the following:

Corollary 1. *If Condition 1A holds, FTAs act as strong building blocks whenever* $\zeta^{\phi} < \zeta < \zeta^{ab}$.

The above result hinges on the insight that when free trade is not feasible due to the reluctance of the high-cost country, the fact that the low-cost countries are free to form a bilateral FTA can make the high-cost country a more willing participant in global free trade since such an FTA is worse from its perspective than free trade. It is worth noting here that Baldwin (1995) argued that the expansion of a regional trade bloc can induce outsiders to join since their export profits suffer if they stay outside. In our model, a similar logic operates but there are several important differences. First, our logic does not rely on the presence of economies of scale. Second, the formation of FTAs is fully endogenous in our approach. Third, and more importantly, our model highlights the fact that under a purely multilateral approach, a country that is reluctant to liberalize can effectively prevent liberalization between its trading partners and the removal of such "veto power" may sometimes be necessary to achieve global free trade.

When $\zeta > \zeta^{ab}$ free trade is not feasible under either game. However, the second statement of Proposition 7 implies that there is still a sense in which the freedom to pursue bilateral FTAs proves beneficial. More specifically, the option to form FTAs can lead to welfare-improving trade liberalization that is ruled out by the No FTA game: when $\zeta > \zeta^{ab}$, the FTA game yields $\langle ab \rangle$, whereas the No FTA game yields $\langle \Phi \rangle$. Under such circumstances, we say that FTAs act as *partial building blocks*—the option to pursue bilateral FTAs delivers partial trade liberalization, whereas the multilateral approach delivers none. The policy implication here is that insisting only on multilateral trade liberalization can sometimes run the risk of ending up with no trade liberalization.

What happens when Condition 1A fails? If so, country c prefers $\langle ab, ac \rangle$ to $\langle ab \rangle$ and the equilibrium outcome depends on how it ranks $\langle ab, ac \rangle$ and $\langle \Phi \rangle$:

Proposition 8. *Suppose Condition 1A fails. If* $\zeta \leq \zeta^{ab,ac}$ *then free trade is a stable equilibrium of the FTA game; otherwise, the hub-and-spoke arrangement* $\langle ab, ac \rangle$ *is stable.*

Propositions 5 and 8 imply the following:

Corollary 2. *If Condition 1A fails, FTAs act as strong building blocks when* $\zeta^{\phi} < \zeta < \zeta^{ab,ac}$ *and they act as partial building blocks when* $\zeta^{ab,ac} < \zeta$.

However, we should note that when Condition 1A fails, FTAs are not necessarily a force for the good. In particular, when $\zeta^{ab,ac} < \zeta < \zeta^{\phi}$ FTAs act as weak stumbling blocks because the hub-and-spoke arrangement $\langle ab, ac \rangle$ is stable under the FTA game while free trade is stable under the No FTA game. On other hand, even when Condition 1A fails, so long as the high-cost country prefers $\langle ab, ac \rangle$ to $\langle \Phi \rangle$, there is another sense in which FTAs act as partial building blocks—the FTA game delivers $\langle ab, ac \rangle$, whereas the No FTA game yields $\langle \Phi \rangle$.

We next provide a graphical illustration of our main results under asymmetry using linear demand.

6. A Linear Demand Illustration

Suppose $u(x_i) = x_i - (x_i^2/2) + y$ so that $p_i(x_i) = 1 - x_i$. To ensure that the high-cost firm has positive sales in all markets under all trade regimes, we need $\zeta < \bar{\zeta} = \frac{1}{3} - t$: this boundary defines the feasible parameter space in all figures.

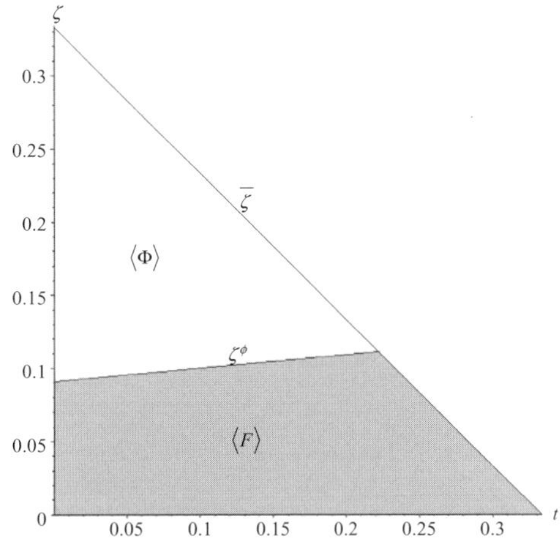

Figure 1. Stable Agreements under the No FTA Game

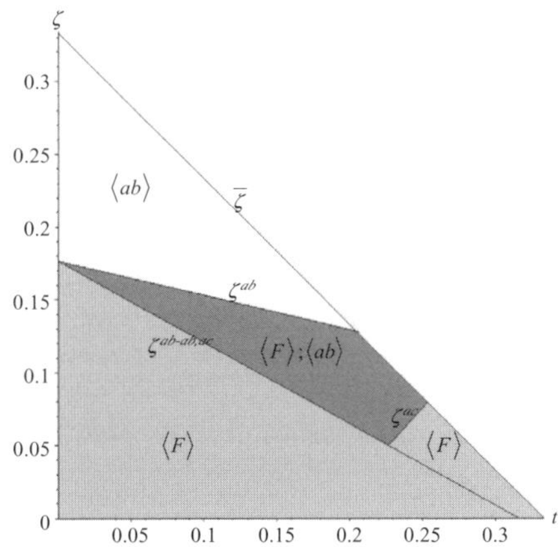

Figure 2. Stable Agreements under the FTA Game

We now illustrate stable agreements under the two games of trade liberalization. As is clear from Figure 1, free trade is stable under the No FTA game when $\zeta \le \zeta^{\phi} = (1 + t)/11$.

Figure 2 illustrates stable agreements under the FTA game. In Figure 2, free trade is stable under the FTA game when $\zeta \le \zeta^{ab} = (3 - 4t)/17$. Multiple stable equilibria arise over the darker region: both $\langle ab \rangle$ and $\langle F \rangle$ are stable. Straightforward calculations yield the relevant boundaries illustrated in Figure 2:

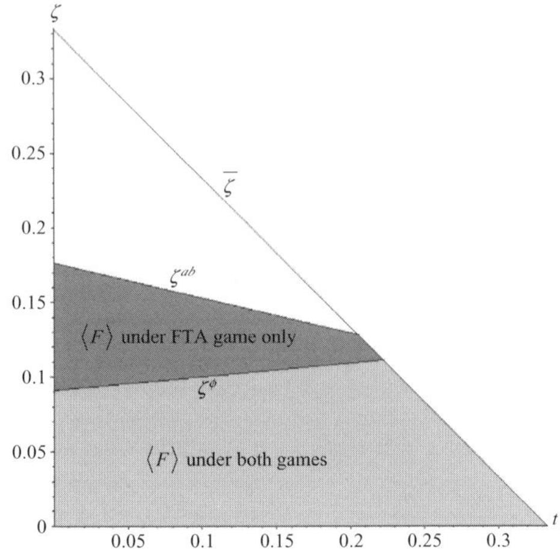

Figure 3. FTAs as Strong Building Blocks

$$\zeta^{ac} = \frac{11t-2}{10} \quad \text{and} \quad \zeta^{ab-ab,ac} = \frac{6-19t}{34}. \tag{27}$$

Figures 1 and 2 together imply that free trade is stable when production technologies are relatively similar across countries. Furthermore, Figure 2 shows that when country c is sufficiently high-cost FTAs act as partial building blocks: multilateral free trade is infeasible and $\langle \Phi \rangle$ obtains under the No FTA game, whereas $\langle ab \rangle$ emerges under the FTA game. When there exist multiple stable equilibria, there are two distinct scenarios to be considered. In scenario I, we assume that over the darker region in Figure 2, free trade is stable, whereas in scenario II the bilateral FTA $\langle ab \rangle$ is stable. We consider each in turn.

Under scenario I, Figure 3 shows that free trade is stable over a much *larger* region under the FTA game. Since the high-cost country prefers $\langle \Phi \rangle$ to $\langle ab \rangle$, its incentive to unilaterally deviate from free trade is greater under the No FTA game relative to the FTA game. As a result, FTAs act as strong building blocks when $\zeta^{\phi} < \zeta < \zeta^{ab}$. It is worth emphasizing that this result obtains when the cost disadvantage of country c is of an intermediate magnitude. If country c is too high cost, it loses too little in export markets from the preferential trade liberalization that occurs between countries a and b and for domestic surplus considerations it prefers to retain its own tariffs. Similarly, when its cost is quite low it prefers to form FTAs with both its trading partners.

Now consider scenario II where $\langle ab \rangle$ rather than $\langle F \rangle$ obtains as the stable agreement over the darker region of Figure 2. A comparison of the two trade liberalization games under scenario II is presented in Figure 4.

Under scenario II, we highlight three different regions in Figure 4. In region A, $\langle F \rangle$ is a stable agreement of the No FTA game, whereas $\langle ab \rangle$ obtains under the FTA game. As a result, in region A, FTAs act as stumbling blocks for multilateral trade liberalization. However, even under scenario II, FTAs continue to act as building blocks: in region B of Figure 4, they act as strong building blocks, whereas in region C they act as partial

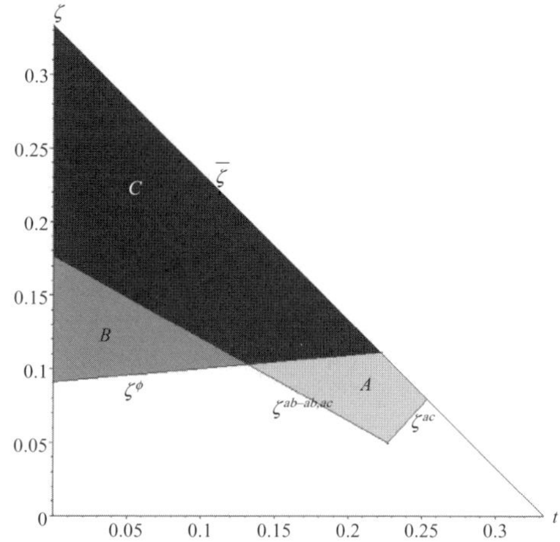

Figure 4. Building and Stumbling Blocks

building blocks (since the bilateral FTA ⟨*ab*⟩ obtains under the FTA game, whereas ⟨Φ⟩ obtains under the No FTA game). How does the option to pursue FTAs affect the welfare of individual countries and that of the world as a whole?

Proposition 9. *Under linear demand, the following obtains: (i) when FTAs act as building blocks (strong or partial), the option to form bilateral FTAs benefits low-cost countries (as well as the world as a whole), whereas it hurts the high-cost country; (ii) when FTAs act as stumbling blocks, all countries lose from being able to form bilateral FTAs.*

Why does the high-cost country lose when FTAs act as building blocks? To see why, first note that, for all $t > 0$, the high-cost country always prefers the status quo to the bilateral FTA ⟨*ab*⟩. Thus when FTAs act as partial building blocks, they necessarily make the high-cost country worse off. Recall that FTAs act as strong building blocks only when $w_c(\Phi) > w_c(F) > w_c(ab)$. So here too the high-cost country loses from the option to form FTAs. Finally, note that when FTAs act as stumbling blocks (as in scenario II), all countries are willing to jointly deviate from ⟨*ab*⟩ to ⟨*F*⟩. However, due to the incentives of countries *a* and *c* to further deviate from ⟨*F*⟩ to ⟨*ac*⟩, the bilateral FTA ⟨*ab*⟩ obtains as a stable equilibrium.

7. Concluding Remarks

Our analysis sharpens the stumbling versus building block debate regarding FTAs by highlighting conditions under which each of the two effects is likely to obtain. More specifically, when countries are relatively symmetric, the option to pursue FTAs might hinder the attainment of global free trade in the sense that free trade is no longer uniquely stable when FTAs are permitted. On the other hand, free trade is harder to sustain under asymmetry and FTAs can actually be desirable from a world welfare perspective. In fact, *we show that there exist circumstances where multilateral free trade obtains as an equilibrium only if countries are free to form bilateral FTAs.* We also find that FTAs can deliver welfare-improving trade liberalization when multilateral free trade is infeasible. Another interesting result of the paper is that a hub-and-spoke-type trading regime is not a stable equilibrium under symmetry.

To allow for greater richness in the modeling of FTA formation, we have kept the underlying model of intraindustry trade as simple as possible. It is important to determine whether our approach to FTA formation can be fruitfully applied to general-equilibrium models of inter- and intraindustry trade (such as the Ricardian model of comparative advantage and the monopolistic competition model of trade in differentiated goods). We leave this for future research.

References

Aghion, Philippe, Pol Antràs, and Elhanan Helpman, "Negotiating Free Trade," *Journal of International Economics* 73 (2007):1–30.

Bagwell, Kyle and Robert W. Staiger, "Multilateral Tariff Cooperation during the Formation of Free Trade Areas," *International Economic Review* 38 (1997):291–319.

Baldwin, Richard, "A Domino Theory of Regionalism," in R. Baldwin, P. Haaparanta, and J. Kiander (eds), *Expanding European Regionalism: The EU's New Members*, Cambridge: Cambridge University Press (1995):25–48.

Bernheim, Douglas B., Bezalel Peleg, and Michael Whinston, "Coalition-Proof Nash Equilibria I. Concepts," *Journal of Economic Theory* 42 (1987):1–12.

Bhagwati, Jagdish, *The World Trading System at Risk*, Princeton, NJ: Princeton University Press (1991).

Bhagwati, Jagdish, Arvind Panagariya, and Pravin Krishna (eds), *Trading Blocs*, Cambridge, MA: MIT Press (1999).

Bond, Eric, Raymond Riezman, and Constantinos Syropoulos, "A Strategic and Welfare Theoretic Analysis of Free Trade Areas," *Journal of International Economics* 64 (2004):1–27.

Brander, James and Paul Krugman, "A 'Reciprocal Dumping' Model of International Trade," *Journal of International Economics* 15 (1983):313–23.

Brander, James and Barbara Spencer, "Tariff Protection and Imperfect Competition," in H. Kierzkowski (ed.), *Monopolistic Competition and International Trade*, Oxford: Oxford University Press (1984):107–19.

Dutta, Bhaskar and Suresh Mutuswami, "Stable Networks," *Journal of Economic Theory* 76 (1997):322–44.

Furusawa, Taiji and Hideo Konishi, "Free Trade Networks," *Journal of International Economics* 72 (2007):310–35.

Goyal, Sanjeev and Sumit Joshi, "Bilateralism and Free Trade," *International Economic Review* 47 (2006):749–78.

Grossman, Gene and Elhanan Helpman, "The Politics of Free-Trade Agreements," *American Economic Review* 85 (1995):667–90.

Jackson, Matthew and Asher Wolinsky, "A Strategic Model of Social and Economic Networks," *Journal of Economic Theory* 71 (1996):44–74.

Krishna, Pravin, "Regionalism and Multilateralism: A Political Economy Approach," *Quarterly Journal of Economics* 113 (1998):227–51.

Levy, Philip, "A Political-Economic Analysis of Free Trade Agreements," *American Economic Review* 87 (1997):506–19.

Ornelas, Emanuel, "Trade Creating Free Trade Areas and the Undermining of Multilateralism," *European Economic Review* 49 (2005a):1717–35.

———, "Rent Destruction and the Political Viability of Free Trade Agreements," *Quarterly Journal of Economics* 120 (2005b):1475–506.

Qiu, Larry, "Lobbying, Multisector Trade and Sustainability of Free Trade Agreement," *Canadian Journal of Economics* 37 (2004):1061–83.
Saggi, Kamal and Halis Murat Yildiz, "Bilateralism, Multilateralism, and the Quest for Global Free Trade," *Journal of International Economics* 81 (2010):26–37.
Yi, Sang-Seung, "Endogenous Formation of Customs Unions under Imperfect Competition: Open Regionalism is Good," *Journal of International Economics* 41 (1996):153–77.

Notes

1. In Saggi and Yildiz (2010), we obtain similar results in a competing exporters model of trade wherein all goods markets are perfectly competitive and internationally integrated.
2. Our terminology follows Dutta and Mutuswami (1997).
3. Grossman and Helpman (1995), Levy (1997), Qiu (2004), and Ornelas (2005b) provide analyses of political economy considerations that arise in the context of FTAs. For simplicity, we abstract from these considerations and assume that governments maximize national welfare.
4. In an environment where countries are fully symmetric, it is reasonable to take the status quo to be a situation where MFN tariffs are equal across countries. However, when countries are asymmetric, MFN tariffs could differ across countries and this assumption is on weaker grounds but we retain it for reasons of tractability. Nevertheless, in our oligopoly model, what matters is the tariff-included marginal cost of exporting to a foreign market. We expect our analysis of asymmetric countries in section 6 to go through with minor modifications if countries were symmetric with respect to production costs but asymmetric with respect to tariffs.
5. Of course, Article XXIV does not prevent FTA members from *lowering* their tariffs on nonmembers, something that is not allowed by our model. Indeed, the lowering of tariffs by FTA members on nonmembers is a feature of many existing models of FTAs—see, for example, Bagwell and Staiger (1997) and Bond et al. (2004).
6. As is well known, assuming second-order conditions for profit maximization hold, these comparative statics obtain when the Cournot–Nash equilibrium is stable and output levels of firms are strategic substitutes.
7. Under our approach, the formation of a bilateral FTA requires consent from both sides. This is in contrast to the open membership rule analyzed by Yi (1996) where existing members cannot prevent others from joining.
8. See Bernheim et al. (1987) for the formal definition of a coalition-proof Nash equilibrium.
9. Note that $ww(ab, ac) = ww(ab, bc)$ and $ww(ac) = ww(bc)$.
10. When $\zeta = \zeta^{\phi}$, both no agreement and free trade are stable. An analogous statement applies to the remainder of the propositions under asymmetry.
11. To conserve space, we omit the proofs of Propositions 6, 7, and 8. These proofs are available upon request.
12. Note that the threshold ζ^{ac} (similarly ζ^{bc}) exists only when $w_c(ac) < w_c(F)$ under symmetry. Otherwise, it is immediate from assumption A2 that $w_c(ac) > w_c(F)$ for all ζ.

CHAPTER 9

American Economic Journal: Microeconomics 2013, 5(1): 63–99
http://dx.doi.org/10.1257/mic.5.1.63

On the Relationship between Preferential and Multilateral Trade Liberalization: The Case of Customs Unions†

By Kamal Saggi, Alan Woodland, and Halis Murat Yildiz*

This paper compares equilibrium outcomes of two games of trade liberalization. In the Bilateralism game, countries choose whether to liberalize trade preferentially via a customs union (CU), multilaterally, or not at all. The Multilateralism game is a restricted version of the Bilateralism game in that countries cannot form CUs and can only undertake non-discriminatory trade liberalization. When countries have symmetric endowments, global free trade is the only stable equilibrium of both games. Allowing for endowment asymmetry, we isolate circumstances where the option to form CUs helps further the cause of multilateral liberalization as well as where it does not. (*JEL* F12, F13)

The General Agreement on Tariffs and Trade (GATT) permits member countries of the World Trade Organization (WTO) to form preferential trade agreements (PTAs) such as free trade agreements (FTAs) and customs unions (CUs), under which PTA members can grant tariff reductions to each other that they do not extend to other WTO members. This freedom is provided under Article XXIV of GATT, and empirical evidence indicates that WTO members have made rather liberal use of it: as per the WTO's official website, as of January 2012, the WTO had received notification of 511 such arrangements, of which 370 were notified under Article XXIV.[1] While FTAs constitute an overwhelming majority of PTAs, the existing CUs involve some of the major economies of the world: for example, the Latin American customs union Mercosur counts Argentina, Brazil, Paraguay, and Uruguay as its members, while the European Union (EU)—a CU that extends across both goods and services—comprises most major European economies. As a result, it is important to obtain a better understanding of the factors that give rise to CUs, and the effect CUs have on the multilateral trading system.

* Saggi: Department of Economics, Vanderbilt University, PMB 351828, 2301 Vanderbilt Place, Nashville, TN 37235-1828 (e-mail: k.saggi@vanderbilt.edu); Woodland: School of Economics, Australian School of Business, The University of New South Wales, NSW 2052, Australia (e-mail: a.woodland@unsw.edu.au); Yildiz: Department of Economics, Ryerson University, 350 Victoria Street, Toronto, ON, Canada M5B 2K3 (e-mail: hyildiz@ryerson.ca). Parts of this paper were written during Saggi's visit to the Stanford Center for International Development (SCID), Stanford University, Palo Alto, CA. Saggi is grateful to SCID researchers and its administrative staff for providing an excellent research environment. Woodland gratefully acknowledges the financial support for this research provided under a discovery grant from the Australian Research Council.

† To comment on this article in the online discussion forum, or to view additional materials, visit the article page at http://dx.doi.org/10.1257/mic.5.1.63.

[1] About 319 such agreements are already in force and Mongolia is the only WTO member that does not participate in any PTA. Most WTO members belong to multiple PTAs and one even observes major PTAs in discussion with each other regarding mutual liberalization.

The sanctioning of discriminatory trade agreements by GATT and the complicated web of global tariffs that has resulted from their pursuit by WTO member countries raises some uncomfortable questions about the nature of the multilateral trading system. Indeed, Article XXIV appears to be in direct conflict with the first and the most fundamental Article of GATT—i.e., the most favored nation (MFN) clause that forbids WTO members from pursuing discriminatory trade liberalization. Bhagwati (1991) has argued quite forcefully that PTAs are fundamentally incompatible with the WTO's stated goal of multilateral trade liberalization, and many observers have wondered whether the multilateral trading system would function more effectively if the GATT allowed no exceptions to non-discriminatory trade liberalization.

While GATT sanctions PTAs, it does so only under certain conditions. In particular, Article XXIV requires that (i) a PTA should cover "substantially all trade" between members; (ii) a PTA should result in significant trade liberalization among members almost to the point that it leads to free trade amongst them; and (iii) that PTA members not raise tariffs on nonmembers—a condition that appears to be an attempt to safeguard the interests of those left outside such discriminatory trade agreements. Of course, these conditions do not succeed in fully protecting the interests of nonmembers. It is also not necessarily the case that PTAs satisfying these requirements are consistent with multilateral trade liberalization.

The goal of this paper is to isolate the consequences of the *option* to pursue bilateral/discriminatory trade liberalization in the form of CUs for the ultimate objective of achieving multilateral free trade. To this end, we derive and compare the stable (or coalition proof) Nash equilibria of two games of trade liberalization between three countries with potentially asymmetric endowments. Under the first game (called *Bilateralism*), countries are free to liberalize trade bilaterally, multilaterally, or not at all. The bilateral option takes the form of a CU under which members eliminate tariffs on each other while imposing common external tariffs on the nonmember. Under the second game, countries must either liberalize multilaterally or not at all. This restricted game—called *Multilateralism*—is an attempt to capture a world without Article XXIV of GATT. By comparing equilibrium outcomes under Bilateralism with those under Multilateralism, we isolate the consequences of the exception to nondiscriminatory trade liberalization provided by GATT. The most attractive feature of our approach is that it endogenizes both the *nature* and the *degree* of trade liberalization—something that has been done rather infrequently in the rather vast literature on PTAs.[2]

Consistent with actual trade negotiations and the WTO's MFN principle, under our Multilateralism game a pair of countries undertaking reciprocal trade liberalization are required to extend their respective tariff reductions to the third country. We denote such an *MFN-consistent trade agreement* between countries i and j by $\langle ij\rangle^m$. By contrast, under a discriminatory CU $\langle ij\rangle$ members i and j impose their optimal external tariffs on the non-member country. In our model, the tariff implemented by a country as a participant in the MFN-consistent agreement $\langle ij\rangle^m$ is lower than its optimal external tariff as a member of the CU $\langle ij\rangle$. As a result, the non-participating

[2] See Bhagwati, Panagariya, and Krishna (1999) for a collection of important but somewhat dated papers in the area.

country (i.e., k) is worse off under the CU $\langle ij \rangle$ relative to the MFN-consistent agreement $\langle ij \rangle^m$ due to two separate reasons. First, it faces discriminatory tariffs in both export markets under $\langle ij \rangle$ whereas no such discrimination exists under $\langle ij \rangle^m$. Second, the external tariffs of countries i and j under $\langle ij \rangle$ are higher than those under $\langle ij \rangle^m$.

When countries are fully symmetric with respect to their endowments, we find that multilateral free trade emerges as the unique stable equilibrium under both Bilateralism and Multilateralism. In other words, under symmetry, a CU does not arise in equilibrium so that the option to discriminate available under Bilateralism simply goes unexercised. This result suggests that heterogeneity across countries is likely to be a crucial determinant of why WTO members sometimes end up preferring discriminatory trading arrangements to non-discriminatory ones. Indeed, we show that when endowments are asymmetric across countries, the option to form CUs has important ramifications for the types of agreements that emerge in equilibrium. Furthermore, the nature of underlying asymmetry plays a rather subtle role in determining the relationship between bilateral and multilateral trade liberalization.

We first examine a scenario where one country (called country s) has a relatively smaller endowment than the other two (called l and l'). Under such a pattern of asymmetry, we find that the option to form CUs can actually increase the likelihood of achieving global free trade. The intuition for this result is as follows: opting out of global free trade is relatively costlier for a country when it faces a discriminatory CU between the other two countries—as it does under Bilateralism—than when it faces an MFN-consistent agreement between them—as it does under Multilateralism. As a result, absent the threat of a discriminatory CU, the smaller country is less willing to liberalize multilaterally. However, if endowments are not too symmetric across countries, global free trade fails to arise under both Bilateralism and Multilateralism. If so, the equilibrium agreement reached under Multilateralism is welfare-superior to Bilateralism due to its non-discriminatory nature. An important practical implication of this result is that if global free trade is truly infeasible (i.e., cannot be reached under either Bilateralism or Multilateralism), then a purely multilateral approach to trade liberalization is preferable since it delivers a superior trade agreement.

When we consider a pattern of asymmetry where one country is relatively bigger (called l) than the other two (called s and s'), the argument in favor of Multilateralism becomes even stronger. First, even under this type of asymmetry, Multilateralism yields a superior trade agreement when free trade is infeasible under both games. Perhaps more interesting is the fact that, under this alternative pattern of asymmetry, global free trade arises over a larger parameter space under Multilateralism (i.e., when countries cannot form bilateral CUs). The intuition is that under Bilateralism each of the smaller countries has a joint incentive to exclude the larger country in order to impose optimal external tariffs on its relatively large volume of exports. This result lends support to the view that discriminatory trade agreements can end up supplanting multilateral liberalization.

In the existing literature on PTAs, perhaps the two most closely related papers to ours are Aghion, Antràs, and Helpman (2007) and Saggi and Yildiz (2010).[3] While

[3] In a recent paper, Seidmann (2009) develops a three-country bargaining model of trade negotiations in which bilateral agreements arise only if members gain more than outsiders and this alters the status quo in favor of PTA

Aghion, Antràs, and Helpman (2007) also provide a comparison of bilateral and multilateral liberalization, their approach is fundamentally different from ours. In particular, in their multilateral bargaining protocol countries must choose between global free trade and no agreement, whereas in our approach two countries can undertake reciprocal trade liberalization so long as each extends its respective tariff reduction to the third country on an MFN basis. This implies that in Aghion, Antràs, and Helpman (2007), by voting against free trade any country (say country k) can ensure that the status quo continues to prevail under multilateral bargaining. Under our approach to multilateral negotiations, a country that does not wish to liberalize ends up facing the MFN-consistent agreement $\langle ij \rangle^m$. Thus, unlike in their model, the relative effects of the non-discriminatory agreement $\langle ij \rangle^m$ and the discriminatory CU $\langle ij \rangle$ play a crucial role in our analysis.

Our analysis of CUs complements and builds on that of Saggi and Yildiz (2010) who address related questions in the context of FTAs, the second major type of PTAs sanctioned by GATT.[4] The two types of PTAs differ in an important way: while FTA members impose individually optimal tariffs on nonmembers, CUs coordinate their external tariffs.[5] Naturally, this suggests that the potential adverse impact of a CU on nonmembers might be larger. This fear finds some support in the existing literature: in many models, the tariff complementarity effect—i.e., the tendency of PTA members to lower their tariffs on nonmembers—is generally weaker for a CU relative to a FTA. As a result, one of the key conditions of GATT Article XXIV—i.e., PTA members should not raise tariffs on nonmembers—is more likely to bind for a CU relative to a FTA.[6]

The results of the present paper, together with those of Saggi and Yildiz (2010), imply that the freedom to pursue PTAs may prevent the attainment of global free trade when such agreements take the form of CUs but not when they take the form of FTAs.[7] In general, in a three-country model of trade agreements, two scenarios can prevent the attainment of free trade: (i) two countries may decide to *exclude* the third country from their mutual trade liberalization, even though the third country wants to be included; (ii) a country may choose not to engage in trade liberalization

members during subsequent negotiations. Thus, PTAs can help improve the strategic position of members during future negotiations. Such a strategic incentive for PTA formation does not arise in our simultaneous game. Another important difference between his approach and ours is that, by design, PTAs cannot be conducive to the cause of global free trade in his model.

[4] Several papers have considered the relationship between an endogenously determined FTA between two countries and its impact on incentives for multilateral liberalization—see, for example, Krishna (1998), and Ornelas (2005a, b). Our contribution is to provide an equilibrium theory in which the choice between bilateral CUs and multilateral liberalization itself is endogenous.

[5] An important consequence of this difference between the two types of PTAs is that a FTA member is free to sign *another* FTA with an existing nonmember *without* needing consent of an existing FTA partner whereas a CU member cannot do so.

[6] An earlier version of this paper also derived equilibrium trade agreements under the assumption that the maximum tariff a CU member can charge equals its tariff prior to the formation of the CU. We found that, in our model, such a tariff restriction on CU members does not make the attainment of multilateral free trade any more likely, although it does yield a CU that is preferable from an aggregate welfare perspective. By contrast, in the oligopoly trade model of Mrázová, Vines, and Zissimos (2010), such a constraint on a CU's external tariff can lead to a reduction in world welfare when free trade fails to obtain.

[7] This finding complements the traditional perspective that CUs are likely to be more distortionary due to the fact the member countries of a CU coordinate their market power while choosing external tariffs whereas members of an FTA do not.

with the other two countries who end up undertaking mutual trade liberalization with each other (even though they are open to including the third country).

In Saggi and Yildiz (2010), a country's unilateral incentive to opt out of multilateral liberalization determines the stability of free trade. Since this unilateral incentive to deviate from free trade is larger when the deviating country faces the MFN-consistent agreement $\langle ij \rangle^m$ as an outsider relative to when it faces a discriminatory FTA, in Saggi and Yildiz (2010) the freedom to form FTAs facilitates the achievement of global free trade by making it costlier for a country to opt out of multilateral liberalization, i.e., FTAs act as pure building blocks. As we show in the current paper, the freedom to pursue CUs is not necessarily conducive to the goal of reaching free trade. Exactly why this happens in our model illuminates a key difference between a FTA and a CU. Being an outsider is actually more costly for a country when it faces a CU between the other two countries rather than a FTA since the external tariffs of CU members are higher than those of FTA members. Thus, the reason that the results of Saggi and Yildiz (2010) differ from ours is not because CUs and FTAs affect outsiders differently. Rather, when the pursuit of bilateralism takes the form of CUs, the stability of free trade hinges on the joint incentive of two countries to exclude the third country from the agreement. Because of the tariff coordination involved in a CU, *this exclusion incentive under Bilateralism is stronger when the PTA takes the form of a CU as opposed to a FTA*.

We next briefly discuss three strands of existing literature that overlap to some degree with our paper. The first related stream of literature comprises of models of repeated interaction that examine how the exogenous formation of a PTA affects incentives for self-enforcing multilateral tariff cooperation on the part of members and nonmembers—see Bagwell and Staiger (1997a, 1997b, and 1998), Bond and Syropoulos (1996), Hadjiyiannis (2004), and Saggi (2006).[8] A second closely related line of research examines the type of trading blocs that emerge as stable equilibria when the number and the sizes of trading blocs are endogenously determined—see Yi (1996), Goyal and Joshi (2006), and Furusawa and Konishi (2007).[9] Finally, the third related strand studies the endogenous formation of CUs using a cooperative game theory approach—see Riezman (1985), Kennan and Riezman (1990), Riezman (1999), and Melatos and Woodland (2007b). While we depart from these lines of research in several ways, perhaps the most important difference is that we evaluate the relative pros and cons of preferential and multilateral trade liberalization in a model where the choice between the two types of liberalization is endogenous.

[8]Unlike others, Bagwell and Staiger (1997a) also consider the period of transition during which a CU arises and find that while the early stages of CU formation facilitates multilateral liberalization, the harmony between CUs and multilateral trade liberalization is only temporary. Hadjiyiannis (2004) extends the Bagwell and Staiger (1998) competing-exporters model of trade to allow for asymmetric discount factors across countries. He examines a scenario where two countries are patient, relative to the third, and finds that the impact of a PTA depends on which countries form the PTA. Finally, Freund (2000) takes the multilateral tariff as exogenous and asks how it affects incentives for cooperation among PTA members.

[9]In a three-country framework, Furusawa (2002) examines the choice between preferential arrangement and open regionalism when countries form a single trading bloc.

I. Trade Model

To endogenize the formation of trade agreements among asymmetric countries, we make use of an adapted version of the competing exporters model of Bagwell and Staiger (1997b, 1998).[10] There are three countries—a, b, and c—and three (non-numeraire) goods—A, B, and C. Each country's market is served by two competing exporters and I denotes the good that corresponds to the upper case value of i. For example, if $i = a$ then $I = A$. Country i is endowed with zero units of good I and e_i units of the other two goods.

The demand for good z in country i is specified as[11]

$$d(p_i^z) = \alpha - p_i^z, \quad \text{where} \quad z = A, B, \text{ or } C. \tag{1}$$

Since each country possesses only two goods while it demands all three, country i must import good I in order to consume it and can import it from either trading partner. For example, country a imports good A from both countries b and c while it exports good B to country b and good C to country c.

Let t_{ij} be the tariff imposed by country i on its imports of good I from country j. By design, our model abstracts from export taxes. We do so for several reasons. First, much of the existing literature on PTAs makes the same assumption and following this approach makes it easier to compare our results with previous analyses. Second, there are good practical grounds for not considering export taxes. Compared to import tariffs, which are used by basically every country in the world, the use of export taxes is relatively infrequent. In general, trade policy across the world seems to reflect mercantilist tendencies which led Krugman (1991) to assert that the mind-set of trade negotiators at the WTO is essentially that "exports are good; imports are bad; and other things equal, an equal increase in imports and exports is good." [12] Perhaps these tendencies are partly why export taxes are used a lot less frequently than import tariffs and are actually outright illegal in the United States.

Ruling out prohibitive tariffs yields the following no-arbitrage conditions for good I

$$p_i^I = p_j^I + t_{ij} = p_k^I + t_{ik}, \tag{2}$$

[10] The trade model underlying our two games of trade liberalization and the nature of Nash equilibrium tariffs is the same as that in Saggi and Yildiz (2010), who focus on FTAs as opposed to CUs. Rather than referring the reader to Saggi and Yildiz (2010), for the sake of completeness, we have chosen to include the details of this common trading structure developed in equations (1) through (6), and the derivation of optimal tariffs reported in equations (11), (20), and (24). We should note that to properly highlight the consequences of the various institutional differences between FTAs and CUs, it is crucial to retain that same trading structure as Saggi and Yildiz (2010).

[11] As is well known, the above demand functions can be derived from a utility function of the form $\sum_z u(c^z) + w$, where $u(\cdot)$ is quadratic, c^z denotes consumption of good z and $z = A, B$, or C, and w is the consumption of the numeraire good.

[12] Bagwell and Staiger (2000) argue that the economics underlying this viewpoint (or simply "GATT-Think") is consistent with a model in which trade agreements help neutralize terms of trade externalities that countries impose on each other in their pursuit of nationally optimal policies.

where $i, j, k = a, b, c$, and $i \neq j \neq k$. Let m_i^I be country i's imports of good I. Since country i has no endowment of good I, we have

$$m_i^I = d(p_i^I) = \alpha - p_i^I. \tag{3}$$

Each country's exports of a good must equal its endowment of that good minus its local consumption:

$$x_j^I = e_j - [\alpha - p_j^I]. \tag{4}$$

Market clearing for good I requires that country i's imports equal the total exports of the other two countries:

$$m_i^I = \sum_{j \neq i} x_j^I. \tag{5}$$

Equations (2) through (5) imply that the equilibrium price of good I in country i equals

$$p_i^I = \frac{1}{3}\left(3\alpha - \sum_{j \neq i} e_j + \sum_{j \neq i} t_{ij}\right). \tag{6}$$

Using these prices, the volume of trade is easily calculated. As is clear from equation (6), the price of good I in country i increases in its tariffs and decreases in the endowment levels of the other two countries. The effect of a country's tariff on its terms of trade is evident from equation (6): only a third of a given increase in either of its tariffs is passed on to domestic consumers with exactly two third of the tariff increase falling on the shoulders of foreign exporters.[13]

Each country's welfare is defined as the sum of consumer surplus, producer surplus, and tariff revenue over all such goods and given by

$$w_i = \sum_z CS_i^z + \sum_z PS_i^z + TR_i. \tag{7}$$

By using equations (2) through (6), welfare of country i as a function of endowment levels and global tariffs can easily be calculated. Let aggregate world welfare be defined as the sum of each country's welfare:

$$ww = \sum_i w_i. \tag{8}$$

We proceed as follows. First, we consider a three-stage game of trade liberalization (which we refer to as *Bilateralism*), under which each country is free to pursue either (a) no trade liberalization, (b) bilateral trade liberalization, or

[13] By design, the model examines country j's trade protection towards only good J (i.e., the only non-numeraire good that it imports).

(c) multilateral trade liberalization.[14] After deriving Nash equilibria of this game and isolating those equilibria that are stable (more on this below), we next ask how equilibrium outcomes are affected if countries can choose only between options (a) and (c). This restricted game is called *Multilateralism*. Next, we compare these two games when countries are asymmetric in their endowments, first when one country is smaller and then when one country is larger than the other two. These two analyses shed light on the consequence of country asymmetry upon equilibrium policy regimes that arise under the two alternative policy games.

II. Equilibria under Bilateralism

The Bilateralism game proceeds as follows. In the first stage, each country announces the names of countries with whom it wants to form a customs union (CU). Country i's announcement is denoted by σ_i, and its strategy set Ω_i consists of four possible announcements

$$\Omega_i = \{\{\phi\}, \{j\}, \{k\}, \{M\}\}, \tag{9}$$

where the announcement $\{\phi\}$ by country i is in favor of the status quo (or no trade liberalization); $\{j\}$ is in favor of a CU with only country j; $\{k\}$ is in favor of a CU with only country k; and $\{M\}$ is in favor of multilateral free trade. This announcement stage determines the global policy regime. Next, given the policy regime, countries impose their optimal external tariffs. Finally, given trade agreements and tariffs, international trade and consumption take place.

The Bilateralism game can yield the following policy regimes: (i) the status quo $\langle\Phi\rangle$ prevails when no two announcements match or when everyone announces $\{\phi\}$; (ii) the CU $\langle ij\rangle$ is formed if countries i and j announce each other's name $\sigma_i = \{j\}$ and $\sigma_j = \{i\}$; (iii) free trade $\langle F\rangle$ obtains if $\sigma_i = \{M\}$ for all $i, j, k = a, b, c$.

One aspect of our Bilateralism game deserves comment. The CU $\langle ab\rangle$ obtains as long as country a and b call each other and neither of them calls country c, *regardless* of the nature of country c's announcement. This means that if $\sigma_a = \{b\}$ and $\sigma_b = \{a\}$, the excluded country (i.e., c) is indifferent between $\sigma_c = \{\phi\}$, $\sigma_c = \{a\}$, $\sigma_c = \{b\}$, or $\sigma_c = \{M\}$ since the outcome under any of these announcements on its part is the CU $\langle ab\rangle$. We settle such indifference on the part of the excluded country in favor of the most parsimonious announcement among the three—i.e., $\sigma_c = \{\phi\}$. This is reasonable since a proposal to form a CU is unlikely to be costless in the real world and a country facing no proposals from others would be better off not making any proposals of its own.[15]

[14]Note that all countries have market power in the competing exporters model of Bagwell and Staiger (1997b and 1998) that we utilize. As a result, allowing for unilateral liberalization is not necessary—no country will choose to pursue it in this model.

[15]Even if announcements were costless, the set of stable agreements under both games remains the same. However, the set of Nash equilibria is quite sensitive to this assumption. We assume that the excluded country chooses to make the parsimonious announcement since this helps reduce the deviation possibilities that need to be considered.

We next derive equilibrium trade agreements. Throughout the remainder of this section, as well as in Section III, we maintain the following assumption:[16]

ASSUMPTION 1 (Symmetry): $e_i = e$ *for all* $i = a, b, c$.

Let country i's welfare as a function of trade regime r be denoted by $w_i(r)$, where $r \in \{\langle\Phi\rangle, \langle ab\rangle, \langle ac\rangle, \langle bc\rangle, \langle F\rangle\}$. Also, let $\Delta w_i(r - v)$ denote the difference between country i's welfare under trade regimes r and v:

$$(10) \qquad \Delta w_i(r - v) \equiv w_i(r) - w_i(v).$$

In accordance with Article I of GATT, we assume that, under the status quo, each country imposes a non-discriminatory tariff on its trading partners: $t_{ij} = t_{ik} = t_i^{\phi}$ for all $i, j, k = a, b, c$. Country i's optimal MFN tariff is easily calculated as

$$(11) \qquad t_i^{\phi} \equiv \text{Arg max } w_i(\Phi) = \frac{e}{4}.$$

Under symmetry, $t_i^{\phi} = t^{\phi}$ for all $i = a, b, c$. If two countries form a CU, they remove tariffs on each other and impose jointly optimal external tariffs (denoted by t_i^u and t_j^u) on the non-member country.[17] The tariff pair (t_i^u, t_j^u) is chosen to solve the joint welfare maximization problem[18]

$$(12) \qquad \max_{t_i^u, t_j^u} w_i(ij) + w_j(ij) \quad \text{subject to} \quad t_{ij} = t_{ji} = 0.$$

Since each country is the unique importer of a good in our competing exporters model, the "market power effect" of a CU emphasized by Bagwell and Staiger (1997a) does not arise here since that effect arises only when CU members "compete" for imports.[19] As a result, the coordination of tariffs is beneficial to CU members only because each member internalizes the effect of its tariff on the export surplus of the other member. Furthermore, note that the constraint of zero internal tariffs does not bind for a CU since free internal trade is actually optimal for members.

[16]Calculations supporting the results reported in the rest of the paper are contained in the Mathematical Appendix.

[17]Our simple formulation of a CU's tariff choice problem is intuitively appealing and in line with much of existing literature. However, Syropoulos (2003) has shown that the nature of the sharing rule of a CU with respect to tariff revenue can affect tariff preferences as well as the trade patterns of CU members in ways that can prevent the implementation of jointly optimal tariffs. An important insight of his analysis is that CU members have an incentive to influence their common tariffs, not just for external terms-of-trade reasons, but also for internal distributional purposes. Given the focus of our paper, we abstract from such considerations.

[18]The assumption that the CU maximizes the sum of national utilities is commonly employed in the literature. Issues of the delegation of tariff-setting authority and the choice of weights in the social welfare function are discussed by Gatsios and Karp (1991) and Melatos and Woodland (2007a, b).

[19]In Bagwell and Staiger (1997a), countries forming a CU do not trade with each other at all and the CU is attractive to them only because it allows them to pool their market power and extract a larger terms of trade gain from nonmembers.

When countries are symmetric, we have $t_i^u = t_j^u = t^u$ and the optimal external tariff of each CU member is given by

$$t^u = \frac{e}{5}. \quad (13)$$

Note that, under symmetry, the formation of a CU induces each member country to *lower* its tariff on the nonmember relative to the status quo (i.e., the model exhibits tariff complementarity): $t^u < t^\phi$.[20] Furthermore, since tariffs are independent across countries, the nonmember continues to impose its optimal MFN tariff on the member countries of the CU.

We are now ready to derive equilibrium trade agreements under Bilateralism. It is straightforward that the status quo is a Nash equilibrium since no country has an incentive to announce another's name if the latter does not announce its name in return. Which of the other two policy regimes—i.e., a CU $\langle ij \rangle$ and global free trade—are Nash equilibria? We address this next.

Denote the welfare of a country under a regime r with the relevant optimal tariffs substituted by $w^*(r)$. For example, when each country's tariff equals its optimal MFN tariff, the welfare of country i is given by $w_i^*(\Phi)$. Using calculations reported in the Mathematical Appendix, it is easy to show that a CU member has no unilateral incentive to defect from the agreement since

$$\Delta w_i^*(ij - \Phi) = \Delta w_j^*(ij - \Phi) > 0, \quad (14)$$

so that a CU is a Nash equilibrium. It is worth clarifying here that our model differs in an important way from the usual one-stage model of trade agreements where countries simply choose tariffs. In our model, the tariffs chosen by countries at the second stage depend upon the agreements reached in the first stage. In particular, if two countries agree to form a CU in the first stage, they essentially commit to choosing jointly optimal tariffs at the next stage. To see why this matters, suppose first-stage announcements are given by $\sigma_a = \{b\}$, $\sigma_b = \{a\}$, and $\sigma_c = \{\phi\}$. Then, if country a unilaterally deviates and alters its announcement to $\sigma_a = \{\phi\}$, it does so with the understanding that at the tariff setting stage *all* countries will impose their optimal MFN tariffs on each other.

It is noteworthy that the tariff complementarity effect in our model is not large enough to make the nonmember better off under a CU relative to the status quo since

$$\Delta w_k^*(ij - \Phi) < 0. \quad (15)$$

[20] Bagwell and Staiger (1998) derive the tariff-complementarity effect under symmetry and show that it is not large enough to make the non-member country better off under a customs union than under Nash tariffs. However, unlike us, they do not offer an analysis of stable equilibria for the Bilateralism and Multilateralism games, which is the primary focus of the present paper. Incidentally, tariff complementarity is also a feature of the general equilibrium model of Bond, Riezman, and Syropoulos (2004). For empirical evidence regarding tariff complementarity in the context of the Latin American customs union Mercosur, see Estevadeordal, Freund, and Ornelas (2008).

Free trade is also a Nash equilibrium since no country has an incentive to unilaterally deviate from it:

$$(16) \qquad \Delta w_k^*(F - ij) > 0.$$

To capture the process of CU formation in a more realistic fashion, we now refine the set of Nash equilibria by isolating those Nash equilibria that are *stable* or *coalition proof*—i.e., are immune to self-enforcing coalitional deviations as defined in Bernheim, Peleg, and Whinston (1987).[21] Which, if any, of the Nash equilibrium agreements described above are stable? For free trade to be stable, we need to rule out two joint deviations:

(JF1): Deviation of i and j from $\langle F \rangle$ to $\langle ij \rangle$.
(JF2): Deviation of i and j from $\langle F \rangle$ to $\langle \Phi \rangle$.

The first of these deviations–i.e., (JF1)—is easily dismissed since

$$(17) \qquad \Delta w_i^*(F - ij) > 0.$$

Under symmetry, no two countries have a joint incentive to exclude the third country by forming a bilateral CU, since the terms of trade gain enjoyed by each CU member by excluding the nonmember is more than offset by the loss it suffers in the nonmember's market. As we shall see later, this is not necessarily the case when endowments are asymmetric.

Furthermore, it is immediate from (14) and (17) that joint deviation (JF2) will also not occur. In fact, $\langle \Phi \rangle$ is *not* a stable equilibrium because inequality (14) implies that the joint deviation of countries i and j from $\langle \Phi \rangle$ to $\langle ij \rangle$ is self-enforcing: any *further* deviation from $\langle ij \rangle$ on the part of either member reverts them back to $\langle \Phi \rangle$ under which both are worse off. The CU $\langle ij \rangle$ also fails to be stable since all three countries have an incentive to jointly deviate from $\langle ij \rangle$ to $\langle F \rangle$ and this joint deviation is self-enforcing since each country's welfare under $\langle F \rangle$ is higher than that under the CU $\langle ij \rangle$ or the status quo.[22]

Thus, bringing these results together, we have:

PROPOSITION 1: *Given symmetry, the status quo, a CU between two countries, and free trade are all Nash equilibrium trade agreements under Bilateralism. However, the only stable trade agreement is free trade.*

An important point to note is that when countries are symmetric, a CU between two countries is *not* a stable equilibrium. Under symmetry, the move from the status quo of optimal MFN tariffs to global free trade confers equal gains on all countries.

[21] In our three-country model, a coalitional deviation is credible or self-enforcing if, taking the nonmember's announcement as given, no member of the deviating coalition has an incentive to *further* deviate from its announcement as a part of the deviating coalition.

[22] Note that under symmetry even the members of a CU are better off under free trade.

As a result countries have an incentive to communicate with each other to attain the Pareto optimal outcome of global free trade. When countries make unilateral decisions and such communication is not possible, while free trade can arise as a Nash equilibrium, so can the status quo and a CU—outcomes that are decidedly worse from a global welfare perspective.

Proposition 1 raises the following question: can a bilateral CU arise as a stable equilibrium when countries are not symmetric in some respect? Before addressing this important question, we analyze the Multilateralism game under symmetry.

III. Equilibria under Multilateralism

Under the *Multilateralism* game, the strategy set of country i consists of four possible announcements

$$\Omega_i = \{\{\phi\}, \{j_m\}, \{k_m\}, \{M\}\}, \tag{18}$$

where the announcement $\{\phi\}$ by country i is in favor of no trade liberalization; $\{j_m\}$ is in favor of an MFN-consistent agreement with only country j; $\{k_m\}$ is in favor of an MFN-consistent agreement with only country k; and $\{M\}$ is in favor of multilateral free trade.

As under the Bilateralism game, the status quo $\langle\Phi\rangle$ prevails when no two announcements match or when everyone announces $\{\phi\}$. The MFN-consistent agreement $\langle ij^m\rangle$ is formed if countries i and j announce each other's name $\sigma_i = \{j_m\}$ and $\sigma_j = \{i_m\}$ and under such a regime member countries jointly choose their optimal tariffs subject to the constraint that they *cannot* discriminate against country k.[23] Formally, under the agreement $\langle ij\rangle^m$, countries i and j choose the tariff pair (t_i^m, t_j^m) to solve

$$\max_{(t_i^m, t_j^m)} w_i(ij^m) + w_j(ij^m) \quad \text{subject to} \quad t_{ij} = t_{ik} = t_i^m \text{ and } t_{ji} = t_{jk} = t_j^m. \tag{19}$$

Finally, if all three countries announce in favor of multilateral free trade ($\sigma_i = \{M\}$), they implement the jointly optimal set of tariffs which, in our model, are all equal to zero—i.e., a three-country agreement implies free trade.

As in the previous section, we maintain the assumption that countries are symmetric: $e_i = e$ for all $i = a, b, c$. Under symmetry, we must have $t_i^m = t_j^m = t^m$ and this jointly optimal MFN tariff is given by

$$t^m = \frac{e}{7}, \quad \text{where} \quad t^m < t^\phi. \tag{20}$$

Since $t^m < t^\phi$, it is immediate that countries that sign the MFN-consistent agreement $\langle ij\rangle^m$ lower their tariffs on each other as well as on the non-participating country (i.e., k). One aspect of the MFN-consistent agreement $\langle ij\rangle^m$ is noteworthy: since country k retains its optimal Nash tariff t^ϕ under $\langle ij\rangle^m$ while countries i and j cut

[23] Unlike the open membership feature of the Multilateralism game in Saggi and Yildiz (2010), we consider an exclusive membership game in this paper. We thank an anonymous referee for suggesting this appealing formulation of Multilateralism.

tariffs on an MFN basis, it benefits from the trade liberalization undertaken by countries i and j without having to offer any liberalization in return.[24]

Next, note that $t^m < t^u$: i.e., country k faces higher tariffs in export markets when the other two countries implement a CU $\langle ij \rangle$ relative to when they sign the multilateral agreement $\langle ij \rangle^m$. To make matters worse, country k is also subject to *discriminatory treatment* in both its export markets under the CU $\langle ij \rangle$—while countries i and j face zero tariffs in each other's market under $\langle ij \rangle$, country k faces the tariff t^u. By contrast, such discriminatory treatment is absent under the agreement $\langle ij \rangle^m$. Therefore, the welfare of the non-member country (k) is strictly lower under the CU $\langle ij \rangle$ compared to the agreement $\langle ij \rangle^m$. Of course, as noted above, the flip side of this is that countries i and j are strictly better off under the CU $\langle ij \rangle$ relative to the multilateral agreement $\langle ij \rangle^m$ since only under the latter agreement do they have to abide by the non-discrimination constraint. These results are formalized in Section IV as Lemma 1.

We now derive equilibrium agreements under Multilateralism. As under Bilateralism, the status quo $\langle \Phi \rangle$ is a Nash equilibrium under Multilateralism. Next, we note that $\langle ij \rangle^m$ is also Nash since a member country has no incentive to break the multilateral agreement $\langle ij \rangle^m$:

$$\Delta w_i^*(ij^m - \Phi) > 0. \tag{21}$$

The only remaining question is whether free trade is a Nash equilibrium. To this end, we show that no country has an incentive to unilaterally deviate from free trade and become an outsider facing the MFN-consistent agreement $\langle ij \rangle^m$ since

$$\Delta w_k^*(F - ij^m) > 0. \tag{22}$$

Thus, the status quo $\langle \Phi \rangle$, an MFN-consistent agreement $\langle ij \rangle^m$, and free trade $\langle F \rangle$ are all Nash equilibrium trade agreements under Multilateralism.

Next, we examine which of these agreements are stable. First, it is clear from (21) that the status quo $\langle \Phi \rangle$ is not stable since countries i and j benefit from deviating from $\langle \Phi \rangle$ to $\langle ij \rangle^m$ from which there is no further unilateral deviation. Next, we note that countries i and j do not have a joint incentive to deviate from $\langle F \rangle$ to $\langle ij \rangle^m$ and exclude country k since

$$\Delta w_i^*(F - ij^m) = \Delta w_j^*(F - ij^m) > 0. \tag{23}$$

It is immediate from (21) and (23) that all three countries benefit from deviating from $\langle \Phi \rangle$ to $\langle F \rangle$. Therefore, we can argue from (22) and (23) that all countries always

[24] In a competitive general equilibrium model, Raimondos-Møller and Woodland (2006) have shown that if coordinated non-discriminatory tariff reforms by a subset of countries are accompanied by appropriate income transfers between them, reforming members can make themselves strictly better off without having an adverse effect on nonmembers. In our model, while there are no transfers, the MFN-consistent agreement $\langle ij \rangle^m$ makes all countries strictly better off under symmetry. However, as we note below, the more relevant question here is how the nonmember fares under $\langle ij \rangle^m$ relative to the CU $\langle ij \rangle$.

have an incentive to jointly deviate from $\langle ij \rangle^m$ to $\langle F \rangle$ and this joint deviation is self-enforcing since there exists no further unilateral or joint deviation from free trade $\langle F \rangle$.

We thus have:

PROPOSITION 2: *Given symmetry, the status quo* $\langle \Phi \rangle$, *an MFN-consistent agreement* $\langle ij \rangle^m$, *and free trade* $\langle F \rangle$ *are all Nash equilibrium trade agreements under Multilateralism. However, the only stable agreement is free trade.*

A comparison of Propositions 1 and 2 shows that when endowments are symmetric across countries, a multilateral approach to trade liberalization is sufficient to reach global free trade.[25] A powerful implication of this result is that if the gains from global trade liberalization were spread equally across countries (something that necessarily happens when countries have symmetric endowments), the freedom to pursue bilateral CUs is irrelevant for the ultimate objective of achieving global free trade. Two aspects of our model are crucial for delivering this result. First, governments are assumed to maximize national welfare. Second, tariffs are endogenously determined given the trade agreement. We briefly discuss the role of each assumption.

Together with symmetry, the assumption that governments maximize national welfare implies that any terms of trade gain obtained in the domestic market is more than offset by the corresponding losses suffered in foreign markets (i.e., each country's gain from tariff manipulation is smaller than its loss). In general, whether free trade obtains or not would clearly depend upon the assumed objective of the government. For example, our model lacks an import competing sector, the presence of which (especially under lobbying pressure) could result in a stable outcome in which all countries choose positive tariffs even in the Multilateralism game. Similarly, in the presence of political economy considerations, a three-country agreement with positive tariffs could also arise under Bilateralism. However, we expect the *same agreement* (with positive tariffs) to arise under the two games under symmetry. Thus, we believe that Propositions 1 and 2 are special in the sense that they single out free trade as the outcome, but not in the sense that the same outcome arises in the two games.

Furthermore, the endogeneity of tariffs plays a crucial role in our model. If tariffs were controlled by forces outside the model (i.e., were exogenously given), free trade could fail to obtain even between symmetric countries. For example, it is straightforward to show that countries i and j prefer a CU to free trade if the CU's external tariff t^{CU} is sufficiently high relative to the non-member country's tariff t^{ϕ}. A similar result holds in the Multilateralism game: whenever the external tariffs of countries i and j under the MFN-consistent agreement $\langle ij \rangle^m$ are sufficiently high relative to the non-member country's tariff, they prefer $\langle ij \rangle^m$ to free trade.

Given Propositions 1 and 2, the natural question is: do there exist circumstances under which the freedom to pursue bilateral CUs matters? We show next that such a possibility arises when endowments are sufficiently asymmetric across countries.

[25] Saggi and Yildiz (2010) showed that global free trade is uniquely stable even when bilateralism takes the form of FTAs.

IV. Liberalization among Asymmetric Countries

From hereon we drop Assumption 1 and begin by deriving optimal tariffs under asymmetry. If country i does not participate in any trade agreement, it chooses a non-discriminatory (or MFN) tariff t_i^ϕ to maximize its own welfare:

$$t_i^\phi \equiv \text{Arg max } w_i(\Phi) = \frac{e_j + e_k}{8}. \tag{24}$$

Note that country i's optimal tariff t_i^ϕ increases with the endowments of its trading partners.

Similar to (13), when countries i and j form a CU $\langle ij \rangle$, they abolish tariffs on each other and choose their external tariffs to maximize their joint welfare $w_i(ij) + w_j(ij)$.[26, 27] These external tariffs are

$$t_i^u = \frac{2e_k - e_j}{5} \quad \text{and} \quad t_j^u = \frac{2e_k - e_i}{5}. \tag{25}$$

It is easy to see that each CU member's external tariff increases with the endowment of the nonmember whereas it decreases with that of its CU partner. This is intuitive. If the endowment of a CU member country increases, its exports to the partner country's market increase relative to the nonmember and this induces the partner to reduce its tariff on the nonmember.

As noted earlier, to minimize the potential harmful effects of PTAs on nonmembers, Article XXIV of GATT requires that member countries not raise their external tariffs on nonmembers. Such a constraint on the tariff choices of country i as a CU member binds if and only if $t_i^u > t_i^\phi$. Accordingly, we have

$$t_i^u \geq t_i^\phi \Leftrightarrow 11e_k \geq 13e_j. \tag{26}$$

In what follows, we ignore the restriction imposed by Article XXIV and assume that a CU can impose its optimal tariffs.

Under the multilateral agreement $\langle ij \rangle^m$, countries i and j choose the pair (t_i^m, t_j^m) to maximize $w_i(ij^m) + w_j(ij^m)$. As in Saggi and Yildiz (2010), we have

$$t_i^m = \frac{2e_k - e_j}{7} \quad \text{and} \quad t_j^m = \frac{2e_k - e_i}{7}. \tag{27}$$

As under symmetry, the comparison of the external tariffs under $\langle ij \rangle$ and $\langle ij \rangle^m$ implies that (i) the nonmember faces lower tariffs under $\langle ij \rangle^m$ relative to $\langle ij \rangle$: $t_i^m < t_i^u$

[26] It is worth noting that under asymmetry it is still optimal for the CU member countries to reduce the internal tariffs to zero.

[27] Under symmetry, the choice of the common external tariff by custom union members is independent of the country weights in the union's social welfare function. However, when countries are asymmetric this independence disappears. Accordingly, the custom union's external tariffs will now depend upon the country weights in the joint welfare function and our assumption of equal weights may be regarded as rather special. Consideration of alternative weighting schemes, such as along the lines of Melatos and Woodland (2007a), would significantly complicate the analysis and so we retain the equal weights assumption.

and $t_j^m < t_j^u$; and (ii) the non-member country is subject to *discriminatory treatment* in each member country's market under the CU $\langle ij \rangle$ relative to the agreement $\langle ij \rangle^m$. This implies the following result.[28]

LEMMA 1: *The welfare comparison of $\langle ij \rangle$ and $\langle ij \rangle^m$ from the perspective of members and the nonmember is as follows*:

(i) *The nonmember is strictly worse off under $\langle ij \rangle$ relative to $\langle ij \rangle^m$: $w_k^*(ij) < w_k^*(ij^m)$; and*

(ii) *if $e_i = e_j$, the member countries are strictly better off under $\langle ij \rangle$ relative to $\langle ij \rangle^m$: $w_i^*(ij) = w_j^*(ij) > w_i^*(ij^m) = w_j^*(ij^m)$.*

As explained before, part (i) of Lemma 1 is an immediate consequence of the higher external tariff under $\langle ij \rangle$ relative to $\langle ij \rangle^m$ and the discriminatory nature of the CU $\langle ij \rangle$. Part (ii) of Lemma 1 says that symmetric member countries are strictly better off under the CU $\langle ij \rangle$ relative to the MFN-consistent agreement $\langle ij \rangle^m$. The intuition for this is transparent: only under the latter agreement do they have to abide by the non-discrimination constraint. The restriction $e_i = e_j$ is sufficient, but not necessary, for this result. Indeed, along with Lemmas 2 and 3, this restriction also delivers a clear ranking of the preferences of individual countries under Multilateralism relative to Bilateralism for the two types of endowment asymmetries later considered in the paper.

It is worth asking why it is possible under asymmetry for a member country to be better off under the MFN-consistent agreement $\langle ij \rangle^m$, relative to the CU $\langle ij \rangle$, even though their joint welfare is always higher under the latter agreement. The intuition is that if one member country is substantially smaller than the other, the maximization of joint welfare by a CU can lead to a situation where the pair of coordinated tariffs imposed by the CU is less attractive for the small country relative to the tariffs imposed under the MFN-consistent agreement $\langle ij \rangle^m$.

In this context, an important aspect of our model deserves comment. Since member countries of a CU import different goods from the non-member country, the formation of a CU requires member countries to alter their tariffs *solely* because they internalize the export surplus of the partner country, and not due to any enhanced market power on their part since their tariffs apply to different goods. As a result, the gains from tariff coordination are not evenly split across CU member countries when their endowments differ. Indeed, the larger exporter in a CU gains relatively more from the formation of the CU since the tariff it faces in the other member's market is relatively higher under the status quo.

Before proceeding further, we note that a restriction on the degree of endowment asymmetry must be imposed for the underlying pattern of trade assumed in the model (i.e., the competing exporters structure) to remain valid. To this end, let $x_j^I(r)$ denote the export of country j of good I to country i under regime r. We show

[28] Welfare levels under all possible regimes are reported in the Mathematical Appendix, and these can be used to prove Lemmas 1–3.

in the Appendix that country j exports good I to country i under all trade regimes if and only if $3e_k \leq 5e_j$ or

(28) $$x_j^I(r) \geq 0 \quad \text{if and only if} \quad 3e_k \leq 5e_j.$$

From hereon we assume that this condition holds.

To derive equilibrium agreements, it is useful to briefly examine the incentives of asymmetric countries for bilateral and multilateral trade liberalization.[29] We begin by stating the following lemma.[30]

LEMMA 2: *Let country j be either a CU or free trade partner of country i under regime r, where $r = \langle ij \rangle$ or $\langle F \rangle$, but not under regime v, where $v = \langle \Phi \rangle$, $\langle ik \rangle$, or $\langle jk \rangle$. Then, the following hold*:

(i) $$\frac{\partial \Delta w_i^*(r - v)}{\partial e_j} < 0 < \frac{\partial \Delta w_i^*(r - v)}{\partial e_i}; \textit{ and}$$

(ii) $$\frac{\partial \Delta w_i^*(ij - \phi)}{\partial e_k} > 0 \quad \textit{and} \quad \frac{\partial \Delta w_i^*(F - ij)}{\partial e_j} > 0.$$

The intuition for part (i) of Lemma 2 is as follows. The smaller a country's endowment, the lower its volume of exports and the less it benefits from tariff reductions granted by others. Similarly, the larger the endowment of a country's partner, the larger the terms of trade loss suffered by it from granting the partner free access to its market. Thus, a country's willingness to eliminate its tariff on a trading partner depends positively on its own endowment and negatively on that of its partner. The second part of the lemma captures two related points. The inequality $\partial \Delta w_i^*(ij - \phi)/\partial e_k > 0$ says that, beginning at the status quo $\langle \Phi \rangle$, the advantage gained by country i in country j's market from signing the CU $\langle ij \rangle$ increases in country k's size, making such a CU more valuable from its welfare perspective. Recall that both countries i and k export the same good to country j (i.e., they are competing exporters). Thus, a country always prefers to form a CU with the smaller of its two trading partners since

(29) $$w_i^*(ij) \geq w_i^*(ik) \quad \text{if and only if} \quad e_k \geq e_j.$$

[29]In the competing exporters model of Bagwell and Staiger (1997b and 1998) utilized by us, asymmetry in endowments translates directly into asymmetries of export volumes: an increase in a country's endowment increases its exports of non-numeraire/protected goods without affecting its imports of such goods since the model lacks any income effects. Indeed, the country with the largest endowment of non-numeraire goods faces the smallest imports of such goods.

[30]The results reported in part (i) of Lemma 2 are analogous to lemma 2a of Saggi and Yildiz (2010). Together they show that the effects that variations in the underlying endowment structure have on the incentive of an individual country to sign a PTA with another are qualitatively similar across the two major types of PTAs (i.e., FTAs and CUs).

The inequality $\partial \Delta w_i^*(F - ij)/\partial e_j > 0$ says that when country *j* is already a CU partner of country *i*, country *i*'s welfare gain from moving to multilateral free trade increases with the endowment of country *j*. This is because the value of the preferential treatment enjoyed by country *i* in country *j*'s market under $\langle ij \rangle$ decreases with the endowment of the competing exporter *j*.

How do the incentives of countries to form (or join) an MFN-consistent trade agreement depend on the underlying endowment structure?

LEMMA 3: *Under Multilateralism, the following hold*:

(i) $$\frac{\partial \Delta w_i^*(ij^m - \phi)}{\partial e_i} > 0, \quad \frac{\partial \Delta w_i^*(ij^m - \phi)}{\partial e_j} < 0 \quad \textit{and} \quad \frac{\partial \Delta w_i^*(ij^m - \phi)}{\partial e_k} < 0; \textit{ and}$$

(ii) $$\frac{\partial \Delta w_i^*(F - ij^m)}{\partial e_i} > 0, \quad \frac{\partial \Delta w_i^*(F - ij^m)}{\partial e_j} < 0 \quad \textit{and} \quad \frac{\partial \Delta w_i^*(F - ij^m)}{\partial e_k} < 0.$$[31]

Part (i) of Lemma 3 implies that two forces underlie the formation of an MFN-consistent agreement. On the one hand, a country prefers to form an agreement with a smaller partner. On the other hand, the joint determination of external tariffs makes it attractive for each country to form an MFN-consistent agreement with a similar sized country. These two effects together imply that the country with the smallest endowment prefers an MFN-consistent agreement with the smaller of its two trading partners, while the preference of the other countries depends on the degree of asymmetry between countries:

(30) $$w_i^*(ij^m) \geq w_i^*(ik^m) \quad \text{if and only if} \quad e_k \geq e_j \geq e_i.$$

To highlight the crucial role played by asymmetry in our model and to facilitate a comparison of our results with those of Saggi and Yildiz (2010), it proves instructive to focus on two special cases: (i) two countries (denoted by l and l') have larger endowments than the third (denoted by s); and (ii) two countries (denoted by s and s') have smaller endowments than the third (denoted by l). We consider each in turn.

V. If One Country Is Smaller

Let the pattern of endowment asymmetry be given by:

ASSUMPTION 2a: $e_s = \frac{e}{\theta} < e_l = e_{l'} = e \quad \textit{and} \quad 1 \leq \theta \leq \frac{5}{3}.$

The restriction $\theta \leq 5/3$ is necessary to ensure that the pattern of trade assumed by the competing exporters structure remains valid under asymmetry. In all of the results reported in this section, endowments are as specified under Assumption 2a.

[31] Since the nature of the multilateral agreement in the present model is the same as that in Saggi and Yildiz (2010), Lemma 3 is essentially a restatement of lemma 4 in Saggi and Yildiz (2010). We include it here for completeness.

A. *Equilibrium Agreements under Bilateralism*

To avoid redundancy, we focus directly on stable agreements under Bilateralism (i.e., we skip the discussion of Nash equilibria). First consider the perspective of the larger countries. We know from (14) and (17) that starting from global free trade, under symmetry, two countries have no incentive to jointly deviate from $\langle F\rangle$ to $\langle\Phi\rangle$. Lemma 2 implies that $\partial w_l^*(F-\phi)/\partial\theta = \partial\Delta w_{l'}^*(F-\phi)/\partial\theta > 0$, and thus it follows that the larger countries have no incentive to deviate from $\langle F\rangle$ to $\langle\Phi\rangle$:

$$\text{(31)} \qquad \Delta w_l^*(F-\Phi) = \Delta w_{l'}^*(F-\Phi) > 0 \quad \text{for all } \theta.$$

Similarly, we know from (16) that under symmetry ($\theta = 1$), a country has no incentive to unilaterally deviate from free trade to become an outsider facing a CU. From Lemma 2, we have $\partial\Delta w_l^*(F-sl')/\partial\theta = \partial\Delta w_{l'}^*(F-sl)/\partial\theta > 0$. Thus, it follows that

$$\text{(32)} \qquad \Delta w_l^*(F-sl') = \Delta w_{l'}^*(F-sl) > 0 \quad \text{for all } \theta.$$

Do the larger countries have an incentive to exclude the small country by deviating from $\langle F\rangle$ to $\langle ll'\rangle$? We know from (17) that this is not the case under symmetry ($\theta = 1$). Further, note from Lemma 2 that $\partial\Delta w_l^*(F-ll')/\partial\theta = \partial\Delta w_l^*(F-ll')/\partial\theta > 0$. This implies that

$$\text{(33)} \qquad \Delta w_l^*(F-ll') = \Delta w_{l'}^*(F-ll') > 0 \quad \text{for all } \theta.$$

Only two possible defections from free trade remain to be considered:

(UF): Unilateral deviation of country s from $\langle F\rangle$ to $\langle ll'\rangle$;

(JF): Joint deviation of countries s and l (or l') from $\langle F\rangle$ to $\langle sl\rangle$ (or $\langle sl'\rangle$).

Let $\theta_i(r-v)$ denote the critical degree of endowment asymmetry at which country i is indifferent between regimes r and v. Direct calculations show that the deviation (UF) occurs when country s is sufficiently smaller than others:

$$\text{(34)} \qquad \Delta w_s^*(F-ll') \leq 0 \quad \text{if and only if} \quad \theta \geq \theta_s(F-ll').$$

Now consider deviation (JF). It turns out that a larger country (say l) has an incentive to jointly deviate with the smaller country provided it is sufficiently small:

$$\text{(35)} \qquad \Delta w_l^*(F-sl) \leq 0 \quad \text{if and only if} \quad \theta \geq \theta_l(F-sl).$$

Similarly, we have

$$\text{(36)} \qquad \Delta w_s^*(F-sl) \leq 0 \quad \text{if and only if} \quad \theta \geq \theta_s(F-sl).$$

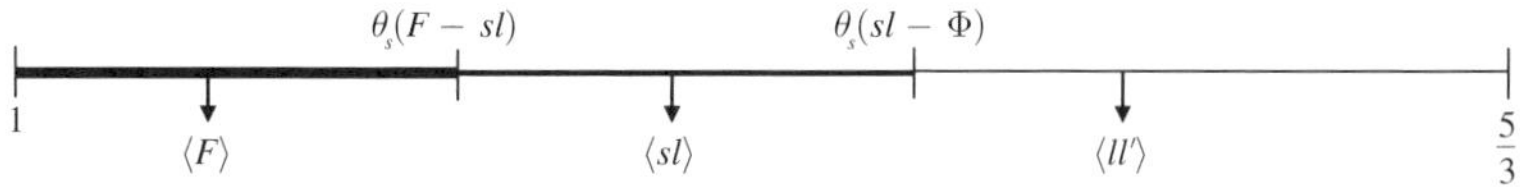

FIGURE 1. STABLE AGREEMENTS UNDER BILATERALISM: ONE COUNTRY IS SMALLER

We show in the Appendix that $\theta_l(F - sl) < \theta_s(F - sl)$ so that deviation (JF) occurs when $\theta \ge \theta_s(F - sl)$. Note further that this joint deviation is self-enforcing only when $\theta \le \theta_s(sl - \Phi)$; otherwise, the smaller country has an incentive to further deviate unilaterally from $\langle sl \rangle$ to $\langle \Phi \rangle$:

$$\Delta w_s^*(sl - \Phi) \le 0 \quad \text{if and only if} \quad \theta \ge \theta_s(sl - \Phi). \tag{37}$$

The deviation conditions specified in (34), (35), (36), and (37) imply that *free trade is stable only when* $\theta \le \theta_s(F - sl)$. By considering the stability of each of the other remaining Nash equilibria, we prove the following result in the Appendix.

PROPOSITION 3: *Stable equilibria under Bilateralism are as follows*:

(i) *free trade obtains over* $\theta \le \theta_s(F - sl)$;

(ii) *the CU* $\langle sl \rangle$ *obtains over* $\theta_l(F - sl) \le \theta \le \theta_s(sl - \Phi)$;[32] *and*

(iii) *the CU* $\langle ll' \rangle$ *obtains over* $\theta \ge \theta_s(sl - \Phi)$.

Figure 1 illustrates the results in Proposition 3 by showing the ranges of θ over which the various agreements are stable under Bilateralism.

Proposition 3 relates the degree of underlying asymmetry to the nature of stable agreements. Part (i) simply says that if the degree of endowment asymmetry is sufficiently small, free trade is uniquely stable. Part (ii) says that if the degree of endowment asymmetry is moderate, a CU between two asymmetric partners is stable. When the degree of endowment asymmetry is sufficiently large, only a CU between the two larger countries is stable. Over this range, the smaller country faces relatively low tariffs under the CU $\langle ll' \rangle$ and it prefers to remain an outsider.

B. *Multilateral Liberalization*

We now analyze the Multilateralism game when the pattern of endowments is given by Assumption 2a. Using arguments similar to those employed under symmetry, it can be shown that there are four possible Nash equilibria under

[32] Note that when $\theta_l(F - sl) \le \theta \le \theta_s(F - sl)$, both $\langle F \rangle$ and $\langle sl \rangle$ or $\langle sl' \rangle$ are stable. Since theory offers no guidance about which of these equilibria might be observed, we examine both of these possibilities hereafter. However, for the sake of illustrative clarity, Figure 1 does not show that a CU between the small country and one of the larger countries, i.e., $\langle sl \rangle$ or $\langle sl' \rangle$, is also stable when $\theta_l(F - sl) \le \theta \le \theta_s(F - sl)$.

Multilateralism: $\langle\Phi\rangle$, $\langle sl\rangle^m$, $\langle ll'\rangle^m$ and $\langle F\rangle$. Before proceeding with the stability discussion, we state an immediate extension of Lemma 3.

LEMMA 4: *There exist no unilateral or coalitional deviation from free trade that involves larger countries under the Multilateralism game.*

The above lemma implies that the unilateral incentive of the smaller country to deviate from free trade to $\langle ll'\rangle^m$ determines the stability of free trade. It turns out this deviation occurs only when the degree of endowment asymmetry is sufficiently large since

(38) $$\Delta w_s^*(F - ll'^m) \leq 0 \quad \text{if and only if} \quad \theta \geq \theta_s(F - ll'^m).$$

It immediately follows that *free trade is stable under Multilateralism when* $\theta \leq \theta_s(F - ll'^m)$.

Which agreements are stable when $\theta > \theta_s(F - ll'^m)$ holds (when free trade is not feasible)? We turn to this question next. We know from inequality (21) that $\Delta w_l^*(ll'^m - \Phi) > 0$ under symmetry ($\theta = 1$). Since $\partial \Delta w_l^*(ll'^m - \phi)/\partial\theta > 0$ (Lemma 3) we have

(39) $$\Delta w_l^*(ll'^m - \Phi) > 0 \quad \text{for all } \theta.$$

Since there exists no further unilateral deviation, the joint deviation of the two larger countries from $\langle\Phi\rangle$ to $\langle ll'\rangle^m$ is self-enforcing. Thus, $\langle\Phi\rangle$ *is not stable.*

Next, we show that the smaller country has no incentive to jointly deviate with one of the large countries (say country l) from $\langle ll'\rangle^m$ to $\langle sl\rangle^m$:

(40) $$\Delta w_s^*(ll'^m - sl^m) > 0 \quad \text{for all } \theta.$$

Then, it is immediate from (38), (39), and (40) that *the multilateral agreement* $\langle ll'\rangle^m$ *is stable over the range* $\theta \geq \theta_s(F - ll'^m)$.

Finally, consider the stability of $\langle sl\rangle^m$. First note that $\langle sl\rangle^m$ is a Nash equilibrium only when the degree of endowment asymmetry is sufficiently small since

(41) $$\Delta w_s^*(sl^m - \Phi) > 0 \quad \text{if and only if} \quad \theta \leq \theta_s(sl^m - \Phi).$$

When $\theta \leq \theta_s(sl^m - \Phi)$, the only deviation that can occur from $\langle sl\rangle^m$ is the joint deviation of all countries to $\langle F\rangle$. It is immediate from (38) that this deviation is self enforcing only when $\theta < \theta_s(F - ll'^m)$. Thus, $\langle sl\rangle^m$ is stable when $\theta_s(F - ll'^m) \leq \theta \leq \theta_s(sl^m - \Phi)$.

The following proposition summarizes the above findings.

PROPOSITION 4: *The following hold under Multilateralism: (i) free trade is the unique stable equilibrium when* $\theta \leq \theta_s(F - ll'^m)$; *(ii) both MFN-consistent agreements* $\langle ll'\rangle^m$ *and* $\langle sl\rangle^m$ *are stable when* $\theta_s(F - ll'^m) \leq \theta \leq \theta_s(sl^m - \Phi)$; *and (iii) the MFN-consistent agreement* $\langle ll'\rangle^m$ *is the unique stable equilibrium when* $\theta \geq \theta_s(sl^m - \Phi)$.

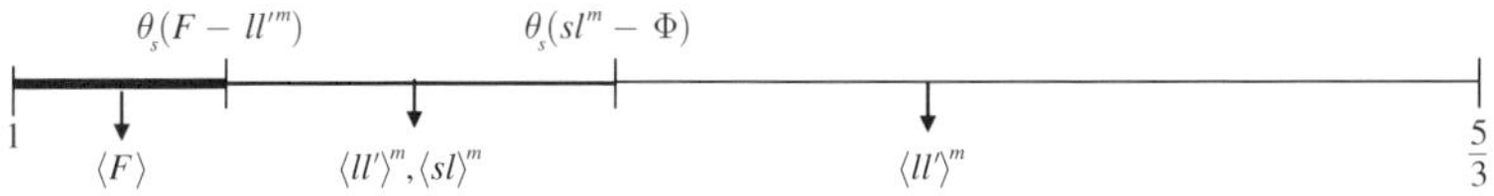

FIGURE 2. STABLE AGREEMENTS UNDER MULTILATERALISM: ONE COUNTRY IS SMALLER

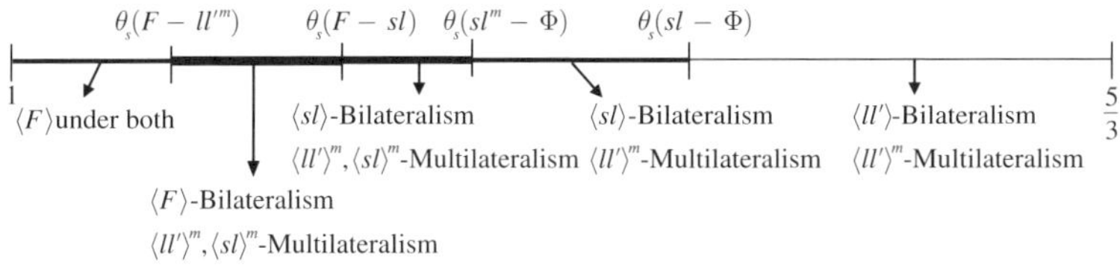

FIGURE 3. BILATERALISM VERSUS MULTILATERALISM: ONE COUNTRY IS SMALLER

Figure 2 shows stable agreements under Multilateralism.

Recall that under Bilateralism, global free trade is stable when $\theta < \theta_s(F - sl)$, whereas it is stable under Multilateralism only when $\theta \leq \theta_s(F - ll'^m)$. A straightforward comparison of these critical thresholds along with Figures 1 and 2 delivers a central result of our paper in the following proposition, which is illustrated in Figure 3.

PROPOSITION 5: *A comparison of equilibrium outcomes under Bilateralism and Multilateralism shows that:*

(i) $\theta_s(F - ll'^m) < \theta_s(F - sl)$; *and*

(ii) *over the parameter range* $\theta_s(F - ll'^m) < \theta \leq \theta_s(F - sl)$ *the unique stable agreement under Bilateralism is free trade, whereas under Multilateralism both MFN-consistent agreements* $\langle ll' \rangle^m$ *and* $\langle sl \rangle^m$ *are stable.*

Part (i) of Proposition 5 says that free trade is stable over a *larger* parameter space when countries are free to form CUs relative to when they cannot. Part (ii) isolates the parameter range over which the freedom to pursue CUs is *necessary* for achieving global free trade. Over this range, because $\theta > \theta_s(F - ll'^m)$, the smaller country has an incentive to unilaterally deviate from free trade to $\langle ll' \rangle^m$ under Multilateralism whereas there exist no such incentive (either unilateral or coalitional) under Bilateralism. It is important to note that, under Multilateralism, the stability of free trade hinges on the *unilateral* deviation incentive of the smaller country whereas under Bilateralism it depends on the *coalitional* deviation incentive of the smaller country and one of the larger countries. As indicated earlier, the smaller country faces a higher tariff under a CU $\langle ll' \rangle$ relative to the agreement $\langle ll' \rangle^m$. Moreover, under the CU $\langle ll' \rangle$ the smaller country is discriminated against in its export markets whereas it suffers no such disadvantage under the agreement $\langle ll' \rangle^m$.

The joint effect of these two factors—a higher tariff and the discriminatory nature of the CU—makes opting out of global free trade relatively costlier for the smaller country.[33]

What if global free trade fails to obtain under both Bilateralism and Multilateralism? Under such a situation, one possible way forward is to ask how global welfare compares under the equilibrium agreements that obtain under these two games. To compare Bilateralism and Multilateralism when free trade fails to materialize, first consider the range $\theta_s(F - sl) \leq \theta \leq \theta_s(sl^m - \Phi)$. Over this range, the CU $\langle sl \rangle$ is stable under Bilateralism while both $\langle sl \rangle^m$ and $\langle ll' \rangle^m$ obtain under Multilateralism. Comparing global welfare under these agreements using the formulae reported in the Mathematical Appendix, we find that Multilateralism yields a superior outcome since

$$\text{(42)} \qquad \Delta ww^*(sl^m - sl) > 0 \quad \text{and} \quad \Delta ww^*(ll'^m - sl) > 0 \quad \text{for all } \theta.$$

The intuition for this result is straightforward: unlike the multilateral agreement $\langle sl \rangle^m$ and $\langle ll' \rangle^m$, the CU $\langle sl \rangle$ diverts trade from country l' to country s and this is problematic because, under nondiscriminatory tariffs, country l' has a lower relative price of the good exported to country l.

Similarly, when $\theta_s(sl^m - \Phi) \leq \theta \leq \theta_s(sl - \Phi)$, the CU $\langle sl \rangle$ is stable under Bilateralism while $\langle ll' \rangle^m$ obtains under Multilateralism and it is immediate from the second part of (42) that MFN-consistent agreement $\langle ll' \rangle^m$ yields higher world welfare than CU $\langle sl \rangle$.

Finally, when $\theta > \theta_s(sl - \Phi)$ the CU $\langle ll' \rangle$ arises under Bilateralism while the agreement $\langle ll' \rangle^m$ obtains under Multilateralism which is once again a superior outcome since

$$\text{(43)} \qquad \Delta ww^*(ll'^m - ll') > 0 \quad \text{for all } \theta.$$

Thus, when free trade is infeasible, the option to pursue CUs leads to inferior outcomes. What are the policy implications of this result? As any observer of the global policy landscape can see, international trade barriers are very much present today, have been with us essentially forever, and might always be part of the global policy landscape. If global free trade is truly out of reach, then there is an argument to be made in favor of excluding CUs from Article XXIV of GATT since non-discriminatory multilateral liberalization avoids the type of distortions that result from the formation of CUs.

Of course, aggregate world welfare does not necessarily speak to the fate of individual countries. In this regard, we can state the following result.

[33] It is also important to note that Proposition 5 focuses only on the parameter range where free trade is uniquely stable under Bilateralism. However, we know from Proposition 3 that both free trade and an asymmetric CU are stable over $\theta_l(F - sl) \leq \theta \leq \theta_s(F - sl)$. Thus, one can argue that when $\theta_l(F - sl) \leq \theta \leq \theta_s(F - sl)$, the freedom to pursue CUs acts as a force in favor of trade liberalization in a weaker sense.

PROPOSITION 6: *From the viewpoint of individual countries, the relative attractiveness of Bilateralism and Multilateralism depends upon the underlying asymmetry in endowments in the following manner:*

(i) *When $\theta_s(F - ll'^m) < \theta \leq \theta_s(F - sl)$, the two larger countries are better off under Bilateralism whereas the smaller country is worse off.*

(ii) *When $\theta_s(F - sl) \leq \theta \leq \theta_s(sl^m - \Phi)$, the larger country that ends up as a member of the CU is better off under Bilateralism whereas the excluded larger country is worse off. The smaller country is better off under Bilateralism when $\langle sl \rangle^m$ is stable under Multilateralism while the opposite holds when $\langle ll' \rangle^m$ is stable.*

(iii) *When $\theta_s(sl^m - \Phi) \leq \theta \leq \theta_s(sl - \Phi)$, the smaller country and the larger country that is excluded from the CU are better off under Multilateralism whereas the other larger country is worse off.*

(iv) *When $\theta > \theta_s(sl - \Phi)$, the two larger countries are better off under Bilateralism whereas the smaller country is worse off.*

Since world welfare is higher under free trade relative to $\langle ll' \rangle^m$, the first part of the proposition is a direct implication of inequality (38). Next, consider the second part. When $\theta_s(F - sl) \leq \theta \leq \theta_s(sl^m - \Phi)$, the CU $\langle sl \rangle$ is stable under Bilateralism while either $\langle sl \rangle^m$ or $\langle ll' \rangle^m$ obtains under Multilateralism. Suppose first that $\langle sl \rangle^m$ is stable under Multilateralism. Under such a case, over the given range of endowment asymmetry, member countries prefer CU to an MFN-consistent agreement, while the excluded larger country has the opposite preferences since it faces discriminatory treatment as well as higher external tariffs under the CU $\langle sl \rangle$ relative to the MFN-consistent agreement $\langle sl \rangle^m$.

Now consider the case where $\langle ll' \rangle^m$ is stable under Multilateralism. Using Lemma 1 and (29), we note that $w_l^*(sl) > w_l^*(ll') > w_l^*(ll'^m)$. This implies that the larger country that ends up as a CU member (i.e., country l) is better off under Bilateralism relative to Multilateralism. The flip side of this is that the excluded larger country under Bilateralism prefers Multilateralism: $w_{l'}^*(sl) < w_{l'}^*(ll'^m)$. But why is the smaller country worse off under Bilateralism even though it is a willing member of the CU $\langle sl \rangle$? Direct calculations establish that when $\theta_s(F - sl) \leq \theta \leq \theta_s(sl - \Phi)$ we have $w_s^*(sl) < w_s^*(ll'^m)$. *In other words, over this range, the smaller country would prefer to be an outsider facing an MFN-consistent agreement between the two larger countries rather than being a member of a CU*, which is what ends up happening under Bilateralism. The same intuitive explanation applies to the third part of the above proposition.

Finally, the last part of the proposition is a direct implication of Lemma 1 since (i) the smaller country faces discriminatory treatment and higher external tariffs under $\langle ll' \rangle$ relative to $\langle ll' \rangle^m$, and (ii) the large countries, provided they are symmetric, are better off under CU $\langle ll' \rangle$ relative to the agreement $\langle ll' \rangle^m$, since only under the latter agreement do they have to abide by the non-discrimination constraint.

The combination of Proposition 4 and Proposition 5 implies that, when the freedom to pursue bilateral CUs is *necessary* for achieving global free trade, Bilateralism leads to higher world welfare and larger countries' preferences are consistent with the world welfare ranking. However, when free trade is not feasible under either regime, Multilateralism leads to higher world welfare and the smaller country's preference for Multilateralism is consistent with the world welfare ranking as long as $\langle sl \rangle^m$ does not arise under Multilateralism.

The careful reader will note that our Bilateralism game does not allow countries to undertake MFN-consistent liberalization of the type that is considered in the Multilateralism game. One might want to consider a comparison between our Multilateralism game and an *expanded* Bilateralism game, which has all the options available under Multilateralism plus the option to form a CU.[34] However, even if one allows for MFN-consistent agreements in the Bilateralism game, Proposition 3 (which reports stable agreements under Bilateralism) remains intact since countries always have incentives to coalitionally deviate from any MFN-consistent agreement to some type of a CU. *Thus, MFN-consistent agreements do not arise as stable outcomes under the Bilateralism game when it is expanded to allow for such agreements.*

We next consider the case where one country is larger than the other two.

VI. If One Country Is Larger

Let the pattern of endowments be given by

ASSUMPTION 2b:

$$e_s = e_{s'} = \frac{e}{\theta} < e_l = e \quad \textit{and} \quad 1 < \theta \leq \frac{5}{3}.$$

In other words, the endowments of countries s and s' are smaller than that of country l. To avoid redundancy, we directly state the main results of this section and relegate the supporting calculations to the Mathematical Appendix. In all of the results reported in Section VI, endowments are as specified under Assumption 2b.

PROPOSITION 7: *The following hold under Bilateralism:* (i) *there exist no unilateral or coalitional deviation from free trade that involves the large country, and* (ii) *free trade is stable if* $\theta \leq \theta_s(F - ss')$; *otherwise, the CU* $\langle ss' \rangle$ *is stable.*

The above proposition, illustrated in Figure 4, informs us that it is the joint incentive of the two smaller countries to exclude the larger country that determines the stability of free trade.

As before, in order to examine how the ability to form CUs matters, consider next the equilibrium outcomes of the Multilateralism game. As under Bilateralism, it is straightforward to show that even under Multilateralism there exist no unilateral or

[34] We thank an anonymous referee for suggesting this formulation of Bilateralism.

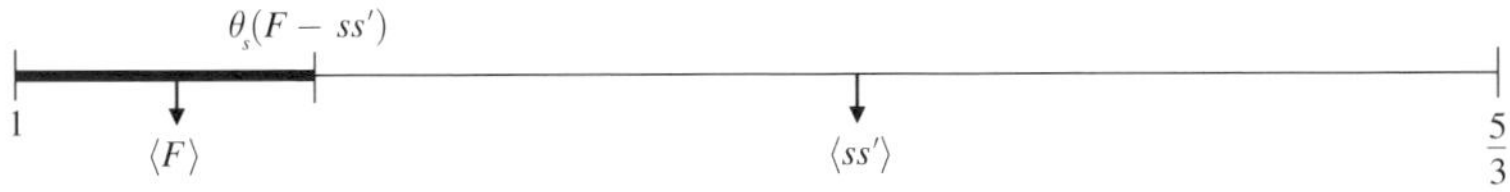

FIGURE 4. STABLE AGREEMENTS UNDER BILATERALISM: ONE COUNTRY IS LARGER

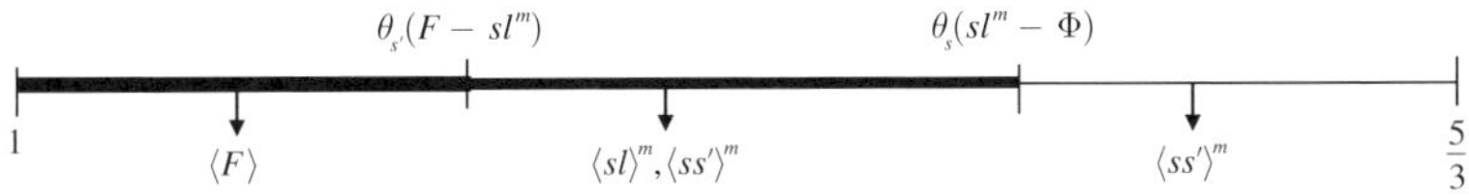

FIGURE 5. STABLE AGREEMENTS UNDER MULTILATERALISM: ONE COUNTRY IS LARGER

coalitional deviations from free trade that involve the larger country. The following result, illustrated in Figure 5, is proved in the Mathematical Appendix.

PROPOSITION 8: *The stable agreements under Multilateralism are as follows:*

(i) *free trade obtains over* $\theta < \theta_{s'}(F - sl^m)$; *and*

(ii) *the MFN-consistent agreement* $\langle sl \rangle^m$ *and* $\langle ss' \rangle^m$ *obtains over* $\theta_{s'}(F - sl^m) \leq \theta \leq \theta_s(sl^m - \Phi)$ *while* $\langle ss' \rangle^m$ *obtains over* $\theta \geq \theta_s(sl^m - \Phi)$.

The above proposition and Proposition 7 together show that while joint deviation incentives of the two smaller countries from free trade determine the stability of free trade under Bilateralism, the unilateral deviation incentive of one of the smaller countries does that under Multilateralism.

What light does our model shed on the effects of Article XXIV when two countries are relatively smaller? We directly state our main result in the following proposition.

PROPOSITION 9: *If* $\theta_s(F - ss') < \theta \leq \theta_{s'}(F - sl^m)$, *Multilateralism yields free trade as the stable equilibrium, whereas Bilateralism yields the CU* $\langle ss' \rangle$.

Proposition 9, illustrated in Figure 6, argues that, unlike the case of two larger countries and one smaller country, free trade is stable over a *larger* parameter space when countries *cannot* form bilateral CUs. Thus, over the parameter range $\theta_s(F - ss') < \theta \leq \theta_{s'}(F - sl^m)$, the freedom to pursue CUs prevents the attainment of global free trade. This is in sharp contrast to the results of Saggi and Yildiz (2010) who analyzed the case of FTAs. Together, these results suggest that the concern that PTAs might undermine the multilateral trading system maybe more relevant for CUs than for FTAs.

When countries are free to pursue CUs and $\theta_s(F - ss') < \theta \leq \theta_{s'}(F - sl^m)$, the smaller countries have a joint incentive to exclude the larger country via deviating from $\langle F \rangle$ to $\langle ss' \rangle$ and this deviation is self-enforcing, since neither of the smaller

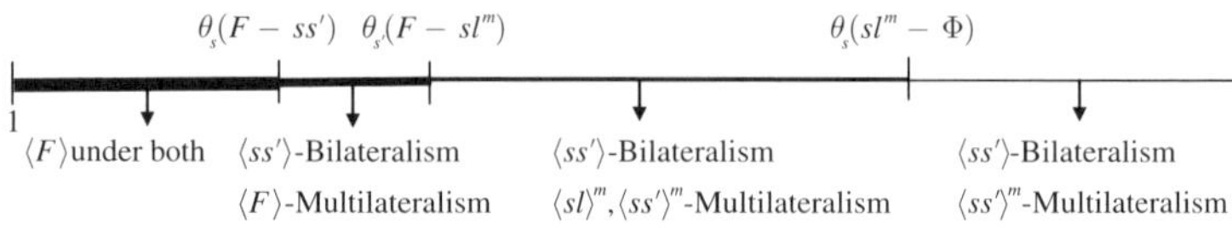

Figure 6. Bilateralism versus Multilateralism: One Country Is Larger

countries has a unilateral incentive to further deviate. On the other hand, over the same range, there exists no unilateral or joint deviation from free trade under Multilateralism.

Why does the freedom to pursue CUs supplant free trade when the pattern of asymmetry is given by Assumption 2b (one country is smaller), whereas it has the opposite effect under Assumption 2a (one country is larger)? The intuition behind this result can be built in steps. First, note that regardless of the pattern of asymmetry, under Multilateralism it is the *unilateral deviation incentive* of a smaller country that determines the stability of free trade. Second, the benefit of the external tariff reduction enjoyed by the smaller country under the agreement $\langle ll' \rangle^m$—relevant under Assumption 2a—is larger than that under $\langle sl \rangle^m$—applicable under Assumption 2b. This, in turn, implies that when the pattern of asymmetry is given by Assumption 2a, the smaller country is less willing to participate in free trade relative to the case when it is given by Assumption 2b—i.e., $\theta_{s'}(F - sl^m) > \theta_s(F - ll'^m)$.

The third point to note is that in the Bilateralism game, it is the *joint deviation incentive* of two countries to exclude the larger country from free trade—of countries s and l under Assumption 2a, and countries s and s' under Assumption 2b—that determines the stability of free trade. In this regard, we find that this joint incentive to exclude is stronger under Assumption 2b (when two countries are smaller than the third) relative to that under Assumption 2a because, in the former scenario, each of them benefits relatively more from being able to impose its optimal CU tariff on the relatively large volume of imports supplied by the nonmember. This implies that the region over which free trade is stable under Bilateralism is larger under Assumption 2a: $\theta_s(F - ss') < \theta_s(F - sl)$.

These three points together help explain how the underlying pattern of endowment asymmetry ends up determining the role of Article XXIV. Relative to Assumption 2a, the pattern of asymmetry under Assumption 2b yields free trade over a *larger* parameter space in the Multilateralism game, while it yields free trade over a *smaller* parameter space under the Bilateralism game. This is why Article XXIV ends up harming the prospects for global free trade under Assumption 2b, whereas it has the opposite effect under Assumption 2a.

Finally, what if $\theta > \theta_{s'}(F - sl^m)$ and global free trade fails to obtain under both Bilateralism and Multilateralism? As before, under such a situation, we can ask how global welfare compares under the equilibrium agreements that obtain under the two games. We know from Proposition 7 and Proposition 8 that: (i) when $\theta_{s'}(F - sl^m) \leq \theta \leq \theta_s(sl^m - \Phi)$, the MFN-consistent agreements $\langle sl \rangle^m$ and $\langle ss' \rangle^m$ are stable under Multilateralism, while the CU $\langle ss' \rangle$ is stable under Bilateralism;

and (ii) when $\theta > \theta_s(sl^m - \Phi)$, the MFN-consistent agreement $\langle ss' \rangle^m$ is stable under Multilateralism, while the CU $\langle ss' \rangle$ is stable under Bilateralism. Comparing global welfare under these agreements over the given range yields

$$\Delta ww^* (sl^m - ss') > 0 \quad \text{for all } \theta \tag{44}$$

and

$$\Delta ww^* (ss'^m - ss') > 0 \quad \text{for all } \theta. \tag{45}$$

Once again, Multilateralism yields the more preferred outcome from an aggregate welfare perspective. The preferences of individual countries are as stated in the following proposition.

PROPOSITION 10: *The larger country is better off under Multilateralism relative to Bilateralism, whereas the smaller countries are worse off.*

When $\theta_s(F - ss') < \theta \leq \theta_{s'}(F - sl^m)$, the joint deviation of the smaller countries determines the stability of free trade and they are better off under the CU $\langle ss' \rangle$ relative to free trade. Since world welfare is higher under free trade relative to the CU $\langle ss' \rangle$, this automatically implies that the larger country is better off under Multilateralism relative to Bilateralism over this parameter range. Proposition 6 and Proposition 10 together imply that, irrespective of the type of asymmetry, larger countries' preferences are consistent with the world welfare ranking: when CUs facilitate global free trade larger countries prefer bilateralism, while the large country prefers multilateralism when CUs act as stumbling blocs. When $\theta_{s'}(F - sl^m) \leq \theta \leq \theta_s(sl^m - \Phi)$, recall that either $\langle sl \rangle^m$ or $\langle ss' \rangle^m$ is stable under Multilateralism, while the CU $\langle ss' \rangle$ is stable under Bilateralism. Suppose first that $\langle sl \rangle^m$ is stable over the given range. It is immediate from Lemma 1 and Lemma 3 that $w_s^*(ss') > w_s^*(ss'^m) > w_s^*(sl^m)$, implying that country s is better off under Bilateralism relative to Multilateralism. When $\theta > \theta_{s'}(F - sl^m)$, the same result obtains for country s', i.e., $w_{s'}^*(ss') > w_{s'}^*(sl^m)$, while the opposite result obtains for the larger country, which is better off under Multilateralism relative to Bilateralism. Similarly, as indicated above, if $\langle ss' \rangle^m$ is stable under Multilateralism, small countries prefer Bilateralism relative to Multilateralism, since they face the MFN constraint only under the latter game. Since world welfare is higher under $\langle ss' \rangle^m$ relative to $\langle ss' \rangle$, the larger country must be better off under Multilateralism.

VII. Conclusion

Ever since Viner (1950) first drew attention to the issue, the economics of preferential trade agreements, such as CUs, has received intense scrutiny from economists and policymakers alike. In this paper, we conduct an analysis that sheds light on whether and how the freedom to pursue CUs provided under Article XXIV of

GATT affects the process of multilateral trade liberalization. Our model is novel in that both the type of trade liberalization (preferential versus multilateral), and the magnitude of tariff cuts undertaken by countries under each type of liberalization, are endogenously determined.

We provide an analytical comparison of two alternative games of trade liberalization. Under the Bilateralism game, countries are free to liberalize trade bilaterally via the formation of a CU, multilaterally, or not at all, whereas under the Multilateralism game they can either liberalize multilaterally or not at all. This is in sharp contrast to the much of the existing literature that has tended to take either preferential trade agreements or multilateral liberalization as exogenously given. Comparing equilibrium outcomes of these two games helps provide an evaluation of GATT Article XXIV—perhaps the most important exception to the principle of nondiscrimination available to WTO members today.

Our analysis shows that if governments base decisions on national welfare, no two countries would choose to form a preferential CU if endowment levels are relatively symmetric across countries. Instead, under such a scenario, global free trade would obtain as the unique stable equilibrium and the freedom to pursue discriminatory CUs would go unused. This result implies that some type of heterogeneity across countries may be necessary to induce countries to opt out of multilateral liberalization. To verify this intuition, we consider two scenarios: one where one country is smaller than the other two and another where it is larger. Under the former scenario, the key result is that the freedom to form CUs can actually further the cause of global free trade by changing the outside option facing the country that is reluctant to liberalize multilaterally—i.e., the smaller country. However, under the latter scenario, the relationship between the preferential and multilateral routes is much more strained: the concern that CUs can serve as exclusionary devices that undermine the prospects of multilateral free trade is indeed borne out in this scenario.

An important assumption of our analysis is that countries intervene in free trade only via import tariffs. In particular, like much of the existing literature, we do not permit the use of export taxes. We conjecture that allowing for such taxes should not affect our result that free trade is the only stable agreement under Bilateralism and Multilateralism under symmetry. However, under asymmetry, export taxes are likely to matter and potentially have more subtle consequences. In particular, the relative value of a CU as well as that of a MFN-consistent agreement to both member and nonmember countries will change if export policies are available. For example, an outside country will have an additional instrument with which to counter some of the harmful effects of exclusion. On the other hand, members of a CU would also potentially stand to gain more from coordination, if such coordination were to involve both import tariffs and export taxes. How exactly these types of incentives play out in equilibrium is a topic worthy of future research.

Mathematical Appendix

In this Mathematical Appendix, we provide the necessary supporting calculations and proofs.

A. *Welfare Levels*

We begin by reporting welfare levels under different policy regimes as a function of tariffs. Let $\mathbf{t}=(t_i, t_j, t_k)$. Since countries i and j impose MFN-consistent tariffs under both the status quo and the agreement $\langle ij^m \rangle$, for a *given* vector of tariffs $\mathbf{t}$, we can write

$$\text{(A1)} \qquad w_i(\Phi) = w_i(ij^m) = w_i(jk^m) = CS_i(ij^m) + PS_i(ij^m) + TR_i(ij^m),$$

where

$$CS_i(ij^m) = \frac{1}{18}\left[(e_i + e_j + t_k)^2 + (e_i + e_k + t_j)^2 + (e_j + e_k - 2t_i)^2\right]$$

and

$$PS_i(ij^m) = e_i\left(2\alpha - \frac{2e_i + \sum_{z \neq i}(e_z + t_z)}{3}\right)$$

and

$$TR_i(ij^m) = \frac{t_i}{3}\left(\sum_{z \neq i} e_z - 2t_i\right).$$

Under the status quo $\langle \Phi \rangle$, country i chooses its non-discriminatory tariff t_i to maximize its own welfare. Accordingly, we have that

$$\text{(A2)} \qquad \frac{\partial w_i(\Phi)}{\partial t_i} = \frac{e_j + e_k - 8t_i}{9} = 0 \Rightarrow t_i^{\phi} = \frac{e_j + e_k}{8}.$$

Note further that $t_i(jk^m) = t_i^{\phi}$, since the excluded country under the MFN-consistent agreement $\langle jk \rangle^m$ continues to impose its optimal MFN tariff on its trading partners.

Under the agreement $\langle ij \rangle^m$, countries i and j jointly choose their nondiscriminatory tariffs (t_i^m, t_j^m) to maximize $w_i(ij^m) + w_j(ij^m)$. The relevant first-order conditions and the associated optimal tariffs are

$$\text{(A3)} \qquad \frac{\partial(w_i(ij^m) + w_j(ij^m))}{\partial t_i} = \frac{2e_k - e_j - 7t_i}{9} = 0 \Rightarrow t_i^m = \frac{2e_k - e_j}{7}$$

$$\frac{\partial(w_i(ij^m) + w_j(ij^m))}{\partial t_j} = \frac{2e_k - e_i - 7t_j}{9} = 0 \Rightarrow t_j^m = \frac{2e_k - e_i}{7}.$$

Under the CU $\langle ij \rangle$, members abolish tariffs on each other $(t_{ij} = t_{ji} = 0)$ and impose jointly optimal tariffs on the nonmember. Let t_i and t_j denote member countries' external tariffs and t_k denote the nonmember's non-discriminatory tariff. Then, the welfare of member i equals

(A4) $$w_i(ij) = CS_i(ij) + PS_i(ij) + TR_i(ij),$$

where

$$CS_i(ij) = \frac{1}{18}\left[(e_i + e_j + t_k)^2 + (e_i + e_k - t_j)^2 + (e_j + e_k - t_i)^2\right]$$

and

$$PS_i(ij) = e_i\left(2\alpha - \frac{2e_i + \sum_{z\neq i}(e_z + t_k - t_j)}{3}\right)$$

and

$$TR_i(ij) = \frac{t_i}{3}(2e_k - e_j - 2t_i).$$

Member countries choose their external tariffs to maximize their joint welfare $w_i(ij) + w_j(ij)$. This gives

(A5) $$\frac{\partial(w_i(ij) + w_j(ij))}{\partial t_i} = \frac{4e_k - 2e_j - 10t_i}{9} = 0 \Rightarrow t_i^u = \frac{2e_k - e_j}{5}$$

$$\frac{\partial(w_i(ij) + w_j(ij))}{\partial t_j} = \frac{4e_k - 2e_i - 10t_j}{9} = 0 \Rightarrow t_j^u = \frac{2e_k - e_i}{5}.$$

Now consider the welfare of a non-member country i under $\langle jk\rangle$, given by

$$w_i(jk) = CS_i(jk) + PS_i(jk) + TR_i(jk) = w_i(\Phi),$$

where $CS_i(jk)$. Thus, the non-member country i's tariff under the CU $\langle jk\rangle$ equals t_i^ϕ and is given by

$$\frac{\partial w_i(jk)}{\partial t_i} = \frac{e_j + e_k - 8t_i}{9} = 0 \Rightarrow t_i(jk) = t_i^\phi = \frac{e_j + e_k}{8}.$$

Finally, by imposing $t_i = t_j = t_k = 0$ in (A1), we obtain $w_i^*(F)$, the welfare of country i under free trade, as

(A6) $$w_i^*(F) = w_i(\Phi)\big|_{t_i=t_j=t_k=0}.$$

Using the welfare and tariff levels reported above, we can easily obtain the formulae for welfare levels under all possible regimes. Lemmas 2 and 3 and the various inequalities reported in the main text follow from a direct application of the relevant formulae. For example, consider the world welfare comparisons reported in (42) and (43). A direct application of the relevant formulae yields $\Delta ww^*(ll'^m - sl) \geq 0$ if and only if $\theta \leq 5/3$. Indeed, the same parameter restriction (i.e., $\theta \leq 5/3$) ensures that: (1) $\Delta ww^*(ll'^m - ll') \geq 0$; (2) $\Delta w_s^*(ll'^m - sl) \geq 0$; (3) $\Delta w_{l'}^*(ll'^m - sl) \geq 0$; and (4) $\Delta ww^*(sl^m - ss') \geq 0$. To save space, we do not include the algebraic details underlying these straightforward calculations.

B. *Inequality (28)*

We have $x_j^l(\Phi) = x_j^l(jk) = x_j^l(jk^m) = 5e_j - 3e_k/8 \geq 0$ if and only if $e_k \leq 5e_j/3$. Furthermore, under the CU $\langle ij \rangle$ we have $x_j^l(ij) = 3e_j - e_k/5 \geq 0$ if and only if $e_k \leq 3e_j$ and $x_j^l(ik) = 2e_j - e_k/5 \geq 0$ if and only if $e_k \leq 2e_j$. Next, under the MFN-consistent agreement $\langle ij \rangle^m$ we have that $x_j^l(ij^m) = 5e_j - 3e_k/7 \geq 0$ if and only if $e_k \leq 5e_j/3$ and $x_j^l(ik^m) = 4e_j - 2e_k/7 \geq 0$ if and only if $e_k \leq 2e_j$. Finally, under free trade, we have that $x_j^l(F) = 2e_j - e_k/3 \geq 0$ if and only if $e_k \leq 2e_j$.

C. *Critical θ values in Propositions 4–6, 8 and 9*

In the multilateralism game, $\theta_s(sl^m - \Phi) \cong 1.12$ and $\theta_s(F - ll'^m) \cong 1.015$ obtain under Assumption 2a, while $\theta_s(F - ss'^m) \cong 1.375$, $\theta_{s'}(F - sl^m) \cong 1.03$ and $\theta_s(sl^m - \Phi) \cong 1.15$ obtain under Assumption 2b.

D. *Proofs of Propositions and Lemmas*

PROOF OF PROPOSITION 3:

Consider first the CU $\langle ll' \rangle$. There are three possible defections from it:

(ULL): Unilateral deviation of l or l' from $\langle ll' \rangle$ to $\langle \Phi \rangle$.

(JLL1): Joint defection of s and l (or l') from $\langle ll' \rangle$ to $\langle sl \rangle$ (or $\langle sl' \rangle$).

(JLL2): Joint defection of s, l, and l' from $\langle ll' \rangle$ to $\langle F \rangle$.

We know from (14) that under symmetry no member country has an incentive to unilaterally deviate from a CU to the status quo. From Lemma 2, we have $\partial \Delta w_l^*(ll' - \Phi)/\partial\theta = \partial \Delta w_{l'}^*(ll' - \Phi)/\partial\theta < 0$. Next note that

$$\Delta w_l^*(ll' - \Phi) = \Delta w_{l'}^*(ll' - \Phi) > 0 \quad \text{when} \quad \theta = \frac{5}{3}.$$

Thus, we can argue that (ULL) never occurs since

(D1) $$\Delta w_l^*(ll' - \Phi) = \Delta w_{l'}^*(ll' - \Phi) > 0 \quad \text{for all} \quad \theta.$$

Now consider (JLL1). From (29), we know that a larger country (say l) always has an incentive to deviate from $\langle ll' \rangle$ to $\langle sl \rangle$, while the smaller country deviates only when the degree of endowment asymmetry is not large since

$$\text{(D2)} \qquad \Delta w_s^*(sl - ll') \geq 0 \quad \text{if and only if} \quad \theta \leq \theta_s(sl - ll') \cong 1.28,$$

and that this joint deviation is self-enforcing when $\theta \leq \theta_s(sl - \Phi) \cong 1.27$.

Now consider (JLL2). It is immediate from (33) and (34) that (JLL2) occurs when $\theta \leq \theta_s(F - ll') \cong 1.23$ and it is self enforcing if and only if $\theta \leq \theta_s(F - sl) \cong 1.048$. These deviations together imply that $\langle ll' \rangle$ is stable when $\theta \geq \theta_s(sl - \Phi)$.

Now consider the stability of $\langle sl \rangle$. Note from (37) that country s has an incentive to unilaterally deviate from $\langle sl \rangle$ to $\langle \Phi \rangle$ when $\theta > \theta_s(sl - \Phi)$. It is straightforward from (29) that there exist no joint deviations from $\langle sl \rangle$ to $\langle ll' \rangle$. Furthermore, all countries deviate to free trade when $\theta < \theta_l(F - sl) \cong 1.045$ and this joint deviation is self-enforcing. As a result, $\langle sl \rangle$ or $\langle sl' \rangle$ is stable when $\theta_l(F - sl) \leq \theta \leq \theta_s(sl - \Phi)$.

Finally, we examine the stability of the status quo under Bilateralism. Note from (D1) that two larger countries jointly deviate from $\langle \Phi \rangle$ to $\langle ll' \rangle$ and this deviation is self-enforcing. Thus $\langle \Phi \rangle$ is not stable.

PROOF OF LEMMA 4:

Under Assumption 2a in the Multilateralism game, there are three possible defections from free trade that involves larger countries:

(ULF): Unilateral deviation of l (or l') from $\langle F \rangle$ to $\langle sl'^m \rangle$ (or $\langle sl^m \rangle$).

(JLLF): Joint defection of l and l' from $\langle F \rangle$ to $\langle ll'^m \rangle$.

(JSLF): Joint defection of s and l (or l') from $\langle F \rangle$ to $\langle sl^m \rangle$ (or $\langle sl'^m \rangle$).

We first show that (ULF) never occurs since

$$\text{(D3)} \qquad \Delta w_l^*(F - sl'^m) = \frac{e^2(55 + 471\theta^2 - 514\theta)}{84^2} > 0 \quad \text{for all} \quad \theta.$$

Now consider (JLLF). From (23), we know that larger countries have no incentive to jointly deviate from $\langle F \rangle$ to $\langle ll'^m \rangle$ under symmetry. From Lemma 3, we have $\partial \Delta w_l(F - ll'^m)/\partial\theta > 0$. Therefore, we can argue that (JLLF) never occurs since

$$\text{(D4)} \qquad \Delta w_l^*(F - ll'^m) = \Delta w_{l'}^*(F - ll'^m) > 0 \quad \text{for all} \quad \theta.$$

PROOF OF PROPOSITION 7:

(i) It is immediate from (16) and Lemma 2 that

$$\text{(D5)} \qquad \Delta w_l^*(F - ss') > 0 \quad \text{for all} \quad \theta.$$

Moreover, we know from Lemma 2 that $\partial \Delta w_l^*(F - sl)/\partial\theta > 0$. Then, combining this with inequality (17) yields

$$\text{(D6)} \qquad \Delta w_l^*(F - sl) > 0 \quad \text{for all} \quad \theta.$$

Finally, combining (14) and Lemma 2 implies that $\Delta w_l^*(sl - \Phi) > 0$. Then, from this inequality and (D6) it is immediate that $\Delta w_l^*(F - \Phi) > 0$.

(ii) Consider the perspective of countries s and s'. Direct calculations yield

$$\text{(D7)} \qquad \Delta w_s^*(F - ss') \le 0 \quad \text{if and only if} \quad \theta \ge \theta_s(F - ss') \cong 1.02.$$

Moreover, Lemma 2 and (14) together imply that

$$\text{(D8)} \qquad \Delta w_s^*(ss' - \Phi) > 0 \quad \text{for all} \quad \theta.$$

Thus, the joint deviation from $\langle F\rangle$ to $\langle ss'\rangle$ is self enforcing. Inequality (D8) also implies that the status quo is not stable since the smaller countries jointly deviate from $\langle \Phi\rangle$ to $\langle ss'\rangle$ and this deviation is self-enforcing.

Further note that

$$\text{(D9)} \qquad \Delta w_s^*(F - \Phi) \le 0 \quad \text{if and only if} \quad \theta \ge \theta_s(F - \Phi) \cong 1.39.$$

However, $\theta_s(F - \Phi) > \theta_s(F - ss')$ and thus the above deviation is not binding for the stability of $\langle F\rangle$. Finally, note from (14), (15), and Lemma 2 that the smaller countries have an incentive to jointly deviate from $\langle sl\rangle$ to $\langle ss'\rangle$ and this deviation is a self-enforcing deviation—see (D8). Thus, the CU between a small country and the large country $\langle sl\rangle$ is not stable.

PROOF OF PROPOSITION 8:

(i) Under Assumption 2b in the Multilateralism game, there are three possible defections from free trade that involves larger countries:

(ULF-b): Unilateral deviation of l from $\langle F\rangle$ to $\langle ss'^m\rangle$.

(JSLF-b): Joint defection of l and s (or s') from $\langle F\rangle$ to $\langle sl^m\rangle$ (or $\langle s'l^m\rangle$).

We first show that (ULF-b) never occurs since

$$\text{(D10)} \qquad \Delta w_l^*(F - sl'^m) = \left(\frac{e}{420\theta}\right)^2 [3 + 208\theta(1-\theta)] > 0 \quad \text{for all} \quad \theta.$$

Now consider (JSLF-b). From (23), we know that the large country has no incentive to jointly deviate with a smaller country from $\langle F\rangle$ to $\langle sl^m\rangle$ under symmetry. From

Lemma 3, we have $\partial \Delta w_l(F - sl^m)/\partial\theta > 0$. Therefore, we can argue that (JSLF-b) never occurs since

(D11) $$\Delta w_l^*(F - sl^m) = \Delta w_l^*(F - s'l^m) > 0 \quad \text{for all} \quad \theta.$$

Thus, the unilateral and joint incentives of the smaller countries to deviate from free trade determine the stability of free trade. The unilateral deviation of a smaller country (say country s') from $\langle F\rangle$ to $\langle sl\rangle^m$ occurs unless the degree of endowment asymmetry is sufficiently small since

(D12) $$\Delta w_{s'}^*(F - sl^m) \leq 0 \quad \text{if and only if} \quad \theta \geq \theta_{s'}(F - sl^m).$$

Similarly, two smaller countries have incentives to jointly deviate from $\langle F\rangle$ to $\langle ss'\rangle^m$ when the degree of endowment asymmetry is sufficiently large since

(D13) $$\Delta w_s^*(F - ss'^m) = \Delta w_{s'}^*(F - ss'^m) \leq 0 \quad \text{if and only if} \quad \theta \geq \theta_s(F - ss'^m).$$

Finally, the smaller countries have incentives to jointly deviate from $\langle F\rangle$ to $\langle\Phi\rangle$ provided they are sufficiently small relative to the larger country since

(D14) $$\Delta w_s^*(F - \Phi) = \Delta w_{s'}^*(F - \Phi) \leq 0 \quad \text{if and only if} \quad \theta \geq \theta_s(F - \Phi).$$

However, since $\theta_s(F - \Phi) > \theta_s(F - ss'^m) > \theta_{s'}(F - sl^m)$, the unilateral deviation (and thus self-enforcing) of a smaller country (say country s') from $\langle F\rangle$ to $\langle sl\rangle^m$ determines the stability of free trade: *$\langle F\rangle$ is stable when $\theta \leq \theta_{s'}(F - sl^m)$.*

(ii) First note that $\langle\Phi\rangle$ *is never stable* since the smaller countries have a joint incentive to deviate from $\langle\Phi\rangle$ to $\langle ss'\rangle^m$ and it is a self-enforcing deviation since

(D15) $$\Delta w_s^*(ss'^m - \Phi) > 0 \quad \text{for all} \quad \theta.$$

Now consider the stability of MFN-consistent agreement of smaller countries $\langle ss'\rangle^m$. It is immediate from Lemma 3 that the joint deviation of countries s and l from $\langle ss'\rangle^m$ to $\langle sl\rangle^m$ never happens, as the smaller country s always prefers the other smaller country to the larger country as a partner under an MFN-consistent agreement since

(D16) $$\Delta w_s^*(ss'^m - sl^m) > 0 \quad \text{for all} \quad \theta.$$

Then, the only possible deviation from $\langle ss'\rangle^m$ is the joint deviation of all countries to free trade. Note from (D13) and (D12) that this deviation happens when $\theta < \theta_s(F - ss'^m)$ and it is self enforcing only when $\theta \leq \theta_{s'}(F - sl^m)$. Thus, *$\langle ss'\rangle^m$ is stable when $\theta \geq \theta_{s'}(F - sl^m)$.* Finally, consider the stability of $\langle sl\rangle^m$. Country s has an incentive to unilaterally deviate from $\langle sl\rangle^m$ to $\langle\Phi\rangle$ if θ is sufficiently large since

$$\Delta w_s^*(sl^m - \Phi) < 0 \quad \text{if and only if} \quad \theta > \theta_s(sl^m - \Phi).$$

Moreover, country s' always prefers to be outsider under $\langle sl \rangle^m$ relative to being a member under $\langle ss' \rangle^m$ and thus has no incentive to jointly deviate with country s from $\langle sl \rangle^m$ to $\langle ss' \rangle^m$. Thus, $\langle sl \rangle^m$ is stable if and only if $\theta_{s'}(F - sl^m) < \theta \leq \theta_s(sl^m - \Phi)$ holds.

REFERENCES

Aghion, Philippe, Pol Antràs, and Elhanan Helpman. 2007. "Negotiating Free Trade." *Journal of International Economics* 73 (1): 1–30.

Bagwell, Kyle, and Robert W. Staiger. 1997a. "Multilateral Tariff Cooperation during the Formation of Customs Unions." *Journal of International Economics* 42 (1–2): 91–123.

Bagwell, Kyle, and Robert W. Staiger. 1997b. "Multilateral Tariff Cooperation during the Formation of Free Trade Areas." *International Economic Review* 38 (2): 291–319.

Bagwell, Kyle, and Robert W. Staiger. 1998. "Regionalism and Multilateral Tariff Cooperation." In *International Trade Policy and the Pacific Rim*, edited by John Piggott and Alan Woodland, 157–85. London: MacMillan.

Bagwell, Kyle, and Robert W. Staiger. 2000. "GATT-Think." National Bureau of Economic Research (NBER) Working Paper 8005.

Bernheim, Douglas B., Bezalel Peleg, and Michael Whinston. 1987. "Coalition-Proof Nash Equilibria I. Concepts." *Journal of Economic Theory* 42 (1): 1–12.

Bhagwati, Jagdish. 1991. *The World Trading System at Risk*. Princeton: Princeton University Press.

Bhagwati, Jagdish, Arvind Panagariya, and Pravin Krishna, eds. 1999. *Trading Blocs*. Cambridge, MA: MIT Press.

Bond, Eric W., Raymond G. Riezman, and Constantinos Syropoulos. 2004. "A Strategic and Welfare Theoretic Analysis of Free Trade Areas." *Journal of International Economics* 64 (1): 1–27.

Bond, Eric W., and Constantinos Syropoulos. 1996. "The Size of Trading Blocs: Market Power and World Welfare Effects." *Journal of International Economics* 40 (3–4): 411–37.

Estevadeordal, Antoni, Caroline Freund, and Emanuel Ornelas. 2008. "Does Regionalism Affect Trade Liberalization toward Nonmembers?" *Quarterly Journal of Economics* 123 (4): 1531–75.

Freund, Caroline. 2000. "Multilateralism and the Endogenous Formation of Preferential Trade Agreements." *Journal of International Economics* 52 (2): 359–76.

Furusawa, Taiji. 2002. "Preferential Trade Arrangements versus Open Regionalism: A Theoretical Analysis of APEC." In *Issues and Options for US-Japan Trade Policies*, edited by Robert M. Stern, 253–67. Ann Arbor: University of Michigan Press.

Furusawa, Taiji, and Hideo Konishi. 2007. "Free Trade Networks." *Journal of International Economics* 72 (2): 310–35.

Gatsios, Konstantine, and Larry Karp. 1991. "Delegation Games in Customs Unions." *Review of Economic Studies* 58 (2): 391–97.

Goyal, Sanjeev, and Sumit Joshi. 2006. "Bilateralism and Free Trade." *International Economic Review* 47 (3): 749–78.

Hadjiyiannis, Costas. 2004. "Regionalism and Multilateral Trade Liberalization with Asymmetric Countries." *Review of International Economics* 12 (3): 395–411.

Kennan, John, and Raymond Riezman. 1990. "Optimal Tariff Equilibria with Customs Unions." *Canadian Journal of Economics* 23 (1): 70–83.

Krishna, Pravin. 1998. "Regionalism and Multilateralism: A Political Economy Approach." *Quarterly Journal of Economics* 113 (1): 227–51.

Krugman, Paul R. 1991. "The Move Toward Free Trade Zones." Paper presented at the Federal Reserve Bank of Kansas City Symposium: Policy Implications of Trade and Currency Zones, Jackson Hole, August 22–24.

Melatos, Mark, and Alan D. Woodland. 2007a. "Pareto-Optimal Delegation in Customs Unions." *Review of International Economics* 15 (3): 441–61.

Melatos, Mark, and Alan D. Woodland. 2007b. "Endogenous Trade Bloc Formation in an Asymmetric World." *European Economic Review* 51 (4): 901–24.

Mrázová, Monika, David Vines, and Ben Zissimos. 2010. "Is the WTO's Article XXIV Bad?" http://www.monikamrazova.com/ArtBad.pdf.

Ornelas, Emanuel. 2005a. "Trade Creating Free Trade Areas and the Undermining of Multilateralism." *European Economic Review* 49 (7): 1717–35.

Ornelas, Emanuel. 2005b. "Rent Destruction and the Political Viability of Free Trade Agreements." *Quarterly Journal of Economics* 120 (4): 1475–1506.

▶**Raimondos-Moller, Pascalis, and Alan D. Woodland.** 2006. "Non-Preferential Trading Clubs." *Journal of International Economics* 68 (1): 79–91.
▶**Riezman, Raymond.** 1985. "Customs Unions and the Core." *Journal of International Economics* 19 (3–4): 355–65.
▶**Riezman, Raymond.** 1999. "Can Bilateral Trade Agreements Help to Induce Free Trade?" *Canadian Journal of Economics* 32 (3): 751–66.
▶**Saggi, Kamal.** 2006. "Preferential Trade Agreements and Multilateral Tariff Cooperation." *International Economic Review* 47 (1): 29–57.
▶**Saggi, Kamal, and Halis Murat Yildiz.** 2010. "Bilateralism, Multilateralism, and the Quest for Global Free Trade." *Journal of International Economics* 81 (1): 26–37.
▶**Seidmann, Daniel J.** 2009. "Preferential Trading Arrangements as Strategic Positioning." *Journal of International Economics* 79 (1): 143–59.
▶**Syropoulos, Constantinos.** 2003. "Rules for the Disposition of Tariff Revenues and the Determination of Common External Tariffs in Customs Unions." *Journal of International Economics* 60 (2): 387–416.
Viner, Jacob. 1950. *The Custom Union Issue*. New York: Carnegie Endowment for International Peace.
▶**Yi, Sang-Seung.** 1996. "Endogenous Formation of Customs Unions under Imperfect Competition: Open Regionalism Is Good." *Journal of International Economics* 41 (1–2): 153–77.

CHAPTER 10

Journal of International Economics 99 (2016) 105–119

Contents lists available at ScienceDirect

Journal of International Economics

journal homepage: www.elsevier.com/locate/jie

External trade diversion, exclusion incentives and the nature of preferential trade agreements☆

Paul Missios [a,1], Kamal Saggi [b,*,2], Halis Murat Yildiz [a,3]

[a] Department of Economics, Ryerson University, 350 Victoria Street, Toronto, ON M5B 2K3, Canada
[b] Department of Economics, Vanderbilt University, Nashville, TN 37235-1828, United States

ARTICLE INFO

Article history:
Received 19 September 2014
Received in revised form 14 September 2015
Accepted 21 January 2016
Available online 29 January 2016

JEL classification:
F11
F12

Keywords:
Free trade agreement
Customs union
Hub and spoke agreements
Free trade
Optimal tariffs

ABSTRACT

In a game of endogenous trade agreements between three countries, we show that while the pursuit of customs unions (CUs) prevents global free trade from emerging as a coalition-proof Nash equilibrium, the pursuit of free trade agreements (FTAs) does not. This result reflects the relatively *flexible* nature of FTAs: whereas each FTA member can independently undertake further trade liberalization with respect to the non-member, CU members must do so as a group due to their common external tariff. By diverting members' exports away from the non-member, both types of trade agreements induce the non-member to voluntarily lower its import tariffs.

1. Introduction

Preferential trade agreements (PTAs) are more popular than ever before while multilateral trade liberalization seems to have come to a standstill. The ever increasing popularity of PTAs can be gauged from the fact that as of April 7, 2015, 612 notifications of PTAs (counting goods and services separately) had been received by the GATT/WTO. Of these notifications, 406 PTAs are already in force with the rest scheduled for implementation in the near future. By contrast, despite fourteen years of fitful negotiations, the Doha Round of multilateral trade negotiations has failed to yield a bargain that is acceptable to all sides. Economists and policy-makers have long suspected that the contrasting fortunes of these two types of trade liberalization may be interrelated. More specifically, there is widespread concern that the formation of PTAs may undermine multilateral liberalization. Our objective in this paper is to investigate this issue with a finer lens by comparing the implications of the two most popular types of PTAs – i.e. free trade agreements (FTAs) and customs unions (CUs) – for the prospects of global free trade.[4]

As is well known, the central difference between an FTA and a CU is that members of a CU impose common external tariffs on non-members whereas FTA members adopt individually optimal tariffs. This difference in tariff setting behavior between the two types of PTAs has two important consequences. First, while an FTA member is free to enter into additional trade agreements with non-member countries without requiring consent from its existing FTA partners, a CU member can only do so if all other members also agree to participate in the new agreements.[5] In other words, FTA members enjoy more *flexibility* than CU members. Second, as noted in Bagwell and Staiger (1997a) and Bond and Syropoulos (1996), the coordination of tariffs within a CU allows members to *pool their market power*, thereby leading them to impose relatively higher external tariffs than FTAs.

☆ For helpful comments and discussions, we thank Kyle Bagwell, Rick Bond, Bill Ethier, Henrik Horn, Murat Kirdar, James Lake, Petros Mavroidis, Sezgin Polat, Andrey Stoyanov, Mustafa Ulus, two anonymous referees, and especially Bob Staiger. All errors are our own.

* Corresponding author.
E-mail addresses: pmissios@ryerson.ca (P. Missios), kamal.saggi@vanderbilt.edu (K. Saggi), hyildiz@ryerson.ca (H.M. Yildiz).
[1] Tel.: +1 416 979 5000x6186.
[2] Tel.: +1 615 322 3237.
[3] Tel.: +1 416 979 5000x6689.

[4] Roughly 90% of the existing PTAs take the form of FTAs, with CUs comprising the rest (Freund and Ornelas, 2010). However, the existing CUs do involve major trading areas of the world: the EU and much of Latin America (where MERCOSUR resides).

[5] For example, the United States has signed several FTAs since the ratification of NAFTA in 1995 that do not include Mexico and Canada as partners whereas the FTAs that the European Union has entered into over the years have required the approval and participation of all its existing members.

http://dx.doi.org/10.1016/j.jinteco.2016.01.002
0022-1996/

The objective of this paper is to isolate the implications of these fundamental differences between FTAs and CUs for the prospects of free trade in the global economy. Our modeling approach follows that of Saggi and Yildiz (2010) and Saggi et al. (2013) under which PTAs emerge endogenously as the outcome of a game of trade liberalization between three countries that are free to pick their PTA partners as well as their tariff levels. We derive Nash equilibria of two games of PTA formation (called the FTA game and the CU game) and then isolate their set of coalition proof Nash equilibria (CPNE). Thus, our focus is on Nash agreements that are immune to self-enforcing coalitional deviations. As in Bernheim et al. (1987), all countries are free to arrange mutually beneficial deviations from Nash agreements and an initial coalitional deviation of two countries from a Nash equilibrium is self-enforcing if, taking the strategy of the third country as fixed, neither member of the deviating coalition has an incentive to further deviate to make itself better off.

In the first stage of either game, each country simultaneously announces the names of countries with whom it wants to sign a PTA. Next, given the trade policy regime, countries choose their optimal tariffs. In the final stage of the game, production, consumption and international trade take place. The mapping between first stage announcements and trade agreements is as follows. If no announcements match or the only matching announcement is in favor of no agreement, then no PTA is formed. A bilateral PTA arises if two countries announce each others' names and there is no other matching announcement. Since FTA members choose their external tariffs independently, two independent FTAs (or a hub and spoke trading regime) can arise in the FTA game and this happens if (*i*) a country (call it the hub) announces in favor of signing an FTA with the other two countries and (*ii*) the other two countries (spokes) announce in favor of signing an FTA with the hub country and at least one of them does not announce in favor of the other. By contrast, since CU members impose common external tariffs, a hub and spoke type of trading arrangement is *infeasible* in the CU game. In either game, free trade emerges only if each country seeks a PTA with both its trading partners.

Our paper addresses the important issue of when and why countries prefer to liberalize preferentially as opposed to doing so multilaterally. By contrast, existing literature generally takes one of two approaches: (*i*) it either takes PTAs to be exogenously given and compares incentives for multilateral liberalization in their presence to those in their absence or (*ii*) it simply asks whether a pair of countries benefit from entering into a PTA given that there exists no trade agreement between them, a comparison that does not tell us much about when and why they might deliberately choose to *exclude* others from their mutual trade liberalization. To address the exclusion incentive in a convincing manner, one needs a model that gives all countries an active voice in negotiations so that one can determine whether some countries prefer to exclude others from their mutual trade liberalization even though they wish to be included. We provide such a model and use it to assess the strength of the exclusion incentive under our two games as well as the ability of member countries to exercise it in equilibrium.

The fact that external trade liberalization by a CU member is conditional on the approval of other members implies that, relative to a CU, an FTA is more susceptible to opportunistic unilateral deviations by member countries. To see this clearly, consider the FTA game and suppose countries *i* and *j* announce in favor of an FTA with each other. Then, country *i* is free to seek a *separate* FTA with country *k* in order to create a pair of independent bilateral FTAs (i.e. a hub and spoke arrangement) with itself as the hub and countries *j* and *k* as the spokes. By contrast, in the CU game, if countries *i* and *j* announce in favor of a CU with each other, the only way one of them can undertake further trade liberalization with country *k* is if they *both agree* to reduce their common external tariff. We show that this crucial difference between a CU and an FTA has important consequences for multilateral trade liberalization. In particular, in our three country model of symmetric countries, while free trade obtains as the unique CPNE of the FTA game, a CU between only two countries emerges as the unique CPNE of the CU game. Thus, in our model, the pursuit of CUs undermines global free trade whereas that of FTAs does not even though the exclusion incentive exists under both types of PTAs in the sense that the welfare of members of both types of PTAs is strictly higher than that under free trade.

The intuition behind this key result is as follows. Suppose each country announces in favor of forming an FTA with both other countries so that the resulting outcome is free trade. Due to the existence of an exclusion incentive in our model, two of these countries (say *i* and *j*), taking the announcement of their complement as fixed (i.e. country *k* still announces in favor of FTAs with both *i* and *j*), benefit if they jointly deviate to announcements wherein they call for an FTA with only each other. As per the concept of a CPNE, for this joint deviation to be self enforcing, a proper subset of the initially deviating countries (i.e. *i* or *j*) should not have an incentive to deviate to another announcement, taking the announcement of the complement (country *k*) as fixed. However, in the FTA game, each of the initially deviating country (*i* or *j*) indeed has an incentive to deviate to an announcement in favor of FTAs with both countries since the welfare of a hub country exceeds that of the member of a single FTA. Therefore, the initial joint deviation of countries *i* and *j* from free trade is not self-enforcing and the CPNE of the FTA game yields free trade. By contrast, since members of a CU impose a common external tariff, two independent CUs (a hub and spoke type arrangement) are infeasible and the initial joint deviation of two countries that converts free trade to a bilateral CU is self-enforcing so that the CPNE of the CU game yields a bilateral CU. Thus, whereas the exclusion incentive is reflected in the equilibrium of the CU game, it goes unexpressed in the FTA game due to the lure of a hub and spoke arrangement and the flexibility that FTA members have to pursue such an arrangement.

Our underlying trade model is an adapted version of the two-country comparative advantage based framework of Horn et al. (2010) where each country exports a unique good to the other two. This *competing importers* framework delivers a novel type of tariff complementarity: when two countries form a PTA (either an FTA or a CU), the excluded country voluntarily *reduces* its tariffs on them.[6] As a result, PTA members benefit not only from their mutual trade liberalization but also from the unilateral liberalization induced in the non-member country. This finding is reminiscent of the reciprocated unilateralism result of Krishna and Mitra (2005) who showed that unilateral tariff liberalization by a (large) country can result in a reciprocal tariff reduction by its smaller trading partner.[7] In their model, unilateral liberalization by the large country encourages the formation of an export lobby in the small country which then competes effectively with the import-competing lobby to lower tariffs and export taxes.

The competing importers framework highlights a type of trade diversion that has generally been overlooked in the literature. Traditionally, trade diversion is defined as the increase in trade between PTA members that occurs at the expense of exports of non-members to the PTA, i.e., the traditional notion of trade diversion refers to the reduction in the volume of *imports* that PTA members source from non-members. By contrast, in our model, the formation of a PTA reduces the volume of *exports* of member countries to the non-member — a phenomenon we refer to as *external trade diversion*. Indeed, such trade diversion is precisely what makes it optimal for the non-member to reduce its tariffs on PTA members.[8] To the best of our knowledge, our model is the first

[6] By contrast, existing literature has tended to focus on how the formation of a PTA can induce member countries to reduce their external tariffs. See Bagwell and Staiger (1997a, 1997b and 1998); Bond et al. (2004), and Estevadeordal et al. (2008).

[7] See also Coates and Ludema (2001) for a theory of trade policy leadership based on repeated interaction between a large and a small country. In their model, a large country can undertake unilateral liberalization in order to induce reciprocal trade liberalization by the small country.

[8] In our model, this logic would also apply to unilateral liberalization by any country so long as it is preferential in nature (i.e. extended only to one country).

to capture the effects of such external trade diversion on the import tariffs of the non-member country and the associated welfare implications of such a change, issues that cannot be addressed by models that take the tariffs of non-members to be exogenously given or assume a trading structure under which PTA formation does not affect them.[9]

To isolate the market power effect of a CU from their relative lack of flexibility, in Section 4.1 we also consider a scenario where CU members are not allowed to raise their tariffs above pre-existing levels. This experiment is well motivated on policy grounds: Article XXIV of GATT – the key clause that sanctions PTAs in the WTO – forbids member countries of a PTA from raising tariffs on non-members. When CUs are constrained in this manner, we find that a bilateral CU continues to arise in the CPNE of the CU game thereby thwarting global free trade. This finding implies that while the restriction on external tariffs mandated by Article XXIV softens the negative impact of a CU on outsiders, it does not eliminate the exclusion incentive that gives rise to a CU in the first place. Thus, it is the relative flexibility of FTAs over CUs that helps the prospects of global free trade and not their weaker market power.

While the present paper follows the analytical approach of Saggi and Yildiz (2010) and Saggi et al. (2013), it highlights an important conceptual difference between the two types of PTAs that has not been explored in these papers (or in the rest of the literature on PTAs). More specifically, the conceptual point that the relative inflexibility of a CU makes it coalitionally more stable than an FTA has never really been explicitly proven in the literature since most existing papers generally focus on only one type of a PTA.

Unlike the present paper, both Saggi and Yildiz (2010) and Saggi et al. (2013) analyze PTA formation in a *competing exporters* model of trade in which each country imports the same good from two other countries. Both of these papers primarily focus on the issue of whether PTAs are building or stumbling blocs for free trade by comparing outcomes of two games – one where discriminatory PTAs are allowed and another where only non-discriminatory multilateral agreements are permitted. This is not an issue that we address here. Saggi and Yildiz (2010) focus on FTAs and find that in their competing exporters framework, no two countries have an incentive to exclude the third country from their mutual trade liberalization. In their model, under symmetry the outcome is global free trade whereas under asymmetry the outcome is an agreement between the two larger countries not because they wish to exclude the third country but rather because the third country *chooses* to stay out on its own accord. In other words, the exclusion incentive never arises in Saggi and Yildiz (2010). By contrast, when the model in the present paper is extended to an asymmetric setting, in the FTA game the two larger countries deliberately choose to exclude the smaller country even though it would be better off being included in the agreement.

The CU game analyzed by Saggi et al. (2013) in a competing exporters model of trade delivers free trade under symmetry. By contrast, in the present paper, the outcome of the CU game even under symmetry is a bilateral CU. Furthermore, the present paper shows that the exclusion incentive of a CU exists even when its members are not allowed to fully exercise their market power by raising their tariffs above preexisting levels. This result shows that it is the relative lack of flexibility of CUs relative to FTAs that prevents the obtainment of global free trade in the CU game, as opposed to their higher market power. Finally, note that though the exclusion incentive plays a role in the CU game of Saggi et al. (2013) when countries are asymmetric, the magnitude of this incentive is quite different in the present paper: in our competing importers framework, the reduction in the external tariff of the non-member induced by external trade diversion reinforces the exclusion incentive whereas no such effect arises in a competing exporters framework.

The rest of the paper is organized as follows. Section 4.1 examines the CU game under the restriction that CU members cannot raise their tariff above preexisting levels. In Section 4.2, we consider a game where countries can choose between the two types of PTAs and show that the unique CPNE of this game delivers a bilateral CU. In Section 4.3, we show that this basic insight holds even when countries are not fully symmetric. Section 5 contains concluding remarks.

2. Tariffs and trade

Our underlying economic framework is an adapted version of the two-country model of Horn et al. (2010). We consider a perfectly competitive world with three large countries: $z = i, j$, and k, three (non-numeraire) goods: $g = I, J$, and K and a numeraire good v_0. On the demand side, the representative citizen's utility function is linear in the numeraire good and separable in the non-numeraire goods:

$$U(\mathbf{v}, v_0) = u(\mathbf{v}) + v_0, \tag{1}$$

where $v = [v_I, v_J, v_K]$ is the consumption vector for the three non-numeraire goods, v_0 denotes the consumption of the numeraire good, and $u(\mathbf{v})$ is quadratic and additively separable in the three non-numeraire goods. The demand for good g in country z is then given by

$$d_z^g(p_z^g) = \alpha - p_z^g \tag{2}$$

where p_z^g denotes the consumer price of good g in country z. Assuming that the population in each country is a continuum of measure one, we can write the consumer surplus associated with good g in country z as:

$$CS_z^g(p_z^g) = u_z^g[d_z^g(p_z^g)] - p_z^g d_z^g(p_z^g). \tag{3}$$

On the supply side, as in Horn et al. (2010), labor (l) is the only factor of production which is employed in the production of the numeraire good that is produced one-for-one from labor. The supply of labor is assumed to be large enough that the numeraire good is always produced in a positive amount; therefore the equilibrium wage is equal to one.

Each non-numeraire good is produced from labor with diminishing returns. In particular, we assume the following production function for non-numeraire good g in country $z: Q_z^g = \sqrt{2\lambda_z^g l_g}$, where Q_z^g is the production of good g in country z and l_g is the labor employed in the production of good g. The supply function of good g in country z is as follows:

$$s_z^g(q_z^g) = \lambda_z^g q_z^g \tag{4}$$

where q_z^g denotes the producer price for good g in country z.

We assume that there exists a symmetric comparative advantage structure across countries: $\lambda_i^I = \lambda_j^J = \lambda_k^K = 1 + \lambda$ while $\lambda_i^J = \lambda_i^K = \lambda_j^I = \lambda_j^K = \lambda_k^I = \lambda_k^J = 1$. In other words, each country has a comparative advantage in one good while having a comparative disadvantage in the other two: each country exports the good that is indexed by the same uppercase letter as the identity of the country. For example, country i exports good I while importing good J from country j and good K from country k. Thus, there are two *competing importers* for each non-numeraire good and the model is Ricardian in nature with diminishing returns in the production of each good. Country z's producer surplus in good g as follows:

$$PS_z^g(q_z^g) = \int s_z^g(q_z^g) dq_z^g = \frac{1}{2}\lambda_z^g (q_z^g)^2. \tag{5}$$

[9] See, for example, Bagwell and Staiger (1997a, 1997b, 1998); Krishna (1998); Ornelas (2005a and 2005b), and Saggi and Yildiz (2010). In general, the literature has tended to focus on the reduction of market access experienced by non-members due to the formation of a PTA.

As a representative scenario for all goods and countries, consider good I (i.e. the good in which country i has a comparative advantage). Let t_{ji} be the tariff imposed by country j on its imports of good I from country i.[10] Given that all countries are large, the world price of good I depends on the tariffs chosen by countries j and k but to simplify notation we suppress the dependence of prices on tariffs and simply denote the price of good I by p_i^I.

Due to the absence of any tariff in country i on good I, the consumer and producer prices of good I in country i are equal: $q_i^I = p_i^I$. As there is no domestic taxation for the import competing sectors, producer and consumer prices are also equal: $q_i^g = p_i^g$, where $g \neq I$. Finally, ruling out prohibitive tariffs yields the following no-arbitrage conditions for good I:

$$p_j^I = p_i^I + t_{ji} \text{ and } p_k^I = p_i^I + t_{ki}. \tag{6}$$

Let m_j^I and m_k^I be the imports of good I by countries j and k:

$$m_j^I\left(p_j^I\right) = d\left(p_j^I\right) - s_j^I\left(p_j^I\right) \text{ and } m_k^I(p_k^I) = d(p_k^I) - s_k^I(p_k^I). \tag{7}$$

Similarly, let x_j^I and x_k^I denote country i's exports (of good I) to countries j and k where

$$x_j^I = s_i^I(p_i^I) - d(p_i^I) - m_k^I(p_k^I) \tag{8}$$

and

$$x_k^I = s_i^I(p_i^I) - d(p_i^I) - m_j^I\left(p_j^I\right). \tag{9}$$

Market clearing for good I requires that country i's exports to a country equals the imports of that country:

$$x_z^I = m_z^I \text{ where } z = j, k. \tag{10}$$

Before proceeding with the derivation of optimal tariffs, it is useful to highlight some important features of the model. Since each country exports a unique good in the model, a country's tariff on one of its trading partners has no impact on the volume of its imports from its second trading partner. This implies that a country's external tariffs are independent of one another (since they apply to different goods, each with its own demand function).[11] Second, if two countries liberalize trade only towards one another, they import more from each other and start exporting less to the third country — a phenomenon which we call *external trade diversion*. As we will see below, this reduction in the volume of exports to the third country in turn has implications for its optimal tariffs.

2.1. Optimal Nash tariffs

Country z's welfare is defined as the sum of consumer surplus, producer surplus, and tariff revenue over all goods:

$$w_z = \sum_g CS_z^g(p_z^g) + \sum_g PS_z^g(q_z^g) + \sum_{h \neq z} t_{zh} m_z^H \tag{11}$$

where H corresponds to the good exported by country h.

In the absence of any trade agreement, each country chooses its tariffs to maximize its welfare. To derive optimal tariffs, we follow the approach of Feenstra (2004) and Broda et al. (2008).

Consider country k's tariff problem. Differentiating w_k with respect to t_{ki}, we obtain:

$$\frac{\partial w_k}{\partial t_{ki}} = t_{ki} \frac{\partial m_k^I}{\partial p_k^I} \frac{\partial p_k^I}{\partial t_{ki}} - m_k^I \frac{\partial p_i^I}{\partial t_{ki}}. \tag{12}$$

The first term of the above first order condition is the efficiency cost of the tariff (i.e. the marginal deadweight loss from the tariff) while the second term is the terms of trade effect, that is, the reduction in the price of good i that accrues to country $i(p_i^I)$ multiplied by the quantity of country k's imports from country i.

The optimal ad-valorem tariff is computed where Eq. (12) equals zero:

$$\frac{\partial w_k}{\partial t_{ki}} = 0 \Rightarrow \frac{t_{ki}}{p_i^I} = \frac{\frac{\partial p_i^I}{\partial t_{ki}} \frac{m_k^I}{p_i^I}}{\frac{\partial m_k^I}{\partial p_k^I} \frac{\partial p_k^I}{\partial t_{ki}}} \tag{13}$$

The above expression can be interpreted in two different ways. Note first that since $m_k^I = x_k^I$ we must have

$$\frac{\partial m_k^I}{\partial p_k^I} \frac{\partial p_k^I}{\partial t_{ki}} = \frac{\partial x_k^I}{\partial t_{ki}}.$$

Substituting this into Eq. (13) shows that country k's optimal ad-valorem tariff equals the inverse of the elasticity of the export supply curve of country i to country k, denoted by ε_{ik}:

$$\frac{t_{ki}}{p_i^I} = \frac{1}{\varepsilon_{ik}} = \left[\frac{\partial x_k^I}{\partial p_i^I} \frac{p_i^I}{x_i^I}\right]^{-1}. \tag{14}$$

For an alternative interpretation of the optimal tariff, we can rearrange Eq. (13) and write the optimal tariff formula for country k as follows:

$$\frac{t_{ki}}{p_i^I} = \frac{1}{\mu_k^I} \frac{\partial p_i^I}{\partial t_{ki}} \left[\frac{\partial p_k^I}{\partial t_{ki}}\right]^{-1} \text{ where } \mu_k^I = \frac{\partial m_k^I}{\partial p_k^I} \frac{p_k^I}{m_k^I}. \tag{15}$$

As can be seen from above, the optimal tariff is also equal to the inverse of the elasticity of import demand of good I in $k(\mu_k^I)$, times the ratio of the change in the relative world price and domestic price of imports. Given that import demand elasticity $\mu_k^I < 0$, the fact that country k's tariff on good I drives down the local price of the good in country i (i.e. $\frac{\partial p_i^I}{\partial t_{ki}} < 0$) while raising it locally ($\frac{\partial p_k^I}{\partial t_{ki}} > 0$), the optimal tariff imposed by country k is positive. Note that the term $\frac{\partial p_i^I}{\partial t_{ki}}$ captures the *terms of trade gain* of the tariff since it informs us how country k's tariff on good I affects the price collected by country i while $\frac{\partial p_k^I}{\partial t_{ki}}$ refers to the *pass through* of the tariff since it tells us how the domestic price of good I in country k varies with its tariff on country i.[12]

---

[10] We assume that tariff revenues for each good are redistributed uniformly to all individuals.

[11] One consequence of this feature is that the MFN principle of non-discrimination plays no role in our model.

[12] Broda et al. (2008) provide evidence that the importers with market power indeed use it in setting their non-cooperative trade policy.

Using the demand and supply functions in Eqs. (2) and (4) as well as Eq. (6) through Eq. (10), the equilibrium prices of good l in country i and in importing country j equal:

$$p_i^l = \frac{3\alpha - 2\sum_{z \neq i} t_{zi}}{\lambda + 6} \text{ and } p_j^l = \frac{3\alpha - 2t_{ki} + (4+\lambda)t_{ji}}{\lambda + 6}. \tag{16}$$

As is clear from Eq. (16), the price of good l in country i decreases in the degree of comparative advantage λ (supply effect) and the tariffs it faces in export markets (terms of trade effect). Similarly, the prices of good l in country j increases with its own tariff whereas it decreases with the tariff of the rival importer (i.e. country k). Using the above price equations, we can explicitly calculate the terms of trade gain and the pass through of import tariffs.[13] We have:

$$\frac{\partial p_i^l}{\partial t_{ji}} = \frac{\partial p_i^l}{\partial t_{ki}} < 0 \tag{17}$$

i.e. the tariffs imposed by countries j and k lower the price collected by country i's exporters and

$$\frac{\partial p_j^l}{\partial t_{ji}} = \frac{\partial p_k^l}{\partial t_{ki}} < 1 \tag{18}$$

i.e. the pass through from tariffs to local prices in importing countries is incomplete – i.e. the local price in a country does not increase one-to-one with its import tariff.

The first order condition in Eq. (12) can be written as:

$$\frac{\partial w_k}{\partial t_{ki}} = \frac{2[\alpha\lambda - t_{ki}(\lambda+4)(\lambda+8) + 4t_{ji}]}{(\lambda+6)^2}. \tag{19}$$

It is immediate from the above first order condition that we have positively sloped reaction functions, i.e., tariffs imposed by different countries on the same good (i.e. their common import) are *strategic complements* in our model:

$$\frac{\partial t_{ki}}{\partial t_{ji}} > 0. \tag{20}$$

The intuition for why tariffs of different countries end up being strategic complements in our model is easy to see: an increase in the tariff country j imposes on country i increases the volume of country i's exports to country k thereby increasing the latter's ability to manipulate its terms of trade. Simultaneous solution of first order conditions for countries j and k leads to the following optimal Nash tariffs (which are equal due to symmetry):

$$t_{ji}^* = t_{ki}^* = t^* = \frac{\alpha\lambda}{\lambda^2 + 12\lambda + 28}. \tag{21}$$

2.2. How PTA formation affects tariffs

If countries i and j form an FTA $\langle ij \rangle$, they remove their tariffs on each other ($t_{ij} = t_{ji} = 0$) and impose their individually optimal external tariffs on the non-member country by solving:

$$\left.\frac{\partial w_i}{\partial t_{ik}}\right|_{t_{ij}=0} = 0 \text{ and } \left.\frac{\partial w_j}{\partial t_{jk}}\right|_{t_{ji}=0} = 0. \tag{22}$$

Since member countries i and j are competing importers of good K, the elimination of their internal tariffs due to the FTA has *no impact* on their tariffs on imports of good K and thus the optimal external tariff of FTA members, denoted by $t(ij)$, is the same as that under no agreement, denoted by t^*. We have $t(ij) = t^*$.[14]

On the other hand, since countries compete over imports, the formation of an FTA between two countries changes the first order conditions of the tariff choice problem of the non-member country. We have:

$$\left.\frac{\partial w_k}{\partial t_{ki}}\right|_{t_{ji}=0} = \frac{2[\alpha\lambda - t_{ki}(\lambda+4)(\lambda+8)]}{(\lambda+6)^2} \tag{23}$$

Since we know from Eq. (20) that tariffs on the same good imposed by different importers are strategic complements, the reduction of t_{ij} and t_{ji} to zero induces country k to lower its external tariff on the imports from country i and country j. We have:

$$t_k(ij) = \frac{\alpha\lambda}{(\lambda+4)(\lambda+8)} < t^*$$

We can now state:

Proposition 1A. *The external trade diversion caused by a bilateral FTA induces the non-member to lower its tariffs on members* (i.e. $t_k(ij) < t^*$) *while it has no effect on the external tariffs of members* (i.e. $t(ij) = t^*$).

The general intuition behind the above proposition is as follows. Since the removal of internal tariffs under the FTA $\langle ij \rangle$ leads to an increase in the imports of country j from country i, the export supply curve of country i to country k shifts to the left. As a result, the equilibrium world price of good l rises while the equilibrium exports of country i to country k decline. Since export supply curves are linear in our model, the elasticity of export supply curves of countries i and j facing country k rises due to the formation of the bilateral FTA $\langle ij \rangle$:

$$\varepsilon_{ik}(ij) - \varepsilon_{ik}(\Phi) = 2/\lambda > 0 \tag{24}$$

which in turn implies that country k's optimal tariff on imports from countries i and j under the FTA $\langle ij \rangle$ is lower than its optimal Nash tariff t^*.

For an alternative interpretation of Proposition 1A, consider the optimal tariff formula in Eq. (15). Note that the FTA $\langle ij \rangle$ leads to an upward movement along the import demand curves of country k for goods i and j leading to a higher elasticity of import demand (common due to symmetry). Thus, the removal of the internal tariffs under the FTA $\langle ij \rangle$ leads to a lower terms of trade gain and a higher tariff pass through in country k:

$$\left.\frac{\partial p_i^l}{\partial t_{ki}}\right|_{t_{ji}=0} > \left.\frac{\partial p_i^l}{\partial t_{ki}}\right|_{t_{ji}=t*} \text{ and } \left.\frac{\partial p_k^l}{\partial t_{ki}}\right|_{t_{ji}=0} > \left.\frac{\partial p_k^l}{\partial t_{ki}}\right|_{t_{ji}=t*}$$

both of which tend to lower its optimal tariff. Analogous reasoning explains why the two spoke countries end up imposing lower tariffs on each other relative to the status quo: under the hub and spoke arrangement, each spoke exports more to the hub and less to the other spoke relative to the status quo, which in turn lowers the ability of both spokes to manipulate their terms of trade vis-à-vis one another.

Next, we consider the formation of a CU between countries i and j, denoted by $\langle ij_u \rangle$. Like FTA members, CU members remove tariffs on each other. However, unlike FTA members, CU members impose a jointly optimal external tariff on the non-member. Under the CU $\langle ij_u \rangle$ members solve:

$$\max_t w_i(ij^u) + w_j(ij^u) \text{ subject to } t_{ij} = t_{ji} = 0. \tag{25}$$

[13] Using the prices in Eq. (16), the volume of trade as a function of tariffs can be easily calculated.

[14] Thus, the model does not exhibit the type of tariff complementarity described in Bagwell and Staiger (1997a, 1997b) and some other models of PTAs.

As the common market of a CU is larger than that of its members, the combined market power of the CU exceeds that of the individual member countries. Since the terms-of-trade externalities across members are internalized by a CU and tariffs on the same good across countries are complementary in our model, the optimum external tariffs of members rise following the formation of CU.[15]

To gain further insight, let m^K be the total import demand of good K in countries i and j:

$$m^K = \sum_{z=i,j} [d(p_z^K) - s_z^K(q_z^K)] \tag{26}$$

while x^K denote the exports of good K (from country k) to the common market of countries i and j:[16]

$$x^K = s_k^K(q_k^K) - d(p_k^K). \tag{27}$$

The equilibrium world price of good K is determined by the market clearing condition:

$$x^K = m^K \tag{28}$$

Using the market clearing prices and quantities, the first order condition for the welfare maximization problem in Eq. (25) can be written as:

$$\frac{\partial[w_i(ij^u) + w_j(ij^u)]}{\partial t} = \frac{4[2\alpha\lambda - t(\lambda+2)(\lambda+10)}{(\lambda+6)^2} = 0. \tag{29}$$

Solving this yields the optimal tariff of the CU $\langle ij_u \rangle$:[17]

$$t(ij^u) = \frac{2\alpha\lambda}{\lambda^2 + 12\lambda + 20}. \tag{30}$$

Since both countries import the same good from the non-member country, the market power effect of a CU emphasized by Bagwell and Staiger (1997a) arises here. A CU allows members to pool their market power and extract a larger terms of trade gain from the non-member leading to an increase in their tariffs:

$$t(ij^u) > t(ij) = t^*. \tag{31}$$

It is also immediate that since member countries reduce their internal tariffs to zero, like an FTA, a bilateral CU also induces the non-member to lower its tariffs on members (and exactly to the same level):

$$t_k(ij^u) = t_k(ij) < t^*. \tag{32}$$

It is straightforward to establish that the external trade diversion caused by a CU has qualitative similar effects as an FTA:

Proposition 1B. *The formation of a CU induces members to raise their external tariffs* (i.e. $t(ij^u) > t^*$) *and the non-member to lower them:* $t_k(ij^u) < t^*$.

To see the general picture behind the above result more clearly, suppose that we start with the status quo where all countries impose the optimal tariff t^* on each other. It is obvious that the export supply of country k to the CU's common market lies to the right of its individual export supply curves to the markets of countries i and j since it applies to a common larger market. Similarly, following the formation of the CU $\langle ij_u \rangle$, the common import demand of member countries is larger relative to individual import demands. Therefore, market clearing under the CU $\langle ij_u \rangle$ occurs at a lower p_k^K/x_k^K ratio relative to the status quo. Since export supply curves are linear, the elasticity of country k's export supply curve falls due to the formation of the CU $\langle ij_u \rangle$. As a result, the optimal common external tariff under CU $\langle ij_u \rangle$ is higher than the individually optimal tariffs of countries i and j.

It is worth noting that Article XXIV of GATT requires PTA members to not raise their external tariffs on non-member countries. For now, we ignore this tariff restriction imposed by Article XXIV and assume that a CU can impose its optimal tariffs. In Section 4.1, we examine the implications of this tariff restriction on welfare and on the prospects of global free trade.

3. Endogenous preferential trade agreements

We now describe our three stage game of trade liberalization. In the first stage, each country simultaneously announces the names of countries with whom it wants to sign a PTA. This stage determines the underlying trade policy regime. Next, given the trade policy regime, countries choose their optimal tariffs. Finally, consumption, production and international trade take place. As noted before, a key difference between the two types of PTAs is the relative flexibility of FTAs: while an FTA member is free to sign another FTA with a non-member without needing consent of an existing FTA partner, a CU member cannot do so since all CU members must have a common external tariff. To capture the implications of this important difference between an FTA and a CU, we now derive and compare the equilibrium outcomes of the two games.

3.1. Free trade agreements

In the first stage of the FTA game, each country simultaneously announces the names of countries with whom it wants to sign an FTA. Country i's announcement is denoted by σ_i and its strategy set S_i consists of four possible announcements:

$$S_i = \{\{\phi,\phi\}, \{j,\phi\}, \{\phi,k\}, \{j,k\}\}$$

where $\{\phi,\phi\}$ denotes an announcement in favor of no FTA with either trading partners, $\{j,\phi\}$ in favor of an FTA with only country j; $\{\phi,k\}$ in favor of an FTA with only country k; and $\{j,k\}$ in favor of FTAs with both of them.

It is important to note that we employ a game of announcements or proposals. In our game, a country does not announce in favor of a specific trade agreement but rather names partners with whom it wants to form such agreements. Furthermore, since a trade agreement requires consent from both sides, we posit the following mapping between various announcements profiles and the types of trade agreements that countries can form:

(i) No two announcements match or the only matching announcements are $\{\phi,\phi\}$. All of these announcement profiles lead to no agreement $\langle \Phi \rangle$ wherein all countries impose their optimal Nash tariffs on one another.

(ii) Two countries announce each others' name and there is no other matching announcement: i.e., the following three conditions hold: (*a*) $j \in \sigma_i$ and $i \in \sigma_j$; (*b*) $i \notin \sigma_k$ and/or $k \notin \sigma_i$ and (*c*) $j \notin \sigma_k$ and/or $k \notin \sigma_j$. All announcements satisfying these three conditions yield an FTA between countries i and j denoted by $\langle ij \rangle$ under which members impose zero tariffs on each other and the optimal external tariff t^* on the non-member.

(iii) Country i announces in favor of signing an FTA with countries j and k while countries j and/or k announce only in favor of signing an FTA with country i: i.e. $\sigma_i = \{j,k\}$; $i \in \sigma_j$; and $i \in \sigma_k$ while $k \notin \sigma_j$ and/or $j \notin \sigma_k$. This set of announcements yields a pair of

[15] Olarreaga et al. (1999) provide evidence that the terms-of-trade externalities among Mercosur's members were internalized in its external tariffs.

[16] Note that with a CU we are back to two country set-up of Feenstra (2004) and Broda et al. (2008).

[17] It is straightforward to confirm that the optimal ad-valorem tariff of the CU equals the inverse of the elasticity of country k's export supply curve: $t/p_k^K = 1/\varepsilon_k(ij_u)$.

independent FTAs (i.e. a hub and spoke trading regime) with i as the common member denoted by $\langle ij, ik\rangle$ (or simply $\langle ih\rangle$) under which countries j and k impose the optimal external tariff on each other while imposing no tariffs on country i who also imposes no tariffs on either of them.

(iv) All countries announce each others' names. These announcements yield global free trade $\langle F\rangle$ under which all countries eliminate their tariffs on each other.[18]

Note that since an FTA between two countries can arise only if it is mutually acceptable to both sides, multiple announcement profiles can map into the same agreement. For example, the FTA $\langle ij\rangle$ obtains when (i) countries i and j call only each other, *regardless* of the nature of country k's announcement: if $\sigma_i=\{j,\phi\}$ and $\sigma_j=\{i,\phi\}$, then $\langle ij\rangle$ obtains for all four possible announcements on the part of country k, i.e., for $\sigma_k=\{\phi,\phi\}$, $\{i,\phi\}$, $\{\phi,j\}$ and $\{i,j\}$ so that country k's announcement has no bearing upon the outcome when neither of the other two countries' announces its name; (ii) countries i and j announce each other's name and either one or both of them also announce country k but country k does not reciprocate: i.e. all of the following types of announcements map into the FTA $\langle ij\rangle$: (a) $\sigma_i=\{j,k\}$ and $\sigma_j=\{i,\phi\}$ but $i\notin\sigma_k$ or (b) $\sigma_i=\{j,\phi\}$ and $\sigma_j=\{i,k\}$ but $j\notin\sigma_k$ or (c) $\sigma_i=\{j,k\}$ and $\sigma_j=\{i,k\}$ but $\sigma_k=\{\phi,\phi\}$.

3.1.1. Welfare effects of various trade agreements

Let country i's welfare as a function of the underlying trade agreement a be denoted by $w_i(a)$ and let $\Delta w_i(a\text{-}b)$ denote the difference between country i's welfare under trade agreements a and b: $\Delta w_i(a\text{-}b)\equiv w_i(a)-w_i(b)$. Also, let m denote a member country of the bilateral FTA $\langle ij\rangle$ so that $m=i$ or j.

We first state the following preliminary result that explains the welfare effects of various types of trade agreements:

Lemma 1. *Let $m,\widetilde{m}=i,j$ denote member countries of the FTA $\langle ij\rangle$. The welfare impact of various types of trade agreements on members and nonmembers is as follows:*

(i) $\Delta w_k(ij\text{-}\Phi)<0<\Delta w_m(ij\text{-}\Phi)$.
(ii) $\Delta w_m(F\text{-}ij)<0<\Delta w_k(F\text{-}ij)$.
(iii) $\Delta w_{\widetilde{m}}(mh-ij)<0<\Delta w_m(mh-ij)$.
(iv) $\Delta w_k(mh\text{-}ij)>0$.
(v) $\Delta w_m(F-mh)<0<\Delta w_{\widetilde{m}}(F-mh)$.

Part (i) says that, given that there exists no trade agreement, a pair of countries have an incentive to form a bilateral FTA and the formation of such an FTA makes the non-member country worse-off. In our model, the formation of a bilateral FTA does not affect the non-member's producer surplus in export markets since external tariffs of FTA members are the same as those under the status quo (i.e. $t(ij)=t^*$). But since the external trade diversion caused by an FTA lowers the non-member's ability to manipulate its terms of trade vis-à-vis member countries (which is reflected, in turn, in its reduced external tariff), the non-member becomes worse off relative to the status quo. Since aggregate world welfare increases due to the trade liberalization undertaken by FTA member countries, it follows that the formation of an FTA makes member countries better off at the expense of the non-member.

The result stated in part (ii) of Lemma 1 establishes the existence of an *exclusion incentive* since a pair of countries prefer a bilateral FTA to free trade. Furthermore, since world welfare under free trade is higher than that under a bilateral FTA, it follows that the non-member country is better off under free trade relative to a bilateral FTA. The forces that give rise to the exclusion incentive can be understood as follows. Relative to free trade, each member country of an FTA has the ability to manipulate its terms of trade vis-à-vis the non-member while also being able to free ride on the terms of trade effect of the non-member's tariff on its FTA partner. These benefits of exclusion are somewhat tempered by the fact that, relative to free trade, an FTA member faces positive tariffs in the non-member's market (but recall that these tariffs are lower than those under the status quo owing to the external trade diversion caused by the FTA). All in all, the two positive effects of exclusion on FTA members dominate the negative effect so that a pair of countries benefit if they can successfully exclude the third country from their bilateral trade agreement.

Part (iii) says the welfare of a hub country is higher than that of the member of a single bilateral FTA whereas that of a spoke country is lower. It is important to note that, starting from a single FTA, the external trade diversion caused by the hub country's second FTA reduces the volume of exports flowing from the original non-member (who becomes a spoke) to the original member (who becomes the other spoke). This trade diversion reduces the original non member's ability to manipulate its terms of trade which shows up as a reduction in its optimal external tariff.

Part (iv) simply says that it is better to be a spoke than to be a nonmember facing a bilateral FTA. When the non-member country forms an FTA with one of the member countries, it not only obtains free access to the hub country's market but also faces lower tariffs in the other spoke country due to external trade diversion. However, it also gives free access to its market to the hub country while keeping its tariff on the other spoke country unchanged. Overall, the former positive effects dominates the latter negative effect.

Finally, part (v) says that while each spoke country is better off under free trade, the hub country is worse off. A comparison of hub country m's welfare under $\langle mh\rangle$ relative to $\langle F\rangle$ yields the following: (i) the hub country's producer surplus is equal under the two regimes since its producers face zero tariffs under both regimes and are afforded no protection in the home market (ii) its domestic welfare is higher under $\langle mh\rangle$ relative to $\langle F\rangle$ since it benefits from the positive terms of trade effects of tariffs that the spokes impose on each other – indeed, it is able to import goods from both spokes at prices that are *lower* than those under free trade. As a result, the hub country is strictly better off relative to free trade. To see why the spokes are worse off relative to free trade, first note that aggregate global welfare is strictly higher under free trade. Given that the hub country is strictly better off relative to free trade and the fact that the welfare of the two spokes is equal (due to symmetry), both spokes are worse off relative to free trade.

3.1.2. Nash equilibria of the FTA game

Using the welfare comparisons stated in Lemma 1, we can show that the Nash equilibria of the FTA game are as follows:

Proposition 2A. *The Nash equilibrium announcement profiles of the FTA game and the associated trade agreements are as follows:*

Announcement Profiles	*Trade Agreement*
$\Omega^{\Phi}\equiv\{\sigma_i=\{\phi,\phi\},\sigma_j=\{\phi,\phi\},\sigma_k=\{\phi,\phi\}\}$	$\langle\Phi\rangle$
$\Omega^{ij}\equiv\{\sigma_i=\{j,\phi\},\sigma_j=\{i,\phi\},\sigma_k=\{\phi,\phi\}\}$	$\langle ij\rangle$
$\Omega^{ih}\equiv\{\sigma_i=\{j,k\},\sigma_j=\{i,\phi\},\sigma_k=\{i,\phi\}\}$	$\langle ih\rangle$
$\Omega^{F}\equiv\{\sigma_i=\{j,k\},\sigma_j=\{i,k\},\sigma_k=\{i,j\}\}$	$\langle F\rangle$

The logic behind Proposition 2A is as follows. It is straightforward that the announcement profile Ω^{Φ} is a Nash equilibrium since no country has an incentive to announce another's name if the latter does not announce its name in return. Next consider Ω^{ij}. Note from part (i) of Lemma 1 that neither member country (i or j) has an incentive to unilaterally change its announcement from that which it makes under Ω^{ij}

[18] We should note here that while a scenario under which each country signs an FTA with both its trading partners is institutionally distinct from global free trade, from the perspective of applied tariffs the two are the same since all countries set their tariffs to zero under both scenarios.

since doing so only leads to no agreement $\langle\Phi\rangle$, under which its welfare is lower. Similarly, given that neither country i nor country k announces its name, country k has no incentive to alter its announcement from $\sigma_k = \{\phi,\phi\}$ since doing so has no bearing on the resulting trade agreement. Thus, the announcement profile Ω^{ij} yielding a bilateral FTA is a Nash equilibrium.

Now consider the announcement profile Ω^{ih} associated with the hub and spoke regime $\langle ih\rangle$. First note that the hub country i has no incentive to unilaterally change its announcement from $\{j,k\}$ to $\{j,\phi\}$ or $\{\phi,k\}$ since doing so translates into a deviation from the hub and spoke regime $\langle ih\rangle$ where i is the hub country to $\langle ij\rangle$ or $\langle ik\rangle$ respectively. Similarly, the hub country has no incentive to alter its announcement to $\{\phi,\phi\}$ since doing so yields $\langle\Phi\rangle$ under which it is also worse off. Now consider the incentive of a spoke country to deviate from Ω^{ih}. Neither spoke country (say j) has an incentive to unilaterally deviate from its announcement $\{i,\phi\}$ to $\{\phi,\phi\}$ or $\{i,k\}$ since the former deviation translates into a deviation from $\langle ih\rangle$ where j is a spoke country to $\langle ik\rangle$ where j is a non-member country while the latter deviation does not alter the trading regime, i.e., it remains $\langle ih\rangle$. As a result, neither the hub nor the spokes have an incentive to unilaterally alter their announcements from Ω^{ih} that yields the hub and spoke regime $\langle ih\rangle$.

Finally, consider the announcement profile Ω^F that yields global free trade $\langle F\rangle$. Since world welfare is the highest under $\langle F\rangle$, each country is better off under $\langle F\rangle$ to $\langle\Phi\rangle$ and this preference together with part (*ii*) of Lemma 1 implies that a country (say k) has no incentive to unilaterally deviate from its announcement $\{i,j\}$ to $\{\phi,\phi\}$ since doing so alters the trade regime from $\langle F\rangle$ to $\langle ij\rangle$ under which it is worse off.

Moreover, we know from part (*v*) of Lemma 1 that a country (say k) has no incentive to unilaterally change its announcement from $\{i,j\}$ to $\{i,\phi\}$ or $\{\phi,j\}$ since this translates into a deviation from $\langle F\rangle$ to $\langle ih\rangle$ or $\langle jh\rangle$ under both of which country k is a spoke country. Thus, Ω^F is also a Nash equilibrium.

Observe from Proposition 2A that there is a unique announcement profile that supports each agreement as a Nash equilibrium and that the profile itself is the most *parsimonious* one. For example, even though $\{\sigma_i = \{\phi,j\},\sigma_j = \{\phi,\phi\},\sigma_k = \{\phi,\phi\}\}$ also maps to $\langle\Phi\rangle$, such an announcement profile does not constitute a Nash equilibrium. To see why, simply note that given these announcements, country j has an incentive to alter its announcement from $\sigma_j = \{\phi,\phi\}$ to $\sigma_j = \{i,\phi\}$ in order to form the bilateral FTA $\langle ij\rangle$. Similarly, it is worth considering briefly as to why $\{\sigma_i = \{j,\phi\},\sigma_j = \{i,\phi\},\sigma_k = \{i,\phi\}\}$ is not a Nash equilibrium profile even though, just as the announcement profile Ω^{ij}, it also maps into the FTA $\langle ij\rangle$. Under this announcement profile, given the announcements of countries j and k, as per part (*iii*) of Lemma 1, country i has an incentive to alter its announcement to $\sigma_i = \{j,k\}$ so as to obtain the trade agreement $\langle ij\rangle$ under which it is the hub. Using analogous reasoning, we rule out all other non-parsimonious announcements as candidates for Nash equilibria in the Appendix A.

It is worth noting that except for Ω^{Φ} – which is Pareto dominated by the announcement profile Ω^F that supports global free trade – the *other three Nash equilibria are all Pareto efficient*. To see why, simply note from part (*ii*) of Lemma 1 that Ω^F does not Pareto dominate Ω^{ij} since FTA members prefer the FTA $\langle ij\rangle$ to global free trade. Similarly, part (*v*) of Lemma 1 implies that Ω^F also fails to Pareto dominate Ω^{ih} since the hub country is worse off under free trade while the spokes are better off. Finally, to see why Ω^{ih} and Ω^{ij} cannot be Pareto ranked, observe from part (*iii*) of Lemma 1 that while country i is better off under $\langle ih\rangle$ relative to $\langle ij\rangle$, country j is worse off.

3.1.3. Coalition proof Nash equilibria

In what follows, we refine the set of Nash equilibria by isolating those Nash equilibria that are coalition proof. Bernheim et al. (1987) state that "in an important class of "noncooperative" environments, it is natural to assume that players can freely discuss their strategies, but cannot make binding commitments. In such cases, any meaningful agreement between the players must be self-enforcing. Although the Nash best-response property is a necessary condition for self-enforceability, it is not sufficient – it is in general possible for coalitions to arrange plausible, mutually beneficial deviations from Nash agreements." Allowing countries to discuss their strategies regarding which trade agreements they intend to form is eminently desirable in the present context since countries considering bilateral trade agreements certainly have the capacity to communicate with one another without necessarily having the ability to make binding commitments regarding their future plans. Following Bernheim et al. (1987): "... *an agreement is coalition-proof if and only if it is Pareto efficient within the class of self-enforcing agreements. In turn, an agreement is self-enforcing if and only if no proper subset (coalition) of players, taking the actions of its complement as fixed, can agree to deviate in a way that makes all of its members better off.*" Therefore, a coalition proof Nash equilibrium (CPNE) is immune to all self-enforcing coalitional deviations.

We are now ready to state one of our key results (see the Appendix A for its proof):

Proposition 3A. *The only coalition proof Nash equilibrium of the FTA game is the announcement profile Ω^F that yields global free trade.*

The key message of this result is that even though a pair of countries benefit from excluding the third country from their trade agreement, *they are unable to exercise this exclusion incentive in equilibrium*. The flexible nature of FTAs plays a crucial role in ensuring that the exclusion incentive goes unexercised in the FTA game. To see why, suppose the announcement profile is Ω^F – i.e. each country announces in favor of an FTA with both its trading partners. Starting at Ω^F, as part (*ii*) of Lemma 1 indicates, two countries (say i and j) have an incentive to exclude the third country by jointly altering their announcements in way that the announcement profile changes from Ω^F to $\{\sigma_i = \{j,\phi\},\sigma_j = \{i,\phi\},\sigma_k = \{i,j\}\}$ thereby altering the associated trade regime from free trade to the bilateral FTA $\langle ij\rangle$. However, from Lemma 1 we know that the most preferred trading arrangement from each country's perspective is a hub and spoke regime under which it is the hub. It follows then that, holding constant the announcement of the excluded country at $\sigma_k = \{i,j\}$, each member of the deviating coalition has an incentive *to alter its announcement to form a separate FTA with the excluded country*. For example, country i has an incentive to alter its announcement from $\sigma_i = \{j,\phi\}$ to $\sigma_i = \{j,k\}$ which alters the announcement profile from $\{\sigma_i = \{j,\phi\},\sigma_j = \{i,\phi\},\sigma_k = \{i,j\}\}$ to $\{\sigma_i = \{j,k\},\sigma_j = \{i,\phi\},\sigma_k = \{i,j\}\}$ and the associated trade regime from $\langle ij\rangle$ to $\langle ih\rangle$. Since the welfare of a hub is higher than that of a member country of a single FTA – see part (*iii*) of Lemma 1 – the original coalitional deviation of countries i and j from is not self-enforcing. Thus, the lure of a hub and spoke trading arrangement ends up delivering free trade as the only CPNE of the FTA game.

It is important to acknowledge that when evaluating whether a particular coalitional deviation is self-enforcing or not, the concept of a CPNE holds the announcement of the excluded country constant. Thus, when country i alters its announcement from $\sigma_i = \{j,\phi\}$ to $\sigma_i = \{j,k\}$ in order to secure the hub and spoke regime $\langle ih\rangle$, the CPNE concept rules out the possibility of a pact between countries j and k to enter into an FTA with each other. Thus, by imposing this type of a restriction, the concept of a CPNE captures a relatively limited type of self-enforceability. Is such a restriction plausible in our model of FTAs?[19] As Bernheim et al. (1987) note, one possible justification for this approach is as follows: "...informational problems may cripple any attempt to form coalitions consisting of both members and nonmembers from

[19] We thank an anonymous referee for raising this point. While the concept of CPNE suffers from this limitation, alternative equilibrium concepts – such as Strong Nash – have problems of their own. As Bernheim et al. (1987) note, the concept of Strong Nash gives coalitions too much freedom in choosing their deviations since a Strong Nash equilibrium has to be immune to *all* coalitional deviations, even to those that are not self-enforcing in nature. As a result, Strong Nash equilibria rarely exist. Indeed, the set of Strong Nash equilibria of our FTA game is empty.

some other deviating coalition." This justification is fairly reasonable in our set-up since discussions among a pair of countries regarding a potential FTA between them are likely to be private and an excluded country may lack verifiable information about the content of such discussions. Real world FTAs are relatively complex and multi-faceted arrangements and third parties may not have the means to uncover what exactly is being negotiated between potential member countries. The full details of an FTA generally become public knowledge only after it has been ratified by member countries and the actual signing of an FTA by two countries is rather different from early negotiations between them, detailed information about which may not be easily available to outsiders.

An alternative way of understanding Proposition 3A is as follows. In our three player game, to isolate the CPNE of the FTA game we only need to consider coalitional deviations from each Nash equilibrium to other Nash equilibria since, by definition, any coalitional deviations from a Nash equilibrium announcement profile to other profiles that are not Nash equilibria are susceptible to unilateral deviations on the part of at least one member of the deviating coalition and therefore do not need to be considered. A Nash equilibrium profile from which no coalition wishes to deviate to another Nash equilibrium profile would then be coalition proof. Using this logic, we can immediately rule out the announcement profile Ω^{Φ} as a CPNE since countries i and j benefit from a joint deviation to Ω^{ij}, which is a Nash equilibrium. Next, note that Ω^{ij} also cannot be coalition proof since parts (*iii*) and (*iv*) of Lemma 1 imply that countries i and k benefit by jointly deviating to the Nash equilibrium profile Ω^{ih}. Furthermore, Ω^{ih} is also not coalition proof since, as per part (*v*) of Lemma 1, countries j and k benefit if they jointly deviate from Ω^{ih} to Ω^{F}, which is a Nash equilibrium. Finally, Ω^{F} is indeed coalition proof because any joint deviation from Ω^{F} to an alternative Nash announcement profile *makes at least one member of the deviating coalition worse off*. For example, as per part (*ii*) of Lemma 1, the deviation from Ω^{F} to Ω^{ij} makes country k worse off; that from Ω^{F} to Ω^{ih} makes countries j and k worse off; and that from Ω^{F} to Ω^{Φ} makes all countries worse off. As a result, Ω^{F} is immune to all coalitional deviations.

We now analyze the CU game.

3.2. The CU game

Suppose the PTA under consideration is a CU as opposed to an FTA. As under the FTA game, at the first stage of the CU formation game each country announces the names of countries with whom it wants to form a CU. Country i's announcement is denoted by σ_i and its strategy set S_{iu} consists of four possible announcements:

$$S_{iu} = \{\{\phi,\phi\},\{j_u,\phi\},\{\phi,k_u\},\{j_u,k_u\}\} \tag{33}$$

where $\{\phi,\phi\}$ denotes an announcement in favor of no CU with either trading partners, $\{j_u,\phi\}$ in favor of a CU with only country j; $\{\phi,k_u\}$ in favor of a CU with only country k; and $\{j_u,k_u\}$ in favor of a CU that includes both its trading partners.

The mapping between various announcements profiles and the CUs that can arise is as follows: (*i*) when no two announcements match or the only matching announcements are $\{\phi,\phi\}$ we obtain no agreement $\langle\Phi\rangle$; (*ii*) a CU between countries i and j denoted by $\langle ij_u\rangle$ is formed if they announce each others' names and there is no other matching announcement, i.e., $\langle ij_u\rangle$ is formed if the following three conditions hold: (*a*) $j_u\in\sigma_i$, $i_u\in\sigma_j$ and (*b*) $k_u\notin\sigma_i$ and/or $i_u\notin\sigma_k$ and (*c*) $k_u\notin\sigma_j$ and/or $j_u\notin\sigma_k$; (*iv*) free trade $\langle F\rangle$ obtains iff all countries announce each other's names. Recall that the equivalent of a hub and spoke trading regime cannot arise under the CU game due to the fact that CU members coordinate their external tariffs.

In order to derive Nash equilibria of the CU game, we first summarize the relevant welfare comparisons:

Lemma 2. *Let $m=i,j$ denote a member country of the CU $\langle ij_u\rangle$. Then we have: (i) $\Delta w_k(ij_u\text{-}\Phi)<0<\Delta w_m(ij_u\text{-}\Phi)$ and (ii) $\Delta w_m(ij_u\text{-}F)>0$.*

Lemma 2 can be interpreted much like Lemma 1. Part (*i*) simply says that the formation of a CU makes members better off and the non-member worse off. In fact, since CU members *pool their market power* and extract a larger terms of trade gain from the non-member, the welfare of a CU member is higher than that of an FTA member while that of the non-member is lower:

$$\Delta w_k(ij_u-ij)<0<\Delta w_m(ij_u-ij).$$

Part (*ii*) of Lemma 2 says that the exclusion incentive is very much at play in the CU game. In fact, *the exclusion incentive of a CU is stronger than that of an FTA*, which is another implication of the higher market power of a CU:

$$0<\Delta w_m(ij-F)<\Delta w_m(ij_u-F).$$

3.2.1. Equilibria of the CU game

We can now state:

Proposition 2B. *The Nash equilibrium announcement profiles of the CU game and the associated trade agreements are as follows:*

(i) $\Omega_u^{\Phi}=\{\sigma_i=\{\phi,\phi\},\sigma_j=\{\phi,\phi\},\sigma_k=\{\phi,\phi\}\}$ *which yields no agreement* $\langle\Phi\rangle$.
(ii) *All announcement profiles satisfying $j_u\in\sigma_i$, $i_u\in\sigma_j$ and any one of the following three conditions yield the bilateral CU $\langle ij_u\rangle$: (1) $k_u\notin\sigma_i$ and $k_u\notin\sigma_j$ or (2) $k_u\notin\sigma_i$ and $j_u\notin\sigma_k$ or (3) $k_u\notin\sigma_j$ and $i_u\notin\sigma_k$.*
(iii) $\Omega_u^{F}=\{\sigma_i=\{j_u,k_u\},\sigma_j=\{i_u,k_u\},\sigma_k=\{i_u,j_u\}\}$ *which yields global free trade* $\langle F\rangle$.

The logic underlying Proposition 2B follows directly from Lemma 2. The announcement profile Ω_u^{F} is a Nash equilibrium since no country has an incentive to unilaterally alter its announcement because doing so results in free trade being replaced by a bilateral CU between the other two countries under which it is worse off. Furthermore, Ω_u^{Φ} is a Nash equilibrium since no country has an incentive to announce another's name given that the latter does not reciprocate. The key difference relative to the FTA game is described in part (*ii*) of Proposition 2B. Note that as long as countries i and j announce each other's names but not that of country k, the resulting agreement is the bilateral CU $\langle ij_u\rangle$ regardless of what country k announces. When countries i and j announce each other's names and one of them announces country k but country k does not make any matching announcement, the resulting agreement is again $\langle ij_u\rangle$. As such, a variety of different announcement profiles are consistent with a bilateral CU. Following Lemma 2, $\langle ij_u\rangle$ is the most preferred trade regime of member countries. Therefore, neither country i nor j has an incentive to unilaterally change its announcement and a unilateral change in country k's announcement does not alter the existing trade agreement $\langle ij_u\rangle$ since a CU member cannot have an independent trade agreement with the third country due to the requirement of a common external tariff.

Following our discussion of the FTA game, it is easy to see that Ω_u^{Φ} is not a CPNE of the CU game. To see why, simply note that starting at Ω_u^{Φ}, countries i and j benefit by altering their announcements to $\sigma_i=\{j,\phi\}$ and $\sigma_j=\{i,\phi\}$ which converts no agreement $\langle\Phi\rangle$ to the bilateral CU $\langle ij_u\rangle$ under which both of them are better off (see Lemma 2). Since the announcement profile $\{\sigma_i=\{j,\phi\},\sigma_j=\{i,\phi\},\sigma_k=\{\phi,\phi\}\}$ is a Nash equilibrium of the CU game, it is immune to unilateral deviations on the part of countries i and j.

We now argue that Ω_u^F is also *not* a CPNE of the CU game. To see why, simply consider the coalitional deviation of countries i and j from Ω_u^F to $\Omega_u^1 \equiv \{\sigma_i = \{j,\phi\}, \sigma_j = \{i,\phi\}, \sigma_k = \{i,j\}\}$. Observe from Proposition 2B that this coalitional deviation alters the trade regime from free trade to $\langle ij_u \rangle$ and since CU members enjoy higher welfare than that under free trade, neither member country has an incentive to unilaterally alter its announcements from that which it makes under Ω_u^1. The key difference relative to the FTA game is that the joint deviation of countries i and j from each of them announcing both their trading partners names' to calling only each other is now self-enforcing since, holding constant country k's announcement, neither of them has an incentive to further deviate unilaterally. Thus, Ω_u^F fails to be a CPNE of the CU game.

Thus, the only remaining candidate for a CPNE is the CU $\langle ij_u \rangle$. To see why it must be a CPNE, simply note that, starting with any Nash equilibrium announcement profile that yields $\langle ij_u \rangle$, member countries have no incentive to jointly alter their announcements to either obtain $\langle \Phi \rangle$ or $\langle F \rangle$ since they are worse off under either of these outcomes. Furthermore, since at least one of the members does not announce the non-member's name in any announcement profile that supports $\langle ij_u \rangle$, no coalition of a member and a non-member can obtain free trade by jointly altering their announcements. Thus, we can state the following:

Proposition 3B. *Only those announcement profiles that yield a bilateral CU constitute the coalition proof Nash equilibria of the CU game.*

The difference between results reported in Propositions 3A and 3B is driven by the relatively flexible nature of FTAs compared to CUs. In the FTA game, if two countries (i and j) try to jointly exclude the third country by forming a bilateral FTA then each of them has an incentive to sign an independent FTA with the excluded country thereby making itself a hub. The ability to act on this incentive acts as a deterrent for the other initially deviating country (say j) since it is worse off as a spoke under $\langle ih \rangle$ relative to free trade and thus the initial joint deviation from the announcement profile Ω^F to Ω^{ij} does not occur. However, unlike the FTA game, no such deterrent exists under the CU game since a CU member cannot form an independent agreement with the excluded country without the consent of its CU partner. Therefore, our model suggests that while the pursuit of FTAs is compatible with the goal of achieving global free trade, the pursuit of CUs is not.

We should note here that our non-cooperative approach rules out transfers between countries. It is worth discussing briefly the case where the use of such transfers is permitted. Since joint welfare is maximized under global free trade, if international transfers could be freely used then the outcome of the CU game would also be free trade. In the real world, it is probably the case that countries can use transfers but they also face some constraints regarding how large such transfers can be. If this is the case, our analysis shows that while the FTA game would yield free trade, the CU game will fail to do so if the benefit of the exclusion to two countries exceeds the maximum level of transfer that the non-member can provide to induce CU members to move to global free trade — i.e. free trade would not arise if the maximum level of the transfer that an excluded country can provide to each CU member to induce it to move to free trade falls below $\Delta w_m(ij_u - F)$.

4. Further analysis and discussion

In what follows, motivated by Article XXIV of GATT, we first examine the consequences of restricting CU members from raising their external tariff above the pre-existing level t^*.[20] Next, holding this restriction in place, we analyze two different extensions. In the first extension, we analyze a more general game where countries can choose between FTAs and CUs. In the second extension, we consider a scenario where demand is asymmetric across countries in order to examine how allowing for such type of asymmetry alters our key results.

4.1. Article XXIV restriction on external tariffs

We now isolate the implications of the pooling of market power under a CU from its relative inflexibility compared to an FTA. We do this by holding the external tariff of the CU constant at the pre-existing level t^*. This is well motivated experiment since the key WTO clause that sanctions PTAs, i.e. Article XXIV of GATT, forbids member countries of a PTA from raising tariffs on non-members. In our model, in the absence of such a restriction, CU members indeed raise their tariffs on outsiders due to the pooling of their market power whereas FTA members do not. What is the equilibrium outcome of the CU game when CU members are unable to raise their tariffs above the levels that prevail in the absence of any trade agreements?[21]

If CU members are prohibited from raising tariffs on non-members, the external tariffs under a CU and FTA are equal:

$$t_i(ij) = t_i(ij_u) = t^*. \tag{34}$$

Given that they impose equal external tariffs and face the same tariffs in export markets, the welfare levels of a CU member is the same as that as an FTA member: $w_m(ij_u) = w_m(ij)$ for $m = i,j$. It turns out that countries i and j still have an incentive to jointly deviate from their respective announcements $\{j_u,k_u\}$ and $\{i_u,k_u\}$ to the announcements $\{j_u,\phi\}$ and $\{i_u,\phi\}$ (converting free trade $\langle F \rangle$ to a bilateral CU $\langle ij_u \rangle$) even when the external tariffs are restricted by Article XXIV:

$$\Delta w_m(F - ij_u) < 0 \text{ for } m = i,j. \tag{35}$$

As before, this deviation is self-enforcing and thus free trade fails to be coalition-proof under the restricted CU game. Thus, even when CU members are prevented from raising their tariffs on outsiders, a bilateral CU still emerges in coalition-proof Nash equilibria of the CU game. The only consequence of the tariff restriction is that it reduces the external tariff of the CU. Thus, though the restriction on external tariffs of CU members fails to further the cause of global free trade, it makes the resulting CU more attractive from a global welfare perspective by softening the adverse impact of the CU on the non-member country.[22] Hereafter, we assume that a CU must abide by the external tariff restriction imposed by GATT Article XXIV. A useful implication of abiding by GATT Article XXIV in our model is that the welfare of members of a CU becomes equal to that of FTA members (since their external tariffs become equal and internal tariffs are zero in both cases). As a result, the two types of PTAs differ from one another only in terms of the flexibility available to members.

4.2. The choice between FTAs and CUs

Thus far, we have required countries to form either FTAs or CUs without allowing them to pick between the two. What if both types of

[20] Part 5(a) of Article XXIV of GATT states that "with respect to a customs union, or an interim agreement leading to a formation of a customs union, the duties and other regulations of commerce imposed at the institution of any such union or interim agreement in respect of trade with contracting parties not parties to such union or agreement shall not on the whole be higher or more restrictive than the general incidence of the duties and regulations of commerce applicable in the constituent territories prior to the formation of such union."

[21] Answering this question also allows us to highlight the value of flexibility enjoyed by FTA members since a CU whose external tariff equals that of an FTA differs from it in only one key respect: while FTA members can form independent FTAs with the non-member, CU members cannot. Thus, imposing the external tariff restriction of GATT Article XXIV allows us to utilize some relevant institutional features of the world trading system to isolate the value of the flexibility enjoyed by FTA members.

[22] In a recent paper, Mrázová et al. (2013) compare CU formation with and without the constraint on external tariffs imposed by Article XXIV. In their multi-country oligopoly model, holding constant the structure of the CU, the constraint imposed by Article XXIV improves world welfare. But this positive effect is counterbalanced by a negative compositional effect since Article XXIV encourages the formation of more symmetric CUs and thereby causes a greater volume of trade to be subject to tariffs.

PTAs were permitted simultaneously in the same game? To address this question, consider the following PTA game. In the first stage, each country simultaneously announces the names of countries with whom it wants to sign a PTA as well as the nature of the PTA it seeks. For an agreement to arise between two countries, they need to not only announce each other's names but also call in favor of the same type of PTA (i.e. an FTA or a CU).

Country i's strategy set Ω_i consists of seven possible announcements:

$$\Omega_i = \{\{\phi,\phi\},\{j,\phi\},\{j_u,\phi\},\{\phi,k\},\{\phi,k_u\},\{j,k\},\{j_u,k_u\}\}$$

where $\{\phi,\phi\}$ denotes an announcement in favor of no FTA or CU with either trading partners, $\{j,\phi\}$ in favor of an FTA with only country j; $\{j_u,\phi\}$ in favor of a CU with country j;$\{\phi,k\}$ in favor of an FTA with only country k; $\{\phi,k_u\}$ in favor of a CU with country k; $\{j,k\}$ in favor of FTAs with both of them and $\{j_u,k_u\}$ in favor of a CU that includes all three countries which is tantamount to announcing in favor of global free trade. Here, it is important to re-emphasize that, due to the common external tariff requirement of a CU, a country cannot announce in favor of (*i*) two independent CUs with its trading partners or (*ii*) in favor of a bilateral CU and a bilateral FTA simultaneously. Finally, note that announcing $\{j_u,k_u\}$ is not equivalent to announcing in favor of a bilateral CU with either partner.

The mapping between announcements and trade agreements in the extended PTA game follows naturally from our previous two games. To avoid redundancy, we simply note two novel aspects of the mapping between announcements and agreements in the extended game. First, no agreement $\langle\Phi\rangle$ obtains in the PTA game whenever no announcements match or the only matching announcements are $\{\phi,\phi\}$ where two announcements can fail to match just because two countries desire a different type of a PTA with each other. For example, no agreement $\langle\Phi\rangle$ obtains when $\sigma_i=\{j,\phi\}$; $\sigma_j=\{i_u,\phi\}$; and $\sigma_k=\{\varphi,\phi\}$. In this case, although countries i and j announce each other's names, country i calls in favor of an FTA whereas country j announces in favor of a CU. No agreement obtains because countries i and j call in favor of different types of PTAs with each other and neither of them calls country k. The second point to note about the PTA game is that both of the following announcements map into global free trade: $\{\sigma_i=\{j,k\},\sigma_j=\{i,k\},\ \sigma_k=\{i,j\}\}$ and $\{\sigma_i=\{j_u,k_u\},\sigma_j=\{i_u,k_u\},\ \sigma_k=\{i_u,j_u\}\}$. In other words, if all countries announce in favor of the same type of PTA with both their trading partners, the resulting outcome is free trade regardless of whether the PTA is an FTA or a CU. Other than these two aspects, the mappings between various announcements and trade agreements described in the FTA game and the CU game carry over naturally to the PTA game.

Combining the proofs of Propositions 3A and 3B, we first argue that free trade does not arise in the CPNE of the PTA game. As before, it is immediate that countries i and j have an incentive to coalitionally deviate from their free trade announcements to the announcements $\{j_u,\phi\}$ and $\{i_u,\phi\}$ (thereby converting $\langle F\rangle$ to $\langle ij_u\rangle$) and it is a self-enforcing deviation since, taking country k's announcement as fixed at $\{i_u,j_u\}$, neither of them has an incentive to further deviate unilaterally.

It is straightforward from part (*i*) of Lemmas 1 and 2 that $\langle\Phi\rangle$ is not a CPNE since a pair of countries have an incentive to coalitionally deviate in order to form an FTA or a CU and such a joint deviation is self-enforcing. It is immediate from the inequalities reported in parts (*iii*) and (*iv*) of Lemma 1 that a member country and the non-member country facing a bilateral FTA have an incentive to engage in a coalitional deviation that would convert the FTA to a hub and spoke regime. Furthermore, this initial coalitional deviation is self-enforcing since no proper subset of the initially deviating countries has an incentive to further alter its announcement unilaterally. Therefore, announcement profiles that yield a bilateral FTA are not a CPNE of the PTA game.

Next, we show that a hub and spoke regime such as $\langle ih\rangle$ also does not arise in the CPNE of the PTA game. Note from the inequality in part (*v*) of Lemma 1 that two spoke countries have incentives to coalitionally change their announcements, converting a hub and spoke regime to free trade. This initial coalitional deviation is self-enforcing since the announcement profile supporting free trade is a Nash equilibrium. Therefore, $\langle ih\rangle$ cannot arise in a CPNE. Finally, since member countries under a bilateral CU obtain the highest possible individual welfare, they have no incentive to unilaterally or coalitionally deviate, and thus, only those announcement profiles that yield $\langle ij_u\rangle$ constitute a CPNE.

Based on our previous discussions of the FTA game and CU game, it is clear then that when countries are free to choose between the two types of PTAs, the CPNE of the PTA game yield a bilateral CU $\langle ij_u\rangle$. One way of interpreting this result is that if the CU game is expanded to allow additional strategies that allow players to call in favor of an FTA, the result stated in Proposition 3B remains unaffected. This finding further supports the intuitive idea underlying the paper – i.e. owing to its relatively inflexible nature, a CU is a more coalitionally stable agreement than an FTA. However, it also seems fair to acknowledge that, while our model does a nice job of capturing this fundamental difference between FTAs and CUs, we do not think that the PTA game analyzed above captures some important real-world factors that are likely to determine the choice between FTAs and CUs. For example, by design, the model abstracts from the difficulties that actual CU members face in reaching agreement on and then enforcing a common external tariff. Similarly, the sharing of tariff revenue among CU members does not occur as seamlessly in the real world as is assumed in the model. Finally, the underlying trading structure assumed by us is one in which the exclusion incentive of a CU ends up driving equilibrium outcomes. While such an incentive is likely to arise in other types of trading structures, its magnitude may not be large enough to yield a CU as an equilibrium outcome. For example, in the competing exporters framework of Saggi et al. (2013), the exclusion incentive of a CU is weaker and the equilibrium outcome of the CU game is global free trade.

4.3. Implications of asymmetry: an illustration

Thus far, we have assumed that countries are symmetric in every respect except for the fact that each country has a comparative advantage in a unique good. It is natural to wonder whether our key results extend to a setting where countries differ from one another in some respect. To gain some insight into how asymmetry might matter, it proves instructive to focus on the following case: suppose two countries (denoted by l and l') have larger market demands than the third (denoted by s). More specifically, let the pattern of demand asymmetry be captured by the demand intercept α (see Eq. (2)) in the following fashion: $\alpha_s = 1<\alpha_l=\alpha_{l'}=\alpha$. In order to guarantee interior solutions to the optimal tariff problems of all countries, we assume that $\alpha<\bar{\alpha}(\lambda)=1+\lambda/4$.

How does a country's incentive to form a bilateral PTA with another depend on the distribution of market sizes across countries? We address this key question in the following lemma:

Lemma 3. *Let country j be a PTA partner of country i under regime r but not regime v, where* $r,v=\langle\Phi\rangle,\langle ij\rangle,\langle ij_u\rangle,\langle ih\rangle$ *or* $\langle F\rangle$ *and* $r\neq v$. *Then, the following holds:* $\frac{\partial\Delta w_{i(r-v)}}{\partial\alpha_i}<0<\frac{\partial\Delta w_{i(r-v)}}{\partial\alpha_j}$.

First, observe that the countries with larger markets have greater market power, and therefore gain more from their optimal tariffs than the smaller country. The intuition underlying the $\frac{\partial\Delta w_{i(r-v)}}{\partial\alpha_i}<0$ is as follows. Due to the smaller volume of their exports, countries with larger markets benefit less from tariff reductions granted by the smaller country. Similarly, larger countries have relatively more to lose from eliminating their own optimal tariffs since these tariffs apply to relatively larger import volumes (or to relatively inelastic export supply curves). Thus, a country's willingness to enter into a bilateral trade agreement with another depends negatively on its own market size.

A similar intuition underlies the other inequality (i.e. $\frac{\partial\Delta w_{i(r-v)}}{\partial\alpha_j}>0$). The larger the market size of a country's partner, the larger the increase in its export surplus from the elimination of its partner's optimal tariff and the smaller the loss due to its own trade liberalization since the tariff reduction applies to a smaller volume of imports (due to the larger market size of its partner). The two inequalities reported in Lemma 3 imply that a country prefers to form a bilateral PTA with the larger of its two trading partners:

$$w_i(ij_u) = w_i(ij) \geq w_i(ik) = w_i(ik_u) \text{ iff } \alpha_j \geq \alpha_k. \tag{36}$$

Let $\alpha_i(r\text{-}v)$ denote the critical threshold of market size asymmetry at which country i is indifferent between regimes r and v so that $\Delta w_i(r\text{-}v) = 0$. For example, consider the following two regimes: $\langle ll' \rangle$ and $\langle lh \rangle$ from the perspective of countries s and l. Using the above lemma, we know that $(i)\ \frac{\partial \Delta w_s(lh-ll')}{\partial \alpha_s} < 0$ and $(ii)\ \frac{\partial \Delta w_l(lh-ll')}{\partial \alpha_s} > 0$. We know from the discussion under symmetry that a country prefers being a spoke to being a non-member facing an FTA ($\Delta w_s(lh\text{-}ll') > 0$). As country s becomes smaller in size relative to the other two countries, using (i) we can show that $w_s(lh\text{-}ll') > 0$ for all α – i.e. the result that it is better to be a spoke than to be an outsider extends to the asymmetric setting for the smaller country. Furthermore, there exists a critical threshold of market size asymmetry ($\alpha_l(lh\text{-}ll')$) at which country l is indifferent between regimes $\langle ll' \rangle$ and $\langle lh \rangle$. Recall that under symmetry a country prefers being a hub to being a member under an FTA. Using (ii), we can show that the incentive to become a hub decreases as country s becomes smaller in size relative to the other two countries. At the limit when $\alpha = \bar{\alpha}(\lambda)$, we have $\Delta w_l(lh\text{-}ll') < 0$ and thus it follows that country l prefers $\langle ll' \rangle$ to $\langle lh \rangle$ when $\alpha > \alpha_l(lh\text{-}ll')$. Using this logic and utilizing the results under symmetry as well as Lemma 3, we prove the following proposition, illustrated in Fig. 1, in the Appendix A:

Proposition 4. *Let $\alpha_s = 1 < \alpha_l = \alpha_{l'} = \alpha < \bar{\alpha}(\lambda)$. Then, the following hold:*

(i) ***FTA game**: When $\alpha < \alpha(mh\text{-}ll')$ for $m = l, l'$, the strategy profile that yields global free trade $\langle F \rangle$ is the unique CPNE of the FTA game whereas when $\alpha > \alpha(mh\text{-}ll')$ those announcement profiles that yield the bilateral FTA between the two larger countries $\langle ll' \rangle$ constitute the set of CPNE.*[23]

(ii) ***CU game**: Only those announcement profiles that yield the bilateral CU between the two larger countries $\langle ll'_u \rangle$ constitute the CPNE of the CU game.*[24]

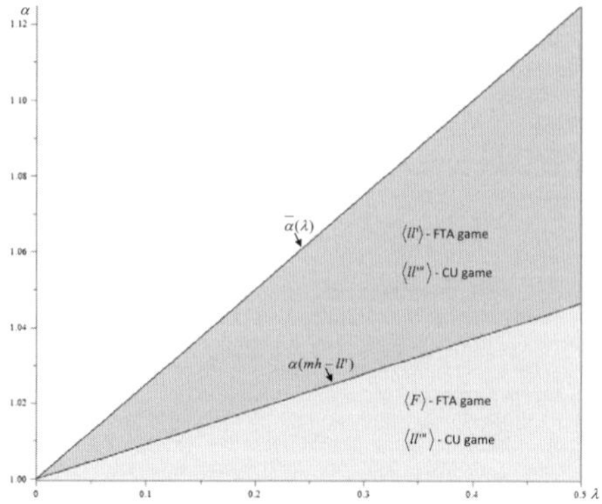

Fig. 1. Equilibrium outcomes under asymmetry.

The intuition behind the first statement in part (i) of Proposition 4 is very similar to Proposition 3A. The two larger countries benefit from excluding the smaller country from their trade agreement: $\Delta w_l(F\text{-}ll') = \Delta w_{l'}(F\text{-}ll') < 0$. Thus, taking the announcement of country s as fixed, countries l and l' have an incentive to jointly deviate from $\sigma_l = \{l', s\}$ and $\sigma_{l'} = \{l, s\}$ to $\sigma_l = \{l', \phi\}$ and $\sigma_{l'} = \{l, \phi\}$ respectively. However, this joint deviation turns out to be not self-enforcing when the degree of market size asymmetry is sufficiently small ($\alpha < \alpha_l(lh\text{-}ll')$) since each larger country, taking the announcement of the smaller country fixed at $\sigma_s = \{l, l'\}$, has an incentive to deviate from its announcement under the coalitional deviation by altering its announcement to include the smaller country's name in order to position itself as a hub. For example, given $\sigma_l = \{l, \phi\}$ and $\sigma_k' = \{l, l'\}$, country l has an incentive to alter its announcement from $\sigma_l = \{l', \phi\}$ to $\sigma_l = \{l, s\}$ so as to obtain the hub and spoke arrangement $\langle lh \rangle$. Thus the result stated in Proposition 3A does not require symmetry; it continues to hold as long as the degree of demand asymmetry between countries is not too pronounced.

When the market size of two larger countries is sufficiently large relative to the smaller country (i.e. $\alpha > \alpha_l(lh\text{-}ll')$), the degree of external trade diversion caused by the bilateral FTA $\langle ll' \rangle$ is high and this tends to lower the optimal tariffs of the smaller country. Therefore, from the perspective of each larger country, starting at the bilateral FTA $\langle ll' \rangle$ the benefit of an additional FTA with the smaller country is limited while the domestic surplus loss incurred by giving up its own optimal tariff is sizeable. Under such a scenario, each larger country prefers to be the member of the bilateral FTA $\langle ll' \rangle$ relative to becoming a hub with two independent FTAs. As a result, the joint announcement deviation of the larger countries from their announcements $\sigma_l = \{l', s\}$ and $\sigma_{l'} = \{l, s\}$ to $\sigma_l = \{l', \phi\}$ and $\sigma_{l'} = \{l, \phi\}$ is self-enforcing and free trade fails to be a CPNE. Thus, when the degree of demand asymmetry exceeds the critical threshold $\alpha(lh\text{-}ll')$, the announcement profile $\{\sigma_l = \{l', \phi\}, \sigma_{l'} = \{l, \phi\}, \sigma_s = \{\phi, \phi\}\}$ leading to the bilateral FTA $\langle ll' \rangle$ is the unique CPNE of the FTA game.

Finally, consider part (ii) of Proposition 4, which states that the result under symmetry (Proposition 3B) extends without any modifications to the asymmetric setting examined here. As in the FTA game, the two larger countries benefit from excluding the smaller country – i.e. $\Delta w_l(F\text{-}ll'_u) = \Delta w_{l'}(F\text{-}ll'_u) < 0$ – and the inability of a CU member to enter into an independent trade agreement with the outsider implies that the exclusion incentive is exercised in equilibrium. Since the larger countries prefer the bilateral CU $\langle ll'_u \rangle$ to no agreement $\langle \Phi \rangle$, there exist no coalitional deviation incentive on their part from the announcements that support $\langle ll'_u \rangle$.

The analysis above shows that the lure of a hub and spoke arrangement that undermines a bilateral FTA is not as strong when the excluded country is sufficiently small relative to the other two countries. This is a fairly intuitive result and it provides useful perspective on when and why the pursuit of bilateral FTAs may not necessarily end up in global free trade. It also fits well with related existing literature that generally finds free trade to be more likely to obtain when countries are relatively symmetric to one another.

5. Conclusion

At a time when multilateral trade liberalization at the WTO seems to have come to a grinding halt, the question whether PTAs have a useful role to play in the global trading system seems to have acquired a greater degree of urgency. After all, other than unilateral trade liberalization, over the last decade or so PTAs appear to be the only game in town for countries interested in undertaking international trade liberalization. Of course, the concern that the pursuit of PTAs might undermine whatever

[23] All strategy profiles with the following two properties yield $\langle ll' \rangle$: (i) $l \in \sigma_{l'}$ and $l' \in \sigma_l$ and (ii) $s \notin \sigma_l$ and $s \notin \sigma_{l'}$.

[24] All strategy profiles with the following two properties yield $\langle ll'_u \rangle$: (i) $l^u \in \sigma_{l'}$ and $l'_u \in \sigma_l$ and (ii) $s^u \notin \sigma_l$ and/or $s^u \notin \sigma_{l'}$.

appetite remains in the global trading system for multilateral trade liberalization remains a real one.

In this paper, we attempt to isolate the implications of the two commonly occurring PTAs, i.e. FTAs and CUs, for the prospects of global free trade. The starting point of our analysis is a well understood difference between these two types of PTAs: while CU members impose common external tariffs, FTA members are free to implement external tariffs of own choosing. This difference in tariff setting behavior between the two PTAs implies that while FTA members have less market power than CU members, they enjoy a greater degree of flexibility in the sense that they are free to enter into further trade agreements with outsiders whereas CU members can only do so with consent of existing members.

An important result of this paper is that the formation of either type of PTA induces the non-member to lower its tariffs on PTA members: the external trade diversion – i.e. the reduction in the volume of exports flowing from PTA members to the non-members – reduces the ability of the non-member to manipulate its terms of trade thereby making it optimal for it to lower its tariffs. Thus, PTA formation not only benefits members because of the internal trade liberalization that they undertake but also because of the external trade liberalization induced abroad.

The central result of the paper is that the flexible nature of FTAs (which in turn emanates from independent external tariff setting on the part of FTA members) helps in the attainment of global free trade. Specifically, in the CPNE of the FTA game, each country ends up entering into FTAs with both its trading partners, an outcome under which all countries impose zero tariffs on each other. By contrast, a bilateral CU is the outcome of all announcement profiles that constitute the CPNE of the CU game. We show that this result holds even when demand, and therefore market power, is asymmetric across countries. This result crisply captures the intuition that, once formed, CUs constrain their members in a way that FTAs do not. Finally, we also find that the tariff restriction imposed by Article XXIV of the GATT fails to further the cause of global free trade although it makes the resulting CU more attractive from a global welfare perspective. Thus, our model shows that while the two key attributes of a CU – i.e. the pooling of market power by its members and the inability of any one member to enter into independent trade agreements with outsiders – both impose welfare costs on the world trading system, the latter is a more important obstacle in path of global free trade.

Appendix A. Appendix

A.1. Supporting calculations

Here we report the key formulae that are necessary for proving our results. For an arbitrary tariff vector $\mathbf{t}=(t_{ij},t_{ik},t_{ji},t_{jk},t_{ki},t_{kj})$, we can write country *i*'s welfare as

$$w_i = CS_i + PS_i + TR_i$$

where consumer surplus in country *i* equals

$$CS_i = \frac{1}{2}\left[(\alpha_i - p_i^I)^2 + \left(\alpha_i - p_j^J - t_{ij}\right)^2 + (\alpha_i - p_k^K - t_{ik})^2\right],$$

whereas its producer surplus equals

$$PS_i = \frac{(\lambda+1)}{2}(p_i^I)^2 + \frac{1}{2}\left[\left(p_j^J + t_{ij}\right)^2 + (p_k^K + t_{ik})^2\right]$$

and the tariff revenue is given by

$$TR_i = t_{ij}(2t_{kj} - \alpha_k) + t_{ik}(2t_{jk} - \alpha_j) + \sum_{z \neq i} t_{iz}(4+\lambda_z)p_z^Z - \alpha_z.$$

Equilibrium prices are given by

$$p_i^I = \frac{\sum\limits_{z=i,j,k}\alpha_z - 2\sum\limits_{z\neq i} t_{zi}}{\lambda+6};\ p_j^J = \frac{\sum\limits_{z=i,j,k}\alpha_z - 2\sum\limits_{z\neq j} t_{zj}}{\lambda+6};\ \text{and}\ p_k^K = \frac{\sum\limits_{z=i,j,k}\alpha_z - 2\sum\limits_{z\neq k} t_{zk}}{\lambda+6}.$$

Finally, optimal tariffs under each trade regime are given by:

$$t_{ll'}^* = t_{ll'}(sl) = \frac{\alpha\lambda^2 + 8\alpha\lambda + 8\alpha - 2\lambda - 8}{(\lambda+6)\left(\lambda^2 + 12\lambda + 28\right)}$$

$$t_{ls}^* = t_{ls}(ll') = \frac{\alpha\lambda + 2\alpha - 2}{\left(\lambda^2 + 12\lambda + 28\right)}$$

$$t_{sl}^* = t_{sl}(sl') = \frac{\lambda^2 + 10\lambda + 20 - 4\alpha(\lambda+5)}{(\lambda+6)\left(\lambda^2 + 12\lambda + 28\right)}$$

$$t_{sl}(ll') = t_{sl}(l'h) = \frac{\lambda + 4(1-\alpha)}{(\lambda+4)(\lambda+8)}$$

$$t_{ll'}(sl') = t_{ll'}(sh) = \frac{\alpha(\lambda+2) - 2}{(\lambda+4)(\lambda+8)}.$$

Note that $t_{sl}(ll') = t_{sl}(l'h) \geq 0$ only when $\alpha < \bar{\alpha}(\lambda) = 1 + \lambda/4$. Using the above formulae and the optimal tariff levels reported in the text, we can easily calculate welfare levels under all possible trade agreements for both cases of symmetry and asymmetry. To save space, we do not include the algebraic details underlying these straightforward calculations. The proofs of Lemmas 1–3 follow immediately from these welfare comparisons.

A.2. Proof of Proposition 2A

In the text, we showed that parsimonious announcement profiles leading to $\langle\Phi\rangle$, $\langle ij\rangle$, and $\langle ih\rangle$ are Nash equilibria of the FTA game. We next consider non-parsimonious announcement profiles and show that these are not Nash equilibria.

First note that, in any non-parsimonious announcement profile leading to no agreement $\langle\Phi\rangle$, it must be the case that countries' announcements do not match with each other. Under such a case, since countries always benefit from FTA formation (from Lemma 1), a country whose name is announced has an incentive to unilaterally change its announcement, leading to a bilateral FTA. Therefore, any non-parsimonious announcement profile that leads to $\langle\Phi\rangle$ cannot be a Nash equilibrium.

Now consider the non-parsimonious announcement profiles leading to a bilateral FTA $\langle ij\rangle$. First, consider the following scenario: $\sigma_i = \{j,\phi\}$ and $\sigma_j = \{i,\phi\}$ while $\sigma_k = \{i,\phi\}$ or $\{\phi,j\}$ or $\{i,j\}$. Under such a case, depending on country *k*'s announcement, either country *i* or country *j* has an incentive to unilaterally change its announcement to include *k* in order to become a hub under a hub and spoke regime. Second, suppose (*a*) $\sigma_i = \{j,k\}$ and $\sigma_j = \{i,\phi\}$ but $i \notin \sigma_k$ or (*b*) $\sigma_i = \{j,\phi\}$ and $\sigma_j = \{i,k\}$ but $j \notin \sigma_k$ or (*c*) $\sigma_i = \{j,k\}$ and $\sigma_j = \{i,k\}$ but $i,j \notin \sigma_k$. Under all three cases, since country *k* prefers being spoke to being a non-member under a bilateral FTA (from Lemma 1), it has an incentive to unilaterally change its announcement in order to become a spoke under a hub and spoke regime. As a result, any non-parsimonious announcement leading to a bilateral FTA $\langle ij\rangle$ cannot be a Nash equilibrium.

Finally, suppose that $\sigma_i = \{j,k\}, \sigma_j = \{i,k\}, \sigma_k = \{i,\phi\}$ or $\sigma_i = \{j,k\}, \sigma_j = \{i,\phi\}, \sigma_k = \{i,j\}$. Under both scenarios, the spoke country that does not announce the other spoke has an incentive to unilaterally change its announcement to also call the other spoke which leads to free trade $\langle F\rangle$. Therefore, the initial announcement profiles are not Nash equilibrium.

A.3. Proof of Proposition 2B

In the text, we showed that parsimonious announcement profile leading to $\langle \Phi \rangle$ is a Nash equilibrium of the CU game. We next consider non-parsimonious announcement profiles and show that these are not Nash equilibria. As in the FTA game, in any non-parsimonious announcement profile leading to no agreement $\langle \Phi \rangle$, it must be the case that countries' announcements do not match with each other. Under such a case, since countries always benefit from CU formation (from Lemma 2), a country whose name is announced has an incentive to unilaterally change its announcement, leading to a bilateral CU. Therefore, any non-parsimonious announcement profile that leads to $\langle \Phi \rangle$ cannot be a Nash equilibrium.

Next, we show that the following announcement profile that yields a bilateral CU $\langle ij_u \rangle$: $\sigma_i = \{j_u, k_u\}, \sigma_j = \{i_u, k_u\}, \sigma_k = \{\phi, \phi\}$ is not a Nash equilibrium. Under such a case, since country k prefers free trade to being a non-member under $\langle ij_u \rangle$ (from Lemma 2), it has an incentive to unilaterally change its announcement from $\{\phi, \phi\}$ to $\{i_u, j_u\}$ that would convert $\langle ij_u \rangle$ to $\langle F \rangle$.

A.4. Proof of Proposition 3A

We begin by considering whether the announcement profile Ω^F that leads to $\langle F \rangle$ is a CPNE. Since world welfare is the highest under $\langle F \rangle$ and countries have equal welfare due to symmetry, each country is better off under $\langle F \rangle$ relative to $\langle \Phi \rangle$ and thus we can immediately rule out any coalitional announcement deviations that would lead to $\langle \Phi \rangle$ replacing $\langle F \rangle$. Similarly, we know that no two countries (say j and k) have incentives to jointly alter their announcements from $\{i,k\}$ to $\{i,\phi\}$ and $\{i,j\}$ to $\{i,\phi\}$, respectively since doing so would lead to a deviation from $\langle F \rangle$ to $\langle ih \rangle$ where both become spokes (and spokes are worse of relative to free trade). Finally, taking the announcement of their complement (country k) as fixed, consider the joint deviation of two countries (say i and j) from their announcements $\{j,k\}$ and $\{i,k\}$ to $\{j,\phi\}$ and $\{i,\phi\}$ respectively. This joint deviation implies a coalitional deviation from $\langle F \rangle$ to $\langle ij \rangle$. From Lemma 1 part (*ii*) we know that $\Delta w_m(F\text{-}ij) < 0$. This implies that, taking the announcement of their complement (country k) fixed at $\sigma_k = \{i,j\}$, the above coalitional deviation in announcements would occur. The question then becomes whether this joint deviation is self-enforcing. We next argue that *it is not*. This is because given that $\sigma_k = \{i,j\}$, we know from Lemma 1 part (*iii*) that country i has an incentive to alter its announcement $\{j,\phi\}$ to $\{j,k\}$ in order to create the trading regime $\langle ih \rangle$ where it becomes the hub. Similarly, country j has an incentive to alter its announcement $\{i,\phi\}$ to $\{i,k\}$ so as to itself become the hub. Thus, the initial coalitional deviation that can cause $\langle F \rangle$ to be replaced by $\langle ij \rangle$ is not self-enforcing. As a result, the announcement profile Ω^F is a CPNE.

Next, we consider whether the announcement profile Ω^{Φ} is a CPNE. Note from Lemma 1 part (*i*) that starting at Ω^{Φ} any two countries (say i and j) have an incentive to coalitionally change their announcements from $\{\phi,\phi\}$ and $\{\phi,\phi\}$ to $\{j,\phi\}$ and $\{i,\phi\}$ respectively, taking country k's announcement fixed: $\sigma_k = \{\phi,\phi\}$. This initial deviation is self-enforcing since no proper subset of the initially deviating countries (neither i nor j) has an incentive to alter its announcement unilaterally (i.e. announcement profile that leads to $\langle ij \rangle$ is a Nash equilibrium). Therefore, the announcement profile that leads to $\langle \Phi \rangle$ is not a CPNE.

We next show that Ω^{ij} is not a CPNE. From parts (*iii*) and (*iv*) of Lemma 1 we know that starting at Ω^{ij} countries i and k have an incentive to coalitionally change their announcements from $\{j,\phi\}$ and $\{\phi,\phi\}$ to $\{j,k\}$ and $\{i,\phi\}$ respectively, taking country j's announcement fixed at $\sigma_j = \{i,\phi\}$. This initial coalitional deviation would convert $\langle ij \rangle$ to $\langle ih \rangle$ where i is the hub and j and k are spokes. Furthermore, this initial coalitional deviation is self-enforcing since no proper subset of the initially deviating countries (neither i nor k) has an incentive to unilaterally alter its announcement since the announcement profile Ω^{ih} that leads to $\langle ih \rangle$ is a Nash equilibrium. Therefore, the announcement profile Ω^{ij} is not a CPNE.

Finally, we show that Ω^{ih} is not a CPNE. Note from Lemma 1 part (v) that starting at Ω^{ih} countries j and k have an incentive to coalitionally change their announcements from $\{i,\phi\}$ and $\{i,\phi\}$ to $\{i,k\}$ and $\{i,j\}$ respectively, taking country i's announcement fixed at $\sigma_i = \{j,k\}$. This coalitional deviation converts the trade regime from $\langle ih \rangle$ to $\langle F \rangle$. Furthermore, this initial coalitional deviation is self-enforcing since no proper subset of the initially deviating countries (neither j nor k) has an incentive to deviate unilaterally since Ω^F is a Nash equilibrium. Therefore, the announcement profile Ω^{ih} is not a CPNE.

A.5. Proof of Proposition 4

Note first that, since the external tariff restriction of Article XXIV is assumed to be binding, the welfare level of a member of a bilateral FTA is the same as that of member of a CU, i.e. $w_i(ij) = w_i(ij^u)$ for all $i,j = l, l', s$. Using the welfare levels reported above, we can easily show the following inequalities:

(i) $\Delta w_l(ll' - \Phi) > 0$ *for all* α
(ii) $\Delta w_l(ll' - sl) = \Delta w_l(ll'_u - sl'_u) > 0$ for all α
(iii) $\Delta w_s(lh - ll') > 0$ for all α while $\Delta w_l(lh - ll') > 0$ when $\alpha < \alpha_l(lh - ll')$
(iv) $\Delta w_l(sh - ll') < 0 < \Delta w_s(sh - ll')$ for all α
(v) $\Delta w_l(F - ll') = \Delta w_l(F - ll'_u) < 0 < \Delta w_s(F - ll') = \Delta w_s(F - ll'_u)$ for all α
(vi) $\Delta w_s(sl - \Phi) > 0$ for all α while $\Delta w_l(sl - \Phi) > 0$ when $\alpha < \alpha_l(sl - \Phi)$
(vii) $\Delta w_l(lh - sl) > 0$ and $\Delta w_{l'}(lh - sl) > 0$ for all α
(viii) $\Delta w_s(sh - sl') > 0$ for all α while $\Delta w_l(sh - sl') > 0$ when $\alpha < \alpha_l(sh - sl')$
(ix) $\Delta w_s(F - \Phi) > 0$ for all α while $\Delta w_l(F - \Phi) > 0$ when $\alpha < \alpha_l(F - \Phi)$
(x) $\Delta w_s(F - sl) > 0$ for all α while $\Delta w_l(F - \Phi) > 0$ when $\alpha < \alpha_l(F - sl)$
(xi) $\Delta w_l(F - sh) > 0$ for all α
(xii) $\Delta w_s(F - l'h) > 0$ for *all* α while $\Delta w_l(F - l'h) > 0$ when $\alpha < \alpha_l(F - l'h)$
(xiii) $\Delta w_s(F - ll') > 0$ and $\Delta w_l(F - sl') > 0$ forall α

We first consider the FTA game and prove Proposition 4(i).

A.5.1. CPNE of the FTA game under asymmetry

To avoid redundancy, we focus on parsimonious Nash announcements. Our proof extends to the case of non-parsimonious Nash announcements (which can arise in the FTA game under asymmetry).

First note from inequality (i) that starting at $\Omega^{\Phi} = \{\sigma_s = \{\phi,\phi\}, \sigma_l = \{\phi,\phi\}, \sigma_{l'} = \{\phi,\phi\}\}$ the two large countries l and l' have an incentive to coalitionally change their announcements from $\{\phi,\phi\}$ to $\{l',\phi\}$ and $\{l,\phi\}$ respectively, taking country s's announcement fixed at $\{\phi,\phi\}$. This initial deviation is self-enforcing since no proper subset of the initially deviating countries (neither l nor l') has an incentive to alter its announcement unilaterally. Therefore, the announcement profile Ω^{Φ} that leads to $\langle \Phi \rangle$ is not a CPNE.

We next show that the announcement profile $\Omega^{sl} = \{\sigma_s = \{l,\phi\}, \sigma_l = \{\phi,s\}, \sigma_{l'} = \{\phi,\phi\}\}$ that leads to $\langle sl \rangle$ is not a CPNE. Note first that $\alpha_l(sh\text{-}sl') > \alpha_l(sl\text{-}\Phi)$ for all λ. From part (vi) we know that, when $\alpha > \alpha_l(sl\text{-}\Phi)$ country l has an incentive to unilaterally change its announcement from $\{\phi,s\}$ to $\{\phi,\phi\}$ and thus the announcement profile Ω^{sl} is not even a Nash equilibrium when $\alpha > \alpha_l(sl\text{-}\Phi)$. Moreover, we know from part ($viii$) that, when $\alpha < \alpha_l(sh\text{-}sl')$, countries s and l have an incentive to coalitionally change their announcements from $\{l,\phi\}$ and $\{\phi,\phi\}$ to $\{l,l'\}$ and $\{\phi,s\}$ respectively, taking country l''s announcement fixed at $\{\phi,s\}$. This initial coalitional deviation would convert $\langle sl' \rangle$ to $\langle sh \rangle$ and it is self-enforcing in nature. Since $\alpha_l(sh\text{-}sl') > \alpha_l(sl\text{-}\Phi)$ for all λ, it is immediate that the announcement profile Ω^{sl} is not a CPNE.

Consider now the announcement profile $\Omega^{sh} = \{\sigma_s = \{l,l'\}, \sigma_l = \{\phi,s\}, \sigma_{l'} = \{\phi,s\}\}$. We know from part ($xi$) that countries l and l' have an incentive to coalitionally change their announcements from $\{\phi,s\}$ and $\{\phi,s\}$ to $\{l',s\}$ and $\{l,s\}$ respectively, taking country s's announcement fixed at $\{l,l'\}$. This initial coalitional deviation would convert $\langle sh \rangle$

to $\langle F \rangle$. From parts (*xii*) and (*xiii*), we know that, when $\alpha<\alpha_l(F\text{-}l'h)$, this coalitional deviation is self-enforcing since neither large country has an incentive to unilaterally alter its announcement. Moreover, we know from part (*iv*) that countries l and l' have an incentive to coalitionally change their announcements from $\{\phi,s\}$ and $\{\phi,s\}$ to $\{l',\phi\}$ and $\{l,\phi\}$ respectively, taking country s's announcement fixed at $\{l,l'\}$. This initial coalitional deviation would convert $\langle sh \rangle$ to $\langle ll' \rangle$. From part (*iii*) we know that this coalitional deviation is self-enforcing when $\alpha>\alpha_l(lh\text{-}ll')$. Since $\alpha_l(lh\text{-}ll')<\alpha<\alpha_l(F\text{-}l'h)$ for all λ, the announcement profile that Ω^{sh}. is not a CPNE.

We next consider the announcement profile $\Omega^{l'h}=\{\sigma_s=\{\phi,l'\},\sigma_l=\{l',\phi\},\sigma_{l'}=\{l,s\}\}$. Note from part (*iii*) that $\Delta w_l(lh-ll')<0$ when $\alpha>\alpha_l(lh-ll')$. Thus, under such a case, country l has an incentive to unilaterally change its announcement from $\{l',\phi\}$ to $\{\phi,\phi\}$ and thus $\Omega^{l'h}$ is not even a Nash equilibrium when $\alpha>\alpha_l(lh-ll')$. Moreover, we know from part (*xii*) that, when $\alpha<\alpha_l(F-l'h)$, countries s and l have an incentive to coalitionally change their announcements from $\{\phi,l'\}$ and $\{l',\phi\}$ to $\{l',s\}$ and $\{l,l'\}$ respectively, taking country l''s announcement fixed at $\{l,s\}$. This initial coalitional deviation would convert $l'h$ to F and it self-enforcing in nature. Given that we have $\alpha_l(F-l'h)>\alpha_l(lh-ll')$ for all λ, it follows that the announcement profile $\Omega^{l'h}$ is not a CPNE.

It is immediate from the above discussion that the only remaining candidates for being a CPNE under the FTA game are the announcement profiles $\Omega^{ll'}$ and Ω^F. We first consider the announcement profile $\Omega^{ll'}=\{\sigma_s=\{\phi,\phi\},\sigma_l=\{l',\phi\},\sigma_{l'}=\{l,\phi\}\}$. On one hand, we know from parts (*i*), (*ii*), (*iv*) and (*v*) that there exist no unilateral or coalitional announcement deviations that alters the trade regime from ll' to Φ, sl, sh and F. On the other hand, it is immediate from part (*iii*) that, when $\alpha<\alpha_l(lh-ll')$, countries l and s have an incentive to change their respective announcement profiles $\{l',\phi\}$ and $\{\phi,\phi\}$ to $\{l',s\}$ and $\{l,\phi\}$ respectively, taking country l''s announcement fixed at $\sigma_{l'}=\{l,\phi\}$. This initial coalitional deviation would convert ll' to lh and it is self-enforcing in nature. As a result, the announcement profile that leads to ll' is a CPNE when $\alpha\geq\alpha_l(lh-ll')$.

We now show when and why Ω^F is a CPNE of the FTA game. Note from part (*v*) that starting at $\Omega^F=\{\sigma_s=\{l,l'\},\sigma_l=\{l',s\},\sigma_{l'}=\{l,s\}\}$ countries l and l' have an incentive to coalitionally change their announcements from $\{l',s\}$ and $\{l,s\}$ to $\{l',\phi\}$ and $\{l,\phi\}$ respectively, taking country s's announcement fixed at $\{l,l'\}$. This initial coalitional deviation would convert F to ll'. From part (*iii*), we know that the initial coalitional deviation is self-enforcing only when $\alpha>\alpha_l(lh-ll')$. Note also that when $\alpha\leq\alpha_l(lh-ll')$ there exist no unilateral or self-enforcing coalitional announcement deviations from Ω^F since $\alpha_l(lh-ll')<\alpha_l(F-\Phi)$ and $\alpha_l(lh-ll')<\alpha_l(F-l'h)$. As a result, the announcement profile $\Omega^F$is a CPNE when $\alpha\leq\alpha_l(lh-ll')$.

We now prove Proposition 4(*ii*).

A.5.2. CPNE of the CU game under asymmetry

It is immediate from parts (*i*), (*ii*) and (*v*) that there exist no unilateral or coalitional announcement deviations from the various announcement profiles that lead to ll'_u. Therefore, all announcement profiles leading to ll'_u are not just CPNE of the CU game but also constitute its strong Nash equilibria. Moreover the announcement profiles that lead to Φ, sl_u, and F fail to be CPNE since the coalitional announcement deviations to the announcement profiles that lead to ll'_u occur and they are self-enforcing in nature.

References

Bagwell, Kyle, Staiger, Robert.W., 1997a. Multilateral Tariff cooperation during the formation of customs unions. J. Int. Econ. 42, 91–123 (Elsevier).

Bagwell, Kyle, Staiger, Robert.W., 1997b. Multilateral tariff cooperation during the formation of free trade areas. Int. Econ. Rev. 38, 291–319.

Bagwell, Kyle, Staiger, Robert.W., 1998. Regionalism and multilateral tariff cooperation. In: Piggott, John, Woodland, Alan (Eds.), International Trade Policy and the Pacific Rim. MacMillan, London.

Bernheim, Douglas B., Peleg, Bezalel, Whinston, Michael, 1987. Coalition-proof Nash equilibria I. Concepts. J. Econ. Theory 42, 1–12.

Bond, Eric W., Constantinos Syropoulos, 1996. The size of trading blocs: market power and world welfare effects. J. Int. Econ. 40, 411–437.

Bond, Eric W., Riezman, Raymond G., Constantinos Syropoulos, 2004. A strategic and welfare theoretic analysis of free trade areas. J. Int. Econ. 64, 1–27.

Broda, Christian, Limao, Nuno, Weinstein, David E., 2008. Optimal tariffs and market power: the evidence. Am. Econ. Rev. 98 (5), 2032–2065.

Coates, Daniel, Ludema, Rodney, 2001. A theory of trade policy leadership. J. Dev. Econ. 65, 1–29.

Estevadeordal, Antoni, Freund, Caroline, Ornelas, Emanuel, 2008. Does regionalism affect trade liberalization toward non Members? Q. J. Econ. 123 (4), 1531–1575.

Feenstra, Robert, 2004. Advanced International Trade. Princeton University Press.

Freund, Caroline, Ornelas, Emanuel, 2010. Regional trade agreements. Annu. Rev. Econ. 2, 139–167.

Horn, Henrik, Maggi, Giovanni, Staiger, Robert W., 2010. Trade agreements as endogenously incomplete contracts. Am. Econ. Rev. 100 (1), 394–419.

Krishna, Pravin, 1998. Regionalism and multilateralism: a political economy approach. Q. J. Econ. 113, 227–251.

Krishna, Pravin, Mitra, Devashish, 2005. Reciprocated unilateralism in trade policy. J. Int. Econ. 65, 461–487.

Mrázová, Monika, Vines, David, Zissimos, Ben, 2013. Is the GATT/WTO's article XXIV bad? J. Int. Econ. 89 (1), 216–232.

Olarreaga, Marcelo, Soloaga, Isidro, Winters, Alan, 1999. What's behind MERCOSUR's common external tariff? Policy Research Working Paper Series 2231. World Bank

Ornelas, Emanuel, 2005a. Trade creating free trade areas and the undermining of multilateralism. Eur. Econ. Rev. 49, 1717–1735.

Ornelas, Emanuel, 2005b. Rent destruction and the political viability of free trade agreements. Q. J. Econ. 120, 1475–1506.

Saggi, Kamal, Yildiz, Halis M., 2010. Bilateralism, multilateralism, and the quest for global free trade. J. Int. Econ. 81, 26–37.

Saggi, Kamal, Woodland, Alan, Yildiz, Halis M., 2013. On the relationship between preferential and multilateral trade liberalization: the case of customs unions. Am. Econ. J. Microecon. 5 (1), 63–99.

CHAPTER 11

American Economic Journal: Applied Economics 2018, 10(3): 128–170
https://doi.org/10.1257/app.20150360

Do Free Trade Agreements Affect Tariffs of Nonmember Countries? A Theoretical and Empirical Investigation†

By Kamal Saggi, Andrey Stoyanov, and Halis Murat Yildiz*

We investigate the effects of free trade agreements (FTAs) on tariffs of nonmember countries. In our multi-country model, the formation of an FTA leads members to reduce their exports to the rest of the world. Such external trade diversion weakens the ability of nonmembers to manipulate their terms of trade vis-à-vis FTA members, a mechanism that induces them to lower their tariffs on FTA members. We empirically confirm this insight using industry-level trade data for 192 importing and 253 exporting countries, along with information on all FTAs formed in the world during 1989–2011. (*JEL* F13, F14)

Preferential trade agreements (PTAs) are a feature of the global trade policy landscape like never before. Much attention has been devoted to how such trade agreements might affect tariff policies of member countries toward not only each other but also nonmembers. However, to the best of our knowledge, we know little about whether and how the formation of PTAs affects the trade policies of nonmember countries. In fact, in both theoretical and empirical analyses of PTAs, it is customary to either completely ignore the trade policies of nonmembers or assume that they are unaffected by PTA formation. For reasons we explain below, this is an important omission from a conceptual as well as a practical perspective. In this paper, we investigate both theoretically and empirically the effects of free trade agreements (FTAs)—the most commonly occurring type of PTA—on the tariffs of nonmember countries. Our empirical work is motivated by a simple theoretical framework based on Horn, Maggi, and Staiger (2010).

Existing literature has shown that the formation of an FTA can induce member countries to lower their tariffs on nonmembers: this is the so-called *tariff complementarity* effect (Bagwell and Staiger 1997). The intuition underlying this surprising effect is quite robust and clean. As Maggi (2014) notes, if two countries possessing

*Saggi: Department of Economics, Vanderbilt University, Nashville, TN 37235 (email: kamal.saggi@vanderbilt.edu); Stoyanov: Faculty of Liberal Arts and Professional Studies, York University, Toronto, Canada (email: andreyst@yorku.ca); Yildiz: Department of Economics, Ryerson University, 350 Victoria Street, Toronto, ON, Canada (email: hyildiz@ryerson.ca). We are very grateful to Kyle Bagwell, Eric Bond, Giovanni Maggi, Vadim Marmer, Paul Missios, Emanuel Ornelas, Joel Rodrigue, Ben Sand, and Yoto Yotov for helpful discussions. We are also greatful for seminar and conference participants at Drexel University, McMaster University, Vanderbilt University, York University, University of Ottawa, University of Waterloo, Canadian Economics Association Meetings, European Economic Association Congress, Stanford Institute for Theoretical Economics, and Trade, Integration, and Growth Network Conference for helpful comments.

†Go to https://doi.org/10.1257/app.20150360 to visit the article page for additional materials and author disclosure statement(s) or to comment in the online discussion forum.

market power sign an FTA, they start to import more from each other and less from nonmembers and this trade diversion reduces their incentives to manipulate their terms of trade vis-à-vis nonmembers, which ultimately results in lower external tariffs on their part. Empirical support for this type of tariff complementarity has been provided by Bohara, Gawande, and Sanguinetti (2004); Estevadeordal, Freund, and Ornelas (2008); Calvo-Pardo, Freund, and Ornelas (2009); and Mai and Stoyanov (2015).[1]

The key insight of our paper is that the logic underlying the tariff complementarity effect for member countries ought to apply to the optimal tariffs of nonmember countries as well. If tariffs set by a country on imports from different sources are complementary to each other, as is the case for FTA member countries, then the tariffs applied by different countries on imports from the same source should also be complementary. In such a case, a reduction in tariff by one importer should induce the other importers of the same good to lower their tariffs. In a world with increasing production costs, if two countries undertake bilateral trade liberalization via an FTA, their mutual trade increases while their exports to other countries fall. This change in the pattern of international trade reduces the ability and the incentive of nonmember countries to manipulate their terms of trade vis-à-vis FTA members, a mechanism that ought to induce nonmembers to voluntarily *lower* their tariffs on FTA members. To the best of our knowledge, this insight regarding the effect of FTAs on tariffs of nonmember countries has been generally overlooked in the literature.[2]

In this paper, we first formally develop this insight in a simple economic framework based on Missios, Saggi, and Yildiz (2016) that uses an adapted version of Horn, Maggi, and Staiger (2010) and then provide empirical evidence in its support. The theoretical framework is a classical partial equilibrium set-up comprising an arbitrary number (n) of countries who produce a single numeraire good v_0 and n non-numeraire goods, where the marginal cost of production of each non-numeraire good increases with output. The pattern of comparative advantage is such that each country exports a unique good to all its trading partners, i.e., the underlying trade pattern is one in which there are $n - 1$ *competing importers* of each non-numeraire good. An important feature of this economic framework is that if two countries liberalize trade toward one another, their mutual imports increase while the exports (of their respective comparative advantage goods) to the rest of the world decrease—a phenomenon we call the *external trade diversion.*

We first derive optimal tariffs in the absence of any trade agreement and then consider how the formation of an FTA amongst m countries, $m < n$, affects the tariffs of a typical nonmember country. We show that the export supply elasticities facing nonmember countries increase with the size of the FTA (as measured by the

[1] The review by Limão (2016) describes strong evidence for substitution for developed countries and weak evidence of complementarity for some developing countries, including Latin America. Crivelli (2016) uses the data and basic approach in Estevadeordal, Freund, and Ornelas (2008) and finds that the strength of the tariff complementarity depends on the initial tariff levels.

[2] Chang and Winters (2002) investigate the effects of the Latin American customs union MERCOSUR on excluded countries. They find that the excluded countries' firms' export prices to Brazil were influenced not only by the tariffs faced by them but also by the tariffs faced by their rival exporters. More importantly, they show that excluded countries suffered a decline in their terms of trade since their firms reduced export prices in response to the improved market access enjoyed by their rival exporters due to the preferential treatment accorded to them.

number of FTA partners *m*) as well as the external tariff preference margin enjoyed by a typical FTA member. Thus, the formation of an FTA reduces the export supply elasticities facing nonmember countries which in turn induces them to lower their tariffs on FTA members.

However, bringing this prediction from the theoretical model directly to the data is problematic because we do not observe variation in export supply elasticities across countries and industries over time. Thus, we base our empirical framework on another related prediction of the model which links unobservable changes in export supply elasticities to observable changes in trade flows between FTA member countries. Specifically, the model predicts that the increase in the export supply elasticities of nonmembers is bigger and the reduction in their external tariffs deeper when the effect of an FTA on preferential trade between member countries is larger. To operationalize this prediction, for every country in our sample we construct a measure of a trade-weighted average change in preferential trade flows of its main trade partners. This measure, which we call *preferential export share*, has a strong theoretical relationship to the elasticities of export supply, and the data reveals that it indeed reflects over time variation in export supply elasticities. In particular, when we split our sample of countries into two halves by time, we find that an increase in the preferential export share of a country's average partner between the two periods is associated with an increase in its export supply elasticity, estimated using the Broda and Weinstein (2006) methodology.

Building on the insights of the model, we empirically investigate whether countries indeed adjust trade policies in response to FTA formation by other countries. Our main empirical focus is on the relationship between changes in MFN tariff rates of countries and preferential export shares. To construct a measure of the annual change in the preferential export share of a country's average trade partner, we use industry-level bilateral trade data for 192 importing and 253 exporting countries, along with the information on all FTAs formed between 1989 and 2011.

Our estimation results support the external trade diversion hypothesis. We find that the formation of an FTA by a group of countries and the associated increase in the share of trade between them induces other countries to lower MFN tariffs. The results are both statistically significant and economically sizable. For example, in our benchmark specification, if a country's preferential exports increase by 10 percent as a result of a new FTA, and its share in imports of a nonmember country is 10 percent, the latter reduces its MFN tariff by 0.08 percentage points. This result is remarkably robust to the inclusion of a broad set of fixed effects, including country-year and country-industry fixed effects. Moreover, the effect is the most pronounced for trade-creating FTAs which increase the share of preferential trade between members and, according to the theory, result in greater increase in the export supply elasticities for nonmembers.

We pay close attention to endogeneity issues and use several instrumental variables strategies to determine whether the effect of FTAs on tariffs of nonmember countries is causal. The first endogeneity concern arises from the simultaneity between MFN tariffs and import shares. We address this problem by instrumenting for a country's export pattern using a geography-based gravity model in the spirit of Frankel and Romer (1999). The second source of endogeneity is the presence of omitted variables that could affect trade flows between FTA member countries for reasons unrelated to agreement formation. In order to better isolate variation in preferential trade shares that is driven by the formation of preferential trade agreements, we instrument preferential export shares with predetermined geographic variables using the insights of Baier and Bergstrand (2004). Overall, our IV estimates point to an even stronger external trade diversion effect of FTAs. Moreover, the dynamics of the effect are also consistent with our expectations: we find external trade diversion to be the strongest in the second and the third years of FTA implementation—the period of the most intense trade liberalization for most agreements—but not in the subsequent years when the effect of preferential liberalization on trade have largely been exhausted. Also, the effect of FTAs on tariffs of nonmembers is insignificant in the first year, suggesting that countries do not immediately adjust their trade policies in response to changes in trade patterns induced by policy changes in rest of the world.

The policy implications of our results are clear as well as important. If the formation of FTAs can cause trade liberalization to spill over to excluded countries, an important welfare gain accruing from their formation has been ignored thus far in not just the academic literature but also in policy analysis. For example, the important and influential literature addressing whether FTAs are building or stumbling blocks for further liberalization in the world economy has tended to focus primarily on the effects FTAs have on the incentives for further liberalization of member countries.[3] Our analysis shows that the scope of this line of inquiry needs to be broadened to also include the effects that FTAs might have on the policies of nonmember countries.

Terms of trade effects play a central role in our analysis, and the results of our study complement the empirical research investigating the role of terms of trade motives in determining trade policy. Broda, Limão, and Weinstein (2008) confirm that non-WTO countries indeed manipulate their terms of trade by setting higher tariffs on goods that are supplied inelastically. Several recent studies identify the terms of trade effect from trade policy renegotiations imposed by multilateral agreements. Bagwell and Staiger (2011) focus on changes in tariff rates resulting from a country's accession to the WTO and Ludema and Mayda (2013) examine variation in MFN tariffs resulting from the Uruguay round of trade negotiations. In line with the predictions of the terms of trade theory, both studies find that countries reduce tariffs to a deeper degree in industries in which they have greater market power. Using data on import tariffs imposed by the United States on 49 countries during 1997–2006 period under anti-dumping and safeguard laws, Bown and Crowley (2013) provide an empirical confirmation of the managed trade theory of Bagwell and Staiger (1990) in which countries play a repeated game and any trade agreement between them has to be self-enforcing. Our paper contributes to this literature by identifying FTAs as a source of exogenous shocks to the terms of trade of all nonmember countries. We demonstrate that nonmember countries reduce their MFN tariffs in response to negative terms of trade shocks associated with FTAs. By so doing, we uncover a new empirical domain within which implications of terms of trade theory

[3] See, for example, Krishna (1998), Bagwell and Staiger (1997), Saggi and Yildiz (2010), and Stoyanov and Yildiz (2015).

for optimal tariffs can be investigated. This is important because the formation of an FTA between a few countries can be reasonably interpreted as an exogenous event from the perspective of the rest of the world.

I. Theoretical Model

Our motivating economic framework is a suitably adapted version of the two-country model of Horn, Maggi, and Staiger (2010). We consider a perfectly competitive world comprising n large countries that produce n (non-numeraire) goods and a single numeraire good v_0. We first describe the underlying economic structure and then derive optimal tariffs in the absence as well as the presence of a free trade agreement (FTA) comprised of an arbitrary number of countries.

On the demand side, the representative citizen's utility function is given by

$$U(\mathbf{v}, v_0) = u(\mathbf{v}) + v_0, \tag{1}$$

where $\mathbf{v}$ is the consumption vector for the n non-numeraire goods, and v_0 denotes consumption of the numeraire good. We assume $u(\mathbf{v})$ is quadratic and additively separable in non-numeraire goods so that demand for good g in country z is given by

$$d_z^g(p_z^g) = \alpha - p_z^g, \tag{2}$$

where p_z^g is the consumer price of good g in country z. Assuming that population in each country is a continuum of measure one, we can write the consumer surplus associated with good g in country z as

$$CS_z^g(p_z^g) = u_z^g\left[d_z^g(p_z^g)\right] - p_z^g d_z^g(p_z^g). \tag{3}$$

On the supply side, as in Horn, Maggi, and Staiger (2010), the production of one unit of the numeraire requires one unit of labor (l). The supply of labor is assumed to be large enough that the numeraire good is always produced in a positive amount and the equilibrium wage is equal to one.

The production technology for non-numeraire goods is subject to diminishing returns. In particular, the production function for (non-numeraire) good g in country z is $Q_z^g = \sqrt{2\lambda_z^g l_g}$, where Q_z^g is the output of good g in country z and l_g is employment in industry g. The corresponding supply function of good g in country z is as follows:

$$s_z^g(q_z^g) = \lambda_z^g q_z^g, \tag{4}$$

where q_z^g denotes the producer price for good g in country z.[4]

The structure of comparative advantage is assumed to be symmetric across countries: $\lambda_z^Z = 1 + \lambda$, while $\lambda_z^g = 1$ for $g \neq Z$. In other words, each country has a

[4] In Appendix B, we extend the model to allow for more general demand and supply functions.

comparative advantage in a single good that is indexed by the same uppercase letter as the identity of the country (i.e., country z has comparative advantage in good Z), while having a comparative disadvantage in the remaining $n - 1$ goods. Thus, there are $n - 1$ *competing importers* for each non-numeraire good. Country z's producer surplus in good g is equal to

$$PS_z^g(q_z^g) = \int s_z^g(q_z^g)\, dq_z^g = \frac{1}{2}\lambda_z^g(q_z^g)^2. \tag{5}$$

As a representative case, consider good Z, i.e., the good in which country z has a comparative advantage. Let t_z^g be the MFN tariff imposed by country z on its imports of good $g \neq Z$.[5] Given that all countries are large, the world price of good g depends on tariffs of all importing countries. However, to simplify notation, we suppress the dependence of prices on tariffs and simply denote the price of good g in country z by p_z^g.

Since country z imposes no tariff on good Z, the consumer and producer prices of good Z in country z are equal: $q_z^Z = p_z^Z$. Similarly, as there is no domestic taxation of the import competing sectors, producer and consumer prices are also equal: $q_z^g = p_z^g$, where $g \neq Z$. Ruling out prohibitive tariffs yields the following no-arbitrage conditions for good Z in importing country c:

$$p_c^Z = p_z^Z + t_c^Z, \quad c \neq z. \tag{6}$$

Let m_c^Z be imports of good Z by country c:

$$m_c^Z = d(p_c^Z) - s_c^Z(p_c^Z), \quad c \neq z. \tag{7}$$

Similarly, let x_z^Z denote country z's exports of good Z to country c:

$$x_{zc}^Z = s_z^Z(p_z^Z) - \sum_{\tilde{c}\neq z,c} d(p_{\tilde{c}}^Z). \tag{8}$$

Market clearing for good Z requires that country z's export to country c equals the imports of that country:

$$x_{zc}^Z = m_c^Z. \tag{9}$$

Country c's welfare is defined as the sum of consumer surplus, producer surplus, and tariff revenue over all goods:

$$w_c = \sum_g CS_c^g(p_c^g) + \sum_g PS_c^g(p_c^g) + \sum_{g\neq C} t_c^g m_c^g. \tag{10}$$

[5] We assume that tariff revenues for each good are redistributed uniformly to all individuals.

In the absence of any trade agreements, each country chooses its tariffs to maximize its welfare.[6] To derive optimal tariffs, we follow the approach of Feenstra (2004) and Broda, Limão, and Weinstein (2008). Consider country c's tariff problem for good Z. Differentiating w_c with respect to t_c^Z, we obtain

$$\frac{\partial w_c}{\partial t_c^Z} = t_c^Z \frac{\partial m_c^Z}{\partial p_c^Z} \frac{\partial p_c^Z}{\partial t_c^Z} - m_c^Z \frac{\partial p_z^Z}{\partial t_c^Z}. \tag{11}$$

The first term of the above first-order condition captures the efficiency cost of the tariff (i.e., the marginal deadweight loss of the tariff) and the second term captures the terms of trade effect, that is, the reduction in the world price of good Z that accrues to country z multiplied by the quantity of country c's imports from country z.

The optimal tariff is computed where (11) equals zero:

$$\frac{\partial w_c}{\partial t_c^Z} = 0 \Rightarrow \frac{t_c^Z}{p_z^Z} = \frac{\frac{\partial p_z^Z}{\partial t_c^Z} \frac{m_c^Z}{p_z^Z}}{\frac{\partial m_c^Z}{\partial p_c^Z} \frac{\partial p_c^Z}{\partial t_c^Z}}. \tag{12}$$

Since $m_c^Z = x_{zc}^Z$, we must have

$$\frac{\partial m_c^Z}{\partial p_c^Z} \frac{\partial p_c^Z}{\partial t_c^Z} = \frac{\partial x_{zc}^Z}{\partial t_c^Z}.$$

Substituting this into (12) shows that country c's optimal ad valorem tariff on good Z equals the inverse of the elasticity of the export supply curve faced by country c for that good, denoted by ε_c^Z:[7]

$$\frac{t_c^Z}{p_z^Z} = \frac{1}{\varepsilon_c^Z} = \left[\frac{\partial x_{zc}^Z}{\partial p_z^Z} \frac{p_z^Z}{x_{zc}^Z}\right]^{-1}. \tag{13}$$

Using the demand and supply functions in equations (2) and (4), as well as the no arbitrage and market clearing conditions in (6) and (9), we can obtain the equilibrium price, exports, and imports of good Z.

To derive the implications of FTA formation on MFN tariffs of excluded countries, suppose country z forms an FTA with $m - 1$ countries, so that the FTA is of size m, and country c is a nonmember.[8] Let $\hat{t}^Z$ denote the preferential internal tariff on good Z within the FTA imposed by country z's FTA partners; $t_{\bar{c}}^Z$ denotes the tariff of a typical nonmember country other than country c, and φ_{ext}^Z denotes the external

[6] In Appendix C, we show that the main predictions of our model continue to hold when countries set trade policies cooperatively (in the sense that each country takes the effects of its tariffs on other countries into account), so long as each country weighs foreign welfare less than domestic welfare.

[7] In the empirical section, we use an equivalent ad valorem tariff.

[8] When $m = 1$, we are back to the status quo of optimal tariffs in the absence of an FTA.

tariff preference margin enjoyed by members within an FTA relative to tariffs they face in nonmember countries: $\varphi_{ext}^{Z} \equiv t_{\bar{c}}^{Z} - \hat{t}^{Z}$.[9]

It is easy to show that country z's export supply function of good Z to country c is as follows:

$$x_{zc}^{Z} = [2(n-1)+\lambda]p_{z}^{Z} - (n-1)\alpha + 2(n-2)t_{\bar{c}}^{Z} - 2(m-1)\varphi_{ext}^{Z}. \quad (14)$$

Before deriving optimal tariffs in the presence of an FTA, it is useful to highlight an important feature of our economic framework. If two countries liberalize trade toward one another in our model, they import more from each other and start exporting *less* to other countries owing to the fact that the marginal cost of production is increasing—a phenomenon we call *external trade diversion*. As we demonstrate below, this reduction in the volume of exports of members to excluded countries has implications for their optimal tariffs.

It is immediate from (14) that the formation of an FTA affects country z's export supply function through two key channels: the size of the FTA (as measured by the number of FTA partners m) and the external tariff preference margin φ_{ext}^{Z}. These two channels represent the extensive and intensive margins of preferential trade liberalization, respectively. Along the extensive margin, the export supply of country z to country c decreases with the size of FTA: $\partial x_{zc}^{Z}/\partial m < 0$. Similarly, along the intensive margin, the export supply of country z to country c also decreases in the FTA's external tariff preference margin φ_{ext}^{Z}: $\partial x_{zc}^{Z}/\partial \varphi_{ext}^{Z} < 0$.

Given the export supply function above, the export supply elasticity ε_{c}^{Z} faced by the nonmember country c can be calculated as follows:

$$\varepsilon_{c}^{Z} = \frac{[2(n-1)+\lambda]\left[n\alpha + 2(m-1)\varphi_{ext}^{Z} - 2(n-2)t_{\bar{c}}^{Z} - 2t_{c}^{Z}\right]}{\alpha\lambda - [4(n-1)+2\lambda]t_{c}^{Z} - 4(m-1)\varphi_{ext}^{Z} + 4(n-2)t_{\bar{c}}^{Z}}. \quad (15)$$

Note that the export supply elasticity ε_{c}^{Z} increases in both m and φ_{ext}^{Z}:

$$\frac{\partial \varepsilon_{c}^{Z}}{\partial m} > 0 \quad \text{and} \quad \frac{\partial \varepsilon_{c}^{Z}}{\partial \varphi_{ext}^{Z}} > 0. \quad (16)$$

It also proves useful to consider how the two main attributes of an FTA (i.e., m and φ_{ext}^{Z}) affect its overall trade pattern. Suppose country z negotiates an FTA with $m-1$ other countries. The share of country z's exports of good Z flowing to its $m-1$ FTA partners equals

$$PXS_{z}^{Z} = \frac{\sum_{j\in(m-1)} x_{zj}^{Z}}{\sum_{j\neq z} x_{zj}^{Z}}. \quad (17)$$

[9] Here, for the sake of clarity, we report country c's optimal tariff as a function of exogenously given internal and external tariffs of other countries. We report the export supply elasticity and optimal tariff expressions in Appendix A.

We refer to PXS_z^Z as country z's *preferential export share.*

In the absence of any FTA (which we denote as regime ϕ), due to symmetry, the share of country z's exports of good Z flowing to any $m-1$ countries is $PXS_z^Z(\phi) = \frac{m-1}{n-1}$. In other words, when country z is not a participant in any FTA, the share of its exports going to any $m-1$ countries equals $PXS_z^Z(\phi)$.

Following the formation of the FTA (letting $\hat{t}^Z = 0$), it is straightforward to show that the preferential export share of country z in good Z becomes

$$PXS_z^Z = \frac{(m-1)\left[\lambda\alpha + 4(n-m)\varphi_{ext}^Z\right]}{\alpha\lambda(n-1) - 2(\lambda+2)(n-m)\varphi_{ext}^Z}, \tag{18}$$

where direct calculations show that

$$\frac{\partial PXS_z^Z}{\partial m} > 0 \quad \text{and} \quad \frac{\partial PXS_z^Z}{\partial \varphi_{ext}^Z} > 0. \tag{19}$$

Therefore, both the preferential export share of a typical FTA member country z and the export supply elasticities facing nonmember countries increase with both the size of the FTA (m) and the tariff preference margin (φ_{ext}^Z).

From here on, we utilize parameters m and φ_{ext}^Z to capture changes in both the preferential export share and the export supply elasticity. The change in the preferential export share of country z due to the formation of an FTA equals

$$\begin{aligned} \Delta PXS_z^Z &= PXS_z^Z - PXS_z^Z(\phi) \\ &= \frac{2(m-1)(n-m)(\lambda+2n)\varphi_{ext}^Z}{(n-1)\left[\alpha\lambda(n-1) - \varphi_{ext}^Z[2(\lambda+2)(n-m)]\right]} > 0. \end{aligned} \tag{20}$$

Note that for any given FTA of size m, the greater the external tariff preference margin, the larger the increase in the preferential export share: $\partial \Delta PXS_z^Z / \partial \varphi_{ext}^Z > 0$.[10] A similar analysis holds for country c's optimal tariff. Using (13) and (15), nonmember country c's optimal tariff when country z forms an FTA with $(m-1)$ other countries is equal to

$$t_c^Z(t_{\bar{c}}^Z) = \frac{2\alpha\lambda + 8\left[(n-2)t_{\bar{c}}^Z - m\varphi_{ext}^Z\right]}{[2(n-1)+\lambda][4(n+1)+2\lambda]}. \tag{21}$$

It is immediate from above that the tariffs imposed by different nonmember countries on the same good are *strategic complements* in our model:

$$\frac{\partial t_c^Z}{\partial t_{\bar{c}}^Z} > 0. \tag{22}$$

[10]Note that PXS_z^Z rises with m at increasing rate when m is sufficiently small. As m approaches $n-1$, we approach the global free trade in good Z and thus PXS_z^Z converges to $PXS_z^Z(\phi) = \frac{m}{n-1}$.

The intuition for why tariffs of different countries end up being strategic complements is that an increase in $t_{\tilde{c}}^{Z}$ increases the volume of country z's exports to country c, thereby increasing the latter's ability to manipulate its terms of trade.

Note that as the preferential export share rises either due to an increase in either the size of the FTA (m) or the preference margin (φ_{ext}^{Z}), the external trade diversion caused by the FTA induces the nonmember country to lower its tariffs on members:

$$\text{(23)} \qquad \frac{\partial t_c^Z}{\partial m} < 0 \quad \text{and} \quad \frac{\partial t_c^Z}{\partial \varphi_{ext}^Z} < 0.$$

The optimal pre-FTA MFN tariff of country c can be found by setting $\varphi_{ext}^{Z} = 0$ in (21), which yields

$$\text{(24)} \qquad t_c^Z(\phi) = \frac{2\alpha\lambda + 8\left[(n-2)t_{\tilde{c}}^{Z}\right]}{[2(n-1)+\lambda][4(n+1)+2\lambda]}.$$

Using (21) and (24), we can directly calculate the response of the optimal MFN tariff of nonmember country c to FTA formation by its trade partners a function of m and φ_{ext}^{Z}:

$$\text{(25)} \qquad \Delta t_c^Z = t_c^Z(\phi) - t_c^Z = \frac{m\varphi_{ext}^{Z}}{[2(n-1)+\lambda][4(n+1)+2\lambda]},$$

where $\partial \Delta t_c^Z/\partial m > 0$ and $\partial \Delta t_c^Z/\partial \varphi_{ext}^{Z} > 0$. The following proposition summarizes our central theoretical finding.

PROPOSITION 1: *The larger the increase in the preferential export share of FTA member countries, the greater the reduction in the external tariffs of nonmember countries.*

The intuition for this proposition is clear: the greater the degree of external trade diversion caused by an FTA, the weaker the ability of nonmembers to manipulate their terms of trade via import tariffs. Proposition 2 in Appendix B shows that the same result holds under a general demand and supply structure as long as the inverse supply function is log-concave. Moreover, Appendix C extends our theoretical model to allow for tariff cooperation. Specifically, we have derived optimal trade policy for the case when each governments' objective function is a weighted average of national welfare and the welfare of other countries. We find that our main result in Proposition 1 fully extends into the cooperative tariff setting and holds for all levels of cooperation.

II. Empirical Framework

Our main empirical specification is based on Proposition 1, which builds a theoretical relationship from unobservable changes in elasticities to observable changes in trade shares. Intuitively, a greater increase in trade between FTA member countries implies stronger external trade diversion and therefore a larger increase in ε_{cit}, which translates into reductions in tariffs of nonmember countries. Using this insight, the simplest structure to study the relationship between FTA formation and MFN tariffs of excluded countries is

$$\Delta MFN_{cit} = \beta \Delta \overline{PXS}_{cit} + \upsilon_{cit}, \tag{26}$$

where ΔMFN_{cit} is the change in the MFN tariff rate of country c in industry i at time t, and $\Delta \overline{PXS}_{cit}$ is the change in the preferential export share of country c's average trade partner.

Given that each country has multiple trading partners, we construct $\overline{PXS}_{cit}$ as a weighted average of preferential exports of country c's partners using their import shares as weights:

$$\Delta \overline{PXS}_{cit} = \left(\sum_{p \neq c} imp\_share_{cpi} \cdot \Delta PXS_{pit}\right); \tag{27}$$

$$\Delta PXS_{pit} = \sum_{j \neq i} FTA_{pjt} \cdot \Delta exp\_share_{pjit},$$

where imp_share_{cpi} is the share of country p in total imports of industry i by country c, exp_share_{pjit} is the share of country p's exports of good i to country j, FTA_{pjt} is a binary variable that takes the value of one if countries p and j have an FTA in year t and zero otherwise, and PXS_{pit} is the share of country p's exports of good i to its FTA partner countries excluding c. Note that import shares, used as weights in equation (27), are constructed as averages over the entire sample period for each country-pair and industry. This is done in order to reduce measurement error and to bring the empirical specification closer to our theoretical model, which predicts that the effect of trade agreements operates through changes in preferential export share of a country's trade partners. Therefore, the variation in $\overline{PXS}_{cit}$ measure over time for each country-pair-industry is driven only by the variation in preferential export shares of a country's trade partners rather than by the variation in its own trade structure.

In equation (26), $\beta < 0$ would provide support for the argument that countries lower their import tariffs in response to an increase in the share of preferential exports of their trade partners. However, equation (26) only captures contemporaneous correlation between the change in the MFN tariff and the change in preferential export share of an average partner country. To capture the dynamic response of MFN tariffs to FTA formation by other countries, we analyze the differential effect of the change in preferential export shares by trade partners within the first five years of FTA formation:

$$(28) \qquad \Delta MFN_{cit} = \sum_{T=-3}^{6} \beta_T \, \Delta \overline{PXS}(T)_{cit-T-1} + \gamma_{ct} + \gamma_{cI} + \upsilon_{cit};$$

$$(29) \quad \Delta \overline{PXS}(T)_{cit-T-1} = \Big(\sum_{p} imp\_share_{cpi} \cdot \Delta PXS(T)_{pit-T-1} \Big);$$

$$(30) \quad \Delta PXS(T)_{pit-T-1} = \sum_{j \neq c} FTA(T)_{pjt} \cdot \big(exp\_share_{pjit} - exp\_share_{pjit-T-1} \big),$$

where $FTA(T)_{pjt}$ is a binary variable that takes the value of one if an FTA between countries p and j came into force in year $(t - T)$. Thus, for all countries that formed FTAs with country p in year $(t - T)$, $\Delta PXS(T)_{pit-T-1}$ measures the change in p's exports of product i to these countries relative to the reference year $(t - T - 1)$. The effect of agreements formed more than five years ago is combined into one general category, $\overline{PXS}(T = 6)$. We also include two leads of the explanatory variable in equation (28) and use pretrends to confirm that the effect of an FTA on nonmembers' tariffs materializes after commencement of the agreement.[11]

The benchmark specification (28) includes country × year fixed effects γ_{ct} to control for general episodes of country-specific trade liberalization, accession to the WTO and regional trade agreements, changes in fiscal and monetary policies, and other macroeconomic characteristics that affect general changes in tariff policies in specific countries and periods. Country × industry-group fixed effects γ_{cI} control for economic and political factors that may affect the average changes in the level of protection in different industries within a country. In particular, γ_{ci} capture a government's potential reluctance to liberalize trade in certain sensitive industries and the possibility for more rapid tariff reductions in other industries.

A. *Addressing Endogeneity of Import Shares*

The key assumption underlying identification of β_T coefficients from equation (28) is that the decision to form an FTA is independent of future changes in trade policies of other countries.[12] However, the other two components of $\overline{PXS}(T)$ variables—import shares and preferential export shares—may not be fully exogenous. Although the broad set of fixed effects allows us to control for many possible unobservables and remove most of the omitted variables, this does not resolve all potential endogeneity issues with various components of the explanatory variables. Using import shares as weights in the construction of $\overline{PXS}(T)$ variables is particularly problematic because of simultaneity with import tariffs. This concern would be even more serious if reductions in import tariffs were to have differential impact

[11] In the Appendix Table 3A we show results with six leads of the explanatory variable.

[12] We believe this is a plausible assumption because trade agreements usually take many years to negotiate. By the time an agreement is implemented, MFN tariffs of third countries would have already responded to any shocks that could have potentially triggered those negotiations.

on imports from partners with different preferences for regional trade liberalization. For example, if countries that are more actively involved in preferential trade benefit more from trade liberalization by others, than a reduction in import tariffs will increase the share of imports from those countries, thus raising the value of our explanatory variables and causing simultaneity bias in β_T. Another concern with using import shares is that they may partially offset the effect of FTAs on preferential export shares. If an FTA between a pair of countries redirects their exports from third countries toward each other's markets, as the theory predicts, an increase in preferential export shares of the FTA member countries will go hand-in-hand with a decrease in import shares of other countries from that FTA, reducing the value of $\overline{PXS}(T)$ and causing a bias in the estimates.

We address the endogeneity of import shares via an instrumental variable strategy and construct the following instruments, one for each $\Delta_{T-1}\overline{PXS}(T)$:

$$IV^S(T)_{cit} = \left(\sum_p \widehat{imp\_share}_{cpi} \cdot \Delta PXS(T)_{pit-T-1}\right). \tag{31}$$

The terms $\widehat{imp\_share}_{cpi}$ in (31) are the import shares predicted from various versions of the gravity model that help isolate variation in import shares stemming from changes in either expected MFN tariff changes or preferential trade shares of partner countries. Constructed this way, instruments $IV^S(T)$ allow us to obtain estimates of β_T, which are based on the variation in import shares arising from the geographical determinants of trade flows only, and thus are free from any policy influences.

Our benchmark gravity specification to obtain $\widehat{imp\_share}_{cpi}$ is based on Do and Levchenko (2007), who extend the methodology of Frankel and Romer (1999) to industry-level data. Frankel and Romer (1999) rely on the gravity equation to predict trade flows between a pair of countries using their predetermined geographic characteristics, such as distance, population, and other standard covariates of trade costs used in the gravity model literature:

$$\ln X_{cpit} = Z_{cpit}\beta_i + \varepsilon_{pjit}, \tag{32}$$

where X_{cpit} is exports of good i from country c to country p in year t, and the vector Z_{cpit} includes the log of distance between countries c and p, log of population in each country, log of land size, landlock and common border indicators, and the interactions of all of the above variables with the common border dummy variable. These are reasonable instruments because, on one hand, they are powerful determinants of trade flows, as the gravity literature demonstrates.[13] On the other hand, it is difficult to think of any reasons why country's geographic characteristics could affect product-specific tariff changes other than through changes in trade flows. As in Do and Levchenko (2007), we generate cross-industry variation in import shares by allowing the coefficients on the covariates in the gravity model to vary across industries. This approach exploits differential response of trade volumes to geographic

[13] The F-test for the joint significance of Z in regression (32) has the p-value of less than 0.01 for all industries and the average R^2 is 0.2.

characteristics across industries.[14] Following this methodology, we obtain predicted values of trade flows between every country pair for every industry, and use them to construct the predicted "natural" import shares, $\widehat{imp\_share}_{cpi}$. With these values, we use (31) to form the first set of instruments, $IV_1^S(T)$, for $\Delta\overline{PXS}(T)$ variables.

Instruments constructed with trade flows predicted from the gravity model (32) have two limitations. First, Silva and Tenreyro (2006) argue that not accounting for zero trade flows and heteroskedasticity in the log linear gravity models can lead to inconsistent OLS estimates. The authors advocate estimating equation (32) with Poisson pseudo-maximum likelihood (PPML), which they demonstrate to address the above two problems in Monte Carlo simulations. Our second set of instruments, $IV_2^S(T)$, is constructed from (31), for which the import shares are predicted from the gravity model (32) estimated with PPML.

The second limitation of the model (32), illustrated by Anderson and van Wincoop (2003), is that it can produce inconsistent estimates of the gravity variables coefficients due to the omitted multilateral price terms. The standard solution to this problem in the gravity literature is to control for the price terms with two sets of country-industry-year fixed effects. However, this approach prevents separate identification of all country-specific geography variables in equation (32) and reduces the strength of the instruments. As a robustness test for the benchmark IV specification, we introduce the full set of exporter-industry-year and importer-industry-year fixed effects into the gravity model (32), and use the information contained in both the fixed effects and in the remaining gravity variables to construct two sets of instruments—$IV_3^S(T)$ from the OLS estimates of the extended gravity model and $IV_4^S(T)$ from the PPML estimates. Such IV strategy not only allows obtaining consistent estimates of the gravity variables coefficients but also results in stronger instruments that can predict the actual trade shares better. The drawback of this IV approach is that the fixed effects introduce economic factors into the predicted trade shares, and the validity of the instruments constructed in such a way relies on a strong identification assumption relative to $IV_1(T)$ and $IV_2^S(T)$.

III. Data and Preliminary Evidence

The bilateral trade data for this project are taken from the World Integrated Trade Solutions (WITS) database, maintained by the World Bank, and cover the time period from 1989 to 2011. The data that we use to construct trade share variables is a four-dimensional unbalanced panel covering 192 importing countries, 253 exporting countries, 98 2-digit HS industries, and spanning 22 years.[15]

The binary variable that measures the presence or absence of an FTA in a given year is constructed for all pairs of countries in our sample using the WTO database on Regional Trade Agreements, which includes information on the date of notification and the date when the agreement entered into force. We record FTA as being

[14] On our model, 70 percent of variation in predicted trade values comes from within country-pair-year cells, close to 59 percent observed in the actual data.

[15] We exclude China from the sample because China's increasing ability to penetrate other markets results in a reduction in trade shares between members of most FTAs. However, keeping China in the sample does not materially affect our results, as we show below in the robustness Section VI.

formed in year t if it came into force between July of $(t-1)$ and June of t. Since the membership structure of some FTAs varies over time and the WTO database does not always keep track of those changes, the data on bilateral FTA structure was complemented with information from other sources, such as official websites of these agreements. The resulting database covers all complete FTAs that were formed between 1989 and 2011 and includes 2,513 country-pairs trading under an FTA clause in 2011, or 9 percent of all country-pairs in our sample. Without information on coverage of each FTA, we assume that FTAs apply to trade in all industries between their members. Using equation (29) and the data on bilateral trade flows and FTA membership, we construct nine measures for changes in preferential export shares of an average partner for every country, industry, and year. We combine this information on preferential trade of an average partner country with the MFN and preferential tariff data from the WITS. In the analysis that follows we remove observations with an 11 or more percentage point change in the MFN tariffs in a single year (approximately 1 percent of observations in each tail of the ΔMFN distribution).

In order to construct instruments for import and preferential export shares, we merge trade data with geography variables obtained from the Centre d'Etudes Prospectives et d'Informations Internationales (CEPII). This database contains information on bilateral distance between each pair of countries, land size of each country, and information on whether two countries are landlocked and share a border. The data on population are taken from the Penn World Tables.

Table 1 reports the basic descriptive statistics for our key variables on the estimation sample. The mean ad valorem MFN tariff is 10.35 percentage points and is decreasing annually by 0.2 percentage points. The average country in our sample does not experience any substantial change in preferential export shares of its average trade partner. Changes in $\overline{PXS}(T)$ variables fluctuate around 0 during the first 5 years of FTAs formed by its trade partners, and is equal to -0.24 for older trade agreements. This pattern reflects the regularity, observed in most country-pairs and industries, that the share of trade between FTA member countries, averaged across industries, does not change much over time despite preferential access to each other's markets.

Figure 1 displays the dynamics of MFN tariffs and FTA prevalence over our sample period.

The time period of study overlaps with intense multilateral tariff reductions, negotiated during the Uruguay Round (UR) of the WTO and phased in between 1996 and 2001. Because countries committed to these tariff reductions in the early 1990s, they are predetermined relative to subsequent FTAs. However, Figure 1 shows that decrease in the global trade-weighted average MFN tariff was more intense in the decade after the UR: a 1.74 percentage point reduction from 2002 to 2011 versus 0.95 from 1992 to 2001, and the pattern is similar for a simple unweighted average MFN rate (that is independent of compositional changes in trade flows). This observation suggests that a substantial part of tariff reductions in our sample, especially after 2001, were not affected by institutional constraints implied by the WTO. Figure 1 also shows a steady increase in FTA formation throughout the sample period, measured by the share of country-pairs trading under an FTA, although

TABLE 1—SUMMARY STATISTICS

	Mean	Median	SD	Minimum	Maximum
MFN tariff (level)	10.20	9.27	10.43	0.00	349.5
Annual changes:					
ΔMFN	−0.163	0	2.76	−11.0	11.0
$\Delta PXS(T = -3)$	−0.029	0	0.74	−26.9	16.1
$\Delta PXS(T = -2)$	−0.010	0	0.61	−26.4	28.4
$\Delta PXS(T = 0)$	0.024	0	0.65	−43.0	38.6
$\Delta PXS(T = 1)$	0.024	0	0.84	−31.8	42.1
$\Delta PXS(T = 2)$	−0.014	0	1.00	−45.0	50.5
$\Delta PXS(T = 3)$	−0.001	0	0.90	−31.5	59.3
$\Delta PXS(T = 4)$	−0.013	0	0.86	−36.6	36.9
$\Delta PXS(T = 5)$	−0.014	0	1.05	−55.5	44.1
$\Delta PXS(T \geq 5)$	−0.242	0	2.52	−62.7	66.9

Note: $\Delta PXS(T)$ is the change in preferential export share of a country's average trade partner due to FTAs formed T years ago.

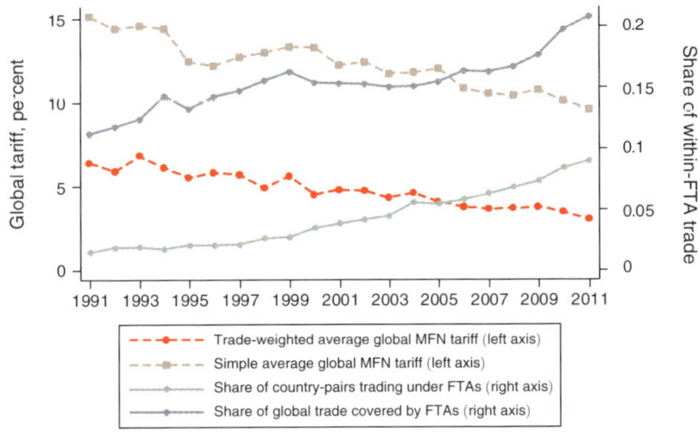

FIGURE 1. EVOLUTION OF MFN TARIFFS AND FTA PREVALENCE

the process intensified after 1999. In terms of the share of global trade covered by FTAs, the increase was particularly pronounced after 2004 and coincided with the rapid decline in the simple average MFN tariff rate.

Figure 2 plots kernel densities for changes in MFN tariffs in industries with various exposure to changes in partner countries' preferential exports (PPX). We measure this exposure with a cumulative change in preferential exports of a country's average trade partner over the first five years of FTA formation.

The figure shows that in industries with negative and zero changes in the PPX, the distributions of ΔMFN_{cit} are very similar. In contrast, for industries with positive changes in the PPX, the distribution of tariff changes shifts slightly to the left. Furthermore, for industries that are exposed to the greatest increases in partner's preferential exports (top decile of the PPX distribution), the distribution of tariff changes shifts further to the left: the probability of a tariff reduction in industries in the top decile of PPX distribution is 27 percent, as opposed to only 19 percent in

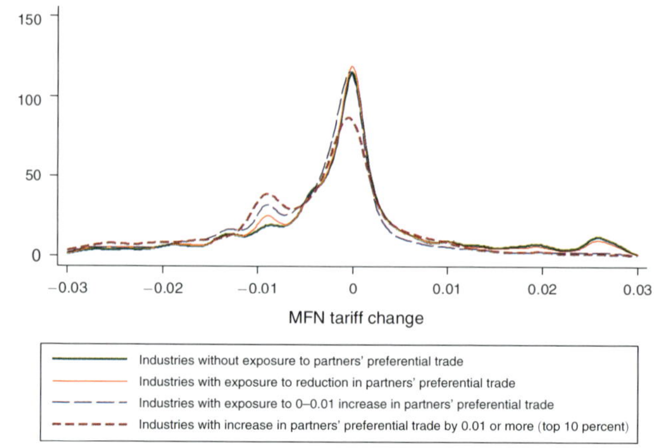

FIGURE 2. KERNEL DENSITY FOR MFN TARIFF CHANGES IN INDUSTRIES WITH VARIOUS EXPOSURES TO CHANGE IN PREFERENTIAL EXPORT SHARE IN TRADE PARTNER COUNTRIES

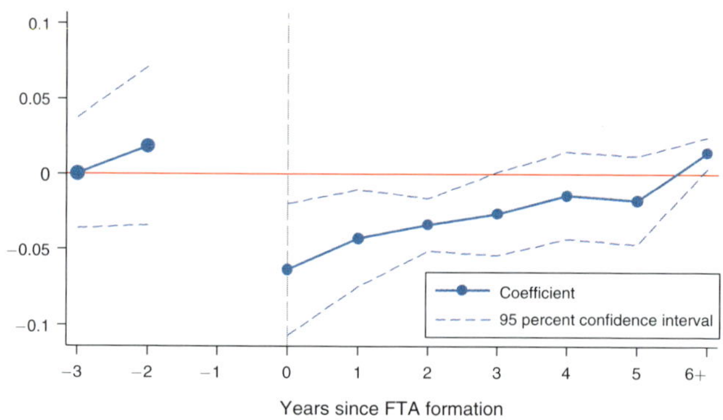

FIGURE 3. RELATIONSHIP BETWEEN FTA FORMATION AND TARIFFS OF NONMEMBER COUNTRIES

Note: > y-year fixed effects are controlled for.

industries with no change in the PPX. This suggests that an increase in preferential trade between FTA member countries is associated with a subsequent reduction in MFN tariffs by nonmember countries.

To demonstrate how this association evolves over time, we plot the OLS estimates of β_T coefficients from model (28) in Figure 3, where T stays for the number of years since FTA formation.

Because changes in the partner country's preferential exports are measured relative to the year before FTA came into force, the coefficient estimates for $T = -1$ are

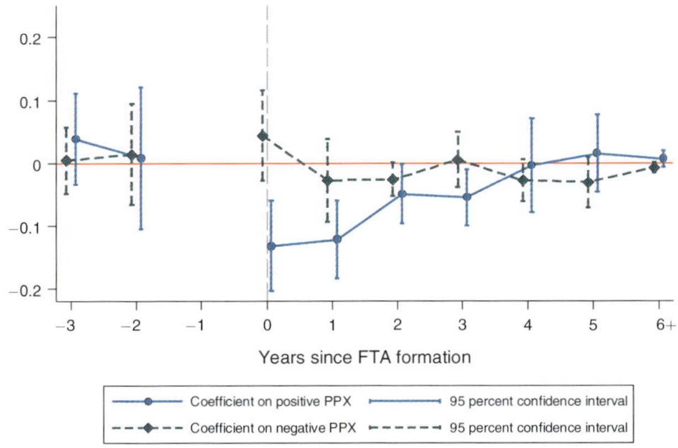

Figure 4. Relationship between FTA Formation and Tariffs of Nonmember Countries—by FTAs That Increase and Decrease Trade between Members

unavailable. Figure 3 shows a clear pattern. In the first four years after the formation of an FTA, the MFN tariffs of nonmember trading partners tend to decline, before leveling off in the following years.

As a demonstration of the importance of trade creation within FTAs for our results, in the next exercise we focus on FTAs that lead to more trade between members. The baseline specification (28) assumes that both positive and negative changes in preferential export shares are equally important for tariffs of other countries, i.e., $\beta_T < 0$ in equation (28) implies that a decline in trade following an FTA formation would induce other countries to increase their tariffs. This result cannot be rationalized by our theoretical framework, which predicts that preferential trade liberalization always redirects FTA members' trade flows toward each other. In practice, however, various other determinants of trade flows between member countries may outweigh trade agreement's potential to generate new trade between members, in which case there will be no increase in the export supply elasticities and no effect on tariffs of other countries. Therefore, we are more likely to observe countries lowering their tariffs in response to FTAs that result in stronger trade creation.

Figure 4 illustrates this point by plotting OLS regression coefficients for equation (28), but with changes in partner countries' preferential export shares calculated separately for positive and negative changes.[16] Specifically, each circle point in Figure 5 corresponds to a regression coefficient on variables analogous to (29), but calculated only over those country pairs and industries for which FTAs resulted in a positive change in preferential share. Similarly, the diamond points represent regression coefficients on $\Delta\overline{PXS}(T)$ constructed only for observations with negative changes in preferential export shares. If only trade-creating FTAs lead to a long-run

[16]Later, we address the issue of identification of the effect of FTAs on tariffs more formally with an IV strategy.

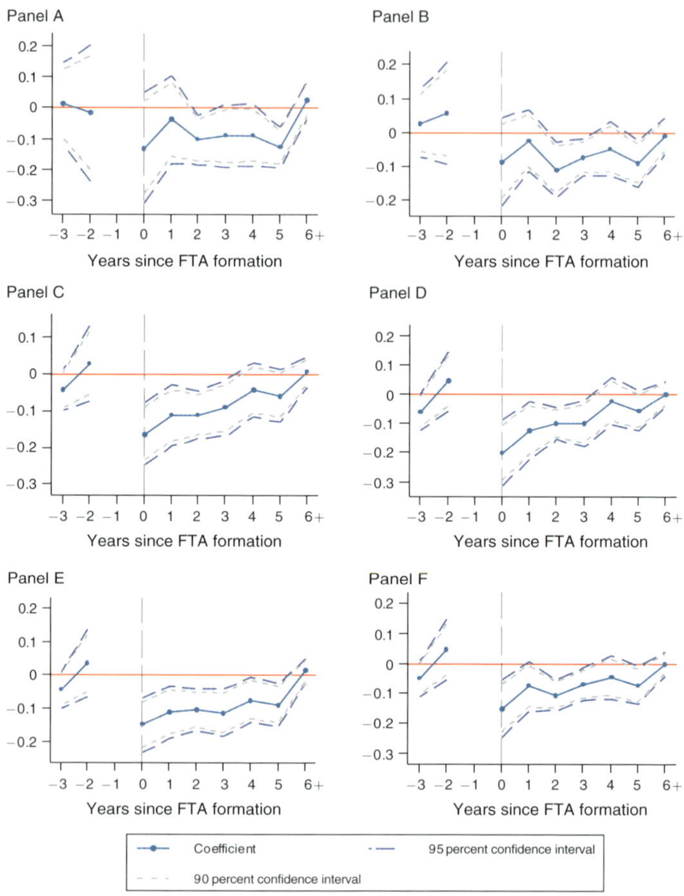

FIGURE 5. BASELINE RESULTS WITH INSTRUMENTED IMPORT SHARES

Note: Trade shares are predicted from: OLS gravity model without fixed effects (panel A); PPML gravity model without fixed effects (panel B); OLS gravity model with country-industry-year fixed effects (panel C); PPML gravity model with country-industry-year fixed effects (panel D); OLS gravity model with and without fixed effects (panel E); PPML gravity model with and without fixed effects (panel F).

increase in the export supply elasticity, as the theory predicts, then we would expect the coefficients on positive changes in $\Delta PXS(T)$ to be negative and larger in absolute value than the coefficients on the negative changes.

Figure 4 shows that the relationship between the formation of an FTA and the tariff reductions implemented by nonmembers is stronger in those cases when the FTA triggers an increase in the share of preferential trade between member countries. The figure illustrates three points consistent with our expectations. First, the effect of future changes in $\overline{PXS}$ variables, constructed for both positive and negative changes in preferential export shares, has no relationship with past changes in nonmembers tariffs. Second, tariffs tend to decline only in response to FTAs that increase the share of trade within an agreement: the coefficients on $\Delta\overline{PXS}(T)$ constructed only for positive changes in preferential export share are negative and statistically significant for the first four years of the agreement, while the coefficients negative $\Delta\overline{PXS}(T)$ are never statistically different from zero. And lastly, the effect of trade agreements occurs on impact and lasts for four years. The finding that not all FTAs lead to trade policy adjustments by outside countries also highlights the importance of isolating the effect of FTAs on preferential export shares from other influences, which we do in a more structural manner in Section V.

IV. Baseline Results

Figure 5 presents the IV-GMM estimation results for equation (28). Full estimation results, including some first-stage diagnostic statistics, are provided in Table 2. All standard errors are clustered both at country-industry level to correct for serial correlation in the error term and at country-year level to correct for country-wide policy changes correlated across industries.

Panel A of Figure 5 plots β_T coefficient estimates from (28) for $-3 \leq T \leq 6$, using the benchmark instruments $IV_1^S(T)$. The instruments perform well in the first stage of the estimation procedure. The t-statistics from the test of the significance of $IV_1^S(T)$ in the first-stage regressions for $\Delta\overline{PXS}(T)$ range from 4.7 for $T = 2$ to 13.8 for $T = 6$. Since we have multiple endogenous variables, we use Angrist-Pischke statistics, designed specifically to address this issue, to assess the strength of our instruments (Angrist and Pischke 2009). The associated p-values for all endogenous regressors are always below 0.05, indicating that the weak instrument is unlikely to be a problem. However, the conventional F-statistics for instrument exclusion, reported in the lower part of Table 2, are fairly low.[17]

The second-stage estimates show that an increase in preferential exports of a product by a country's trade partners is associated with a subsequent reduction in its MFN tariffs. As shown in panel A of Figure 5, there is no indication of a negative trend in coefficients on $\Delta\overline{PXS}(T)$ prior to FTA formation, and a clear pattern for the coefficients to decrease right after. For all $0 \leq T \leq 5$, β_T coefficients are negative, and three of them are statistically significant at least at the 90 percent confidence level. The pattern is very similar in panel B, where trade share instruments are obtained from the gravity model estimated with the PPML. It should be noted that the estimation results are robust to the inclusion of various fixed effects and the magnitude of the coefficients is fairly stable across specifications.[18]

[17] We cannot apply Stock-Yogo weak identification test since the critical values for this test are only available when the number of endogenous regressions does not exceed three. Using the conventional "rule of thumb" by Staiger and Stock (1997), all F-statistics are close or above 10, suggesting that weak identification could in fact be a problem.

[18] A possible alternative to using $IV^S(T)$ instruments to break simultaneity of import shares of MFN tariffs is to use import shares from the first year of the sample. In Appendix D we show that such approach provides only partial solution to endogeneity problem.

TABLE 2—ESTIMATION RESULTS

	(1)	(2)	(3)	(4)	(5)	(6)	(7)	(8)	(9)
$\Delta PXS(T=-3)$	0.014	0.027	−0.042	−0.061	−0.045	−0.052	0.045	−0.148	−0.017
	(0.068)	(0.050)	(0.029)	(0.031)	(0.028)	(0.031)	(0.081)	(0.076)	(0.031)
$\Delta PXS(T=-2)$	−0.016	0.057	0.029	0.046	0.036	0.046	0.322	0.121	−0.029
	(0.113)	(0.077)	(0.052)	(0.052)	(0.052)	(0.052)	(0.183)	(0.117)	(0.069)
$\Delta PXS(T=0)$	−0.130	−0.086	−0.162	−0.201	−0.150	−0.150	−0.012	−0.279	−0.107
	(0.092)	(0.067)	(0.044)	(0.058)	(0.042)	(0.049)	(0.113)	(0.104)	(0.076)
$\Delta PXS(T=1)$	−0.037	−0.023	−0.113	−0.123	−0.111	−0.076	−0.256	−0.504	−0.145
	(0.073)	(0.047)	(0.043)	(0.051)	(0.040)	(0.042)	(0.163)	(0.309)	(0.084)
$\Delta PXS(T=2)$	−0.103	−0.109	−0.110	−0.099	−0.104	−0.105	−0.305	−0.290	−0.096
	(0.041)	(0.042)	(0.033)	(0.028)	(0.032)	(0.026)	(0.106)	(0.108)	(0.035)
$\Delta PXS(T=3)$	−0.090	−0.072	−0.091	−0.100	−0.113	−0.068	−0.329	−0.101	−0.042
	(0.052)	(0.028)	(0.039)	(0.040)	(0.036)	(0.027)	(0.093)	(0.172)	(0.045)
$\Delta PXS(T=4)$	−0.088	−0.048	−0.042	−0.022	−0.074	−0.045	0.022	−0.086	−0.091
	(0.052)	(0.041)	(0.038)	(0.041)	(0.035)	(0.037)	(0.124)	(0.203)	(0.065)
$\Delta PXS(T=5)$	−0.127	−0.091	−0.058	−0.057	−0.089	−0.072	0.116	−0.121	−0.078
	(0.033)	(0.035)	(0.036)	(0.034)	(0.033)	(0.033)	(0.077)	(0.129)	(0.036)
$\Delta PXS(T>5)$	0.028	−0.010	0.007	0.003	0.014	−0.002	0.032	0.000	−0.046
	(0.032)	(0.027)	(0.021)	(0.023)	(0.019)	(0.020)	(0.077)	(0.104)	(0.030)
Observations	51,658	51,658	51,658	51,658	51,658	51,658	51,658	51,658	51,658
Instrument set:	IV_1^S	IV_2^S	IV_3^S	IV_4^S	IV_1^S, IV_3^S	IV_2^S, IV_4^S	IV_1^X	IV_1^X	IV_2^X
Gravity equation for import share instruments:									
Estimator	OLS	PPML	OLS	PPML	OLS	PPML	PPML	PPML	PPML
Ind. specific coef.	YES	YES	YES	YES	YES	YES	YES	YES	YES
Imp/exp-ind-yer FE	NO	NO	YES	YES	YES	YES	NO	YES	YES
Gravity equation for preferential export share instruments:									
Estimator							OLS	OLS	PPML
Dep. var.							Pref. share	Pref. share	log imports
Anderson-Rubin test	0.001	0.010	0.000	0.000	0.000	0.000	0.004	0.018	0.019
Hansen J-test, p-value					0.322	0.190			
F-stat:									
$PXS(T=-2)$	13.87	11.10	49.47	45.96	26.94	29.42	12.25	13.46	47.81
$PXS(T=-1)$	6.83	10.03	18.07	20.60	13.80	18.01	6.37	7.45	19.27
$PXS(T=0)$	10.88	6.74	17.91	5.16	23.95	10.43	10.84	16.55	3.79
$PXS(T=1)$	5.44	15.30	9.68	16.13	7.59	13.23	5.82	6.00	17.77
$PXS(T=2)$	4.55	4.76	9.79	25.00	9.20	16.14	5.50	5.57	19.56
$PXS(T=3)$	4.95	7.04	8.32	9.20	7.41	6.26	7.98	7.16	11.23
$PXS(T=4)$	11.98	15.23	22.66	37.45	22.72	24.72	9.73	3.91	31.88
$PXS(T=5)$	12.47	10.29	17.50	19.99	14.69	15.47	11.99	4.43	27.73
$PXS(T>5)$	14.54	16.50	16.29	27.07	18.58	23.90	6.07	4.62	27.58

Notes: The dependent variable is the change in the MFN tariff between years t and $(t-1)$. $\Delta PXS(T)$ is the change in preferential export share of a country's average trade partner due to FTAs formed in year $(t-1)$. Standard errors in parentheses are obtained using two-way clustering at country-industry and country-year levels. All specifications include country-year and country-industry fixed effects. For the Hansen test of overidentifying restrictions, the null hypothesis is that all instruments are jointly uncorrelated with the error term of the second-stage regression and correctly excluded from the estimated equation. For the Anderson-Rubin test, the null hypothesis is that the coefficients of the endogenous regressors in the second-stage equation are jointly equal to zero.

Results with instruments $IV_3^S(T)$ and $IV_4^S(T)$, illustrated in panels C and D, respectively, reveal even more pronounced discontinuity in β_T coefficients around the year of FTA establishment—the coefficient drops sharply in the year of FTA formation and then increases gradually until becoming insignificant in the fifth year of an FTA. As previously discussed, the main advantage of $IV_3^S(T)/IV_4^S(T)$ instruments over

$IV_1^S(T)/IV_2^S(T)$ is the inclusion of the country-industry-year fixed effects in the gravity equation that predicts trade shares for the former. Not only do these fixed effects correct the omitted variable bias in the gravity variables, but they also substantially improve the fit of the gravity model itself, making the relationship between the instruments and the endogenous regressors much stronger. One can see that the first stage F-statistics in columns 3 and 4 of Table 2 are substantially greater than those in columns 1 and 2. However, the disadvantage of this approach is that the fixed effects can absorb potentially endogenous unobservable determinants of trade. In column 5 of Table 2 we use both $IV_1^S(T)$ and $IV_3^S(T)$ to instrument changes in preferential export shares, and perform a standard Hansen-J overidentification test to assess the quality of instruments. The test passes easily, and we cannot reject the hypothesis of exogeneity of instruments. The same is true in column 6 when $IV_2^S(T)$ and $IV_4^S(T)$ are used jointly as instruments for $\Delta\overline{PXS}(T)$.

The dynamic response of tariff changes to FTA formation in Figure 5 relies on two sources of data variation, captured by the two components of $\Delta\overline{PXS}(T)$ variables in equation (30). The first component, $FTA\,(T)_{pjt}$, captures the delay in tariff response to an FTA shock. The second component, $(exp\_share_{pjit} - exp\_share_{pjit-T-1})$, captures the intensity of the external trade diversion of an FTA, and measures the strength of the FTA shock for each country and industry. As T increases in Figure 5, $\Delta\overline{PXS}(T)$ changes because both the time elapsed since FTA formation and the strength of trade diversion within an FTA change. In the next exercise we isolate the first effect from the second by fixing the change in preferential trade share within an FTA. Specifically, we fix the second component in equation (30) to the cumulative change over the first five years of the agreement: $(exp\_share_{pj,T=5} - exp\_share_{pji,T=-1})$. The three panels of Figure 6 reproduce results of panels B, D, and E of Figure 5 using fixed preferential export shares to construct $\Delta\overline{PXS}(T)$. The figure confirms that tariff reductions are the most pronounced in years two to four after FTA formation, and the magnitude of the effect is similar to the previous estimates.

The estimates from Figure 6 and Table 3 point to a potentially nonnegligible economic impact of FTAs on tariffs of nonmembers. For ease of interpretation of the magnitudes of the effects, we estimate the cumulative effect of FTAs over the first five years of implementation using the variation of equation (30):

$$(33) \qquad \Delta_5 MFN_{cit} = \beta\Delta_6\overline{PXS}\,(T = 5)_{cit} + \gamma_{ct} + \gamma_{cI} + \upsilon_{cit},$$

where the dependent variable is the change in the MFN tariff between years t and $(t-5)$, and $\Delta_5\overline{PXS}(T = 5)$ is the change in preferential export share between t and $(t-6)$ resulting from FTAs formed in year $(t-5)$. The estimation results for equation (33) using different sets of instruments, presented in Table 3, confirm that the cumulative effect of FTAs on nonmember tariffs is negative and significant for all but one specification. Taking -0.401 as the estimate of β from column 1, it implies that if a country's preferential exports increase by 10 percent as a result of a new FTA, and the share of this country in imports of another country is 10 percent, the latter will reduce its MFN tariff by 0.401 percentage points in the first 5

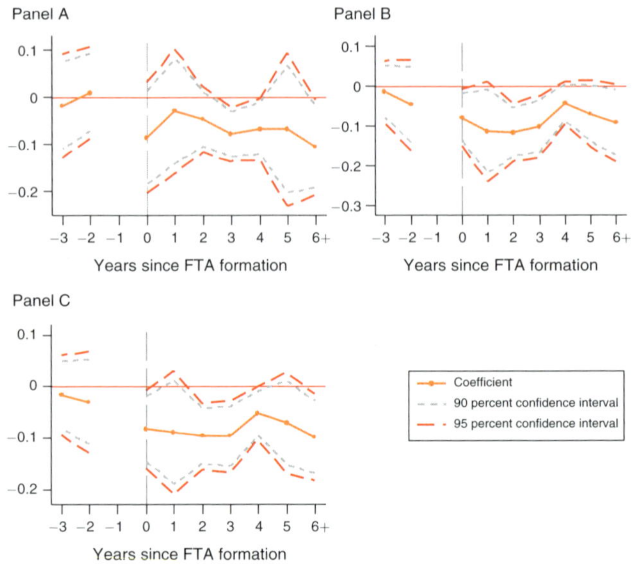

FIGURE 6. BASELINE RESULTS WITH INSTRUMENTED IMPORT SHARES AND FIXED PREFERENTIAL EXPORT SHARES

Notes: Trade shares are predicted from: PPML gravity model without fixed effects (panel A); PPML gravity model with country-industry-year fixed effects (panel B); PPML gravity model with and without fixed effects (panel C).

TABLE 3—ESTIMATION RESULTS IN LONG DIFFERENCES

Dependent variable: The change in the MFN tariff over the first five years after FTA formation	(1)	(2)	(3)	(4)	(5)	(6)	(7)
$PXS(T = 5)$	−0.401	−0.352	−0.235	−0.178	−0.556	−0.243	−0.273
	(0.199)	(0.172)	(0.104)	(0.093)	(0.334)	(0.183)	(0.103)
Instrument set:	IVS1	IVS2	IVS3	IVS4	IVX1	IVX1	IVX2
Anderson-Rubin Wald test	0.031	0.035	0.006	0.040	0.081	0.161	0.003
First stage F-statistic	56.6	71.4	51.9	100.0	55.3	53.8	74.0
Observations	32,171	32,171	32,171	32,171	32,171	32,171	32,171

Notes: Standard errors in parentheses are clustered by country-industry. All specifications include country-year and country-industry fixed effects. For the Anderson-Rubin test the null hypothesis is that the coefficients of the endogenous regressors in the second-stage equation are jointly equal to zero.

years of the agreement. This result is comparable to what we obtain from Table 2 by summing statistically significant coefficients for β_0–β_5 ($0.103 + 0.090 + 0.088 + 0.127 = 0.408$). However, because most FTAs do not lead to substantial increase in trade shares between member countries,[19] the link between preferential

[19] For 89 percent of all country-pairs and industries in our sample, an increase in the share of preferential trade in total trade of FTA member countries does not exceed 1 percentage point in the first four years of the agreement.

trade shares of FTA members and MFN tariff reductions by an average nonmember country in our sample is quantitatively not very strong. In particular, a 1 standard deviation increase in the $\Delta_6\overline{PXS}(T = 5)$ variable is associated with a reduction in the MFN tariff by 0.03–0.04 standard deviations, or by 0.1 percentage points, and industries in ninetieth percentile of $\Delta_6\overline{PXS}(T = 5)$ distribution have on average 0.076 percentage points lower MFN tariff relative to industries in the tenth percentile.

V. Results with Instruments for Preferential Export Shares

The empirical strategy of the previous section addresses endogeneity concerns that may arise if import shares are correlated with the error term in equation (28). Another identification issue with equation (28) relates to the preferential export shares that are used in the construction of the main explanatory variables as proxies for unobservable changes in the export supply elasticities. The theoretical model predicts that FTAs affect both the export supply elasticities and the preferential export shares positively, so that changes in the latter can be used to infer changes in the former. However, a change in the share of a country's exports to its FTA trade partners is an imperfect measure of a change in the export supply elasticity since trade shares may vary for a variety of other reasons.

In the presence of the measurement error in the export supply elasticities, identification of the effect of trade agreements on trade policies of excluded countries in model (28) rests on two assumptions. First, the variation in preferential export shares must to some extent reflect changes in the export supply elasticities. We provide some evidence in support of this assumption in Appendix D where we use Feenstra's (1994) methodology to estimate country-industry-specific export supply elasticities for two time periods: 1988–2001 and 2002–2011. Consistent with our theory, we find a positive and statistically significant relationship between changes in the export supply elasticities and changes in preferential export shares over these two periods.

The second assumption that is necessary to obtain consistent estimates of β_T from model (28) is that the portion of variation in preferential export shares that is unexplained by changes in the export supply elasticities must be unrelated to the error term in (28). In particular, this assumption requires that there are no shocks that affect both the trade structure within FTAs and the MFN tariffs of excluded countries other than country-industry and country-year specific shocks.[20] Furthermore, large measurement error in preferential export shares may lead to the attenuation bias in β_T estimates.

[20] This assumption also requires that preferential trade shares of FTA member countries do not respond to future changes in trade policies of third countries. For example, one may argue that future reductions in MFN tariffs can divert trade flows of third countries away from their FTA partners to the extent that those changes are expected.

To address these endogeneity concerns, we instrument for $\Delta\overline{PXS}(T)$ using the following IVs:

$$(34)\qquad IV^X(T)_{cit} = \left(\sum_p \widehat{imp\_share}_{cpi} \cdot \Delta\widehat{PXS(T)}_{pit-T-1}\right);$$

$$\Delta\widehat{PXS(T)}_{pit-T-1} = \sum_{j \neq c} FTA(T)_{pjt} \cdot \Delta\widehat{exp\_share}_{pjit},$$

where $\Delta\widehat{exp\_share} = \left(\widehat{exp\_share}_{pjit} - \widehat{exp\_share}_{pjit-T-1}\right)$ capture the part of variation in preferential trade shares that is orthogonal to the error term in (28). We build on theoretical frameworks to obtain $\Delta\widehat{exp\_share}$ measures, and then use these measures to construct two alternative sets of instruments $IV^X(T)$ that rely on different sources of identifying variation in preferential export shares. For $\widehat{imp\_share}$ we can use any of the gravity models discussed in Section II, but our most favored specifications are the ones estimated with the PPML, both with and without country-industry-year fixed effects.

Obtaining $\Delta\widehat{exp\_share}$ requires instruments for changes in preferential export shares that are correlated with the effect of trade agreements on trade flows between member countries, but uncorrelated with both the MFN tariffs of third countries and possible common shocks. The first sets of instruments that isolate the variation in preferential export shares due to regional trade agreements is motivated by Baier and Bergstrand (2004), who constructed a general equilibrium model of trade with two monopolistically competitive industries, two factors of production, six countries, and three continents. Using this model, Baier and Bergstrand identify several factors that contribute to larger effect of an FTA on trade volumes between member countries. Specifically, they find that FTAs lead to more trade between member countries when trade partners are "natural" (i.e., when trade costs between them are low), more remote from the rest of the world, are larger, and more similar in size. They also show that FTAs create more trade when the difference in factor endowments is large between member countries and small between members and the rest of the world. As with the instrumental variables strategy for import shares, we begin by focusing on geographic determinants of trade only, and add differences in factor endowments in our analysis later.

To control for trade costs between FTA member countries p and j we use three gravity model variables: logarithm of the bilateral distance ($\ln D_{pj}$), the common border indicator (B_{pj}), and the common language indicator (L_{pj}). The remoteness measure for a pair of countries p and j with respect to the rest of the world is constructed as the simple average of the log of mean distance of country p to its trade partners except for j and the log of mean distance of country j to its trade partners except for p:

$$REMOTE_{pj} = \frac{1}{2}\left[\ln\left(\frac{\sum_{k\neq j} D_{pk}}{N-2}\right) + \ln\left(\frac{\sum_{k\neq p} D_{jk}}{N-2}\right)\right],$$

where N is the total number of countries. As in Baier and Bergstrand (2004), we use the interaction of the remoteness measure with the same continent indicator variable

$(CREMOTE_{pj})$ in order to distinguish inter-continental and intra-continental trade costs. We use the sum of logarithms of two countries' populations as a measure of their economic size $(SIZE_{pj})$ and the absolute difference in the logarithms of population of two countries as a measure of size asymmetry $(DSIZE_{pj})$.

Because we need instruments for preferential export shares at country-pair-industry-year level while the geography variables do not vary within country pair cells, our point of departure is to estimate the dynamic effect of those variables on trade volumes within an FTA. We allow several years for trade volumes between trade partners to converge to the new equilibrium levels in the presence of an FTA. There are at least two reasons to expect a delayed response of trade flows to FTA formation. First, it may take some time for producers to adjust their production plans and capacities to changes in market conditions. Second, many FTAs do not lead to free trade in the first year of the agreement but rather liberalize trade policy gradually by phasing-out preferential tariff reductions over several years. In the presence of dynamic response of trade flows to FTA formation, we allow for the effect of the instruments for preferential trade shares to be time-specific during the first five years of the agreement. We also allow for the effect of these geography instruments on within-FTA trade to vary by industry. As a result, for every industry i we estimate the following regression:[21]

$$(35) \quad \Delta\ exp\_share_{pjit} = \beta^0_{iT} + \beta^1_{iT}\ln D^T_{pjt} + \beta^2_{iT}B^T_{pjt} + \beta^3_{iT}L^T_{pjt} + \beta^4_{iT}REMOTE^T_{pjt} + \beta^5_{iT}CREMOTE^T_{pjt} + \beta^6_{iT}SIZE_{pj} + \beta^7_{iT}DSIZE_{pj} + v_{pjit},$$

where $x^T_{pjt} = FTA(T)_{pjt}x_{pj}$ and $-3 \leq T \leq 6$. As before, we combine all FTAs formed prior to year $(t-5)$ into one category of $T = 6$. Using fitted values from model (35), $\Delta\widehat{exp\_share}$, we predict the effect of FTAs on trade between members from the geography variables only, and this prediction is plausibly independent from other determinants of trade policies of nonmember countries. We then use $\Delta\widehat{exp\_share}$ in equation (34) to construct the first set of instruments, $IV^X_1(T)$, for $\Delta\overline{PXS}(T)$ variables in model (28). These instruments are functions of predetermined geographic characteristics of a country's trade partners and FTA dummy variables, and provide consistent estimates under the condition that the decision of a pair of third countries to form an FTA is independent of the error term in (28).

Estimation results for model (35) indicate that trade costs, remoteness, and the level and asymmetry in populations of two countries are reasonably good predictors of the effect of an FTA on preferential trade shares. For 94 industries out of 97 we reject the null that the explanatory variables have no effect on changes in preferential export shares at the 99 percent confidence level.[22] The mean F-statistics for the test $\beta^k_{iT} = 0\ \forall k = 1, \ldots, 7$ is 9.26, the mean R^2 is 0.21, and the correlation between predicted and actual preferential trade shares is 0.27.

[21] The model by Baier and Bergstrand (2004) also proposes economic determinants of trade creation within FTA, such as relative and absolute difference in physical and human capital endowments. However, because these determinants have little predictive power for trade effects of FTAs in the data, we do not use them in our analysis.

[22] For the remaining three industries the explanatory variables in (35) are jointly significant at 95 percent.

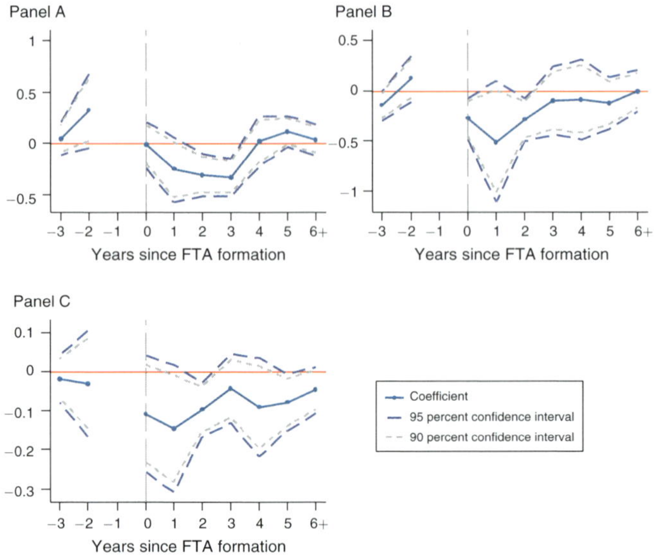

FIGURE 7. RESULTS WITH INSTRUMENTED IMPORT SHARES AND PREFERENTIAL EXPORT SHARES

Notes: Preferential export shares are predicted from: OLS gravity model with geography variables (panels A and B); PPML gravity model with geography variables (panel C). Import shares are predicted from: PPML gravity model without fixed effects (panel A); PPML gravity model with fixed effects (panels B and C).

Three points about equation (35) need to be emphasized. First, allowing for the effect of FTAs to be dynamic generates variation in $\widehat{\Delta exp\_share}$ over time. This variations captures delayed economic response to terms-of-trade shocks, as well as the possibility of a "phased-in" implementation of the agreement. Second, with the coefficients on the right-hand side variables varying by industry, we obtain cross-industry variation in the predicted preferential trade shares even though the geography variables in (35) vary only by country-pair. To develop intuition for this approach, consider the distance variable. We know that the effect of an FTA on trade flows depends on trade costs and is decreasing in distance. Our earlier results also show that the effect of distance and other gravity model measures of trade costs vary across industries. Therefore, one would expect the effect of an FTA on trade to be stronger in those industries where transportation costs and distance play lesser role. The relevance of variation in coefficients in equation (35) is supported by the fact that 65 percent of variation in $\widehat{\Delta exp\_share}$ is coming from the variation within country-pair-year cells and 51 percent is coming from the variation within country-pair-industry cells. Lastly, we are not trying to predict changes in preferential trade between countries which are not members of any preferential trade agreement. For this reason, equation (35) is estimated only for country pairs which were part of an FTA in year $(t - T)$.

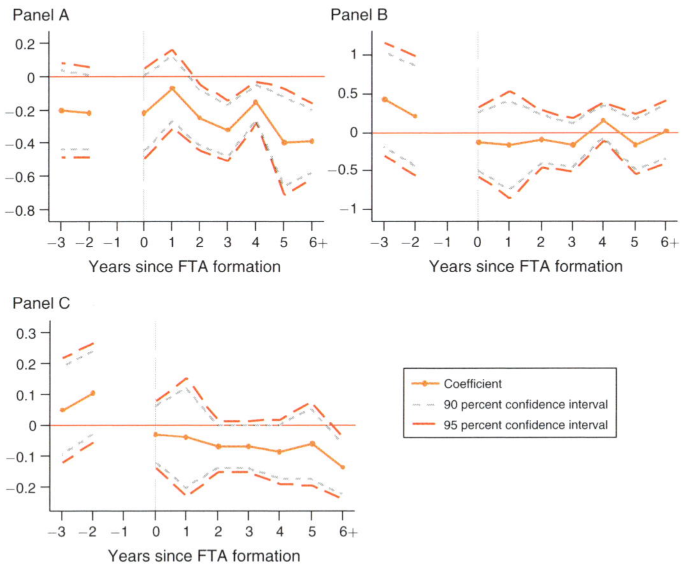

FIGURE 8. RESULTS WITH FIXED EXPORT SHARES AND INSTRUMENTS FOR IMPORT SHARES AND PREFERENTIAL EXPORT SHARES

Notes: Preferential export shares are predicted from: OLS gravity model with geography variables (panels A and B); PPML gravity model with geography variables (panel C). Import shares are predicted from: PPML gravity model without fixed effects (panel A); PPML gravity model with fixed effects (panels B and C).

Estimation results with $IV_1^X(T)$ instruments are presented in Figure 7, while Table 2 reports the first-stage statistics.

We report results with import shares obtained from the gravity model (32) without fixed effects (panel A of Figure 8; column 7 of Table 2) and with country-industry-year fixed effects (panel B of Figure 7; column 8 of Table 2). In this way, $IV_1^X(T)$ instruments not only isolate variation in preferential export shares changes, which can be attributed to the effect of FTAs, but also address the problem of endogeneity of import shares. Although the first-stage F-statistics are somewhat low, the results of Angrist-Pischke test indicate strong correlation between our instruments and the endogenous regressors.

The dynamics of β_T coefficients over the life of an FTA is similar to what was obtained previously without instrumenting for preferential export shares. The MFN tariffs of nonmember countries exhibit a negative response to an FTA immediately after the agreement formation. Of the eight second-stage coefficients on $\overline{PXS}(T)$ variables, three remain negative and statistically significant at the 90 percent confidence level. Specifically, the estimated effect of FTAs on tariff reduction by outside countries is the strongest in years one to three of FTA formation. Although the overall pattern in β_T coefficients is similar to what we obtained previously, the point estimates of these coefficients are notably larger when the changes in preferential export shares are instrumented for, which is consistent with the presence of attenuation bias in the benchmark estimates. Since changes in preferential export shares is an imperfect measure of changes in export supply elasticities, noisy data may bias the coefficient estimates towards zero. Hence, isolating variation in $\overline{PXS}(T)$ variables which is related to trade agreements and changes in export supply elasticity may improve identification of the effect of our interest.

To build the second set of instruments for preferential export shares, we utilize a structural gravity model instead of (35) to obtain predicted changes in preferential export shares. We follow Anderson and Yotov (2016) and estimate the following gravity model with PPML:

$$(36) \qquad X_{pjit} = \exp\left[Z_{pjit} \cdot FTA\,(T)_{pjt}\beta_{iT} + \gamma_{pit} + \gamma_{jit} + \gamma_{pji} + \varepsilon_{pjit}\right],$$

where X_{pjit} is exports of product i from country p to country j in year t. The term Z_{pjt} is a set of geography variables that may affect the strength of an FTA on internal trade flows. Specifically, Z_{pjt} includes a constant term, the logarithm of bilateral distance between countries p and j, the common border and the common language indicators, the measure of remoteness of p and j from the rest of the world, the sum of logarithms of the two countries' populations, and the absolute difference in the logarithms of populations of the two countries. Thus, $Z_{pjit} \cdot FTA\,(T)_{pjt}$ interactions estimate the dynamic effect of FTAs on bilateral trade. Variables γ_{pit} and γ_{jit} denote importer-industry-year and exporter-industry-year fixed effects that account for multilateral price terms, output, and expenditure. Further, γ_{pji} capture importer-exporter-industry fixed effects, which not only control for time-invariant trade costs at country-pair-industry level, but also alleviate potential endogeneity of $FTA\,(T)_{pjt}$ binary variables arising from non-random selection of partner countries for preferential trade liberalization (Baier and Bergstrand 2007).

We use model (36) to predict both the counterfactual value of trade in the absence of FTAs,

$$\hat{X}^{0}_{pjit} = \exp\left[\hat{\gamma}_{pit} + \hat{\gamma}_{jit} + \hat{\gamma}_{pji}\right],$$

and trade flows with FTAs,

$$\hat{X}^{1}_{pjit}(T) = \exp\left[Z_{pjit} \cdot FTA\,(T)_{pjt}\hat{\beta}_{iT} + \hat{\gamma}_{pit} + \hat{\gamma}_{jit} + \hat{\gamma}_{pji}\right],$$

and construct the second set of instruments, $IV^{X}_{2}(T)$, using (34) and the predicted changes in preferential exports,[23]

$$(37) \qquad \Delta\,\widehat{PXS(T)}_{pit-T-1} = \sum_{j \neq c}\left(\frac{\hat{X}^{1}_{pjit}(T) - \hat{X}^{0}_{pjit-T-1}}{\hat{X}^{0}_{pjit-T-1}}\right).$$

[23] Due of the perfect collinearity problem, we have to drop one of the importer-industry-year fixed effects and one of the exporter-industry-year fixed effects. As a result, all γ_{pit} and γ_{jit} are estimated relative to these omitted categories. However, this normalization does not affect the quality of our instruments because the relative ranking of partner countries in their preferential trade shares is preserved.

Because the gravity model (36) accounts for several identification issues that the model (35) cannot address—such as the omitted variables bias, the endogeneity of trade agreements, and the truncation of trade flows at zero—the main advantage of $IV_2^X(T)$ instruments over $IV_1^X(T)$ is the more reliable estimates of the FTA effect on trade. However, the disadvantage is that $IV_2^X(T)$ rely on aggregate trade flows predicted from the structural gravity equation (36). Since these predicted trade flows incorporate information on price indices, expenditure, and other potentially endogenous economic variables, the exclusion restriction for $IV_2^X(T)$ is more likely to fail.

Results with $IV_2^X(T)$ instruments are presented in panel C of Figure 7 and column 9 of Table 2. The first thing to note is that the instruments $IV_2^X(T)$ are highly relevant. The correlation between preferential export shares predicted from (37) and the actual shares is 0.53, and the F-statistics for joint significance of the instruments in the first-stage regressions substantially greater than with $IV_1^X(T)$ instruments. The estimation results from the second stage are close to the benchmark specification, both in terms of the magnitudes and the overall pattern. All post-FTA coefficients are negative with a sharp reduction in the first year of agreement formation, while the pre-FTA coefficients are close to zeroes. However, estimating equation (28) with $IV_2^X(T)$ instruments gives less precisely estimated regression coefficients, with three out of seven the post-FTA coefficients being statistically significant at 10 percent and only one of them being significant at 1 percent.

In Figure 8 we reproduce the results of Figure 7 using time-invariant changes in preferential export shares, as in Figure 6 before. Specifically, we use the change in preferential export shares over the first five years of an FTA, both actual and predicted, to construct $\Delta\overline{PXS}(T)$ variables and their instruments. While in panel A the effect of FTAs on tariff changes by nonmembers become stronger and statistically significant in year two and all following years, in panel B all coefficients become insignificant. With $IV_2^X(T)$ as instruments in panel C, the estimates have similar magnitudes to those in Figures 5–8 and are statistically significant at 10 percent confidence level in years 2 to 4.

VI. Robustness Tests

We conduct a series of robustness tests for the effect of FTAs on nonmembers' tariffs. First, the time frame of our sample overlaps with the major episode of multilateral tariff reductions, negotiated during the Uruguay round of the WTO negotiations and phased in between 1996 and 2001. One might be concerned that tariff reductions during 1996–2001 period were predetermined and correlated with some unobservable characteristics of countries' trade partners through multilateral bargaining process. To verify that our explanatory variables pick up the effect of preferential trade liberalization rather than the WTO-induced tariff reductions, we report the estimation results separately for 1988–2001 and 2002–2011 time periods. We also exclude from the sample all WTO accession countries, which may have negotiated different timing for tariff reductions. Figure 9 shows that the dynamics in β_T coefficients on the two subsamples is similar to the benchmark results.

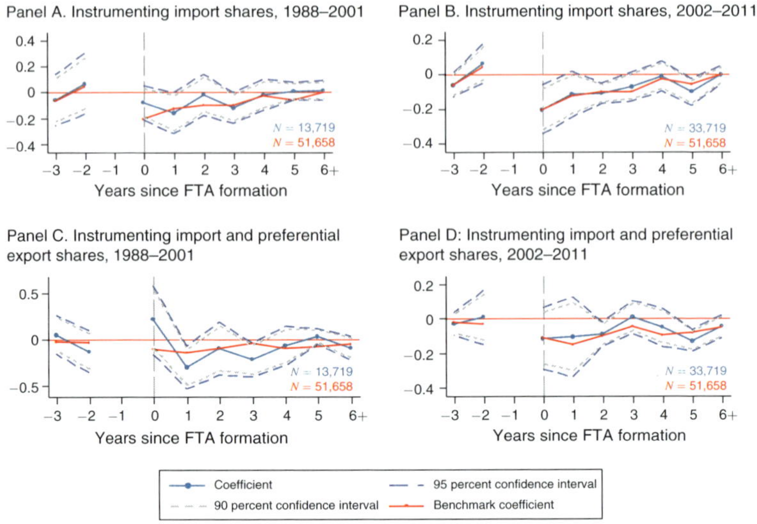

FIGURE 9. RESULTS FOR PRE- AND POST-URUGUAY ROUND SAMPLES

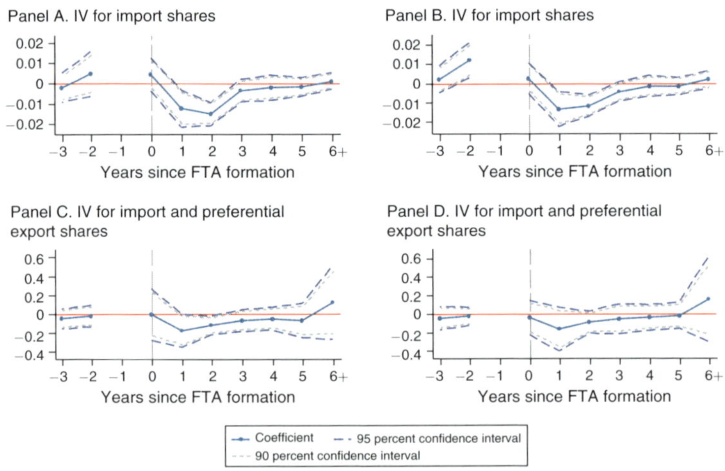

FIGURE 10. RESULTS WITH FOUR-DIGIT HS INDUSTRY CODES

Notes: Trade shares are predicted from: PPML gravity model without fixed effects (panel A); PPML gravity model with country-industry-year fixed effects (panels B, C, D). Preferential export shares are: original (panels A and B); predicted from the OLS gravity model with geography variables (panel C); predicted from the PPML gravity model with geography variables (panel D).

In Figure 10, we show that our results are robust at a higher level of product disaggregation. Specifically, we show that tariffs respond negatively to an increase in partner countries' preferential trade in 4-digit HS trade and tariff data. The effect is still the strongest in the second and the third years of a trade agreement but the magnitudes are lower with more disaggregated data. When import shares are instrumented for, the coefficient estimates obtained with the 4-digit HS data are smaller than those obtained with 2-digit data, but remain highly significant in the second and third years of the agreement. When both import and preferential export shares are instrumented, the estimates are comparable in magnitude to our previous results but are estimated less precisely, with the coefficients β_1 and β_2 significant only at 10 percent level. Overall, the results with more disaggregated trade data confirm our previous findings that FTAs stimulate other countries to lower their tariffs.

We perform many additional sensitivity tests and tabulate the key estimates for alternative samples of the data to verify that our results remain stable. We show that the main result remains qualitatively similar when China is included in the sample. Although rapid increase in Chinese exports since 2001 has a strong negative impact on the average change in preferential export share, this effect does not vary systematically across FTAs and keeping China in the sample does not affect the estimates. Results are similar when the model is estimated for countries with different income levels and for different industry groups. Finally, results are also robust to excluding African countries from the sample. Most African countries export mostly primary goods, and regional integration has little potential for trade creation. Yet there are many multilateral trade agreements in Africa and nearly 15 percent of all country-pairs with FTAs in our sample are between African countries. Excluding those trade agreements from the analysis does not change any of the results.

VII. Welfare Implications

In this section, we examine quantitatively the importance of tariff adjustments by nonmember countries for the welfare effects of FTAs. Although our empirical results show that the FTA-induced tariff reduction undertaken by an individual nonmember country is fairly small, in this section, we show that the combined tariff reductions of all nonmember countries can deliver substantial welfare gains.

Let w_z^{adj} and w_z^{no-adj} denote the welfare levels of an FTA member country when nonmembers do and do not adjust their tariffs, respectively. Then using our theoretical model the welfare gain to member countries from tariff reductions undertaken by nonmembers can be written as

$$\begin{aligned}\Delta w_z^{adj} &= w_z^{adj} - w_z^{no-adj} \\ &= \frac{2(n-m)^2 \Delta t_c^Z t_c^Z(\phi)\left[\alpha\lambda - (\lambda+2m)\, t_c^Z(\phi)(2-\Delta t_c^Z)\right]}{(\lambda+2n)^2}.\end{aligned}$$

The effect of an FTA on members' welfare in the absence of tariff adjustments by nonmembers is

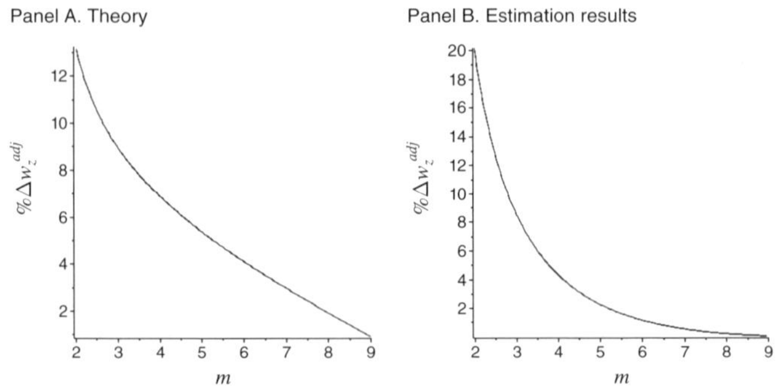

FIGURE 11. THE EFFECT OF TARIFF ADJUSTMENTS BY NONMEMBERS ON WELFARE OF FTA MEMBER COUNTRIES ($n = 10, \lambda = 0.5$)

$$\Delta w_z^{FTA-noadj} = w_z^{no-adj} - w_z(\phi)$$

$$= \frac{(m-1)t_c^Z(\phi)\left[2(n-m)\alpha\lambda + t_c^Z(\phi)\left(\lambda^2 + 2(m+1)\lambda + 4(n+(n-m)(n-m-1))\right)\right]}{(\lambda+2n)^2}$$

where $w_z(\phi)$ is welfare under no agreement.

The welfare gain of a member country from an FTA when nonmembers impose optimal tariffs is the sum of the above welfare gains:

$$\Delta w_z^{FTA} = \Delta w_z^{FTA-noadj} + \Delta w_z^{adj}.$$

Consider a single FTA of size m. Using the optimal tariff expressions (24) and (25), we can calculate the welfare gain for member countries from the implied tariff adjustments by nonmembers as a fraction of the total welfare gain: $\%\Delta w_z^{adj} = 100 \times \frac{\Delta w_z^{adj}}{\Delta w_z^{FTA}}$. Figure 11 plots $\%\Delta w_z^{adj}$ for different sizes of an FTA m, assuming $n = 10$ and $\lambda = 1/2$.[24]

Panel A of Figure 11 demonstrates that tariff adjustments by nonmember countries account for over 12 percent of FTA welfare gains to members when the FTA is small relative to the rest of the world, and this share falls gradually as size of the FTA relative to the rest of the world goes up. In panel B of Figure 11, we repeat the same exercise, but this time we use the elasticity of nonmembers' tariffs with respect to an FTA estimated from the data rather than the one implied by our model. Specifically, we use the change in the PXS predicted by the model and assume that nonmember countries lower their pre-FTA MFN tariffs by 0.319 percent of the increase in the PXS of their average trade partner, which is the elasticity estimate from our most preferred specification (the sum of all statistically significant coef-

[24] The simulation results reported below are not particularly sensitive to variations in λ.

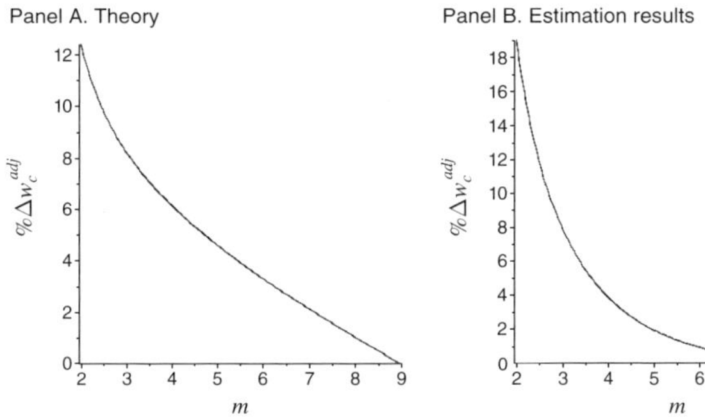

FIGURE 12. THE EFFECT OF TARIFF ADJUSTMENTS BY FTA NONMEMBERS ON THEIR WELFARE ($n = 10, \lambda = 0.5$)

ficients in column 9 of Table 2). This exercise yields very similar results for the contribution of tariff adjustments to welfare gains for member countries.

Next, we analyze the role of tariff adjustments by nonmember countries for the effect of FTAs on their welfare. For nonmember country c, the welfare loss from tariff adjustment by all nonmember countries equals

$$\begin{aligned}\Delta w_c^{adj} &= w_c^{adj} - w_c^{no-adj}\\ &= \frac{m\Delta t_c^Z t_c^Z(\phi)\left[(\lambda + 2m)(\lambda + 4n - 2m)t_c^Z(\phi)\left(2 - \Delta t_c^Z\right) - 2(n - m)\alpha\lambda\right]}{(\lambda + 2n)^2} < 0.\end{aligned}$$

It is important to note here that while each nonmember country optimally reduces its tariff noncooperatively, the simultaneous reduction in tariffs by other nonmember countries increases the price of the imported good and weakens the terms of trade effect, thus lowering the welfare of a typical nonmember country.

The welfare effect of an FTA when nonmembers keep their original tariffs is

$$\begin{aligned}\Delta w_c^{FTA-noadj} &= w_c^{no-adj} - w_c(\phi)\\ &= -\frac{2m(m - 1)t_c^Z(\phi)\left[\alpha\lambda + 2(n - m - 1)\,t_c^Z(\phi)\right]}{(\lambda + 2n)^2} < 0,\end{aligned}$$

and the total welfare loss for a nonmember country from an FTA when nonmember countries optimally adjust tariffs is the sum of the above welfare changes: $\Delta w_c^{FTA} = \Delta w_c^{FTA-noadj} + \Delta w_c^{adj}$. Similar to the discussion for member countries, the welfare loss of nonmember countries due to tariff adjustment relative to total loss from an FTA is $\%\Delta w_c^{adj} = 100 \times \frac{\Delta w_c^{adj}}{\Delta w_c^{FTA}}$. Panel A of Figure 12 plots $\%\Delta w_c^{adj}$ for different m.

The results show that when FTA is comprised of only 2 countries, tariff adjustments by nonmembers account for 12 percent of the total negative impact of the FTA on nonmembers' welfare, and the share goes up to 17 percent when we use the estimated elasticity of nonmembers tariff with respect to FTAs. Overall our simple simulation exercise reveals that tariff adjustments by individual nonmembers induced by the formation of an FTA, albeit small in absolute values, can have a substantial collective effect on the welfare of member and nonmember countries.

VIII. Conclusions

We develop a simple theoretical model of endogenous tariffs with an arbitrary number of countries and analyze the effect that the formation of an FTA between a subset of countries has on the import tariffs of excluded countries. This model predicts that an FTA redirects export flows of member countries away from the rest of the world toward each other and thereby reduces the elasticities of export supply curves faced by nonmembers. As a result, the ability of nonmembers to manipulate their terms-of-trade via import tariffs is weakened which, in turn, induces them to lower their MFN tariffs on FTA members. We show that this trade liberalization effect of an FTA on nonmember countries is stronger when the increase in trade flows between members resulting from the agreement is larger.

Bringing this prediction to the data, we find considerable support for the hypothesis that FTAs reduce the terms-of-trade motive for protection of nonmember countries. Using tariff data for 136 countries and information on all FTAs formed in the world between 1990 and 2011, we find that larger trade flows between member countries indeed lead to reductions in MFN tariffs of their nonmember trade partners.

In conclusion, we wish to emphasize two fundamental points. First, since the evidence presented in this paper shows that the formation of FTAs can cause trade liberalization to spill over to excluded countries, an important channel of welfare gains resulting from their formation has been overlooked in the existing literature. For example, the literature addressing whether FTAs are building or stumbling blocks for multilateral liberalization has tended to focus primarily on how FTA formation affects the incentives of member countries to undertake further liberalization with respect to excluded countries. Our analysis shows that we also need to pay attention to the effects that FTAs might have on trade policies of nonmember countries. The second major point to note is that, by examining the impact of FTAs on tariffs of nonmember countries, our results provide rather novel and convincing support for the terms of trade theory of optimal tariffs since the formation of an FTA between a few countries can be reasonably interpreted as an exogenous event from the perspective of the rest of the world.

Appendix

In this section, we provide the necessary supporting calculations, proofs, and discussions.

Appendix A: Welfare Components and the Optimal Tariff

In this section, consistent with the Article XXIV of the GATT, we assume that member countries under an FTA remove their internal tariffs ($\hat{t}^g = 0$) while imposing external tariffs on the nonmember countries independently. As before, suppose that country z forms an FTA with $(m - 1)$ countries and country c is a nonmember country while $\tilde{c}$ denotes nonmembers other than country c. Let F denote the set of goods produced by FTA member countries. Next, we report individual welfare components for country c. Consumer surplus equals

$$\begin{aligned} CS_c =& \frac{1}{2}\left[\alpha - \frac{n\alpha - 2mt_m^C - 2(n-m-1)t_{\tilde{c}}^C}{\lambda + 2n}\right]^2 \\ &+ \frac{1}{2}\sum_{J\in F}\left[\alpha - \frac{n\alpha - 2t_c^J - 2(n-m-1)t_{\tilde{c}}^J}{\lambda + 2n} - t_c^J\right]^2 \\ &+ \frac{1}{2}\sum_{J\notin F, J\neq C}\left[\alpha - \frac{n\alpha - 2t_c^J - 2mt_m^J - (n-m-1)t_{\tilde{c}}^J}{\lambda + 2n} - t_c^J\right]^2, \end{aligned}$$

while producer surplus is

$$\begin{aligned} PS_c =& \frac{1+\lambda}{2}\left[\frac{n\alpha - 2mt_m^C - 2(n-m-1)t_{\tilde{c}}^C}{\lambda + 2n}\right]^2 \\ &+ \frac{1}{2}\sum_{J\in F}\left[\frac{n\alpha - 2t_c^J - 2(n-m-1)t_{\tilde{c}}^J}{\lambda + 2n} + t_c^J\right]^2 \\ &+ \frac{1}{2}\sum_{J\notin F, J\neq c}\left[\frac{n\alpha - 2t_c^J - 2mt_m^J - (n-m-1)t_{\tilde{c}}^J}{\lambda + 2n} + t_c^J\right]^2. \end{aligned}$$

Furthermore, tariff revenue equals

$$\begin{aligned} TR_c =& \frac{\sum_{J\in F} t_c^J\left[\alpha\lambda - 2\lambda t_c^J - 4(n-1)t_c^J + 4(n-m-1)t_{\tilde{c}}^J\right]}{\lambda + 2n} \\ &+ \frac{\sum_{J\notin F, J\neq C} t_c^J\left[\alpha\lambda - 2\lambda t_c^J - 4(n-1)t_c^J + 4mt_m^J + 4(n-m-2)t_{\tilde{c}}^J\right]}{\lambda + 2n}. \end{aligned}$$

Under optimal tariffs, the export supply elasticity ε_c^Z is found as

$$\varepsilon_c^Z = \frac{n\lambda + 2[n(n-1) + m]}{\lambda}. \tag{A1}$$

Note that the intensive margin is internalized with optimal tariffs and only extensive margin appears in capturing the preferential export share. The formation of an FTA raises ε_c^Z relative to no agreement and it rises more as the FTA has more members (as the preferential export share rises): $\partial\varepsilon_c^{g_z}/\partial m > 0$. Country c's optimum external tariff on good Z is found as follows:

$$t_c^Z = \frac{\alpha\lambda}{(\lambda + 2n)^2 - 4(n-m)}. \tag{A2}$$

Consistent with the export supply elasticity discussion, we find that nonmember countries impose lower tariffs with the formation of an FTA and as the size of the FTA expands (i.e., as the preferential export share of a typical FTA member rises), the result gets stronger: $\partial t_c^Z/\partial m < 0$.

Appendix B: General Demand and Supply

In this section, we examine whether the results obtained under a linear demand and supply framework extend to a more general setting. To this end, we make two fairly unobjectionable assumptions: (i) import demand functions are negatively sloped while export supply functions are positively sloped; (ii) there exist at least one member country exporting good z while at least one other member country and one nonmember country (country c) importing good Z. At a given world price, the formation of an FTA increases the preferential export shares of member countries while simultaneously reducing their export supply to all importing nonmember countries. As a result, FTA formation leads to a decrease in $x_{zc}^Z(p_z^Z)$, shifting it parallel leftward and the equilibrium world price of good Z rises while the equilibrium exports of good Z to country c fall.[25] Note that the larger the volume of preferential trade among FTA members relative to the rest of the world, the greater the magnitude of the leftward shift of $x_{zc}^Z(p_z^Z)$.

The following result, confirms that the main findings of our theoretical model hold under a fairly general setting.

PROPOSITION 2: *Suppose that the (inverse) export supply function $p_z^Z(x_{zc}^Z)$ is log-concave.*[26] *Then the following holds: (i) the formation of an FTA raises ε_c^Z,*

[25] The same results would obtain even when the shift is nonparallel as long as there is a greater magnitude of shift at higher prices.

[26] Note from its definition that $p_z^{g_z}(x_{zc}^{g_z})$ is log-concave if and only if $\frac{d^2 \log p_z^{g_z}(x_{zc}^{g_z})}{dx_{zc}^{g_z 2}} < 0$ holds. This condition implies that $\frac{dp_z^{g_z}(x_{zc}^{g_z})}{dx_{zc}^{g_z}} \frac{1}{p_z^{g_z}}$ falls as $x_{zc}^{g_z}$ rises, or we can rearrange and argue that $\frac{dx_{zc}^{g_z}}{dp_z^{g_z}(x_{zc}^{g_z})} p_z^{g_z}$ rises as $x_{zc}^{g_z}$ rises. It is important to note that log-concavity of the inverse export supply function is the sufficient but not the necessary condition for our result.

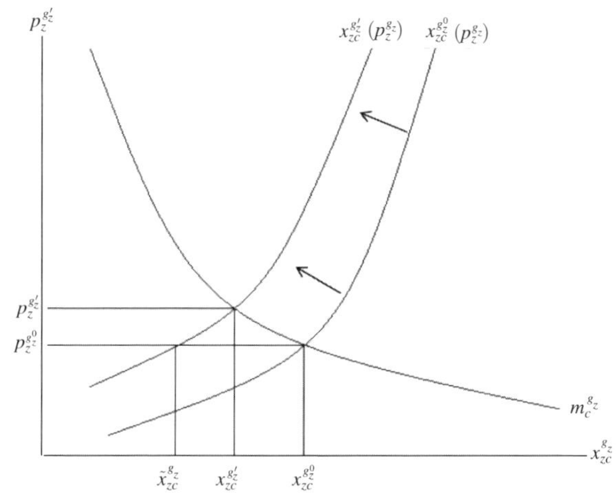

FIGURE B1. FTA FORMATION AND LOG CONCAVE EXPORT SUPPLY

which in turn leads to a reduction in the optimal tariff t_c^Z of a typical nonmember country (i.e., country c), and (ii) the larger the increase in the volume of preferential trade among FTA members relative to the rest of the world, the larger is the reduction in the tariffs of nonmember countries.

As mentioned above, following the formation of an FTA, the export supply curve of country z, i.e., $x_{zc}^{Z^0}(p_z^Z)$, shifts parallel leftward to $x_{zc}^{Z'}(p_z^Z)$. As represented in Appendix Figure B1, at the original equilibrium price $p_z^{Z^0}$, the outputs supplied are $x_{zc}^{Z^0}$ and $\tilde{x}_{zc}^{g_z}$ along the supply curves $x_{zc}^{Z^0}(p_z^Z)$ and $x_{zc}^{Z'}(p_z^Z)$, respectively.[27] Note that we have the same slope at $p_z^{Z^0}$ along both $x_{zc}^{Z^0}(p_z^Z)$ and $x_{zc}^{Z'}(p_z^Z)$ and thus $\frac{dx_{zc}^Z}{dp_z^Z(x_{zc}^Z)}\,p_z^Z$ is the same at both $x_{zc}^{Z^0}$ and $\tilde{x}_{zc}^Z$. Furthermore, the new equilibrium quantity of exports $(x_{zc}^{Z'})$ is smaller relative to the original $(x_{zc}^{Z^0})$: $x_{zc}^{Z'} < x_{zc}^{Z^0}$. Since the inverse export supply function is log-concave, moving from $\tilde{x}_{zc}^Z$ to new equilibrium export supplied $x_{zc}^{Z'}$, $\frac{dx_{zc}^Z}{dp_z^Z(x_{zc}^Z)}\,p_z^Z$ rises. As a result, the export supply elasticity at $x_{zc}^{Z'}$ is larger than that at $x_{zc}^{Z^0}$ which in turn induces the nonmember country c to reduce its optimal tariff t_c^Z. Finally, the larger the increase in the volume of preferential trade among FTA members relative to the rest of the world, the greater the magnitude of the leftward shift in the export supply curve $x_{zc}^{Z^0}(p_z^Z)$ of member country z and the larger the increase in the export supply elasticity facing nonmembers.

[27] Note that when the inverse export supply function is concave or linear, log-concavity always holds. Therefore, we represent only the case of strictly convex inverse export supply in our figure.

Appendix C: Cooperative Tariff Setting

In this section, we demonstrate that Proposition 1 continues to hold even when countries do not set their tariffs noncooperatively. Let $\mu \in [0, 1]$ denote the weight each country assigns to the welfare of other countries in setting its optimal tariffs under any trade policy regime, where μ captures the degree of cooperation across countries. The case where countries set tariffs noncooperatively arises when $\mu = 0$ while $\mu = 1$ captures full cooperation in tariff setting. The latter case of complete cooperation is uninteresting because when $\mu = 1$, countries fully internalize the effect of their trade policies on their trade partners, and the optimal tariff of every country is equal to zero under any trade regime. In such a situation, there is no need for trade agreements and FTAs would simply not arise. Thus, in what follows, we assume that $\mu \in [0, 1)$.

Focusing on the response of nonmember countries' tariffs to formation of FTA of size *m*, we can calculate the tariff reduction implemented by nonmember country *c* as

$$\Delta t_c^Z(\mu) = -\frac{2(1-\mu)\alpha\lambda(m-1)[\alpha\lambda + 2[1+(n-1)\mu]]}{[(\lambda+2n)^2 - 2(n-1)[2(n-1)\mu + \mu\lambda + 2]][(\lambda+2n)^2 - 2(n-m)[2(n-1)\mu + \mu\lambda + 2]]}.$$

Note that $\Delta t_c^Z(\mu) < 0$ for all $\mu \in [0, 1)$. This implies that FTAs reduce export supply elasticities for nonmember countries, inducing them to lower tariffs even when countries act cooperatively. Therefore, our main result in Proposition 1 fully extends into the cooperative tariff setting and holds for all levels of cooperation.[28]

Appendix D: Relationship between Changes in Export Supply Elasticities and Preferential Export Shares

In the main text, we emphasize one key assumption required for the identification of the effect of FTAs on import tariffs of excluded countries using explanatory variables (29) and instruments (31) in the model (28). Specifically, the variation in the trade-weighted average of the preferential export share of a country's trade partners should reflect the variation in the export supply elasticity. In this Appendix, we provide some evidence in support of this assumption. We do so by estimating export supply elasticities for every country-industry pair in our sample for two time periods and relating the change in the elasticity to the observed change in preferential export shares of a country's average trade partner.

We use the approach of Feenstra (1994) and its extension by Broda and Weinstein (2006) to separately identify import demand and export supply elasticities. The

[28] In fact, we can go one step further and argue that, when the extent of tariff cooperation is not too large, an increase in the degree of cooperation leads to a greater reduction in tariff of nonmember countries:

$$\frac{\partial|\Delta t_c^Z(\mu)|}{\partial\mu} > 0 \quad \text{when} \quad \mu < \bar{\mu},$$

where $\frac{\partial\bar{\mu}}{\partial n} > 0$ and $\frac{\partial\bar{\mu}}{\partial m} < 0$.

presentation here draws heavily on the treatment in Broda and Weinstein (2006), which can be used for a more detailed reference. The approach is based on the following parametrization of the system of import demand and export supply equations:

(D1)
$$x_{civt} = \left(\frac{p_{civt}}{\phi_{it}}\right)^{1-\sigma_{ci}} \frac{d_{civt}E_{ct}}{p_{civt}};$$
$$p_{civt} = \exp(\upsilon_{civt})x_{civt}^{\omega_{ci}},$$

where x_{civt} in the first equation is the demand for variety v of good i consumed in country c in year t derived from the CES utility function, which depends on the price (p_{civt}), aggregate income (E_{ct}), the elasticity of substitution between varieties of good i (σ_{ci}), price index for good i (ϕ_{it}), and the random taste parameter (d_{civt}). The export supply function depends on the inverse export supply elasticity (ω_{ci}) and the random technology factor (υ_{civt}) assumed to be independent of d_{civt}. Rewriting quantities in (D1) in terms of market shares, taking logs, and time differencing yields

$$\Delta \ln s_{civt} = \varphi_{it} - (\sigma_{ci} - 1)\Delta \ln p_{civt} + u_{civt};$$
$$\Delta \ln p_{civt} = \omega_{ci}\Delta \ln x_{civt} + \delta_{civt},$$

where $\varphi_{it} = (\sigma_{ci} - 1)\ln[\phi_{it}/\phi_{it-1}]$. In order to eliminate this good-specific unobservable term from the demand equation, both equation are differences with respect to a reference country k. Using superscript k to denote the reference difference operator, the system becomes

(D2)
$$\Delta^k \ln s_{civt} = -(\sigma_{ci} - 1)\Delta^k \ln p_{civt} + u_{civt}^k;$$
$$\Delta^k \ln p_{civt} = \omega_{ci}\Delta^k \ln x_{civt} + \delta_{civt}^k.$$

Solving for the error terms in (D2) and multiplying them through, we obtain

(D3)
$$Y_{civt} = \theta_{1ci}X_{1civt} + \theta_{2ci}X_{2civt} + u_{civt},$$

$$Y_{civt} = (\Delta^k \ln p_{civt})^2, \quad X_{1civt} = (\Delta^k \ln s_{civt})^2, \quad X_{2civt} = (\Delta^k \ln p_{civt})(\Delta^k \ln s_{civt}),$$

$$u_{civt} = \frac{u_{civt}^k \delta_{civt}^k}{(1 - \rho_{ci})}, \quad \rho_{ci} = \frac{\omega_{ci}(\sigma_{ci} - 1)}{1 + \omega_{ci}\sigma_{ci}}.$$

Feenstra (1994) demonstrates that equation (D3) estimated with the 2SLS for every country and industry using indicator variables for varieties as instruments will

TABLE D1—RELATIONSHIP BETWEEN CHANGES IN THE EXPORT ELASTICITIES AND CHANGES IN PREFERENTIAL EXPORT SHARES

Dependent variable: Change in the average partner's preferential export share between 1988–2001 and 2002–2011 for						
	All FTAs			FTAs formed in 2001–2002		
	(1)	(2)	(3)	(4)	(5)	(6)
Δ Inverse exp. elast.	−0.038 (0.017)	−0.037 (0.017)	−0.027 (0.012)	−0.006 (0.002)	−0.008 (0.002)	−0.006 (0.002)
Industry fixed effects	No	Yes	Yes	No	Yes	Yes
Country fixed effects	No	No	Yes	No	No	Yes
R^2	0.001	0.137	0.320	0.001	0.090	0.254
Observations	4,785	4,785	4,785	4,785	4,785	4,785

Note: Standard errors are clustered by country.

produce consistent estimates of θ_{1ci} and θ_{2ci}. This estimates, $\hat{\theta}_{1ci}$ and $\hat{\theta}_{2ci}$, can be used to calculate elasticity parameters from

$$\text{(D4)} \qquad \hat{\theta}_{1ci} = \frac{\hat{\omega}_{ci}}{(1+\hat{\omega}_{ci})(\hat{\sigma}_{ci}-1)};$$

$$\hat{\theta}_{2ci} = \frac{\hat{\omega}_{ci}(\hat{\sigma}_{ci}-2)-1}{(1+\hat{\omega}_{ci})(\hat{\sigma}_{ci}-1)}.$$

The identification of import demand and export supply elasticities in Feenstra (1994) rests on a number of strong assumptions which make it impossible to use them directly in our work. Most importantly for this study, the estimator is asymptotically consistent as the number of time periods approaches infinity. Therefore, changes in the elasticities cannot be obtained for every country-industry-year observation in our sample and are proxied by changes in preferential export shares. In order to assess the quality of this proxy we need to obtain a measure of a change in the export supply elasticity that can be related to changes in preferential export shares. We thus proceed by estimating export supply elasticity ω_{ci} for every country-industry pair in two time periods, 1988–2001 and 2002–2011. Denoting the two periods with T_1 and T_2, we then calculate the change in the average preferential export share between the two periods and regress it on the change in the inverse export supply elasticity:[29]

$$\text{(D5)} \qquad \Delta\overline{PXS}_{ci} = \beta_0 + \beta_1 \Delta\omega_{ci} + e_{ci};$$

$$\overline{PXS}_{ciT_k} = \left(\frac{1}{T_k}\sum_{p} imp\_share_{cpi} \cdot \sum_{t\in T_k} \Delta PXS_{pit}\right), \quad k = 1,2;$$

$$\Delta\overline{PXS}_{ci} = \overline{PXS}_{ciT_2} - \overline{PXS}_{ciT_1}, \quad \Delta\omega_{ci} = \omega_{ciT_2} - \omega_{ciT_1}.$$

[29] In this regression, we use only observations with $\hat{\theta}_{1ci} > 0$. We also drop 1 percent of the observations with the highest and the lowest changes in ω_{ci} in order to minimize the effect of outliers.

Table D1 presents estimation results for equation (D4). The coefficient in column 1 is negative and statistically significant at the 5 percent confidence level. This result implies that, as the theory predicts, a reduction in the inverse export supply elasticity (increase in the level of the export supply elasticity) is associated with an increase in the preferential export share of a country's trade partners. Adding industry fixed effects in column 2 to control for industry-specific trends in preferential trade shares does not affect the results. Column 3 includes country fixed effects to control for country-year specific characteristics, such as size and the general structure of trade. Results are broadly similar to the basic specification. Finally, in columns 4–6, we reestimate equation (D4) using only FTAs formed in 2001–2002 in construction of the dependent variable. These are the FTAs that do not affect the estimate of ω_{ci} in period T_1 and have potentially the strongest impact on ω_{ci} in period T_2. Although the coefficient β_1 is smaller than in columns 1–3, it becomes statistically significant at 1 percent confidence level.[30]

While the above evidence is consistent with our assumption that changes in preferential export shares reflect changes in the export supply elasticities, these results should be treated with caution. The average number of time periods in the two subsamples are 6.4 and 7.1, respectively, and the estimates of ω_{ciT_2} and ω_{ciT_1} may not be very precise. Indeed, Soderbery (2010) show that in samples of that size the estimates of the export supply elasticity are biased upward by more than 60 percent.

REFERENCES

Anderson, James E., and Eric van Wincoop. 2003. "Gravity with Gravitas: A Solution to the Border Puzzle." *American Economic Review* 93 (1): 170–92.

Anderson, James E., and Yoto V. Yotov. 2016. "Terms of trade and global efficiency effects of free trade agreements, 1990–2002." *Journal of International Economics* 99: 279–98.

Angrist, Joshua D., and Jörn-Steffen Pischke. 2009. *Mostly Harmless Econometrics: An Empiricist's Companion.* Princeton: Princeton University Press.

Bagwell, Kyle, and Robert W. Staiger. 1990. "A Theory of Managed Trade." *American Economic Review* 80 (4): 779–95.

Bagwell, Kyle, and Robert W. Staiger. 1997. "Multilateral Tariff Cooperation during the Formation of Free Trade Areas." *American Economic Review* 38 (2): 291–319.

Bagwell, Kyle, and Robert W. Staiger. 2011. "What Do Trade Negotiators Negotiate About? Empirical Evidence from the World Trade Organization." *American Economic Review* 101 (4): 1238–73.

Bagwell, Kyle, and Robert W. Staiger. 1999. "Regionalism and Multilateral Tariff Co-operation." In *International Trade Policy and the Pacific Rim*, edited by John Piggott and Alan Woodland, 157–85. London: Macmillan.

Baier, Scott L., and Jeffrey H. Bergstrand. 2004. "Economic determinants of free trade agreements." *Journal of International Economics* 64 (1): 29–63.

Baier, Scott L., and Jeffrey H. Bergstrand. 2007. "Do free trade agreements actually increase members' international trade?" *Journal of International Economics* 71 (1): 72–95.

Bohara, Alok K., Kishore Gawande, and Pablo Sanguinetti. 2004. "Trade diversion and declining tariffs: Evidence from Mercosur." *Journal of International Economics* 64 (1): 65–88.

Bown, Chad P., and Meredith A. Crowley. 2013. "Self-Enforcing Trade Agreements: Evidence from Time-Varying Trade Policy." *American Economic Review* 103 (2): 1071–90.

Broda, Christian, Nuno Limão, and David E. Weinstein. 2008. "Optimal Tariffs and Market Power: The Evidence." *American Economic Review* 98 (5): 2032–65.

[30] The variation in $\Delta\overline{PXS}_{ci}$ in columns 4–6 is only one-sixth of that in columns 1–3. For both dependent variables the change in ω_{ci} explains the same share of variation.

▶**Broda, Christian, and David E. Weinstein.** 2006. "Globalization and the Gains from Variety." *Quarterly Journal of Economics* 121 (2): 541–85.

Calvo-Pardo, Hector, Caroline Freund, and Emanuel Ornelas. 2009. "The ASEAN Free Trade Agreement: Impact on Trade Flows and External Trade Barriers." Centre for Economic Performance (CEP) Discussion Paper dp0930.

▶**Chang, Won, and L. Alan Winters.** 2002. "How Regional Blocs Affect Excluded Countries: The Price Effects of MERCOSUR." *American Economic Review* 92 (4): 889–904.

▶**Crivelli, Pramila.** 2016. "Regionalism and falling external protection in high and low tariff members." *Journal of International Economics* 102: 70–84.

▶**Do, Quy-Toan, and Andrei A. Levchenko.** 2007. "Comparative advantage, demand for external finance, and financial development." *Journal of Financial Economics* 86 (3): 796–834.

▶**Estevadeordal, Antoni, Caroline Freund, and Emanuel Ornelas.** 2008. "Does Regionalism Affect Trade Liberalization toward Nonmembers?" *Quarterly Journal of Economics* 123 (4): 1531–75.

Feenstra, Robert C. 1994. "New Product Varieties and the Measurement of International Prices." *American Economic Review* 84 (1): 157–77.

Feenstra, Robert C. 2004. *Advanced International Trade: Theory and Evidence*. Princeton: Princeton University Press.

▶**Frankel, Jeffrey A., and David H. Romer.** 1999. "Does Trade Cause Growth?" *American Economic Review* 89 (3): 379–99.

▶**Horn, Henrik, Giovanni Maggi, and Robert W. Staiger.** 2010. "Trade Agreements as Endogenously Incomplete Contracts." *American Economic Review* 100 (1): 394–419.

▶**Krishna, Pravin.** 1998. "Regionalism And Multilateralism: A Political Economy Approach." *Quarterly Journal of Economics* 113 (1): 227–51.

Limão, Nuno. 2016. "Preferential Trade Agreements." National Bureau of Economic Research (NBER) Working Paper 22138.

▶**Ludema, Rodney D., and Anna Maria Mayda.** 2013. "Do terms-of-trade effects matter for trade agreements? Theory and evidence from WTO Countries." *Quarterly Journal of Economics* 128 (4): 1837–93.

Maggi, Giovanni. 2014. "International Trade Agreements." In *Handbook of International Economics*, Vol. 4, edited by Gita Gopinath, Elhanan Helpman, and Kenneth Rogoff, 317–90. Amsterdam: North-Holland.

▶**Mai, Joseph, and Andrey Stoyanov.** 2015. "The effect of the Canada-US Free Trade Agreement on Canadian multilateral trade liberalization." *Canadian Journal of Economics* 48 (3): 1067–98.

▶**Missios, Paul, Kamal Saggi, and Halis Murat Yildiz.** 2016. "External trade diversion, exclusion incentives and the nature of preferential trade agreements." *Journal of International Economics* 99: 105–19.

▶**Saggi, Kamal, and Halis Murat Yildiz.** 2010. "Bilateralism, multilateralism, and the quest for global free trade." *Journal of International Economics* 81 (1): 26–37.

Saggi, Kamal, Andrey Stoyanov, and Halis Murat Yildiz. 2018. "Do Free Trade Agreements Affect Tariffs of Nonmember Countries? A Theoretical and Empirical Investigation: Dataset." *American Economic Journal: Applied Economics*. https://doi.org/10.1257/app.20150360.

▶**Silva, J. M. C. Santos, and Silvana Tenreyro.** 2006. "The Log of Gravity." *Review of Economics and Statistics* 88 (4): 641–58.

▶**Soderbery, Anson.** 2010. "Investigating the asymptotic properties of import elasticity estimates." *Economics Letters* 109 (2): 57–62.

▶**Staiger, Douglas, and James H. Stock.** 1997. "Instrumental Variables Regression with Weak Instruments." *Econometrica* 65 (3): 557–86.

▶**Stoyanov, Andrey, and Halis Murat Yildiz.** 2015. "Preferential versus multilateral trade liberalization and the role of political economy." *European Economic Review* 80: 140–64.

PART III

SUSTAINING INTERNATIONAL TARIFF COOPERATION

CHAPTER 12

ELSEVIER

Journal of Development Economics 83 (2007) 141–156

JOURNAL OF Development ECONOMICS

www.elsevier.com/locate/econbase

Tariff bindings and bilateral cooperation on export cartels

Bernard Hoekman [a,*], Kamal Saggi [b,1]

[a] *The World Bank, 1818 H Street, N.W., Washington, DC 20433, USA*

[b] *Department of Economics, Southern Methodist University, Dallas, TX 75275-0496, USA*

Received 17 August 2004; received in revised form 12 January 2006; accepted 13 January 2006

Abstract

Despite the negative international externalities that they generate, export cartels are legal in many countries. We use a repeated game approach to analyze cooperation between a low-income country (LIC) and its high-income country (HIC) trade partner where the HIC agrees to prevent its industry from organizing as an export cartel in return for a combination of improved market access (i.e. a tariff reduction) and a transfer from the LIC. If the LIC is subject to a tariff binding (say because of an existing trade agreement), the transfer it pays to the HIC increases and the scope for bilateral cooperation declines.

JEL classification: F1; L4; O1
Keywords: Tariff bindings; Trade agreements; Export cartels; Oligopoly; Economic development; Issue linkage

1. Introduction

During the 1990s, both the European Union (EU) and the United States (US) investigated a number of cartels in products such as vitamins, steel, and animal feeds.[2] Many such international cartels were found to be illegal and fined by the relevant competition authorities because of their detrimental effects on *domestic* consumers in the investigating jurisdictions. However, such fines

* Corresponding author. Tel.: +1 202 473 1185; fax: +1 202 676 9810.
E-mail addresses: bhoekman@worldbank.org (B. Hoekman), ksaggi@smu.edu (K. Saggi).
[1] Tel.: +1 214 768 3274; fax: +1 214 768 1821.

[2] International cartel-type arrangements also exist in air and maritime transport services (Francois and Wooton, 2001). Fink et al. (2002) estimate that restrictive trade and anti-competitive practices raise maritime liner transport costs by up to $3 billion on goods carried to the US.

0304-3878/$ - see front matter
doi:10.1016/j.jdeveco.2006.01.003

failed to account for the global nature of the cartels in question. For example, according to Levenstein, Oswald, and Suslow (2002), in 1997 developing countries imported US $36.4 billion worth of goods that had been subject to a price-fixing conspiracy during the 1990s. These imports equaled 2.9% of their total imports and 0.7% of their gross domestic product. Even so, national competition laws in most countries explicitly permit collusion in export markets. In fact, the legal status of export cartels constitutes a national policy whose *sole purpose* is to benefit local firms at the expense of foreign consumers.[3]

Two recent antitrust cases illustrate the difficulties of seeking recourse against anti-competitive behavior by firms when the adverse effects of such behavior are international in nature. The first case concerned maritime transport services between the EU and West Africa, which operates under a so-called block exemption from EU antitrust rules.[4] The exemption is premised on the argument that price-fixing and supply regulation stabilize freight rates and assure shippers of reliable maritime transport services. In this case, the European Commission found that behavior of shippers constituted an abuse of market power and harmed EU consumers/shippers. More interestingly, the fact that African buyers were also injured was *not* considered relevant—the EU competition law focuses squarely on effects in and on the EU, not on foreign buyers and consumers. Thus, to bring an antitrust case against EU firms one would need to prove that their anti-competitive behavior negatively affects EU interests, something that might be difficult to achieve for small developing countries.

Consider now the more well known case F. Hoffmann-LaRoche Ltd. versus Empagran S.A that involved US vitamin producers. This case revolved around a claim by purchasers of vitamin products from Ukraine, Australia, Panama, and Ecuador that they were harmed by the inflated prices charged by Hoffman-LaRoche and other chemical firms. It is noteworthy that these firms operated a global price fixing cartel and had *already* been subjected to large fines by both the US and the EU. However, these fines were based on the respective *domestic harm* incurred by the EU and US, and *not the global effects* of the cartel. The foreign plaintiffs sought treble damages under US law. The case ended before the Supreme Court in 2004 and the Court held that antitrust claims based entirely on "independent foreign harm" were not covered by US antitrust statutes (Supreme Court, 2004).[5] The implication is that foreign plaintiffs cannot bring a case in the US based solely on "independent" foreign injury. To do so, they would need to establish a link *between foreign anti-competitive behavior and adverse effects in the US market*.

One might suppose that developing countries should be able to use their own antitrust law to combat foreign export cartels. However, few (if any) developing countries can break up an international cartel, even if they have the capacity to discover and document collusive behavior. Thus, it is worth knowing whether international cooperation can help alleviate some of the spillovers generated by international cartels. Accordingly, this paper investigates the idea that developed countries should prohibit their firms from colluding and raising prices in developing countries (see Hoekman and Mavroidis, 2003; Stiglitz and Charlton, 2005). Of course, such a course of action is unlikely to be adopted unilaterally by developed countries. So the question becomes: what can developing countries do to induce developed countries to implement such a

[3] See Bhattacharjea (2004) for a comprehensive survey of the literature on export cartels, how they are exempted in national competition laws, arguments for and against such exemptions, and recent antitrust cases involving them.

[4] See French–West African liner shipping, OJ 1992 L 134/1, and UKWAL, OJ 1992, L 121/45.

[5] The relevant law, the Federal Trade Improvement Antitrust Act (FTAIA) of 1982 (15 U. S. C. § 6a) states that US antirust only applies to foreign conduct if it has (i) a direct, substantial, and reasonably foreseeable effect on the US domestic market (including imports and exports), and (ii) such effect gives rise to a claim under the US antirust law (the Sherman Act).

policy? More specifically, is a bargain linking market access commitments (such as tariff reductions) and transfers by developing countries in return for antitrust enforcement (i.e. a ban on export cartels) by developed ones feasible? Building on the work of Auquier and Caves (1979) and Brander and Spencer (1984), we develop a two-country model to address this question.[6]

In the model, a low-income country (LIC) that does not have the capacity to enforce national antitrust law against foreign exporters from a high-income country (HIC) is confronted with the possibility of cartelization by those exporters. Using a repeated game approach, we focus on the incentives the LIC has to offer a tariff reduction and a transfer in exchange for the prohibition of an export cartel by the HIC.[7] In addition, we compare this scenario with a situation where the LIC's use of trade policy is constrained due to prior international commitments–such as membership in bilateral free trade agreements or in the World Trade Organization (WTO)–that either preclude tariffs above some bound level or require its tariff to be set at zero.

We show that the use of two instruments (i.e. a tariff and a transfer) maximizes the scope for bilateral cooperation and that the required transfer is lower if the LIC has the ability to limit access to its market via a tariff. Thus, taking away the LIC's ability to punish cartelization via a tariff increase–a direct consequence of a tariff binding–not only makes it less likely that the globally efficient outcome is realized, but it also increases the 'price' that must be paid by the LIC to 'purchase' antitrust enforcement from the HIC.

The paper is organized as follows. Section 2 presents the one shot policy game. Section 3 considers the benchmark repeated game when the LIC can use both tariffs and transfers to sustain cooperation. Section 4 studies the impact of a tariff binding on the scope for bilateral cooperation. Section 5 shows that our analysis is applicable even when firms compete in prices. Section 6 concludes.

2. Basic model

Consider a two-country world comprised of a high-income country (indexed by subscript H and referred to as the HIC) and a low-income country (indexed by subscript L and referred to as the LIC). There are two goods (x and y) and preferences in the LIC over these goods are quasi-linear. Good y is the numeraire and it is produced under perfect competition with constant returns to scale technology in both countries.

There are n firms that produce good x in the HIC, where $n \geq 2$. The marginal cost of production of each firm is set to zero for expositional ease. To focus on the "pure" case for cooperation on the basis of consumer welfare, we assume that good x is consumed only in the LIC and produced only by the HIC.[8] Ruling out domestic production of good x in the LIC allows us to ignore protectionist and strategic motives for the use of a tariff.[9] With regards to local

---

[6] Despite their practical importance, export cartels have not received much attention in the rather large literature on trade and competition policy (see Dixit, 1984; Horn and Levinsohn, 2001; Bagwell and Staiger, 2001; Richardson, 1999, for prominent examples).

[7] Our model abstracts from domestic policies that may help sustain cooperation. Ederington (2002) analyses linkages between domestic and trade polices in the context of self-enforcing trade agreements. See also Bagwell and Staiger (2001).

[8] Note that the HIC has an incentive to employ an export tax and that such a tax acts as a substitute for cartelization. Since at present there are exist no multilateral disciplines on export taxes, any agreement involving a ban on export cartels would need to be complemented by a ban on export taxes or else it could be easily undermined.

[9] The assumption also implies the LIC may have no incentive to create a domestic antitrust agency.

consumption in the HIC, Auquier and Caves (1979) have noted that the cartelization of an export industry might not raise domestic welfare if the cartel also raises prices at home. However, antitrust laws in many developed countries (such as the United States) permit local firms to form export cartels only if they do *not* raise prices at home. In our model, if the HIC were to enforce such a condition on its export cartel, allowing for consumption of good x in the HIC would not alter our analysis.

Let t denote the specific import tariff imposed by the LIC on good x. We assume that firms are organized enough to successfully cartelize production so long as the HIC permits them to do so. Also, the LIC is assumed to lack the institutional capacity needed to prevent the HIC's export cartel from charging high prices. In effect, the import tariff is the only instrument through which the LIC can effectively reduce the benefits of cartelization to the HIC (if it finds it optimal to do so).

Consider the following two stage policy game. In the first stage, the two countries simultaneously make their policy decisions: the HIC decides whether or not to permit its firms to form an export cartel while the LIC chooses the level of its tariff. Given the policy choices of the two countries, HIC firms decide how much to export and consumption takes place. We next derive the (sub-game perfect) Nash equilibrium of this policy game. To facilitate analytical derivations, assume that $u(X)$ is quadratic so that the (inverse) demand curve for good x in the LIC is given by:

$$p = \alpha - X \tag{1}$$

where X denotes the HIC's total exports of good x.

Suppose n HIC firms export to the LIC at the second stage of the game (where $n=1$ corresponds to the case of a cartel). Firm i's first order condition is given by

$$p + p'\, x_i = t \tag{2}$$

where x_i denotes the output of firm i and $i=1\ldots n$. Since firms are symmetric, in equilibrium, we have $x_i=x$ for all i and $X=nx$.

At the trade policy stage, the LIC chooses its tariff t to maximize its own welfare (defined as the sum of consumer surplus and tariff revenue):

$$\max_t W_{\mathrm{L}}(t) \equiv u(X) - pX + tX \tag{3}$$

Using the consumer optimization condition $u'(X)=p$ and Eq. (1), the first order condition for the above problem can be written as:

$$\frac{\partial W_{\mathrm{L}}}{\partial t} = -\frac{nX(t)}{n+1} + X(t) - \frac{nt}{n+1} = 0 \tag{4}$$

which yields

$$nt = X(t) \tag{5}$$

The above equation defines the optimal LIC tariff t^* and it implies that as long as $X(t^*)>0$ it must be that $t^*>0$. In fact, using Eq. (1), we have:

$$t^* = \frac{\alpha}{n+2} \tag{6}$$

Lemma 1. *The LIC's optimal tariff t^* decreases with the number of competing HIC firms.*

Intuitively, as the mark-up charged by HIC firms shrinks, the LIC's incentive to extract rents also diminishes. Lemma 1 implies that if the HIC were to permit cartelization, the tariff imposed by the LIC would increase thereby partially undermining the effectiveness of the export cartel. Let

$$t^c \equiv t^*(n=1) = \frac{\alpha}{3} \tag{7}$$

be the optimal LIC tariff under cartelization, where $t^c > t^*$ for all $n \neq 1$.

The objective of the HIC is to maximize the total profits of its exporters. Given this, it is immediate that *given* the tariff rate chosen by the LIC, the HIC always permits cartelization. Thus, in equilibrium, HIC firms organize into an export cartel and the LIC imposes the optimal tariff t^c. However, we argue below that this outcome–denoted by the pair $(1, t^c)$–constitutes a Prisoner's dilemma for a large range of parameter values.

As expected, the LIC prefers competition (n, t^*) to cartelization $(1, t^c)$:

$$\frac{\partial W_L(t^*(n), n)}{\partial n} = \frac{\alpha^2}{(n+2)^2} > 0. \tag{8}$$

In other words, the increase in its optimal tariff in response to cartelization is not sufficient to make cartelization more attractive than competition to the LIC. Given the tariff response of the LIC, the HIC prefers competition (n, t^*) to cartelization $(1, t^c)$ iff

$$n\pi(n, t^*) > \pi(1, t^c) \Leftrightarrow n < 4 \tag{9}$$

Proposition 1. *The HIC prefers competition amongst its exporters under the (low) LIC tariff t^* to cartelization of its exporters subject to the high tariff t^c iff $n<4$.*

Proposition 1 says that cartelization subject to the high LIC tariff t^c is not preferred by the HIC iff its market structure is relatively concentrated to begin with. On the other hand, when its market structure is highly competitive, cartelization results in a large increase in profits and is attractive to the HIC even if it is accompanied by the high LIC tariff t^c. Thus, cartelization combined with the tariff t^c is a Prisoner's dilemma whenever $n<4$. Of course, aggregate world welfare under (n, t^*) is always higher relative to $(1, t^c)$. As a result, cooperation between the two countries is desirable.

Before analyzing the scope for such cooperation in a repeated game context, we comment on the timing of decisions in the one shot policy game. If the decision to ban cartels were more long-term in nature relative to the imposition of a tariff, it would be reasonable to allow the HIC to move first.[10] In the sub-game perfect equilibrium of such a sequential game, the HIC would enforce the ban and the LIC would respond via its (low) optimal tariff t^* whenever $n<4$ (whereas in the simultaneous move game, the HIC always permits cartelization). To see this, suppose the HIC were to ban cartelization in the first stage. Then, the LIC would impose the tariff t^* and the payoff to the HIC would equal $n\pi(n, t^*)$. On the other hand, were the HIC to allow cartelization, the LIC's tariff in the next stage would be t^c and the HIC's payoff would be $\pi(1, t^c)$. Given that the HIC has the first move, competition would obtain iff $\pi(1, t^c) < n\pi(n, t^*)t \Leftrightarrow n<4$—in this range, the sequential game delivers a superior outcome than the simultaneous game. However,

[10] We thank the co-editor and an anonymous referee of this journal for this suggestion.

regardless of the order of moves, it remains the case that competition under free trade (i.e. $t=0$) is the efficient outcome and this cannot be obtained in the one-shot policy game. Furthermore, as long as the Nash tariff t^c is used to sustain cooperation over the efficient outcome, the following analysis will continue to apply regardless of whether the one-shot policy game is simultaneous or sequential in nature.

We now explore whether the socially desirable outcome can be sustained under repeated interaction between the two countries.

3. International cooperation

Repeated interaction allows the two countries to cooperate over free trade whereas in the one-shot policy game the lowest (credible) tariff imposed by the LIC is t^*. Since free trade maximizes social welfare, it is natural to examine the scenario where cooperation involves the LIC practising free trade and the HIC forbidding cartelization. In Hoekman and Saggi (2004) we show that while bilateral cooperation can also be sustained when the LIC has access to only a tariff, the use of an additional instrument (i.e. a transfer) enhances the scope for cooperation. Given this result and the fact the LIC has a lot to gain from preventing cartelization, in what follows we assume that it can use both instruments (i.e. a tariff and a per period transfer T). While the transfer can be thought of in financial terms, in practice it will likely involve action or commitments by the LIC in other areas of interest to the HIC.

By assumption, countries sustain cooperation via *trigger strategies*: defection by any country results in a *policy war* where in both countries revert to their Nash equilibrium policies, i.e. the HIC government permits cartelization and the LIC imposes the tariff t^c and stops paying the transfer T. The two instruments available to the LIC play complementary roles: the tariff acts as a *stick* whereas the transfer acts as a *carrot*. We refer to the case where the LIC has access to both a tariff and a transfer as the (t, T) case.

The HIC prohibits cartelization under cooperation and permits it under defection. The per period welfare of the HIC under cooperation equals the sum of industry profits under free trade and the LIC transfer $n\pi(n, 0)+T$ whereas under defection it equals the sum of its export cartel's profit under free trade and the LIC transfer $\pi(1, 0)+T$. Sustained bilateral cooperation requires that the (current) benefit of defection be dominated by the present discounted value of future costs of defection for both countries. Thus, cooperation is incentive compatible for the HIC iff

$$[\pi(1,0) + T] - [n\pi(n,0) + T] \le \frac{\delta}{1-\delta}[n\pi(n,0) + T - \pi(1,t^c)] \tag{10}$$

where δ denotes the discount factor. The above incentive constraint can be written as:

$$T > T_H \equiv \frac{(1-\delta)\pi(1,0) - n\pi(n,0)}{\delta} + \pi(1,t^c) \tag{11}$$

$$= \frac{1-\delta}{\delta}\frac{\alpha^2}{4} - \frac{n\alpha^2}{\delta(n+1)^2} + \frac{\alpha^2}{9} \tag{12}$$

This implies that the HIC requires a positive transfer (i.e. $T_H>0$) iff

$$\delta < \delta_H \equiv \frac{9(n-1)^2}{5(n+1)^2} \tag{13}$$

That is, when the discount factor is sufficiently small, the HIC requires a transfer from the LIC in order to abide by cooperation.

Proposition 2. *Bilateral cooperation over the prohibition of its export cartel in return for free access to the LIC's market and the payment of a per period transfer T from the LIC is acceptable to the HIC iff the LIC's transfer is sufficiently high (i.e. $T \geq T_H$). Furthermore, the minimum transfer required by the HIC to cooperate with the LIC increases as its market structure becomes more competitive (i.e. $\frac{dT_H}{dn} > 0$).*

Now consider the viewpoint of the LIC. Let X^0 denote total output sold in the LIC under free trade and competition and p^0 the associated price: $X^0 \equiv X(n,0)$ and $p^0 \equiv p(X^0)$. The LIC's per period welfare under cooperation (gross of the transfer T) equals:

$$W_L^0 \equiv u(X^0) - p^0 X^0 \tag{14}$$

Let (p^*, X^*) denote the price quantity pair under competition and the optimal LIC tariff t^*. The LIC's welfare under defection equals the sum of consumer surplus and tariff revenue under the pair (p^*, X^*) and its optimal tariff t^*:

$$W_L^D \equiv u(X^*) - p^* X^* + t^* X^* \tag{15}$$

Let the pair (p^c, X^c) denote the price quantity pair under the policy war, where $X^c \equiv X(1, t^c)$ and $p^c \equiv p(X^c)$. The LIC's welfare under the policy war equals

$$W_L^W \equiv u(X^c) - p^c X^c + t^c X^c \tag{16}$$

Cooperation is incentive compatible for the LIC iff

$$W_L^D - \left[W_L^0 - T\right] \leq \frac{\delta\left(W_L^0 - T - W_L^W\right)}{1-\delta} \Leftrightarrow (1-\delta) W_L^D + \delta W_L^W \leq W_L^0 - T \tag{17}$$

This can be rewritten as

$$T \leq T_L \equiv W_L^0 - (1-\delta) W_L^D - \delta W_L^W \tag{18}$$

$$= \frac{n^2 \alpha^2}{2(n+1)^2} - \frac{(1-\delta) n \alpha^2}{2n+4} - \frac{\delta \alpha^2}{6} \tag{19}$$

This implies that the LIC is willing to pay a transfer (i.e. $T_L > 0$) iff

$$T_L > 0 \Leftrightarrow \delta > \delta_L \equiv \frac{3n}{2(n-1)(n+1)^2} \tag{20}$$

Proposition 3. *Bilateral cooperation over prohibition of the HIC's export cartel in return for the payment of a per period transfer T and free access to its market is acceptable to the LIC iff $T \leq T_L$. Furthermore, the maximum transfer the LIC is willing to pay increases as the HIC's market structure becomes more competitive (i.e. $\frac{dT_L}{dn} > 0$).*

Propositions 2 and 3 together imply that the LIC is willing to cooperate so long as the transfer paid to the HIC falls below the critical threshold T_L whereas the HIC is willing to cooperate iff the transfer paid by the LIC exceeds the critical threshold T_H. Thus, bilateral cooperation occurs over the range $T_H \leq T \leq T_L$.

Up to this point we have assumed that the LIC is completely free to restrict access to its market via a tariff both when it deviates from cooperation itself and when it punishes the HIC for doing so. The ad-valorem equivalent of the optimal specific tariff t^* evaluated in terms of the tariff ridden price $p(t^*)$ equals

$$\frac{t^*}{p(t^*)} = \frac{t^*}{\alpha + nt^*} = \frac{\alpha(n+1)}{\alpha(n+2)+n\alpha} = \frac{\alpha(n+1)}{2\alpha(n+1)} = 50\% \tag{21}$$

Since an ad-valorem tariff of 50% may not be always feasible given WTO tariff bindings or due to a bilateral free trade agreement with the HIC, in the next section we consider how a tariff binding affects the scope for international cooperation.

4. Effects of a tariff binding

Denote the maximum tariff that the LIC can impose by $\bar{t}$ where $0 \leq \bar{t} < t^*$. The one shot policy game under a tariff binding is modified in only one way. At the second stage, regardless of the number of HIC firms, the LIC always imposes the tariff $\bar{t}$. The main question we address below is how a tariff binding alters the incentives for cooperation of both countries.

Let $(\bar{p}, \bar{X})$ denote the price quantity pair under competition and the constrained LIC tariff $\bar{t}$. The LIC's welfare under defection equals the sum of consumer surplus and tariff revenue under the pair $(\bar{p}, \bar{X})$ and the tariff $\bar{t}$:

$$W_{\rm L}^{\rm D}(\bar{t}) \equiv u(\bar{X}) - \bar{p}\bar{X} + \bar{t}\bar{X} \tag{22}$$

Let the pair $(p^{\rm c}(\bar{t}), X^{\rm c}(\bar{t}))$ denote the price quantity pair under the policy war subject to the tariff binding $\bar{t}$, where $X^{\rm c}(\bar{t}) \equiv X(1, \bar{t})$ and $p^{\rm c}(\bar{t}) \equiv p(X^{\rm c}(\bar{t}))$. The LIC's welfare under a policy war equals

$$W_{\rm L}^{\rm W}(\bar{t}) \equiv u(X^{\rm c}(\bar{t})) - p^{\rm c}(\bar{t})X^{\rm c}(\bar{t}) + \bar{t}X^{\rm c}(\bar{t}) \tag{23}$$

As before, the LIC is willing to cooperate iff

$$T \leq T_{\rm L}(\bar{t}) \equiv W_{\rm L}^0 - (1-\delta)W_{\rm L}^{\rm D}(\bar{t}) - \delta W_{\rm L}^{\rm W}(\bar{t}) \tag{24}$$

Since $\bar{t}$ is less than the *optimal* LIC tariff t^*, it follows that the LIC's welfare under a policy war as well as that under a unilateral defection is lower at $\bar{t}$ relative to t^*: $W_{\rm L}^{\rm D}(\bar{t}) < W_{\rm L}^{\rm D}$ and $W_{\rm L}^{\rm W}(\bar{t}) < W_{\rm L}^{\rm W}$. From Eqs. (18) and (24), it immediately follows that $T_{\rm L}(\bar{t}) > T_{\rm L}$—a tariff binding that does not permit the LIC to impose its optimal tariff t^* *increases* the transfer the LIC is willing to pay to sustain bilateral cooperation.[11]

[11] Note that we restrict attention to the case where the tariff binding is strict, i.e., $\bar{t} < t^*$. An alternative scenario to consider is one where $t^* < \bar{t} < t^{\rm c}$—i.e. the LIC is able to impose its optimal tariff when the HIC firms compete but is constrained from doing so when they act as an export cartel. Since the LIC can charge its optimal unconstrained tariff while defecting, we have $W_{\rm L}^{\rm D}(\bar{t}) = W_{\rm L}^{\rm D}$. However, since the LIC is constrained by the tariff binding during a policy war (i.e. $\bar{t} < t^{\rm c}$), we have $W_{\rm L}^{\rm W}(\bar{t}) < W_{\rm L}^{\rm W}$. Thus, even when $t^* < \bar{t} < t^{\rm c}$, the tariff binding still increases the transfer that the LIC is willing to pay to induce cooperation because its per period welfare during the policy war is lower.

Now consider the HIC's perspective. As before, the per period welfare of the HIC under cooperation equals the sum of its industry's profits under free trade and the LIC transfer $n\pi(n, 0)+T$ whereas its welfare under defection equals $\pi(1, 0)+T$. If the HIC defects, a policy war results in which the LIC stops paying the transfer T and imposes the maximum permissible tariff $\bar{t}$. The per period payoff of the HIC under a policy war equals $\pi(1, \bar{t})$. Since $\bar{t}<t^*$, $\pi(1, \bar{t})>\pi(1, t^c)$: when the LIC cannot charge its optimal tariff t^c, profits of the HIC's cartel under a policy war are higher. This implies that a tariff binding *reduces* the LIC's ability to punish a defection by the HIC.

Under a tariff binding, cooperation is incentive compatible for the HIC iff:

$$[\pi(1,0) + T] - [n\pi(n,0) + T] \leq \frac{\delta}{1-\delta}[n\pi(n,0) + T - \pi(1,\bar{t})] \tag{25}$$

Thus, the HIC is willing to cooperate iff the per period LIC transfer T exceeds the critical threshold $T_H(\bar{t})$:

$$T > T_H(\bar{t}) \equiv \frac{(1-\delta)\pi(1,0) - n\pi(n,0)}{\delta} + \pi(1,\bar{t}) \tag{26}$$

From Eqs. (11) and (26), we conclude that the minimum transfer required by the HIC is higher when the maximum tariff that the LIC can use is $\bar{t}$ (which is less than t^*). The logic of this statement is as follows. The only difference between the transfer levels required by the HIC under a tariff binding relative to before is that the term $\pi(1, t^c)$ in Eq. (11) is replaced by the term $\pi(1, \bar{t})$ in Eq. (26). Since $\pi(1, \bar{t})>\pi(1, t^c)$, defection is more attractive to the HIC under a tariff binding and it therefore requires a larger transfer from the LIC to cooperate. The following proposition summarizes the central result of this section:

Proposition 4. *The minimum transfer required by the HIC to co-operate with the LIC is higher when the LIC is constrained via a tariff binding: $T_H(\bar{t})>T_H$. Furthermore, the LIC itself is willing to pay a higher transfer under a tariff binding: $T_L(\bar{t})>T_L$.*

The main messages of this proposition are worth emphasizing. First, if the LIC is limited in its ability to punish cartelization via a tariff, the HIC requires a higher transfer from the LIC to abide by cooperation. Second, the LIC finds itself in a weaker position if its tariff is bound and *is itself willing to pay more* to induce the HIC to prohibit cartelization. The fact that the required transfer is less if the LIC faces no restrictions on the use of its tariff provides a motivation for developing countries to not bind tariffs through trade agreements, or, to negotiate an exception that permits the use of trade policy instruments to combat foreign export cartels. Adoption of a binding prohibition on the formation of export cartels by developed countries would encourage developing countries to move forward in reducing and binding their tariffs, as multilateral dispute settlement procedures–which can authorize retaliation against violations of rules–can be used to enforce the export cartel ban.

The last part of the above proposition shows that the LIC's higher willingness to pay a transfer under a tariff binding does not imply that the transfer is necessarily acceptable to the HIC, as it too requires a higher transfer when the LIC tariff is bound. To make further analytical progress on this issue, below we consider the case where the LIC must practice free trade (i.e. $\bar{t}=0$). It is worth emphasizing that such a constraint actually confronts many developing countries because of the free trade agreements that they have signed with the EU and US.

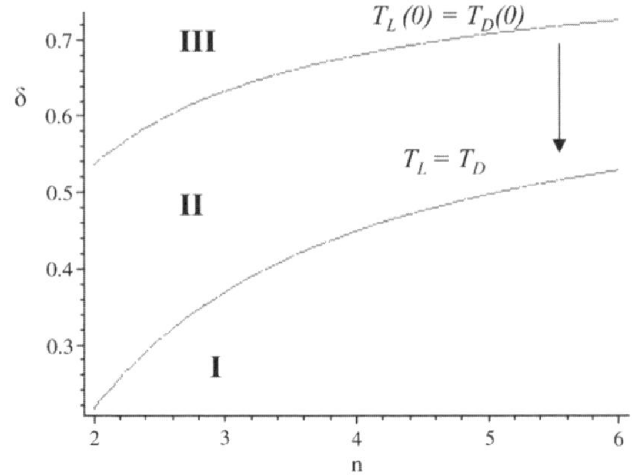

Fig. 1. Effects of a tariff binding: T versus (t, T).

When $\bar{t}=0$, the LIC is willing to cooperate iff:

$$T \leq \frac{\delta}{1-\delta}\left[W_{\mathrm{L}}^{0} - T - W_{\mathrm{L}}^{\mathrm{W}}\Big|_{\bar{t}=0}\right] \tag{27}$$

The above constraint binds at the critical threshold $T_{\mathrm{L}}(0)$:

$$T < T_{\mathrm{L}}(0) \equiv \delta\left(W_{\mathrm{L}}^{0} - W_{\mathrm{L}}^{\mathrm{W}}\big|_{\bar{t}=0}\right) = \frac{\delta\alpha^2(n-1)(3n+1)}{8(n+1)^2} > 0 \tag{28}$$

Similarly, when $\bar{t}=0$, the HIC is willing to cooperate iff

$$T > T_{\mathrm{H}}(0) \equiv \frac{\pi(1,0) - n\pi(n,0)}{\delta} = \frac{\alpha^2(n-1)^2}{4(n+1)^2\delta} > 0$$

As expected, $T_{\mathrm{L}}(0) > 0$: in equilibrium, the LIC is indeed willing to pay the HIC to sustain cooperation. Furthermore, as the market structure becomes more competitive, the maximum transfer the LIC is willing to pay, $T_{\mathrm{L}}(0)$, and the minimum transfer required by the HIC, $T_{\mathrm{H}}(0)$, both increase:

$$\frac{dT_{\mathrm{L}}(0)}{dn} = \frac{n\delta\alpha^2}{(n+1)^3} > 0 \text{ whereas } \frac{dT_{\mathrm{H}}(0)}{dn} = \frac{(n-1)\alpha^2}{\delta(n+1)^3} > 0 \tag{29}$$

A key question is then whether there are circumstances under which the transfer the LIC is willing to pay is acceptable to the HIC? It follows from above that

$$T_{\mathrm{L}}(0) > T_{\mathrm{H}}(0) \text{ iff } \delta > \delta^{T} \equiv \sqrt{\frac{2(n-1)}{3n+1}} \tag{30}$$

Furthermore, δ^T increases in n:

$$\frac{1}{\delta^T}\frac{\mathrm{d}\delta^T}{\mathrm{d}n} = \frac{2}{3(n+1)(n-1)} > 0 \quad (31)$$

so that cooperation becomes harder to sustain as competition in the HIC market increases.

How does the complete removal of the tariff as an instrument affect incentives for cooperation? To address this, Fig. 1 compares the T only case with the (t, T) case. The constraint $T_{\mathrm{H}} = T_{\mathrm{L}}$ (for the (t, T) case) lies below the constraint $T_{\mathrm{H}}(0) = T_{\mathrm{L}}(0)$ (for the T only case), and the figure can be divided into three regions: I, II, and III.[12] Cooperation can be sustained under a transfer only in region III, while under both instruments cooperation occurs in regions II and III. Thus, when the LIC has both a stick (t) and a carrot (T) at its disposal, cooperation is more likely. Furthermore, in Fig. 1, region II primarily obtains because the transfer required by the HIC falls.

Thus far, the analysis assumes that, in the absence of cartelization, firms compete in quantities (Cournot competition). There are two reasons for considering how our results change when firms compete in prices (Bertrand competition). First, as is well known, results under oligopoly can be quite sensitive to the choice of strategic variable (price versus quantity). Second, since the Nash equilibrium under price competition results in marginal cost pricing, the Bertrand case also applies to a scenario where the potential cartelization of a perfectly competitive industry in the HIC is considered.

5. Price competition

Under price competition, the equilibrium price charged by HIC firms equals their marginal cost c. In the one shot policy game, the optimal LIC tariff t^* would equal zero: when price equals marginal cost there are no rents to be extracted and an import tariff t merely inflicts a deadweight loss on the LIC by raising the price in its market from c to $c+t$.[13] On the other hand, if the HIC firms cartelize, the optimal LIC tariff is t^{c} (i.e. it is the same as that under Cournot competition).

Since price competition erodes all rents, the HIC would *always* permit its export industry to organize into a cartel.[14] Such a beggar-thy-neighbor policy creates room for international cooperation since aggregate world welfare is lower under cartelization.

The LIC constraint under the (t, T)case is given by

$$(1-\delta)W_{\mathrm{L}}^{\mathrm{D}} + \delta W_{\mathrm{L}}^{\mathrm{W}} \leq W_{\mathrm{L}}^{0} - T \quad (32)$$

The above constraint implies that the LIC is willing to cooperate iff

$$T \leq T_{\mathrm{L}}^{\mathrm{B}} \equiv \frac{\delta\alpha^2}{3} \quad (33)$$

[12] A function analogous to δ^T can be derived for the (t, T) case but the analytical expression for it is rather cumbersome. It is easy to show that this function is increasing in n and approaches 0.68 when n approaches infinity.

[13] In this situation, LIC welfare would equal total consumer surplus.

[14] If HIC firms had asymmetric production costs, the HIC would prefer competition under free trade to cartelization as long as one of the firms is sufficiently more efficient than its competitors. Under such a scenario, the firm with the lowest cost would monopolize the market by charging a limit price equal to the cost of its most efficient rival. The mark-up of the efficient firm would then create room for the LIC to charge a positive tariff.

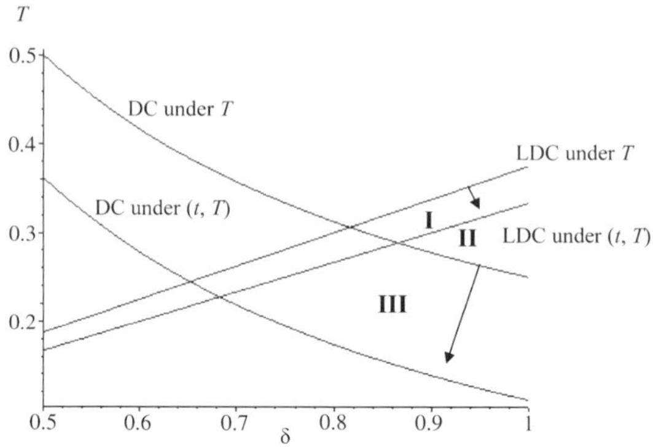

Fig. 2. Cooperation under price competition.

The HIC constraint for cooperation under the two instruments is given by

$$(1-\delta)\pi(1,0)+\delta\pi(1,t^{c})\leq\delta T \tag{34}$$

Solving for the critical transfer $T_{\mathrm{H}}^{\mathrm{B}}$, above which cooperation is acceptable to the HIC, gives

$$T_{\mathrm{H}}^{\mathrm{B}}=\frac{(9-5\delta)\alpha^{2}}{36\delta} \tag{35}$$

Thus, policy cooperation succeeds iff $T_{\mathrm{L}}^{\mathrm{B}}>T_{\mathrm{H}}^{\mathrm{B}}\Leftrightarrow\delta(12\delta+5)>9$ which happens when $\delta>0.68$.[15]

Finally, how does the scope for policy cooperation change under price competition when the LIC has only a transfer at its disposal (i.e. $\bar{t}=0$)?[16] The incentive constraints of the HIC under the T only case is given by:

$$T>T_{\mathrm{H}}^{\mathrm{B}}(0)\equiv\frac{\pi(1,0)}{\delta}=\frac{\alpha^{2}}{4\delta}>0 \tag{36}$$

whereas for the LIC we have

$$T<T_{\mathrm{L}}^{\mathrm{B}}(0)\equiv\delta\left(W_{\mathrm{L}}^{0}-W_{\mathrm{L}}^{\mathrm{W}}\big|_{\bar{t}=0}\right)=\frac{3\delta\alpha^{2}}{8}>0 \tag{37}$$

It immediately follows that the LIC transfer is sufficient to induce cooperation if $T_{\mathrm{L}}^{\mathrm{B}}(0)>T_{\mathrm{H}}^{\mathrm{B}}(0)\Leftrightarrow\delta>\sqrt{\frac{2}{3}}=0.82$.

To see what difference the removal of the tariff makes, Fig. 2 plots 3 the incentive constraints of the two countries under price competition for the T only and the (t, T) case. The LIC constraint under the T only case is upward sloping because as the discount factor increases, i.e. the LIC's willingness to pay a transfer is higher if it values the future more. Similarly, the HIC

[15] The same holds true under Cournot competition when n approaches infinity.

[16] We ignore the case of a general tariff binding here since its main effects have already been described in detail under Cournot competition.

constraint is downward sloping because the transfer it requires to prevent cartelization is lower if it places a bigger weight on future periods. In the absence of a tariff, cooperation occurs in regions I and II where the discount factor is relatively high and the transfer required by the HIC is acceptable to the LIC.

Now consider the incentive constraints under the (t, T) case (also plotted in Fig. 2). Each country's incentive constraint under the (t, T) case lies below its corresponding constraint under the T only case. The LIC constraint shifts down when the tariff is available because its willingness to pay a transfer is lower when cartelization can be punished by a tariff increase. Similarly, the HIC constraint under the (t, T) case is lower because the transfer it requires to prohibit cartelization is smaller when the LIC is free to raise its tariff. Fig. 2 shows that the HIC constraint shifts down substantially more than the LIC constraint. The net effect is that when the transfer is the only available instrument, cooperation occurs in region I whereas if both instruments are available it occurs in regions II and III but *not* in region I. Since region III is much larger than region I, cooperation occurs over a larger range of parameter values when both instruments are available to the LIC.

Incidentally, because the LIC has no incentive to impose a tariff when HIC firms compete in prices, the price competition case helps to isolate the punishment effect of a tariff.[17] This is because, under Cournot competition, the LIC has an incentive to defect from cooperation to raise revenue via its tariff, so that the punishment effect is not the sole reason for using a tariff.

As was the case under Cournot competition, if the LIC cannot use a tariff, it is willing to make a larger transfer to the HIC who also requires a bigger transfer to cooperate. A comparison of price and quantity competition can also be used to highlight the main implications of these alternative assumptions regarding firm behavior. In general, we can show that the transfer levels (both the minimum required by the HIC and the maximum the LIC is willing to pay) are higher under price competition relative to the Cournot case. The intuition underlying these results is that price competition results in marginal cost pricing and is highly attractive to the LIC. For the same reason, under price competition, the HIC suffers a lot from banning an export cartel and therefore requires a large transfer to adopt such a policy.

6. Conclusion

Institutional capacity constraints in many LICs restrict their ability to apply national antitrust actions against international cartels. As a result, several researchers have proposed that developed countries with sophisticated antitrust authorities alter their legislation so as to ban export cartels (and similar practices), even if these cartels have no overt effects on their own markets (see Hoekman and Mavroidis, 2003; Stiglitz and Charlton, 2005).

In principle, developed countries can ban export cartels unilaterally. However, realism suggests that the principle of reciprocity will require LICs to make concessions in order to obtain such a policy change. The most obvious deal would involve LICs offering a mix of market access commitments and transfers in return for HIC agreement to discipline export cartels (and similar practices). We show that a mutually beneficial deal of this type can indeed be struck, and that the scope for cooperation is higher when LICs can use both carrots (transfers) as well as sticks (tariffs). The more constrained the access of LICs to tariffs, the larger the transfers they

[17] The punishment effect of a tariff under price competition can be quantified by $T_{\rm D} - T_{\rm D}^{\rm B} = \frac{5\alpha^2}{36}$.

would need to make to sustain international cooperation. Our analysis implies that LICs should be allowed conditional access to tariffs to enforce international cooperation over a (potential) ban on export cartels. Any tariff commitments/bindings (whether past or new) could then be reversed in cases where HICs violate their obligations to ban export cartels.

Acknowledgement

We thank Aditya Bhattacharjea, Simon Evenett, Gordon Hanson, Nuno Limao, Aaditya Mattoo, Santanu Roy, and an anonymous referee for helpful comments and suggestions. All errors are our own.

Appendix A

Here we present the calculations underlying the main results of the paper.

A.1. Optimal LIC tariff

After appropriate substitutions, welfare in the LIC can be written as

$$W_{\mathrm{L}}(t) = \frac{X^2(t)}{2} + tX(t) \text{ where } X = nx = \frac{(\alpha - t)n}{n+1}$$

The first order condition for the optimal tariff is $X(t) = nt$, which is the same as $\frac{\alpha - t}{n+1} = t \Leftrightarrow t^* = \frac{\alpha}{n+2}$

A.2. Profit and welfare expressions

Profits of a Cournot oligopolist equal

$$\pi(n,t) = (\alpha - t - nx)x = x^2 = \frac{(\alpha - t)^2}{(n+1)^2}.$$

Substituting $t=0$ in the above gives $\pi(n,0) = \frac{\alpha^2}{(n+1)^2}$ whereas setting $n=1$ gives profits $\pi(1,0) = \frac{\alpha^2}{4}$. Similarly, setting $t=t^*$ and $n=1$, gives $\pi(1,t^{\mathrm{c}}) = \frac{\alpha^2}{9}$.

Next we derive the welfare expressions. We have

$$X^0 = \frac{n\alpha}{n+1} \text{ and } p^0 = \frac{\alpha}{n+1} \text{ which gives } W_{\mathrm{L}}^0 = \frac{(X^0)^2}{2} = \frac{1}{2}\left(\frac{n\alpha}{n+1}\right)^2$$

Similarly

$$X^* = \frac{n(\alpha - t^*)}{n+1};\ p^* = \frac{\alpha + t^*}{n+1};\ \text{and } W_{\mathrm{L}}^{\mathrm{D}} = \frac{[X^*]^2}{2} + t^*X^* = \frac{n\alpha^2}{2(n+2)}$$

Substituting $n=1$ in the expressions in the above equation gives

$$X^{\mathrm{c}} = \frac{\alpha - t^{\mathrm{c}}}{2};\ p^{\mathrm{c}} = \frac{\alpha + t^{\mathrm{c}}}{2};\ \text{and } W_{\mathrm{L}}^{\mathrm{W}} = \frac{[X^{\mathrm{c}}]^2}{2} + t^{\mathrm{c}}X^{\mathrm{c}} = \frac{\alpha^2}{6}$$

A.3. Proposition 2

We have

$$\frac{dT_H}{dn} = \frac{n-1}{\delta(n+1)^3} > 0.$$

A.4. Proposition 3

We have

$$\frac{dT_L}{dn} = \frac{\delta n(3n + n^2 + 3) + \delta + n^2 + n - 1}{(n+1)^3(n+2)^2} > 0.$$

A.5. Calculations for Section 4

We have:

$$T_H(0) - T_H = \frac{\alpha^2(n-1)^2}{4(n+1)^2\delta} - \frac{9\alpha^2(n-1)^2 - 5\alpha^2\delta(n+1)^2}{36\delta(n+1)^2} = \frac{5\alpha^2}{36} > 0$$

and

$$T_L(0) - T_L = \frac{\delta\alpha^2(n-1)(3n+1)}{8(n+1)^2} - \frac{2\delta\alpha^2 n(n^2+n-1) - (2\delta + 3n)\alpha^2}{6(n+1)^2(n+2)}$$
$$= \frac{1(12n + \delta n^3 + 4\delta n^2 - 7\delta n + 2\delta)\alpha^2}{2(n+1)^2(n+2)} > 0$$

A.6. Price competition

Under price competition, $\pi(n, 0)=0$ and $t^*(n)=0$. When $n=1$, the profit and tariff formulae derived under Cournot competition continue to apply since it makes no difference whether the cartel chooses price or quantity. Consider the welfare expressions next. We have:

$$X^0 = \alpha;\ p^0 = c;\ \text{and}\ W_L^0 = \frac{(X^0)^2}{2} = \frac{\alpha^2}{2}$$

Since $t^*=0$ and $p^0=c=p^*$, we have $W_L^D = W_L^0$. Under cartelization, $n=1$, and the expressions are the same as those derived under the Cournot case so that $W_L^W = \frac{\alpha^2}{6}$ and $W_L^W|_{\bar{t}=0} = \frac{\alpha^2}{8}$.

References

Auquier, Antoine A., Caves, Richard E., 1979. Monopolistic export industries, trade taxes, and optimal competition policy. Economic Journal (Supplemental Issue) 89, 559–581.

Bagwell, Kyle, Staiger, Robert, 2001. Domestic policies, national sovereignty and international economic institutions. The Quarterly Journal of Economics 116, 519–562.

Bhattacharjea, Aditya, 2004. Export cartels—a developing country perspective. Journal of World Trade 38, 331–359.

Brander, James A., Spencer, Barbara J., 1984. Trade warfare: tariffs and cartels. Journal of International Economics 16, 227–242.

Dixit, Avinash, 1984. International trade policy for oligopolistic industries. Economic Journal (Supplemental Issue) 94, 1–16.

Ederington, J., 2002. Trade and domestic policy linkage in international agreements. International Economic Review 43, 1347–1367.

Fink, C., Mattoo, A., Neagu, I., 2002. Trade in international maritime services: how much does policy matter? World Bank Economic Review 16, 81–108.

Francois, J., Wooton, I., 2001. Trade in international transport services: the role of competition. Review of International Economics 9, 49–61.

Hoekman, Bernard, Mavroidis, Petros C., 2003. Economic development, competition policy and the WTO. Journal of World Trade 37, 1–28.

Hoekman, Bernard, Saggi, Kamal, 2004. Trading market access for competition policy enforcement. World Bank Policy Research Working Paper 3188.

Horn, Henrik, Levinsohn, James, 2001. Merger policies and trade liberalization. Economic Journal 111, 244–277.

Levenstein, Margaret, Oswald, Lynda, Suslow, Valerie Y., 2002. "International Price-Fixing Cartels and Developing Countries: A Discussion of Effects and Policy Remedies," University of Massachusetts, mimeo. At http://www-unix.oit.umass.edu/mag-giel/Research.htm.

Richardson, Martin, 1999. Trade and competition policies: concordia discors? Oxford Economic Papers 51, 649–664.

Stiglitz, Joseph, Charlton, Andrew, 2005. The Development Round of Trade Negotiations in the Aftermath of Cancun. Initiative for Policy Dialogue, New York.

Supreme Court of the United States, 2004. "Opinion No. 03-724, F. Hoffmann-LaRoche v. Empagran," June 14.

CHAPTER 13

Journal of International Economics 76 (2008) 48–60

Contents lists available at ScienceDirect

Journal of International Economics

journal homepage: www.elsevier.com/locate/econbase

Tariff retaliation versus financial compensation in the enforcement of international trade agreements ☆

Nuno Limão [a,*,1], Kamal Saggi [b,2]

[a] University of Maryland, Department of Economics, CEPR, NBER, United States
[b] Southern Methodist University, United States

ARTICLE INFO

Article history:
Received 22 February 2006
Received in revised form 18 March 2008
Accepted 26 March 2008

Keywords:
Dispute settlement
WTO
Tariffs
Monetary fines
Bonds
Policy coordination

JEL classification:
F13
F42
K33
H77

ABSTRACT

We analyze whether financial compensation is preferable to the WTO's current dispute settlement system that permits injured member countries to impose retaliatory tariffs. We show that, ex-post, monetary fines are more efficient than tariffs in terms of granting compensation to injured parties but fines suffer from an enforcement problem since they must be paid by the violating country. If fines must ultimately be supported by the threat of tariffs, they fail to yield a more cooperative outcome than the use of tariffs alone. Furthermore, the exchange of bonds between symmetric countries also does not improve enforcement relative to retaliatory tariffs.

1. Introduction

One of the major goals of the World Trade Organization (WTO) is to reduce policy barriers to international trade. Yet, its dispute settlement system allows members to raise tariffs in response to trade violations committed by other members. Although retaliation is permitted only as a last resort, the fact that the WTO even permits tariff increases appears to be a direct contradiction of its goal of freer trade. This contradiction as well as the fact that many small countries cannot effectively retaliate via tariffs have lead to calls for alternative trade dispute remedies.[3]

☆ The views expressed are those of the authors. We thank the editor, two anonymous referees, Stephanie Aaronson, Piyush Chandra, Kyle Bagwell, Chad Bown, Bernard Hoekman and Petros Mavroidis for useful discussions and comments. We gratefully acknowledge the financial support of the UK's Department for International Development.

* Corresponding author. Tel.: +301 405 7842.
E-mail addresses: limao@econ.umd.edu (N. Limão), ksaggi@smu.edu (K. Saggi).

[1] I gratefully acknowledge the financial support of the World Bank and IMF Research Groups, which hosted me during part of this research. The views expressed in this paper are those of the authors and not of these institutions.

[2] Tel.: +214 768 3274.

[3] See Hoekman and Kostecki (2001) for a good overview of the WTO's dispute settlement procedures. Lawrence (2003) notes that WTO rules are designed to preserve the existing balance of concessions (i.e. to maintain reciprocity). Ethier (2003) argues that the role of the WTO's dispute settlement procedure is "not to facilitate punishment: It is to constrain it."

0022-1996/$ – see front matter © 2008 Elsevier B.V. All rights reserved.
doi:10.1016/j.jinteco.2008.03.005

There are at least two possible reasons why the WTO's Dispute Settlement Understanding (DSU) permits tariff retaliation. First, the threat of retaliation might encourage members to comply with WTO rules: in the absence of any fear of foreign retaliation, members would be tempted to raise their trade barriers whenever so urged by their import lobbies. Second, tariff retaliation may allow an injured country to obtain partial compensation by either improving its terms-of-trade and/or by benefiting those import competing sectors that are favored due to political economy considerations. Of course, even if tariff retaliation helps enforce cooperation and/or enable compensation in trade agreements, it may not necessarily be the optimal instrument for achieving these objectives. In principle, monetary fines payable by a country that violates WTO rules could have both a deterrent effect and a compensatory one while simultaneously avoiding the well-known inefficiencies of tariffs. Our goal in this paper is to evaluate whether the use of fines and bonds can improve upon the WTO's current dispute settlement system based on retaliatory tariffs.

The idea that trade disputes be settled via financial compensation has gained substantial attention in recent years with several new proposals to reform the DSU in the Doha Round, which is still under way.[4] Similar proposals were made in the early 1960s by Uruguay and Brazil who wanted less developed countries to be provided with financial compensation for GATT violations committed by developed countries. Moreover, as .Dam (1970) notes, the principle of financial liability to injured parties underlies domestic laws across the world and its use in international law seems natural.

Desirable as it may seem, the implementation of financial compensation faces important hurdles. We address what we think is the major hurdle: *enforcing such a system*. How does one ensure that the required fine, whatever it is ruled to be, is actually paid by a violating country? While an injured country can implement retaliatory tariffs without requiring any cooperation from a violating country, such is not the case for fines. Ultimately, a violating country has to agree to pay the fine and it will only do so when it is in its best interest since there exists no supra-national authority that can enforce the payment of the fine.[5] This enforcement problem with financial compensation is clearly reflected in the current DSU — it allows for compensation but does not specify the form it must take. Article 22.2 of the DSU states that the compensation must be mutually agreed upon and if it is not, an injured country can apply for retaliation. The only case that we know of where a dispute resulted in monetary compensation was when the US was found guilty of non-payment of royalties by US firms to the EU. This shows that while financial compensation is possible under the DSU, it simply has not been agreed to in most trade disputes that have come before the WTO.[6]

An important objective of this paper is to analyze the effectiveness of alternative dispute remedies in maintaining relatively low trade barriers. We also analyze the effectiveness of the different systems from the perspective of compensating injured countries. In so doing, we argue that one needs to account not only for how a remedy is able to enforce cooperation but also *how the remedy itself can be enforced*. For fines to succeed in enforcing low tariffs and providing compensation, it is crucial that they be backed by a supporting instrument that is not controlled by a violating country. Retaliatory tariffs are the obvious choice for such a *supporting* instrument. However, we show that a system where retaliatory tariffs are used to support the payment of fines yields no more cooperation than one that uses tariffs alone to retaliate against violations.

The equivalence of fines and tariff retaliation in terms of enforcement suggests that both mechanisms yield the same payoffs. However, we show that this is only true if there are no deviations from cooperation. When such deviations occur, and they clearly do in practice, we show that fines supported by tariffs have an advantage over tariff retaliation as a primary remedy. Namely, the payoff to an injured country is higher under fines even though the cost of the penalty for a violating country is unchanged. Thus we show that switching to fines generates a Pareto improvement in the presence of shocks that result in disputes. The underlying rationale for this result is that tariffs are an inefficient form of compensation: the welfare gain they generate for an injured country with market power is always less than the welfare cost they impose on the country that commits the original violation.[7]

Given the aforementioned result regarding the equivalence of fines and tariffs from an enforcement perspective, it is important to ask whether alternative financial mechanisms can help sustain greater cooperation. To this end, we ask whether international cooperation can be sustained by a system where countries exchange bonds of a given amount, with the understanding that a country's bond will be forfeited in case it commits a trade violation. We find that the exchange of bonds between symmetric countries does not improve enforcement relative to a system based solely on retaliatory tariffs. This is because a deviating country has no incentive to return the other country's bond and the extra benefit of deviating on bonds is exactly offset by the cost of losing one's own bond.

Our paper is related to the literature on the enforcement of trade agreements, early contributions to which are reviewed in Staiger (1995). Since then there have been several important contributions and here we briefly note some that are particularly relevant for our paper. Park (2000) studies cooperation between a large and a small country (which has no market power) and shows, among other things, that trade agreements where the small country can make direct transfers can enforce lower tariffs. This is because the threat of terminating the transfer payment gives the small country more leverage than a tariff retaliation. The "purchase" of market access to a large country by a small one is an interesting and relevant result when this transfer is understood

---

[4] For example, Bronckers and Van Den Broek have argued strongly in favor of financial compensation as a means of settling trade disputes (see editorial in the Financial Times, 06/24/04 and Bronckers and Van Den Broek, 2005).

[5] Another hurdle might be an informational one: determining the financial loss incurred by an exporter. However, a similar issue occurs under the current tariff retaliation system. For more recent discussions by legal scholars on improvements of the WTO's DSU and use of monetary compensation see Shaffer (2003) and Hudec (2002).

[6] However, monetary fines have recently been introduced by the US in its preferential trade agreements with Singapore, Chile, the central American countries, and Australia. More specifically, in these agreements, monetary fines are typically a preferred form of compensation when there is a violation related to the trade or intellectual property right provisions.

[7] In a different context, Hoekman and Saggi (2007) argue that since most developing countries lack the institutional capacity for fighting foreign export cartels via antitrust enforcement, developed countries ought to ban such cartels in return for tariff concessions or some monetary compensation. Cartelization creates an inefficiency much like the use of a tariff by a large country in that the loss suffered by the injured party exceeds the gain of the other party.

as a concession in a non-trade issue, as invoked by Park and explicitly analyzed by others (e.g. Limão, 2007). However, in this paper we focus on examining alternative enforcement mechanisms in a setting with large symmetric countries.

In addition to proposals to switch to financial compensation, which we analyze, there have also been others. For example, Mexico has proposed injured countries to be allowed to trade their retaliation rights, i.e. to "sell" them to countries that have sufficient market power to credibly threaten tariff retaliation. Bagwell et al. (2007) analyze this proposal in an auction framework where a country has "earned" the right to retaliate against another (offending) country and wants to sell this right as opposed to retaliating itself (perhaps because it has no market power in trade with the offending country). In one of the auctions they consider, the offending country – the target of retaliation – is permitted to bid to retire the right of retaliation, and in effect is induced to pay the injured country cash compensation in order to keep the right of retaliation out of the hands of other countries who would use it. In this way, Bagwell et al argue that such an auction could harness the retaliatory measures in the WTO to make credible the payment of cash compensation by large industrial countries (who have violated WTO rules) to small least-developed countries (who are injured by these violations). This point is related to our findings here, in that both there and here the threat of tariffs is required to make the payments of financial compensation credible. But our emphasis is very different: Bagwell et al do not model the deviation that creates the right of retaliation that is then auctioned, and their focus is on how auctions might multilateralize this threat to facilitate compensatory payments between countries of asymmetric power and size. In contrast, we focus on the potential role of financial compensation in allowing countries of similar size to implement lower tariffs in a self-enforcing agreement.

Yet an alternative role for financial instruments in trade agreements is considered by Bagwell and Staiger (2005). They show that if governments face anticipated political economy shocks that are private information, then allowing for cash transfers helps to enforce more cooperative tariffs. We also extend our model to include private, anticipated shocks and show that the types of fines we consider do not enforce more cooperation in that setting. The difference in the results occurs because we consider fines that are enacted only in the case of a deviation whereas in Bagwell and Staiger (2005) the financial transfers are used only as long as countries cooperate. The fact that different types of "financial instruments" lead to different tariff cooperation highlights the importance of carefully modelling each of their roles in international trade agreements.

Following most of the literature, we model trade agreements as the sub-game perfect equilibria of repeated games. But rather than focusing on infinite Nash reversion in tariffs as a form to punish violations we focus on renegotiation proof agreements, which better captures the WTO as argued by Ludema (2001). He notes that most trade disputes in the WTO have been settled through negotiations and whenever sanctions have been used, their level has been in accordance with the principle of reciprocity. He then shows that this important feature of disputes in the WTO implies that only those trade agreements that are renegotiation proof are sustained in equilibrium.[8]

The structure of the paper is as follows. In Section 2 we introduce the model and derive the tariff levels in the absence of enforcement problems. In Section 3 we introduce the alternative enforcement mechanisms and contrast the degree of trade liberalization that they can each enforce. We also show the ex-post efficiency of fines relative to tariff retaliation as a form of compensation when trade disputes occur after unanticipated shocks. Furthermore, we discuss how the results extend to the case of anticipated shocks and how different types of financial instruments lead to different outcomes when such shocks are private information. In Section 4 we summarize the results and discuss possible extensions.

2. Model

Given that the issue of alternative enforcement mechanisms is not yet well understood we focus on the simple case of two symmetric countries (home and foreign). Each country produces two homogeneous goods, $i=x$, y as well as a numeraire good, n. Individual utility over the consumption level, c, of three goods is given by

$$u \equiv c_n + \sum_i u_i(c_i)$$

Since utility is quasi-linear, the demand function for good i depends only on its own price and is similar for all individuals so we denote aggregate demand at home by $D_i(p_i)$, where $D_i'(p_i)<0$. Each unit of the numeraire good c_n is produced with constant returns to scale technology using only labor, which is available in fixed supply, L. Each good i is produced with a constant returns technology using both labor and a specific factor; each specific factor is available in fixed supply. We denote the supply function for good i by $S_i(p_i)$ where $S_i'(p_i)>0$.

Let x denote home's import. Under trade, domestic import prices are given by $p_x=p^w+\tau$ where p^w is the "world" price and τ is a specific import tariff on x. Home's excess demand is then $M_i \equiv D_i(p_i)-S_i(p_i)$. Denoting foreign variables with an asterisk (*) the world price for home's import is determined by the market clearing condition

$$M_x(p_x^w+\tau)+M_x^*(p_x^w)=0 \tag{1}$$

A similar condition applies to foreign's import good, y. We assume that no export policies are used so that trade policy is simply described by the level of the import tariff in each country, τ and τ^*. Moreover, we assume that countries have market power in trade so

[8] A broader question is why a third party such as the WTO and its dispute system is needed at all if trade agreements are self-enforcing. Maggi (1999) argues that the role of the WTO is to disseminate information about violations. Klimenko, Ramey, and Watson (2008) argue that the WTO can facilitate cooperation by helping countries to condition their negotiations on the history of cooperation. This role is important when there are ongoing negotiations with outcomes that can differ depending on whether the history is one of cooperation or disputes.

that their optimal tariffs are positive. It is then simple to verify that, in this setup, increasing the tariff on good x lowers the world price, $p_x^w(\tau)$, and raises the domestic one. Given the symmetry a similar relationship holds for the effect of τ^* on the prices of good y.[9]

We focus directly on a reduced form objective function for the government that may allow extra weight (measured by $\lambda_i \geq 1$) to be placed on specific factor owners.

$$W\left(\tau,\tau^*\right) = \sum_i \left[\int_{p_i}^{\infty} D_i(p_i)dp_i + \lambda_i \int_0^{p_i} S_i(p_i)dp_i + \tau_i M_i(p_i)\right] + wL \tag{2}$$

where we recall that τ affects W both directly through tariff revenue, the term $\tau_x M_x$, and through its effect on home prices; whereas the effect of τ^* is indirect and occurs only through the world price, $p_y^w(\tau^*)$. The first term in brackets is consumer surplus. The second one captures producer surplus (weighted by λ) or alternatively the quasi-rents accruing to the fixed factor owners. The last term, wL, is the total wage income. We assume that L is large enough to ensure a positive supply of the numeraire and so the wage rate in the economy is fixed by the marginal productivity of labor in the numeraire good, which in the absence of labor taxes we normalize to unity. Therefore, W can be interpreted as a reduced form of a political contributions model such as Grossman-Helpman (1994).[10]

The Nash tariff, denoted by τ^N, is obtained by maximizing (2) while taking the other country's tariff as given. Since we do not model export policies the good subscript, i, can be dropped so any subscripts below denote partial derivatives. Let

$$\tau^N = \arg_\tau \max W\left(\tau,\tau^*\right) \tag{3}$$

Recalling that the equilibrium prices are a function of the tariff, the first order condition is

$$-Dp_\tau + \lambda S p_\tau + M + \tau M_p p_\tau = 0 \tag{4}$$

Using $M=D-S$, $p_\tau = p_\tau^w + 1$ and re-arranging the above we obtain

$$(p_\tau^w + 1)\left[\tau M_p + (\lambda - 1)S\right] - M p_\tau^w = 0, \tag{5}$$

which implies that the Nash tariff in ad-valorem terms, $\tau^N/p^w(\tau)$, is implicitly defined by:

$$\frac{\tau^N}{p^w(\tau)} = \frac{1}{\varepsilon(\tau)} + (\lambda - 1)\frac{S(\tau)/M(\tau)}{\xi(\tau)} \tag{6}$$

We explicitly show the potential dependence of the various terms on the tariff. We do so for clarity in the formula but will omit them below for notational simplicity. The first term, $1/\varepsilon$ is defined as $\frac{M^*}{p^w M_p^*}$ and represents the inverse of the foreign export supply elasticity and it reflects the terms-of-trade motive for the use of tariffs. The second term reflects a political economy motive that is increasing in the extra weight placed on specific factor owners (λ) and decreasing in home's import demand elasticity ξ where $\xi \equiv -\frac{\partial M}{\partial p^w}\frac{p^w}{M} = -M_p p^w/M$. Given symmetry, the foreign country's import tariff is the same, i.e. $\tau^N = \tau^{*N}$.

At the other extreme, if cooperation was not subject to any enforcement problems, countries would choose tariffs that maximize their joint objective $W+W^*$. This is equivalent to maximizing the objective of either one once we employ symmetry and note that $\tau=\tau^*$. Thus we obtain

$$\tau^G \equiv \arg_{\tau^c} \max W\left(\tau^c, \tau^* = \tau^c\right) \tag{7}$$

which implies that the globally optimal ad-valorem tariff $\tau^G/p^w(\tau^G)$ is given by

$$\frac{\tau^G}{p^w(\tau)} = (\lambda - 1)\frac{S(\tau)/M(\tau)}{\xi(\tau)} \tag{8}$$

It is clear that the optimal cooperative tariff is lower than the non-cooperative tariff (i.e. $\tau^G/p^w < \tau^N/p^w$). The difference between the Nash and globally cooperative policies confirms that market power in trade leads to international externalities that can potentially be resolved by trade agreements.[11] Moreover, it points out that even in the presence of an international agreement, countries may choose to have positive tariffs due to internal political economy distortions. Since the globally optimum tariff is below the level that is optimal for each *individual* country, each country has an incentive to deviate from it and would do so if it faced no punishment. We now address how countries can enforce cooperation.

[9] Broda, Limão and Weinstein (in press) estimate that several countries have considerable market power in trade and use it to set higher tariffs prior to their WTO accession.

[10] In Grossman-Helpman (1994) the government's objective is $W^{GH} = a\bar{W} + c$, where $\bar{W}$ is social welfare, c is political contributions and a is the marginal rate of substitution between the two. In W the term $\lambda - 1$ can be directly interpreted as the inverse of a when factor ownership is extremely concentrated.

[11] This role for the WTO is argued in Bagwell and Staiger (1999). Bagwell and Staiger (2006) provide evidence for their theory by showing that WTO accession leads to greater tariff reductions in products with higher initial import volumes.

3. Enforcement of trade agreements

The absence of a supra-national authority to punish violators implies that international agreements must be self-enforcing. Cooperative self-enforcing agreements are well characterized by certain repeated games.[12] We begin with the standard approach in the literature of using the threat of tariff retaliation to enforce cooperation and then contrast its outcome with alternative enforcement mechanisms.

3.1. Supporting cooperation via tariff retaliation

Consider an infinitely repeated game where the stage game delivers the Nash tariff in the previous Section. Assume that governments observe each other's actions at the end of each period. The strategy employed by countries is to start by cooperating until one deviates by raising its tariff. Any deviation is followed by a punishment phase of n periods after which cooperation is resumed. We model punishments as being temporary because this is clearly more realistic than infinite Nash reversion. Although the latter is a possibility, we view it as the ultimate punishment corresponding to an unravelling of the GATT/WTO system that results from member countries not following its rules. The more common occurrences are trade disputes that are met with temporary punishments.

To find the lowest cooperative tariff that is renegotiation proof we must first define the payoffs to each government under the alternative situations that can arise. In the absence of cooperation, the payoff to each country equals the government's objective evaluated at the non-cooperative tariffs:

$$W^N \equiv W\left(\tau^N, \tau^{*N}\right) \tag{9}$$

Similarly, when countries cooperate, i.e. set their tariffs at τ^c and τ^{*c} (determined below), the payoff to each is given by:

$$W^C \equiv W\left(\tau^c, \tau^{*c}\right) \tag{10}$$

If a country deviates, it does so by imposing its optimal Nash tariff τ^N on its trading partner who, in that period, still utilizes the cooperative tariff, τ^{*c}. The payoff to a country in the period it deviates is therefore given by

$$W^D \equiv W\left(\tau^N, \tau^{*c}\right) \tag{11}$$

Given the symmetry, in equilibrium $\tau^c = \tau^{*c}$ and $\tau^N = \tau^{*N}$, where τ^N is defined by Eq. (6).[13] Since we allow for renegotiation after a deviation we must model the punishment phase before cooperation is resumed. We assume that countries agree that a deviation will be followed by n periods of punishment where the country that deviated faces τ^{*N} on its exports and must show its willingness to restart cooperation by setting its own import tariff at the cooperative level $\tau^c < \tau^N$. The per-period payoff for the deviating country during the punishment phase is therefore

$$W^P \equiv W\left(\tau^c, \tau^{*N}\right)$$

Given the above payoffs, it is straightforward to show that the static tariff game has a Prisoner's Dilemma structure since the following two sets of inequalities are satisfied:

$$W^D > W^C > W^N > W^P \tag{12}$$

$$W^C + W^{*C} > W^P + W^{*P}\left(\tau^c, \tau^{*N}\right) \tag{13}$$

where $W^{*P}(\tau^c, \tau^{*N})$ is foreign's payoff when home is being punished. The inequality $W^D > W^C$ reflects the incentive to deviate from the static cooperative outcome. It is guaranteed in our model by the fact that when home cooperates its tariff is below its reaction curve so switching to τ^N generates a welfare gain during the deviation period. The inequality $W^C > W^N$ requires a country to prefer the cooperative to the non-cooperative outcome where both countries set τ^N; and this is ensured by the fact that countries are symmetric so the higher non-cooperative tariffs have no impact on their terms-of-trade but introduce a deadweight loss. The inequality $W^N > W^P$ simply says that during the punishment phase of the repeated game, the punished country's payoff is below the static Nash level W^N, which holds since τ^c is not home's best-response to τ^{*N}. Finally, inequality (13) requires that cooperative tariffs yield a higher *joint* welfare than an outcome where either country is being punished thus precluding countries from

[12] See Dixit (1987) and Bagwell and Staiger (1990) for example.

[13] The deviation value of the tariff is independent of the other country's policy, i.e. the best-response functions are horizontal. This is due to the quasilinear demand structure and the fact that there are no export policies. In a different setup, e.g. one with import and export policies, the deviation value of the tariff would be lower or higher than τN depending on whether it was a strategic complement or substitute of the foreign export tax.

optimally choosing to alternate in punishing each other instead of cooperating. This condition, as we will see, is crucial in showing the compensation role for fines. It is automatically satisfied in our setup because the difference between the cooperative and Nash tariffs simply reflects a terms-of-trade motive that involves a deadweight loss so home's cost from being punished $W^C - W^P$ always exceeds foreign's terms-of-trade gain, $W^{*P} - W^{*C}$.[14]

Define the continuation payoff after a deviation as:

$$V^{\tau} \equiv \sum_{t=1}^{n} \delta^t W^P + \sum_{t=n+1}^{\infty} \delta^t W^C \tag{14}$$

Given these payoffs, the following incentive compatibility (IC) constraint must be satisfied

$$W^D + V^{\tau} \leq \frac{W^C}{1-\delta} \tag{15}$$

which is identical for the symmetric countries. That is, the sum of the payoff of a deviation, W^D, and the continuation payoff, V^{τ}, should not exceed the payoff of cooperation, which is discounted by $\delta < 1$.

Since $W^P < W^N$ the punishment phase is subgame perfect only if it is not profitable for the country that is being punished to simply abandon the agreement and revert to Nash forever. So we require that V^{τ} exceed the discounted Nash payoff in order to be *weakly renegotiation* proof (WRP):[15]

$$V^{\tau} \geq \frac{\delta}{1-\delta} W^N \tag{16}$$

Because $W^C > W^P$, the longer the punishment phase, the lower is V^{τ}. Therefore the maximum punishment that is WRP is found by increasing n to lower the continuation payoff until it is equal to the RHS of Eq. (16). We define this value as $n^{\max}$, which is implicitly given by

$$V^{\tau\min} \equiv \delta \frac{1-\delta^{n^{\max}}}{1-\delta} W^P + \frac{\delta^{n^{\max}}+1}{1-\delta} W^C = \frac{\delta}{1-\delta} W^N \tag{17}$$

To confirm that the lowest cooperative tariff that is WRP is identical to the one under infinite Nash reversion we can replace Eq. (17) in Eq. (15) to obtain

$$W^D + \frac{\delta}{1-\delta} W^N \leq \frac{1}{1-\delta} W^C \tag{18}$$

The lowest self-enforcing tariff under infinite Nash reversion or WRP is implicitly defined when Eq. (18) holds with equality. This serves as a convenient benchmark against which alternative enforcement mechanisms can be compared. Since we are interested in cases where the threat of tariff retaliation is insufficient to enforce the global optimum, we consider discount factors δ low enough that tariff retaliation alone cannot sustain τ^G. In the symmetric case above this requires $\delta < \delta_g$, where δ_g is defined when Eq. (18) holds with equality at $\tau = \tau^* = \tau^G$.

3.2. *Fines and tariff retaliation*

We now consider the effect of switching from tariff retaliation to a monetary fine to punish deviations from a trade agreement. One key difference between these options is that the fine must be voluntarily paid by the deviating country whereas retaliatory tariffs are imposed by the other country. This means that if the country that deviates decides *not* to pay the fine, the only thing the other country can ultimately do is to revert to non-cooperation in tariffs, which in our model is equivalent to leaving the agreement altogether. Given this, the most cooperative tariff that can be achieved with fines is determined as follows.

After a deviation, a country must pay a fine equal to f units of the numeraire, which the government collects via a lump-sum tax. Cooperation in tariffs resumes the same period the fine is paid. It is reasonable to suppose that if the fine is paid, the transfer occurs in a single period. Thus we set $n = 1$ without loss of generality since we can always alter the value of the fine, f, to mimic the effects of changes in n. The incentive constraint is then similar to the one we had previously, with the possible exception of the continuation payoff that is now V^f:

$$W^D + V^f \leq \frac{W^C}{1-\delta} \tag{19}$$

[14] Note that under W^P home sets τ^c and faces τ^{*N}, which is also the outcome that occurs if foreign were to deviate. Thus in our setup W^P corresponds exactly to the "sucker" payoff and W^{*P} to foreign's deviation payoff that are more commonly used in defining these inequalities. We thank an anonymous referee for prompting us to include these inequalities explicitly.

[15] Farrell and Maskin (1989) and Van Damme (1989) show that using the following punishment as part of the strategy is WRP: the party that deviates accepts to be punished and during that period it plays cooperatively. In this case clearly $W^P < W^N$. The WRP concept requires the strategy not to be Pareto dominated (i.e. $W^{*P} > W^{*C}$) so that cooperation does not Pareto dominate the punishment phase for the injured party. When this is the case, the foreign country is better off when home is punished than under cooperation but home is worse off.

The continuation payoff V^f is now the cost of the fine, $-\delta f$, plus the stream of cooperative payoffs

$$V^f \equiv -\delta f + \frac{\delta}{1-\delta} W^C \tag{20}$$

If we ignore the renegotiation constraint, there exists a sufficiently large f that delivers the global optimum, τ^G. However, we must ensure that the punishment payoff is WRP. Also, since in the absence of tariff retaliation a deviating country has no incentive to pay the fine, there must be a punishment for not doing so. In the context of our model, the only punishment that the other country can impose is to increase its tariff. Therefore the WRP constraint is defined with respect to the payoff under infinite Nash reversion and it requires that

$$V^f \geq \frac{\delta}{1-\delta} W^N \tag{21}$$

Thus WRP requires the maximum fine, $f^{\max}$, and the resulting minimum payoff that the deviating country can be held to, $V^{f\min}$, to be

$$V^{f\min} \equiv -\delta f^{\max} + \frac{\delta}{1-\delta} W^C = \frac{\delta}{1-\delta} W^N \tag{22}$$

which implies that the maximum fine that is WRP is the present discounted value of cooperation in the trade agreement, i.e.

$$f^{\max} = (W^C - W^N)/(1-\delta) \tag{23}$$

By substituting $V^f = V^{f\min}$ in Eq. (19) we can obtain the lowest cooperative tariff that is WRP when fines are enforced by the threat of abandoning the agreement altogether. This gives

$$W^D + \frac{\delta}{1-\delta} W^N \leq \frac{W^C}{1-\delta} \tag{24}$$

which is identical to the constraint under tariff retaliation in (18). We summarize this result in the following proposition.

Proposition 1. *(Enforcement equivalence of tariffs and fines): In a trade agreement between two symmetric countries, the most cooperative tariff that can be enforced by tariff retaliation is equal to the tariff that can be enforced with WRP fines.*

The basic intuition behind this result becomes clear after we note two points. First, since the fine must be paid by the violating country it must find it in its best interest to do so. Therefore, the fine itself needs to be enforced. In the absence of additional instruments this enforcement must rely on the threat of infinite tariff retaliation, i.e. the breakdown of the trade agreement. Second, the maximum punishment that is WRP is the payoff that the deviating country would get if it abandoned the agreement. This is true of the value of the fine paid and the cost imposed by temporary tariff retaliation. Thus both alternatives yield the same cooperative tariff.

There is one important corollary of Proposition 1. Since the most cooperative tariff is identical under these two mechanisms, the payoffs are also exactly the same. This is because thus far we have not introduced any deviations in equilibrium and, along the equilibrium path, countries always obtain the cooperative payoff W^C (that depends only on the level of the cooperative tariff). In Section 3.4 we show that if deviations do occur, the payoffs under the two mechanisms are different. Before doing so, we analyze whether an alternative enforcement mechanism can improve cooperation relative to the ones analyzed above.

3.3. Exchanging bonds

Fines are not the only financial enforcement mechanism. An interesting alternative to consider is the use of bonds that countries forfeit if they violate a trade agreement. This type of scheme has actually been proposed in the context of trade agreements so we now consider how effective it would be in improving tariff cooperation.[16]

Suppose that at the beginning of every period each country posts a bond of value b (measured in terms of the numeraire good) that it forfeits in case it commits a violation. Assume also that countries observe this and cooperate only if such a bond is posted by both of them. Naturally, once bonds are posted, countries are free to decide whether to cooperate on tariffs or not. If either country does not post a bond, both play Nash in tariffs forever (we later discuss the case where the punishment phase is finite). We assume there is no third party that can hold the bonds so that governments must post them with each other. If at the end of a period both countries have cooperated then they "return" their bonds to each other, otherwise the country that deviated loses its bond. In the

[16] In its bilateral trade agreement with the US, Chile proposed a scheme where each member would fund an escrow account and forfeit some of it if it violated the agreement ("Chile Looks for Monetary Sanctions as Enforcement Mechanism", INSIDE U.S. TRADE 13, 11/11/2002). This effectively amounts to posting a bond with a third party and we discuss this possibility in our working paper. Here we focus on the exchange of bonds, i.e. the case when no outside enforcement institution is available to hold bonds or is too costly to use.

exposition we abstract from the possibility of countries keeping the foreign bond without ever posting their own, since as we discuss at the end of the section and show in the appendix this does not change the key results.

Under infinite Nash reversion, if a country deviates in tariffs it will be optimal for it not to return the other country's bond. In this case, the equilibrium tariff remains unchanged relative to the case of no bonds. To see this, note that the incentive constraint is given by:

$$\left(W^D + b^* - b\right) + \frac{\delta}{1-\delta}W^N \leq \frac{W^C}{1-\delta} \tag{25}$$

where the payoff under Nash reversion is the same as before since under no cooperation both countries simply set their tariffs at τ^N and bonds are irrelevant. The functional form of the cooperation payoff is also unchanged because we assume that if countries cooperate they receive their bond and consume it at the end of the period (and we assume no discounting within the period). The key difference is the deviation payoff, which is now given by the original value, W^D, net of the value of the bond that is lost, $-b$ and the one not returned, b^*. However, if, as we expect due to symmetry and stationarity, the optimal bond is the same for both countries (i.e. $b^* = b$), the constraint in Eq. (25) is identical to the one in Eq. (18) and thus the resulting cooperative tariff is equal to that under infinite Nash reversion.

Now consider the case where the punishment phase is finite. Countries start cooperating by initially posting a bond b with each other. If a country deviates from the cooperative tariff, it loses its bond. For cooperation to resume, the deviating country must return the present discounted value of the bond of the injured country, b^*/δ. If it does so in the period after the deviation occurs, tariffs return to the cooperative level. The incentive constraint for cooperation can be written as:

$$W^D + b^* - b + V^b \leq \frac{W^C}{1-\delta} \tag{26}$$

We can again write the minimum continuation payoff that is WRP:

$$V^{b\min} \equiv -\frac{\delta b^{*\max}}{\delta} + \frac{\delta W^C}{1-\delta} = \frac{\delta}{1-\delta}W^N$$

which implies a maximum bond of

$$b^{*\max} = b^{\max} = \delta\frac{W^C - W^N}{1-\delta} \tag{27}$$

Replacing this in Eq. (26) we obtain an IC for the lowest cooperative tariff under bonds that is exactly the same as in Eq. (25), which we already noted yields the same tariff as infinite Nash reversion. Therefore we have the following proposition:

Proposition 2. *(Enforcement under tariffs versus exchanged bonds): In a trade agreement between two symmetric countries, the most cooperative tariff that can be enforced by tariff retaliation is equal to the tariff enforced by WRP bonds exchanged between them.*

Our formulation regarding the use of bonds deserves further discussion. We assume that if either country does not post a bond, both play Nash in tariffs. What if one country receives a bond and decides not to post any in return so that the agreement breaks down and both countries revert to their Nash tariffs? This possibility does not change the result in the last proposition. In the appendix we provide the additional incentive constraint arising from deviation in bonds and show that it allows for bonds up to $b^{IC} = (W^C - W^N)/(1-\delta)$ to be sustained. As a result this IC does not bind for bonds of lower value such as $b^{\max}$ in Eq. (27).

Alternatively we could have allowed countries the *option* of exchanging bonds without any penalty if they did not do so. Note, however, that while our formulation may not be necessary to obtain Proposition 2, this result is if anything stronger under our approach – i.e. we have shown that even if we "coerce" countries to use bonds the outcome is no better than if tariffs alone are used. Note that we "coerce" countries to use bonds via the threat of Nash reversion in tariffs so this is achieved as an *equilibrium* outcome and in a way that is consistent with the rest of our model. Absence such a tariff threat there would effectively be no punishment for a country that failed to provide (or return) a bond after receiving one. Thus, the alternative specification where countries are simply given the option of posting bonds could not help enforce more cooperation on tariffs than the one we use.

3.4. Compensation under alternative mechanisms

As we note in the Introduction, WTO dispute settlement remedies have both an enforcement and a compensation role. Thus far we have focused only on the enforcement aspect and shown that enforcement cannot be improved by replacing the current system with fines or bonds alone. When the most cooperative tariff under that alternative mechanism is identical so is the payoff to governments. The reason is that our model thus far assumes perfect foresight and no shocks, so that no violations occur in equilibrium – i.e. no disputes actually arise. One consequence of this is that the potential inefficiency of tariffs relative to financial compensation in the event of a trade dispute cannot be addressed. We now extend our model to address this issue and show that if a dispute is triggered by a violation, fines can generate *higher compensation* for the injured country at the same cost to the violator even if the cooperative tariff enforced is identical. For ease of exposition we illustrate this result for the punishments considered thus far but then prove it also holds for the less severe punishments often contemplated by the DSU.

In what follows, we illustrate our point in the simplest possible way. We assume governments believe the set of parameters are fixed and base their policies on those fixed values, e.g. a certain level of political pressure, λ in Eq. (2). We then consider the impact of a shock that is unanticipated by the government and perfectly observable by all. If this shock implies higher political pressure, i.e. $\lambda^H > \lambda$, then it generates an incentive for a higher tariff than the cooperative level previously set. Moreover, we assume the shock is temporary, so in the following period λ returns to the original level and thus the government continues to believe that will be the relevant value to base future policies on. Such a shock and the resulting tariff increase would likely trigger a dispute and a ruling against the country because tariffs are bound at a maximum numerical value in the WTO and not on a contingent set of parameters.[17]

The question we ask is the following: Given that a country deviates from the agreement due to an unanticipated shock, under which mechanism is the continuation payoff higher? We focus on fines supported by tariffs so as to yield the same enforcement outcome as temporary tariff retaliation. Since we focus on the most cooperative tariff, the minimum payoff that the deviating country can be held to is the discounted Nash payoff, $W^N\delta/(1-\delta)$. The question then is whether this alternative yields a higher compensation for the *injured country*. The continuation payoff for the injured country under temporary tariff retaliation when the most cooperative WRP is implemented is

$$V^{*\tau} = \delta W^{*P} \frac{1-\delta^{n^{\max}}}{1-\delta} + \frac{\delta^{n^{\max}+1}}{1-\delta} W^{*C} \tag{28}$$

where we recall that the payoff for the injured country under the punishment phase $W^{*P}(\tau^c, \tau^{*N})$ exceeds $W^{*C}(\tau^c, \tau^{*c})$ because the punishment involves the injured setting its optimal tariff $\tau^* = \tau^N$ and the other country setting its cooperative tariff, τ^c.

Under a fine supported by infinite Nash tariff reversion the payoff analogous to (28) is

$$V^{*f} = \delta f^{\max} + \frac{\delta}{1-\delta} W^{*C} \tag{29}$$

This payoff reflects the received fine and the immediate resumption of cooperation with a payoff W^{*C} per period, identical to the one in Eq. (28) since we derived that both sustain the same cooperative tariff. Therefore the compensation under fines is higher than under tariff retaliation if and only if the expression in Eq. (29) exceeds Eq. (28). This yields the following condition for the fine:

$$f^{\max} > \frac{1-\delta^{n^{\max}}}{1-\delta}\left(W^{*P} - W^{*C}\right) \tag{30}$$

With this condition we are ready to compare the compensation properties of each mechanism and rank them. Since we consider unanticipated shocks we think that a reasonable ranking of the two can be established by comparing their payoffs under cooperation and their continuation payoffs if a shock does occur. Denoting the equilibrium WRP cooperative levels of tariffs under fines and tariff retaliation by τ^{Cf} and $\tau^{C\tau}$ we use the following definition. *A trade agreement enforced by fines generates a Pareto improvement relative to one using tariffs if the following inequalities hold: (i)* $W^C(\tau^{Cf}) \geq W^C(\tau^{C\tau})$; *(ii)* $W^{*C}(\tau^{Cf}) \geq W^{*C}(\tau^{C\tau})$; *(iii)* $V^f \geq V^\tau$; *and (iv)* $V^{*f} \geq V^{*\tau}$ *with at least one holding strictly.* We can now state the following.

Proposition 3. *(Compensation properties and ranking of tariffs versus fines): (a) In the presence of unanticipated shocks, e.g. to the political economy parameter* λ*, a trade agreement between two symmetric countries that is enforced by WRP fines supported by tariffs yields higher compensation for the injured country* ($V^{*f} > V^{*\tau}$) *and generates a Pareto improvement relative to a similar agreement enforced by tariff retaliation alone. (b) The results in (a) are independent of restrictions on the severity of the punishment (i.e. they hold for* $n < n^{\max}$ *or* $f < f^{\max}$*) whenever the tariff retaliation and fine mechanisms enforce the same cooperative tariff.*

The first part of the proposition says that the continuation payoff for the injured country after a shock is higher under fines, i.e. the inequality in Eq. (30) always holds. We show this in the appendix, below we provide the intuition. The Pareto improvement is then a corollary of the higher continuation payoff and of Proposition 1. In Proposition 1 we show that fines and tariffs enforce the same cooperative tariff so $W^C(\tau^{Cf}) = W^C(\tau^{C\tau})$ for home and similarly for foreign due to symmetry. Moreover, we also showed that the WRP continuation payoff that a country is held to in equilibrium is the same under the two alternatives, $V^f = V^\tau$. So fines generate a Pareto improvement. The last part of the proposition shows the same result holds even if punishments are less severe provided we consider punishments that enforce similar tariffs.

To see why inequality (30) always holds, note that when the WRP constraint under fines binds then $f^{\max}$ is given by Eq. (23), which due to symmetry is also equal $(W^{*C} - W^{*N})/(1-\delta)$. Using this and the definition of the payoffs we can rewrite Eq. (30) as

$$\frac{W^{*C} - W^{*N}}{1-\delta} > \frac{1-\delta^{n^{\max}}}{1-\delta}\left(W^*\left(\tau^c, \tau^{*N}\right) - W^*\left(\tau^c, \tau^{*c}\right)\right) \tag{31}$$

The value of the fine received by the injured country (i.e. the left hand side) is equal to the present discounted value of cooperation in the trade agreement relative to infinite Nash reversion. This value needs to exceed any temporary gains that the injured country

[17] A potential reason for this in the WTO is the difficulty of writing an agreement that is conditional on political economy parameters that are likely to be hard to observe by other countries.

can obtain by raising its tariff during the punishment phase of n^{max} periods. The latter gain is simply the terms-of-trade benefit that it obtains from using its Nash tariff relative to the cooperative one. By using the definition for n^{max} in Eq. (17) and simplifying we can show this condition always holds. The underlying reason is that while tariffs can also transfer income by changing the terms-of-trade, they lead to a deadweight loss whereas fines do not.

The objective in this section is to determine if fines have an advantage over tariff retaliation when both enforce the same degree of tariff cooperation. In this context, considering the punishment that leads to the most cooperative tariffs seems a natural benchmark since Proposition 1 shows that under this type of punishment both tariff retaliation and fines deliver identical enforcement. However, since the WTO's DSU can restrict punishment to be less severe, it is worth asking how such a restriction affects our results regarding compensation. The last part of Proposition 3 shows that our results hold for all punishments that yield the same cooperative tariffs under fines and tariff retaliation.

Consider, for example, the case when the tariff punishment period is $n^p \in [1, n^{max}]$ so that it may be less severe than before and can be chosen to match a range of alternative payoffs for either the violating country or the injured one (e.g. n^p can be chosen to allow the injured country to impose higher tariffs for a sufficient period as to "withdraw substantially equivalent concessions"). To hold constant the degree of enforcement across the two mechanisms and to focus on compensation, consider a fine equal to f^p, which delivers the same cooperative tariff as tariff retaliation when $n = n^p$. This fine is easily found by requiring the continuation payoffs for a country that deviates to be identical under the alternative mechanisms, i.e. $V^{\tau}(n^p) = V^{f}(f^p)$. It is then simple to show that compensation for the injured country is higher under fines relative to tariff retaliation if and only if a condition exactly analogous to Eq. (30) holds. The only difference being that it is now evaluated at n^p (and f^p), which can be restricted to fall below the maximum value n^{max} (and f^{max}). Such a condition holds for exactly the same reasons as those described above.

Proposition 3 captures an important insight about the role of fines as a compensation mechanism. We chose the simplest setup to show it, i.e. one where the deviation is caused by a shock to λ that is unanticipated by the government. This means that the government places a zero probability on such a shock and is therefore indifferent between fines and tariffs *ex-ante*. However, this does *not* mean that such a shock has a zero probability of actually occurring, it only means that the government beliefs about λ may be proved wrong at any given point in time and when that occurs fines do generate a Pareto improvement *ex-post*. However, if governments are frequently proved wrong they may learn to anticipate some shocks and we now discuss this possibility.

3.5. Tariffs versus fines under anticipated shocks

Thus far we have shown that fines supported by tariff retaliation do not yield more cooperation than tariff retaliation alone, but fines yield a Pareto improvement in the presence of unanticipated shocks since they are more efficient in compensating the injured party. However, some shocks are anticipated and this raises two questions. First, do our results have any implications for the scenario where shocks are anticipated by governments? Second, are our results robust to changes in model structure that allow it to directly tackle anticipated shocks? We now argue that the answer to both of these questions is a qualified yes.

The compensation result in Proposition 3 is also relevant when political economy shocks are anticipated provided there are contracting costs. To see this suppose that the government knows the true distribution of λ. Let that distribution take $N+1$ possible values, one being λ_p, with probability p, and the remaining N alternative values each having identical probability $(1-p)/N$. Then, if contracting costs are high and increasing in the number of states of nature and if p is sufficiently high, then the governments may optimally choose a simple agreement based on the most likely value, λ_p. In sum, although our compensation result was derived under unanticipated shocks, we think that its insight may also operate under more realistic settings where shocks are anticipated and there are contracting costs. Rather than modeling these new features, which deserve a paper of its own, we now discuss an extension of the model that directly tackles anticipated shocks.

To clearly contrast our results with those in the literature we now describe the impact of fines in the context of a closely related model that considers anticipated shocks; we provide the details in an Appendix available on request. Bagwell and Staiger (2005) (henceforth BS) show that certain types of financial transfers can enhance tariff cooperation by allowing a country with high political pressure to raise its tariff while simultaneously compensating its trading partner. In their model, governments experience anticipated political shocks to λ that create incentives for raising tariffs. They show that when countries can set a tariff-transfer combination in each period, they are able to implement fully efficient tariffs. Their formulation of transfers as an integral part of tariff-setting is conceptually quite different from ours in that we model fines as a retaliation or ex-post compensation. Interestingly, these two alternative formulations of financial compensation require different rules and instruments to be available in trade agreements and, more importantly, lead to rather different outcomes. Indeed, when we integrate our type of retaliatory fines into the setup of BS we find that the use of such fines yields *no* more tariff cooperation than the use of tariff retaliation alone.

Following BS, suppose that each government's political economy parameter, λ, is private information and is identically and independently distributed over time. For simplicity, as in Bagwell (2007), assume that λ equals λ_H with probability π_H and λ_L with probability $\pi_L \equiv 1 - \pi_H$ where $\lambda_H > \lambda_L$. One can then calculate Nash tariff values that depend on λ, $\tau^N(\lambda)$. One difference is that now strong tariff bindings (i.e. fixed levels of the cooperative tariff) are dominated by weak bindings, i.e. setting a maximum tariff (see BS). Intuitively, a weak binding helps address the terms-of-trade externality while *also* providing governments the flexibility to change tariffs to respond to political pressure (up to some maximum). Thus we follow their paper and focus on a weak tariff binding. This means that if a government's Nash tariff falls below the weak binding, denoted by τ^W, it utilizes the Nash value, $\tau^N(\lambda)$, and otherwise it applies the agreed binding.

Now consider a repeated game setting where countries cooperate on the *optimal* weak binding. To examine the alternative enforcement mechanisms we need to define the payoffs under deviation. Bagwell (2007) shows that countries only have an incentive to deviate when $\lambda = \lambda_H$ since the optimal weak binding level turns out to be higher than a country's Nash tariff when $\lambda = \lambda_L$. That payoff is given by

$$W\left(\tau^N(\lambda_H), \tau^{*c}(\lambda, \tau_o^W), \lambda = \lambda_H\right) \tag{32}$$

In the benchmark case when countries use infinite Nash reversion and no transfers, Bagwell (2007) shows there is a discount factor $\delta \equiv \delta^W < 1$ such that the IC below is satisfied with equality at the global cooperative weak binding, $\tau^c(\lambda, \tau_o^w)$.

$$W\left(\tau^N(\lambda_H), \tau^{*c}(\lambda, \tau_o^W), \lambda = \lambda_H\right) + \frac{\delta E_{\lambda,\lambda^*} W\left(\tau^N(\lambda), \tau^{*N}\left(\lambda^*\right), \lambda\right)}{1-\delta} \leq \frac{E_{\lambda,\lambda^*} W\left(\tau^c(\lambda, \tau_o^W), \tau^{*c}\left(\lambda^*, \tau_o^W\right), \lambda\right)}{1-\delta} \tag{33}$$

The discounted Nash payoff (the second term on the LHS) and the cooperation payoff (the term on the RHS) correctly capture the expectation over the political economy parameters.

Instead of facing infinite Nash reversion, we assume that countries that deviate face n periods of punishment. Similarly to what we have seen in Sections 3.1 and 3.2, this implies that the discounted Nash payoff in Eq. (33) should be replaced by a continuation payoff, denoted by $E_{\lambda\lambda^*}V^\tau$ in the case of tariff retaliation and $E_{\lambda\lambda^*}V^f$ in the case of fines. The main difference relative to our earlier definition of these continuation payoffs is that we must now take expected values over any terms that depend on λ.[18]

In equilibrium it must still be the case that the minimum expected continuation payoff that can be imposed on a country that deviates is the expected discounted Nash payoff (otherwise the country would be better off by simply abandoning the agreement). This ensures that the IC under WRP tariffs or fines would be identical to Eq. (33) and so, when $\delta = \delta^W$, those IC hold with equality at $\tau^c(\lambda, \tau_o^w)$, i.e. either enforcement mechanism leads to the exact same cooperative tariff even with anticipated shocks.

To contrast our result with the one in BS note that at δ^W countries set their optimal cooperative tariffs when $\lambda = \lambda^H$ but still set their Nash tariffs along the equilibrium path when $\lambda = \lambda_L$. The latter are jointly inefficient but, in the absence of other instruments being used along the equilibrium path, this inefficiency is a necessary cost to pay to enforce a weak binding where $\tau_o^w > \tau^N(\lambda_L)$.[19] Since in our setup fines are used only when the weak binding is broken they do not affect the level of the applied tariff when $\lambda = \lambda_L$ (so that inefficiency remains). By contrast, BS allow governments to make transfers to each other at the time that they apply their individual tariffs and show that these transfers can help sustain the efficient tariffs even if $\lambda = \lambda_L$.

Intuitively, the existence of the transfer in BS expands the number of available instruments that can be used to sustain cooperation and thus the set of feasible payoffs (something that does not happen with the retaliatory fines considered by us) and this allows for more tariff cooperation. Furthermore, in BS if a country violates the tariff binding it reverts to its Nash tariff without needing to pay any fine or transfer. By contrast, in our model, a fine is stipulated to be paid *only* when a country breaks the tariff binding, i.e. the fine is used as a punishment for sustaining the cooperative equilibrium. As a result, the enforcement of the fine itself becomes a central issue in our model. The fact that different types of "financial instruments" lead to different levels of tariff cooperation highlights the importance of carefully modelling each of their role in international trade agreements.

4. Conclusion

The opinion that the WTO's dispute settlement system needs improvement is widespread. In particular, there is much concern about the use of tariff retaliation as the sole mechanism for dealing with member countries that fail to comply with a WTO ruling against them. In this paper, we analyze alternative mechanisms based on financial compensation and argue that one of the major problems in their implementation is enforcement.

Ultimately, the enforcement of monetary fines may require some type of retaliatory instrument and in that case, fines fail to yield any more cooperation than tariffs. Thus, despite their problems, a desirable aspect of retaliatory tariffs is that they are controlled by injured parties and can be used in the event a violating country fails to comply with the ruling of a WTO panel. We also analyze whether bonds can improve cooperation relative to tariff retaliation and show they cannot do so when exchanged between symmetric countries. An interesting question to address in future research is how this result changes with asymmetric countries.[20]

We also showed that fines have an advantage over tariff retaliation as a primary remedy: if a violation does occur, the payoff to an injured country is higher under fines even though the cost of the penalty for a violating country is unchanged. The intuition is simple: tariffs are an inefficient form of compensation because the welfare gain they generate for an injured country with market power is always less than the welfare cost for the country facing the tariff punishment. We established this ex-post efficiency of

[18] The other difference is that now they are defined over the weak binding tariffs.

[19] Since $\tau^G(\lambda_H) > \tau^N(\lambda_L)$ and $T^G(\lambda_L) = 0$, the low type country has no incentive to cheat – it is free to use its optimal Nash tariff and has to pay no transfer for doing so. Thus cooperation hinges on the high type country.

[20] Posting bonds with a third party may improve cooperation between symmetric countries. As we discuss in our working paper if bonds are deposited in an escrow fund (i.e. with a third party), tariff retaliation is no longer necessary since the bond posted by the violating country can be used to compensate the injured country. As we noted earlier, such an escrow scheme was proposed by Chile in its bilateral trade agreement with the US. Future research should develop a model that fully accounts for the role of a third party in this context.

fines in the case of unanticipated shocks and argued it could be extended to more realistic cases. Moreover, we discussed how different types of financial compensation leads to different outcomes under private information, which illustrates the importance of carefully modelling alternative instruments.

Future research should build on these insights to determine whether the WTO's dispute system should move to financial compensation as the primary remedy. In our view, several aspects related to the ex-ante efficiency of tariffs as an enforcement mechanism deserve to be modelled carefully in the future. First, the level of compensation under fines deserves attention. If fines were required to deliver the exact same level of compensation to the injured country as it would obtain under tariff retaliation, then equilibrium tariffs would actually be higher under fines. The logic is similar to Proposition 3 but now it applies to the violating country: a given amount of compensation received is less costly to the violating country if it can pay it with a fine instead of having to face higher tariffs on its exports during the punishment period. Second, the enforcement advantage of tariff retaliation would be even stronger if injured countries can select the goods on which they retaliate, as observed in recent cases where retaliating parties chose products concentrated in swing states. By targeting states with greater political influence, tariffs may be more effective in generating pressure through exporters for the violating government to comply with the WTO's ruling. As Lawrence (2003) notes, parties often retaliate in a fashion that maximizes incentives for compliance. Third, this advantage of tariffs relative to fines can be further reinforced when fines are raised via general taxation because then the punishment for violating the trade agreement is dispersed and can go unnoticed. Future research on the optimal design of enforcement mechanisms should extend our analysis to incorporate these ex-ante efficiency arguments of tariffs relative to fines.

Appendix A. Proofs

A.1. Proposition 2 (robustness to bond deviation)

The basic proposition is proved in the text but here we prove the claim in the text that its result is robust to deviations in bonds. More specifically, we show that deviations in bonds that lead to a breakdown of the agreement, i.e. infinite reversion to Nash tariffs, do not affect the result in Proposition 2. The additional IC if a country keeps the foreign bond, b^*, and does not post its own, reflects the fact that both immediately go to Nash in tariffs, i.e.

$$\left(W^N + b^*\right) + \frac{\delta}{1-\delta}W^N \leq \frac{W^C}{1-\delta}$$

this implies that the maximum bond that satisfies this IC is equal to

$$b^{*IC} = \frac{W^C - W^N}{1-\delta}$$

It is then immediate to see that the maximum bond that is WRP in Eq. (27) is lower than b^{*IC} and thus it also satisfies the "bond" IC above, that is

$$b^{*\max} = \delta\frac{W^C - W^N}{1-\delta} \leq b^{*IC} = \frac{W^C - W^N}{1-\delta}$$

So the extra IC for deviating in bonds alone does not bind under the WRP case and the proposition in the text remains unchanged. □

We can also add that the result under infinite reversion described earlier in that section holds, with a slight qualification requiring that the maximum bond countries would ever choose would be b^{*IC}. Any higher (symmetric) bonds do not affect the original IC in Eq. (25) but increase the incentive to deviate in bonds and would thus require a higher cooperative tariff in equilibrium for the bond IC to be satisfied, thus bonds above b^{*IC} would actually lead to less cooperation in tariffs.

A.2. Proposition 3: Higher compensation: $V^{*f}(f) > V^{*\tau}(n)$

Proposition 1 shows that we obtain $\tau^{Cf}(f=f^{\max}) = \tau^{C\tau}(n=n^{\max})$. Consider now some arbitrary $n^p \in [1, n^{\max}]$ and a corresponding fine f^p defined by $V^f(f^p) = V^\tau(n^p)$, as given in Eqs. (14) and (20). These punishments also imply the equilibrium cooperative tariff is identical across enforcement mechanisms, i.e. $\tau^{Cf}(f=f^p) = \tau^{C\tau}(n=n^p)$, as is clear from the constraints in Eqs. (15) and (19). When $n^p = n^{\max}$ we have $f = f^{\max}$ since $V^f(f^{\max}) = \frac{\delta}{1-\delta}W^N = V^\tau(n^{\max})$, so $n^p = n^{\max}$ is a special case and we prove the general result for n^p. For a given n^p we obtain the following f^p by employing the definitions in Eqs. (14) and (20) and $\tau^{Cf}(f=f^p) = \tau^{C\tau}(n=n^p)$

$$V^\tau(n^p) = V^f(f^p)$$
$$f^p = \frac{1-\delta^{n^p}}{1-\delta}(W^C - W^P)$$

The payoffs $V^{*\tau}(n)$ and $V^{*f}(f)$ are defined in Eqs. (28) and (29) when $f=f^{\max}$ and $n=n^{\max}$. The definition is the same at $f=f^p$ and $n=n^p$ and so $V^{*f}(f^p)>V^{*\tau}(n^p)$ iff

$$\delta f^p+\frac{\delta}{1-\delta}W^{*C}\left(\tau^{Cf}\right)>\delta W^{*P}\left(\tau^{C\tau},\tau^{*N}\right)\frac{1-\delta^{n^p}}{1-\delta}+\frac{\delta^{n^p+1}}{1-\delta}W^{*C}\left(\tau^{C\tau}\right)$$

Since $\tau^{Cf}(f=f^p)=\tau^{C\tau}(n=n^p)$ we simplify this to obtain the expression in (30) in the text and now show it must hold for the general case.

$$f^p>\frac{1-\delta^{n^p}}{1-\delta}\left(W^{*P}-W^{*C}\right)\Leftrightarrow W^C-W^P>W^{*P}-W^{*C}$$

where the second line uses the value of f^p found above. The last line can be re-arranged to obtain inequality (13). As we describe in the text this holds because the difference between the cooperative and Nash tariffs simply reflects a terms-of-trade motive that involves a deadweight loss so home's cost from being punished, W^C-W^P, always exceeds foreign's terms-of-trade gain, $W^{*P}-W^C$.

Pareto improvement. Our definition of Pareto improvement in the text is satisfied if (*i*) $W^C(\tau^{Cf})=W^C(\tau^{C\tau})$; (*ii*) $W^{*C}(\tau^{Cf})=W^{*C}(\tau^{C\tau})$; (*iii*) $V^f=V^\tau$; and (iv) $V^{*f}>V^{*\tau}$. Since the last inequality was just shown we need only show the first three equalities. From Proposition 1 we know that $\tau^{Cf}=\tau^{C\tau}$ for $n^{\max}$ and $f^{\max}$. Therefore $W^C(\tau^{Cf})=W^C(\tau^{C\tau})$. Given symmetry we also have $W^{*C}(\tau^{Cf})=W^{*C}(\tau^{C\tau})$. As we show in Section 3.1, Eq. (17), $V^\tau=V^{\tau\min}=\frac{\delta}{1-\delta}W^N$. In Section 3.2, Eq. (22) shows that V^f is also equal to that value. Thus, under the most cooperative tariff we have $V^\tau=V^f$. By definition of n^p and f^p we have $V^\tau(n^p)=V^f(f^p)$ and as shown above this implies $\tau^{Cf}(f=f^p)=\tau^{C\tau}(n=n^p)$ so conditions (*i*); (*ii*) and (*iii*) also hold for the general case. □

References

Bagwell, K., 2007. Self-Enforcing Trade Agreements and Private Information. Mimeo.
Bagwell, K., Staiger, R., 1990. A theory of managed trade. American Economic Review 80, 779–795.
Bagwell, K., Staiger, R., 1999. An economic theory of GATT. American Economic Review 89 (1), 215–248.
Bagwell, K., Staiger, R., 2005. Enforcement, private political pressure, and the GATT/WTO Escape Clause. Journal of Legal Studies 34 (2), 471–513.
Bagwell, K., Staiger, R., 2006. What do trade negotiators negotiate about? Empirical Evidence From the World Trade Organization, NBER Working Paper Series No. 12727. National Bureau of Economic Research, Cambridge, MA.
Bagwell, K., Mavroidis, P., Staiger, R., 2007. Auctioning countermeasures in the WTO. Journal of International Economics 73 (2), 309–332.
Broda, C., N. Limão, Weinstein, D., in press. Optimal tariffs and market power: the evidence. American Economic Review.
Bronckers, M., Van Den Broek, N., 2005. Financial compensation in the WTO: improving the remedies of WTO dispute settlement. Journal of International Economic Law 8, 101–126.
Dam, K.W., 1970. The GATT Law and International Economic Organization. The University of Chicago Press, Chicago.
Dixit, A., 1987. Strategic aspects of trade policy. In: Bewley, T. (Ed.), Advances in Economic Theory. Cambridge University Press, pp. 329–362.
Ethier, W.J., 2003. Intellectual Property Rights and Dispute Settlement in the World Trade Organization. Mimeo.
Farrell, J., Maskin, E., 1989. Renegotiation in repeated games. Games and Economic Behavior 1 (4), 327–360.
Grossman, G., Helpman, E., 1994. Protection for sale. American Economic Review 84 (4), 833–850.
Hoekman, B.M., Kostecki, M., 2001. The Political Economy of the World Trading System. Oxford University Press, New York, NY.
Hoekman, B., Saggi, K., 2007. Tariff bindings and bilateral cooperation on export cartels. Journal of Development Economics 83, 141–156.
Hudec, R., 2002. The adequacy of WTO dispute settlement remedies: a developing country perspective. In: Mattoo, Aaditya, Hoekman, Bernard, English, Philip (Eds.), Development, Trade, and the WTO: A Handbook. The World Bank, Washington, D.C.
Klimenko, M., Ramey, G., Watson, J., 2008. Recurrent trade agreements and the value of external enforcement. Journal of International Economics 74 (2), 475–499.
Lawrence, R., 2003. Crimes and punishments? Retaliation under the WTO. Institute of International Economics, Washington, D.C.
Limão, N., 2007. Are preferential trade agreements with non-trade objectives a stumblingblock for multilateral liberalization? Review of Economic Studies 74 (3), 821–855.
Ludema, R., 2001. Optimal international trade agreements and dispute settlement procedures. European Journal of Political Economy 17, 355–376.
Maggi, G., 1999. The role of multilateral institutions in international trade cooperation. American Economic Review 89 (1), 190–214.
Park, J.-H., 2000. International trade agreements between countries of asymmetric size. Journal of International Economics 50, 473–495.
Shaffer, G., 2003. How to make the WTO dispute settlement system work for developing countries: some proactive developing country strategies. International Centre for Trade and Sustainable Development, Working Paper No. 5.
Staiger, R., 1995. In: Grossman, Gene, Rogoff, Kenneth (Eds.), International rules and institutions for trade policy. . Handbook of international economics, vol. 3. Elsevier, North-Holland, pp. 1495–1551.
Van Damme, E., 1989. Renegotiation-proof equilibria in repeated prisoners' dilemma. Journal of Economic Theory 47, 206–217.

CHAPTER 14

ELSEVIER

Journal of Development Economics 88 (2009) 132–143

JOURNAL OF Development ECONOMICS

www.elsevier.com/locate/econbase

The MFN clause, welfare, and multilateral cooperation between countries of unequal size ☆

Kamal Saggi *

Department of Economics Southern Methodist University, United States

Received 25 January 2006; received in revised form 10 September 2007; accepted 29 January 2008

Abstract

This paper analyzes MFN in a "competing exporters" model of trade between three countries with unequal endowments and shows that MFN yields higher aggregate welfare than tariff discrimination even as it makes low income countries worse off. Furthermore, in a repeated game of tariff cooperation, multilateral free trade is easier to sustain under MFN punishments relative to discriminatory ones. This conclusion holds even when tariff discrimination takes the form of bilateral trade agreements. Overall, the analysis shows that from the viewpoint of low income countries, MFN and multilateral tariff cooperation are complementary in nature.

JEL classifications: F13; F10; F15
Keywords: Most favored nation clause; Country income; Welfare; Multilateral tariff cooperation; Tariff discrimination

1. Introduction

The most favored nation (MFN) clause is the most important principle underlying multilateral trade agreements such as the General Agreement on Tariffs and Trade (GATT).[1] MFN requires that when choosing their trade policies, member countries of the World Trade Organization (WTO) treat all other members in a non-discriminatory fashion. Given that there exist myriad differences across countries, it is unlikely that such a non-discrimination requirement affects all countries in a similar fashion. Accordingly, this paper asks: from the perspective of an individual country, how does the desirability of MFN depend upon the size of its economy relative to others? Under repeated interaction, how does MFN affect the prospects of multilateral tariff cooperation? The present paper pushes forward the rich body of literature on the economics of the multilateral trading system by addressing these questions in a model that gives a central role to heterogeneity in country size.[2]

The model is a simple generalization of the three-country "competing exporters" framework of Bagwell and Staiger (1998). Countries have asymmetric endowments of three non-numeraire goods and equal endowments of the numeraire good. Each country imports a different non-numeraire good from the other two. Since trade in the numeraire good is assumed to be free whereas non-numeraire goods are potentially subject to tariffs, such goods are also referred to as *protected* goods. Throughout the paper, the free trade income levels of countries are used to rank countries in terms of the size of their economies.[3] An important result of the model is that under tariff discrimination, each country levies a higher tariff on the country from whom it imports a greater

☆ I thank Caroline Freund, Gordon Hanson, Bernard Hoekman, Aaditya Mattoo, Marcelo Olarreaga, Caglar Ozden, Faruk Sengul, Maurice Schiff, Bob Staiger, seminar audiences at Georgia Tech and the World Bank and two anonymous referees for helpful comments. All errors are my own.

* Dallas, TX 75275-0496, United States. Tel.: +214 768 3274; fax: +214 768 1821.
E-mail address: ksaggi@smu.edu.

[1] See Hoekman and Kostecki (2001) for a good overview of the WTO and the multilateral trading system.

[2] Important analytical contributions in this area include Bagwell and Staiger (1999, 2004), Caplin and Krishna (1988), Choi (1995), Gatsios (1990), Ludema (1991), McCalman (2002), and Saggi (2004). A comprehensive survey of the literature on MFN is provided by Horn and Mavroidis (2001).

[3] In the model, a country's endowment of protected goods basically determines its income relative to others.

0304-3878/$ - see front matter © 2008 Elsevier B.V. All rights reserved.
doi:10.1016/j.jdeveco.2008.01.006

volume of protected goods. Furthermore, since demand functions are assumed to be linear each country's optimal MFN tariff is simply the average of its optimal discriminatory tariffs. As a result, MFN adoption by a country benefits its richer trading partner whereas it hurts the poorer one.[4] Despite its adverse distributional impact, MFN yields higher aggregate world welfare than tariff discrimination because it eliminates the global inefficiency caused by the international price differentials that prevail under tariff discrimination.

The widespread use of MFN in trade agreements suggests that it might be expected to play a positive role in facilitating multilateral cooperation. To address this issue, this paper follows the approach of Riezman (1991), Bagwell and Staiger (1997, 1998), Bond et al. (2001), and Saggi (2006) wherein multilateral cooperation is modeled as a self-enforcing trade agreement. The main question motivating this analysis is: are MFN punishments more effective in sustaining cooperation relative to discriminatory ones? In a recent paper, Ederington and McCalman (2003) have argued that this is indeed the case. The approach here is similar to that of Ederington and McCalman (2003) but the focus is on how underlying differences in endowment/income levels across countries impact incentives for multilateral cooperation. In particular, since countries are symmetric in Ederington and McCalman (2003), static Nash tariffs are equal across countries (and these in fact are the MFN punishment tariffs in their model). By contrast, in the present model, each country's optimal Nash trade policy in the absence of MFN is a discriminatory tariff vector.[5]

Analysis of the repeated game of multilateral tariff cooperation shows that a country's benefit of defection under tariff discrimination depends upon the volume of its imports (*volume effect*) and on the degree of endowment heterogeneity between its trading partners (*discrimination effect*). The *volume effect* works as follows: when demand is symmetric across countries, the smaller a country's endowment, the larger its imports of protected goods and the stronger its incentive to raise tariff revenue. Simply put, the *discrimination effect* captures the idea that the larger the endowment asymmetry between two competing exporters, the stronger the importing country's incentive to tariff discriminate between them. Of course, a country's incentive to defect from the multilateral agreement also depends upon the (future) cost it suffers during a trade war and this cost turns out to be positively related to its size due to two reasons. First, the loss in export surplus that a country suffers from foreign tariffs is proportional to the volume of its exports. Second, since tariff discrimination is biased against bigger exporters, they suffer relatively larger tariffs under a trade war. Given that the benefit of defection is negatively related to a country's endowment level (when the discrimination effect is not too strong) whereas the cost of defection is positively related, the low income country is the least willing participant in multilateral cooperation when such cooperation is sustained on the basis of discriminatory tariffs.

What if countries punishing a deviation must abide by MFN?[6] How does such a restriction alter the costs and benefits of defection for individual countries? Note that since a deviating country is free to tariff discriminate, the benefit of defection under MFN punishments is the same as that under discriminatory ones. Furthermore, just as under discrimination, the cost of defection increases with country size. Thus, even under MFN punishments, incentives for multilateral cooperation are negatively related to country size. More importantly, I find that the range of parameter values over which the free trade can be sustained under MFN tariffs is larger than the corresponding range under discriminatory tariffs.[7] While numerical simulations are used to illustrate this result in the basic model, an illuminating special case that eliminates the volume effect (and therefore isolates the discrimination effect) permits a remarkably clear graphical demonstration of MFN's contribution to multilateral cooperation (see Fig. 2).

Taken together, the results of this paper show that from the viewpoint of low income countries, MFN and multilateral tariff cooperation are complementary in nature. Absent tariff cooperation, MFN has an adverse effect on low income countries. However, if repeated interaction gives countries the opportunity to cooperate multilaterally then MFN benefits all countries by facilitating the obtainment of free trade.[8] Of course, for high income countries, MFN is beneficial even if the scope for multilateral tariff cooperation is limited or missing altogether.

The rest of this paper is organized as follows. The next section presents the basic model and contrasts tariff discrimination and MFN from a static perspective. Section 3 studies a stationary repeated game to evaluate how MFN affects multilateral tariff cooperation. Section 4 considers several extensions: Section 4.1 considers a special case of the basic model that helps isolate the role of MFN in the absence of the volume effect; Section 4.2 investigates how the formation of a bilateral free trade agreement affects multilateral tariff cooperation relative to MFN; and Section 4.3 considers the role of demand asymmetry. Section 5 concludes while Section 6 constitutes Appendix A.

2. Basic model

The model builds on the partial equilibrium framework of Bagwell and Staiger (1997, 1998). There are three countries:

[4] It is worth noting that developing countries have been granted special and differential (S&D) treatment within the WTO ever since the Generalized System of Preferences (GSP) came into existence in the 1970s. One possible interpretation of these exceptions to MFN is that receiving MFN status from others is simply not sufficient compensation for developing countries to be willing to grant MFN to others.

[5] Furthermore, in Ederington and McCalman (2003) discriminatory punishments refer to the notion that only a deviating country is punished by cooperating countries.

[6] Bown (2004) finds that in actual trade disputes between countries one observes both discriminatory as well as non-discriminatory trade violations. Interestingly, Article XXIII of GATT allows affected member countries to tariff discriminate against a country that is officially found to be in violation of GATT rules.

[7] In Section 4.2, I show that this result holds even when tariff discrimination takes the form of a bilateral trade agreement that, by definition, discriminates against the non-member country. Thus, the present model does not support the well-known exception to MFN provided under Article XXIV of GATT that, under certain conditions, permits WTO members to form preferential trade agreements.

[8] I thank an anonymous referee for suggesting this interpretation of the main results of this paper.

A, B, and C denoted by $J=\{A, B, C\}$; three (non-numeraire) goods a, b, and c denoted by $i=\{a, b, c\}$; and a numeraire good n whose price is normalized to 1. Each country's market is served by two competing exporters and j denotes the good that corresponds to the lower case value of J. For example, if $J=A$, then $j=a$. Country A is endowed with $x/2$ units of goods b and c and zero units of good a; country B is endowed with $y/2$ units of goods a and c and zero units of good b; and country C is endowed with $z/2$ units of goods a and b and zero units of good c. In addition, each country's endowment of the numeraire good n equals e and this endowment is big enough to ensure that trade is balanced.

The demand for good i in country J is given by

$$D(P_i^J) = \alpha - \beta P_i^J. \tag{1}$$

As is well known, the above demand functions can be derived from a utility function of the form $U(c_i)=u(c_i)+n$ where c_i denotes consumption of good i; n denotes the numeraire good; and $u(c_i)$ is quadratic and additively separable in each of the three goods. Since each country possesses only two goods while it demands all three, country J must import good j in order to consume it and it can import it from either trading partner. Fig. 1 illustrates the pattern of trade: each country imports a single good from the other two and exports different goods to each of them. For example, country A imports good a from both countries B and C while it exports good b to country B and good c to country C.

Without loss of generality, let $x<y<z$. Since demand functions are symmetric across goods and countries, prices of all non-numeraire goods are equal across countries under free trade. Let this common free trade price of good i be denoted by P_i. Since $x<y<z$, the free trade national income of country A (which equals $P_b x/2+P_c x/2+e$) is the lowest while that of country C is the highest and it equals $P_a z/2+P_b z/2+$e. Accordingly, from hereon, country A is called the low income country; country B the middle income one; and country C the high income one.

2.1. Tariff-ridden trade equilibrium

Let t_i^J be the tariff imposed on country J's exports of good i. For example, t_a^B is the tariff faced by country B's exports of good a to country A. Thus, country A's tariff vector is given by

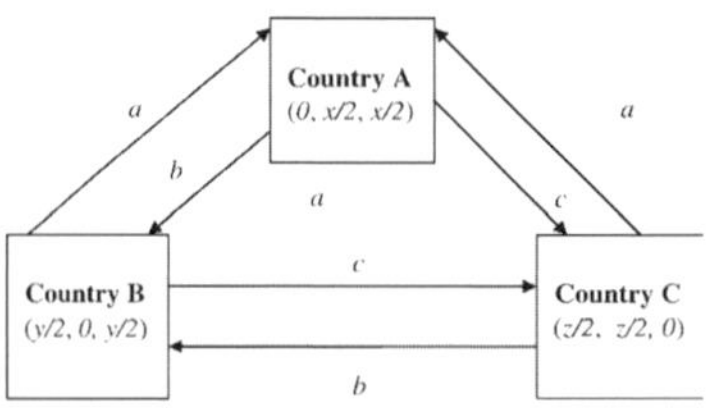

Fig. 1. The pattern of trade.

(t_a^B, t_a^C). Ruling out prohibitive tariffs yields the following no-arbitrage conditions for good a:

$$P_a^A = P_a^B + t_a^B = P_a^C + t_a^C. \tag{2}$$

Similar no-arbitrage conditions hold for the other two goods. Let M_a^A be country A's imports of good a. Since country A has no endowment of good a, we have

$$M_a^A = \alpha - \beta P_a^A. \tag{3}$$

Country B's exports of good a equal its endowment of that good minus its local consumption:

$$X_a^B = y/2 - [\alpha - \beta P_a^B]. \tag{4}$$

Similarly, country C's exports of good a to country A equal:

$$X_a^C = z/2 - [\alpha - \beta P_a^C]. \tag{5}$$

Market clearing for good a requires that country A's imports equal the total exports of countries B and C:

$$M_a^A = X_a^B + X_a^C. \tag{6}$$

Conditions analogous to (2) through (6) hold for the other two goods.

Eqs. (2)–(6) imply that

$$\alpha - \beta P_a^A = y/2 - [\alpha - \beta P_a^B] + z/2 - [\alpha - \beta P_a^C]. \tag{7}$$

Using the non-arbitrage condition (2), we have

$$\alpha - \beta P_a^A = y/2 - [\alpha - \beta(P_a^A - t_a^B)] + z/2 - [\alpha - \beta(P_a^A - t_a^C)] \tag{8}$$

which yields the equilibrium price of good a in country A:

$$P_a^A = \frac{6\alpha - y - z}{6\beta} + \frac{t_a^B + t_a^C}{3}. \tag{9}$$

As expected, the price of good a in country A increases in its tariffs and decreases in the endowment levels of the other two countries. From Eqs. (2) and (9) we have,

$$P_a^B = \frac{6\alpha - y - z}{6\beta} - (2t_a^B - {}_a^C) \text{ and } P_a^C = \frac{6\alpha - y - z}{6\beta} - (2t_a^C - t_a^B). \tag{10}$$

Using these prices, the volume of trade is easily calculated. Country A's imports of good a equal:

$$M_a^A = \frac{y+z}{6} - \frac{\beta(t_a^B + t_a^C)}{3} \tag{11}$$

where the exports of each of its trading partners are

$$X_a^B = \frac{2y - z}{6} - \frac{\beta(2t_a^B - t_a^C)}{3} \text{ and } X_a^C = \frac{2z - y}{6} - \frac{\beta(2t_a^C - t_a^B)}{3}. \tag{12}$$

As expected, country A's total imports decrease with either tariff and country B's exports to country A decrease with t_a^B whereas they increase with t_a^C.

By design the model examines country J's trade protection towards only good j (i.e. the only non-numeraire good that it imports). Since countries have asymmetric endowments, under free trade (i.e. when $t_i^J=0$ for all i and J), country A faces the largest volume of imports of protected goods (it imports $(y+z)/6$ units of good a) whereas country C faces the lowest volume of imports of such goods (it imports $(x+y)/6$ units of good c).[9] Note also that country J's imports of good j do *not* equal its exports of other non-numeraire goods. For example, under free trade, country A exports $(2x-z)/6$ units of good b to country B and $(2x-y)/6$ units of good c to country C and these are lower than its imports of good a from either country: $0<2x-z<2x-y<y+z$. In order to balance trade, in addition to exporting goods b and c, country A exports the numeraire good to both countries B and C. Similarly, country C imports the numeraire good from both its trading partners.

2.2. Discriminatory tariffs in Nash equilibrium

In what follows, to keep the analysis tractable it is assumed that the pattern of trade does not change with the nature of the tariff regime (MFN or discrimination). As Bagwell and Staiger (1998) note, in practice there are likely to be significant fixed costs involved in exporting and small tariff changes will typically alter only the volume of trade without changing the underlying pattern of world trade.

Each country chooses its tariff vector to maximize its welfare. Given the partial equilibrium nature of the model, it suffices to consider only protected goods and welfare can be defined as the sum of consumer surplus, producer surplus, and tariff revenue over all such goods. Furthermore, also note that country J is policy active in only good j. As a result, tariff policies are independent across countries in this model. This feature of the model is a bit unrealistic but it greatly simplifies the analysis. It also fits with the argument made by Staiger (1995) that strategic independence of tariffs across countries is a reasonable assumption since it is not clear whether tariffs ought to be strategic substitutes or complements.

Given the structure of the model, it is sufficient to consider Country A's tariff problem in isolation:

$$\max_{t_a^B,t_a^C} W^A(t_a^B,t_a^C)=\sum_i \mathrm{CS}_i^A(t_a^B,t_a^C)+\sum_i \mathrm{PS}_i^A(t_a^B,t_a^C)+\mathrm{TR}^A(t_a^B,t_a^C) \tag{13}$$

where country A's consumer surplus over imports and exports equals:

$$\sum_i \mathrm{CS}_i^A=\frac{1}{2\beta}\left[(M_a^A)^2+(\alpha-\beta P_b^A)^2+(\alpha-\beta P_c^A)^2\right] \tag{14}$$

its producer surplus equals over local sales and exports equals:

$$\sum_i \mathrm{PS}_i^A=(x/2-X_b^A)P_b^A+(x/2-X_c^A)P_c^A+X_b^A(P_b^B-t_b^A)+X_c^A(P_c^C-t_c^A) \tag{15}$$

and its tariff revenue equals

$$\mathrm{TR}^A=t_a^BX_a^B+t_a^CX_a^C. \tag{16}$$

Maximization of the welfare function in (13) delivers country A's optimal discriminatory tariff schedule:

$$t_a^B=\frac{3y-z}{16\beta}\ \text{and}\ t_a^C=\frac{3z-y}{16\beta}. \tag{17}$$

Inspection reveals that $t_a^B<t_a^C$ *since* $y<z$:

Proposition 1. *Under optimal tariff discrimination, each country levies a higher tariff on its relatively bigger trade partner.*

To see why such discrimination is optimal from each country's perspective, suppose country A were to treat countries B and C symmetrically by setting $t_a^B=t_a^C$. Under symmetric tariffs, due to endowment asymmetry country A would import more of good a from country C than from country B. Now suppose country were to increase t_a^C by a small amount ε and decreases t_a^B by the same amount such that even under the new tariff schedule country A continues to import more from country C. Since demand is linear, such a change in tariff levels does not alter country A's total imports of good a: from Eq. (11) note that M_a depends only upon the sum of country A's tariffs (i.e. on $t_a^B+t_a^C$). However, since $X_a^C>X_a^B$, this policy change *increases* country A's total tariff revenue without altering any other component of its welfare. Thus, beginning at $t_a^B=t_a^C$, country A's tariff revenue increases if it raises its tariff on country C by a small amount and lowers its on country B by the same amount. In fact, the larger the difference between the volume of imports sourced from the two countries under symmetric treatment, the stronger the degree of tariff discrimination against the bigger exporter (this is called the *discrimination effect*).

An alternative perspective on Proposition 1 — and one that is in line with the traditional optimal tariff argument — can be obtained by considering the elasticity of the export supply curve for each country. Under free trade, the elasticity of country B's export supply curve with respect to country A is given by

$$f^B\equiv\frac{dX_a^B/X_a^B}{dP_a^B/P_a^B}=\beta\frac{P_a^B}{X_a^B}=\frac{2\alpha-y}{2X_a^B}+1. \tag{18}$$

Similarly, the elasticity of country C's export supply curve to country A equals

$$f^C\equiv\frac{2\alpha-z}{2X_a^C}+1. \tag{19}$$

Now note that if both countries B and C face the same tariff (which is zero under free trade) then $X_a^C>X_a^B$ since $y<z$. It follows then that starting at $t_a^B=t_a^C$, we have $f^C<f^B$: i.e. the country with the bigger endowment of good a has a less elastic

[9] The same ranking applies with respect to the value of imports $P_j^J mjJ$ so long as $\alpha>x+y+2z$, which is a very minor condition and it is assumed to be satisfied. Given this condition, value of country A's imports (of good a) exceeds the value of country B's imports (of good b) and country C's value of imports (of good c).

export supply curve. As a result, country A has an incentive to impose a higher tariff on country B relative to country C.[10]

2.3. Nash MFN tariffs

Under MFN, each country imposes the same tariff on the other two. For example, under MFN Country A solves:

$$\operatorname*{Max}_{t_a} W^A(t_a) = \sum_i \mathrm{CS}_i^A(t_a) + \sum_i \mathrm{PS}_i^A(t_a) + \mathrm{TR}^A(t_a). \quad (20)$$

Straightforward calculations yield country A's optimal MFN tariff t_a^M:

$$t_a^M = \frac{y+z}{16\beta}. \quad (21)$$

A comparison of country A's optimal MFN tariff with its optimal discriminatory tariff schedule yields the following:

Proposition 2. *Each country's optimal MFN tariff is the average of its two optimal discriminatory tariffs:* $2t_a^M = t_a^B + t_a^C$.[11]

Thus, relative to tariff discrimination, MFN benefits each country's bigger trade partner while it hurts the smaller one. As was noted earlier, this result suggests that MFN treatment by itself may be insufficient to induce small developing countries to participate in an MFN based organization such as the WTO and that S&D treatment accorded to such countries might have been necessary to induce (or retain) their WTO membership.

Having clarified the distributional impact of MFN, it is time now to turn to its aggregate effect.

2.4. A welfare comparison of the two regimes

To conserve space, let $\mathbf{t^J}$ denote country J's optimal discriminatory tariff schedule. For example, $\mathbf{t^A} = (t_a^B, t_a^C)$. Prices of good a in the two exporting countries (B and C) differ from the price in country A only by the respective tariffs (t_a^B, t_a^C) faced by each country. Since $2t_a^M = t_a^B + t_a^C$, the equilibrium price of good a in country A is the same under MFN and discrimination. Thus, the total volume of imports of country A (and therefore local producer and consumer surplus) does not change with its MFN adoption. As a result, the only effect of MFN on the welfare of the adopting country is to lower its tariff revenue and (therefore) its total welfare. Accordingly, country A's loss from MFN adoption equals:

$$\Delta W^A(t_a^M, \mathbf{t^A}) \equiv W^A(t_a^M) - W^A(\mathbf{t^A}) = -\frac{(z-y)^2}{32\beta} < 0. \quad (22)$$

As is obvious from the above equation, if countries B and C were completely symmetric (i.e. $y=z$) then MFN adoption by country A does not affect its welfare.

How does MFN adoption by country A affect welfare of countries B and C? We know that

$$P_a^B(\mathbf{t^A}) + t_a^B = P_a^C(\mathbf{t^A}) + t_a^C \text{ and } t_a^B < t_a^C \Rightarrow P_a^B(\mathbf{t^A}) > P_a^C(\mathbf{t^A}) \quad (23)$$

i.e. the price of good a under discrimination is higher in country B relative to country C. By contrast, under MFN we have

$$P_a^B(t_a^M) + t_a^M = P_a^C(t_a^M) + t_a^M \Rightarrow P_a^B(t_a^M) = P_a^C(t_a^M) \quad (24)$$

i.e. the price of good a under MFN is equal in countries B and C even though they do not directly trade this good with each other. The higher price of good a in country B relative to that in country C under tariff discrimination creates a global inefficiency that is remedied by MFN.[12] Straightforward calculations (contained in the Appendix A) lead to

Proposition 3. *MFN adoption by country J (i) lowers its own welfare by decreasing its tariff revenue; (ii) increases (decreases) producer surplus and decreases (increases) consumer surplus in the country from whom it imports relatively more (less) of good j while it increases (reduces) its total welfare; and (iii) it increases aggregate world welfare.*

Following the derivations outlined for country A, two additional results can be shown. First, *the biggest welfare gain for the world comes from the MFN adoption of country B (the middle income country).* In fact, it is straightforward to show that

$$\Delta \mathrm{WW}^B(t_b^M, \mathbf{t^B}) \equiv \mathrm{WW}(t_b^M) - \mathrm{WW}(\mathbf{t^B}) = \frac{|\Delta W^B(t_b^M, \mathbf{t^B})|}{2} = \frac{(z-x)^2}{64\beta} > 0. \quad (25)$$

The intuition is that country B's discriminatory tariffs create a bigger inefficiency relative to those of the other two countries since the difference between equilibrium prices of good b between countries A and C is larger than the analogous price differentials between the other two countries. The equilibrium price differentials have this feature because the gap between A and C's respective endowments of good b (i.e. $z-x$) is larger than the gap between B and C's endowments of good a (i.e. $z-y$) and A and B's endowments of good c (i.e. $y-x$).

A second result that follows from the independence of tariffs across countries is that the *world welfare gain from MFN adoption is additive in the number of countries that adopt MFN*:

$$\Delta \mathrm{WW}^M(\mathbf{t^M}, \mathbf{t^D}) \equiv \mathrm{WW}(\mathbf{t^M}) - \mathrm{WW}(\mathbf{t^D}) = \frac{(y-z)^2 + (x-z)^2 + (x-y)^2}{64\beta} > 0 \quad (26)$$

where $\mathbf{t^D} = (\mathbf{t^A}, \mathbf{t^B}, \mathbf{t^C})$ is the vector of optimal discriminatory tariffs of all countries and $\mathbf{t^M} = (t_a^M, t_b^M, t_c^M)$ that of optimal MFN tariffs.

[10] Of course, since each country imports from multiple sources, its optimal tariff on another country no longer exactly equals the inverse of the elasticity of that country's export supply curve (see Ederington and McCalman, 2003, for a more in-depth discussion of this issue).

[11] Linearity delivers this precise relationship between tariffs under the two regimes. In the absence of linearity, one would expect that the optimal MFN tariff would be bound by the two discriminatory tariffs and not necessarily lie at the midpoint.

[12] Recall that the price of good a in country A is the same under MFN and discrimination.

The analysis above has shown that MFN adoption is beneficial for world welfare. The key point here is that MFN constrains the pursuit of "beggar-thy-neighbor" trade policies on the part of individual countries: each country's optimal discriminatory tariffs impose deadweight losses on its trade partners that outweigh its own benefits. Although MFN does not eliminate the aggregate terms of trade losses suffered by exporters, it reduces their magnitude. Furthermore, while MFN increases aggregate world welfare, it does have distributional consequences in that it makes the smaller exporter to each country worse off. Having said that, it is worth noting that strategic independence of tariffs across countries is an important driving force behind Propositions 1–3. Whether or not such results can be obtained when tariffs are interdependent across countries is difficult to determine without having an analytically tractable model of interdependent tariffs.

3. Role of MFN in sustaining free trade

This section evaluates the contribution of MFN to multilateral cooperation over free trade. As in much of the existing literature, multilateral cooperation is modeled as the infinite repetition of the basic tariff game. Defection by any country results in a trade war wherein all countries revert to their static Nash tariffs (i.e. countries use trigger strategies) that vary with the underlying policy regime (MFN or tariff discrimination). Every period, each country weighs the current benefit of defecting from cooperation against the future cost of the breakdown of such cooperation.

3.1. Cooperation under discriminatory tariffs

Suppose the three countries agree to cooperate on multilateral free trade (denoted by the 1×3 vector $\mathbf{0}\equiv(0,0,0)$). Each country practices free trade until anyone defects, in which case cooperation breaks down with all countries imposing their optimal discriminatory tariffs on each other. Let $W^J(\mathbf{0})$ denote the per period welfare of country J under multilateral free trade:

$$W^J(\mathbf{0}) = S^J(0) + X^J(\mathbf{0}_{-J}). \tag{27}$$

where (*i*) $S^J(0)$ is the sum of country J's domestic producer surplus, consumer surplus, and tariff revenue when it practices free trade and (*ii*) $X^J(\mathbf{0}_{-J})$ is country J's export surplus when it faces no tariffs abroad (the 1×2 vector $\mathbf{0}_{-J}\equiv(0,0)$ denotes zero tariffs of countries other than J).

Let $W^J(\mathbf{t^J}, \mathbf{0}_{-J})$ denote the welfare of country J when it defects from cooperation over free trade to its optimal discriminatory tariff vector $\mathbf{t^J}$ given that other countries practice free trade:

$$W^J(\mathbf{t^j}, \mathbf{0}_{-J}) = S^J(\mathbf{t^j}) + X^J(\mathbf{0}_{-J}). \tag{28}$$

An important feature of the model that greatly simplifies the analysis is that when a country changes its tariffs, its export surplus remains unchanged. Recall that since good j is imported only by country J, when country J changes its tariffs, prices of other goods are unaffected in all countries. As a result, own defection benefits a country by increasing its domestic surplus but has no effect on its export surplus. Thus, country J's one time payoff of defecting from free trade to its optimal discriminatory tariff schedule equals:

$$B^J(\mathbf{t^J}, \mathbf{0}_{-J}) = W^J(\mathbf{t^J}, \mathbf{0}_{-J}) - W^J(\mathbf{0}) = S^J(\mathbf{t^J}) - S^J(\mathbf{0}_{-J}). \tag{29}$$

Now consider the cost of defection. Defection by any country leads to a permanent trade war in which all countries impose their optimal discriminatory tariffs. Recall that $\mathbf{t^D}$ denotes the vector of optimal discriminatory tariffs under the trade war where $\mathbf{t^D}=(\mathbf{t^A}, \mathbf{t^B}, \mathbf{t^C})$. Let country J's surplus from exports under a trade war be denoted by $X^J(\mathbf{t^D})$. The per period cost to country J of a trade war is given by

$$C^J(\mathbf{t^D}, 0) = W^J(\mathbf{0}) - W^J(\mathbf{t^D}) = S^J(\mathbf{0}) - S^J(\mathbf{t^D}) + X^J(\mathbf{0}) - X^J(\mathbf{t^D}). \tag{30}$$

The above equation shows that a country's cost of defection is comprised of two components. The first component is the increase in domestic surplus caused by the breakdown of cooperation whereas the second is the loss in export surplus that results from an increase in foreign tariffs. Domestic surplus under a trade war exceeds that under free trade due to two reasons. First, total domestic surplus derived by country J from good j is higher under a trade war than under free trade (due to own tariffs). Second, foreign tariffs increase domestic supply of exported goods thereby lowering local prices of those goods.

For cooperation to succeed, the current benefit of defection must be less than the discounted life-time cost of defection for each country. In other words, the following incentive compatibility (IC) constraint must hold for each country:

$$B^J(\mathbf{t^J}, \mathbf{0}_{-J}) \le \frac{\delta}{1-\delta} C^J(\mathbf{t^D}, 0) \tag{31}$$

where δ denotes the discount factor so that $\frac{\delta}{1-\delta} C^J(\mathbf{t^D}, 0)$ measures the trade war's cost to country J. It is shown in Appendix A that

$$B^B(\mathbf{t^B}, \mathbf{0}_{-B}) > B^C(\mathbf{t^C}, \mathbf{0}_{-C}) \tag{32}$$

Furthermore,

$$B^B(\mathbf{t^B}, \mathbf{0}_{-B}) > B^A(\mathbf{t^A}, \mathbf{0}_{-A}) \text{ iff } 34z > 19(x+y) \tag{33}$$

and that

$$B^A(\mathbf{t^A}, \mathbf{0}_{-A}) > B^C(\mathbf{t^C}, \mathbf{0}_{-C}) \text{ iff } 19(x+z) > 34y. \tag{34}$$

Proposition 4. *If inequality* (33) *holds, the middle income country has the highest benefit of defection:* $B^B(\mathbf{t^B}, \mathbf{0}_{-B}) > \text{Max}\{B^A(\mathbf{t^A}, \mathbf{0}_{-A}), B^C(\mathbf{t^C}, \mathbf{0}_{-C})\}$. *Furthermore, the high income country has the smallest benefit of defection* ($B^C(\mathbf{t^C}, \mathbf{0}_{-C}) < B^A(\mathbf{t^A}, \mathbf{0}_{-A})$) *iff inequality* (34) *holds.*

Proposition 4 can be understood as follows. A country's benefit of defection is determined by two effects both of which arise from the underlying asymmetry across countries. First is the *volume effect*: the larger a country's volume of imports, the stronger its current benefit of raising tariffs on its trade partners. Second is the *discrimination effect*: larger the size asymmetry between two countries, the stronger the third country's incentive to discriminate between them. Recall that low income country (i.e. A) faces the largest volume of imports of protected goods while the middle income country (i.e. B) gains the most from being able to discriminate. If the discrimination effect dominates (as it does when inequality 33 holds) then the middle income country has the strongest incentive to defect. On the other hand, when the volume effect dominates, the low income country (i.e. A) gains the most from defection.

Proposition 5A. *When defections are punished by discriminatory tariffs, the low income country's cost of defection is the smallest while that of the high income country is the largest:* $C^A(\mathbf{t^D}, 0) < C^B(\mathbf{t^D}, 0) < C^C(\mathbf{t^D}, 0)$.

The above result holds due to two reasons. First, since country A's volume of exports of protected goods is the smallest, any given tariff increases by its trade partners implies a smaller loss in its export surplus. Second, since discriminatory tariffs are biased against bigger exporters, country A suffers the smallest tariff increases during a trade war. Propositions 4 and 5A together imply that, *under tariff discrimination, the low income country has the weakest incentive for multilateral cooperation* (if inequality (33) does not hold then the middle income country has the weakest incentive). Thus, multilateral cooperation can succeed only if the two relatively smaller countries find it incentive compatible to cooperate multilaterally: i.e. iff $\delta > \max\{\delta^A(\mathbf{t^D}), \delta^B(\mathbf{t^D})\}$.

We are now in a position to consider multilateral cooperation under MFN tariffs.

3.2. *Sustaining cooperation via MFN tariffs*

Recall that $\mathbf{t^M}$ denotes the vector of MFN tariffs of all three countries. Let $\mathbf{t^M_{-J}}$ denote the vector of MFN tariffs of countries other than J. As under discrimination, if country J defects, it switches to its optimal discriminatory tariff vector $\mathbf{t^J}$. Defection by any one country results in a trade war under which the non-defecting countries adopt their respective MFN tariffs. It is obvious that even if cooperation is sustained via MFN tariffs, each country's benefit of defecting from cooperation is the same as that when it is sustained by discriminatory tariffs so that Proposition 4 continues to apply.

Consider next the costs of defection. As under discrimination, we can write

$$C^J(\mathbf{t^M}, \mathbf{0}) = S^J(\mathbf{0}) - S^J(\mathbf{t^M}) + X^J(\mathbf{0}) - X^J(\mathbf{t^M}). \qquad (35)$$

Proposition 5B. *When cooperation is sustained via MFN tariffs, the low income country's cost of defection is the smallest while that of the high income country is the largest:* $C^A(\mathbf{t^M}, \mathbf{0}) < C^B(\mathbf{t^M}, \mathbf{0}) < C^C(\mathbf{t^M}, \mathbf{0})$.

The intuition for this result is that, under a trade war, the low income country benefits the most from the increase in its own tariff (which is the highest) and is hurt the least in export markets because the tariff increases inflicted by its trade partners are relatively smaller. As a result, it faces the lowest cost of defection on both counts: the loss in domestic consumer surplus is shielded to a greater degree by the benefits of a tariff increase on a larger volume of imports whereas the loss in export surplus is muted due to smaller tariff increases abroad. Propositions 4 and 5A imply that even under MFN punishments, either the low or the middle income has the strongest incentive to defect from multilateral cooperation. Under what type of tariffs is cooperation more likely to succeed? We turn to this next.

Table 1
Critical discount factors under discrimination and MFN

Endowments	$\delta^J(\mathbf{t^D})$	$\delta^J(\mathbf{t^J}, \mathbf{t^M})$
(*i*) $x=2, y=2, z=2$	.57, .57, .57	.57, .57, .57
(*ii*) $x=2, y=2, z=2.2$	.78, .78, .36	.66, .66, .45
(*iii*) $x=2, y=2.1, z=2.2$	.87, .59, .41	.70, .58, .48
(*iv*) $x=2, y=2.1, z=2.25$	.95, .64, .37	.73, .61, .45

3.3. *MFN versus discriminatory punishments*

Whether or not MFN facilitates multilateral cooperation can be determined by a comparison of $\delta^A(\mathbf{t^A}, \mathbf{t^M})$ and $\max\{\delta^A(\mathbf{t^D}), \delta^B(\mathbf{t^D})\}$. Unfortunately, a ranking of these critical discount factors proves analytically difficult. However, numerical simulations show that countries are indeed more willing to multilaterally cooperate under MFN relative to tariff discrimination. Table 1 below shows the results of a typical simulation.[13]

Note from Table 1 that when countries are fully symmetric, as expected, the degree of multilateral cooperation under both discriminatory and MFN tariffs is identical and free trade occurs in the range $\delta \in (.57, 1)$. However, in cases (*ii*) through (*iv*), free trade can be sustained for a *larger* range of parameter values under MFN tariffs relative to discriminatory tariffs. Table 1 also illustrates that the range of discount factors over which the low income country is willing to cooperate is the smallest. A few additional observations regarding the role played by the other two countries in multilateral tariff cooperation can be made from Table 1. First, a comparison of cases (*ii*) and (*iii*) indicates that as the middle income country's endowment increases, its willingness to cooperate (under both discrimination and MFN) increases whereas that of the low income country decreases substantially.[14]

Second, the high income country is always more willing to cooperate under discrimination relative to MFN. However, since it is the incentive constraint of the low income country that determines whether multilateral cooperation succeeds or not, the high income country's lower willingness to cooperate under MFN turns out not to matter.

[13] While the above simulations are illustrative rather than definitive, a counterexample to the findings in Table 1 could not be found despite extensive explorations.

[14] Interestingly, under discrimination, an increase in the size of the middle income country makes the high income country less willing to cooperate since its incentive to discriminate between its trading partners increases.

4. Extensions

In this section, I consider three extensions of the basic model. First, I consider a model that separates the discrimination effect from the volume effect. Second, I examine how the formation of a bilateral free trade agreement affects multilateral tariff cooperation. Third, I briefly study the role of potential demand asymmetry across countries.

4.1. Isolating the discrimination effect

In the model considered thus far, each country's optimal discriminatory tariffs depend upon its incentive to discriminate across its trading partners as well as the total volume of its trade. Since MFN is essentially a non-discrimination clause, it is worth asking how the analysis in this paper is modified if only the discrimination incentive is in operation. This can be addressed by considering the following endowment structure: let country A's endowment vector be $(0, x, 1-x)$, that of B be $(1-x, 0, x)$ and that of C be $(x, 1-x, 0)$ where $0 \leq x \leq 1$.[15] As is clear, under this endowment structure the total global supply of each good equals 1 unit and when $x=1/2$, each country faces two symmetric suppliers (and therefore has no incentive to tariff discriminate). Furthermore, since the total volume of each country's imports under free trade is the same, the volume effect plays no role in determining optimal tariffs and the effects of MFN. Following earlier derivations, it is straightforward to show that the optimal discriminatory tariff vector is the same for all countries

$$t^J = \frac{3-4x}{8\beta} \quad \text{and} \quad t^K = \frac{4x-1}{8\beta} \quad \text{where} \quad J \neq K \tag{36}$$

and that each country's optimal MFN tariff equals

$$t^M = \frac{1}{8\beta} = \frac{t^J + t^K}{2}. \tag{37}$$

As before, since demand is linear, each country's optimal MFN tariff is the average of its optimal discriminatory tariffs and MFN adoption increases aggregate global welfare relative to tariff discrimination.

This alternative endowment structure proves especially useful in isolating the value of MFN in sustaining cooperation. To see this, note that since each country faces two exporters with endowments of x and $1-x$, the incentive compatibility constraints for all three countries are now identical. This simplifies the analysis of tariff cooperation tremendously since it reduces the number of incentive constraints that need to be satisfied from three to one.

In fact, it is straightforward to show that tariff cooperation succeeds under MFN iff $\delta > \delta^M \equiv 4/7$ whereas it succeeds under discrimination iff

$$\delta > \delta^D \equiv \frac{4(19-72x(1-x))}{115-432x(1-x)}. \tag{38}$$

[15] I thank an anonymous referee for making this valuable suggestion since it helps isolate the role of non-discrimination in an elegant manner.

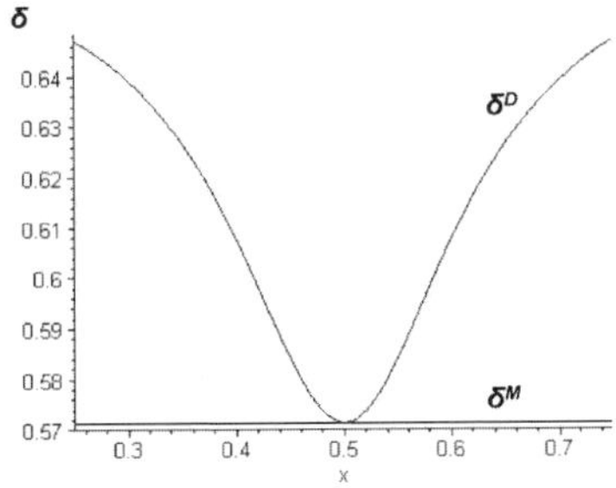

Fig. 2. MFN facilitates multilateral cooperation.

Plotting δ^D and δ^M over the permissible parameter range delivers Fig. 2.

As is clear from Fig. 2, $\delta^D \geq \delta^M$. More specifically, δ^D lies *above* δ^M (which is a horizontal line just above the x axis) everywhere except when $x=1/2$ at which point $\delta^D=\delta^M$. At $x=1/2$, each country faces identical exporters and therefore has no incentive to discriminate. For *any* other endowment distribution, each country has a unilateral incentive to tariff discriminate and MFN blunts the gains of tariff defection while raising the costs of such defection. More specifically, we have:

$$B^M(t^M, \mathbf{0}_{-J}) - B^J(\mathbf{t}^J, \mathbf{0}_{-J}) = -\frac{(2x-1)^2}{8\beta} < 0 \tag{39}$$

whereas

$$C^M(t^M, \mathbf{0}_{-J}) - C^J(\mathbf{t}^J, \mathbf{0}_{-J}) = \frac{(2x-1)^2}{16\beta} < 0 \tag{40}$$

But note that

$$|B^M(t^M, \mathbf{0}_{-J}) - B^J(\mathbf{t}^J, \mathbf{0}_{-J})| = 2|C^M(t^M, \mathbf{0}_{-J}) - C^J(\mathbf{t}^J, \mathbf{0}_{-J})| > 0. \tag{41}$$

Thus, MFN reduces the benefits of defection by double the amount by which it reduces the costs of defection thereby making the overall incentive constraint easier to satisfy. As a result, MFN facilitates multilateral tariff cooperation relative to tariff discrimination.

Thus far, the paper has asked whether MFN yields tariff cooperation over free trade for a larger set of discount factors than discrimination. An alternative way of specifying the gains from MFN adoption is to quantify the explicit welfare gains that MFN yields for a given discount factor.[16] It is clear that when both regimes can sustain free trade, the issue is whether or not MFN sustains free trade for a larger parameter range. However, the question of quantifying long run welfare gains from MFN is interesting even when free trade cannot be sustained under either regime. Under such circumstances, the lowest sustainable tariffs under the two regimes assume an important role. As

[16] Once again I thank an anonymous referee for posing this question.

might be expected, analytical results in this regard are hard to come by but numerical examples show that when free trade cannot be sustained under either regime, MFN delivers slightly higher world welfare than tariff discrimination. An example illustrates the point. Suppose $\delta=0.55$. Then it is easy to show that that free trade cannot be sustained under either regime. Let $\alpha=\beta=1$ and $x=0.6$. Calculating aggregate world welfare under the lowest sustainable tariffs under the two regimes yields that the welfare gain from MFN adoption is of the order of .03%.

4.2. Bilateral trade agreements

In the real world, tariff discrimination often arises in the form of bilateral trade agreements under which member countries grant each other preferential treatment relative to non-members. Do such agreements hinder or facilitate multilateral tariff cooperation relative to MFN? To address this issue, suppose countries B and C form a bilateral FTA wherein they agree to impose no tariffs on each other. Their individual tariffs on country A are chosen independently to maximize their respective welfare. Thus, under a bilateral FTA, member countries practice constrained tariff discrimination: each imposes a zero tariff on the other member and its individually optimal external tariff on the non-member.

Under multilateral cooperation, countries impose no tariffs on each other. However, if cooperation breaks down, FTA members continue to impose no tariffs on each other but impose their optimal external tariffs on the non-member. The major question of interest is: Is multilateral cooperation in the presence of a bilateral FTA easier or harder to sustain relative to MFN? As before, a direct answer to this question can be obtained by solving the critical discount factor for each country under an FTA and then identifying the country whose incentive constraint is hardest to satisfy. It turns out that in the present model, it is the *non-member country* whose incentive to cooperate is most weakened due to the formation of a bilateral FTA. The intuition for this is that the statically optimal Nash tariffs of FTA members B and C on non-member country A are lower than their respective MFN tariffs (i.e. there is tariff complementarity). As a result, the welfare loss suffered by the non-member due to the breakdown of cooperation is *lower* in the presence of an FTA relative to MFN. This in turn implies that it is less willing to cooperate multilaterally relative to MFN. Rather than present repetitive calculations, I show the above result in Fig. 3.

Fig. 3 shows the critical discount factors of the two members (countries B and C) as well as that of the non-member (country A) and compares them with the critical discount factor under MFN. As is clear, the critical discount factor under MFN is always dominated by that of the non-member (which in turn lies below the critical discount factor of a member when x is quite near $1/2$). The crucial point is that multilateral tariff cooperation necessarily declines due to the formation of an FTA. This result accords well with the existing literature on preferential trade agreements and multilateral tariff cooperation (such as Bagwell and Staiger, 1997; Saggi, 2006). This literature has shown that when countries are symmetric and multilateral cooperation is self-enforcing in nature, the decline in the external tariffs of member countries relative to MFN can undermine the cooperation incentive of the non-member country by reducing the punishment it faces in the event of a trade war.[17]

4.3. Role of demand asymmetry

The focus of this paper is on how the effects of MFN depend upon endowment asymmetries across countries. But this is not the only dimension along which countries might to be asymmetric. Surely, demand asymmetries can also play an important role in determining this context.[18] To isolate the role of demand asymmetry, retain the endowment structure of Section 4.1 and suppose the demand function for good i in country J is given by $D(P_i^J)=\alpha^J-\beta P_i^J$. For expositional simplicity, let $\alpha^A=\alpha^B=\alpha\leq\alpha^C$ and $\Delta\alpha\equiv\alpha^C-\alpha\geq 0$. In other words, country C is the high demand country relative to countries A and B. It is clear that country C has a tendency to import a higher quantity of good c relative to the imports of goods a and b by the other two countries and this has a bearing on the effects of MFN. To avoid redundancy, in what follows, I make note of the main points that emerge from the analysis of this demand driven model without delving into detailed derivations.

First note that Country A's optimal discriminatory tariffs are now given by[19]

$$t_a^B=\frac{3-4x+\Delta\alpha}{8\beta} \quad \text{and} \quad t_a^C=\frac{4x-1-3\Delta\alpha}{8\beta} \tag{42}$$

It follows from above that

$$t_a^C-t_a^B=-\frac{(1-2x+\Delta\alpha)}{2\beta}. \tag{43}$$

At $x=1/2$, the endowment structure provides no incentive for tariff discrimination but demand asymmetry does. It is immediate from above that at $x=1/2$, $t_a^C<t_a^B$. Intuitively, country C's higher demand translates into a reduced willingness on its part to export to foreign markets which is then reflected in relatively smaller tariffs on its exports. This basic force is in operation even when the endowment pattern is asymmetric across countries except that it can be dominated by supply side considerations thereby reversing the pattern of tariff discrimination. In fact, it is immediate from above that $t_a^C>t_a^B$ iff

$$1-2x+\Delta\alpha<0\Leftrightarrow x-(1-x)>\Delta\alpha. \tag{44}$$

Intuitively, the left hand side of the above inequality measures the degree to which country C's endowment of

[17] Note that in the present model, as well as in most of the existing literature, the formation of an FTA does not alter the optimal Nash tariffs of non-member countries (because of tariff independence across countries). In a richer model where national tariffs are interdependent, cooperation incentive of the non-member country need not necessarily decline.

[18] I thank an anonymous referee for making this suggestion.

[19] Since demand is symmetric across countries A and B, exactly the same conclusions hold with respect to its tariffs.

good a exceeds that of country B while the right hand side measures the extent to which its own demand for the same good is higher. Only when asymmetry on the supply side dominates that on the demand side is country C the relatively bigger exporter to country A and therefore ends up facing the higher tariff under discrimination.

Consider now the optimal tariffs of the high demand country (i.e. C). We have:

$$t_c^B = \frac{4x - 1 + 2\Delta\alpha}{8\beta}; t_c^A = \frac{3 - 4x + 2\Delta\alpha}{8\beta}. \quad (45)$$

As might be expected, the fact that its own demand is higher affects the level of country C's optimal tariffs but *not* their qualitative pattern — its tariff on country B exceeds that on A iff $x > 1/2$ (exactly the same condition holds under demand symmetry).

I now briefly summarize the results under repeated interaction. First, it turns out that under tariff discrimination, while country C does not always have the largest benefit of defection, its cost of defection is lower than that of the other two countries. However, the incentive constraints under MFN can be ranked unambiguously: country C has the lowest cost and the highest benefit of defection. This result corresponds quite well to the earlier result under symmetric demand that the country with the smallest endowment is the least willing participant in multilateral cooperation. Intuitively, high demand at home translates into smaller exports and larger imports of protected goods. Finally, extensive numerical simulations yield a figure quite similar to Fig. 3: the critical discount factor above which country C is willing to cooperate under MFN is smaller than its corresponding discount factor under discrimination, i.e., MFN facilitates multilateral cooperation under the type of demand asymmetry explored above.

5. Conclusion

This paper explores the economics of MFN along two dimensions: it investigates the welfare effects of MFN and evaluates its contribution to multilateral cooperation. An important result is that while MFN has beneficial effects on world welfare, its adoption alone does not benefit the low income country since it faces lower tariffs under tariff discrimination. However, the paper also shows that multilateral cooperation over free trade is easier to sustain when defections are punished by MFN tariffs relative to discriminatory ones and this aspect of MFN benefits all countries.

The results of this paper regarding the static welfare effects of MFN fit well with the existing explorations of MFN in the oligopoly model of trade (see Gatsios 1990, Choi, 1995, Saggi, 2004): in such models, high cost countries are worse off under MFN relative to discrimination. Such close correspondence between the two sets of models is encouraging since whether one views developing countries as having smaller economies or as having inferior production technologies does not appear to matter. From the perspective of trade theory, these results are also reassuring because the nature of trade and the motive for tariffs differ fundamentally in two types of models: in the oligopoly model, trade is intraindustry in nature and tariffs serve to extract rents from firms with market power whereas in the model presented here, trade is interindustry and tariffs are motivated by terms of trade considerations.

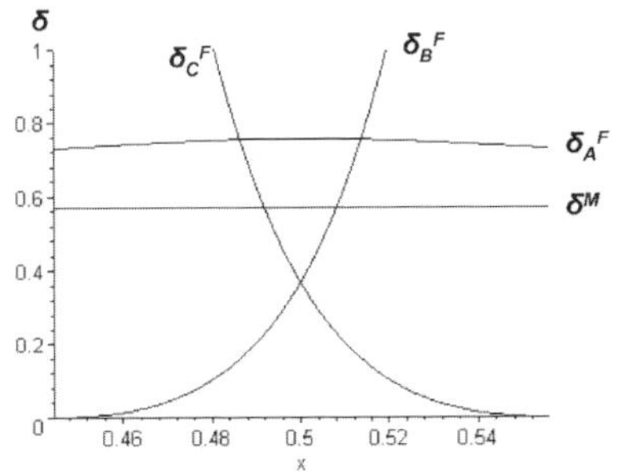

Fig. 3. An FTA between countries B and C hampers multilateral cooperation.

Appendix A

The appendix contains all derivations and proofs not included in the text.

Proposition 3. Welfare effects of MFN

MFN adoption by country A impacts countries B and C via its effects on both consumer welfare and producer surplus.[20] Consider first the effect on producers. It is straightforward to show that

$$\mathrm{PS}^C(t_a^M) - \mathrm{PS}^C(\mathbf{t}^A) = \frac{z(z-y)}{16\beta} > 0 \quad (46)$$

whereas

$$\mathrm{PS}^B(t_a^M) - \mathrm{PS}^B(\mathbf{t}^A) = -\frac{y(z-y)}{16\beta} < 0. \quad (47)$$

However, since $z > y$, the total producer surplus in countries B and C increases with country A's MFN adoption:

$$\sum_{J \neq A} \mathrm{PS}^J(t_a^M) - \sum_{J \neq A} \mathrm{PS}^J(\mathbf{t}^A) = \frac{(z-y)^2}{16\beta} = 2|\Delta W^A(t_a^M, \mathbf{t}^\mathbf{A})| > 0 \quad (48)$$

Consider next the effect on consumers in countries B and C. We have:

$$\mathrm{CS}^B(t_a^M) - \mathrm{CS}^B(\mathbf{t}^A) = -\frac{(2y+z)(z-y)}{64\beta} > 0 \quad (49)$$

[20] There is no effect on the tariff revenue of countries B and C because these countries do not import good a (so that their tariffs are independent of country A's tariffs).

whereas

$$\mathrm{CS}^C(t_a^M) - \mathrm{CS}^C(\mathbf{t}^A) = -\frac{(2z+y)(z-y)}{64\beta} < 0 \tag{50}$$

The last two equations imply that

$$\sum_{j \neq A} \mathrm{CS}^J(t_a^M) - \sum_{J \neq A} \mathrm{CS}^J(\mathbf{t}^A) = -\frac{(z-y)^2}{64\beta} = \frac{\Delta W^A(t_a^M, \mathbf{t}^\mathbf{A})}{2} < 0 \tag{51}$$

Let aggregate world welfare be defined as the sum of each country's welfare:

$$\mathrm{WW} \equiv \sum_J W^J = \sum_J \left[\sum_i \mathrm{CS}_i^J + \sum_i \mathrm{PS}_i^J + \mathrm{TR}^J \right].$$

Calculating aggregate world welfare under tariff discrimination by country A and comparing it to that under MFN adoption by country A yields:

$$\Delta \mathrm{WW}^A(t_a^M, \mathbf{t}^\mathbf{A}) \equiv \mathrm{WW}(t_a^M) - \mathrm{WW}(\mathbf{t}^\mathbf{A}) = \frac{|\Delta W^A(t_a^M, \mathbf{t}^\mathbf{A})|}{2} = \frac{(z-y)^2}{64\beta} > 0. \tag{52}$$

i.e. MFN adoption by country A increases total world welfare even though it immiserizes the adopting country, consumers in country C, and producers in country B. As expected, MFN delivers no welfare gains if the endowments of countries B and C are the same.

Proposition 4. Benefits of defection

Straightforward calculations yield

$$B^B(\mathbf{t}^B, \mathbf{0}_{-B}) - B^C(\mathbf{t}^C, \mathbf{0}_{-C}) = \frac{(z-y)(19(y+z) - 34x)}{576\beta} \tag{53}$$

which implies that

$$B^B(\mathbf{t}^B, \mathbf{0}_{-B}) > B^C(\mathbf{t}^C, \mathbf{0}_{-C}) \quad \text{iff} \quad 19(y+z) > 34x$$

which necessarily holds since $z > y > x$.

Similarly,

$$B^B(\mathbf{t}^B, \mathbf{0}_{-B}) - B^A(\mathbf{t}^\mathbf{A}, \mathbf{0}_{-A}) = \frac{(y-x)(34z - 19(y+x))}{576\beta} > 0 \quad \text{iff} \quad 34z > 19(y+x). \tag{54}$$

Finally,

$$B^A(\mathbf{t}^\mathbf{A}, \mathbf{0}_{-A}) - B^C(\mathbf{t}^C, \mathbf{0}_{-C}) = \frac{(z-x)(-34y + 19(z+x))}{576\beta} > 0 \quad \text{iff} \quad 34y < 19(z+x). \tag{55}$$

Proposition 5A. Costs of defection under discriminatory tariffs

It is easy to show that

$$C^B(\mathbf{t}^\mathbf{D}, \mathbf{0}) - C^A(\mathbf{t}^\mathbf{D}, \mathbf{0}) = \frac{(y-x)(-158z + 149(y+x))}{1536\beta} > 0 \quad \text{since} \quad 158z < 149(y+x) \tag{56}$$

Similarly,

$$C^B(\mathbf{t}^\mathrm{D}, \mathbf{0}) - C^C(\mathbf{t}^\mathrm{D}, \mathbf{0}) = -\frac{(z-y)(-158x + 149(z+y))}{1536\beta} < 0 \tag{57}$$

since $158x < 149(z+y)$ and $z > y$. Finally,

$$C^A(\mathbf{t}^\mathbf{D}, 0) - C^C(\mathbf{t}^\mathbf{D}, 0) = -\frac{(z-x)(-158y + 149(z+x))}{1536\beta} < 0 \tag{58}$$

since $158y < 149(z+x)$ and $z > x$.

Proposition 5B. Costs of defection under MFN tariffs

We have:

$$C^B(\mathbf{t}^\mathbf{M}, \mathbf{0}) - C^A(\mathbf{t}^\mathbf{M}, \mathbf{0}) = \frac{(y-x)(29(y+x) - 10z)}{1536\beta} > 0 \tag{59}$$

and

$$C^C(\mathbf{t}^\mathbf{M}, \mathbf{0}) - C^B(\mathbf{t}^\mathbf{M}, \mathbf{0}) = \frac{(z-y)(29(y+z) + 10x)}{1536\beta} > 0. \tag{60}$$

References

Bagwell, K., Staiger, R.W., 1997. Multilateral cooperation during the formation of free trade areas. International Economic Review 38, 291–319.

Bagwell, K., Staiger, R.W., 1998. Regionalism and multilateral tariff cooperation. In: Pigott, John, Woodland, Alan (Eds.), International Trade Policy and the Pacific Rim. Macmillan, London.

Bagwell, K., Staiger, R.W., 1999. An economic theory of GATT. American Economic Review 89, 215–248.

Bagwell, K., Staiger, R.W., 2004. Multilateral trade negotiations, bilateral opportunism and the rules of GATT/WTO. Journal of International Economics 67, 268–294.

Bond, Eric W., Syropoulos, C., Winters, L.A., 2001. Deepening of regional integration and multilateral trade agreements. Journal of International Economics 53, 335–362.

Bown, C., 2004. Trade policy under the GATT/WTO: empirical evidence of the equal treatment rule. Canadian Journal of Economics 37, 678–720.

Caplin, A., Krishna, K., 1988. Tariffs and the most favored nation clause: a game theoretic approach. Seoul Journal of Economics 1, 267–289.

Choi, J.P., 1995. Optimal tariffs and the choice of technology: discriminatory tariffs vs. the most favored nation clause. Journal of International Economics 38, 143–160.

Ederington, J., McCalman, P., 2003. Discriminatory tariffs and international negotiations. Journal of International Economics 61, 397–424.

Gatsios, K., 1990. Preferential tariffs and the 'most favoured nation' principle: a note. Journal of International Economics 28, 365–373.

Hoekman, B.M., Kostecki, M.M., 2001. The Political Economy of the World Trading System. Oxford University Press, New York, NY.

Horn, H., Mavroidis, P.C., 2001. Economic and legal aspects of the most-favored nation clause. European Journal of Political Economy 17, 233–279.

Ludema, R., 1991. International trade bargaining and the most-favored nation clause. Economics and Politics 3, 1–20.

McCalman, P., 2002. Multi-lateral trade negotiations and the most favored nation clause. Journal of International Economics 27, 151–176.

Riezman, R., 1991. Dynamic tariffs with asymmetric information. Journal of International Economics 30, 267–283.

Saggi, K., 2004. Tariffs and the most favored nation clause. Journal of International Economics 63, 341–368.

Saggi, K., 2006. Preferential trading agreements and multilateral tariff cooperation. International Economic Review 47, 29–57.

Staiger, R.W., 1995. International rules and institutions for trade policy. In: Grossman, G.M., Rogoff, K. (Eds.), The Handbook of International Economics, vol. 3. Elsevier Science, Amsterdam.

CHAPTER 15

INDIA AT THE WTO: FROM URUGUAY TO DOHA AND BEYOND

Kamal Saggi

1. Introduction

India's voice in international trade negotiations has often been a loud one, often louder than one would expect given its limited participation in world trade over the years. But the small scale of India's international trade prior to its 1991 economic reforms is partly what makes its current role at the WTO so important. It is so because during the first five or so decades after gaining independence from British rule in 1947, India essentially chose to shut off its economy from the rest of the world by enacting extremely restrictive trade and foreign-investment policies. As one might expect, the nature of India's involvement in multilateral negotiations reflected its pursuit of an inward-looking development strategy. During GATT years, India was widely perceived as a player that invariably took negative (i.e. antiliberalization) positions on most issues. Indeed, the default position of Indian ambassadors to GATT was generally assumed to be just "no."

One could argue that at least during the initial decade or so of its existence as an independent country, India's isolationist policies and its pursuit of "self-sufficiency" were not entirely unreasonable responses to its colonial experience — after all, the British rule of India began via the arrival of the British East India Company, a private multinational firm that sought to profit from exporting Indian goods to world markets. However, India's colonial hangover can hardly justify its prolonged pursuit of protectionist policies, not least because these policies significantly slowed down its economic progress relative to those countries that adopted a more outward-looking approach.

Given India's size and the fact that its historical colonial legacy was shared by a host of developing countries, its voice in the international arena has often been seen as representative of the developing world at large. It seems fair to say that India appears to have been rather willing to play this leadership role, a role most clearly on display during the negotiation of the agreement on trade-related aspects of intellectual property rights (TRIPS) under the Uruguay Round (1986–1993), the successful completion of which led to the establishment of the WTO and the single undertaking system of today. The general feeling among developing countries, certainly in India, seems to have been that the TRIPS agreement was not in their interest in and of itself but was acceptable, perhaps barely so, as part of a larger package wherein developed countries would remove or lower trade barriers in areas of interest to developing countries. But 17 years after the conclusion of the Uruguay Round, progress on this front has been disappointing. Indeed, when the Doha Round was launched in 2001, it was hailed as the round that would put the interests of developing countries at the forefront — a corrective action of sorts to restore the perceived imbalance that resulted from the Uruguay Round.

Consider the following quotation from the Doha ministerial declaration of November 2001 (with italics added for emphasis):

> The majority of WTO members are developing countries. *We seek to place their needs and interests at the heart of the Work Programme adopted in this Declaration.* Recalling the Preamble to the Marrakesh Agreement, we shall continue to make positive efforts designed to ensure that developing countries, and especially the least-developed among them, secure a share in the growth of world trade commensurate with the needs of their economic development.[1]

Of the nine GATT/WTO rounds of trade negotiations, the Doha Round was the first to put the interests of developing countries at center stage; so at least was the claim. The lofty declaration above notwithstanding, progress during the Doha Round has been rather slow. Indeed, some doubt that there has been any progress at all. In this latter view, somewhat ironically this "Development Round" has so far been a round without any significant developments at all!

One taking a cynical perspective might suggest that stalemate is precisely what we should expect of a round that purports to put the interests of the WTO's weaker members first. This might be too harsh a judgment. Hoekman *et al.* (2009) argue that the relevant issue is not whether there is sufficient liberalization contained in the package currently on the table at Doha. According to their view, the world would do well to bind the current level of openness and to secure commitments that countries are willing to make. While their pragmatic perspective calls for a speedy conclusion to the Doha Round, they also acknowledge that the current deal on the table does not go far enough to justify calling the Doha Round a development round.

A reasonable argument can be made that the slow progress of Doha does not necessarily imply that the deck is stacked against developing countries. Rather, it is more likely that the relatively easier part of the journey of global trade liberalization is behind us and the issues that remain on the table are simply harder to tackle, particularly insofar as trade in agriculture is concerned. As a result, progress may be slow and fitful during all future WTO negotiations; the Doha Round might simply mark the change in the underlying negotiating environment of world trade. This perspective suggests that the Doha Round is progressing slowly not because it is a development round but rather because we are simply in a new, stickier regime of global trade negotiations.

This viewpoint finds further support in the changing architecture of the multilateral trading system. When GATT came into existence, it was a club of 23 countries, of which many were at rather similar levels of economic development. Furthermore, the aftermath of World War II had contributed to the emergence of a common worldview among these countries regarding the benefits of world trade and international economic engagement. While India was a founding member of GATT, its policy choices suggest that it did not view the economic benefits of participating in the multilateral trading system in the same way as most other founding members. India did recognize the importance of staying engaged globally, even if it were only for its political and strategic benefits.

Developing countries are now a part of the multilateral system as never before. Consider that of the 153 members of the WTO, over two-third are developing countries, of which roughly half are classified by UNCTAD as being "least-developed countries" (i.e. their per capita income is below $750). These numbers imply that whenever broad consensus or unanimity is required, developing countries have the ability to influence the WTO's proceedings. Of course, in most matters economic size trumps country numbers. But in this regard, too, developing countries have become increasingly influential, not least because of the recent emergence of China, Brazil, and India. During 2009, all three countries ranked in the top ten in terms of gross domestic product, with China having the third largest economy in the world (after the European Union and the United States) and India the fifth largest. The fact that the combined economic clout of developing countries at the WTO is sizable and is increasing fast will undoubtedly affect the pace and nature of future WTO negotiations.

The remainder of this chapter is organized as follows. Section 2 provides a brief overview of India's trade policies and the evolution of its role in world trade. Section 3 provides a discussion of how and why the ratification of TRIPS led to the view among developing countries (particularly India and Brazil) that the outcome of the Uruguay Round was tilted in favor of the developed world. Section 4 discusses how the Doha Round has attempted to address some of these concerns and provides an overview of the two major areas currently being negotiated at Doha: agriculture and market access in nonagricultural goods. Finally, by way of conclusion, Section 5 argues that India should use its increasing clout in global trade negotiations, not to stall liberalization, but to secure more favorable terms for itself.

2. India in World Trade

As was noted earlier, during the first five decades or so of its existence as a modern nation, India implemented extremely restrictive policies toward international trade and foreign direct investment. The economic costs of its strategy of import substitution have been studied widely — see Panagariya (2008) for a comprehensive overview of the issues involved

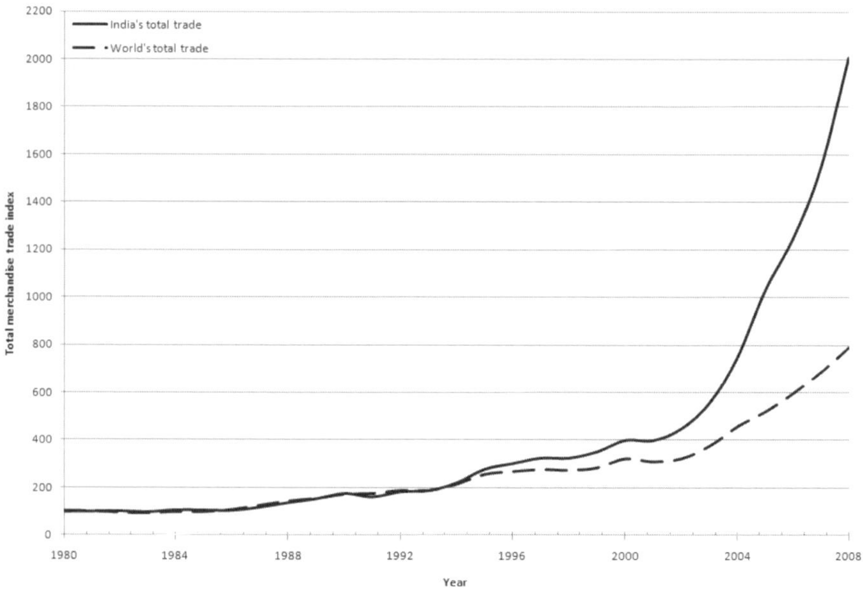

Figure 14.1. India's total merchandise trade value index, 1980–2008.

and Bhagwati and Desai (1970) for an early and influential critique of these policies.[2] It is fair to say that India's experience vis-à-vis the East Asian tigers — South Korea, Hong Kong, Singapore, and Taiwan — is perhaps the most damning evidence for the case against import substitution. Few economists would disagree that these policies had pernicious effects on India's economic development and on the well-being of its citizens.

Figure 14.1 plots India's total merchandise trade from 1980 to 2008, with the value of trade in 1980 being set equal to 100.[3]

The figure points to three important observations. First, from 1980 to 1992, the value of India's total trade roughly doubled. Second, from 1992 to 2002, trade once again trade roughly doubled. Third, from 2002 to 2008, India's trade with the rest of the world virtually exploded: *trade in 2008 was five times that in 2002 and twenty times what it was in 1980*. As Figure 14.1 shows, even compared to the growth in world trade, this is impressive: global trade in 2008 was eight times what it was in 1980.

Part of the explanation behind the recent surge in India's trade is that in 1991, spurred on by a record current-account deficit and large debt-service payments, India lifted some of its restrictions on trade and foreign investment, thereby opening the door for the Indian economy to assume its natural place in the world trading order. In an in-depth analysis of the Indian economy, Srinivasan and Tendulkar (2003) note that in 1990 India's current-account deficit stood at a record 3.2% of GDP, and its debt-service payments were as high as 35.3% of foreign-exchange receipts. The urgency of these external pressures as well as the emerging realization among its policymakers that an isolationist stance in the world economy had hardly been conducive to India's economic development finally led India to undertake a set of fairly substantial economic reforms in 1991.

On the trade side, Srinivasan and Tendulkar point out that in 1990, 65% of all imports were subject to nontariff barriers, the import-weighted average tariff stood at 87%, and the unweighted tariff at a whopping 128%. These high tariff levels had effectively turned India into one of the most closed economies of the world. Fortunately, the liberalization package of 1991 went some way to lowering its tariffs: the import-weighted tariff was reduced to 64% in 1992/93, to 47% the next year, and then to 24.6% in 1996.[4] While such liberalization helped better integrate the Indian economy with that of the rest of the world, India continues to be a minor player in world markets. Figure 14.2 plots India's share in world merchandise trade. As can be seen from this figure, while India's share has increased rather sharply since the year 2000 or so, in absolute terms it is still rather small: in 2008, India accounted for just over 1.4% of world merchandise trade.[5]

While tariffs have been gradually reduced over the last two decades or so, Indian trade policy has of late acquired another undesirable trait: India is now the world's leading user of antidumping (AD) duties. While AD legislation was introduced in India in 1985, India did not initiate its first AD case until 1992. This suggests that the trade liberalization that resulted from the economic reforms of 1991 has been partially undone by the increased use of AD measures, generally considered to be worse than tariffs due to their discriminatory nature and the magnitude of the duties imposed.[6] Furthermore, as Irwin (2007) notes, once imposed, AD duties

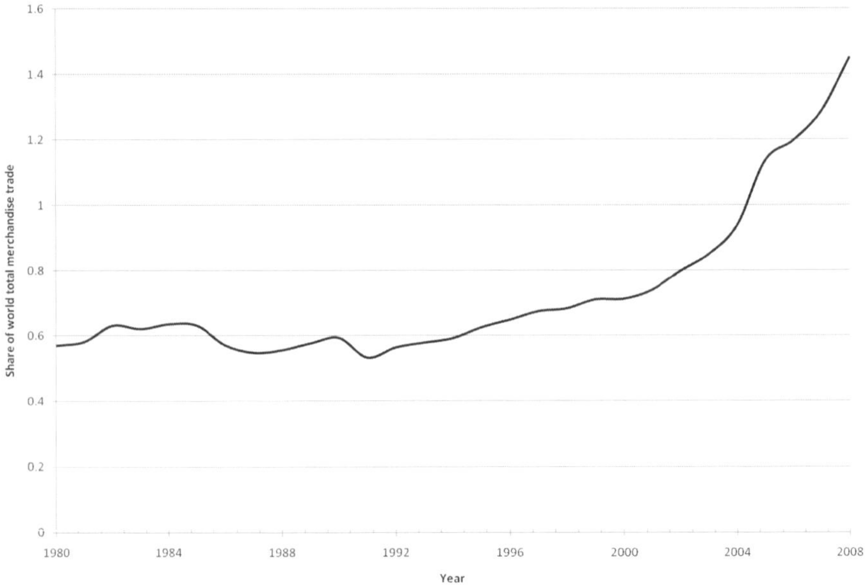

Figure 14.2. India's share in world total merchandise trade, 1980–2008.

are notoriously hard to remove, and the very existence of AD law ends up yielding collusive outcomes in the product market: knowing that low pricing might result in the imposition of AD duties, foreign firms have an incentive to charge higher prices to prevent such an outcome.

Figure 14.3 plots the AD measures implemented by India during the period 1995–2008.

While there has been some decline in the use of AD in recent years, there was a steady and sharp increase in India's AD activity during the period 1995–2002 and a peak in 2002, when India implemented 64 AD measures; the next biggest user during 2002 being the United States, with 26. As might be expected, the major targets of India's AD measures were some of the largest exporters to India: China, the European Union, and the United States.[7]

Cumulatively, between 1995 and 2008, India accounted for 386 AD measures, substantially more than the 286 implemented by the United States, the next biggest user. Figure 14.4 plots India's share of these as a percentage of the world total. During 2002, India alone implemented

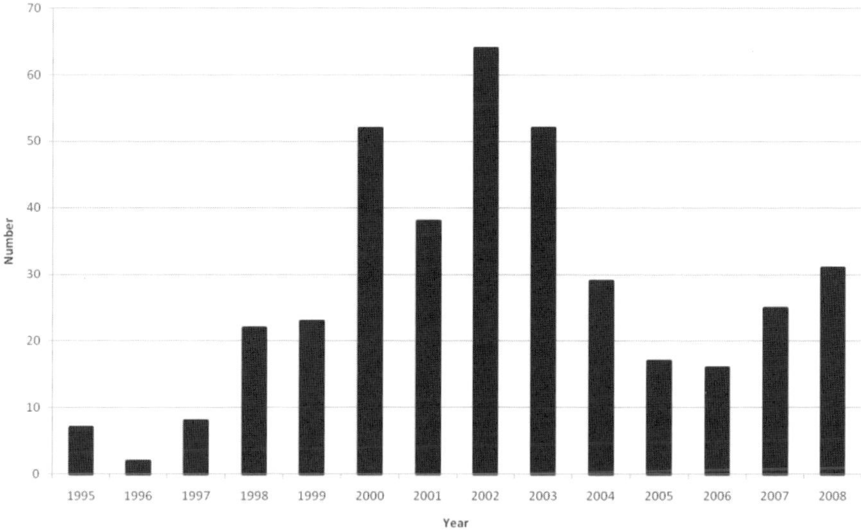

Figure 14.3. India's anti-dumping measures.

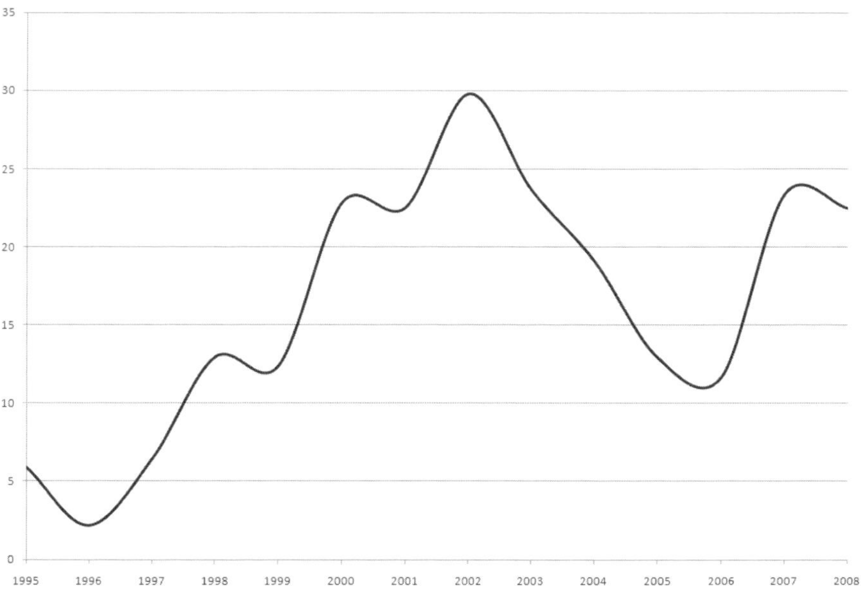

Figure 14.4. India's anti-dumping measures as a percentage of the world's total.

roughly one-third of the AD measures in the world (recall that India's share of world trade was only about 1.4% in 2008). When viewed against this backdrop, India's AD activity is simply off the charts.

The pace at which India has taken to the use of antidumping is nothing short of alarming; it raises serious questions about the degree to which tariff reductions have simply been replaced by the increased use of AD duties. This issue has been investigated in some detail by Bown and Tovar (2009). They exploit cross-product variation to examine whether there is a product-level link between the size of the initial tariff cut enacted by India during its 1991 reforms and its subsequent use of AD and safeguard protection. Their analysis is motivated by the simple observation that it was only after the tariff reform program of 1991 that India went from being a nonuser of antidumping to becoming its most frequent user in the world — hardly the sort of distinction India needs. Their econometric analysis shows that products with larger tariff cuts between 1990 and 1997 were associated with a substitution toward AD and safeguards in the early 2000s.[8]

Another perspective on the nature of India's multilateral engagement can be obtained by examining its participation in the dispute-settlement process of the WTO. Since 1995, India has been involved in 18 WTO disputes as a complainant and 20 as a respondent — relatively few compared to the number of disputes involving the European Union or the United States. But India is a much smaller participant in world trade relative to them; after all, the less a country trades, the fewer the opportunities for it to get entangled in disputes with its trading partners.

Does India dispute more than it trades? The answer depends upon one's point of view. As noted earlier, India's AD activity is surely out of proportion to its trade level. Additional evidence is found in Table 14.1, which shows the ten biggest cumulative users of the WTO's dispute-settlement system from 1995 to 2010, along with the absolute level of their trade in 2008 and their share in world merchandise trade.

For example, while India's share of world merchandise trade in 2008 was 1.4%, it was involved in 6.11% of all disputes among WTO members between 1995 and 2010. However, India's involvement in disputes is comparable with that of Brazil (38 disputes) and Mexico (35), as is its share in world trade.[9]

Table 14.1. Disputes and total merchandise trade by country (1995–2010).

Country name	Disputes as complainant	Disputes as respondent	Total disputes	Share of world merchandise exports in 2008 (%)	Share of world merchandise imports in 2008 (%)	Total share in world merchandise trade (%)	Total merchandise exports, f.o.b. (million US$) 2008	Total merchandise imports, c.i.f. (million US$) 2008
Argentina	15	16	31	0.44	0.35	0.79	70,023	57,423
Brazil	24	14	38	1.23	1.11	2.34	197,942	182,408
Canada	33	15	48	2.84	2.55	5.39	456,464	418,311
China	7	17	24	8.89	6.90	15.78	1,428,332	1,132,488
European Communities	81	68	149	36.70	38.09	74.80	5,898,440	6,255,765
India	18	20	38	1.10	1.79	2.89	177,499	293,374
Japan	13	15	28	4.87	4.64	9.51	782,047	762,589
Korea	14	14	28	2.63	2.65	5.28	422,007	435,275
Republic of Mexico	21	14	35	1.82	1.97	3.78	291,729	323,151
United States	94	109	203	8.01	13.21	21.22	1,287,442	2,169,487

3. The Legacy of Uruguay and Implications for Doha

The Uruguay Round constituted the longest and perhaps the most far-reaching multilateral trade negotiations ever conducted. It took over seven years (1986–1993) to complete and involved 125 countries; its coverage of trade was unusually broad in that it included services as well as issues related to intellectual property. A full review of Uruguay Round negotiations is clearly beyond the scope of this chapter. Yet to understand India's positions going forward, it is imperative to obtain a clearer understanding of exactly why the Uruguay Round was seen as having created a "development deficit." In this regard, the Uruguay Round agreement that stands out above all others is TRIPS.[10]

Like all multilateral agreements, TRIPS is complex and far-reaching. It is unique in that it does not deal directly with trade but with the protection of intellectual property rights (IPRs). TRIPS made it mandatory (after some time lags) for developing countries to reform their IPR regimes so as to harmonize them with those of developed countries. Of course, the asymmetry inherent in this change is easy to see: much of the world's existing intellectual property — as measured by patents, trademarks, and copyrights — is held by the developed world, so that any strengthening of IPR protection by developing countries could impose significant short-run welfare losses on them by increasing the monopoly power of rights holders.

With regard to TRIPS, three important questions merit attention. First, is there any need for a multilateral agreement on IPRs? Second, is there any relationship between IPRs and international trade? And third, is the WTO the right organization within which to implement an international agreement on IPRs?

Let us take the questions in order. To the extent international agreements are meant to internalize international externalities created by the pursuit of beggar-thy-neighbor policies, there is little doubt that some type of international IPR coordination is necessary. The logic is as follows: each country would like to pay as little as possible for foreign innovations while charging as much as possible in foreign markets for its own. These clashing objectives create strong national incentives to discriminate against foreign residents with respect to the enforcement of IPRs. As a result, the pursuit of IPR policies based on narrow self-interest can create an outcome where each country offers too little protection to foreign residents relative to its own. Indeed, the key principles contained in TRIPS, including MFN and national treatment, are targeted at curbing the pursuit of policies that attempt the improvement of one nation's welfare at the expense of others.

The second question raised above is also relatively easy to answer; that is, do IPRs have anything to do with trade? The answer would have to be in the affirmative. To see why, suppose that a patent holder in one country is unable to successfully export its product to a foreign country because its technology is imitated by a local firm in that country. Then, in effect, such imitation is equivalent to a prohibitive tariff (or a complete ban) on its exports to that country. It is difficult to argue that prohibitive tariffs are problematic but outright theft of intellectual property is not. Research in international trade has established beyond doubt that IPRs are "trade-related" (see Maskus 2000). Indeed, if trade and IPRs were orthogonal issues, it would be impossible to make sense out of the large amount of international patenting that goes on in the world economy today.

Despite its opposition to TRIPS, the single-undertaking nature of the WTO implied that India had little choice but to sign TRIPS in 1994. Not signing TRIPS was equivalent to opting out of the WTO, something India certainly was not prepared to do. By 2005 India had altered its patent regime to make it fully compliant with TRIPS, the most important change being the recognition of product patents in pharmaceuticals. A frequently voiced fear was that these changes in IPR laws would substantially increase drug prices in India by causing the exit of local firms producing imitations of drugs patented abroad. While recent empirical evidence indicates that this concern is not without merit, a longer time horizon is needed to accurately estimate the welfare costs of TRIPs, since the response of foreign multinational firms is crucial and the necessary adjustments in market structure will take time to materialize.[11]

Static welfare losses that might result from the shutting down of local firms producing imitated foreign goods are not the only concern that India and other developing countries have with respect to TRIPS. These countries are equally concerned, if not more so, about the impact of TRIPS on technology transfer; they have voiced this concern forcefully at the WTO. While TRIPS includes some nominal clauses that encourage developed countries to facilitate technology transfer to developing countries, it is far from clear how these statements, in and of themselves, can alter the incentives of private agents and governments involved in this process. These clauses on technology transfer appear to be mainly lip service.

As Branstetter *et al.* (2011) note, the key trade-off with respect to technology transfer facing countries such as India is clear: clamping down on imitation and reverse engineering slows down technology transfer to the local economy, but its effects can perhaps be offset by increased flows of foreign direct investment from abroad. A full evaluation of the trade-off will become clearer only with time, but the emerging evidence, at least with respect to U.S. multinationals, is that the scale of activities undertaken by such firms in India and other countries that undertook serious IPR reform has increased substantially. More specifically, Branstetter *et al.* (2011) investigate the impact of IPR reform on multinational production by analyzing the responses of U.S. multinationals to 16 countries' IPR reforms during the 1980s and 1990s. They find that U.S.-based multinationals expanded the scale of their production and employment in reforming countries after IPR reform. They also show that industry-level value added increased after reforms, particularly in technology-intensive industries.[12]

Consider now the third, perhaps the hardest, question with respect to TRIPS: does TRIPS belong at the WTO? India's position on this question notwithstanding, it is worth noting that if there exist international externalities in the enforcement of IPRs and such externalities affect global trade flows, an argument can certainly be made that TRIPS indeed belongs at the WTO. But IPRs are by no means unique in this regard. Even TRIPS proponents must concede that the set of "trade-related" economic activities in today's globalized world is very large. In some senses, almost any economic activity and associated laws and regulations are trade-related. For example, labor laws, competition laws, and investment laws are all obviously trade-related. Should the WTO negotiate, implement, monitor, and help enforce multilateral agreements in these areas, too? To have an effective and manageable agenda, the WTO has to draw the line somewhere. A WTO that included every trade-related activity would likely be a cumbersome and ineffective organization.

In this regard, it is notable that India has consistently opposed an expansion of the multilateral trading system in the direction of negotiating and implementing multilateral agreements on investment, competition policy, and government procurement — a possibility created by the

Singapore ministerial declaration of 1996. The Indian position was articulated by Murasoli Maran in his November 2001 statement at the Doha ministerial conference (italics added).

> In the areas of Investment, Competition, Trade Facilitation or Transparency in Government Procurement, *basic questions remain even on the need for a multilateral agreement.* Most importantly, do the developing countries have the capacity to deal with them? Will we be able to say that they do not impinge strongly on domestic policies that are well removed from trade? We are doubtful that if we can give affirmative replies to all these questions. In any case, the Singapore Declaration requires an explicit consensus for any decision to move to negotiations. Let us therefore wait till an explicit consensus emerges on these issues.[13]

As Panagariya (2008) notes, Indian opposition to the Singapore issues was instrumental in removing investment, competition, and government procurement from the negotiating agenda of the Doha Round. Of the four original Singapore issues, only trade facilitation remains on the table at Doha.

4. The Doha Round and India's Role in Ongoing Negotiations

The Doha Round began in 2001 against a backdrop of dissatisfaction among developing countries with respect to the results of the Uruguay Round. Indeed, part of the "development" focus of the Doha Round, at least in terms of the stated intentions, resulted from the widely held view that the multilateral bargain achieved during the Uruguay Round was tilted strongly in favor of the developed world. Before discussing ongoing Doha negotiations, it is important to get a better understanding of the legacy of the Uruguay Round.

4.1. The Uruguay round TRIPS hangover

At the Doha ministerial conference of November 2001, India's then minister of commerce and industry, Murasoli Maran, made an appeal: "WTO has to recognize the existing *development deficit* in various WTO agreements and take necessary remedial action" (italics added). Furthermore, he drew attention to the "the asymmetries and imbalances in the Uruguay Round agreements" and noted that "TRIPS has invited strong reactions from developing country stakeholders."

Criticism of TRIPS by India and others, particularly with respect to its potential adverse effect on access to medicines in developing countries, was not entirely ineffectual. Recognizing the seriousness of the public health problems afflicting many developing and least-developed countries, the Doha Ministerial Conference of 2001 acknowledged that TRIPS should not hinder members from taking measures to protect public health and to promote access to medicines. Drawing attention to the flexibilities available to WTO members under TRIPS, it noted that a member country could issue compulsory licenses of necessary pharmaceuticals to local firms in order to deal with public health crises such as HIV/AIDS, tuberculosis, and malaria.[14]

Most importantly, the 2001 declaration recognized that countries with inadequate manufacturing capacity in the pharmaceutical sector would be unable to avail themselves of the compulsory licensing option and might need to import medicines from countries that had the ability to produce them. Since TRIPS only authorized domestic production under compulsory licensing and not imports from third parties, the declaration called on the TRIPS Council to find an expeditious solution to this problem. The solution agreed to by WTO members was announced on the eve of the Cancún ministerial meeting in 2003: the domestic market requirement of compulsory licensing was waived, and least-developed countries, as well as those that lacked sufficient manufacturing capacity, were permitted to use compulsory licensing to import pharmaceuticals for "HIV/AIDS, malaria, tuberculosis and other epidemics" from third parties.[15]

As of March 8, 2010, 54 countries (including India) had ratified this amendment. Once the amendment is ratified by two-thirds of WTO members, it will become a formal part of the TRIPS agreement; until then, the waiver for domestic production made by the 2003 decision will continue in force.[16] This is welcome news for developing countries, perhaps particularly for India. With large and well-developed pharmaceutical industries, India and Brazil especially are in prime position to take advantage of the 2003 decision and export needed pharmaceuticals to countries that lack the ability to produce them locally. Yet while such an outcome is possible and may even be plausible, the 2003 decision has so far had little impact on improving actual access to medicines in developing countries. In the seven years that have elapsed since the decision, only one WTO member — Rwanda — has made use of the decision to import the HIV/AIDS drug TriAvir from Canada.[17]

After the relatively quick action on the public health issue, progress at Doha has been slow and limited. The initial ministerial conference of 2001 was followed by similar conferences at Cancún (2003), Geneva (2004), Hong Kong (2005), and Geneva (2006 and 2008). But a multilateral bargain acceptable to all parties has still not been reached. Though the Doha Round has gone on longer than any previous round, it had not yet concluded even late in 2011.

The duration of the Doha Round has led Ronald Kirk, the current U.S. trade representative, to proclaim that the Doha Round "is like a cricket match. You don't know the score and it takes a long time, but it does end, and there is a winner."[18] There is one sense, though perhaps only one, in which this analogy is correct: like a cricket test match that sometimes seems never ending — it can last up to 5 days; an eternity in sports — the Doha Round has been ongoing for simply too long. But in every other regard, the statement is quite misleading. In fact, it is rather revealing of the mind-set of trade negotiators, who often incorrectly view such negotiations as a zero-sum-game. As economists have been pointing out since the days of David Ricardo, greater openness to trade does not produce a single winner. Rather, all participating countries stand to gain from mutual trade liberalization.

Leaving aside the rhetoric of politicians and trade negotiators, why has the Doha Round stagnated? The first major setback occurred in 2003 at the Cancún ministerial meeting. Ismail (2009) argues that the catalyst for this breakdown was the approach undertaken by the European Union and the United States, which proceeded to negotiate a bilateral agreement accommodating each other's interests and then presented it almost as a fait accompli to the rest of the WTO members. As several observers have noted, this approach galvanized the developing countries into action, many of them forming an alliance that came to be called the G20 group.

The emergence of this coalition and the breakdown of the Cancún negotiations perhaps indicated that fundamental changes had occurred in the multilateral trading system during recent decades, a theme to which we will later return.

After the failure at Cancún, the 2005 ministerial meeting at Hong Kong helped narrow some of the differences among countries but only to the extent that members agreed to a new timetable for completing negotiations. At this meeting, Kamal Nath, then India's minister of commerce, sustained the position taken by his predecessor in 2001. He stated, "[W]e are mandated to correct the 'development deficit' bequeathed to us by the Uruguay Round."[19] But this rhetoric seems a bit out of touch with on-the-ground realities in India and with India's positions at the WTO. In particular, as Ray and Saha (2009) have noted, India's stance with respect to the TRIPS agreement has shifted over time. As noted above, during the Uruguay Round negotiations, India was a leading opponent of strengthening IPR protection in developing countries. Indeed, its 1970 patent act did not even recognize product patents on pharmaceuticals. Since then, however, India's position and interests have changed considerably. Ray and Saha (2009) note that domestic business interests in India were never uniformly opposed to TRIPS; the major Indian pharmaceutical companies (such as Ranbaxy and Dr. Reddy) were in fact favorably disposed to it.

In addition to the use of compulsory licensing for public health concerns, India raised two other IPR-related issues during the ongoing Doha negotiations. First, it argued that IPR protection under geographical indication should not be limited only to wine and spirits but be extended to include other products (such as Basmati rice). Second, it pushed for restrictions on the use or misuse of biological and genetic resources and traditional knowledge. As Ray and Saha (2009) point out, these are demands in favor of increasing rather than lowering IPR protection.

4.2. Agriculture at Doha and India's stand

We now turn to India's role in the ongoing Doha negotiations. At the 2005 Hong Kong ministerial meeting, Mr. Nath argued that the structure of international trade in agriculture was severely distorted and that the development outcome of the Doha Round would hinge on its achievement in this area, since many developing countries have a natural comparative advantage in agriculture. He further voiced the view that developing countries were "shut out from world markets by a complex edifice of protection, built on high tariff walls, domestic and export subsidies, and an intricate maze of non-tariff barriers." As might be expected given India's relatively strong position in services exports, he also argued that liberalization of professional services needed to figure high on the development agenda — a claim that is sure to ring hollow among those developing countries that are uncompetitive in services.

It is appropriate here to make the general point that not all developing countries are the same. Despite India's desire or willingness to act as a leader of the developing world at the WTO, its negotiating positions cannot automatically be taken as representative of that world at large. Sometimes India's interests converge with those of a majority of developing countries; sometimes they diverge. As is well known, services exports, particularly in software, constitute an area where India has more at stake than almost any other developing country. This divergence of interest is likely to increase over time: India's exports of services, which tripled from \$20 billion to \$60 billion between 2002/03 and 2005/06, are expected to continue increasing sharply (Panagariya 2008).[20]

The timetable set at the Hong Kong ministerial meeting was not met, and negotiations were actually suspended in Geneva in July 2006, when the WTO Director-General Pascal Lamy asked members to "prepare the ground for fully fledged negotiations to take place when the conditions are right." Prior to the Geneva summit, in an effort to try to bring the round to closure, Pascal Lamy had put forward the "20-20-20" proposal, which called for (i) the United States to accept a ceiling of \$20 billion on domestic farm subsidies; (ii) developed countries to accept the G20 proposal of 54% as the minimum average cut to agricultural tariffs in developed countries; and (iii) developing countries to accept 20% as the tariff ceiling on industrial goods. However, his proposal was criticized by all sides and not adopted.[21]

Negotiations are ongoing on several issues, but most of the action is in two key areas: agriculture and NAMA (non-agricultural market assess). Indeed, agriculture has widely been seen as the linchpin of the Doha Round. Meaningful reform in agriculture requires sizable reductions in tariffs and other trade barriers, as well as cuts in subsidies and other means of government support to agriculture, especially in the European Union and the United States. As Elliott (2006) notes, the Uruguay Round required rich countries to cut agricultural tariffs by an average of 36% and other trade-distorting support by 20%, but these targets were not met, and overall trade barriers and subsidy levels remain very high. From this perspective, the prospects of a successful conclusion of the Doha Round and the actual implementation of the proposals currently on the table do not appear very bright.[22] Elliott (2006) points out that even if development was not the stated focus of the Doha Round, agriculture would have to occupy center stage at current WTO negotiations since it is the "major unfinished business" from previous trade rounds and it is in agriculture that the developed countries have the most to give in terms of improved market access.

According to Hoekman *et al.* (2009), proposals under discussion at Doha would reduce the average bound tariff on agricultural goods from 40% to 30% and on nonagricultural goods from roughly 8% to 5%. While these reductions in bound rates are not overwhelming, they are also not meaningless, since trade liberalization in agriculture has evaded the multilateral system ever since the inception of GATT in 1947. Most importantly, the successful conclusion of Doha would result in a complete ban on agricultural export subsidies as well as sharp reductions in the maximum-allowed levels of government support (by 70% in the European Union and 60% in the United States), policy changes that are likely to raise prices of agricultural goods in world markets.

Is a significant reduction in agricultural subsidies by the European Union and the United States necessarily good for all developing countries? Clearly the answer is not in the affirmative. While countries that are net exporters of agricultural goods (such as India) would stand to gain from an increase in the prices of such goods, net importers (of which there are many) would likely lose.[23] In 2008, while India accounted for roughly 1.6% of world exports of agricultural products, its share of imports of such products was only half that — that is, about 0.8%. Figure 14.5 plots the share of agricultural products in India's merchandise exports from 1980 to 2008. As can be seen from this figure, the share of agricultural exports in total merchandise exports has steadily fallen over this time

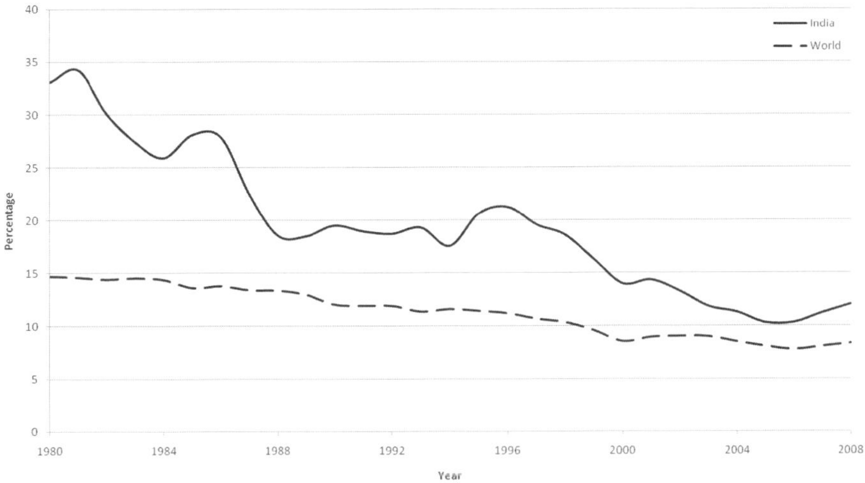

Figure 14.5. Share of agricultural products in merchandise exports.

period, from 35% to roughly 15%, which approximates the share of agriculture in world exports. Of course, the decline in the relative importance of agricultural exports is a reflection of the emergence of India's nonagricultural sectors over this time period. Nevertheless, 15% is still a fairly large share of exports, and agriculture is of especial importance to India since it is a source of livelihood for millions of India's poorer citizens.

If the elimination of EU and U.S. agricultural subsidies does raise prices of agricultural goods, the outcome would not necessarily be development friendly, since the world's poorest countries tend to be net importers of agricultural goods, especially food.[24] Indeed, Elliott (2006) argues that, while necessary, progress in agriculture would be insufficient to realize the development ambitions of the Doha Round simply because higher food prices would hurt the poorest countries the most. The exporting opportunities resulting from reduction in trade barriers may go unrealized due to inadequate infrastructure and poor access to necessary inputs in many such countries.[25]

Elliott (2006) also notes that key developing-country exports are not those that the rich countries support most generously. More specifically, she points out that while reductions in EU subsidies in temperate products and in U.S. cotton subsidies are important for many poor countries, subsidy cuts in dairy, meat, and sugar are unlikely to benefit the poorest developing countries. Of course, the effect on world prices of the reduction in agricultural subsidies by the European Union and the United States depends in part on the existing level of these subsidies and the cuts actually implemented. How large are these subsidies? While Oxfam has popularized the figure of $1 billion a day in subsidies, Pascal Lamy has asserted that actual subsidies are probably one-third the Oxfam figure. Elliott (2006), agreeing that the Oxfam figure is somewhat of an exaggeration, argues that the relevant figure is the level of support available to agricultural producers in developed countries — about $250 billion a year.

Within agriculture, negotiations over the special safeguard mechanism (SSM) have frequently been mentioned as a potentially important roadblock to successful completion of the Doha Round. If implemented, the SSM would provide developing countries with a safeguard under which they could raise tariffs temporarily to deal with import surges or price declines in agricultural goods. But the centrality of the SSM to the ongoing negotiations seems questionable, since the main disagreement with respect to SSM is over whether developing countries would have the freedom to raise tariffs above the levels they committed to in the Uruguay Round in order to protect domestic agriculture. Furthermore, one might wonder why the SSM is needed at all, since a safeguard clause already exists in the agreement on agriculture reached during the Uruguay Round. The key difference is that the special agricultural safeguard (SSG) of the Uruguay Round is available only in those goods that had been "tarrified" — goods in which nontariff barriers such as import quotas had been converted to equivalent tariffs. Since many developing countries did not adopt this tariffication approach in agriculture, they are not able to make use of the SSG.

What role has India played during the agricultural negotiations at the Doha Round? At the failed Cancún Ministerial Conference of 2003, Arun Jaitley, then India's minister of commerce and industry and law and justice, stressed that "the commitment by developed countries to eliminate distortions in world agriculture caused by their policies holds the key to resolving differences amongst us in the area." He correctly drew attention to the high levels of agricultural subsidies in developed countries and noted that the level of these subsidies was far greater than what these countries spent on official development assistance.

As a member of the G20, India is widely recognized as an essential interlocutor in the difficult and drawn-out agricultural negotiations.[26] Overall, India's position in agriculture has been largely defensive. Like many other countries, India seeks to maintain agricultural self-sufficiency and has been reluctant to make concessions that may potentially undermine this goal. But at the same time, India has demanded reductions in trade-distorting domestic support from other WTO members, particularly the European Union and the United States. India has pushed for the abolition of export subsidies and insisted on the principle of proportionality, according to which developing countries should be asked to make fewer concessions than developed countries, an argument in line with the "special and differential treatment" provisions of the WTO.[27]

4.3. Non-agricultural market access (NAMA) negotiations at Doha

Turning to NAMA, consider paragraph 16 of the Doha ministerial declaration of 2001, which states (italics added),

> We agree to negotiations which shall aim, by modalities to be agreed, to reduce or as appropriate eliminate tariffs, including the reduction or *elimination of tariff peaks, high tariffs, and tariff escalation, as well as non-tariff barriers, in particular on products of export interest to developing countries*. Product coverage shall be comprehensive and without a priori exclusions. The negotiations shall take fully into account the *special needs and interests of developing and least-developed country participants*, including through less than full reciprocity in reduction commitments, in accordance with the relevant provisions of Article XXVIII bis of GATT 1994 and the provisions cited in paragraph 50 below.

Once again, the declaration of intent is clear: special effort was to be made at Doha to accommodate the interests and needs of developing countries. But, as we shall see below, negotiations have dragged on partly because developing countries have argued that the actual bargain on the table has not lived up to this declaration of intent.

While tariff reductions can be implemented by a variety of methods — see the lucid discussion in Low and Santana (2009) — much of the focus in the NAMA negotiations has been on the application of the Swiss formula for tariff reductions, a nonlinear formula that seeks to reduce high tariffs by a bigger percentage than low tariffs.[28] Given that the Doha declaration called for a focus on "tariff peaks, high tariffs, and tariff escalation," the use of the Swiss formula during NAMA negotiations seems natural. The Swiss formula requires that the new (or reduced) tariff t' be related to the existing tariff t as follows: $t' = c.t/(c+t)$, where c is the tariff coefficient to be negotiated by the participants. The Swiss formula implies that (i) the new tariff levels always lie below the coefficient c; and (ii) the tariff cut for a good exceeds 50% if and only if the existing tariff level is above the coefficient c. An attractive feature of this formula is that negotiations can be centered on a single parameter — that is, the coefficient c — with developing countries permitted to have higher coefficients than developed ones.

It is worth noting that there was broad and strong support for the use of the Swiss formula. India and Brazil actually favored using the ABI formula, under which $t' = (b.t_a.t)/(b.t_a+t)$, where t_a is the average tariff and b is the coefficient that countries negotiate. As is clear, the ABI formula differs from the Swiss formula in only way: the coefficient under negotiation also applies to a country's average tariff. Both the Swiss and the ABI formula approaches remained on the table until the 2005 Hong Kong ministerial meeting, but eventually discussions centered on the Swiss formula since there was broader support for it.

Initially, developed countries argued for a Swiss-formula coefficient of 10 for themselves and 15 for developing countries, while the NAMA-11 group, of which India is a member, insisted that the development mandate of the Doha Round calls for a minimum spread of 25 points between the coefficients for the two groups (Low and Santana 2009). A coalition at NAMA comprising mostly middle income countries and accordingly called the Middle Ground Group attempted to bridge the gap between these positions by proposing a coefficient of 8 to 9 for developed countries and 19 to 23 for developing ones.[29] However, this intermediate proposal was resisted by the NAMA-11 on the ground that it failed to deliver on the "less than full reciprocity" mandate of the Doha declaration.

As if to remind the participants of the original Doha declaration, India argued that the negotiations had to effectively deal with "tariff peaks, tariff escalation, high tariffs and nontariff measures" since "tariff peaks imposed by developed countries are often concentrated in products that are of export interest to developing countries such as in textiles and clothing; leather, rubber, footwear and travel goods; transport equipment; fish and fish products" and that "the approach should fully integrate the 'less than full reciprocity' concept in reduction commitments. Formulae effectively seeking to drastically reduce the tariffs generally prevailing in a developing country schedule while being comparatively less demanding on developed country counterparts will not be in keeping with the mandate."[30]

Generally, an important aspect of multilateral tariff negotiations is that countries agree to bind their tariffs to levels above which they cannot raise them. A widely known major achievement of the Uruguay Round was that many countries, especially developing ones, substantially increased their binding coverage. However, Low and Santana (2009) note that a lot still remains to be done in this area: while 82 WTO members have bound more than 95% of their tariff lines, 29 members have bound less than 35% of them. Note, too, that in 2001, 38.8% of India's imports occurred under tariff lines that were subject to absolutely no binding. If NAMA negotiations conclude successfully according to the current bargain on the table, the binding coverage of developing countries would increase from 81.5% to 96%. Among developing countries, paragraph 6 countries — a group comprising 12 developing countries (not including India) — that currently have very low binding coverage would have to substantially increase their coverage.

As might be expected, NAMA negotiations have become increasingly intertwined with those in agriculture. India and other developing countries are unwilling to commit on NAMA without progress in agriculture. For their part, developed countries are insisting that progress on agriculture will be tied to how much the developing countries are willing to do on NAMA. Such issue linkage aside, India's position within NAMA has been defensive, perhaps too much so given its relatively high tariffs and limited bindings.

Finally, as might be expected, India has proactively pushed for trade liberalization in services. In particular, it is bargaining for better market access, especially in mode 1 (cross-border supply) and mode 4 (presence of natural persons). The cross-border supply of services directly impacts software services and business-process outsourcing, areas in which India possesses a clear comparative advantage.[31] India has also called for abolition of numerical visa quotas and visa restrictions.[32] But services liberalization does not appear to be a major part of the Doha agenda; in this regard the limited commitments that countries made during the Uruguay Round suggest that India's demands in this area, despite their considerable merit, are unlikely to be met in this round of negotiations.

5. Today's Multilateral Landscape and India's Role Going Forward

Its original inclusion in GATT in 1947 notwithstanding, the economic policies pursued by India during its first five decades or so of independence effectively shut off its economy from the rest of the world. After British rule ended, India embarked on an ambitious path of import substitution, the benefits of which petered out rather quickly. Worse still, this path brought decades of low growth and denied opportunities to a large segment of humanity. Reflecting its inward-looking development strategy, India's negotiating positions at the GATT during these years were essentially negative in nature: reluctant to open its borders to trade and investment, India was really not in a position to be an effective participant in the multilateral trading system. Fortunately, starting in 1991, India began a process of economic liberalization that has already paid significant dividends in terms of higher economic growth and increased integration with the world economy.

In terms of multilateral negotiations, the single-undertaking nature of the WTO left India and other developing countries no choice but to sign on to all multilateral agreements of the WTO that emerged from the Uruguay Round, including GATS and TRIPS, agreements to which India was quite opposed. There is a strong argument to be made that the WTO should stick to its core competence of negotiating trade barriers down multilaterally instead of spreading into intellectual property, competition, investment, labor standards, and other areas. Indeed, such prominent economists as Jagdish Bhagwati and T. N. Srinivasan have consistently argued in favor of this position, and so have Indian trade negotiators. But the fact of the matter is that TRIPS is here to stay, and there is not much India or any other developing country can do about it.

The perceived asymmetry of the Uruguay Round bargain has had implications for the Doha Round from the very beginning. This legacy continues to loom large, as is obvious from the stands India and other major developing countries have taken during the ongoing negotiations. Furthermore, the very nature of the multilateral trading system has changed substantially over the years. For example, during most GATT negotiations the United States and the European Union, along with a few other countries, negotiated matters of mutual interest and then extended the resulting concessions to other GATT members on an MFN (most-favored nation) basis — a process that allowed the developing countries to free ride to some degree but also implied that issues that were primarily of interest to them were excluded from multilateral negotiations. As a result, during the early GATT rounds developing countries were essentially nonparticipants in the multilateral trading system: whatever they received came their way due to MFN, but they did not have to, and mostly did not, reciprocate with concessions of their own.[33]

The WTO has 153 members today, and economic growth in large developing countries such as Brazil, China, and India is far outpacing that in the developed world. With the growth in the size of these economies increasing their stake in the system, nonparticipation is no longer a viable option. Furthermore, growth has altered the balance of economic power in their favor. Finally, the increase in the number of WTO members has led to the emergence of several subgroups, such as the G20. As Schott (2004) has noted, the formation of coalitions complicates the nature of multilateral bargaining. Given these factors' combined weight and the fact that the "easy" part of global trade liberalization is most likely in the past, perhaps one should not be too critical of the glacial pace of the Doha Round.

For its own part, India should use its growing leverage not to stall liberalization but rather to secure more favorable terms in the emerging bargain. For that, it has to be willing to concede as well as receive concessions, and this requires that the notion of self-sufficiency, which shaped the first decades of its independent existence, needs to be deemphasized or perhaps dispensed with altogether (Mattoo and Subramanian 2000).

Indeed, relative to its historical participation in the multilateral trading system, India appears to be playing a more constructive role on the global stage. It took an important step forward when, in an attempt to bring the ongoing Doha negotiations to a conclusion, it played host to a meeting of the world's trade ministers in September 2009. (Past international meetings in India had typically involved only developing countries with similar interests and positions.) It remains to be seen whether this event was a one-off or a sign of things to come.

Increased multilateral engagement backed by a true intent toward greater openness is in India's long-term interest. One hopes that the ever-changing coalitional politics of India's vibrant democracy and the pursuit of short-term gain by its political leaders will not lead it astray from the path of constructive multilateral engagement — something it must continue to follow if it is to achieve its rightful place in the world economic order.

Endnotes

1. The text of this declaration is at http://www.wto.org/english/thewto_e/minist_e/min01_e/mindecl_e.htm.
2. See also Bhagwati and Srinivasan (1975).
3. Data for all figures have been taken from the official database of the WTO. The data on trade flows are taken from Time Series, the WTO statistics database on international trade, at http://stat.wto.org/StatisticalProgram/WSDBStatProgramHome.aspx?Language=E; the data on antidumping are from the WTO Antidumping Gateway, at http://www.wto.org/english/tratop_E/adp_e/adp_e.htm.
4. The WTO's 2007 Trade Policy Review of India notes that in 2006/07: (i) tariff revenue accounted for 23% of net tax revenue in India; (ii) the overall average for applied MFN tariffs was 15.8%, with 12.1% for nonagricultural products and 40.8% for agricultural products; (iii) manufacturing continues to have high tariffs, especially in textile and clothing (22.5%) and autos (33.65%); and (iv) over 75% of India's tariff were bound, but the bindings were rather high: 100% for agriculture and 71.6% for nonagricultural goods; and (v) the difference between bound and applied rates was substantial.
5. During 2008, 21.6% of India's exports went to the EU, 11.8% to the USA, 10.5% to the UAE, 5.6% to China, and 4.9% to Singapore. On the import

side, India sourced 13.9% of its imports from the EU, 10% from China, 7.8% from the USA, 7.3% from Saudi Arabia, and 6.2% from the UAE. India's trade-to-GDP ratio stood at 47.6%, and while India ran a trade deficit in goods of roughly $113 billion, it ran a trade surplus in services of roughly $15 billion.

6. For example, as per Irwin (2007), from 1995 to 1998, the average AD duty imposed by the USA stood at almost 59%. As one might expect, such large duties result in significant welfare costs. Irwin (2007) reports that during 1993 alone, the net welfare costs of AD and CVD duties imposed by the USA was $4 billion.
7. As per Bown and Tovar (2009), the dominant user of AD within India's manufacturing sector is the chemical industry. Other important users include iron and steel, as well as machinery.
8. Furthermore, they find that the degree of import reduction associated with India's use of antidumping is similar in magnitude to the initial import expansion associated with its tariff reform and that there is a negative relationship between the length of protection granted under an antidumping measure and the size of the original tariff cut. Needless to say, all this is pretty strong evidence of substitution among alternative instruments of trade protection.
9. During the period 1995–2010, while China accounted for more than 14% of world trade, it was involved in less than 4% of WTO disputes. However, China did not become a WTO member until November 10, 2001. Since China's accession, there have been 162 WTO disputes, 24 (14%) of which have involved China while 12 (7%) have involved India.
10. India was also opposed to the negotiations on services that culminated in the General Agreement on Trade in Services (GATS). Panagariya (2008) notes that this opposition stemmed from India's fear that liberalization in services would inevitably require opening up to foreign investment to a degree for which India was not prepared.
11. Using detailed product-level data from India (1999/2000), Chaudhuri, Goldberg, and Jia (2006) estimate that even if the implementation of TRIPS has no price effects, the withdrawal of the four domestic antibiotics in the fluoroquinolone subsegment in India (implied by TRIPS compliance) would result in a consumer-welfare loss equal to 65% of the sales of the entire antibiotic market in India in 2000. Two points are worth noting. First, their analysis assumes that the exit of local producers would not be offset by the entry of multinationals. Second, as they note, since most antibiotic drugs were not under patent in 1990, the actual negative effect of TRIPS in the antibiotic market might be quite small.

12. Branstetter *et al.* (2011) also analyze the impact of IPR reform on the annual count of "initial export episodes" — the number of ten-digit commodities for which U.S. imports from a given country exceed zero for the first time. They find that the count of such episodes increased sharply after IPR reform, suggesting that the decline in indigenous imitation resulting from IPR reform was more than offset by the increase in the range of local production undertaken by multinational affiliates. For direct evidence on the response of intrafirm technology transfer to IPR reforms, see Branstetter *et al.* (2006).
13. See WTO document WT/Min(01)/ST/10, dated November 10, 2001.
14. Compulsory licensing occurs when a government permits someone other than the patent holder to produce the patented good without the permission of the rights holder. It is one of the so-called "flexibilities" available under the TRIPS agreement. However, this flexibility comes with some conditions (listed in article 31 of TRIPS). In particular: the person or company applying for a license is first required to negotiate a voluntary license with the patent holder on "reasonable commercial terms." Only if such negotiations fail can a compulsory license be issued. Furthermore, the patent owner has to be compensated; the TRIPS agreement says "the right holder shall be paid adequate remuneration in the circumstances of each case, taking into account the economic value of the authorization." In addition, compulsory licenses cannot be exclusive in nature and have to be subject to legal review.
15. See "Implementation of Paragraph 6 of the Doha Declaration on the TRIPS Agreement and Public Health," IP/C/W/405, August 30, 2003, and the accompanying chairman's statement at http://www.wto.org/english/news_e/pres03_e/pr350_e.htm.
16. The WTO maintains the list of countries that have ratified the 2003 decision at http://www.wto.org/english/tratop_e/trips_e/amendment_e.htm.
17. One aspect of the Rwanda case is encouraging, however: it took only two weeks for the Canadian drug company Apotex to obtain the compulsory license for exporting TriAvir to Rwanda. For more details, see http://www.wto.org/english/news_e/news10_e/trip_02mar10_e.htm.
18. Also, as in other sports, in cricket you do know the score at all times!
19. See WTO document WT/Min(05)/ST/17.
20. Such divergence of interests among developing countries is not unique to services. As we will argue below, the elimination of export subsidies and other government support to agriculture in the EU and the USA might be in the interest of India but not in the interest of some of the poorest members of the WTO, which usually tend to be net importers of food and other agricultural products.

21. See Fergusson (2008).
22. Elliott (2006) emphasizes that not all types of subsidies do equal damage. In particular, she notes that to be effective, reform has to limit the discretion available to policymakers to shift subsidies among the various categories; that is, from the less harmful subsidies in the green and blue categories to the more harmful subsidies that lie in the amber category — a classification system that originated in the Uruguay Round.
23. Of course, even those countries that are net importers would respond to changes in world prices by stepping up domestic production of agricultural goods, and this production response could dampen the adverse effect on them, perhaps even convert some of them from being net importers to net exporters.
24. Analyzing data on 115 developing countries, Elliott (2006) finds that 76 are net importers of agricultural products, of which 37 have an overall deficit in agriculture but export at least one of the three among cereals, other foods, and agricultural raw materials.
25. Indeed, most existing studies suggest that it is the middle income countries such as Brazil, Argentina, and Thailand that will be the big winners from liberalization of trade in agriculture (Anderson *et al.* 2006).
26. The G20 group consists of China, almost all of Latin and Central America, India, Pakistan, Philippines, Thailand, and several African countries. The group's combined negotiating clout is substantial, and its emergence is an unmistakable sign of the fundamental changes that have occurred in the landscape of the multilateral trading system since the early GATT days.
27. Briefly speaking, these provisions grant special rights and privileges to developing countries that are not accorded to other WTO members. These special provisions manifest themselves in several different ways; they include longer time periods for implementing WTO agreements such as TRIPS and other commitments, measures to enhance their trading opportunities, special efforts to safeguard the trade interests of developing countries, and assistance in building the infrastructure necessary for WTO work, handling disputes, and implementing technical standards.
28. As Low and Santana (2009) note, the Swiss formula is not the only modality in use for tariff reductions; members have agreed to apply several different methods for achieving these reductions.
29. The Middle Ground Group at NAMA comprises Chile, Colombia, Costa Rica, Hong Kong China, Israel, Malaysia, Mexico, Morocco, Pakistan, Peru, Singapore, and Thailand. See WTO document TN/MA/W/98.

30. See WTO document TN/MA/W/10/Add.1.
31. As Brummer (2005) notes, India demands commitments from WTO members in various services segments, such as computer-related services, financial data processing, research and development, management consulting, environmental services, and the provision of financial information.
32. I thank an anonymous referee for pointing out that while India opposed the inclusion of services in the Uruguay Round, it has pushed for services liberalization in the Doha Round because it has undertaken unilateral liberalization in this area while it continues to face trade barriers in major foreign markets (such as the United States), especially in the area of mode 4. Similarly, India's unilateral liberalization has lessened pressure from export interests in the United States and other countries to undertake reciprocal services liberalization where mode 4 liberalization is a politically sensitive issue.
33. This interpretation is not universally accepted; in a provocative paper, Wilkinson and Scott (2009) argue that developing countries have always participated actively at the GATT and that their attempts to secure more favorable treatment for themselves were more a result of the underlying structure of GATT — such as the use of bargaining based on the principal supplier rule, the reliance on reciprocity as a negotiating condition, and the virtual exclusion of agriculture from the agenda — than an attempt to free ride on their part. Along similar lines, Ismail (2009) has argued that the collapse of the July 2008 talks of the Doha Round can in part be traced to the principal-supplier method of negotiations, with the imbalanced nature of the bargain between NAMA and agriculture being the other major factor.

Acknowledgments

This chapter was written during a visit to the Stanford Center for International Development, Stanford University, Palo Alto, California. I thank the center's director, Nicholas Hope, and its staff for their hospitality and support. I also thank Jingting Li for her excellent research assistance and for useful comments on an early draft. Helpful comments from an anonymous referee and from the editor, Chetan Ghate, are also acknowledged.

References

Anderson, Kym, Will Martin, and Dominique van der Mensbrugghe. 2006. "Market and Welfare Implications of the Doha Reform Scenarios." In *Agricultural Trade Reform and the Doha Development Agenda*, edited by Kym Anderson and Will Martin. London and Washington: Palgrave Macmillan / World Bank.

Bhagwati, Jagdish, and Padma Desai. 1970. *India: Planning for Industrialization*. Oxford: Oxford University Press.

Bhagwati, Jagdish, and T. N. Srinivasan. 1975. *Foreign Trade Regimes and Economic Development: India*. New York: National Bureau of Economic Research.

Bown, Chad P., and Patricia Tovar. 2009. "Trade Liberalization, Antidumping, and Safeguards: Evidence from India's Tariff Reform." Mimeo. World Bank and Brandeis University.

Branstetter, Lee, Raymond Fisman, and Fritz Foley. 2006. "Does Stronger Intellectual Property Rights Increase International Technology Transfer? Empirical Evidence from U.S. Firm-Level Data." *Quarterly Journal of Economics* 121, 321–349.

Branstetter, Lee, Raymond Fisman, Fritz Foley, and Kamal Saggi. 20011. "Does Intellectual Property Rights Reform Spur Industrial Development?" *Journal of International Economics* 83, 27–36.

Brummer, Julia. 2005. "India's Negotiation Positions at the WTO." Briefing paper, FES Geneva.

Chaudhuri, Shubham, Pinelopi K. Goldberg, and Panle Jia. 2006. "Estimating the Effects of Global Patent Protection in Pharmaceuticals: A Case Study of Quinolones in India." *American Economic Review* 96, 1477–1514.

Elliott, Kimberly A. 2006. *Delivering on Doha: Farm Trade and the Poor*. Washington, DC: Peterson Institute of International Economics.

Fergusson, Ian F. 2008. "World Trade Organization Negotiations: The Doha Development Agenda." CRS Report for Congress. Washington, DC: Congressional Research Service.

Hoekman, Bernard, Aaditya Mattoo, and Will Martin. 2009. "Conclude Doha: It Matters!" Policy Research Working Paper 5135. Washington, DC: World Bank.

Irwin, Douglas. 2005. *Free Trade under Fire*. Princeton, NJ: Princeton University Press.

Ismail, Faizel. 2009. "An Assessment of the WTO Doha Round July–December 2008 Collapse." *World Trade Review* 8, 579–605.

Low, Patrick, and Roy Santana. 2009. "Trade Liberalization in Manufactures: What Is Left after the Doha Round?" *Journal of International Trade and Diplomacy* 3, 63–126.

Maskus, Keith E. 2000. *Intellectual Property Rights in the Global Economy*. Washington, DC: Institute for International Economics.

Mattoo, Aaditya, and Arvind Subramanian. 2000. "India and the Multilateral Trading System Post-Seattle: Defensive or Proactive?" World Bank Policy Research Working Paper 2379.

Panagariya, Arvind. 2008. *India: The Emerging Giant*. New York: Oxford University Press.

Schott, Jeffrey J. 2004. "Reviving the Doha Round." Washington, DC: Peterson Institute of International Economics.

Srinivasan, T. N., and Suresh D. Tendulkar. 2003. *Reintegrating India with the World Economy*. Washington, DC: Institute of International Economics.

Wilkinson, Rorden, and James Scott. 2009. "Developing Country Participation in the GATT: A Reassessment." *World Trade Review* 7, 473–510.

CHAPTER 16

European Economic Review 63 (2013) 10–27

Contents lists available at SciVerse ScienceDirect

European Economic Review

journal homepage: www.elsevier.com/locate/eer

Size inequality, coordination externalities and international trade agreements

Nuno Limão [a], Kamal Saggi [b,*]

[a] University of Maryland, NBER and CEPR, United States
[b] Vanderbilt University, United States

ARTICLE INFO

Article history:
Received 24 February 2012
Accepted 24 May 2013
Available online 15 June 2013

JEL classification:
F13
F42
K33
O1
O24

Keywords:
Trade agreements
Tariffs
Bonds
Fines

ABSTRACT

Developing countries now account for a significant fraction of world trade and two-thirds of the membership of the World Trade Organization (WTO). However, many are still individually small and thus have a limited ability to bilaterally extract and enforce trade concessions from larger developed economies even though as a group they would be able to do so. We show that this coordination externality generates asymmetric outcomes under agreements that rely on bilateral threats of trade retaliation – such as the WTO – but not under agreements extended to include certain financial instruments. In particular, we find that an extended agreement generates improvements in global efficiency and equity if it includes the exchange of bonds prior to trading but not if it relies solely on ex post fines. Moreover, a combination of bonds and fines generates similar improvements even if small countries are subject to financial constraints that prevent them from posting bonds.

1. Introduction

International trade relations between developed and developing countries have often been adversarial. As early as 1947, some developing countries were denouncing the United States' proposals for the predecessor of the World Trade Organization (WTO) as "serving the interests of developed countries and undermining the development prospects of poor countries" (Srinivasan, 1999, p. 1050). More recently, the Uruguay Round was seen by most developing countries as having produced a multilateral bargain that is biased heavily in favor of developed countries. Partly to rectify the perceived imbalance of the Uruguay Round outcome, the Doha *Development* Round was launched in 2001 with the idea that it would put the interests of developing countries at the forefront.[1]

Developing countries now account for two-thirds of the 157 WTO members (up from 11 in the GATT) and over a third of world trade and have increasingly begun to demand a more active voice in multilateral negotiations. However, they still face considerable challenges in translating such demands into tangible outcomes: despite having been launched over a decade ago, the Doha Round has yet to be concluded. In this paper we analyze a key problem that developing countries face in

* Corresponding author. Tel.: +615 322 3237.
E-mail addresses: Limao@econ.umd.edu (N. Limão), k.saggi@Vanderbilt.Edu, ksaggi@gmail.com (K. Saggi).

[1] The Doha ministerial declaration of November 2001 states: "We recognize the need for all our peoples to benefit from the increased opportunities and welfare gains that the multilateral trading system generates. The majority of WTO members are developing countries. We seek to place their needs and interests at the heart of the Work Programme adopted in this declaration."

0014-2921/$ - see front matter
http://dx.doi.org/10.1016/j.euroecorev.2013.05.006

trying to achieve a more favorable outcome in international trade negotiations—i.e. the presence of a *coordination externality* among themselves. Even though developing countries are now large on aggregate, most are still individually small and thus have a limited ability to bilaterally extract and enforce trade concessions from larger developed economies. We show that under standard agreements that rely on bilateral threats of trade retaliation – such as the WTO – this coordination externality generates asymmetric outcomes that are less favorable to developing countries (as well as globally) than those obtained under an agreement extended to include certain types of financial instruments.

The traditionally dominant role of large countries in the world trading system is partly due to the bilateral and reciprocal nature of negotiations in international trade agreements such as the GATT/WTO. The key idea is the following: if the European Union (EU) wants the United States (US) to lower its tariffs on EU exports then it must reciprocate with lower tariffs on goods it imports from the US. However, this reciprocal exchange relies on the presence of relatively symmetric market power on both sides: while a tariff reduction by a country with a sufficiently high import share and market power increases the price received by foreign exporters, no significant bilateral concessions occur when the reduction is undertaken by a small country.[2] Market power is also essential in enforcing cooperation since the threat to abandon the agreement and increase tariffs on the part of a country that lacks such power is not credible and therefore fails to act as a useful deterrent. Thus, *bilateral asymmetries* in market power undermine international cooperation and may explain why some exports from (smaller) developing countries (e.g. in agriculture, textiles, some manufactures) have historically faced relatively higher tariffs in (larger) developed countries. By undermining cooperation, this asymmetry can also lead to higher tariffs by developing countries but, as long as they remain small as a group, the large countries do not lose much from this, which may explain why the latter have not pushed developing countries to liberalize further until recently.[3]

Most formal analyses of the GATT/WTO focus on two large countries.[4] The focus on this canonical case has yielded important insights and was a reasonable approximation until the Uruguay Round since up to that point GATT/WTO negotiations were led primarily by the US and Europe (cf. Schott, 2009). However, the global economic landscape has changed significantly with the emergence of the BRICs—Brazil, Russia, India and China. From 2000 to 2009 alone the world import share of the largest traders, the US and EU, fell from 43% to 34% (54–42% if we also include Japan and Canada) and their bilateral trade accounts for less than 20% of their total trade.[5] The relative decline of the US and EU in world trade suggests that it is important to analyze international trade agreements between multiple countries of asymmetric size, something that we focus on in this paper.

While some of the recent decline of the US and EU in world trade is mirrored in the rise of the BRICs – particularly China – there is also a longer trend driven by other developing countries' trade liberalization and growth.[6] This is important in motivating the coordination externality underlying our model since this externality is most relevant if several countries jointly account for a non-negligible amount of exports of a larger country. For example, if we exclude Japan, Australia and China, the next top 10 Asian destinations in 2009 accounted for 13% of total US exports but their median share was only 1.3% (the largest is Korea with less than 3%). Another case in point is South and Central America: while the region jointly accounts for 10% of US exports all but one country accounts for less than 1% (the only exception is Brazil, whose share is 2.5%). More broadly, if the US were to negotiate only with the top five destinations for its products it would cover only 64% of its exports, with the analogous figure for the EU being even smaller, 44%.[7]

Our model highlights the role of *bilateral size asymmetry* in international trade agreements by focusing on two "regions" of equal size with one containing a single country (Large) and the other multiple countries, each of whom individually has less market power in trade. Large exports a single good, x, to all small countries and imports a different good in return. The bilateral size asymmetry generates lower tariffs and welfare for the smaller countries in the absence of an agreement because their tariff choices are subject to a coordination externality, i.e. when setting its tariff on good x each small country ignores any positive terms-of-trade effect that its tariff has on all other *importers* of the same good. We then show that this

---

[2] For evidence of the positive relationship between market power and either import shares or GDP see Broda et al. (2008).

[3] In fact, if the asymmetry is sufficiently large, the large country would be strictly better off by not cooperating (cf. Johnson, 1953–1954). An additional explanation for relatively higher tariffs by the large developed countries on exports of small developing countries is that historically the latter have tended not to take an active role in multilateral trade negotiations. One reason for such non-participation and higher tariffs by large countries arises when, as in our setup, a large country imports the same good from many small countries. Ludema and Mayda (2009) show how the WTO's MFN rule requiring the importer to set the same tariff on all exporters lowers the incentive for the latter to participate in reciprocal negotiations in an attempt to minimize reductions in their own tariffs. Since this incentive is well understood theoretically we abstract from it (by assuming all exporters either participate or not) and focus instead on the coordination externality.

[4] See for example Mayer (1981), Grossman and Helpman (1995) and Bagwell and Staiger (1999). The latter also considers a third large country to study tariff discrimination.

[5] Authors calculations based on data from the WTO's "International trade statistics 2010". We treat the EU as a single country since it has a common tariff and negotiates as a block. Thus, world imports exclude flows within EU-27.

[6] As the Director General of the WTO notes "Between 1973 and 1997 the developing countries' share of manufactured imports in developed markets tripled—from 7.5% to 23%. What these figures reflect is the developing world's truly remarkable integration into the global economy over the past three decades." Source: Ruggiero (1999) accessed at ⟨http://www.wto.org/english/news_e/pres99_e/pr122_e.htm⟩. Besedes and Prusa (2011) examine the sources of export growth for 46 countries between 1975 and 2003.

[7] Moreover, the recent increases in this dispersion measure suggest an increasingly important role for the coordination externality among importers of US goods. For example, the top five US destinations in 2000 accounted for 70% of its exports but those in 2009 only accounted for 64%. At the industry level we see a similar trend with over 2/3 of HS 2 industries showing declines averaging 7 percentage points in the share of top five destinations (the average for those with an increase was about 4 p.p.).

imbalance remains even if countries cooperate through a standard trade agreement that relies on the threat of tariff retaliation because cooperation is ultimately sustained by the threat of non-cooperative tariffs, which are subject to the coordination externality.[8] The small countries would gain from jointly threatening higher tariffs to punish any deviation by Large but this threat is not credible: in the event the agreement breaks down, each small country has an individual incentive to free ride on the others if they were to try punishing the large country via a jointly optimal Nash tariff.

In the model all countries have identical *income per capita* in the absence of trade policies. When trade policy is used it generates an asymmetry in income per capita: increasing it for the larger country and reducing it for the smaller ones when cooperation is based on tariff retaliation alone. The most parsimonious way to show this result involves a "developing" region with K countries and a "developed" one with a single large country, but a similar insight should hold as long as the representative country in the developed region was larger. Given this, and the current distribution of world trade – where about half is accounted for by a large number of developing countries – we think it is reasonable to identify the region with more countries as the developing one.[9] Moreover, as we discuss next, the type of reforms proposed to standard trade agreements to address the size asymmetry issue have mainly originated with developing countries.

Next, we examine how standard agreements – i.e. those based on tariff retaliation alone – can be reformed to counter the coordination externality and generate more efficient and equitable (i.e. symmetric) outcomes. More specifically, we extend the standard trade agreement to include financial instruments such that a country that deviates must incur a monetary cost, such as paying a fine or losing a bond that it previously posted. Some such instruments have been proposed in the WTO, particularly by developing countries arguing that their limited market power prevents them from using tariffs to obtain proper compensation in case of a violation.

Before explaining why and how such extended agreements may generate more efficient and equitable outcomes, we describe some of the ongoing debate surrounding the use of financial instruments in trade agreements. The situation confronting developing countries is well illustrated by the case in which Ecuador challenged the preferential treatment that the EU accorded to banana exporting nations that were its former colonies. The US too had challenged the EU's regime and, like Ecuador, was authorized to impose retaliatory tariffs on the EU. However, while the US was in a good position to make use of this authorization, Ecuador simply did not import enough from the EU to be able to effectively retaliate in tariffs. If it had done so it would have simply imposed a distortion on itself without much harm to the EU. Given this, Ecuador went so far as to seek WTO approval to cross-retaliate in the area of intellectual property by not allowing local producers of red wine to use the 'Bordeaux' label and by allowing local firms to produce unauthorized copies of hit European recordings.[10]

The idea that financial compensation could be used as means for settling international trade disputes has a long history—in fact it was discussed during the original GATT 1947 negotiations. While the GATT did not adopt this idea, calls for its usage have resurfaced periodically. For example, in 1964 Brazil and Uruguay formally suggested its consideration and the idea was floated and discussed also during the Uruguay Round negotiations (Mercurio, 2009). While the dispute settlement system of the WTO has yet to embrace financial compensation as a mandatory trade remedy, it does allow for 'voluntary compensation' as an alternative to trade retaliation. Financial compensation was actually used in the *US-Copyright* dispute between the US and the EU. This case was filed by the EU to challenge US laws that exempted small businesses such as restaurants and bars from paying royalties when playing copyrighted music (Grossman and Mavroidis, 2004). The EU challenged these laws on the grounds that they were inconsistent with Article 9.1 of the Trade Related Intellectual Property Agreement (TRIPS). The WTO panel ruled that at least part of the exemptions granted by the US were indeed in conflict with TRIPS. Instead of amending its laws to make them WTO compliant, the US entered into discussions with the EU in order to find a mutually agreeable level of financial compensation.[11]

In recent years, the use of financial compensation has also become more common in bilateral trade agreements. For example, Mercurio (2009) notes that in several recent free trade agreements involving the United States – and countries such as Australia, Chile, and Singapore – the signatories have agreed to a format under which a non-compliant country can stop the complainant country from instituting retaliatory measures by paying an annual 'monetary assessment', much like in the *US-Copyright* case between the US and the EU.

In case of a trade dispute it is typically more efficient to use financial compensation than a distortionary instrument such as a tariff, provided the compensation can be enforced. What existing proposals and their analyses typically neglect however, and what we focus on, is the more difficult question of how financial compensation can be enforced and whether such instruments can deter deviations and generate more cooperation ex ante.[12] We show that agreements extended to

[8] We should note that tariff retaliation at the WTO is permitted as a last resort after negotiations between the affected parties have failed and any panel ruling calling for compliance has gone unheeded by the defendant.

[9] About 51% of world imports in 2009 were accounted for by the US, EU and eight other high income countries (Japan, Canada, Korea, Australia, Switzerland, Norway, New Zealand and Israel). The remaining half of world imports was accounted for by a very large number of developing countries since the BRICs together accounted for only about 16% of world imports.

[10] For an elaborate discussion of the legal and economic arguments in favor of financial compensation as a means for settling trade disputes see Bronckers and Van Den Broek (2005). A comprehensive overview of the various aspects of the dispute settlement process in the WTO is provided by Lawrence (2003).

[11] Ultimately, the two sides could not come to agreement and had to resort to binding WTO arbitration, which determined the annual level of compensation that the US would have to pay to the EC so long as its laws remained incompatible with TRIPS.

[12] The financial transfers do not have to come directly from the country that violates the agreement. For example, Mexico has proposed that countries should be allowed to sell their right to retaliate to others that possess more market power to retaliate. This proposal has been analyzed by Bagwell et al.

include specific financial instruments can enhance cooperation and generate outcomes that are more symmetric relative to a standard trade agreement. In particular, we show these improvements occur when countries exchange bonds *prior to trading and agree to forfeit them in case of a violation*. The use of bonds in this fashion accomplishes two important tasks. First, by requiring a high enough bond to be posted ex ante, we remove the incentive of the large country to deviate (so as not to forfeit its bond). Second, the use of bonds neutralizes the tariff coordination externality amongst small countries. It does so because if the large country deviates then any one of the small countries can, and will, keep the bond that the large country posted with it and doing so has *no effect on the values of bonds held by any other small countries*.[13]

We also show that the specific choice of the financial instrument is crucial since the obvious alternative, i.e. a monetary fine, does *not* improve on the standard agreement *when used in isolation*. The reason is that for the fine to be paid by the violating country it must still be enforced by small countries through the threat of tariff retaliation, which is subject to the coordination externality. Relative to Limão and Saggi (2008), the crucial novel element in our present paper is the presence of the coordination externality among small countries, each of which is not in a position to credibly threaten tariff retaliation. As noted earlier, this scenario is an apt description of the situation confronting developing countries at the WTO.

There are potentially important obstacles in reforming standard agreements to include financial instruments. The main obstacle that we consider is the limited ability countries might have to post bonds with trading partners. We show that our main results are robust to the presence of some bond constraints even if they are severe for small countries provided the extended agreement includes both bonds (posted by the large country) *and* fines that are paid in the event of a deviation. However, if the bond constraint is also severe for the large country then this extended agreement must rely on fines alone and it yields the same outcome as the standard trade agreement that relies only on tariff retaliation. The intuition for this result is that the payment of fines can ultimately only be enforced by the threat of tariffs (if no bonds were posted).[14]

Our basic approach is common in the literature on trade agreements: we model such agreements as an equilibrium outcome of repeated interaction between governments. However, most of this literature ignores the role of financial instruments. An exception is Bagwell and Staiger (2005) who show that if governments face private anticipated shocks then cash transfers can help enforce more cooperative tariffs. However, Limão and Saggi (2008) show that their result will not hold if we instead consider fines enacted in the case of a deviation. The fact that different types of financial instruments lead to different levels of tariff cooperation highlights the importance of carefully modeling each of their roles in international trade agreements. Unlike these two papers, we examine countries that are asymmetric in their market power and show this generates a role for bonds, that is absent in Limão and Saggi (2008). Park (2000) also examines cooperation between asymmetric countries but focuses on a case where there is a single small country with *no* market power and one large country; he shows that cash transfers from the former to the latter can help enforce lower tariffs. This purchase of market access by a single infinitesimally small country is fundamentally different from the coordination externality among many small countries that we analyze and argue is empirically relevant. Thus the results we find are naturally different, e.g. we find that cooperation in tariffs can be achieved without requiring the small countries to purchase market access from the large country.

The paper is structured as follows. In Section 2 we set up the model and describe the policy externalities. In Section 3 we derive the policy and welfare impacts of standard agreements, contrast them with the extended agreements and analyze the implementation issues that may arise. We conclude in Section 4. All proofs are in the Appendix.

2. Setup and trade policy externalities

2.1. Setup

The economic structure within each country is a standard one in the analysis of trade agreements (cf. Limão and Saggi, 2008). However, instead of focusing on two symmetric countries, we allow for multiple asymmetric countries. To clearly highlight the role of size asymmetries we focus on a single large country trading with a finite number of small countries, $K > 1$, where the latter are identical among themselves.

Given that preferences and technologies are identical across countries, we describe the setup in detail for the large country (using variables without asterisks), and then point out any modification for the small ones. Each country can produce two homogeneous goods, $i = x, y$ and a numeraire, n. Individual utility over the consumption levels, c, of these goods is given by $u \equiv c_n + \sum_i u_i(c_i)$. Since utility is quasi-linear and separable, the demand function for good i depends only on its own price and is the same for all individuals so we denote aggregate demand by $D_i(p_i)$.

(*footnote continued*)
(2007) in an auction framework that assumes the violation has already occurred and a country has "earned" the right to retaliate against another (offending) country. They show that in some cases it is the offending country that wins that auction so the transfer is direct but that is not always the case.

[13] We further show that this benefit of bonds relative to the standard agreement is eliminated when there are just two symmetric countries, which is the special case that Limão and Saggi (2008) study. Thus, the underlying asymmetry among trading partners is necessary for bonds to enhance the scope for cooperation.

[14] This extends one of the basic insights in Limão and Saggi (2008) – that allowing for fines does not improve cooperation relative to standard agreements – to a setting with asymmetric countries.

Each unit of the numeraire, c_n, is produced with a constant returns to scale technology using only labor. Each non-numeraire good is also produced with a constant returns technology but it uses both labor and a specific factor. We denote the supply function for non-numeraire goods by $S_i(p_i)$, omitting its dependence on the specific factor endowment since both labor and specific capital endowments are assumed constant and inelastically supplied.

We assume that the large country is a mirror image of the set of small countries so it imports one of the non-numeraire goods, which we label y, and exports the other, x. Under trade, the domestic import price in the large country is then $p_y = p_y^w + \tau$ where p^w is the "world" price and τ is a specific import tariff on y, which satisfies an MFN constraint, i.e. it does not discriminate by country of origin. The large country's imports of y are then $M_y \equiv D_y(p_y) - S_y(p_y)$ and its world price is determined by the market clearing condition

$$M_y(p_y^w + \tau) + \sum_k M_y^{*k}(p_y^w) = 0 \tag{1}$$

where M_y^{*k} denote exports of good y by each of the k small countries. An analogous condition applies to good x.

We assume that no export policies are available so trade policy is described by the level of the import tariff in each country. Reductions in the large country's import demand affect the world price of y and it is simple to verify that in this setup an increase in the large country's tariff lowers the world price, $p_y^w(\tau)$, and raises the domestic one. Similarly, if the K small countries jointly increased their tariffs on x they would reduce its world price; i.e. small countries as a whole also have market power in trade.

The government chooses trade policies that maximize the political objective function below, which reflects social welfare and allows for extra weight ($\lambda_i \geq 1$) on specific factor owners[15]

$$W(\tau, \boldsymbol{\tau}^*) \equiv \sum_i \left[\int_{p_i}^{\infty} D_i(p_i)\, dp_i + \lambda_i \int_0^{p_i} S_i(p_i)\, dp_i + \tau_i M_i(p_i) \right] + L \tag{2}$$

where we recall that the tariff τ affects W both directly through tariff revenue, the term $\tau_y M_y$, and through its effect on home prices; whereas the effect of small countries' import tariffs, $\boldsymbol{\tau}^*$, is indirect and occurs only through the world price, $p_x^w(\boldsymbol{\tau}^*)$. In Eq. (2), the first term in parenthesis is consumer surplus; the second term can be interpreted as producer surplus or the quasi-rents accruing to the fixed factor owners; and the last term, L, is simply the total wage income of the large country when the wage is unity. This objective function is concave in τ and decreasing in each of the elements of $\boldsymbol{\tau}^*$.[16]

Each of the individual small countries has an objective function, which is denoted by W^{*k}. It has the same functional form as (2) so we do not rewrite it but simply note that it is evaluated using the prices and endowments in each k. To simplify the exposition and focus on the size asymmetry we now describe some restrictions. Each of these K small countries owns a constant fraction $(1/K)$ of its region's population (L^*) so $L^{*k} = L^*/K$ and of its specific inputs. Moreover, given identical preferences, technologies and political parameters in the region ($\lambda_i^{*k} = \lambda_i^*$), the only potential difference that can arise across W^{*k} is if some k faces different prices because it sets or faces different tariffs than the others. It will often be useful to focus on equilibria where all small countries set the same tariff, $\tau^* = \tau^{*k}$ for all k and face the same tariff exporting to Large, τ, which can be different from τ^*. In this case prices and quantities are identical for all k so, given constant returns, the aggregate variables for the region are $Z_i^* \equiv \sum_k Z_i^{*k}(p_i^{*k}) = KZ_i^{*k}(p_i^*)$ (where $Z^* = D^*, S^*, M^*$). Moreover, the aggregate political welfare in the region when $\tau_i^{*k} = \tau_i^*$ and $\lambda_i^{*k} = \lambda_i^*$ is $W^* \equiv \sum_k W^{*k} = KW^{*k}$.

We also assume that the two regions as a whole have equal populations ($L = L^*$) and equal supplies of fixed factors in their respective import and export sectors. This symmetry assumption implies that the "aggregate" import market power of small countries is no different from that of the large country. This underlying symmetry across regions simplifies our exposition but is not crucial for our results; the same is true of our assumption of equal political weights in each region ($\lambda_y = \lambda_x^* = \lambda$) and their absence in the respective export sectors ($\lambda_x = \lambda_y^* = 1$).[17]

2.2. *Trade policy externalities among asymmetric countries*

The large country's Nash tariff is obtained by maximizing (2) while taking the small countries' tariffs as given. Since we do not model export policies we drop the good subscript, i, and any subscripts below denote partial derivatives. The large country's Nash tariff on y solves

$$\tau^N \equiv \underset{\tau}{\operatorname{argmax}}\ W(\tau, \boldsymbol{\tau}^*) \tag{3}$$

Recalling that the equilibrium prices are a function of tariffs, the first order condition for τ is

$$-Dp_\tau + \lambda S p_\tau + M + \tau M' p_\tau = 0 \tag{4}$$

---

[15] This can be obtained as the reduced form of a political economy model such as Grossman and Helpman (1994).

[16] We assume that there is sufficient labor to ensure a positive supply of the numeraire so that the wage rate in the economy is fixed by the marginal productivity of labor in the numeraire, which is normalized to unity.

[17] A more important assumption we make is that the political economy parameter is fixed and public information. For an interesting analysis of the role of the WTO where that is not the case see Beshkar (2010).

Using $M = D - S$, $M' \equiv dM(p)/dp$ and $p_\tau = p_\tau^w + 1$ and the elasticity expressions defined below we obtain a Nash tariff in ad-valorem terms, $\tau^N/p^w(\tau)$, implicitly defined by

$$\frac{\tau^N}{p^w(\tau)} = \frac{1}{\varepsilon(\tau)} + (\lambda - 1)\frac{S(\tau)/M(\tau)}{\xi(\tau)} \tag{5}$$

We show the potential dependence of the endogenous variables on the tariff. We do so for clarity in the formula but will omit it below for notational simplicity. The first term, $1/\varepsilon \equiv M^*/(p^w M'^*)$, is the inverse of the elasticity of the aggregate export supply curve of small countries (since τ applies to all small countries) and it reflects the large country's terms-of-trade (TOT) motive for the use of tariffs. The second term reflects a political economy motive that is increasing in the extra weight placed on specific factor owners (λ) and decreasing in the large country's import demand elasticity ξ where $\xi \equiv -(\partial M/\partial p^w)(p^w/M) = -M'p^w/M$.

If the small countries cannot successfully coordinate their tariff choices, then the Nash tariff of an individual small country in its import sector (x) is

$$\frac{\tau^{*Nk}}{p^w} = \frac{1}{\varepsilon^{*k}} + (\lambda - 1)\frac{S^{*k}/M^{*k}}{\xi^{*k}} \tag{6}$$

where all the variables are defined similarly to τ^N in (5) but from the perspective of country k, as detailed in the Appendix.

A country's import tariff lowers the price received by exporters of that good, this is the standard negative *terms-of-trade externality*, which we will confirm below is a central reason for a trade agreement. However, the outcome of that agreement will depend on another externality that is present when there are several countries importing the same good, what we will refer to as a *coordination externality*. To understand it suppose that small countries could coordinate their tariffs choices in order to maximize their region's aggregate objective, $\sum_k W^{*k}$, then their *coordinated* Nash tariff, denoted by $\tau^{*Ncoord}$, would be given by (6) evaluated at the *aggregate* regional quantities (S^*/M^*) and elasticities, ε^* and ξ^*. We argue that small countries set a higher tariff when acting jointly than individually because their market power is higher under coordination. We show this by contradiction. Suppose τ^{*Nk} and $\tau^{*Ncoord}$ are identical and then evaluate the TOT and political economy components of welfare. Note that given the symmetry across small countries we have the same τ^{*Nk} across all of them and thus the same price, therefore $(S^{*k}/M^{*k})/\xi^{*k} = (S^*/M^*)/\xi^*$, so with $\tau^{*Nk} = \tau^{*Ncoord}$ and thus equal prices the political economy component is also identical. However, at any given tariff and prices we can show that $1/\varepsilon^{*k} < 1/\varepsilon^*$ if $K > 1$. The intuition for this is simple, when small countries set their tariffs independently, each small country does not take into account the positive TOT benefits that accrue to other small countries. As might be expected, this coordination externality is increasing in the number of countries.

The empirical relevance of the expressions above in tariff policy setting requires at least three pieces of evidence. First, countries should have at least some market power in imports. Second, prior to trade agreements countries should set higher tariffs on products with higher market power. Third, larger countries (in terms of GDP or import quantities) should have more market power than smaller countries. Evidence for each of these is provided by Broda et al. (2008).[18] Evidence for the third point is particularly relevant for this paper since as we divide a region of given size each of the resulting K countries will have lower GDP and imports than the whole region and lower market power, $1/\varepsilon^{*k}$.

As we noted before, to highlight the size differences it is useful to keep other factors constant. If we assume symmetry across regions in their respective import and export sectors then two other implications emerge. First, since $\tau^N = \tau^{*Ncoord}$ the lack of coordination among small countries implies that their respective tariffs are lower than that of the large country. Note that the tariff τ^N applies to good y and is independent of the tariffs that small countries set on x because (i) the utility function is quasi-linear and separable and (ii) the only mobile factor is labor and its factor price is pinned down by its productivity in the numeraire sector. The second implication of symmetric regions is as follows. Under an agreement without enforcement problems countries could choose tariffs to maximize their joint objective $W + KW^{*k}$ and, if regions were symmetric, this would be equivalent to maximizing the objective of either region after imposing $\tau = \tau^*$. Thus we obtain

$$\tau^G \equiv \underset{\tau^C}{\operatorname{argmax}}\, W(\tau^C, \tau^* = \tau^C) \tag{7}$$

so the globally optimal ad-valorem tariff $\tau^G/p^w(\tau^G)$ (derived in the appendix) is

$$\frac{\tau^G}{p^w(\tau)} = (\lambda - 1)\frac{S(\tau)/M(\tau)}{\xi(\tau)} \tag{8}$$

It is simple to see that $\tau^G/p^w < \tau^N/p^w$. The difference between the Nash and globally cooperative policies confirms that market power in trade leads to international externalities motivating the need for a trade agreement (Bagwell and Staiger, 1999). Note also that even in the presence of an international agreement, countries may choose to have positive tariffs due to internal political economy distortions (i.e. when $\lambda > 1$).[19]

---

[18] They also find evidence of a positive impact of the political economy component, captured by $(S/M)/\xi$.

[19] Broda et al. (2008) provide evidence that countries set higher protection in goods where they have higher market power if they are either non-WTO members or the policy is not subject to strong WTO discipline. Bagwell and Staiger (2011) find that WTO accession leads to greater tariff reductions in products with higher initial import volumes and market power.

Since the globally optimal tariff τ^G is below the level that is optimal for each *individual* country, each country has an incentive to deviate from it and would do so if it faced no punishment. Before addressing how the threat of tariff retaliation can be used to sustain international cooperation, we make an important observation. Note from (6) that if the number of small countries is sufficiently high and governments face no political pressures (i.e. $\lambda = 1$), the Nash tariff of each small country in the absence of coordination among them, τ^{*Nk}, approaches zero. Under such circumstances, a small country neither can individually offer *any* tariff reduction to the large country nor can it credibly threaten the large country with any tariff retaliation in case the latter reneges on a cooperative trade agreement. Thus, as K increases so does the coordination externality and this lowers the incentive of the large country to enter into any agreement that relies only on uncoordinated tariff retaliation to enforce cooperation. Naturally if K is so high that the value of τ^{*Nk} is close to the global optimum τ^G then the large country would always prefer not to cooperate at all. On the other hand, an individual small country has a much stronger incentive to cooperate since it has limited ability to manipulate its TOT. In what follows, we assume that $K \in (1, \overline{K}]$, i.e. there is more than one "small" country (thus the asymmetry) but not so many of them as to make their cooperation unattractive to the large country.[20]

3. Trade agreements among asymmetric countries

3.1. Standard agreements: asymmetric outcomes under tariff retaliation

We now examine the role of agreements in enforcing tariff cooperation between asymmetric countries. We show that if standard agreements, which rely solely on tariff threats, cannot sustain the globally optimal tariff for all countries then the outcome is an asymmetric one with the large country setting a higher tariff than the small ones (Proposition 1). The asymmetry is driven by the coordination externality previously highlighted. In the next section, we show that if we go beyond the enforcement instruments in standard agreements and include financial ones, namely bonds, then we can both improve cooperation and make the outcome more equitable by sustaining the symmetric global tariff (Propositions 2 and 3).

Consider an infinitely repeated game where the stage game delivers the Nash tariffs previously derived, i.e. τ^N and τ^{*Nk}. Assume that countries observe each other's actions at the end of each period. The strategy for each country is to cooperate until any country deviates by raising its tariff. Any such deviation is followed by a punishment of n periods during which the country that originally deviated faces Nash tariffs on its exports and demonstrates its willingness to restart cooperation by setting a cooperative tariff level. If this occurs then cooperative tariffs are set by all after the n periods, otherwise the agreement breaks down and countries permanently revert to Nash tariffs.

To find the lowest cooperative tariff that is *weakly renegotiation proof* (or simply *WRP*) we first define each country's payoffs under the alternative situations that can arise. We focus on WRP strategies for three reasons. First, taking account of the WRP constraint is intuitively appealing since it ensures that punishing parties actually have an incentive to implement the punishment. Second, temporary punishments are more realistic in the context of disputes in the WTO than infinite Nash reversion after any deviation (the latter is a possibility but we view it as the ultimate punishment corresponding to an unraveling of the GATT/WTO system that results from member countries not following its rules). The third reason is to easily contrast the results with Limão and Saggi (2008) who also employ this approach.[21]

Let $\boldsymbol{\tau}^{*N}$ represent the vector of Nash tariffs composed of each of the (uncoordinated) small countries' equilibrium values, τ^{*Nk}. In the absence of cooperation, the payoff to the large country equals its government's objective evaluated at non-cooperative tariffs

$$W^N \equiv W(\tau^N, \boldsymbol{\tau}^{*N}) \tag{9}$$

The cooperative tariff vector (to be found) for the small countries is represented by $\boldsymbol{\tau}^{*C}$ and its representative element, τ^{*Ck}, will be common to all k during periods of cooperation since these countries are identical. We denote the large country's cooperative tariff by τ^C so the cooperative payoff of the large country is

$$W^C \equiv W(\tau^C, \boldsymbol{\tau}^{*C}) \tag{10}$$

If the large country deviates, it does so by imposing its optimal Nash tariff τ^N, which we recall is non-discriminatory and so applies to all small countries. In that period, the small countries are still setting cooperative tariffs.[22] The deviation payoff to the large country in the period is

$$W^D \equiv W(\tau^N, \boldsymbol{\tau}^{*C}) \tag{11}$$

[20] A sufficient condition for the large country to accept setting a tariff below its Nash and at (or above) its global optimum in exchange for small setting $\boldsymbol{\tau}^{*G}$ is for $W(\tau^G, \boldsymbol{\tau}^{*G}) \geq W(\tau^N, \tau^{*Nk}(K))$, which holds strictly when $K = 1$. There are sufficient free parameters in the model to ensure that the condition also holds for some $K > 1$. But there is some $\overline{K}$ such that $\tau^{*Nk}(K)$ is so low that the condition above holds with equality and thus we assume that $K \in (1, \overline{K}]$.

[21] A further motive is that Ludema (2001) shows that the reliance on reciprocity during dispute settlement at the WTO implies that only trade agreements that are renegotiation proof can be sustained in equilibrium.

[22] The large country's deviation tariff level is independent of the level for the small ones because of the separability across sectors.

According to the strategy we consider if the large country deviates, then in *each* of the n punishment periods its payoff is

$W^P \equiv W(\tau^C, \boldsymbol{\tau}^{*N})$

We can then define the large country's continuation payoff after a deviation as

$$V^{\tau} \equiv \sum_{t=1}^{n} \delta^t W^P + \sum_{t=n+1}^{\infty} \delta^t W^C \qquad (12)$$

i.e. it undergoes punishment for n periods after which cooperation resumes. Given these payoffs, the incentive compatibility (IC) constraint for the large country to cooperate is

$$W^D + V^{\tau} \leq \frac{W^C}{1-\delta} \qquad (13)$$

That is, the sum of the payoff from a deviation, W^D, and the continuation payoff, V^{τ}, should not exceed the present value of the stream of cooperative payoffs.

Since the per period punishment payoff is lower than the Nash payoff, i.e. $W^P < W^N$, the punishment phase is subgame perfect only if it is not profitable for the country that is being punished (in this case the large country) to simply abandon the agreement and revert to Nash tariffs forever. So V^{τ} must be at least as large as the Nash payoff in order for the cooperative equilibrium to be *WRP*

$$V^{\tau} \geq \frac{\delta}{1-\delta} W^N \qquad (14)$$

Because $W^C > W^P$, the longer the punishment phase n, the lower the continuation payoff V^{τ}. Therefore, the maximum punishment phase that is *WRP* is found by equating the continuation payoff V^{τ} to the RHS of (14). We define this maximum punishment period as $n^{\max}$, and it is implicitly given by

$$V^{\tau\ \min} \equiv \delta \frac{1-\delta^{n^{\max}}}{1-\delta} W^P + \frac{\delta^{n^{\max}+1}}{1-\delta} W^C = \frac{\delta}{1-\delta} W^N \qquad (15)$$

Therefore, the lowest cooperative *WRP* tariff is obtained at $n^{\max}$ and implicitly defined when (13) holds with equality. Given the maximum *WRP* punishment it is also simple to see that this cooperative tariff level would also be obtained under an alternative strategy where if any country deviates then they all permanently revert to Nash. To see this clearly, we substitute $V^{\tau\ \min}$ in (13) and use the definitions for W^D, W^N and W^C to obtain

$$W(\tau^N, \boldsymbol{\tau}^{*C}) + \frac{\delta}{1-\delta}(\tau^N, \boldsymbol{\tau}^{*N}) \leq \frac{W(\tau^C, \boldsymbol{\tau}^{*C})}{1-\delta} \qquad (16)$$

which is identical to the large country's incentive constraint under infinite Nash reversion. Thus the lowest self-enforcing tariff under infinite Nash reversion or *WRP* is implicitly defined when (16) holds with equality.

To understand the effect of the coordination externality on cooperation, note that the worst punishment that uncoordinated small countries can inflict on the large one is for each to revert to its individual Nash tariff, τ^{*Nk}, which is lower than their coordinated punishment tariff, $\tau^{*Ncoord}$. Therefore, for any given cooperative tariff, the total payoff of deviating for the large country, as given by the LHS of (16), is greater relative to the case where small countries coordinate their tariff decisions. In other words, the lack of coordination between small countries increases the large country's incentive to deviate, which is one component of the asymmetric outcome. The other component arises because the coordination externality reduces the incentive of each small country to deviate since the short-term gain from such a deviation is smaller relative to coordination.[23] To see this more explicitly we now derive the IC for each small country.

We use $\boldsymbol{\tau}^{*Dk}$ to denote the tariff vector of a small country k when it deviates. To clearly isolate and understand the role of the coordination externality we first describe what are the alternative deviation possibilities one could consider. First, consider a full coordination scenario, that is suppose that we allowed small countries to act as a single country (e.g. if they formed a customs union that maximized their joint welfare under cooperation, deviation and punishment periods). Under this scenario, $\boldsymbol{\tau}^{*Dk}$ is the same for all k and simply reflects their Nash tariff and it would be equal to τ^N, i.e. Large's non-cooperative value (since the regions are symmetric). Therefore, not surprisingly, the IC for each of the k countries and Large would be identical under full coordination and the setting would be the same as in Limão and Saggi (2008), who show there is no role for bonds. Second, consider a scenario where all small countries happen to deviate at the same time but cannot coordinate on the level of the optimal tariff, so they choose the level that maximizes their *individual* government objectives. In this case $\boldsymbol{\tau}^{*Dk} = \boldsymbol{\tau}^{*N}$ so it is the same for all k but evaluated at τ^{*Nk}, the uncoordinated Nash value previously derived. Finally, consider an alternative scenario with individual and uncoordinated deviations where we require all other countries to be cooperating in the period when any small country deviates. In this case $\boldsymbol{\tau}^{*Dk}$ will include the non-cooperative tariff for country k evaluated at the prices that result when the other small countries are still cooperating.

We focus on the second scenario described above for two reasons. First, it allows us to isolate the coordination externality since the only difference relative to the case where the small countries act as a unified decision maker is that

[23] The incentive to deviate by the small countries is also reduced by the fact that reversion to Nash is more costly to them, which implies that if they would deviate the large country would impose a relatively harsher punishment that would still be WRP.

they deviate and punish using $\tau^{*Nk} < \tau^{*Ncoord}$. Second, the results are qualitatively similar if we focus on individual deviations instead.[24]

Following the derivation for the large country, the IC of a small country is given by

$$W^{*k}(\tau^C, \boldsymbol{\tau}^{*Dk}) + \frac{\delta}{1-\delta} W^{*k}(\tau^N, \boldsymbol{\tau}^{*N}) \le \frac{W^{*k}(\tau^C, \boldsymbol{\tau}^{*C})}{1-\delta} \tag{17}$$

We use these incentive constraints to establish the first result, which is a building block to showing that the coordination externality leads to asymmetric tariffs in standard agreements.

Lemma 1 (*Asymmetric cooperation incentives under standard agreements*). *The large country's payoff is higher than the respective aggregate payoff to K uncoordinated small countries under* (i) *a deviation from a given symmetric cooperative tariff, i.e.* $W(\tau^N, \boldsymbol{\tau}^{*C}) > \sum_k W^{*k}(\tau^C, \boldsymbol{\tau}^{*Dk})$ *at* $\tau^C = \tau^{*Ck}$ *and* (ii) *under non-cooperative tariffs, i.e.* $W(\tau^N, \boldsymbol{\tau}^{*N}) > \sum_k W^{*k}(\tau^N, \boldsymbol{\tau}^{*N})$.

It is worth relating Lemma 1 to the recent literature on tariff *wars*. Zissimos (2009) obtains a similar result in a Heckscher–Ohlin model of North–South trade where each region comprises many (similar) countries. In his model, holding constant the number of countries in the North at one, if the number of countries in the South increases then the tariffs set by individual Southern countries falls below their jointly optimal tariff, so that the South necessarily loses from a tariff war when it is composed of many countries. He notes that the asymmetry between the two regions in terms of number of countries is crucial for this result: indeed, in a two-country set-up Syropoulos (2002) has shown that a sufficient condition for a country to be better off under a non-cooperative tariff war relative to free trade is that its relative size be sufficiently large. These papers focus on the outcome of trade wars whereas we use Lemma 1 as a building block to analyze alternative self-enforcing trade agreements.[25]

Lemma 1 fixes the cooperative tariff at a fixed symmetric level to highlight the fact that the larger country may have a weaker incentive to cooperate than the uncoordinated small countries.[26] We now show that this coordination externality not only generates an imbalance in market power across countries but also generates asymmetric cooperative tariffs (and thus unequal welfare outcomes) in a trade agreement enforced by the threat of tariff retaliation. As will be clear enforcement is only an issue if the large country is not sufficiently patient to sustain the global optimum tariff in a standard agreement, i.e. if $\delta < \delta_G$ where δ_G is implicitly defined to ensure that the incentive constraint in (16) is satisfied at τ^G.

Proposition 1 (*Asymmetric outcomes under standard agreements*). *In a standard trade agreement supported by the threat of tariff retaliation, the most cooperative tariff set by a large country exceeds the tariff set by each of the K uncoordinated small countries: i.e.* $\tau^C > \tau^{*Ck}$ *whenever the large country is not sufficiently patient to sustain the globally optimal tariff* ($\delta < \delta_G$) *and thus this agreement yields higher welfare for the large country than for the set of small ones, i.e.* $W(\tau^C, \boldsymbol{\tau}^{*C}) > KW^{*k}(\tau^C, \boldsymbol{\tau}^{*C})$.

Proposition 1 emphasizes the asymmetry in market power across countries and how this asymmetry leads to an outcome that is skewed in favor of the large country when tariff cooperation is sustained solely on the basis of tariff retaliation. We next consider how the use of financial instruments alters the scope for cooperation as well as the welfare of each country.

3.2. *Extended agreements: efficiency and equity with financial instruments*

We now show how the coordination externality can be offset when we extend the set of enforcement instruments to allow for certain type of financial instruments. We show that such an extended trade agreement generates (i) an improvement in global welfare relative to the standard agreement and (ii) more symmetric welfare outcomes across countries.

First, we consider the exchange of bonds as a means for sustaining cooperation when countries pursue the following strategy. Countries start cooperating by posting a bond with each of its import sources. At the end of a period, if the countries have cooperated then they "return" their respective bonds. If a country deviates from the cooperative tariff, it loses

[24] More specifically, in a supplementary appendix we show that the IC for small countries under individual deviations does not bind when evaluated at the solution under simultaneous deviations. Moreover, the type of deviations for small countries does not affect whether or not the IC for the large country binds at the global optimum, which is the source of the inefficiency in the standard agreement. We thank an anonymous referee for suggesting that we clarify this point.

[25] In a recent paper, Syropoulos and Dinopoulos (2012) show that when there are three countries and international income transfers are not possible, a relatively small country may prefer an equilibrium with tariffs over free trade provided that the tariffs used are non-discriminatory in nature, as is required by the core WTO rule of MFN. See also Saggi and Yildiz (2010) where a small country is the one that prevents the obtainment of free trade when liberalizing countries cannot tariff discriminate and must extend any tariff concessions to non-participating countries on an MFN basis. In their model, the possibility of forming FTAs induces the smaller country to vote in favor of free trade since such FTAs are worse from its perspective than MFN based liberalization amongst other countries.

[26] The prediction of higher protection for the larger country in our model would seem to contradict the fact that large developed WTO members typically have lower *average* tariffs. We could easily change the model to replicate this fact if we allowed for lower political pressure for protection, (i.e. λ) in these countries relative to the small ones. We could also introduce an additional block of countries (one large and another K small) and allow for additional goods that are mainly traded between the two large countries, such that the prediction would then be that large countries have relatively higher tariffs on goods that they import from small countries than from large ones, a fact that has been documented. Our model abstracts from these considerations to focus directly on the coordination externality.

its bond. For cooperation to resume, the deviating country must return the present discounted value of the bond of the injured country. If it does so in the period after the deviation occurs, then tariffs return to the cooperative level. If it does not, cooperation breaks down and all countries switch to their optimal Nash tariffs.

To understand the basic insight, consider a situation where each country has a similar discount factor, just below the level required for the large country to sustain the global optimum under a standard agreement, (i.e. δ is just below δ_G). Recall that in that case the small countries are still patient enough to sustain the global optimum so their IC holds with slack. If we then allowed the large country to post a bond with a value exceeding what it receives from the collection of small countries then its incentive to deviate declines (it stands to lose more from forfeiting its bond) so it could sustain a lower cooperative tariff. While this bond would also increase each small country's incentive to deviate, they could still sustain the same cooperation as before since the incentive constraint of each small country had slack at the initial symmetric tariffs $\tau^C = \tau^{*Ck} = \tau^G$ for some $\delta < \delta_G$. We demonstrate this intuition formally below.

Suppose the large country posts a bond of value b^k (in units of the numeraire) with each of the small countries it imports from, and receives $\sum_k b^{*k}$ from them. Since all small countries are ex ante identical we assume from the start that when cooperating they each post a bond of equal value, $b^{*k} = b^*$, and receive an equal share of the large country's bond, $b^k = b/K$. The *WRP* incentive constraint for the large country and *each* of the small countries are respectively given by

$$W(\tau^N, \boldsymbol{\tau}^{*C}) - b + Kb^* + V^b \leq \frac{W(\tau^C, \boldsymbol{\tau}^{*C})}{1-\delta} \tag{18}$$

$$W^{*k}(\tau^C, \boldsymbol{\tau}^{*Dk}) - b^* + b/K + V^{*b} \leq \frac{W^{*k}(\tau^C, \boldsymbol{\tau}^{*C})}{1-\delta} \tag{19}$$

where their respective continuation payoffs are defined as

$$V^b \equiv -\frac{\delta Kb^*}{\delta} + \frac{\delta W(\tau^C, \boldsymbol{\tau}^{*C})}{1-\delta} \tag{20}$$

$$V^{*b} \equiv -\frac{\delta b}{\delta K} + \frac{\delta W^{*k}(\tau^C, \boldsymbol{\tau}^{*C})}{1-\delta} \tag{21}$$

The first term in the large country's continuation payoff V^b equals the present value of the bonds posted by the small countries that must be returned by the large country for cooperation to resume and the second term is the present discounted value of its payoff under cooperation. A similar interpretation applies to a small country's continuation payoff V^{*b}.

We now derive the minimum bond values required to enforce the global optimum assuming the *WRP* constraint is satisfied (which we will verify below). To do so, we substitute these continuation payoffs into (18) and (19) respectively and solve for b^g and b^{*g}

$$b^g = W(\tau^N, \boldsymbol{\tau}^{*G}) - W(\tau^G, \boldsymbol{\tau}^{*G}) \tag{22}$$

$$b^{*g} = W^{*k}(\tau^G, \boldsymbol{\tau}^{*Dk}) - W^{*k}(\tau^G, \boldsymbol{\tau}^{*G}) \tag{23}$$

These bond values are quite intuitive: the minimum bonds required to achieve globally optimal tariffs are equal to each country's TOT gain of deviating from those tariffs. Further note that the large country requires a larger bond than the set of K small countries. That is, $b^g > Kb^{*g}$ since $W(\tau^N, \boldsymbol{\tau}^{*G}) > KW^{*k}(\tau^G, \boldsymbol{\tau}^{*Dk})$ (as proved in Lemma 1) and $W(\tau^G, \boldsymbol{\tau}^{*G}) = KW^{*k}(\tau^G, \boldsymbol{\tau}^{*G})$ (due to symmetry). In sum, since the large country deviates to an optimal tariff, τ^N, that is larger than the optimal tariff of a typical small country (τ^{*Nk}), its TOT gain from deviating is larger than the corresponding total gain of K uncoordinated small countries. Therefore, the large country must post a larger bond, i.e. $b^g > Kb^{*g}$, which reduces its incentive to deviate relative to that under tariff retaliation thereby opening up the possibility of increased cooperation.

The final step is to show that there is some $\delta < \delta_G$ such that tariff retaliation does *not* enforce globally optimal tariffs whereas the bonds b^g and b^{*g} do while also satisfying the *WRP* constraint. Let $b^{\max}$ be the bond value that equates the continuation payoff of a small country V^{*b} in (21) to its payoff from abandoning the agreement $W^{*k}(\tau^N, \boldsymbol{\tau}^{*N})\delta/(1-\delta)$. We have

$$V^{*b} = -\frac{b^{\max}}{K} + \frac{\delta W^{*k}(\tau^C, \boldsymbol{\tau}^{*C})}{1-\delta} = \frac{\delta W^{*k}(\tau^N, \boldsymbol{\tau}^{*N})}{1-\delta}$$

$$b^{\max} = K\frac{\delta[W^{*k}(\tau^C, \boldsymbol{\tau}^{*C}) - W^{*k}(\tau^N, \boldsymbol{\tau}^{*N})]}{1-\delta} \tag{24}$$

In other words, if the bond posted by the large country exceeds $b^{\max}$, then a typical small country is better off cheating on the agreement and abandoning it altogether since its continuation payoff falls below what it gets outside the agreement.

Similarly, let $b^{*\max}$ be the value of the bond posted by a small country that equates the large country's continuation payoff V^b in (21) to $W(\tau^N, \boldsymbol{\tau}^{*N})\delta/(1-\delta)$, i.e. its payoff from abandoning the agreement. We have

$$V^b = -Kb^{*\max} + \frac{\delta W(\tau^C, \boldsymbol{\tau}^{*C})}{1-\delta} = \frac{\delta W(\tau^N, \boldsymbol{\tau}^{*N})}{1-\delta} \tag{25a}$$

$$Kb^{*\max} = \frac{\delta[W(\tau^C, \boldsymbol{\tau}^{*C}) - W(\tau^N, \boldsymbol{\tau}^{*N})]}{1-\delta} \tag{25b}$$

Note that since $W(\tau^N, \boldsymbol{\tau}^{*N}) > KW^{*k}(\tau^N, \boldsymbol{\tau}^{*N})$, we have that $b^{\max} > Kb^{*\max}$ at any symmetric cooperative tariff. The intuition for this is clear: due to its greater market power, abandoning the agreement is relatively more attractive to the large country and therefore a smaller (aggregate) bond on the part of small countries is necessary to ensure that the large country prefers to resume cooperation by returning bonds of small countries as opposed to abandoning the agreement. In other words, since cooperation is relatively less attractive to the large country, it is willing to suffer a relatively smaller punishment to resume cooperation (as measured by the value of bonds it has to repay to resume cooperation).

As before, if the bonds posted by the small countries exceed $Kb^{*\max}$, the continuation payoff of the large country is too low for it to prefer to resume cooperation as opposed to abandoning the agreement altogether. The two *WRP* constraints together ensure that the bonds required to sustain the global optimum $(\tau^G, \boldsymbol{\tau}^{*G})$ are not so high that countries prefer to abandon the agreement altogether

$$b^g \leq b^{\max}(\tau^G, \boldsymbol{\tau}^{*G}) \quad \text{and} \quad b^{*g} \leq b^{*\max}(\tau^G, \boldsymbol{\tau}^{*G})$$

First consider $b^g \leq b^{\max}(\tau^G, \boldsymbol{\tau}^{*G})$. Since $b^g = W(\tau^N, \boldsymbol{\tau}^{*G}) - W(\tau^G, \boldsymbol{\tau}^{*G})$ we can use the definition of δ_G and re-arrange (16) to obtain

$$b^g = \frac{\delta_G[W(\tau^G, \boldsymbol{\tau}^{*G}) - W(\tau^N, \boldsymbol{\tau}^{*N})]}{1-\delta_G}$$

From the symmetry of W and KW^{*k} at the global optimum we can rewrite b^g as

$$b^g = \frac{\delta_G[KW^{*k}(\tau^G, \boldsymbol{\tau}^{*G}) - W(\tau^N, \boldsymbol{\tau}^{*N})]}{1-\delta_G} < K\frac{\delta_G[W^{*k}(\tau^G, \boldsymbol{\tau}^{*G}) - W^{*k}(\tau^N, \boldsymbol{\tau}^{*N})]}{1-\delta_G} = b^{\max}(\tau^G, \boldsymbol{\tau}^{*G}) \tag{26}$$

The last inequality follows from the coordination externality, which implies that $W(\tau^N, \boldsymbol{\tau}^{*N}) > KW^{*k}(\tau^N, \boldsymbol{\tau}^{*N})$ for $K > 1$, as proved in Lemma 1. Since the RHS in the last line is equal to $b^{\max}$ evaluated at the globally optimal tariffs and it is continuous in δ, we have that when $K > 1$ there exist $\delta < \delta_G$ s.t. $b^g \leq b^{\max}(\tau^G, \boldsymbol{\tau}^{*G})$, where we recall that b^g is independent of δ. Intuitively, the inequality above says that at the critical discount factor where the large country's incentive constraint just binds under tariff retaliation, (i.e. at $\delta = \delta_G$), the bond b^g that the large country has to post in order to sustain cooperation over the global optimum is less than the maximum bond $b^{\max}(\tau^G, \boldsymbol{\tau}^{*G})$ that satisfies the *WRP* constraint at globally optimal tariffs (which equals the present discounted value of cooperation to small countries as a whole discounted by one period).

Now consider $b^{*g} \leq b^{*\max}$. Using the value for b^{*g} in (23) on the LHS we have

$$\begin{aligned} Kb^{*g} &= K[W^{*k}(\tau^G, \boldsymbol{\tau}^{*Dk}) - W^{*k}(\tau^G, \boldsymbol{\tau}^{*G})] < W(\tau^N, \boldsymbol{\tau}^{*G}) - W(\tau^G, \boldsymbol{\tau}^{*G}) \\ &= \frac{\delta_G[W(\tau^G, \boldsymbol{\tau}^{*G}) - W(\tau^N, \boldsymbol{\tau}^{*N})]}{1-\delta_G} = Kb^{*\max} \end{aligned} \tag{27}$$

where the first inequality follows from $W(\tau^G, \boldsymbol{\tau}^{*G}) = W^*(\tau^G, \boldsymbol{\tau}^{*G})$ (by symmetry) and $W(\tau^N, \boldsymbol{\tau}^{*G}) > W^*(\tau^G, \boldsymbol{\tau}^{*Dk})$ for $K > 1$, as proved in Lemma 1. The equality on the second line follows from the definition of δ_G. Since the RHS in the last line is equal to $Kb^{*\max}(\tau^G, \boldsymbol{\tau}^{*G})$ in (25b), and is continuous in δ_G, we have that when $K > 1$ there exists a $\delta < \delta_G$ s.t. $b^{*g} \leq b^{*\max}(\tau^G, \boldsymbol{\tau}^{*G})$. Intuitively, the last inequality says that at the critical discount factor where the large country's incentive constraint just binds under tariff retaliation, (i.e. at $\delta = \delta_G$), the collective value of the bonds posted by small countries required to sustain cooperation over the global optimum is less than the present discounted value of cooperation to the large country (discounted by one period).

The main result can now be stated:

Proposition 2 (*Improved cooperation and symmetric outcomes with bonds*). *In a trade agreement extended to include bond exchange as an enforcement instrument the large country and the K uncoordinated small countries can sustain the globally optimal tariffs* ($\tau^C = \tau^{*Ck} = \tau^G$) *even if they cannot enforce it under a standard agreement. Therefore, for some* $\delta < \delta_G$, *the extended agreement generates* (i) *an increase in welfare for the small countries*; (ii) *a global increase in welfare and* (iii) *a more equitable outcome relative to the standard agreement.*

The first part of the proposition follows directly from what we showed above: that there exist WRP bonds that sustain the global optimum for at least some $\delta < \delta_G$. Since the global optimum tariffs are symmetric it follows that the outcome is more equitable than under the standard agreement where the large country sets higher tariffs than the small ones (part iii). Moreover, the tariffs for the large country are lower under the extended agreement and those for the small countries are no higher (at least for some $\delta < \delta_G$) so welfare is higher for small countries (part i) and globally since $W + KW^{*k}$ is concave and decreasing in tariffs above the global optimum.

To understand the intuition behind Proposition 2 it is useful to consider an extreme case where $K=1$ so the asymmetry disappears. In that case the bonds that can support the global optimum can only be *WRP* if $\delta = \delta_G$, as we can see from (26) and (27) but if the two symmetric countries are that patient then they can sustain τ^G in a standard agreement. More generally, if $\delta < \delta_G$ and two symmetric countries exchange bonds then their incentives to deviate remain unchanged because their bonds are of equal value (as shown in Limão and Saggi, 2008). However, if countries are asymmetric then we can require one to post a bigger bond than its smaller partner to offset its incentive to deviate from cooperative tariffs.

This increases the incentive to deviate by the smaller country (to keep the bigger bond) but the threat of future tariff retaliation prevents it from doing so.

This proposition provides an enforcement rationale for why some small countries have advocated for trade agreements to be extended to include financial instruments. In our model, the reason why bonds can help cooperation is that tariffs and bonds have rather different properties from an enforcement perspective. Namely, only tariffs are subject to a coordination externality: their non-cooperative levels reflect the individual small country's TOT motive and ignore the spillover TOT effects on other small countries. So if Large deviates against all small countries then they set a positive tariff that is above the cooperative level but lower than if they were to coordinate their punishment and internalize all the TOT effects on each other; thus the standard agreement fails to enforce the global optimum. The coordination externality is not present with bonds since, conditional on a sufficiently large bond being posted by Large with each of the small countries, if Large deviates then all that each small country has to do is keep the bond that it already received. The decision to keep the bond by a single small country has *no effect on the values of bonds held by others.*

It is worth discussing more broadly why bonds can assist with cooperation when there are asymmetries across countries. While we focus on size asymmetry due to its empirical relevance and in order to highlight the coordination externality that appears to be an important feature of the current world trading system, it is clear that other types of asymmetries could generate a motive for the use of bonds in improving cooperation. For example, bonds can improve cooperation if there are differences in political economy pressures for protection across countries that lead to different non-cooperative tariffs or if patience levels differ across countries so that incentive constraints of relatively impatient countries are harder to satisfy.[27] The basic intuition for the role for bonds in the presence of such type of asymmetries is that bonds posted by those that are less willing to cooperate can help *transfer enforcement power* to countries that are more willing to do so.

We now discuss possible obstacles to reforming standard agreements to include financial instruments.

3.3. *Agreement reform*

There are potentially important obstacles in reforming standard agreements to include financial enforcement instruments. One would be the cost of setting up and administering a system with financial instruments. However, the proposals by different WTO members to implement such schemes suggest that this may not be prohibitively costly. Therefore, the main obstacle we focus on is the limited ability and/or willingness to post bonds with trading partners. We show that even severe "bond constraints" for small countries can be overcome to achieve the outcomes in Proposition 2 if we design the extended agreement to also include fines. However, if the bond constraint is also severe for the large country then this extended agreement will result in the same asymmetric outcome as the standard one. These results highlight the importance of formally modeling alternative instruments to successfully reform standard agreements. We also discuss how to overcome another potential obstacle; namely, that the large country may prefer the standard agreement whereas the small countries prefer the extended one.

It is not difficult to motivate or provide a simple formal model of why certain countries may be unable or unwilling to post a large bond at the start of a period in order to induce another country to set a more cooperative tariff. Therefore, instead of committing to a specific motive for this we instead assume that countries face exogenous "bond constraints", i.e. $b < b^g$ and $b^* < b^{*g}$, and in Proposition 3 we show that the outcome in Proposition 2 can be achieved even if the small countries post *no bond at all* and the large one posts a bond that is of a value smaller than b^g but still positive. So bond constraints may not be an important obstacle to reform a standard agreement even if they are very severe for small countries (if $b^* = 0$). However, in order for agreements to generate efficient and symmetric outcomes in the presence of bond constraints we need to include another financial instrument in the trade agreement, i.e. a fine. The advantage of fines over bonds is that the latter must be posted every period before trading starts whereas fines need only be paid if a deviation ever occurs and are therefore not subject to the same type of financial constraint that bonds are. This raises the question if we need bonds at all in an extended agreement with fines and in Proposition 4 we also constrain $b = 0$ to show that they must be included and posted by the large country.[28]

To understand why fines can overcome bond constraints on small but not large countries we must explain why *WRP* fines face an enforcement issue relative to bonds. Namely, the deviating country has to be induced to pay the fine, whereas the bond is already in the hands of its partner and is thus automatically foregone. Thus fines require some threat of tariff retaliation if they are not paid. We model this tariff threat as a last resort that would only ever materialize if the agreement

[27] As a concrete example, consider cooperation between two countries (Home and Foreign) that are symmetric along all dimensions except their discount factors. Suppose that if both countries had a discount factor of δ_G they could sustain the global optimum in a standard agreement but Home's discount factor is below this critical level while Foreign's is above it, i.e. $\delta < \delta_G < \delta^*$. As a result, Home's IC does not hold at the global optimum but Foreign's IC has some slack in it. This asymmetric situation generates a role for Home to post a bond that would lower its incentive to deviate and thus improve the maximum sustainable cooperation. Suppose Home posts a bond such that its IC just binds at the global optimum. The bond increases Foreign's incentive to deviate, but if Foreign is sufficiently patient, its IC will continue to hold at the global optimum in the presence of the bond.

[28] One simple way to model the "bond constraints" is to assume that production of the numeraire can only take place after policies are set so none of it is available for the initial bonds. If we want the larger country to be able to post some bond we can allow it to have some endowment of the numeraire available at the start of the period. To maintain symmetry we can allow for a similar endowment for the K small countries that is only available after the policies are set so it affects only their ability to post a bond.

breaks down. So, the large country will find it easy to enforce large fines, which prevents small ones from deviating even if they post no bond ($b^* = 0$). But small countries will not have the same ability due to the coordination externality.

Proposition 3 summarizes the results when the extended agreement includes fines and countries face some bond constraints.

Proposition 3 (*Improved cooperation and symmetric outcomes with fines and bond constraints*). *In a trade agreement extended to include WRP fines and constrained bond exchange* ($b \in [\tilde{b}^g, b^g)$; $b^* \in [0, b^{*g})$) *the large country and the K uncoordinated small countries can sustain the globally optimal tariffs* ($\tau^C = \tau^{*Ck} = \tau^G$) *even if they cannot enforce it under a standard agreement. Therefore, for some* $\delta < \delta_G$, *there is a* $\tilde{b}^g > 0$ *such that this agreement generates* (i) *an increase in welfare for the small countries;* (ii) *a global increase in welfare and* (iii) *a more equitable outcome relative to the standard agreement. Furthermore these results hold even if the small countries face severe bond constraints, i.e. if* $b^* = 0$.

A corollary is that if the bond constraints were also severe for the large country, i.e. $b = 0 = b^*$, then Proposition 3 would not hold since $\tilde{b}^g > 0$ unless $\delta = \delta_G$. In fact, under such severe bond constraints, the outcome would be the same as that under the standard agreement. The intuition is straightforward: the outcome under the standard agreement is ultimately determined by the threat of the agreement breaking down and thus infinite tariff reversion, which is the same threat that enforces fines so the two yield the same IC. Proposition 4 summarizes this result.

Proposition 4 (*Equivalence of standard and extended agreements with fines under severe bond constraints*). *A trade agreement extended to include WRP fines and subject to severe constraints on bond exchange* ($b = b^* = 0$) *yields the same outcomes as those in Proposition 1 for a standard trade agreement supported by tariff retaliation.*

This last result makes it clear that an extended agreement has to be carefully designed to include the relevant instruments. In this case, what is needed is a bond posted by the large country that removes the need for small countries to coordinate on a particular tariff level in case a retaliation is required. This result extends Proposition 2 of Limão and Saggi (2008), which showed that fines do not enhance cooperation relative to tariff retaliation between two symmetric countries. Here, we show that in the absence of bonds, fines do not enhance the cooperation even in this setting with asymmetric countries.

We now turn to the choice of agreement. Any of the agreements considered thus far increases the payoffs for *each* of the countries relative to non-cooperation. This should be clear for the small countries. The large country will also be better off relative to non-cooperation if, as we assume throughout, there is a finite number of small countries. However, large and small countries can have different preferred agreements since for some $\delta < \delta_G$ we obtain $\tau^C > \tau^{*Ck} = \tau^G$ under the standard agreement (Proposition 1) and $\tau^C = \tau^{*Ck} = \tau^G$ under the extended agreements with $\tilde{b}^g$ (Propositions 2 and 3). Therefore, the small countries prefer the extended agreement but the large country prefers the standard one since $W(\tau, \boldsymbol{\tau}^{*G})$ is increasing in its own tariff when $\tau < \tau^N$. This raises the question of which agreement would be adopted. If ex ante transfers were available then we would expect the extended agreement to be adopted since it generates the highest global political welfare (Propositions 2 and 3).

One may then ask how to implement this reform in terms of the model and in practice. In this model of agreements with financial instruments, it seems reasonable to allow for transferable utility (via an ex ante transfer of the numeraire good). If we were to then model an initial stage where countries bargain (efficiently) over the type of agreement (standard or extended) and the associated value of the ex ante transfer, then the extended agreement would be adopted. The value of the transfer from each small country would depend on the precise details of the initial bargaining. If the large country had all the bargaining power then it may be able to extract the full additional gain of the extended agreement relative to the standard one. However, there is no reason to believe this is the only distribution of bargaining power. First, small countries are not negligible in size individually and may also be able to exert their collective power at the negotiation stage even if they cannot coordinate their tariffs after a trade war breaks out. Second, in practice negotiation outcomes are affected not only by relative size but also by the fairness of outcomes, which is a goal of the Doha Round. In sum, if ex ante transfers using the numeraire are possible then it is plausible that the extended agreement would be adopted.

The issue is more complicated if, as considered in the last two propositions, small countries are constrained in their transfers of the numeraire. Note that even if these constraints are severe they do not necessarily *eliminate* the possibility that an extended agreement is adopted. As we argued in the last paragraph, the amount of the transfer will reflect not just the benefit of the extended agreement relative to the standard one but also the initial bargaining procedure; so even a small ex ante transfer may be enough to adopt an extended agreement with large benefits.[29] More generally, if transfers are required but the small countries are constrained in terms of the numeraire then a narrow interpretation of our results is that they show the extended agreement provides a potential Pareto improvement. However, we have also clearly identified the potential constraint to implementing this agreement: the ex ante transfer of the numeraire. One way to overcome this constraint is to enrich the model to allow transfers to take the form of an initial concession by small countries in non-trade issues. One example of this was the acceptance by developing countries of the TRIPS agreement in the Uruguay Round, which many viewed as a transfer from developing to developed countries.

[29] In fact, we could consider an alternative initial stage choice mechanisms where the agreements are put to a vote in the WTO such that the larger number of small countries would imply that their preferred outcome is implemented without *any* transfers.

Naturally any transfer that makes the extended agreement more attractive for the large country also reduces some of its attractiveness to the small ones and would not generate symmetric welfare outcomes. But the small countries would still enjoy higher welfare than under non-cooperation or the standard agreement.

4. Conclusion

The multilateral trading system has changed dramatically since 23 founding members signed the GATT in 1947. The WTO now comprises 157 members, many of which are small individually but jointly account for a substantial fraction of trade. The recent emergence of the BRICs and the longer trend of trade liberalization across the developing world has eroded the relative standing of the US and EU in world trade. These salient changes in the global economic landscape have also started to alter the dynamic underlying multilateral trade negotiations. Whereas the first eight rounds of trade negotiations saw limited participation from developing countries and were led primarily by the USA and the EU, the most recent, and currently ongoing, round of negotiations – i.e. the Doha Round – puts (or at least claims to put) the interests of developing countries at center stage.

The increasingly dispersed pattern of world trade along with the increased participation of developing countries at the WTO suggests that the standard two-country paradigm underlying formal models of international trade agreements may no longer adequately capture actual trade negotiations. In this paper we analyze one basic problem that arises under this "new trade order": a *coordination externality* among countries that import a common good. The externality is strongest when each importer is bilaterally small relative to the exporter, but would have a reasonable degree of market power if it were to coordinate its tariff choices with other importers. This coordination externality implies that smaller countries have less of a threat to use tariffs and therefore a limited ability to bilaterally extract and enforce cooperation from larger countries. Thus international cooperation based on the threat of tariff retaliation yields an asymmetric equilibrium outcome that is biased in favor of the large country.

We examine the use of financial instruments as a means for resolving this coordination externality and the asymmetric outcome that results because of it. To this end, we consider an extended trade agreement under which countries post bonds prior to trading, with the understanding that a country violating the agreement would forfeit its bond. We show that the use of bonds in this fashion does not suffer from the coordination externality that characterizes the tariff choices of small countries. Indeed, we find that when the trade agreement is extended to allow for bonds, the resulting outcome is preferable from both an efficiency and equity perspective.[30] Since the implementation of such an extended agreement might be problematic due to the inability to post bonds (especially on the part of small countries) we show that our results hold even if small countries do not post *any* bonds at all provided the extended agreement allows for fines. Furthermore, the use of such fines also allows the large country to post a smaller bond.

The new trade order arising from the decline of the US and EU relative to several smaller developing countries in the world trading system raises a number of interesting questions and challenges. We argue that to adequately address these new issues, one needs to go beyond the canonical economic theories of agreements. In this paper, we construct a model that isolates a specific issue that is arguably central to the new global economic landscape: a coordination externality. Future research should consider the implications of such an externality for WTO rules and for the process via which trade concessions are exchanged, e.g. whether to add other instruments to enforce joint punishments and/or adjust the bilateral reciprocity principle. This externality also highlights the incentive of smaller countries to coordinate on a common external tariff via the formation of a customs unions. Future research could extend our approach by allowing for discriminatory tariffs in order to analyze the interaction between preferential and multilateral liberalization in the presence of bonds.[31] Finally, this new trade order seems to be one where bilateral trade shares and patterns are both dynamic and uncertain, two dimensions that should be better incorporated in future research on trade agreements.

Acknowledgment

We would like to thank Theo Eicher and two anonymous referees for their very useful comments and suggestions.

[30] Although we do not consider this in our model, posting bonds with a third party may also help improve cooperation. For example, if bonds of sufficient value are deposited in an escrow fund, tariff retaliation is no longer necessary for sustaining cooperation since the bond posted by the violating country can be used to compensate the injured country. Such an escrow scheme was in fact proposed by Chile in its bilateral trade agreement with the US. "Chile Looks for Monetary Sanctions as Enforcement Mechanism", INSIDE U.S. TRADE 13, 11/11/2002.

[31] While some countries have tried to do so (e.g. Mercosur) customs unions are difficult to negotiate and are thus unlikely to eliminate the need for alternatives such as financial instruments in the WTO. For an interesting analysis of links between preferential and multilateral liberalization in the absence of other enforcement mechanisms see Ornelas (2005) and Syropoulos and Dinopoulos (2012).

Appendix A

A.1. Nash tariff for smaller countries

The tariff in (6) is obtained by solving the following first-order condition for τ^{*k}, where all variables correspond to their import, x:

$$W^k_{\tau^{*k}} = 0 : (1 + p^w_{\tau^{*k}})[\tau^{*k}M'^{*k} + (\lambda-1)S^{*k}] - p^w_{\tau^{*k}}M^{*k} = 0$$

$$\tau^{*k} = \frac{p^w_{\tau^{*k}}}{1 + p^w_{\tau^{*k}}}\frac{M^{*k}}{M'^{*k}} - (\lambda-1)\frac{S^{*k}}{M'^{*k}}$$

where here and below we use $M'^c \equiv dM^c(p^c)/dp^c$ for each country c's import derivative w.r.t. own price and recall that with a specific tariff $\partial M^{*k}(p^w + \tau^{*k})/\partial\tau^{*k} = \partial M^{*k}(p^w + \tau^{*k})/\partial p^w = M'^{*k}$.

To obtain $p^w_{\tau^{*k}}$ we implicitly differentiate the market clearing condition for x holding all other tariffs constant

$$M(p^w) + \sum_{j\neq k} M^{*j}(p^w + \tau^{*j\neq k}) + M^{*k}(p^w + \tau^{*k}) = 0$$

$$p^w_{\tau^{*k}} = -\frac{M'^{*k}}{M' + \sum_{j\neq k}M'^{*j} + M'^{*k}} \Leftrightarrow \frac{p^w_{\tau^{*k}}}{1 + p^w_{\tau^{*k}}} = \frac{-M'^{*k}}{M' + \sum_{j\neq k}M'^{*j}}$$

Replacing in the first order condition and simplifying we obtain

$$\frac{\tau^{*k}}{p^w} = \frac{-M'^{*k}}{M' + \sum_{j\neq k}M'^{*j}}\frac{M^{*k}}{p^w M'^{*k}} - (\lambda-1)\frac{S^{*k}/M^{*k}}{M'^{*k}p^w/M^{*k}}$$

$$\frac{\tau^{*k}}{p^w} = \frac{1}{\varepsilon^{*k}} + (\lambda-1)\frac{S^{*k}/M^{*k}}{\xi^{*k}}$$

where the last line uses the following definitions of k's import elasticity, ξ^{*k}, and what we refer to as its residual foreign export supply elasticity, ε^{*k} respectively:

$$-\xi^{*k} \equiv -\frac{\partial M^{*k}}{\partial p^w}\frac{p^w}{M^{*k}} = \frac{-M'^{*k}p^w}{M^{*k}}$$

$$1/\varepsilon^{*k} \equiv \frac{M + \sum_{j\neq k}M^{*j}}{p^w(M' + \sum_{j\neq k}M'^{*j})}$$

A.2. Relationship between elasticities of individual small countries and regional aggregate

Notice that if all k have the same tariffs then the individual country and regional import demand elasticities are identical

$$\xi^{*k} = -M'^{*k}p^w/M^{*k} = -(M'^{*}/K)p^w/(M^{*}/K) = \xi^{*}$$

However, the market power of individual small countries, as measured by the inverse of their residual foreign export supply elasticity, is lower than the region's, i.e. $1/\varepsilon^{*k} < 1/\varepsilon^{*}$ whenever $K > 1$ since

$$\frac{1}{\varepsilon^{*k}} \equiv \frac{M + \sum_{j\neq k}M^{*j}}{p^w(M' + \sum_{j\neq k}M'^{*j})} < \frac{M}{p^w M'} \equiv \frac{1}{\varepsilon^{*}} \tag{28}$$

The inequality follows since at any given tariff and world prices (i) the numerator on the LHS of the inequality is lower in absolute value than the one on the RHS (recall that $M < 0$ and $\sum_{j\neq k}M^{*j} > 0$ for the good exported by Large) and (ii) the denominator on the LHS of the inequality is larger in absolute value (since both M' and $\sum_{j\neq k}M'^{*j}$ are negative).

Global optimum tariffs (Eq. (8)): These are obtained by solving the following first-order condition for τ^C:

$$W_\tau(\tau^C) + W_{\tau^*}(\tau^* = \tau^C) = 0 : (1 + p^w_\tau)[\tau^C M' + (\lambda-1)S] = 0$$

Proof of Lemma 1. To see (i) recall that if all small countries set equal tariffs then $\sum_k W^{*k} = KW^{*k}$ and this "regional" welfare measure is mirror symmetric to W so if $\tau^C = \tau^{*Ck}$ and $\boldsymbol{\tau}^* = \tau^N$ for all small countries we have the equality below

$$W(\tau = \tau^N, \boldsymbol{\tau}^* = \tau^C) = KW^{*k}(\tau = \tau^C, \boldsymbol{\tau}^* = \tau^N)$$
$$> KW^{*k}(\tau = \tau^C, \boldsymbol{\tau}^{*Dk})$$

where the inequality arises because $\tau^N = \tau^{*Ncoord}$ maximizes KW^{*k} for a given τ^C and the elements of $\boldsymbol{\tau}^{*Dk}$ are τ^{*Nk}, which are smaller than $\tau^{*Ncoord}$ (from (6) when $K > 1$).

To see (ii) note that symmetry implies that

$$W(\tau^N, \boldsymbol{\tau}^* = \tau^N) = KW^{*k}(\tau^N, \boldsymbol{\tau}^* = \tau^N)$$

which implies that

$$W(\tau^N, \boldsymbol{\tau}^{*N}) > W(\tau^N, \boldsymbol{\tau}^* = \tau^N) = KW^{*k}(\tau^N, \boldsymbol{\tau}^* = \tau^N)$$

This is because $\boldsymbol{\tau}^{*N} = \tau^{*Nk}$ for all K and it is smaller than τ^N (from (6)) and so the export price obtained by the large country is higher relative to when it faces τ^N in all small countries. Furthermore, we have

$$KW^{*k}(\tau^N, \boldsymbol{\tau}^* = \tau^N) > KW^{*k}(\tau^N, \boldsymbol{\tau}^{*N})$$

This is because $\boldsymbol{\tau}^* = \tau^N$ for all K maximizes the aggregate payoff of small countries for any given tariff of the large country, not $\boldsymbol{\tau}^{*N}$ whose elements compose of K tariffs each of which equals $\tau^{*Nk} < \tau^{*Ncoord}$. Combining the last two inequalities we obtain $W(\tau^N, \boldsymbol{\tau}^{*N}) > \sum_k W^{*k}(\tau^N, \boldsymbol{\tau}^{*N})$. □

Proof of Proposition 1. Suppose that $\delta = \delta_G$ so that by definition the incentive constraint of the large country (16) holds with equality when each country sets its tariff to equal the globally optimal tariff τ^G. The incentive constraint for a typical small country is similar to (16), except that small country exporters face a higher tariff relative to that faced by exporters from the large country, i.e. $\tau^N > \tau^{*Nk}$, and the payoff of each small country is divided by K (but K cancels out because it enters similarly on both sides of the IC). Thus, the cooperative payoff for the small countries as a group is equal to that for the large one (due to symmetry) and the payoffs for small countries from deviating are smaller, as shown in Lemma 1. This means that at δ_G, where (16) holds with equality, *there must be slack in the corresponding IC for each small country*. If we lower δ below δ_G then the large country's incentive constraint (16) no longer holds at τ^G. So under tariff retaliation, the global optimum is not feasible for $\delta < \delta_G$. But the corresponding constraint for each small country continues to hold and has slack, at least for some $\delta < \delta_G$.

Since, by definition, for any $\delta < \delta_G$ tariff retaliation cannot sustain τ^G, to prove Proposition 1 we need only to show that when $\delta < \delta_G$ the lowest self-enforcing cooperative tariffs used are such that $\tau^C > \tau^{*Ck}$. We prove this by contradiction. Assume that the lowest self-enforcing cooperative tariffs for all countries are the same, i.e. $\tau^C = \tau^{*Ck}$ and such that the IC of the large country (16) binds.[32] We then show that if $\tau^C = \tau^{*Ck}$ then the IC of a small country (17) has slack implying that such a tariff is not the most cooperative tariff on the part of small countries. Since the RHS of (16) is equal to K times the RHS of (17) at $\tau^C = \tau^{*Ck}$ (due to symmetry) we need only to show that the LHS of (16) exceeds K times the RHS of (17), which is done in Lemma 1. Given this there must be some $\tau^{*Ck} < \tau^C$ for small countries that is still self-enforcing since the reduction in τ^{*Ck} reduces the slack in (17) without violating the large country's IC in (16).

Given the asymmetry in the cooperative tariffs, the large country will have a higher welfare than the collection of small ones even though they are mirror images and there is constant returns to scale in production.[33] □

Proof of Proposition 2. See the text. □

Proof of Proposition 3. To prove Proposition 3 we need only to show that for some $\delta < \delta_G$ the global optimum can be sustained using bonds $b^* = 0 < b^{*g}$ and $b < b^g$. Once that is done the results in (i)–(iii) follow directly from the same arguments in Proposition 2. Consider the following strategy: similarly to before, each country must first post a bond in order for cooperation to begin. We will focus on the case where the total value of this bond is $\tilde{b} > 0$ for the large country (equally divided among the K small countries) whereas b^* is arbitrarily small, in practice $b^* = 0$. If a country deviates, it loses its bond but keeps any foreign bond(s) it may hold. But now, if a deviation were to occur then cooperation resumes only after a fine is paid by the deviating country. The incentive constraints for the large and each of the small countries are respectively

$$W(\tau^N, \boldsymbol{\tau}^{*G}) - \tilde{b} + V^{\tilde{b}} \leq \frac{W(\tau^G, \boldsymbol{\tau}^{*G})}{1-\delta} \tag{29}$$

$$W^{*k}(\tau^G, \boldsymbol{\tau}^{*N}) + \tilde{b}/K + V^{*\tilde{b}} \leq \frac{W^{*k}(\tau^G, \boldsymbol{\tau}^{*G})}{1-\delta} \tag{30}$$

and the minimum continuation payoffs for each are

$$V^{\tilde{b}} \equiv -\delta f + \frac{\delta W(\tau^G, \boldsymbol{\tau}^{*G})}{1-\delta} \quad \text{and} \quad V^{*\tilde{b}} \equiv -\delta f^* + \frac{\delta W^{*k}(\tau^G, \boldsymbol{\tau}^{*G})}{1-\delta}$$

---

[32] It is clear that we need not consider the case where $\tau^C > \tau^{*Ck}$.

[33] This is not to say that the welfare distribution across countries is *more* unequal under the agreement than under non-cooperation since the Nash policies are also asymmetric. In fact, if $\delta = \delta_G$ the agreement sustains the symmetric global optimum and so generates a more equal welfare distribution than non-cooperation. By continuity, this must also be true for at least some $\delta < \delta_G$.

where f and f^* are the fine values paid by the large and small countries respectively. As before, we require the continuation payoff to be *WRP* in that no country prefers to abandon the agreement altogether. This implies that the minimum continuation payoff for each country must be no lower than the payoff obtained under non-cooperation

$$V^{\tilde{b}\ \min} \equiv -\delta f^{\max} + \frac{\delta W(\tau^G, \boldsymbol{\tau}^{*G})}{1-\delta} = \frac{\delta W(\tau^N, \boldsymbol{\tau}^{*N})}{1-\delta} \tag{31}$$

$$V^{*\tilde{b}\ \min} \equiv -\delta f^{*\ \max} + \frac{\delta W^{*k}(\tau^G, \boldsymbol{\tau}^{*G})}{1-\delta} = \frac{\delta W^{*k}(\tau^N, \boldsymbol{\tau}^{*N})}{1-\delta} \tag{32}$$

These constraints pin down the maximum fine that each country is willing to pay and re-arranging them we can interpret that maximum fine to be the net present discounted value of cooperation

$$f^{\max} = \frac{W(\tau^G, \boldsymbol{\tau}^{*G}) - W(\tau^N, \boldsymbol{\tau}^{*N})}{1-\delta}$$

$$f^{*\ \max} = \frac{W^{*k}(\tau^G, \boldsymbol{\tau}^{*G}) - W^{*k}(\tau^N, \boldsymbol{\tau}^{*N})}{1-\delta}$$

Replacing $V^{\tilde{b}\ \min}$ in (29) by $\delta W(\tau^N, \boldsymbol{\tau}^{*N})/(1-\delta)$ allows us to solve for the minimum bond required to sustain globally optimal tariffs

$$\tilde{b}^g = W(\tau^N, \boldsymbol{\tau}^{*G}) + \frac{\delta W(\tau^N, \boldsymbol{\tau}^{*N})}{1-\delta} - \frac{W(\tau^G, \boldsymbol{\tau}^{*G})}{1-\delta}$$

To clearly see the relationship between this and the bond required without fines we rewrite the expression above and use the value of b^g in (22) to obtain

$$\tilde{b}^g = \underbrace{[W(\tau^N, \boldsymbol{\tau}^{*G}) - W(\tau^G, \boldsymbol{\tau}^{*G})]}_{=b^g} - \frac{\delta}{1-\delta}[W(\tau^G, \boldsymbol{\tau}^{*G}) - W(\tau^N, \boldsymbol{\tau}^{*N})[< b^g \tag{33}$$

The inequality $\tilde{b}^g < b^g$ holds because the second term in parenthesis (i.e. $W(\tau^G, \boldsymbol{\tau}^{*G}) - W(\tau^N, \boldsymbol{\tau}^{*N})$) is positive whenever the number of small countries is small enough that the large country prefers a cooperative trade agreement to a trade war, which is our assumption throughout (see footnote 20). Intuitively, when fines can be used in conjunction with bonds, the large country can post a lower bond because the threat of the maximum fine $f^{\max}$ (off the equilibrium path) ensures that its continuation payoff is no higher than when fines are not used (since it equals $\delta W(\tau^N, \boldsymbol{\tau}^{*N})/(1-\delta)$ in either case) while the posting of zero bonds by small countries implies that its short term gain of deviating from cooperation is lower relative to the case without fines. It should also be clear that for $\delta < \delta_G$ we have $\tilde{b}^g > 0$ since if $\delta = \delta_G$ then $\tilde{b}^g = 0$ and reducing δ reduces the gains from cooperation, which is the second term in (33).

To show that $\tilde{b}^g$ does not violate the incentive constraint for small countries in (30) we replace $\tilde{b}^g$ and $V^{*\ b\ \min}$ into (30) and rearrange it to obtain

$$W(\tau^N, \boldsymbol{\tau}^{*G}) + \frac{\delta W(\tau^N, \boldsymbol{\tau}^{*N})}{1-\delta} + K\left[W^{*k}(\tau^G, \boldsymbol{\tau}^{*N}) + \frac{\delta W^{*k}(\tau^N, \boldsymbol{\tau}^{*N})}{1-\delta}\right] \le \frac{W(\tau^G, \boldsymbol{\tau}^{*G})}{1-\delta} + K\frac{W^{*k}(\tau^G, \boldsymbol{\tau}^{*G})}{1-\delta} \tag{34}$$

This is simply the sum of the IC in the standard agreement given by (16) and (17) when evaluated at the global optimum. We know that at δ_G the IC for the large country holds with equality at τ^G (by the definition of δ_G) and the IC for each small country holds with slack (Proposition 1) so (34) holds strictly at δ_G and continuity ensures it must also hold for some $\delta < \delta_G$. □

Proof of proposition 4. Substitute the minimum continuation payoffs for the extended agreement, $V^{\tilde{b}\ \min}$ and $V^{*\tilde{b}\ \min}$, and set $\tilde{b} = 0$ in the IC in (29) and (30). Evaluating these at a general cooperative tariff level (instead of requiring it to be the global optimum) we obtain the IC under the standard agreement, (16) and (17). □

Appendix B. Supplementary data

Supplementary data associated with this article can be found in the online version at http://dx.doi.org/10.1016/j.euroecorev.2013.05.006.

References

Bagwell, K., Staiger, R., 1999. An economic theory of GATT. American Economic Review 89 (1), 215–248.
Bagwell, K., Staiger, R., 2005. Enforcement, private political pressure, and the GATT/WTO escape clause. Journal of Legal Studies 34 (2), 471–513.
Bagwell, K., Staiger, R., 2011. What do trade negotiators negotiate about? Empirical evidence from the world trade organization. American Economic Review 101 (4). 1283–73.
Bagwell, K., Mavroidis, P., Staiger, R., 2007. Auctioning countermeasures in the WTO. Journal of International Economics 73 (2), 309–332.

Besedes, T., Prusa, T., 2011. The role of extensive and intensive margins and export growth. Journal of Development Economics 96 (2), 371–379.
Beshkar, M., 2010. Optimal remedies in international trade agreements. European Economic Review 54 (3), 455–466.
Broda, C., Limão, N., Weinstein, D., 2008. Optimal tariffs and market power: the evidence. American Economic Review 98 (5), 2032–2065.
Bronckers, M., Van Den Broek, N., 2005. Financial compensation in the WTO: improving the remedies of WTO dispute settlement. Journal of International Economic Law 8, 101–126.
Grossman, G., Helpman, E., 1994. Protection for sale. American Economic Review 84 (4), 833–850.
Grossman, G., Helpman, E., 1995. Trade wars and trade talks. Journal of Political Economy 103, 675–708.
Grossman, G., Mavroidis, P.C., 2004. United States—Section 110(5) of the US copyright act, recourse to arbitration under article 25 of the DSU: would've or should've? Impaired benefits due to copyright infringement. World Trade Review 2, 233–249.
Johnson, H.G., 1953–54. Optimum tariffs and retaliation. Review of Economic Studies 21, 142–153.
Lawrence, R., 2003. Crimes and Punishments? Retaliation Under the WTO. Institute of International Economics, Washington, DC.
Limão, N., Saggi, K., 2008. Tariff retaliation versus financial compensation in the enforcement of international trade agreements. Journal of International Economics 76, 48–60.
Ludema, R., 2001. Optimal international trade agreements and dispute settlement procedures. European Journal of Political Economy 17, 355–376.
Ludema, R., Mayda, Anna M., 2009. Do countries free ride on MFN? Journal of International Economics 77 (2), 137–150.
Mayer, W., 1981. Theoretical considerations on negotiated tariff adjustments. Oxford Economic Papers 33, 135–153.
Mercurio, B., 2009. Why compensation cannot replace trade retaliation in the WTO dispute settlement understanding. World Trade Review 8 (2), 315–338.
Ornelas, E., 2005. Trade creating free trade areas and the undermining of multilateralism. European Economic Review 49 (7), 1717–1735.
Park, J.-H., 2000. International trade agreements between countries of asymmetric size. Journal of International Economics 50, 473–495.
Saggi, K., Yildiz, H., 2010. Bilateralism, multilateralism, and the quest for global free trade. Journal of International Economics 81, 26–37.
Schott, J., 2009. America, Europe, and the new trade order. Business and Politics 11 (3), 1–22.
Srinivasan, T.N., 1999. Developing countries in the world trading system: from GATT, 1947, to the third ministerial meeting of WTO, 1999. The World Economy 22 (8), 1047–1064.
Syropoulos, C., 2002. Optimum tariffs and retaliation: how country size matters. Review of Economic Studies 69, 707–727.
Syropoulos, C., Dinopoulos, E., 2012. Multi-country Tariff Wars and Trade Agreements. Mimeo.
Zissimos, B., 2009. Optimum tariffs and retaliation: how country numbers matter. Journal of International Economics 78, 276–286.

PART IV

CASE-STUDIES OF WTO DISPUTES

CHAPTER 17

World Trade Review (2011), 10: 1, 63–86
© Kamal Saggi and Joel P. Trachtman doi:10.1017/S1474745610000455

Incomplete Harmonization Contracts in International Economic Law: Report of the Panel, *China – Measures Affecting the Protection and Enforcement of Intellectual Property Rights*, WT/DS362/R, adopted 20 March 2009

KAMAL SAGGI*
Dedman Distinguished Collegiate Professor of Economics Southern Methodist University, Dallas, TX
JOEL P. TRACHTMAN**
Professor of International Law, The Fletcher School of Law and Diplomacy, Tufts University, Medford, MA

Abstract: In *China – Measures Affecting the Protection and Enforcement of Intellectual Property Rights*, the Panel addressed three main issues:

1. the relationship between China's censorship laws and its obligations to protect copyright under the WTO Agreement on Trade Related Intellectual Property Rights ('TRIPS');
2. China's obligations under TRIPS to ensure that its customs authorities be empowered to dispose properly of confiscated goods that infringe intellectual property rights;
3. whether China's volume and value of goods thresholds for application of criminal procedures and penalties with respect to trademark counterfeiting or copyright piracy comply with TRIPS requirements for application of criminal procedures and penalties.

International trade agreements are generally intended to cause states to internalize policy externalities. The policy externalities that arise from domestic decisions regarding intellectual property protection may deprive foreign intellectual property owners of the monopoly profits that they would otherwise derive from intellectual property protection. In connection with intellectual property protection, even a state that lacks 'traditional' market power on world markets may be able to impose terms-of-trade externalities on other states by reducing its protection of intellectual property below the global optimum. For this reason, and because of the international public-goods aspects of intellectual property, states have incentives to undersupply intellectual property protection. At least in part, TRIPS

* Email: ksaggi@smu.edu
** Email: joel.trachtman@tufts.edu

seems to be an attempt to reduce these policy externalities. All contracts, and all international treaties, are incomplete. This case involves some good examples of treaty incompleteness. Incompleteness can arise from circumstances of uncertainty regarding the possible tradeoffs, and the optimal balance, between different goals, including state autonomy in censorship on the one hand and internalizing policy externalities in intellectual property protection on the other. We analyze the possibility that it might be efficient to allow states broad discretion over censorship. Alternatively, in connection with the requirement for criminal penalties, incompleteness can arise from uncertainty regarding the particular industry structure that might be involved, and what would constitute production of 'commercial scale' for that industry. We also question the rationale for the limitation on the use of nonviolation complaints in connection with the TRIPS, since nonviolation complaints may be used to reduce the possibility that states will use discretion, such as that granted with respect to censorship, in a manner that is inconsistent with the rationale for that discretion so as to defect from the general commitment to provide copyright or other intellectual property rights.

Introduction

In *China – Measures Affecting the Protection and Enforcement of Intellectual Property Rights* ('*China–IP Rights*'),[1] which was not appealed, and therefore was adopted without an Appellate Body review, the Panel addressed three main issues:

1. the relationship between China's censorship laws and its obligations to protect copyright under the WTO Agreement on Trade Related Intellectual Property Rights ('TRIPS');
2. China's obligations under TRIPS to ensure that its customs authorities be empowered to dispose properly of confiscated goods that infringe intellectual property rights;
3. whether China's volume and value of goods thresholds for application of criminal procedures and penalties with respect to trademark counterfeiting or copyright piracy comply with TRIPS requirements for application of criminal procedures and penalties.

This case is not directly about trade in goods or services. Rather, it is about the extent to which China was required to harmonize and enforce its intellectual property law for the benefit of persons of other WTO member states. The TRIPS Agreement, which was part of the WTO single undertaking agreed in 1994, provides for a minimum level of protection of intellectual property rights and enforcement of those rights. Each of the US claims in this case involves a challenge to the implementation by China of its obligations under the TRIPS Agreement; each involves a question of interpretation of the scope of protection required under the TRIPS Agreement. However, these TRIPS claims can be understood in terms of

1 Hereinafter Panel Report.

concerns regarding policy externalities – harm to US firms – and more specifically regarding terms-of-trade externalities.

The establishment of certain minimum levels of IPR protection might be seen as a third level of discipline on domestic, or 'behind the border', regulation. The first level of discipline is a requirement of national treatment, as discussed in Horn.[2] A second level of discipline is a proportionality requirement, as discussed and compared to national treatment in Hoekman and Trachtman.[3] A third level is a requirement for harmonization of IPRs that basically resulted in a significant increase in the degree of IPR protection available in most of the developing world. These three levels do not neatly map into either magnitudes of discipline or degree of specificity of obligation. However, all three may be understood, like much international law in this area, as addressing policy externalities that may arise from actions of the regulating state. National-treatment requirements may be understood as protecting imports from differential treatment motivated by protectionist goals, and proportionality might be understood either as supplementing national treatment or as imposing an additional requirement of rationality in regulation as applied to imports. These disciplines can be understood as 'negative integration' in the sense that they prohibit certain types of national measures. On the other hand, the establishment of minimum levels of IPRs under TRIPS recognizes that each state may have an incentive to enact a level of regulation that falls below the globally efficient level. But the fact that nations have incentives to under-protect intellectual property does not necessarily imply that it is efficient to *equalize* the degree of IPR protection in all nations. Indeed, while such harmonization of IPRs is called for under TRIPS, Grossman and Lai[4] have argued convincingly that such harmonization is neither necessary nor sufficient for achieving global efficiency. In other words, in an open global economy, while each nation will generally undersupply IPR protection and attempt to free-ride on the protection provided by other countries, efficient IPR reform does not require all nations to adopt the same set of IPR policies, since nations are heterogeneous with respect to innovative capacity, market size, and a variety of other relevant variables. Nevertheless, the strengthening of IPR protection in many developing countries that was called for under TRIPS can be viewed as a type of 'positive integration'.

To varying degrees, both negative integration and positive integration can be seen as attempts to internalize what would otherwise be policy externalities imposed by the pursuit of policies based purely on national interest. However, in the case of each of national treatment, proportionality, and harmonization there is always a degree of contractual incompleteness: it is impossible to specify

2 Henrik Horn (2006), 'National Treatment in the GATT', 96 : 1 *The American Economic Review*, 394–404.

3 Bernard Hoekman and Joel P. Trachtman (2010), 'Continued Suspense: *EC–Hormones* and WTO Disciplines on Discrimination and Domestic Regulation', 9 : 01 *World Trade Review*, 151–180.

4 Gene M. Grossman and Edwin L.-C. Lai (2004), 'International Protection of Intellectual Property', 94 : 5 *The American Economic Review*, 1635–1653.

explicitly the treatment of every anticipated circumstance, and it is also impossible *ex ante* to anticipate every possible circumstance. Each of the United States's three claims in the *China–IP* case involves a TRIPS provision that could have been drafted more specifically, with more precision. How can we explain the existing level of incompleteness of the WTO 'contract' with respect to the establishment of minimum standards for enforcement of IPR law? What are the implications of this incompleteness?

Horn, Maggi, and Staiger (referred to as 'HMS')[5] have argued that the WTO can be viewed as an incomplete contract whose form is endogenously determined. They note that the WTO agreement displays both rigidity as well as discretion: while trade instruments are largely bound (and therefore rigid), domestic instruments are largely left to the discretion of governments except that they have to abide by the principle of national treatment. Can this approach be applied to shed some light on the present case?

In Sections 1, 2, and 3, we describe the Panel's analysis in each of the three major issues addressed in this decision. In Section 4, we suggest an incomplete contracts analysis of these issues.

1. Copyright and censorship

As to the first issue of this case, the main question, in summary, is whether China is permitted to deny copyright protection to works that are not permitted to be published in China due to censorship. To some extent, as China argues, it is a moot point: if you lack the right to publish in China, and for reasons of censorship China also prevents others from publishing your work, why would you need copyright protection?[6]

In any event, TRIPS incorporates by reference Article 17 of the Berne Convention, which provides for broad rights for governments to censor. But TRIPS also contains very specific formal obligations to accord copyright protection to works, and to enforce copyright protection, and Article 17 is not structured as an exception to these obligations but as an independent right of states. So, the Panel is called upon to reconcile within TRIPS this set of possibly inconsistent norms. One type of contractual incompleteness is incomplete reconciliation of different values within the WTO treaty.

While this case could be understood as a conflict between the permissive approach (as to state action) to censorship of Article 17 of the Berne Convention and the restrictive approach of human-rights law, the Panel did not mention the

5 Henrik Horn, Giovanni Maggi, and Robert W. Staiger (2010), 'Trade Agreements as Endogenously Incomplete Contracts', 100:1 *The American Economic Review*, 394–419.

6 On the other hand, perhaps copyright protection would protect authors' rights against unauthorized edited versions, or in circumstances in which the censorship is not as fully enforced as copyright would be. Copyright would often be enforced through private claims, whereas censorship is based on government enforcement.

possible application of human-rights norms to limit the scope of censorship by states.[7] Another type of contractual incompleteness is incomplete reconciliation of different values between one treaty regime and another.

The applicable WTO law – the TRIPS Agreement – incorporates by reference certain provisions of the 1971 Berne Convention on Copyright. The relevant portion of the Berne Convention, Article 5(1), protects the rights of authors 'in countries ... other than their country of origin'. Other provisions of the TRIPS Agreement and the Berne Convention set minimum standards for protection of copyright. This harmonization was intended to enhance the protection of the intellectual property rights of foreign persons, not to enhance either the protection of intellectual property rights of domestic persons, or the freedom of expression of anyone. Of course, as a collateral matter, the protection of rights of foreign authors could enhance freedom of expression for domestic persons, and it might be that harmonization for the benefit of foreign authors would naturally lead to a decision to conform national rules for the benefit of domestic authors.

The facts

This case, brought by the United States, did not involve a particular copyright that China was alleged not to have recognized or protected. Rather, it was an 'as such' case, in which the United States claimed that China's copyright law did not, as such, comply with WTO law. Since this is an 'as such' case, the only relevant 'facts' are those about what the Chinese law provides and how it is applied – there was no concrete case before the Panel to assess.[8] So it was incumbent upon the Panel to make an objective assessment of the relevant Chinese law.

Article 4(1) of the Chinese Copyright Law ('CCL'), according to the agreed translation in this case, reads as follows: 'Works the publication and/or dissemination of which are prohibited by law shall not be protected by this Law.' So, the US concern was that this provision would deny copyright protection to works that, under WTO law, are required to be protected. The United States was concerned both about (i) grant of copyright status, and (ii) enforcement of copyright law to protect the copyrighted work.

While Article 4(1) of the CCL on its face seems clear, there were substantial arguments regarding its interpretation and application. China acknowledged that Article 4(1) of the CCL denies protection to certain works due to their content.[9] The Panel found that Article 4(1) denies the protection of Article 10 of the CCL to

7 See Tomer Broude (2009), 'It's Easily Done: The China-Intellectual Property Rights Enforcement Dispute and the Freedom of Expression', Hebrew University International Law Forum Research Paper No. 22-09, October.

8 The Panel referred to the statement by the Appellate Body in *US – Corrosion-Resistant Steel Sunset Review* (WT/DS244/AB/R, adopted 9 January 2004) to the effect that 'When a measure is challenged "as such", the starting point for an analysis must be the measure on its face. If the meaning and content of the measure are clear on its face, then the consistency of the measure *as such* can be assessed on that basis alone' (para. 168).

9 Panel Report, para. 7.30.

certain works.[10] Article 10 of the CCL sets forth the four moral rights and 13 economic rights of copyright holders. Relying on a letter authored by the Chinese Supreme People's Court in connection with the so-called '*Inside Story*' case, the Panel found that Article 4 of the CCL denies copyright protection when the publication or dissemination of a work is prohibited due to its content.[11] However, China argued that only works affirmatively found to be illegal are unprotected.[12] China argued that denial of copyright protection under Article 4(1) requires determination by a court or the National Copyright Administration of China ('NCAC') during enforcement proceedings.[13]

China's first written submission argued that 'illegal' referred to works that are 'completely unconstitutional or immoral'.[14] The NCAC, in a letter to the Supreme People's Court in connection with the *Inside Story* case, had stated that the 'works the publication and dissemination of which are prohibited by law' in Article 4 of the CCL 'refer only to works whose contents are illegal (reactionary, pornographic, or superstitious contents)'. However, China's content review regulations list a number of additional categories of works that are censored, including those that incite hatred, propagate cults, disrupt public order and undermine social stability, propagate obscenity, gambling, or violence, insult or slander others, or infringe upon legitimate rights and interests of others, jeopardize social ethics, and other contents banned by laws.[15] The Panel understood that the NCAC statement referring to 'reactionary, pornographic, or superstitious contents' was a summary reference to this broader list.[16]

The Panel found that works denied protection are those that have already failed content review, and deleted portions of works edited to satisfy content review.[17] It determined that the United States had not made a prima facie case with respect to works never submitted, works awaiting results, and unedited versions of works for which an edited version had been approved.

Legal analysis

The dispute in this case was about the relationship between (i) the obligation to protect the intellectual property rights of foreign authors, on the one hand, and (ii) the scope of discretion of the obligor state to censor that work, on the other hand. The United States claimed that the discretion of the state to censor could not limit the obligation to protect intellectual property rights of foreign authors. China argued first factually that the relevant Chinese law did not restrict the protection of

10 Ibid., para. 7.50.
11 Ibid., para. 7.52.
12 Ibid., para. 7.55.
13 Ibid., paras. 7.64, 7.66.
14 Ibid., para. 7.78, quoting China's first written submission.
15 Ibid., para. 7.79.
16 Ibid., para. 7.81.
17 Ibid., para. 7.103.

these rights, and second that the right to censor either fully satisfied the obligation to protect these rights, or made it moot.

From a broadly theoretical perspective, this dispute demonstrates the difficulty of limiting any legal rule to its intended purpose, and the impossibility of specifying a particular category of obligation so as to isolate its effects from other areas of law or policy. It also shows the difficulty of anticipating and addressing these types of extensions or collisions. International lawyers refer to this problem as the problem of fragmentation, but it can be understood within a broader set of problems categorized by economists as the problem of incomplete contracts.[18]

The United States claimed that under the CCL, authors of unauthorized works do not enjoy minimum rights granted by the Berne Convention, inconsistently with Article 5(1) of the Berne Convention, which is incorporated by reference in the TRIPS via Article 9.1 of TRIPS. Article 5(1) provides as follows:

> Authors shall enjoy, in respect of works for which they are protected under this Convention, in countries of the Union other than the country of origin, the rights which their respective laws do now or may hereafter grant to their nationals, as well as the rights specially granted by this Convention.

The US claim was predicated on the last clause of this provision – the United States argued that the CCL denies 'rights specially granted by [the Berne] Convention'. The Panel found that China's law violated Article 5(1) of the Berne Convention, as incorporated pursuant to Article 9.1 of TRIPS, as to works that have already failed content review, and also as to deleted portions of works edited to satisfy content review.[19]

China offered a defense based on Art. 17 of the Berne Convention, which also is incorporated in TRIPS via Article 9.1 thereof, and provides as follows:

> The provisions of this Convention cannot in any way affect the right of the Government of each country of the Union to permit, to control, or to prohibit, by legislation or regulation, the circulation, presentation, or exhibition of any work or production in regard to which the competent authority may find it necessary to exercise that right.

China understood this provision as broadly ensuring the sovereignty of the state to censor. China claimed that this broad language 'effectively denies WTO jurisdiction in this area'.[20] Indeed, the reference to the determination of the competent authority may be understood as providing a 'self-judging' right to censor, similar to the portion of Article XXI(b) of GATT that has been understood to be 'self-judging' as to the necessity of security measures. The Panel agreed that Article 17

18 For an effort to do so, see Joel P. Trachtman (1999), 'The Domain of WTO Dispute Resolution', 40 *Harvard International Law Journal*, 333.

19 Panel Report, para. 7.117.

20 Ibid., para. 7.120, quoting China's rebuttal submission, paras. 286–287.

of the Berne Convention allows censorship for public-order purposes.[21] Note that, within an incomplete contracts framework, China may be viewed as arguing either that (i) the contract authorizes the obligor state itself to determine the level of protection, or (ii) that there is no effective obligation in this context.

However, while there is broad authority for censorship, this authority does not, according to the Panel, extend to denying copyright protections. The right reserved for states under Article 17 to control 'circulation, presentation, or exhibition' does not include a number of rights granted to copyright holders by the Berne Convention.[22] Furthermore, according to the Panel, censorship may allow governments to interfere with the *exercise* of copyright rights, but not with the *existence* of these rights.[23] This distinction may have limited practical effect.

Indeed, China argued that copyright protection is a 'legal and material nullity' because economic rights are preempted by censorship.[24] In response, the Panel referred to the fact that Article 3.8 of the WTO Dispute Settlement Understanding provides for prima facie nullification or impairment, and that therefore there is no need to show actual economic effects.[25] China argued that public censorship renders private enforcement unnecessary. Again, the problem with this argument is that there is more to copyright than the right to publish. The Panel found assertions by China that it enforces *censorship* against copyright violations in respect of censored works unsubstantiated. It is procedurally interesting, and perhaps questionable that, in an 'as such' case, where there is no actual instance of application of the allegedly illegal national measure, the defending state is required to show actual instances of measures that would obviate the alleged illegality.

The United States made an additional claim that China also violated its obligations to provide enforcement mechanisms for copyright under Article 41.1 of TRIPS. In response, China argued that its censorial ban on publication is a form of 'effective action' – an 'alternative form of enforcement against infringement'. The Panel rejected this argument, finding that Part III of TRIPS requires a broader minimum set of enforcement procedures.[26] This finding is important as it suggests that the existence of alternative forms of protection against violation of IPRs – such as that provided for by the use of censorship – does not mean that a country need not set up the enforcement procedures called for under TRIPS. Thus, the Panel concluded that 'the Copyright Law, specifically the first sentence of Article 4, is inconsistent with China's obligations under Article 41.1 of the TRIPS Agreement'.[27]

21 Ibid., para. 7.126.
22 Ibid., para. 7.127.
23 Ibid., para. 7.132.
24 Ibid., para. 7.134.
25 Ibid., para. 7.138.
26 Ibid., para. 7.180.
27 Ibid., paras. 7.179–7.181.

2. Disposal of infringing goods

The United States claimed that certain Chinese measures relating to customs procedures on the import or export of infringing goods violated TRIPS Articles 46 and 59. Article 59, addressing 'special requirements relating to border measures', provides that 'competent authorities shall have the authority to order the destruction or disposal of infringing goods in accordance with the principles set out in Article 46'.

The Panel found that Article 59, included in Section 4 of TRIPS, only addresses infringing imports, and not exports.[28] While the US claim referred generally to infringing goods, the United States took no position with respect to the question of whether the first sentence of Article 59 also applies to exports, and the Panel found that it did not. The Panel examined Article 51 of TRIPS, as context for Article 59. Article 51 provides states with an option to provide similar procedures to those contained in Section 4 with respect to *exports*, suggesting that the required procedures do not otherwise apply to exports.

Article 46 provides in relevant part as follows:

> In order to create an effective deterrent to infringement, the judicial authorities shall have the authority to order that goods that they have found to be infringing be, without compensation of any sort, disposed of outside the channels of commerce in such a manner as to avoid any harm caused to the right holder, or, unless this would be contrary to existing constitutional requirements, destroyed.

The United States claimed that the relevant authorities lacked the requisite authority to order the destruction or disposal of infringing goods in accordance with the principles set out in Article 46.

The Chinese regulations at issue provided as follows:

> Where the confiscated goods which infringe on intellectual property rights can be used for the social public welfare undertakings, Customs shall hand such goods over to relevant public welfare bodies for the use in social public welfare undertakings. Where the holder of the intellectual property rights intends to buy them, Customs can assign them to the holder of the intellectual property rights with compensation. Where the confiscated goods infringing on intellectual property rights cannot be used for social public welfare undertakings and the holder of the intellectual property rights has no intention to buy them, Customs can, after eradicating the infringing features, auction them off according to law. Where the infringing features are impossible to eradicate, Customs shall destroy the goods.

The United States criticized these regulations as follows:

> *Donation to social welfare bodies* can be harmful to a right holder and nothing appears to prevent such bodies from selling the infringing goods; *sale to the right holder* harms the right holder in the amount that the right holder pays for the

28 Ibid., para. 7.231.

> infringing goods; and *auction* does not constitute disposal outside the channels of commerce and, absent his consent, may harm the right holder. Where any of these three options is available, the authorities are not authorized to order *destruction* of the infringing goods.[29]

The United States argued that the measures at issue created a 'compulsory scheme' limiting the authority of customs officials to destroy infringing goods, and requiring them to give priority to disposal options that allow the infringing goods to enter commerce or otherwise harm the right holder. The focus of the argument, therefore, was on the extent to which China was entitled to condition or prioritize the action of its authorities. In simple terms, where Article 46 says that the 'competent authorities shall have the authority' to take specified actions, (i) are the competent authorities required to take those actions, and (ii) can any conditions be imposed on the ability of the competent authorities to take those actions?

Facts

This also was a challenge of the Chinese measures 'as such', and therefore no specific case of application of these measures was pleaded by the United States.

However, interestingly, the Panel found that during the period 2005–2007, 'all confiscated infringing imports were either donated to the Red Cross Society of China (0.12 %) or destroyed (0.02 %). The volume of infringing imports that was sold to the right holder, or auctioned, was zero.'[30] The percentages in parentheses are calculated against a base of all goods disposed of or destroyed under China's measures at issue; 99.85 % of infringing goods disposed of or destroyed were destined for exportation.[31] Recall that the Panel found that the first sentence of Article 59 of TRIPS only applies to imports, not exports.

Legal analysis

The Panel found that the terms of Article 59 do not indicate that the authority to order the specified types of remedies must be exclusive.[32] The list of remedies is not exhaustive.[33] National authorities are required to be granted certain authority, but are permitted to be accorded the discretion to make other dispositions. Nor does the requirement for the grant of authority imply a requirement that such authority be exercised.[34] Nor does the requirement for the grant of authority imply that conditions cannot be set for the exercise of that authority.[35] Furthermore, the Panel found that the requirement in Article 46 that authority to order a remedy be

29 Ibid., para. 7.197 (emphasis in original).
30 Ibid., para. 7.232.
31 Ibid., para. 7.228.
32 Ibid., para. 7.240.
33 Ibid., para. 7.239.
34 Ibid., para. 7.236.
35 Ibid., para. 7.246.

exercised 'in such a manner as to avoid any harm caused to the right holder' is applicable only to the remedy of disposal outside the channels of commerce.[36]

However, the United States argued that by establishing a mandatory sequence of possible remedies, the Chinese measure denied Chinese authorities the required authority. The Panel agreed that if a different method of disposition is *mandatory*, then this may preclude authority that is required by Article 59.[37]

As noted above, the Chinese measure provided for three disposal methods besides destruction: (i) donation to social-welfare bodies, (ii) sale to the right holder, and (iii) auction.

As to donation to social-welfare bodies, the United States claimed that this method of disposal might cause harm to rights holders, including by virtue of subsequent sale by the social-welfare bodies. The Panel found that if the social-welfare bodies sell the infringing goods into ordinary commerce, this would not constitute disposal outside the channels of commerce.[38]

The United States argued that the Chinese measures failed to provide discretion to the Chinese customs authorities to determine that transfer to a social-welfare body might harm the right holder, and therefore failed to comply with the principles of Article 46, as required by Article 59 of TRIPS. Interestingly, in this 'as such' case, the Panel relied on the fact that 'nothing in the evidence suggests that any harm has ever been caused, or is likely to be caused, to right holders' reputations due to donation of infringing goods under the measures at issue'.[39] Therefore, the Panel found that the United States failed to demonstrate that the Chinese customs officials lacked the requisite authority to dispose of the goods in such a manner as to avoid harm to the right holder.

As to the risk of sale by social-welfare bodies, China pointed out that the implementing measures for the Chinese regulations provide that the customs authorities shall 'carry out necessary supervision'.[40] The Panel found that the United States failed to show that customs authorities lacked the requisite authority in this context to ensure that the right holder is not harmed.[41]

As to sale to the right holder, the Panel found that, since there are always other options available, and sale to the right holder only takes place with the consent of the right holder, 'there appear to be no circumstances in which sale to the right holder is the only option available and could preclude any authority required by Article 59'.[42]

As to the authority of Chinese customs authorities to auction infringing goods, the Panel observed that this is not a method of disposal that is required to be

36 Ibid., para. 7.244.
37 Ibid., para. 7.252.
38 Ibid., para. 7.279.
39 Ibid., para. 7.297.
40 Ibid., para. 7.299.
41 Ibid., para. 7.324.
42 Ibid., para. 7.326.

authorized under Article 59, but recalled its findings that the remedies specified in Article 59 are not required to be exclusive. Therefore, the authorization for auction is not itself inconsistent with Article 59.[43] The United States argued that the Chinese measures treated auction as a 'compulsory prerequisite' to destruction, thereby precluding authority for destruction, in violation of Article 59. However, the Panel found that the Chinese measures only provided authority for auction, rather than a requirement.[44]

Finally, the Panel found that in regard to counterfeit trademark goods, China's measures allow that the 'simple removal' of the trademark unlawfully affixed is sufficient to permit release of the goods into commerce in more than just exceptional cases, and therefore violates the principle stated in the last sentence of Article 46.

3. Thresholds for criminal procedures and penalties

The United States also argued that China had failed to provide appropriate criminal penalties for certain trademark and copyright infringement, as required by the first sentence of Article 61 of TRIPS, which provides as follows: 'Members shall provide for criminal procedures and penalties to be applied at least in cases of wilful trademark counterfeiting or copyright piracy on a commercial scale.' This was another claim regarding the quality of China's implementation of its TRIPS obligations, in which the United States argued that the Chinese thresholds for criminal penalties were higher than those permitted by Article 61.

At stake again was the degree of discretion retained by member states of the WTO under the TRIPS. China argued that the ostensible principle of *in dubio mitius* applies to protect the discretion of member states in the special field of criminal law.[45] The Panel noted that its interpretative mandate is set by Article 3.2 of the WTO Dispute Settlement Understanding. While recognizing 'the sensitive nature of criminal matters and attendant concerns regarding sovereignty', the Panel stated that 'these concerns may be expected to find reflection in the text and scope of treaty obligations regarding such matters as negotiated by States and other Members'.[46] This seems to be an implicit rejection of the argument for special deference, suggesting that to the extent that member states determine that deference is appropriate, they would express the requirement for deference in the specific terms of the treaty text.

China further argued that Article 61 is too general to create legally enforceable obligations,[47] and further asserted that it retains unfettered discretion under Article 1.1 of TRIPS, which provides that 'Members shall be free to determine the

43 Ibid., para. 7.327.
44 Ibid., para. 7.343.
45 Ibid., para. 7.497.
46 Ibid., para. 7.501 (citation omitted).
47 Ibid., paras. 7.508–7.513.

appropriate method of implementing the provisions of this Agreement within their own legal system and practice.' The Panel rejected this argument.

Facts

Here again, the United States challenged China's measures 'as such'. Thus, in order for China to be in breach of the first sentence of Article 61, in this 'as such' case, the United States would be required to show that there is a class of cases of counterfeiting or piracy that are (i) willful, and (ii) of a commercial scale, for which China does not provide criminal penalties. The United States was unable to bear this burden. In particular, the United States offered much evidence in the form of newspaper articles, and the Panel found this evidence to lack sufficient credibility.[48]

The basis for this US complaint was China's Criminal Law, Judicial Interpretation No. 19, and Judicial Interpretation No. 16 – measures that established specific thresholds that had to be met in order for criminal punishments to be imposed. For example, under Judicial Interpretation No. 19, forging of registered trademarks can result in criminal punishments only when the number of forged units is not less than 20,000 pieces or if the 'illegal business operation volume' is not less than 50,000 Yuan, or if the amount of illegal gains is less than 30,000 Yuan.

Legal analysis

The first interpretative question for the Panel involved the determination of the meaning of 'commercial scale' in the first sentence of Article 61. The United States argued that the Chinese thresholds were quantitatively too low, and that, qualitatively, they failed to take into account certain necessary factors. However, the United States accepted that, in principle, numerical thresholds could be acceptable without more.[49]

The essence of the US complaint here was that the use of such thresholds necessarily implied that any act of trademark counterfeiting or copyright piracy that fell below these thresholds was free from the risk of criminal prosecution. The Panel noted that the US complaint with respect to Article 61 had 'two limbs'. The first limb concerned the level and the method of calculating thresholds wherein the threshold levels were argued to eliminate whole classes of criminal activities from risk of prosecution. The second aspect of the complaint was that the use of specific numerical thresholds basically required law-enforcement officials to 'disregard other indicia of counterfeiting and piracy', such as the presence of unfinished products and fake packaging.

The first limb of the US complaint received careful scrutiny from the Panel, whereas the second limb was dismissed summarily on the grounds that the

48 Ibid., para. 7.629.
49 Ibid., para. 7.495.

United States had not made a prima facie case with respect to other indicia of infringement.

It is worth noting that, in and of itself, the use of thresholds by China can hardly be problematic. After all, enforcement costs for criminal prosecution are nontrivial and, either implicitly or explicitly, thresholds are bound to guide enforcement efforts. Indeed, efficiency requires turning a blind eye to trivial occurrences of counterfeiting and piracy. For example, few would argue that photocopying of a few pages (but exceeding an amount considered 'fair use') from a copyrighted textbook for personal use by a student should be subject to criminal prosecution. But, on the other hand, if a student undertook such illegal copying *on a large enough scale* for selling them to classmates, the question becomes more serious. The use of a threshold as guiding principle cannot be avoided: only if the level of copyright piracy exceeds a certain amount would criminal prosecution appear to make legal and economic sense. Indeed, as the Panel Report notes, the United States conceded as much since it did not object to the use of thresholds per se, although it did argue that the fact that China uses thresholds across a range of commercial crimes ought to have no bearing on the Panel's 'assessment of whether China meets its international obligations under the first sentence of Article 61' of TRIPS.[50]

The first limb of the US complaint brought the concept of 'commercial scale' to the forefront, and the Panel Report devoted much space to it. Indeed, from an economic viewpoint, this is a reasonably important aspect of this case and is therefore worth discussing in some detail.

The Panel noted that TRIPS Article 61(1) creates an *obligation* to provide for criminal procedures for all willful acts of counterfeiting and piracy on a commercial scale. In other words, only those acts of piracy and counterfeiting that occur on a 'commercial scale' must be subject to criminal prosecution. Indeed, the Panel clarified the scope of the obligation created by Article 61(1) by noting that it is subject to four different limitations, an emphasis that is likely to prove important for future TRIPS related disputes at the WTO. First, the Panel noted that:

> the obligation applies to trademarks and copyright *rather than to all intellectual property rights* covered by the TRIPS Agreement. The fourth sentence of Article 61 gives Members the *option to criminalize* other infringements of intellectual property rights, in particular where they are committed wilfully and on a

50 See Gene M. Grossman and Petros C. Mavroidis (2003), 'United States – Section 110(5) of the US Copyright Act, Recourse to Arbitration under Article 25 of the DSU: Would've or Should've? Impaired Benefits Due to Copyright Infringement', 2:2 *World Trade Review*, 233–249. Grossman and Mavroidis note that the optimal enforcement policy is not one that ensures 100% compliance (i.e., zero copyright violations in our context) since the costs of enforcing such perfect compliance would far outweigh the benefits. In other words, below some level of thresholds, it would be globally optimal to let IPR violations occur.

commercial scale. Despite the potential gravity of such infringements, Article 61 creates no obligation to criminalize them.[51]

The fact that the obligation applies only to trademarks and copyrights means that there exists a wedge between the degree of protection available under TRIPS to different types of IPRs, with somewhat stronger protection afforded to copyrights and trademarks relative to other IPRs, such as patents. This obviously raises the question of why this might be so. One potential answer is that, with the exception of pharmaceuticals, violations of patents in the form of illegal imitation of products and technologies are relatively costlier to commit than violations of copyrights and trademarks. If so, the legal deterrent required in order to provide equivalent protection to copyrights and trademarks might be greater.

The second limitation of Article 61 noted by the Panel was that the obligation to provide for criminal procedures 'applies to counterfeiting and piracy rather than to all infringements of trademarks and copyright'.[52] Indeed, the Panel went so far as to note that 'the records of the negotiation of the TRIPS Agreement confirm that the term "infringements of trademarks and copyright" on a commercial scale was considered in the draft provision on criminal procedures but ultimately rejected'. In other words, the negotiators found it useful to single out counterfeiting and piracy as serious enough violations worthy of criminal prosecution, although the terms 'counterfeiting' and 'piracy' are not themselves defined under TRIPS.

The third limitation of the obligation singled out by the Panel was that the use of the word 'willful' implies that infringement ought to have been 'intentional' so that there was no obligation 'to make such penalties available with respect to acts of infringement committed without the requisite intent'. In the Panel's view, this focus on intent reflected the criminal nature of enforcement procedures under consideration.

The fourth limitation, and easily the most important one from an economic perspective, is indicated by the use of the words 'commercial scale'. Indeed, the Panel noted that

> The *principal interpretative point in dispute* is the meaning of the phrase 'on a commercial scale'. This phrase functions in context as a qualifier, indicating that wilful trademark counterfeiting or copyright piracy is included in the scope of the obligation provided that it also satisfies the condition of being 'on a commercial scale'. Accordingly, *certain acts of wilful trademark counterfeiting or copyright piracy are excluded from the scope of the first sentence of Article 61.*[53]

After an extensive review of dictionary definitions, and other uses of the terms in the WTO treaties and in other related contexts, the Panel found that '"commercial scale" is the magnitude or extent of typical or usual commercial activity'.

51 Panel Report, para. 7.518 (emphasis added).
52 Ibid., para. 7.519.
53 Ibid., para. 7.525 (emphasis added).

'Therefore, counterfeiting or piracy "on a commercial scale" refers to counterfeiting or piracy carried on at the magnitude or extent of typical or usual commercial activity with respect to a given product in a given market.'[54]

The Panel emphasized that while 'commercial' is a qualitative concept, 'scale' is a quantitative one, noting that it referred to the size of counterfeiting and piracy. The Panel's position was quite different from that of the United States, which initially insisted that any infringer pursuing financial gain in the market was acting on a commercial scale. The Panel also did not agree to the Chinese position that commercial scale was equivalent to 'industrial scale activity'. Instead, *the Panel noted that what constitutes commercial scale depends upon the product or market in question.* This necessarily implies that the Chinese thresholds for criminal prosecution could indeed be too high for certain markets, but the Panel noted that the United States had not provided any hard evidence demonstrating this was the case for any specific market or product in China.

Indeed, the evidence provided by the United States was rather thin in that it was comprised of a few newspaper and magazine articles. Furthermore, the Panel correctly rejected the use of GDP per capita as a measure of commercial scale, since it is too broad a measure that may or may not be relevant for any specific market. Characterizing the evidence submitted by the United States as anecdotal in nature, the Panel ruled that the United States had failed to establish that China's criminal thresholds were inconsistent with its obligations under TRIPS Article 61(1).

While it is easy to fault the United States for not providing sufficient evidence in support of its position that Chinese thresholds were allowing counterfeiting and piracy to occur on a commercial scale in certain markets, it is worth bearing in mind that violations of 'behind the border' rules and commitments are not easy to prove. The collection of such evidence would require the cooperation of Chinese officials responsible for enforcing the law. If such officials enforce TRIPS fully, there would be little evidence to collect. However, if they do not, they certainly have no incentive to cooperate with the United States and provide incriminating evidence against themselves! Indeed, this basic dilemma might partly explain why the United States submitted so little hard evidence in support of its position, choosing to rely more on explicit statements contained in Chinese laws as opposed to the lack of 'enforcement' of those laws.

A potential interpretation of the Panel's definition of 'commercial scale' is that it is a general 'standard', compliance with which is to be determined by dispute-settlement bodies on a case-by-case basis. This standard may be understood as a kind of delegation to Panels to evaluate facts to determine whether they meet the standard's requirements. The Panel noted that, 'what constitutes a commercial scale for counterfeiting or piracy of a particular product in a particular market will

54 Ibid., para. 7.577.

depend on the magnitude or extent that is typical or usual with respect to such a product in such a market, which may be small or large'.[55] In this way, the use of a standard may be seen as a special type of contractual incompleteness, with a special type of institutional mechanism to provide for *ex post* completion. Thus, the Panel noted that the determination of 'commercial scale' cannot be rigidly fixed *ex ante*.

Given that commercial scale is context specific, whether a certain level of illegal copying is deemed to occur on a commercial scale or not is a judgment regarding an appropriate standard that can be made only with the requisite market data in hand for a given work. Thus, the TRIPS contract is incomplete in that it does not include a specific definition of 'commercial scale'. With the Panel's decision, it can be argued that commercial scale is a context-specific standard that is to be determined by future WTO Panels on a case-by-case basis. What this implies, of course, is that the explicit numerical thresholds specified in Chinese law cannot, in and of themselves, be considered too high or too low. Indeed, as we have argued above, even from an efficiency perspective, the existence and use of such thresholds are not inherently problematic.

4. Economic and policy analysis

China has always guarded its sovereignty vigorously. With respect to the claims in the present case regarding copyright protection for prohibited works, and with respect to the claims regarding criminal penalties, China made explicit arguments that the sovereign right to censor, and to determine its own criminal laws, dominates review under WTO law. With respect to the claims regarding disposal of infringing goods, the core argument was also about retained autonomy after harmonization under TRIPS, and in particular the retained discretion to exercise authority that is required to be made available to national authorities under TRIPS. The TRIPS agreement can be characterized in these three contexts as incomplete in its specification of the relationship between the relevant harmonization obligations, and certain areas of retained national autonomy.

Policy externalities in connection with intellectual property rights

Of course, all international law restricts the autonomy of states, and all international trade law may be understood in terms of management of policy

55 The Panel is quite sensible to say that thresholds have to be specific to the context. So in this sense, the Chinese law's specification of rigid thresholds might be a bit odd: infringing sales of 50,000 Yuan might be astronomical (and therefore on a commercial scale) in one market while trivial in another. Furthermore, it is worth noting that the sales revenue lost by the IPR holder and the sales revenue gained by an infringer need not always correlate perfectly. Only when the sales revenue of infringers exceeds that which the IPR holder *would have earned* if infringement were absent does the use of thresholds based on infringing sales work in favor of the rights holder.

externalities. The TRIPS is no exception. As pointed out by Grossman and Mavroidis:

> In a non-cooperative world regime of intellectual property protection, externalities might come in two main forms. *First*, governments may have a national incentive to discriminate against the intellectual property rights of foreign citizens. This explains the requirements for national treatment that are included in *TRIPs*, and in the *Berne Convention* and *Paris Treaty* before it. *Second*, even with national treatment, national governments may choose to provide insufficient protection for intellectual property relative to the strength of protection that would be globally efficient.[56]

The basic calculus of optimal patent protection in a closed economy has been well understood since Nordhaus, who argued that the optimal policy must balance the marginal benefit of inducing more innovation against the marginal static loss imposed by extending monopoly power.[57] More recently, Grossman and Lai[58] have provided a thorough analysis of optimal patent policies in a two-region (North–South) open-economy context. It turns out that the presence of international trade matters a great deal. More specifically, they highlight two reasons why patent protection will be too weak in an open-economy setting when countries choose policies to maximize their own welfare. As was also noted by Grossman and Mavroidis, these two reasons are as follows:

> *First*, national governments do not take into account in their cost–benefit calculus the benefits that accrue to foreign citizens when protection induces additional investments in intellectual property. *Second*, national governments do not consider as an offset to the static cost of granting patent and copyright protection the monopoly profits that accrue to foreign rights holders. For both these reasons, a global regime of independently chosen patent and copyright policies will provide too little incentive for investment in intellectual property relative to the aggregate reward that would maximize world welfare. In effect, countries have an incentive to free ride on the intellectual property rights protection provided by their trading partners.[59]

This is a public-goods problem. Importantly in the present case, it may be that states differ in the extent to which their citizens are benefited by either investment in intellectual property or monopoly profits of rights holders. Importantly also, the magnitudes of (i) the benefits to foreign citizens from investment induced by protection, and (ii) the monopoly profits that accrue to foreign rights holders, are uncertain.

56 See Gene M. Grossman and Petros C. Mavroidis (2003), 'United States – Section 110(5) of the US Copyright Act, Recourse to Arbitration under Article 25 of the DSU: Would've or Should've? Impaired Benefits Due to Copyright Infringement', 2:2 *World Trade Review*, 233–249 (citations omitted).

57 William D. Nordhaus (1969), *Invention, Growth, and Welfare: A Theoretical Treatment of Technological Change*, Cambridge, MA: MIT Press.

58 Grossman and Lai, 'International Protection of Intellectual Property'.

59 Grossman and Mavroidis, 'United States – Section 110(5) of the US Copyright Act'.

To some extent, intellectual property protection below the globally efficient level would impose its policy externality in a way similar to a tariff, although the market mechanism can be rather different. By their very nature, IPRs bestow market power on rights holders. Therefore, any meaningful discussion of the effects of IPR enforcement (or the lack of it) has to recognize the market power of rights holders. This is important because all countries have the ability to affect the degree to which rights holders can exercise their market power locally by controlling the degree of IPR protection available in their respective markets. In other words, the presence of intellectual property-based market power makes the standard distinction between 'small' and 'large' countries somewhat superfluous.

For example, when faced with an import tariff in a foreign market, a monopolist will typically find it optimal to absorb some of the tariff and not pass it on entirely to foreign consumers. While a tariff directly affects the effective price collected by a monopolist or a right holder, the lack of IPR protection can lower the market price for the right holder's good by creating competition in the local market. Sometimes such competition can occur in the form of a lower-quality version of the original good, while at other times the copied version (such as in software or books) might work just as effectively as the original. Regardless, the competition created by the infringing product necessarily implies a reduction in the price of imports, allowing domestic infringers to profit at the expense of foreign intellectual property owners. Indeed, the competition created by the failure to protect IPRs benefits local consumers in the short run and is one reason many analyses of IPR protection in a global economy find that allowing for *some* level of imitative activities can be in the interest of countries that do not possess significant innovative capacity themselves.[60]

Furthermore, for a state like China in which the government continues to own a significant portion of the means of production, the benefits to domestic infringers would in part be captured by the government. Of the two reasons identified by Grossman and Lai[61] as to why IPR protection will generally be too weak, perhaps the second reason is more applicable in the present context since US consumption of Chinese goods that require IPR protection is not nearly as large as the Chinese consumption of US goods that require such protection. The harm inflicted by its weaker IPR protection on US producers would not be internalized by China through narrow reciprocity, resulting in a level of protection that is too low from a global-welfare perspective.

TRIPS as an incomplete contract

TRIPS requires a certain degree of harmonization of intellectual property rights across member countries of the WTO. It sets minimum standards for various types of IPRs, but, as demonstrated in the case at hand, provides a rather incomplete

60 Elhanan Helpman (1993), 'Innovation, Imitation, and Intellectual Property Rights', 61:6 *Econometrica*, 1247–1280.

61 Grossman and Lai, 'International Protection of Intellectual Property'.

specification[62] of its requirements. TRIPS is internally incomplete, but it is also incomplete in an external sense: the relationship between TRIPS and other (incomplete) law – such as on the one hand the human right of expression,[63] and on the other hand the sovereign right to restrict expression – is incompletely specified. In the present case, there is a moderate degree of consistency between the relevant WTO law and human-rights law,[64] but the relevant WTO law was argued by China to be inconsistent with China's sovereign right to restrict expression. Thus, it might be that the incompleteness of TRIPS allows TRIPS rights to be obviated, or nullified or impaired, by a broad national discretion to censor. Furthermore, this is an asymmetric discretion, (i) since the United States censors less than China does, and (ii) to the extent that the United States has more intellectual property to protect than China does.

HMS examine the GATT, finding that it includes an interesting combination of '*rigidity*, in the sense that contractual obligations are largely insensitive to changes in economic (and political) conditions, and *discretion*, in the sense that governments have substantial leeway in the setting of many policies. They observe that 'there is a *wide array of policy instruments* – border measures and especially "domestic" measures – that should be constrained to keep in check each government's incentives to act opportunistically'.[65]

HMS argue that national discretion is likely to be increased where domestic instruments are less available to manipulate the terms of trade, or where the importing country has less market power in connection with the imported good. Under these circumstances, we would expect less use of domestic measures to manipulate the terms of trade.

Intellectual property protection is one type of 'domestic' measure. Interestingly, intellectual property rights protection is different from normal trade measures, insofar as any state, even a state without conventional market power, can impose terms-of-trade externalities on exporters from other states by declining to protect their intellectual property rights. As noted above, this is because IPRs create market power that gives individual sellers the ability to influence prices, and this ability can be manipulated by importing countries by altering the product market

62 Incompleteness is a concept of limited analytical power, insofar as, in effect, all contracts are *completed* by default by letting the costs remain where they fall *except* to the extent that the contract shifts them. The more appropriate concept to refer to is actually specificity: contracts, and treaties, can be expected to vary in their specificity. States may be expected to establish treaties of varying specificity depending on the costs and benefits of specification. One alternative to specificity is implicit delegation to dispute settlement of decisionmaking authority. This institutional alternative can provide *ex post* contract completion, or specification. Considering the role of precedent, it can also, over time, provide greater *ex ante* specification.

63 See, e.g., Article 19 of the International Covenant on Civil and Political Rights, Article 10 of the European Convention on Human Rights, Article 13 of the American Convention on Human Rights, and Article 9 of the African Charter on Human and Peoples' Rights.

64 See Broude, 'It's Easily Done'.

65 Horn, Maggi, and Staiger (2010), 'Trade Agreements as Endogenously Incomplete Contracts', 394.

conditions faced by such sellers in their markets. This fact seems to accentuate the observation of HMS to the effect that, with rising volumes of trade, and consequent increasing costs of allowing discretion, there is an increasing need to constrain domestic policies.[66]

This accentuation would seem to be especially likely in the case of China, which generally has world-class manufacturing capabilities, allowing it to compete with imported intellectual property-based goods. A state without local manufacturing capabilities would not be able to impose terms-of-trade externalities on exporters from other states since it would lack the means of changing market conditions faced by rights holders. In other words, if local providers are incapable of producing competing goods that violate copyrights or trademarks, the lack of local IPR enforcement would not create any competition for rights holders and therefore would not affect their prices. The criminal penalties 'commercial scale' threshold in the present case may be understood as an example of a state contingency related to the question of sufficient manufacturing capabilities – or at least sufficient manufacturing.

Under significant uncertainty as to the future state of affairs, states would wish to establish complex state-contingent contracts. As noted above, the magnitudes of (i) the benefits to foreign citizens from investment induced by protection, and (ii) the monopoly profits that accrue to foreign rights holders, are uncertain. However, contracting is costly, limiting the ability to specify state-contingencies. On the other hand, by specifying general 'standards', and delegating to dispute-settlement bodies the responsibility to apply these standards, states are able to include complex state-contingency in their contracts, with significantly less variable contracting costs. This is a design feature that is not addressed in HMS, but it was clearly at work in the present case.[67]

Consider a simplified version of the HMS model. Suppose an import creates a local externality (like the consumption externality of HMS) that serves to directly lower the government's objective function. In connection with the first claim in this case, that relevant externality could arise because (the government believes) the consumption of the import – such as a novel or an artistic work critical of centralized power – reduces its ability to govern effectively by fomenting dissent or forces it to allocate resources away from other pursuits toward maintaining 'law and order'. Further, assume that the extent of the externality imposed by the import is uncertain and the transactions costs of contracting over censorship are quite large. This is a reasonable assumption in the present context given the long list of types of works that can be potentially subject to censorship and the fact that countries might (and often do) have very different views regarding

66 Ibid., at 406.

67 Ibid., at 416, referring to Giovanni Maggi and Robert W. Staiger (2008), 'On the Role and Design of Dispute Settlement Procedures in International Trade Agreements', National Bureau of Economic Research Working Paper 14067. See Joel P. Trachtman (1999), 'The Domain of WTO Dispute Resolution', 40 *Harvard International Law Journal*, 333.

censorship: what is deemed immoral or worthy of censorship is likely to vary across nations due to very different cultures, religions, and social norms regarding the freedom of expression.[68]

Under such circumstances, the exclusion from the trade agreement of disciplines on the degree of censorship would be optimal, providing governments with a high degree of discretion regarding its use. Indeed, Article 17 of the Berne Convention, incorporated by reference in the TRIPS, permits censorship without detailing any constraints on how and when it can be used.

Nonviolation claims

An alternative mechanism by which to address uncertainty and contracting costs is through a mechanism such as the remedy for nonviolation nullification or impairment developed in the GATT context. We may evaluate the utility of non-violation nullification or impairment (NV) doctrine to complete the WTO contract in areas beyond tariff concessions. We note that WTO member states have determined that, for the time being, member states will not exercise the right to bring NV complaints in connection with TRIPS.[69]

As applied more specifically to the *China–IP Rights* case, the question is whether NV should apply to the obligation of intellectual property protection under TRIPS. If NV claims become available under TRIPS, would it be possible for the United States to make an NV claim against China, on the basis that China's censorship, authorized by Article 17 of the Berne Convention, nullifies or impairs US copyright rights under other provisions of TRIPS? Interestingly, in the *Asbestos* case,[70] the Appellate Body suggested that even where a state took advantage of a policy exception – Article XX of GATT – it might be required to compensate the complainant for nullification or impairment of the complainant's rights. Of course, in the context of the present case, the extent of Chinese censorship was well known prior to China's accession to the WTO, and so it would be difficult for the United States to argue formally that it had 'legitimate expectations' of a noncensorship state of affairs, as required by existing doctrine. But would the availability of a general NV claim in TRIPS otherwise be appropriate?

The case for extending TRIPS to include the possibility of NV claims would appear to be no weaker than that for the original inclusion of NV claims in Article XXIII in GATT. After all, the point of this article under GATT is to prevent the erosion of previously granted market access. The question posed by Bagwell and

68 Recall, for example, that Salman Rushdie's novel *The Satanic Verses* met with critical acclaim in the West but was considered offensive enough by Islamic fundamentalists to have earned him a *fatwā* from Ayatollah Khomeini of Iran in 1989. Indeed, the novel was even banned in India, a secular democracy with a large Muslim population.

69 Article 64.2 of TRIPS specified that NV would not be available with respect to TRIPS for the first five years from the date of entry into force of the WTO Agreement. Paragraph 45 of the 2005 Hong Kong Ministerial Declaration seems to have extended the period of nonapplication of NV indefinitely.

70 Appellate Body Report, *European Communities – Measures Affecting Asbestos and Asbestos-Containing Products* (WT/DS135/AB/R, adopted 5 April 2001).

Staiger is of immediate relevance here.[71] They ask: to what extent must nations cede control over domestic policies (that only affect other countries in a pecuniary manner) in order to achieve economic efficiency in an interdependent world? While their analysis is motivated by the interaction between trade policies (such as tariffs) and domestic policies (such as labor and environmental standards), their findings have implications for the present context as well.

One could view the extent of censorship practiced by a country as a domestic standard that has *no direct economic impact* on its trading partners except for its effects on prices of copyrighted works (i.e., the terms of trade). If so, Bagwell and Staiger's analysis implies that tariff negotiations (analogous to negotiations over the degree of IPR protection in our context) would not be sufficient to achieve efficiency, since each government has an incentive to reclaim a portion of the market access granted under such negotiations via manipulating its domestic standard. In the present context, this result means that TRIPS negotiations regarding copyright protection (i.e., market access) could be undone by the strategic use of censorship.

Perhaps more importantly, Bagwell and Staiger go on to show that an NV complaint procedure (such as that provided for under GATT Article XXIII) that either requires compensation for the trade effects of domestic-policy changes or permits the complainant to withdraw an equivalent market concession of its own can play an important role in helping achieve global efficiency by ensuring that previously granted market-access commitments remain intact. As noted above, while the sovereign right to censor may trump market-access commitments made under TRIPS, the availability of an NV complaint can help ensure that governments do not use this right in an opportunistic manner.

5. Conclusion

International trade agreements are generally intended to cause states to internalize policy externalities. The policy externalities that arise from domestic decisions regarding intellectual property protection may deprive foreign intellectual property owners of the monopoly profits that they would otherwise derive from intellectual property protection. In connection with intellectual property protection, even a state that lacks 'traditional' market power on world markets may be able to impose terms-of-trade externalities on other states by reducing its protection of intellectual property below the global optimum. For this reason, and because of the international public-goods aspects of intellectual property, states have incentives to undersupply intellectual property protection. At least in part, TRIPS seems to be an attempt to reduce these policy externalities, since it basically requires all WTO members to adopt the same level of IPR protection as that which prevails in the

71 Kyle Bagwell and Robert W. Staiger (2001), 'Domestic Policies, National Sovereignty, and International Economic Institutions', 116:2 *The Quarterly Journal of Economics*, 519–562.

industrialized world. As noted earlier, the literature has shown that the global harmonization of IPRs is neither necessary nor sufficient to achieve efficiency, even though individual nations have an incentive to undersupply IPR protection.

All contracts, and all international treaties, are incomplete. This case involves some good examples of treaty incompleteness. Incompleteness can arise from circumstances of uncertainty regarding the possible tradeoffs, and the optimal balance, between different goals, including state autonomy in censorship on the one hand and internalizing policy externalities in intellectual property protection on the other. Following HMS, we analyze the possibility that it might be efficient to allow states broad discretion over censorship. Alternatively, in connection with the requirement for criminal penalties, incompleteness can arise from uncertainty regarding the particular industry structure that might be involved, and what would constitute production of 'commercial scale' for that industry.

We have also questioned the rationale for the limitation on the use of NV complaints in connection with the TRIPS, since NV complaints may be used to reduce the possibility that states will use discretion, such as that granted with respect to censorship, in a manner that is inconsistent with the rationale for that discretion so as to defect from the general commitment to provide copyright or other intellectual property rights.

CHAPTER 18

World Trade Review (2013), 12: 2, 377–408
© Kamal Saggi and Mark WU doi:10.1017/S1474745612000766

Yet Another Nail in the Coffin of Zeroing: *United States – Anti-Dumping Administrative Reviews and Other Measures Related to Imports of Certain Orange Juice from Brazil*

KAMAL SAGGI*
Vanderbilt University
MARK WU**
Harvard Law School

Abstract: This paper analyzes Brazil's WTO challenge to the methods undertaken by the United States in calculating anti-dumping duties in administrative reviews and other investigations of Brazilian orange juice. The dispute resulted in a Panel ruling that conforms with earlier Appellate Body decisions outlawing the use of 'weighted average to transaction' zeroing in such reviews. However, we note that the Panel's stance was driven largely from a desire to preserve 'stability and predictability' within the system, suggesting a practical recognition of the shadow of past Appellate Body decisions on the same legal question. In addition, we argue that to understand fully the effects of zeroing, it is important to account for the underlying reasons behind observed price changes in the market. We show that zeroing is more likely to convert a negative dumping determination into a positive one when price changes are driven by variations in demand relative to when they are driven by variations in the cost of exporting. In the present case, Brazilian exporters of orange juice experienced an increase in (residual) demand for their product since, by reducing the local supply of round oranges, adverse weather conditions in the United States made it difficult for US orange-juice producers to meet local demand.

1. Introduction

Over the past decade, the United States has played a game of 'cat and mouse' when it comes to the use of 'zeroing' in anti-dumping proceedings. As will be described below in greater detail, zeroing is a methodology employed by governments in

* Email: k.saggi@vanderbilt.edu
** Email: mwu@law.harvard.edu
The authors are grateful for comments received from Mark Sanctuary, our discussant, Tom Prusa, and other participants at the 2012 American Law Institute conference on WTO Case Law.

anti-dumping investigations in which transactions with negative dumping margins are not allowed to offset those with positive margins. As a result, when aggregating transactions, the use of zeroing causes the weighted average dumping margin to be higher than it would be without zeroing. This leads to higher anti-dumping margins, much to the chagrin of US trading partners.

Beginning with the *US–Softwood Lumber V*[1] complaint brought forth by Canada in 2002, numerous WTO Appellate Body (AB) decisions have found the US practice of zeroing to be impermissible under WTO rules. The US has consistently interpreted each ruling against it narrowly, eliminating the practice of zeroing in the specific factual context under the legal complaint, but keeping the practice alive in other situations where the context differed ever so slightly. This narrow compliance behavior, in turn, has sparked additional cases, resulting in additional rulings against the use of zeroing. This incrementalist approach toward outlawing zeroing by the AB has resulted in large resource costs, for the litigants as well as the WTO as an institution (Bown and Sykes, 2008). Because of the importance of the US as an export market and the prevalence of zeroing in US anti-dumping investigations, many trading partners have willingly expended litigation resources in an attempt to stop this US practice.

US–Orange Juice (Brazil)[2] is yet another one in this extensive line of cases. At the time the Panel issued its report, 20 zeroing disputes had already come before WTO Panels.[3] All but two of these disputes have involved the US as the defendant (with the EU being the defendant in the remaining two cases). While the EU discontinued the practice of zeroing after losing its cases, the US boldly marched on with its strategy of narrow compliance, changing its use of zeroing in anti-dumping proceedings only to the extent necessary to bring its measure into compliance with the WTO ruling.

However, there is hope that *US–Orange Juice (Brazil)* may indeed be among the last of this long line of WTO litigation involving the US as a defendant on zeroing. On 6 February 2012, US Trade Representative Ron Kirk announced that the US had reached agreements with the EU and Japan to end longstanding WTO disputes

1 *United States – Final Dumping Determination on Softwood Lumber from Canada*, DS264 [*US–Softwood Lumber V*].

2 *United States – Anti-Dumping Administrative Reviews and Other Measures Related to Imports of Certain Orange Juice from Brazil*, DS382 [*US–Orange Juice (Brazil)*]

3 For a review of the WTO cases on zeroing and its impact, see Bown and Prusa (2011). Note that besides the 18 cases listed in Table 14 of Bown and Prusa (2011), two other cases had also come before a WTO panel before the issuance of the panel report: *US – Corrosion-Resistant Carbon Steel Flat Products (Korea)*, DS420 [*US–Carbon Steel Flat Products (Korea)*] and *US – Shrimp and Diamond Sawblades From China*, DS422 [*US–Shrimp and Diamond Sawblades (China)*]. A 21st zeroing dispute was filed after this panel report was issued, *United States – Anti-Dumping Measures on Certain Frozen Warmwater Shrimp from Vietnam*, DS429 [*US – Frozen Warmwater Shrimp (Vietnam)*].

(*US–Zeroing (EC)*,[4] *US–Zeroing (Japan)*,[5] and *US–Continued Zeroing*[6]) over zeroing.[7] Under these recently concluded agreements with the EU and Japan, the US Department of Commerce (DOC) finally completed the process – which began in December 2010 – of ending the use of zeroing in most anti-dumping proceedings.[8] Since the AB has repeatedly found the use of zeroing by the US to be inconsistent with WTO rules, had the US not agreed to end the practice of zeroing, it would have been hit with retaliatory trade measures by the EU and Japan that would have potentially resulted in hundreds of millions of dollars of lost exports. The threat of retaliatory sanctions appears to have put the contentious issue of zeroing mostly to bed, at least for now.[9]

With the EU having already discontinued the practice of zeroing and the US now having committed to do so in most contexts, it is to be hoped that this controversial practice has been consigned to the realm of history. It is hard to imagine other nations, particularly smaller ones, choosing to adopt zeroing, given that two giants of the trading system (the US and EU) have failed to defend its use at the WTO. In our view, the US decision to abandon zeroing in almost all of its anti-dumping proceedings is welcome news. Ridding the WTO system of zeroing removes an onerous burden from the shoulders of the dispute-settlement system. The litigation resource cost of zeroing has been tremendous on an already taxed dispute-settlement system; zeroing has accounted for almost 20% of AB reports (Bown and Prusa, 2011).

Given the stream of commentary about past zeroing cases, both in past studies in this series and elsewhere, what insights then are there to add from the *US–Orange Juice* decision, potentially one of zeroing's last gasps? We offer three points: First, while the Panel in *US–Orange Juice* certainly recognized that zeroing is prohibited in several forms of anti-dumping reviews, it cast doubt as to whether the AB may have overreached in its earlier *US–Zeroing (Japan)* decision when finding zeroing to be a violation of the 'fair comparison' requirement of Article 2.4 of the WTO Anti-Dumping Agreement (ADA). Rather than challenging the AB directly,

4 *United States – Laws, Regulations and Methodology for Calculating Dumping Margins (Zeroing)*, DS294 [*US–Zeroing (EC)*].

5 *United States – Measures Relating to Zeroing and Sunset Reviews*, DS322 [*US–Zeroing (Japan)*].

6 *United States – Continued Existence and Application of Zeroing Methodology*, DS350 [*US–Continued Zeroing*].

7 Press Release, Office of the US Trade Representative, 'United States Trade Representative Ron Kirk Announces Solutions to Years-Old Zeroing Disputes, Demonstrating Commitment to Export Growth and Job Creation' (6 February 2012).

8 Note that in Section 6, we discuss the possibility that the DOC may still have left itself the leeway to use this practice in one particular form of anti-dumping case, that in which there is 'targeted' dumping by a producer in a given region or over a particular time period.

9 As Prusa and Rubini's chapter (forthcoming) discusses, a number of zeroing disputes against the United States remain because the US DOC's new rules on margin calculations applied only prospectively. Thus, several countries have brought disputes concerning zeroed margins in pre-existing cases in order to obtain an adverse finding to force the US DOC to calculate non-zeroed margins for the products.

however, this decision highlights how Panels, at least on longstanding issues such as zeroing where the AB has made its views clear, feel increasingly constrained by the shadow of past AB rulings. Even if Panels are not formally bound by AB rulings, a *de facto* form of vertical *stare decisis* has taken hold in certain areas where panelists are concerned about the systemic costs to the WTO dispute-settlement regime of repeatedly challenging the AB's prior rulings, only then to be overturned.

Second, while the economics of zeroing are transparent and largely well understood, we note that the costs of zeroing differ depending on the context in which the practice is applied. When zeroing eliminates high price observations with larger export volumes, the damage that results is greater than in the case where zeroing eliminates high price observations with lower export volume. In other words, zeroing poses a greater potential problem in situations where the price increase of the exporter's good (which necessitates the importer's use of zeroing) is driven by changes in consumer demand rather than changes in the cost of exporting.

Finally, while we express cautious optimism that the WTO dispute-settlement regime may be seeing its last set of its zeroing challenges,[10] we note that the door remains open for a potential re-emergence of zeroing in a limited context.[11] Nevertheless, despite this opening, it appears that momentous litigation battles over zeroing are winding down, with future battles to be fought in negotiating rooms rather than courtrooms.

2. Background summary of the dispute

2.1 Past WTO challenges on zeroing

To understand the impact of zeroing, one needs to first understand what occurs during the investigation of an anti-dumping case. After a complaint has been filed alleging dumping by a foreign producer, the investigating authority compares the prices of export transactions with the 'normal' value of the product. If the former is lower than the latter, then the foreign producer is found to have 'dumped' its product. The ADA allows 'normal' value to be determined in various ways, depending upon the circumstances. These include reference to home-country prices, third-country prices, and/or a constructed price approach.

Prices will fluctuate with time based on a number of factors, including, but not limited to, input price fluctuations, foreign exchange fluctuations, changes in

10 Given the US strategy of only calculating non-zeroed margins in a pre-existing case following an adverse WTO finding for that particular case, there may still be several zeroing challenges ahead. Nevertheless, these disputes will be fairly easy to resolve, as evidenced by the quick Panel decisions rendered in *United States – Anti-Dumping Measures on Polyethylene Retail Carrier Bags from Thailand*, DS383 [*US–PET Bags (Thailand)*] and *United States – Use of Zeroing in Anti-Dumping Measures Involving Products from Korea*, DS402 [*US–Zeroing (Korea)*].

11 See *supra* note 8 and *infra* Section 6.

market demand conditions, etc. In comparing the price of export transactions with the normal value over a period of time, the investigating authority will encounter fluctuations in the export price over the investigation period. Disputes over zeroing arise from what happens in those instances when the investigating authority finds that the export price is actually higher than the normal value. It can treat such instances as 'negative dumping', meaning that it can use these instances to offset other instances of 'positive' finding (i.e., when the export price is lower than the 'normal value'). Or it can simply set the value to zero for that instance. This latter practice is what is known as 'zeroing'. Its significance is that its use can dramatically alter the results of an anti-dumping investigation and the calculation of anti-dumping margins to be levied.

Why is this? When investigating an allegation of dumping, investigating authorities must consider a series of export price observations over a period of time. The WTO Committee on Anti-Dumping Practices has adopted a recommendation that 'the period of data collection for dumping investigations normally shall be 12 months, and, in any case, no less than six months, ending as close to the date of initiation as is practicable'.[12] Investigating authorities are free to deviate from this investigation, but it is clear that they must consider more than a single observation. Because their dumping determination is based on a series of observations in which prices fluctuate, how these particular observations are treated matters when determining the average of these interactions.

Consider, then, an example series where some observations are ones where the export price is higher than the normal value, but most are instances where they are lower.[13] The former is what is to be expected, whereas the latter constitutes 'dumping' under WTO law. Normally, in determining the average of these observations, the instances of 'negative dumping' would be used to offset those instances of positive dumping. However, where zeroing is deployed, that is not the case. With zeroing, provided there are instances of positive dumping in the series, the investigation will inevitably result in a positive finding of dumping. Moreover, zeroing leads to a higher anti-dumping margin. This is again due to the fact that incidences of 'negative dumping' are set back to zero, so as to minimize their ability to serve as an offset to incidences of positive dumping. As a result, the practice of zeroing has been highly controversial and has been attacked in several prior cases.

To complicate the picture further, investigating authorities have taken different approaches when comparing the price of export transactions with normal value to determine the dumping margin and to calculate anti-dumping duties. Article 2.4.2 of the ADA recognizes three possibilities. The first is to compare 'the weighted

12 Committee on Anti-Dumping Practices, *Recommendation Concerning the Periods of Data Collection for Anti-Dumping Investigations*, adopted 5 May 2000, G/ADP/6, at para. 1(a).

13 Those who prefer to see an example with numbers may wish to skip ahead and read Example 1 in *infra* Section 4.

average normal value with a weighted average of all comparable export transactions'. The second is to compare 'normal value and export prices on a transaction-to-transaction basis'. The former is known as the 'weighted average to weighted average' (W–W) approach, whereas the latter is known as the 'transaction to transaction' (T–T) approach. Either of the two approaches is fine under the ADA. A third approach, however, may be used only in the limited circumstance where 'authorities find a pattern of export prices which differ significantly among different purchasers, regions or time periods, and if an explanation is provided as to why such differences cannot be taken into account by the use of a weighted average-to-weighted average or transaction-to-transaction approach'. Under this condition, investigating authorities are allowed to compare a 'normal value established on a weighted average basis' to 'prices of individual export transactions'. This third possibility, available only under limited circumstances, is known as a 'weighted average to transaction' (W–T) approach.

Prior to the entry into force of the ADA on 1 January 1995, the United States and other major users of anti-dumping generally calculated anti-dumping margins using the W–T approach.[14] However, as noted, the ADA constrained WTO members from using the W–T approach except under exceptional circumstances. In response, the US DOC adopted a new approach, known as 'model' zeroing. Under model zeroing, the product alleged to have been dumped is subdivided into a series of models. For example, a product may be subdivided into models on the basis of differences in physical characteristics, consumer preferences, and/or end use. A 'weighted average-to-weighted average' comparison is then conducted for each model rather than for the product as a whole. This model-specific W–W approach has come to be known as 'model' zeroing. In contrast, where the analysis is not performed on a model-to-model basis, the approach has been described as 'simple' zeroing. By nature, the T–T approach falls under the 'simple' zeroing category. So too does the W–T approach, even where the weighted-average normal value used is one for a model of the product; this is because the export price to which it is being compared is not model-specific.

Thus, the method of comparison which results in the use of zeroing may differ. A complaint brought before the WTO may be attacking one or more of these three different comparison approaches used in determining the dumping margin.

Another area of potential difference in the fact pattern of a WTO zeroing case is the type of investigation in which zeroing is used. So far, we have spoken of an anti-dumping investigation in general terms. However, anti-dumping investigations occur under various different contexts. Specifically, zeroing has been used in five different types of anti-dumping investigations. (1) The first type is the original investigation, i.e. the investigation conducted after the initial petition for anti-dumping remedies is filed. (2) A second type is an interim review or changed-

14 See Prusa and Vermulst (2009) at 222.

circumstance review. Article 11.2 of the ADA stipulates that this must occur 'upon request by any interested party which submits positive information substantiating the need for a review' so long as 'a reasonable period of time has elapsed since the imposition of the definitive anti-dumping duty.' (3) A third type is an administrative review. Under Article 9.3 of the ADA, an investigating authority is permitted, but not required, to determine the amount of the anti-dumping duty assessed on a foreign producer on a retrospective basis. In other words, the duty determined at the end of the original investigation is considered to be only an estimate, but the actual duty levied is determined at a later date retroactively. The administrative review is the process through which the actual duty, calculated retroactively, is determined. Because the US uses this approach, several of the WTO zeroing cases against the US, including this one, have targeted the practice of zeroing in administrative reviews. (4) A fourth type is a sunset review. Article 11.3 of the ADA stipulates that anti-dumping duties be terminated after five years, unless a sunset review initiated before then finds 'that the expiry of the duty would be likely to lead to continuation or recurrence of dumping and injury'. (5) A final type is a new-shipper review. These are reviews, as authorized by Article 9.5 of the ADA, for the purposes of determining individual dumping margins for new exporters that did not export during the period of investigation but are from a country against which anti-dumping duties have been applied.

This complicated web of possibilities has meant that the fact patterns of past WTO zeroing cases will often vary, with the type of comparison methodology and the type of investigation serving as key areas of difference. Unlike the European Union, which eliminated the use of zeroing altogether after losing the *EC–Bed Linens*[15] case, the US has chosen to comply with WTO rulings narrowly, by eliminating the use of zeroing for the particular factual circumstance in which it was challenged and lost. If a trading partner then sought to eliminate the US practice of zeroing in a different fact context, it was forced to bring another case. This has resulted in a series of prior AB rulings on US zeroing practices, which form the backdrop for this dispute. What follows below is a quick review of these cases, with particular attention given specifically to the type of zeroing methodology and the type of investigation at issue in each of the cases in which the AB has ruled against the US.

First, in *US–Softwood Lumber V*, the AB invalidated the use of model zeroing under the W–W methodology in original investigations by the US DOC.[16] The US then deployed simple zeroing under the T–T methodology instead, arguing that it was complying with the ruling by eliminating the offending W–W model zeroing measure. This argument was then challenged in compliance proceedings under

15 *European Communities – Anti-Dumping Duties on Imports of Cotton-Type Bed Linen from India*, DS141 [*EC–Bed Linens*].

16 Appellate Body Report, *US–Softwood Lumber V*, WT/DS264/AB/R, 11 August 2004.

Article 21.5 of the DSU.[17] Again, the US lost. Eventually, this led the US to eliminate the use of zeroing in original investigations.

However, recall that original investigations are but one of the five different types of anti-dumping investigations in which zeroing may be used. The US continued to retain the practice of zeroing in these other contexts, including administrative reviews under Article 9.3 of the ADA as well as new-shipper reviews under Article 9.5 of the ADA. The former is especially important because the US, as noted above, assesses anti-dumping duties retrospectively, as allowed under Article 9.3.1. The original investigation establishes only a deposit rate that the importer must pay, but the actual duty is determined in these subsequent administrative reviews. Thus, what truly matters for most foreign producers is whether the US employs zeroing in the administrative reviews.

US practices in Article 9.3.1 administrative reviews have been challenged in two separate cases, *US–Zeroing (EC)* and *US–Zeroing (Japan)*. In *US–Zeroing (EC)*, the AB addressed the use of W–T simple zeroing in administrative reviews, both as applied and as such. It found that the use of the W–T zeroing as applied by the US in 16 administrative reviews was inconsistent with Article 9.3 of the ADA and GATT Article VI:2.[18] The AB also declared moot the Panel's earlier ruling that the W–T simple-zeroing methodology as such in administrative reviews did not violate provisions of the GATT and the ADA.[19] In *US–Zeroing (Japan)*, the AB again affirmed that W–T simple zeroing is not allowed in administrative reviews. It held that the use of W–T simple zeroing as applied in 11 administrative reviews was inconsistent with several provisions of the ADA (Articles 2.1, 2.4, 9.1, and 9.3) as well as GATT Articles VI:1 and VI:2.[20]

Despite the two AB rulings against it, the US continued to engage in zeroing in administrative reviews. While proceedings challenging US noncompliance progressed, the Europeans filed a follow-up case, *US–Continued Zeroing (EC)*. Again, the Europeans challenged the US practice of using W–T simple zeroing in administrative reviews, along with several other issues. The AB's ruling was circulated in February 2009, after Brazil had already filed its complaint in this case. Just as before, the AB ruled against the US. In 34 of the 37 administrative reviews challenged by the EC, the AB found the use of W–T simple-zeroing methodology violated Article 9.3 of the ADA and GATT Article VI:2.[21] In two instances, the

17 Appellate Body Report, *US–Softwood Lumber V*, Article 21.5, WT/DS264/AB/RW, 15 August 2006.

18 Appellate Body Report, *US–Zeroing (EC)*, WT/DS294/AB/R, 18 April 2006 at para. 135.

19 Ibid., para. 227 (declaring moot the Panel's finding regarding Articles 1, 2.4, 2.4.2, 9.3, 11.1, 11.2, and 18.4 of the ADA and GATT Articles VI:1 and VI:2).

20 Appellate Body Report, *US–Zeroing (Japan)*, WT/DS322/AB/R, 9 January 2007 at para. 176.

21 Appellate Body Report, *US–Continued Zeroing*, WT/DS350/AB/R, 4 February 2009 at paras. 316 and 353.

AB chose not to complete the analysis, and, in the other instance, the AB held that the challenge of a preliminary measure was premature.[22]

In addition to opining on the use of W–T simple zeroing in Article 9.3.1 administrative reviews, the AB used these cases to rule on zeroing in a number of other factual contexts. In *US–Zeroing (Japan)*, Japan also challenged the US DOC's use of W–T simple zeroing in new-shipper reviews; the AB held this practice to be illegal.[23] Japan also challenged US practices in two sunset reviews in which the US relied upon administrative reviews that had used the W–T simple-zeroing methodology. The AB found that such practice violated Article 11.3 of the ADA.[24] In *US–Continued Zeroing (EC)*, the EU also had challenged the US DOC's use of W–W model zeroing in sunset reviews. The AB found the US at fault in eight of 11 sunset reviews in which the US had employed the W–W model-zeroing methodology.[25] In the remaining three instances, the AB again found the challenge of a preliminary measure to be premature.[26]

With the AB consistently ruling against the US on zeroing, why is the beast not yet dead? How is it that we get to yet another zeroing dispute? The main reason is US delay in complying with the AB's rulings. At the time of Brazil's complaint, the US had not yet signaled its intention to comply with the WTO rulings against its zeroing practices. This intransigence led the EU and Japan to press ahead with compliance proceedings under Article 21.5 of the DSU for *US–Zeroing (EC)* and *US–Zeroing (Japan)*; each proceeding was then subsequently appealed to the AB.[27] After winning the compliance proceedings, the EU and Japan sought DSU authorization for retaliation.[28] It was not until February 2012, when the European and Japanese retaliation threats became real, that the US finally backed down. By then, Brazil had already pressed ahead with its own case.

A second reason is the US practice of reading the AB's holding to apply narrowly to only the particular anti-dumping measures being challenged in the case. This meant that even were the US to eliminate the use of W–T simple zeroing with respect to the particular anti-dumping measures challenged by the EU and Japan, its other trading partners lacked confidence that the US would do so in administrative reviews concerning their products. To be certain that the US DOC would stop using W–T simple zeroing in administrative reviews for a particular

22 Ibid., paras. 207–12 and 354–7.

23 Appellate Body Report, *US–Zeroing (Japan)* at paras. 166 and 169 (finding violations of Arts. 2.4, 9.3, and 9.5 of the ADA and Art. VI:2 of the GATT).

24 Ibid., para. 186.

25 Appellate Body Report, *US–Continued Zeroing* at paras. 382–3.

26 Ibid., paras. 207–12.

27 Appellate Body Report, *US–Zeroing (EC)*, Article 21.5, WT/DS294/AB/RW, 14 May 2009; Appellate Body Report, *US–Zeroing (Japan)*, Article 21.5, WT/DS322/AB/RW, 18 August 2009.

28 Request for Recourse to Article 22.2 of the DSU by the European Union, *US–Zeroing (EC)*, Article 22.6, WT/DS294/35, 2 February 2010; Communication from Japan, *US–Zeroing (Japan)*, Article 22.6, WT/DS322/37, 5 May 2010.

Brazilian product, Brazil needed to file its own case. In a way, the US, through its strategy of narrowly interpreting AB rulings on zeroing, was testing its trading partners to see if the cost of zeroing was large enough that it would be willing to burn through costly litigation resources. The Brazilian government, having already tasted the political and economic gains of earlier WTO victories against the US, decided that it was worth forging ahead. Under this context, yet another zeroing dispute arose.

2.2 *The global orange-juice industry*

This particular zeroing case concerns orange juice. The orange-juice market is dominated by producers from two countries – Brazil and the United States. Together, they account for the lion's share of global production. The trade orientation of the industries in the two countries is very different. Domestic demand for pre-squeezed orange juice is small in Brazil.[29] As a result, most of the orange juice produced in Brazil is for export. Brazil supplies over 80% of the global orange-juice exports (USDA, 2007), and Brazilian firms have invested substantial sums in building a fleet of tankers used solely to transport frozen orange juice (Sterns and Spreen, 2010, 170). In contrast, the US is the world's largest consumer of orange juice. Most of the orange juice produced by US firms is for the domestic market, where its major competitors are the Brazilian producers.

The orange-juice industry in Brazil is highly concentrated. In crop year 2004–05, four firms (Coinbra, Cutrale, Citrosuco, and Montecitrus) accounted for approximately 85% of the total production of Brazilian orange juice (USITC, 2006, VII-6). As part of the anti-dumping investigation challenged in this dispute, the US DOC investigated the export practices of three of these firms – Cutrale, Fischer (which owns Citrusco), and Montecitrus – and applied zeroing when calculating the firm's dumping margins. Ironically, while high concentration levels typically raise concerns about monopoly pricing – which tends to be high – the position of the US DOC and the US International Trade Commission (ITC) was that the prices charged by Brazilian firms were *so low* that they caused material injury to the domestic orange-juice industry.[30]

Because the US is the world's largest consumer of orange juice, it is an important export market for Brazilian orange juice. The vast bulk of shipments by Brazilian producers to the US are of frozen orange juice, rather than non-frozen orange juice. Several of the major Brazilian producers have wholly owned or related processing

29 Brazilians prefer to drink orange juice that is freshly squeezed rather than pre-squeezed. They will squeeze oranges themselves at home or purchase from retailers juice that is freshly squeezed before them (USITC, 2006, VII-4 n. 12). Thus, there is little demand for pre-squeezed or frozen orange juice in Brazil.

30 Note that in 2011, long after the ITC determination was made and following the WTO case's conclusion, the Brazilian orange-juice industry further consolidated; a merger between Citrusco and Citrovita has resulted in the creation of the world's largest orange-juice producer. See White and Kassai (2011) and *Hispanically Speaking News* (2011).

affiliates in the US. However, the importance of the US market should not be overstated. In 2003, the year prior to the filing of the anti-dumping petition by the US citrus producers and processors, exports to the US represented only 20% of total Brazilian exports of frozen orange juice.[31] By contrast, exports to the largest and most important export market, the EU, represented over 52% of total Brazilian exports of frozen orange juice.[32]

In the non-frozen orange-juice segment (which represented 18% of total Brazilian orange-juice exports in 2003), the US market was even less important. In 2003, exports of non-frozen orange juice to the US represented a mere 1% of total Brazilian exports.[33] In contrast, 99% of non-frozen exports were destined for the EU.[34] The Brazilian share of the domestic US market in the not-from-concentrate orange-juice market was tiny – rising from a mere 1% in crop year 2001–02 to 3.3% in 2004–05.[35] Even when added with the frozen orange-juice segment, the Brazilian share of the US market was barely over 15% in 2004–05.[36]

Thus, while low-tariff access to the US market affected the business interests of Brazilian orange-juice producers, the zeroing case did not represent a 'make-or-break case' for the Brazilian orange-juice industry. Instead, Brazil's motivation to bring forward this challenge was likely driven by the desire to strike another blow against the US for zeroing, and, in doing so, reap the domestic political gain of another WTO victory against the US. In addition, large US beverage manufacturers (e.g., Coca-Cola and PepsiCo) are important buyers of Brazilian orange juice worldwide and presumably would want the benefit of lower duties for its US imports.[37] One can further speculate whether Brazil may have also been motivated to bring the case in order to cultivate favor with American multinational corporations that operate downstream on the supply chain.

2.3 *Factual aspects of the case*

The specific zeroing practices challenged in this dispute arose out of a 2004 petition filed by a collection of US citrus producers and processors. That petition alleged that Brazilian producers of certain orange juice were dumping their product in the US and materially injuring domestic producers. Upon receiving this petition, the US DOC began an investigation in February 2005, resulting in case number A-351-840.

31 Calculations by authors based on information provided in the UN Comtrade database for HS-200911.

32 Ibid.

33 Calculations by authors based on information provided in the UN Comtrade database for HS-200919.

34 Ibid.

35 See Table IV-5 in USITC (2006).

36 Ibid.

37 For example, Tropicana (owned by PepsiCo) and Minute Maid and Simply Orange (owned by Coca-Cola Co.) are sold not only in the US but also throughout Europe and Asia. See Kiernan and McKay (2012).

On 24 August 2005, the DOC issued a preliminary determination of dumping, which levied anti-dumping duties between 24.62 and 60.29% on Brazilian producers.[38] This was followed by a final determination on 13 January 2006 that revised the final anti-dumping duties downward to between 9.73% and 60.29%.[39]

Because the US employs a retrospective approach to assessing anti-dumping duties, the US collects only a 'security' in the form of a cash deposit at the time of entry. This cash deposit rate (CDR) represents an estimate of the importer's final anti-dumping duty payment.[40] Once a year, interested parties are allowed to request an administrative review to determine the final payment due for the relevant period of review. This payment is known as the importer-specific assessment rate (ISAR). The administrative review is also conducted by the US DOC, pursuant to Article 9.3.1 of the ADA. If no such review is requested, then the final anti-dumping duty assessed is the estimated rate, and the cash deposit collected as security are used to pay the duty owed.[41]

Brazilian orange-juice producers requested such an administrative review. The First Administrative Review was completed on 11 August 2008.[42] During this review, the US DOC employed W–T simple zeroing in calculating the dumping margins, CDRs, and ISARs. On 27 November 2008, Brazil requested consultations with the US at the WTO.[43] Brazil specifically challenged the DOC's use of W–T simple zeroing in calculations for two of the major Brazilian exporters, Cutrale and Fischer.

While the WTO consultations proceeded, Brazilian orange-juice producers requested a second administrative review the following year. On 22 May 2009, before the Second Administrative Review was completed, Brazil requested further consultations with the United States with regard to the use of zeroing in the original anti-dumping duty investigation as well as in the Second Administrative Review.[44] Brazil also requested consultations regarding the continued use of the United States zeroing procedures in successive anti-dumping proceedings pertaining to the imports of certain orange juice from Brazil. The Second Administrative Review was completed on 11 August 2009.[45]

38 'Notice of Preliminary Determination of Sales at Less Than Fair Value, Postponement of Final Determination, and Affirmative Preliminary Critical Circumstances Determination: Certain Orange Juice from Brazil', 70 Fed. Reg. 49557 (24 August 2005).

39 'Notice of Final Determination of Sales at Less Than Fair Value and Affirmative Final Determination of Critical Circumstances: Certain Orange Juice from Brazil', 71 Fed. Reg. 2183 (13 January 2006).

40 Panel Report, *US–Orange Juice (Brazil)*, WT/DS382/1, para. 7.83.

41 Ibid.

42 'Certain Orange Juice from Brazil: Final Results and Partial Rescission of Anti-Dumping Duty Administrative Review', 73 Fed. Reg. 46584 (11 August 2008).

43 Request for Consultations by Brazil, *US–Orange Juice (Brazil)*, WT/DS382/1, 1 December 2008.

44 Request for Consultations by Brazil, *US–Orange Juice (Brazil)*, WT/DS382/1/Add.1, 27 May 2009.

45 'Certain Orange Juice from Brazil: Final Results of Anti-Dumping Duty Administrative Review', 74 Fed. Reg. 40167 (11 August 2009).

The W–T simple-zeroing methodology deployed by the DOC and challenged by Brazil operated as follows.[46] Recall that, in determining whether dumping is occurring and calculating the dumping margin for a given exporter, the investigating authority needs to compare the export price with normal value. The DOC used a computer program to sort through the data necessary to make this comparison. This program computed a weighted-average normal value (WANV) each month for each exporter. The program then performed a series of W–T comparisons for each exporter. In other words, it compared the export price of a specific transaction for a given exporter to the WANV corresponding to that exporter for the month in which the transaction occurred. For every instance in which the normal value was higher than the export price, the computer program was instructed to set the result of this comparison to zero. The results were then aggregated and then divided by the total number of export transactions to figure out the weighted-average dumping margin. Because of the zeroing, the dumping margin was higher than it would have been otherwise.

Brazil's complaint charged that the US DOC's use of W–T simple zeroing in the two administrative reviews violated several WTO treaty provisions, namely Articles 2.4 and 9.3 of the ADA and Article VI:2 of the GATT 1994. Furthermore, Brazil alleged that the US DOC's continued use of W–T simple zeroing in successive anti-dumping proceedings, including the original investigation and subsequent administrative reviews, violated the same WTO provisions as well as Article 2.4.2 of the ADA.

As expected, the ensuing consultations failed to resolve the dispute. The US, as previously mentioned, gave no indication in 2009 of any intention to abandon its practice of zeroing in administrative reviews, despite the AB's rulings against it in *US–Zeroing (EC)* and *US–Zeroing (Japan)*. Therefore, on 20 August 2009, Brazil formally requested that the Dispute Settlement Body (DSB) establish a Panel with regard to the original investigation of the aforementioned dumping case, its two administrative reviews, as well as the continued use of zeroing by the US in anti-dumping proceedings. The Panel was established on 25 September 2009. After conducting its hearings, the Panel issued its report on 25 March 2011.

The Panel, not surprisingly, ruled in favor of Brazil. It held that with respect to the two administrative reviews at issue, the use of W–T simple zeroing by the US violated Article 2.4 of the ADA because it did not allow for a 'fair comparison' between export price and normal value.[47] The Panel further held that the continued use of zeroing under the Orange Juice Order also violated Article 2.4 of the ADA.[48] With respect to Brazil's other claims concerning Articles 2.4.2 and 9.3 of the ADA

46 Panel Report, *US–Orange Juice (Brazil)*, para. 7.85.
47 Ibid., paras. 7.155–7.161.
48 Ibid., para. 7.193.

and GATT Article VI:2, the Panel exercised judicial economy and chose not to examine the claims.[49]

3. The shadow of past Appellate Body rulings

Was the Panel's ruling that the US practice of zeroing violated Article 2.4 of the ADA correct? The provision states:

> A fair comparison shall be made between the export price and normal value. This comparison shall be made at the same level of trade, normally at the ex-factory level, and in respect of sales made at as nearly as possible the same time. Due allowance shall be made in each case, on its merits, for differences which affect price comparability, including differences in conditions and terms of sale, taxation, levels of trade, quantities, physical characteristics, and any other differences which are also demonstrated to affect price comparability.

The key question, as far as Article 2.4 of the ADA is concerned, is whether the practice of W–T simple zeroing allows for a fair comparison to be made.

As the Panel noted, this was the fifth case in which the question of the US DOC's use of W–T simple zeroing in administrative reviews has arisen.[50] Questions over the legality of W–T simple zeroing in periodic administrative reviews have also surfaced in *US–Zeroing (EC), US–Zeroing (Japan), US–Stainless Steel (Mexico)*,[51] and *US–Continued Zeroing*. In all four of these cases, the complainant had alleged that W–T simple zeroing violated Article 2.4 of the ADA. The central legal question, therefore, was anything but novel.

In several of these earlier decisions, the Panel and the Appellate Body (AB) have disagreed in their views on the consistency of W–T simple zeroing with respect to several provisions of the ADA and GATT. We summarize the results of these disagreements in Table 1.

Brazil, like past complainants of the US practice of zeroing in administrative reviews, raised claims that the US practice violated Articles 2.4 and 9.3 of the ADA as well as Article VI:2 of the GATT 1994. A review of the past rulings shows that in each of the four prior decisions, the AB has confirmed that W–T simple zeroing in administrative reviews is inconsistent with Articles 9.3 of the ADA and Article VI:2 of the GATT 1994. On the other hand, in three of the past four cases, the AB has declined to comment fully on the consistency of simple zeroing in periodic administrative reviews with Article 2.4 of the ADA. The AB has refused to endorse the view of several Panels that W–T simple zeroing is not inconsistent with

49 Ibid., para. 7.194.

50 Ibid., para. 7.130.

51 *US – Final Anti-Dumping Measures on Stainless Steel from Mexico*, DS344 [*US–Stainless Steel (Mexico)*].

Table 1. Past rulings on the consistency of simple zeroing in US administrative reviews (i.e., Article 9.3.1 reviews)

	Panel ruling	Appellate Body ruling
US–Zeroing (EC) [DS294] (as applied in 16 reviews)	Found that simple zeroing in administrative reviews is not inconsistent with Articles VI:2 of the GATT 1994 and Articles 2.4, 9.3, 11.1 and 11.2 of the ADA.	Reversed the Panel's finding with respect to Articles VI:2 of the GATT 1994 and Article 9.3 of the ADA, finding instead a violation. Upheld the Panel's finding concerning Articles 11.1 and 11.2 of the ADA, as well as the third to fifth sentences of Article 2.4 of the ADA. Declined to rule on the consistency of simple zeroing with the first sentence of Article 2.4 of the ADA.
US–Zeroing (Japan) [DS322] (as such and as applied in 11 reviews)	Found that simple zeroing in administrative reviews is not inconsistent with Articles VI:1 and VI:2 of the GATT 1994 and Articles 2.1, 2.4, and 9.1–9.3 of the ADA both as such and as applied in 11 periodic reviews.	Reversed the Panel's findings on both the as-such and as-applied claims. Found instead that simple zeroing is inconsistent with Article VI:2 of the GATT 1994 and Articles 2.4 and 9.3 of the ADA for both the as-such and as-applied claims. Declined to complete the analysis on claims regarding Article VI:1 of the GATT 1994 and Articles 2.1, 9.1, and 9.2 of the ADA.
US–Stainless Steel (Mexico) [DS344] (as-such claim and as-applied in five reviews)	Found that simple zeroing in administrative reviews is not inconsistent with Articles VI:1 and VI:2 of the GATT 1994 and Articles 2.1, 2.4, and 9.3 of the ADA both as-such and as-applied in five periodic reviews.	Reversed the Panel's finding on both the as-such and as-applied claims. Found instead that simple zeroing is inconsistent with Article VI:2 of the GATT 1994 and Article 9.3 of the ADA for both the as-such and as-applied claims. Found it unnecessary to rule on the claim concerning Article 2.4 of the ADA.
US–Continued Zeroing [DS350] (as applied in 29 reviews)	Ruled that simple zeroing in administrative reviews violated Article VI:2 of the GATT 1994 and Article 9.3 of the ADA. Applied judicial economy with respect to other claims, including Article 2.4 of the ADA.	Upheld Panel ruling on Article VI:2 of the GATT 1994 and Article 9.3 of the ADA. Declined to make additional findings on Article 2.4 of the ADA.

Article 2.4 of the ADA, overturning such a Panel ruling on three occasions. But more frequently than not, the AB has declined to complete the analysis so as to be able to explain why zeroing in administrative reviews is inconsistent with Article 2.4.

Only in *US–Zeroing (Japan)* did the AB address this issue, albeit briefly. The AB stated, 'If anti-dumping duties are assessed on the basis of a methodology involving comparisons between the export price and the normal value in a manner which results in anti-dumping duties being collected from importers in excess of the amount of the margin of dumping of the exporter or foreign producer, then this methodology cannot be viewed as involving a "fair comparison" within the meaning of the first sentence of Article 2.4.'[52] The AB then implied that the use of W–T simple-zeroing methodology would result in a duty being charged that was higher than the amount of the margin of dumping, because simple zeroing did not allow sales where the export price was higher than normal value to be properly taken into account.[53] Thus, it was 'unfair' and in violation of Article 2.4 of the ADA.

If there is one area where *US–Orange Juice (Brazil)* advances the discussion of the zeroing jurisprudence further, it is with respect to the issue of why exactly W–T simple zeroing is inconsistent with Article 2.4's requirement that a 'fair comparison' be undertaken. Recognizing that past cases had already discussed Article 9.3 of the ADA and Article VI:2 of the GATT 1994 extensively, the Panel chose to pass on those claims, on the ground of judicial economy. Instead, it focused its energy on discussing whether W–T simple zeroing was consistent with Article 2.4 of the ADA.

Yet, even on this question, the Panel did not consider itself entirely free to make up its own mind. Despite the limited discussion in the AB opinion in *US–Zeroing (Japan)*, the AB had clearly answered the question. Use of W–T simple zeroing in administrative reviews for the sake of retrospective duty assessment under Article 9.3.1 of the ADA was not permissible. This was true for both as-such and as-applied claims. The Panel therefore recognized,

> Although adopted panel and Appellate Body reports do not bind WTO Members beyond parties to a particular dispute, the Appellate Body has expressed the view that ensuring 'security and predictability' in the dispute settlement system, as contemplated in Article 3.2 of the DSU, implies that, absent cogent reasons, an adjudicatory body will resolve the same legal question in the same way in a subsequent case. Indeed, the Appellate Body has held that 'following the Appellate Body's conclusions in earlier disputes is not only appropriate, but is what would be expected from panels, especially where the issues are the same'... Institutionally, the fact that all Appellate Body reports overturning panel findings on the question of 'zeroing' have been adopted by the DSB implies acceptance by all WTO Members of their contents, and bestows upon them systemic legitimacy.[54]

52 Appellate Body Report, *US–Zeroing (Japan)*, para. 168.

53 Ibid., paras. 154–55 (cited in para. 168 as a cross-reference explanation for the AB's rationale for its ruling on the claim concerning Article 2.4 of the ADA).

54 Panel Report, *US–Orange Juice (Brazil)*, para. 7.132 (citations omitted).

The Panel, rightly in our opinion, recognized that although it was not bound by *US–Zeroing (Japan)*, the AB's prior proclamation on the very question did serve as a source of legitimate consideration (and constraint) on its deliberations. The excerpt above quoted by the Panel notes the AB's expectation, as stated in *US–Oil Country Tubular Goods Sunset Reviews* and repeated in subsequent cases, that where the legal issues is identical, Panels are expected to follow the AB's prior conclusions.[55] Thus, while the Panel could choose to deviate from the AB's past ruling that W–T simple zeroing in administrative reviews contravened Article 2.4 of the ADA, doing so would largely be a reflection of the Panel's obstinacy. Unless its ruling was crafted in such a way as to convince the AB that its past decision was wrong, it would simply be overruled.

Indeed, in *US–Stainless Steel (Mexico)*, the AB, when discussing a Panel's deviation from an established AB ruling on similar facts, noted, 'Ensuring "security and predictability" in the dispute settlement system, as contemplated in Article 3.2 of the DSU, implies that, absent cogent reasons, an adjudicatory body will resolve the same legal question in the same way in a subsequent case.'[56] In a subsequent zeroing case, *US–Continued Zeroing*, the Panel, while affirming that it was not bound to follow vertical *stare decisis*, nevertheless recognized that neither 'should a panel make a finding different from that in an adopted earlier Panel or Appellate Body report on similar facts and arguments without careful consideration and examination of why a different result is warranted, and assuring itself that its finding does not undermine the goals of the system'.[57]

This Panel appears to have taken these directives seriously. It recognized that it was not bound to follow the past precedent as laid forth by the AB in *US–Zeroing (Japan)*. But if it was to deviate from that ruling, it also recognized that it would need to elaborate on a set of cogent reasons for why such a deviation was necessary, given the costs triggered in terms of undermining 'security and predictability' of the dispute-settlement system. The Panel, therefore, stopped short of deviating and tempting the AB to overrule it. Instead, it simply offered a much more elaborate discussion of the arguments on both sides of the question of whether W–T simple zeroing in administrative reviews under Article 9.3.1 of the ADA was inconsistent with the 'fair comparison' obligation of Article 2.4 of the ADA.

Such a move falls squarely within the range of the Panel's discretion. Article 11 of the DSU directs that a Panel 'should make an objective assessment of the matter before it, including an objective assessment of the facts of the case and the applicability of and the conformity with the relevant covered agreements, and

55 Appellate Body Report, *United States – Sunset Reviews of Anti-Dumping Measures on Oil Country Tubular Goods from Argentina*, WT/DS/268/AB/R, 29 November 2004, para. 188.

56 Appellate Body Report, *US–Stainless Steel (Mexico)*, WT/DS344/AB/R, 30 April 2008, para. 160.

57 Panel Report, *US–Continued Zeroing*, para. 7.180.

make such other findings as will assist the DSB in making the recommendations or in giving the rulings provided for in the covered agreements'. Given the arguments raised by both the US and Brazil on this question, to analyze the various points raised is exactly what is to be expected of a Panel that takes its charge to perform an 'objective assessment' seriously.

The Panel identifies two questions raised by Brazil's challenge: (1) '[W]hether the obligation in the first ... sentence of Article 2.4 to ensure a "fair comparison" between export price and normal value applies outside of the context of what is described in the remainder of the provision, namely beyond the selection of transactions and use of adjustments to account for differences between export price and normal value which affect their comparability'; and (2) If yes, then 'whether the use of "simple zeroing" to calculate a margin of dumping is unfair'.[58]

The first question is whether the 'fair comparison' obligation is a narrow or broad requirement. A narrow reading of the obligation would mean that it is specific to the contexts mentioned in Article 2.4, namely: (a) the selection of transactions to be used for comparing export price to normal value and (b) the use of adjustments when making such a comparison. A broad reading would encompass other contexts beyond Article 2.4, including retrospective duty-assessment proceedings under Article 9.3.1.

On this question, we see the shadow of past AB rulings. In *US–Zeroing (Japan)*, when examining the same question, the Panel declared that 'the requirement of a fair comparison set out in the first sentence of Article 2.4 is an independent legal obligation that is not defined exhaustively by the specific requirements set out in the remainder of Article 2.4 and is not limited in scope to the issue of adjustments to ensure price comparability', noting that a previous Panel in *US–Zeroing (EC)* had reached a similar conclusion.[59] This position was then endorsed implicitly by the AB, as reflected by the fact that the AB then proceeded to assess the compatibility of zeroing in retrospective duty assessment (which is not discussed in the remainder of Article 2.4) with the 'fair comparison' obligation of Article 2.4.[60] Moreover, in *US–Zeroing (EC)*, the AB had explicitly stated that 'the legal rule set out in the first sentence of Article 2.4 is expressed in terms of a general and abstract standard. One implication of this is that this requirement is also applicable to proceedings governed by Article 9.3'.[61] The answer to the first question therefore had been clearly answered by the AB in the past. The obligation applied broadly.

The Panel, in deciding this question, referenced the rationale given in past WTO rulings. It discussed a point noted in the *US–Zeroing (EC)* rulings that the

58 *US–Orange Juice (Brazil)*, para. 7.140.
59 Panel Report, *US–Zeroing (Japan)*, para. 7.157.
60 Appellate Body Report, *US–Zeroing (Japan)*, para. 168.
61 Appellate Body Report, *US–Zeroing (EC)*, para. 146 (citation omitted).

'fair comparison' reference in the first sentence of Article 2.4, which serves as a chapeau to the rest of the provision, must be doing some work beyond addressing the price comparisons expressed in the remainder of the provision.[62] To interpret the provision as not having any independent meaning beyond the scope of price comparison adjustments discussed in Article 2.4 would render the sentence inutile. Hence, the Panel declared that 'fair comparison' obligation 'must apply to discipline the "comparison" between export price and normal value *whenever* undertaken during an anti-dumping proceeding, including during duty assessment'.[63] The obligation therefore extends to the comparisons made in Article 9.3.1 retrospective duty assessment determinations of the sort at issue in this case.

However, while the Panel referenced these past AB rulings, it is not altogether clear that the Panel necessarily agreed fully with the AB's past interpretation. One of its Panel members went so far as to emphasize his view that 'the correct interpretation of the "fair comparison" requirement set out in the first sentence of Article 2.4 is not as clear as previous Panels and the Appellate Body appear to have suggested'.[64] He noted that the first sentence of the chapeau must be interpreted in light of the context of the rest of the chapeau, including the last sentence which also makes reference to a 'fair comparison'. In his opinion, an examination of the fuller context suggests that the scope of Article 2.4 is limited to that of price comparability and adjustments and not that of an enlarged scope encompassing Article 9.3 administrative reviews. As a result, the panelist declared that he 'finds there to be strong grounds to doubt the broad interpretation of the scope of the "fair comparison" requirement made by previous Panels and the Appellate Body'.[65]

Yet, despite apparently holding the view that past Panels and the AB got it wrong on the first question, this panelist did not go so far as to declare his disagreement vehemently. Instead of trying to convince his fellow panelists to join him in challenging the correctness of the past rulings, or expressing a dissent (had he failed in this endeavor), the panelist resigned himself to accepting the subordinate role of the Panel in the WTO dispute-settlement hierarchy. He noted, despite his intellectual objections, 'that, on balance, and in light of the systemic considerations [concerning security and predictability in WTO dispute settlement proceedings], the view of the Appellate Body should be followed on this issue'.[66] This reflects the

62 Panel Report, *US–Orange Juice (Brazil)*, para. 7.142.

63 Ibid (emphasis added). Note that the Panel further added in footnote 240 the clarification that this does not mean 'that a "comparison" between export price and normal value is *required* in *all* anti-dumping proceedings'.

64 Ibid., para. 7.143.

65 Ibid.

66 Ibid.

extent to which the norm of a *de facto* vertical *stare decisis* has taken hold in the mind of panelists, at least with respect to an issue such as zeroing where the AB has made its position adamantly clear.

Is this behavior to be welcomed? On the one hand, where countless litigation resources have been expended on this single topic of zeroing and where the AB has clearly indicated its willingness to overturn Panel rulings that are inconsistent with its prior rulings, perhaps it is the right call. Doing so avoids the cost of yet another appeal on a topic already adjudicated in an earlier case. Yet, on the other hand, in establishing the AB, countries explicitly rejected modeling the WTO dispute-settlement regime along the lines of a common-law regime where the rulings of an appellate court carry the weight of *stare decisis*. Among the advantages of the WTO model is that it gives future Panels the power to reexamine previously decided questions and to highlight ways in which past Panels and the AB may have erred. But this advantage holds only if panelists actually exert this power. Where they find themselves unwilling to do so out of fear that they will be overturned by the AB, then it is the regime itself that suffers.

On balance, we find that on this particular question, the panelist's behavior is, from a pragmatic perspective, the right course of action. By highlighting his intellectual disagreement, he is drawing attention to arguments that the past AB ruling on this question may be wrong. In that sense, he is not abdicating his responsibility to raise questions about the correctness of past rulings. Yet, on this particular question, he recognizes that, even were his view to prevail, this would be immaterial to the outcome of this dispute. Even if the US's actions on simple zeroing were found not to violate Article 2.4 of the ADA because the scope of the provision's 'fair comparison' requirement does not encompass the proceedings at hand, the US zeroing practices are still likely to be inconsistent with other WTO obligations, namely Article 9.3 of the ADA and Article VI:2 of the GATT 1994. Thus, the outcome of this dispute does not turn on this question per se. To flag the issues for the AB to reconsider at a later date, if necessary, seems to be the right call, at least when compared to the alternative of forcing all sides to march yet again down the road of expending resources for an appeal where the overall outcome will not change, even if this question is decided differently. We would disagree, were it the case that we would expect many more future challenges on this same legal question. In that situation, the importance of getting the law right would outweigh any questions of resources. But in this particular instance, the odds of such future challenges appear to be minimal, given the recent changes announced in US zeroing practices.

On the second question of whether the use of W–T simple-zeroing methodology in assessing the anti-dumping duty in Article 9.3.1 administrative reviews actually violated Article 2.4, again, the Panel recognized the shadow of the AB's past ruling in *US–Zeroing (Japan)*. It highlighted the fact that the AB had previously found that the use of W–T simple-zeroing methodology was not fair because it 'would result in duty collection from importers in excess of the margin of dumping established in accordance with Article 2'.[67] This Panel, as a result, decided the question the same way, noting that its decision was based in part on its 'taking into account important systemic concerns'.[68] This, of course, is shorthand for stating that it again did not wish to disturb the 'security and predictability' of WTO jurisprudence on this question, given that the AB had already ruled on it and would likely overrule any disagreement with its ruling.

Yet, again, the Panel expressed some reservation with the correctness of the AB's prior ruling. It signaled its agreement with the US argument that the concept of 'fairness' is highly malleable and context-dependent.[69] The Panel highlighted language from the *US–Softwood Lumber V* Panel suggesting that were the W–T simple zeroing as well as the W–W model-zeroing methodologies both acceptable, then even if the W–T approach resulted in a higher margin than the W–W approach, it could not be deemed inherently unfair.[70] In contrast, were the former prohibited but the latter accepted, then it would be unfair. Thus, according to the Panel, the second question turns on the question whether the W–T simple-zeroing methodology is an acceptable mode of comparison under the ADA.[71]

The Panel then pointed out that the AB, upon examining this question in past disputes, had answered this question in the negative. Yet, the Panel's decision reads more like a resignation of the fact that the Panel is constrained by the AB's prior answer than an enthusiastic affirmation of the AB's interpretation. Relying on the interpretation norms of the Vienna Convention on the Law of Treaties, the Panel first highlighted the fact that there is textual ambiguity. The Panel declared, 'In our view, the language of Article 2.1 of the AD Agreement and Article VI:1 of the GATT 1994 is drafted in such general terms that render both provisions potentially capable of either of the two conceptions of "dumping" advanced by the parties' – with one being that comparisons must be made for a product on the whole (i.e., W–W model zeroing) and the other that they can also be transaction-specific (i.e., W–T simple zeroing).[72]

Given this textual ambiguity, the Panel then turned to the object and purpose of the agreement. The Panel elaborated on several reasons why it thought the drafters of the provision may have viewed a transaction-specific approach as acceptable. First, the Panel noted that GATT negotiators and ADA negotiators may have

67 Ibid, para. 7.146 (citing Appellate Body Report, *US–Zeroing (Japan)*, para. 168).
68 Ibid, para. 7.153.
69 Ibid., para. 7.152.
70 Ibid., para. 7.151 (citing Panel Report, *US–Softwood Lumber V*, para. 5.74).
71 Ibid., para. 7.153.
72 Ibid., para. 7.91.

viewed the term 'product' as having a transaction-specific meaning, since they clearly had expressed such a view when using the term in other treaty provisions outside of the anti-dumping context.[73] Second, the Panel also noted that an approach which required only a product-on-the-whole approach (i.e., W–W model zeroing) for Article 9.3.1 retrospective reviews of anti-dumping duties 'seems to be incongruent and not in keeping with how prospective normal value systems have traditionally operated'.[74] Third, on the historical background to this issue, the Panel expressed 'sympathy for the view that a transaction-specific notion of "dumping" was recognized by the Contracting Parties to the GATT 1947' which subsequently signed the Tokyo Round Anti-Dumping Code.[75] The Panel then concluded that its analysis strongly suggests that the 'Members held, if not accepted, differing views about what "dumping" meant at the time of the closure of the Uruguay Round'.[76]

In short, the Panel was not convinced that W–T simple zeroing was necessarily forbidden and that the only acceptable methodology is the W–W model-zeroing approach. But having seen other Panels challenge the AB's interpretation only to be overturned, the Panel did not dare to pick yet another fight with the AB. It went about as far as it could go in terms of expressing its doubts about the wisdom of the AB's prior judgment, only to then concede that it would follow the AB's prior ruling, since the AB has made its views clear. In short, the Panel acquiesced to the AB's decision on the legal question because doing so would best guarantee the 'security and predictability' of the WTO dispute-settlement system.[77]

Again, while not bound by vertical *stare decisis*, the Panel report in *US–Orange Juice (Brazil)* indicates the influential power that past AB rulings have on future Panel decisions. Even where the Panel may disagree with the AB's past jurisprudence, it may decide that the costs of raising a challenge are too great and damaging to the system for it to bother. This is especially true in an issue such as zeroing, where the questions have been litigated repeatedly and the AB has stuck to its position firmly despite Panel challenges. Instead, as this Panel has done, the panelists may simply articulate their doubts, but, at the end of the day, follow the AB's approach because of the need for 'security and predictability' in dispute settlement.

73 Ibid., para. 7.108 (noting how 'the drafters of the GATT understood the meaning of the word 'product' could have a transaction-specific meaning in the particular context of customs valuation, which in turn also suggests that it cannot be categorically excluded that negotiators may have held the same view about the meaning of 'product' when it appears' in the ADA and GATT Article VI).

74 Ibid., para. 7.112.

75 Ibid., para. 7.124.

76 Ibid., para. 7.126.

77 Ibid., para. 7.133.

4. The economics of zeroing: anything left to say?

The textbook illustration of dumping in international trade usually compares a firm's pricing behavior across two national markets or the price in the export market with the fair value of the product (often measured by its cost of production with a reasonable allowance for profit). As is well known, if a firm is confronted with different demand conditions in two countries (usually captured by differences in the elasticity of demand), then it is optimal for it to engage in international price discrimination. When such discrimination manifests itself as a lower price in the foreign market, the firm is said to be 'dumping'.

The international-price-discrimination-based textbook illustration of dumping is special in many regards. Perhaps its most important limitation is that it presents a *snapshot* comparison of two distinct prices at a point in time. Given only two prices, determining dumping becomes a trivial task: is the price abroad lower than that in the firm's domestic market or not? Of course, in the real world, firms export and sell domestically over multiple time periods, and changes in underlying market conditions often necessitate price adjustments on their part.

In a world of multiple price observations, the most obvious way to define dumping over any particular time period requires a method for aggregating all of the price observations within that time period. At its core, WTO disputes over zeroing – of which there have been many – reflect a disagreement with respect to the method used for *aggregating the information* contained in a particular set of price observations.

An example helps.

Example 1: Suppose a Brazilian firm exports to the US market for four time periods (for instance, months) and alters its price once every period. Furthermore, let the firm's price in Brazil (when converted to dollars) or the fair normal value of its product be constant over this time period at $65 per unit.

Suppose further for simplicity that the firm exports 50 units of output in each time period. The value of total exports over all four periods is easily calculated to be $13,000.

Table 2 shows how the firm's price in the US changes over the relevant time horizon.

Table 2. Effects of zeroing

Time period	US price	Units of US Sales	Dumping margin	Dumping margin with zeroing
1	$50	50	$15	$15
2	$80	50	$–15	$0
3	$80	50	$–15	$0
4	$50	50	$15	$15

According to Table 2, the firm is dumping in the US in periods 1 and 4 but not in periods 2 and 3. The weighted average dumping margin (WADM) can be easily calculated by weighing the DM in each period by the associated export sales and dividing by the value of total export sales. Given the information in Table 2, the WADM equals zero, since the positive dumping margins (DMs) in periods 1 and 4 exactly offset the negative ones in periods 2 and 3 and sales are equal across all periods. Since the WADM is zero (rather than positive), a dumping investigation based on it would find that no dumping has occurred.

How does zeroing fit into the process? The practice of zeroing essentially assigns zeros to all negative dumping margins when calculating the WADM, which in turn has repercussions for both the determination of dumping as well as the level of anti-dumping duty that is eventually imposed. In this example, if the dumping margin in periods 2 and 3 is set to zero, the WADM ends up being 11.54%, which would indicate that the firm is indeed dumping in the US market. Thus, if the dumping investigation incorporates zeroing, then it finds dumping even though the WADM in the absence of zeroing actually equals zero.

For economists, who are generally quite opposed to anti-dumping (and for good reason), the practice of zeroing seems to make a bad policy even worse. As such, it is difficult to conceive of *any* circumstances under which zeroing can help reduce the harm caused by anti-dumping. As Example 1 indicates, it is conceptually clear that zeroing can lead an importing nation to find in favor of dumping even when there is no dumping on average. Furthermore, by inflating the dumping margin, zeroing can also lead to higher anti-dumping duties.

In addition to these well-understood points, Bown and Prusa (2011) make two additional observations about the consequences of zeroing. First, zeroing tends to treat the price in the firm's domestic market (or the fair market value) different from what it actually is. This is because whenever the firm's foreign price is above that in its domestic market, a zeroing policy enacted by the foreign country treats the firm's price there as being the same as its price in its domestic market since, by definition, zeroing sets the dumping margin to zero for such pairs of price observations. Such manipulation of market data is problematic for obvious reasons. Second, they correctly note that 'zeroing is driven by price variations' and that if 'the foreign firm charged exactly the same price for all transactions, then zeroing would not matter'. Thus, to understand the consequences of zeroing, one needs to take a closer look at the causes and consequences of price variations (which we do below).

What arguments do supporters of zeroing make in its defense? Perhaps the most common argument is based on an analogy between zeroing and speeding. Briefly speaking, according to this rationale, it is appropriate to disregard periods of negative dumping margins, since these do no harm to domestic industry, just as driving below the speed limit does not generate undue risks for others (assuming that the speeding limit is optimally chosen by society with that goal in mind to begin with). When a driver speeds by a traffic police car, all previous driving instances where the driver *did not* break the speed limit do not affect the police officer's decision to determine whether or not a traffic violation has occurred at that particular instant. Such a course of conduct on the part of the police officer is reasonable because *each and every speeding incident* has the potential to cause serious harm to others. But is dumping like speeding? In other words, by charging a low price for a day (or even a month), can a foreign firm cause material damage to the local industry? In our view, in their analysis of *Softwood V* zeroing case between Canada and the US, Bown and Sykes (2008) correctly note that 'individual transactions at "dumped" prices are generally of no concern whatsoever. They are simply not analogous to dangerous behaviors such as speeding that are properly subjection to sanction.'

Indeed, for the speeding analogy to be a suitable defense of zeroing, a single instance of dumping ought to be sufficient to do significant damage to domestic. It is difficult to conceive of any real market in which this would be true. Even the typical monopolization concern with respect to dumping (often expressed in the somewhat sensationalistic phrase 'predatory dumping') is not credible in the context of an isolated instance of dumping. As Bown and Sykes (2008) note, 'anti-dumping duties are routinely used in industries where monopolization concerns are fanciful'. Indeed, if a foreign firm were to charge a very low price for a short time with the intention of driving out a domestic competitor, it is unlikely to make much headway, since the domestic competitor will not shut down even when it is suffering losses in the short run, since it would want to avoid having to incur entry/start-up costs in the future. And if the low price charged by the foreign firm were to be permanent, there is again no reason to impose an anti-dumping duty, since a country imports precisely those goods that other countries can produce more cheaply than it can. The possibility of harm exists only in a limited set of circumstances where the foreign firm is able to sustain a low price for a considerable period so as to chase the domestic competitors out of the market and then erect high barriers to entry, so as to preserve a monopoly on the market. In practice, this is difficult to execute, especially with the penalties under competition laws serving a deterrent against any such action.

Despite the fact that most economic commentators tend to agree that anti-dumping is simply another form of protectionism that should be generally avoided and that, if used, dumping ought to be defined on the basis of all price observations that span the relevant time period, the WTO's dispute-settlement process has struggled to come to terms with the appropriate definition of dumping. Indeed, even informed parties have disagreed over this issue: as we noted earlier, the decisions of previous WTO Panels that have decided zeroing disputes have often been over-turned by the Appellate Body (AB), which has repeatedly ruled that the notion of dumping applies to the 'product as a whole' and ought to be based on the *entire set of price observations* over the relevant time period. Thus, the AB has ruled that a country cannot pick and choose price observations in a manner that is unambiguously biased in favor of finding dumping. As should be clear from the discussion above, we are in agreement with this position of the AB, at least generally in contexts where transaction-specific considerations are not mentioned in the ADA, even though several WTO Panels have struggled with the issue and expressed skepticism over the AB's approach.

As we noted above, many analysts have noted that zeroing inflates dumping margins and thereby leads to more affirmative findings of dumping and the eventual application of higher anti-dumping duties. What we want to argue next is that the issue is not just that of ignoring instances where prices are high on average; it may also be important to account for *why* prices fluctuate in the first place. In particular, the consequences of zeroing when price fluctuations are driven by changes in market demand conditions, are likely to be somewhat different than when they are driven by changes in costs of accessing foreign markets (for instance, due to changes in factor markets, technology, transportation costs/trade barriers, or the exchange rate).

As we will demonstrate below, this distinction matters. If high prices in export markets are caused by increases in demand, then they are correlated with high export sales; whereas when they are caused by an increase in costs of exporting, they are correlated with low export sales. We show below that the nature of this correlation between prices and export sales affects the WADM in a way that makes zeroing a relatively more insidious policy than when price fluctuations are driven by changes in market demand as opposed to costs. Thus, the relative harm done by zeroing would be greater in the former scenario.

Consider first the case where prices changes are driven by variations in market demand over time.

Example 2 (when demand changes drive prices): Let the demand curve in the US during periods of low demand (periods 1 and 4) be given by $p = 100 - q$ while that in periods of high demand (periods 2 and 3) by $p = 160 - q$. For simplicity, normalize the marginal cost (MC) of exporting to zero and consider the price decisions of a Brazilian firm.

The profit-maximizing Brazilian firm sets marginal revenue equal to marginal cost, which means that in periods of high demand it solves $MR = 160 - 2q = MC = 0$. This implies that the firm's exports to the US in periods 2 and 3 equal 80 units each. Similarly, in periods 1 and 4 it solves $100 - 2q = 0$, which gives its exports as $q = 50$. As can be observed from Table 3 below, price in the US market equals \$50 in periods 1 and 4 and \$80 in periods 2 and 3 (found by solving the relevant demand curves for p, given the firm's sales). The total value of exports over all four periods equals \$17,800.

As in Example 1, let the firm's price in its home market (i.e., Brazil) be constant at \$65, because demand is assumed to not fluctuate there over time. Given this, the firm's dumping margin (DM) in the US is positive in periods 1 and 4 (it equals \$15), whereas it is negative in periods 2 and 3 and (it equals \$–15). Thus, the firm dumps in periods 1 and 4 but not in periods 2 and 3.

Table 3. Effects of zeroing when demand changes drive price changes

Time period	US price	Units of US sales	Dumping margin	Dumping margin with zeroing
1	\$50	50	\$15	\$15
2	\$80	80	\$–15	\$0
3	\$80	80	\$–15	\$0
4	\$50	50	\$15	\$15

Using the information in Table 3, the WADM is calculated to be –5.1%. Thus, a dumping determination based on either the WADM would find in favor of the firm (i.e., that no dumping occurred in the US).

With zeroing, however, the negative DMs are excluded from the calculation and the ADM as well as the WADM under zeroing end up being 8.4%, which would then indicate that dumping did occur.

A comparison of Examples 1 and 2 yields two insights. First, the WADM is lower in Example 2 even though prices are the same in both cases. This is intuitive: high price observations are accompanied by higher sales levels in Example 2 and therefore carry a greater weight when calculating the WADM. Second, zeroing tends to inflate the WADM to a greater degree in Example 2 (from –5.1% to 8.4%) precisely because it drops observations that carry more weight in the absence of zeroing.

Now consider the case where the changes in export prices are induced by fluctuations in the cost of exporting.

> *Example 3 (when cost changes drive prices):* Suppose US market demand in all periods is given by $p = 100 - q$. Further suppose that the MC of exporting fluctuates over time. In periods 1 and 4, MC equals zero (as in example 1) while in periods 2 and 3 it equals \$60.
>
> From Example 1, we know that the firm's sales in periods 1 and 4 equal 50 units each with the associated price of \$50. In periods 2 and 3, the firm's exports are found by solving $MR = 100 - 2q = 60$ which gives $q = 20$ and $p = 100 - 20 = \$80$.
>
> Observe that, by design, the price levels over the four periods are the same across all three examples: in periods 1 and 4 the price equals \$50, whereas in periods 2 and 3 it equals \$80. However, in the current example, the high prices in periods 2 and 3 are associated with *lower* sales levels of 20 each, whereas in Example 2 they are associated with *higher* sales levels of 80 each.

Table 4 presents the relevant calculations for this example.

Using the information contained in Tables 3 and 4, it is easy to show that even though the price observations are the same in both cases, the WADM is not. When demand variations drive price changes (i.e., in Table 3), the WADM is actually −5.1% (without zeroing), whereas it is 11.0% when price variations are induced by cost changes (i.e., in Table 4). In other words, a dumping investigation based on

Table 4. Effects of zeroing when cost changes drive price changes

Time period	US price	Units of US sales	Dumping margin	Dumping margin with zeroing
1	$50	50	$15	$15
2	$80	20	$–15	$0
3	$80	20	$–15	$0
4	$50	50	$15	$15

the WADM in Example 2 would *not* find dumping, whereas it would find dumping in the current example even though the observed prices are the same in both cases!

Intuitively, when demand increases drive price changes, the high price observations (i.e., those for which the DM is negative) end up receiving a greater weight in the calculation of the WADM relative to the case where cost changes are the driving factor.

An important observation can be made from Tables 3 and 4: while zeroing leads to a reversal in the sign of the WADM under the demand case (from –5.1% to 8.4%), it does not do so under the cost case (where the WADM goes from 11% to 18.3%). *Thus, zeroing is more likely to convert a negative finding regarding dumping into a positive one when price changes result from demand changes as opposed to cost changes.*

While the two examples are rather specific, the insight that they are based on is fairly general: when zeroing eliminates high price observations with larger export volumes, it will tend to do more damage relative to the case where it eliminates high price observations with smaller export volumes.

Which of these two scenarios is more applicable in a particular case would depend upon the context. In the present case, weather shocks in the US reduced the output of local OJ producers, thereby leaving larger residual demand for Brazilian exporters. Thus, it was a negative supply shock to the domestic OJ industry in the US that translated into a larger residual demand curve facing Brazilian exporters, which in turn led to an increase in their exports. Furthermore, it is well known that the material-injury test applied during dumping investigations is often based on rising import volumes doing serious harm to domestic industry (as opposed to falling import volumes). This suggests that the demand scenario described in Example 2 might be more relevant for a typical anti-dumping case relative to the cost scenario described in Example 3.[78] Of course, zeroing tends to have the strongest effect on the outcome of the dumping investigation precisely when it

78 Of course, reductions in the cost of exporting can also lead foreign exporters to increase their sales volumes but such increases in sales would be accompanied by price decreases as opposed to price increases. As a result, such observations would *not* be dropped under a zeroing policy.

eliminates high price observations associated with large export sales by foreign sellers.

5. Resolving the orange-juice dispute

The US chose not to appeal the Panel's rulings. On 28 December 2010, a few months before the Panel decision was rendered, the US DOC had already issued a notice, pursuant to Section 123(g) of the Uruguay Round Agreement Act, seeking comments on a proposal to modify its methodology for calculating anti-dumping margins and duty assessments involving the elimination of zeroing.[79] With this policy shift already underway, the US did not find it necessary to appeal the Panel's decision, especially given that the AB had already made its position on the legal issues clear in prior rulings.

On 17 June 2011, the Dispute Settlement Body adopted the Panel's recommendations and rulings. The US was given until 17 March 2012, to implement the recommendations and rulings. A month prior to this deadline, the US DOC issued its policy change that discontinued the use of zeroing in administrative reviews, new shipper reviews, expedited anti-dumping reviews, and sunset reviews.[80] As noted earlier, the US did so in order to avoid retaliation from the EU and Japan stemming from the earlier WTO zeroing cases. The US then informed the WTO that the policy modification also addressed the outstanding issues in this dispute.

At the same time, the US ITC was engaged in a sunset review of the anti-dumping order against certain Brazilian orange juice. This review resulted in an ITC decision in March 2012 to terminate the anti-dumping duties on Brazilian orange juice altogether; the termination was to be effective as of 9 March 2011.[81] Based on the US DOC policy change on zeroing and the ITC's decision to terminate anti-dumping duties on Brazilian orange juice altogether, the two countries entered into an agreement on 3 April 2012, stating that they had resolved their dispute.[82]

From an economics standpoint, there was little justification for the anti-dumping duties against Brazilian orange juice or the use of zeroing in determining and calculating those duties. At no point did Brazilian orange-juice producers pose an anti-competitive threat. As noted earlier, at the start of the imposition of anti-dumping duties, the Brazilian share of the US domestic orange-juice market

79 'Anti-Dumping Proceedings: Calculation of the Weighted Average Dumping Margin and Assessment Rate in Certain Anti-Dumping Duty Proceedings', 75 Fed. Reg. 81533 (28 December 2010).

80 'Anti-Dumping Proceedings: Calculation of the Weighted-Average Dumping Margin and Assessment Rate in Certain Anti-Dumping Duty Proceedings', Final Modification, 77 Fed. Reg. 8101 (14 February 2012).

81 US International Trade Commission, 'USITC Makes Determination in Five-Year (Sunset) Review Concerning Certain Orange Juice from Brazil, Press Release, 14 March 2012); 'Revocation of Anti-dumping Duty Order: Certain Orange Juice from Brazil', 77 Fed. Reg. 23659 (20 April 2012).

82 'Understanding Between Brazil and the United States Regarding Procedures Under Articles 21 and 22 of the DSU, WT/DS382/11' (10 April 2012).

hovered around 15%. Moreover, the share was not steadily increasing. Instead, it had fluctuated – increasing to 15.9% in crop year 2002–03, before falling to 10.7% in 2003–04, before rising back up again the following year.[83] Nor were the anti-dumping duties particularly effective in stemming the flow of Brazilian orange juice into the American market. Even after the preliminary anti-dumping duties were imposed in 2005, Brazilian orange-juice imports continued to rise. In 2007, the US imported a record $270 million in frozen Brazilian orange juice. This represented more than a doubling from the $129 million imported in 2002, and a more than three-fold increase over the recent low of $85 million in 2004.[84]

Such fluctuations are not surprising given that round oranges, the variety most commonly used for producing orange juice, are a highly perishable commodity. Supply conditions in orange-juice production are intimately linked to variations in the crop volume of round oranges. This link is so strong that growers of round oranges were found by the ITC to be part of the domestic industry when making its injury determination. As the dissenting commissioners in the ITC's injury investigation noted 'the impact of weather and other factors on the US crop resulted in significant volatility in US round orange production during the period examined'.[85] It was this underlying volatility, rather than any anti-competitive behavior, that indirectly led to changes in imports of orange juice from Brazil via its effect on domestic production of orange juice in the US.[86] When crop volumes of domestic round oranges fall, Brazilian orange-juice imports increase, even if anti-dumping duties raise costs. The main effect of the anti-dumping duties in this instance was not protection for American orange-juice producers, but rather higher prices for downstream American consumers.

Therefore, it is clear that the anti-dumping duties against certain Brazilian orange juice were not economically necessary nor were they welfare-enhancing. Moreover, since zeroing in administrative reviews, at least in the early years, was practiced in the face of increasing export volumes due largely to demand changes resulting from exogenous shocks (in the supply of round oranges), we suggest that the damage from zeroing was greater in this context than it would be in others. The termination of anti-dumping duties for certain Brazilian orange juice is therefore welcome news. It has, along with other market forces, brought orange-juice futures down 40% in 2012, which should be welcome news for consumers.[87]

83 See Table IV-5 in USITC (2006).

84 See UN Comtrade database for HS-200911.

85 USITC (2006) at 39.

86 Ibid. This view finds support in the empirical analysis of Carter and Mohapatra (2006) who find that FCOJ imports from Brazil were larger when domestic supplies in the US were relatively low. Similarly, they also find a strong negative correlation between domestic FCOJ inventories in the US and imports from Brazil. Finally, they show that imports of FCOJ from Brazil did not have a significant impact on the price of orange juice in the US over the relevant time period, a finding that is consistent with the position of dissenting USITC commissioners.

87 Wexler (2012).

6. Concluding thoughts: so is this the end of the WTO zeroing disputes?

Does *US–Orange Juice (Brazil)*, along with *US–Shrimp (Vietnam)*,[88] represent the end of the zeroing disputes at the WTO? Technically, the answer remains no. Four cases remain pending before the WTO concerning US zeroing practices: *US–Zeroing (Korea)*, *US–Carbon Steel Flat Products (Korea)*, *US–Shrimp and Diamond Sawblades (China)*, and *US–Frozen Warmwater Shrimp (Vietnam)*.

Yet, the DOC's announcement on 14 February 2012, that it would discontinue the practice of zeroing in administrative reviews (under Article 9.3.1 of the ADA) as well as new shipper reviews, expedited anti-dumping reviews, and sunset reviews will certainly lessen the probability of further conflicts. The era of major substantive battles over US zeroing practices may be drawing to a close.

Two points are worth noting. In order to enjoy the benefits of the DOC's policy eliminating zeroing in administrative reviews, foreign producers subject to anti-dumping duties must request a review during the window of the product's annual review. By placing the impetus on producers rather than making this review automatic, larger foreign producers with the financial means to request and participate in the annual retrospective reviews are placed at an advantage. The smaller producers that fail to expend resources to call for an administrative review in which zeroing is not done will still find themselves subject to CDRs calculated on the basis of zeroing. Countries should therefore seek to ensure that all their exporters subject to anti-dumping duties will seek an administrative review and assist smaller exporters, who may be resource constrained, with such reviews. Otherwise, the effects of zeroing may continue to linger on.

Second, even if the zeroing disputes disappear altogether, the issue is not altogether dead. The US continues to seek, albeit with little or no support, a clarification that zeroing is allowed through Doha Round negotiations. To the extent that the ghost of zeroing continues to hover, it will be increasingly in the rooms of the Rules Negotiation.

Still, in light of the fact that a US negotiating proposal on zeroing is unlikely to succeed, when the history of zeroing is written years from now, what may be most significant about *US–Orange Juice (Brazil)* may not be the decision itself, but the way in which the Panel flagged concerns about past AB decisions without openly disagreeing. On a longstanding issue, the Panel, though not bound by the AB, recognized and accepted its subordinate role. In doing so, it helped deliver yet another nail in the coffin of the WTO's longest-running dispute-settlement drama.

88 *United States – Anti-Dumping Measures on Certain Shrimp from Vietnam*, DS404.

References

Bown, C. P. and A. O. Sykes (2008), 'The Zeroing Issue: A Critical Analysis of Softwood V', *World Trade Review*, 7(1): 121–42.

Bown, C. P. and T. J. Prusa (2011), 'US Anti-dumping: Much Ado About Zeroing', in W. J. Martin and A. Mattoo (eds.), *Unfinished Business? The WTO's Doha Agenda*, London: CEPR and World Bank, pp. 355–92.

Carter, C. and S. Mohapatra (2006), 'The Sunshine State versus Brazil: Economics of Orange Juice Trade', Department of Agricultural and Resource Economics, University of California.

Crowley, M. and R. Howse (2010), 'US–Stainless Steel (Mexico)', *World Trade Review*, 9(1): 117–50.

Hispanically Speaking News (2011), 'Brazil Will Allow Merger of Orange Juice Companies', 15 December 2011, available at http://www.hispanicallyspeakingnews.com/notitas-de-noticias/details/brazil-will-allow-merger-of-orange-juice-companies/12583/.

Kiernan, P. and B. McKay (2012), 'Coke, Pepsi Attempt to Ease O.J. Fears', *Wall Street Journal*, 13 January: B1.

Prusa, T. J. and L. Ribini (forthcoming), 'United States – Use of Zeroing in Anti-Dumping Measures Involving Products From Korea: It's Déjà Vu All Over Again', *World Trade Review*.

Prusa, T. J. and E. Vermulst (2009), 'A One-Two Punch on Zeroing: *US–Zeroing (EC)* and *US–Zeroing (Japan)*', *World Trade Review*, 8(1): 187–241.

Prusa, T. J. and E. Vermulst (2011), 'United States – Continued Existence and Application of Zeroing Methodology: The End of Zeroing?', *World Trade Review*, 10(1): 45–61.

Sterns, J. A. and T. H. Spreen (2010), 'Evaluating Sustainable Competitive Advantages in Brazilian and US Processed Citrus Supply Chains: An Application of Porter's Diamond Framework', *International Journal on Food System Dynamics*, 2: 167–75.

United States Department of Agriculture (USDA) (2007), 'Orange Juice: Foreign Agricultural Service, World Markets and Trade Report.'

US International Trade Commission (USITC) (2006), '*Certain Orange Juice From Brazil*', Publication 3838, Washington, DC.

Wexler, A. (2012), 'Orange Juice Feels Supply–Demand Squeeze', *Wall Street Journal*, 18 May: B4.

White, A. and L. Kassai (2011), 'Citrovita, Citrosuco Win EU Approval For Orange-Juice Deal', May 4, available at http://www.bloomberg.com/news/2011-05-04/citrovita-citrosuco-win-eu-approval-for-orange-juice-deal.html.

CHAPTER 19

World Trade Review (2014), 13: 2, 299–320
 doi:10.1017/S147474561400007X

What is not so Cool about *US–COOL* Regulations? A critical analysis of the Appellate Body's ruling on *US–COOL*

PETROS C. MAVROIDIS*
EUI, Florence
KAMAL SAGGI
Vanderbilt University

Abstract: In *US–COOL*, the Appellate Body (AB) of the World Trade Organization (WTO) found that the US measure imposing country of origin labelling (COOL) requirements on livestock of domestic, foreign, and mixed origin was in violation of the obligation to avoid discrimination embedded in Article 2.1 of the WTO Agreement on Technical Barriers to Trade (TBT). We argue that the AB could not and should not have reached this decision based on the information available to it. The AB adopted an erroneous methodology: under its view, the consistency of a measure coming under the purview of the TBT can be examined under Article 2.1 irrespective of its evaluation under Article 2.2 thereby making the two obligations distinct. The AB also failed to address the central question raised by this dispute: Does there exist an alternative to COOL that is less trade restrictive? We argue that the over-arching issue in this case should have been to determine what, if anything, the TBT Agreement did to alter or enhance the obligation of non-discrimination that was already embedded in the arsenal of the multilateral trading rules. Unless the AB asks this question in subsequent case law pertaining to the TBT, we risk seeing repetitions of similar mistakes in the future.

1. The Facts of *US–COOL*

Up until 2011, *EC–Sardines* was the only dispute that could qualify as a 'core TBT dispute'. While claims under the WTO Agreement on Technical Barriers to Trade (TBT Agreement) had been raised in numerous other disputes that came under the aegis of *General Agreement on Tariffs and Trade* (GATT), these claims were typically of a peripheral nature as opposed to being at the core of such disputes[1]. *EC–Sardines* dealt with some of the key provisions of the

* Email: Petros.Mavroidis@unine.ch
We are highly indebted to Carlo-Maria Cantore, Aaron Cosbey, Bernard M. Hoekman, Rob Howse, Phil Levy, Juan-Alberto Marchetti, and Alan O. Sykes for helpful discussions.
1 Horn *et al.* (2011).

TBT Agreement[2], while leaving some important questions (such as the understanding of the necessity and the non-discrimination disciplines in the TBT Agreement) totally un-interpreted. In 2011, three cases were adjudicated almost simultaneously: *US–Clove Cigarettes*; *US–Tuna II (Mexico)*; and, *US–COOL*. The scope of these disputes was more comprehensive than that of *EC–Sardines*, and WTO adjudicating bodies had to deal with almost all key provisions appearing in the TBT Agreement[3]. The three Panel reports adopted irreconcilable approaches with respect to the interpretation of key terms such as 'like products'.[4] As a result, the task of the Appellate Body (AB) became quite demanding. At the same time, however, *US–COOL* was a good opportunity for the AB to establish a coherent test for consistency with the TBT Agreement. Alas, it seems to have failed to take advantage of this opportunity. In this paper we argue this position by critically evaluating the AB report on *US–COOL*, a dispute filed by Canada and Mexico challenging certain recent US regulations concerning the labelling of meat products.[5]

Via the 2008 Farm Bill, the US adopted legislation (i.e. a technical regulation) aimed at informing consumers about the origin of meat products, and to this effect imposed labelling requirements that distinguished four categories of meat products, two of which referred to meat products wholly obtained from (i.e. born, raised, and slaughtered) within the US (category A) or abroad (category D), and two others that covered meat products originating in more than one country (categories B and C, which cover meat obtained from a cow say raised in Mexico, and slaughtered in the US). While both labels B and C indicate multiple sources of origin, there is an important distinction between them: meat sold under label C is derived from animals imported to the US for immediate slaughter, whereas that under label B is not, with 'immediate' defined as within two weeks of being imported into the US.

As is clear, the information disseminated via COOL concerned three stages in the production of meat: place of birth of the animal, where it had been raised, and where it was slaughtered. The COOL statute permitted the use of a common label if livestock with different labels were 'commingled' in feedlots and/or slaughterhouses on a single production day. For example, label B could be used if there was commingling between livestock with labels A and B. As a result of rules pertaining to commingling, meat sold under label B could actually have come from an animal with 100% US origin. This possibility was seen by the Panel to be relevant for determining whether *US–COOL* conveyed accurate and clear information to consumers.

2 Horn and Weiler (2007) provide an excellent survey and critical analysis of the issues discussed.
3 The only area of the TBT Agreement that case law has not yet dealt with is conformity assessment.
4 Howse and Levy (2012) offer a masterful critical discussion of the three Panel reports.
5 COOL stands for 'country of origin labelling'.

Mexico and Canada successfully challenged the COOL measure, arguing that it was both unnecessary, as well as discriminatory; a claim challenging the legitimacy of the objective pursued was also submitted by the complainants. The Panel found that the COOL measure violated Article 2.1 of the TBT because it afforded 'imported livestock treatment less favourable than that accorded to like domestic livestock' and also Article 2.2 of the same Agreement because it did not 'fulfil the objective of providing consumer information on origin with respect to meat products'. Thus, while the Panel did find that providing consumers more information was a legitimate objective for introducing technical regulations to that effect, its judgement was that the US policy resulted in 'de facto' discrimination by changing the 'conditions of competition' against imports while also failing to meet its intended objective since the 'COOL measure falls short of providing consumers with information on the country of origin of meat products in an accurate and clear manner'.

In Section 2, we explain briefly the legal discipline imposed on WTO Members by the TBT Agreement, as well as the findings of the AB. Section 3 includes our critical evaluation of the AB report. In this section, we adopt the methodology of the AB without questioning its usefulness and/or rationality, and explain why, in our view, the AB should not have decided the case as it did even within the four corners of its preferred methodology. In Section 4, we move to a more normative discussion, and present our own preferred methodology. Here, we argue that the AB should not have imported the GATT method of analysis 'lock, stock, and barrel' into the TBT Agreement, but should have first inquired about the underlying objectives of the TBT Agreement and only then applied its legal test to the facts of the case. Section 5 recaps our main conclusions.

We next discuss the findings of the AB that were called into play because different aspects of the Panels' report invited appeals from the US and Canada.

2. The Findings of the AB

The AB had to address essentially three claims:

(a) whether the US measure pursued a legitimate objective;
(b) if yes, whether the US measure was necessary to achieve that objective; and
(c) whether the US measure was non-discriminatory in nature.

None of the parties appealed the Panel decision to subject the COOL measure under the coverage of the TBT Agreement. Recall that, a WTO Member must, when enacting a measure coming under the purview of the TBT Agreement ensure that it is necessary to achieve the envisaged objective, that it is applied in a non-discriminatory manner, and that it is, in principle, based on an international standard, assuming a relevant international standard exists.

Three classes of measures come under the purview of the TBT Agreement: technical regulations, standards, and conformity assessment procedures. A technical regulation is defined in the Annex to the TBT Agreement as follows:

> Document which lays down product characteristics or their related processes and production methods, including the applicable administrative provisions, with which compliance is mandatory. It may also include or deal exclusively with terminology, symbols, packaging, marking or labelling requirements as they apply to a product, process or production method.

The same Annex contains a definition of the term 'standard':

> Document approved by a recognized body, that provides, for common and repeated use, rules, guidelines or characteristics for products or related processes and production methods, with which compliance is not mandatory. It may also include or deal exclusively with terminology, symbols, packaging, marking or labelling requirements as they apply to a product, process or production method.[6]

In this case, there was no challenge against the Panel decision to classify the labelling requirements provided for in the COOL measure as a 'technical regulation'.

To gain an informed perspective on the findings of the AB (analyzed in detail below), we briefly discuss the nature of the North American market for cattle and hogs. Our discussion is based on the facts presented in Jurenas and Greene (2013). First, in this market, the US exports much less than it imports from its neighbours: in 2012, US exports of cattle and hogs to Canada and Mexico were only $48 million whereas its imports were nearly $2.1 billion (over 40 times). Second, almost all live cattle imports into the US come from its two neighbours: live hog imports come primarily from Canada while feeder cattle (i.e. cattle placed on feed lots or pasture prior to slaughter) come mostly from Mexico. Third, and perhaps most importantly, the market share of domestic meat suppliers is large: since 2000, cattle imports have accounted for only about 6% of total cattle slaughtered in the US with the figure for hogs being roughly the same. As we will see below, the overwhelming dominance of local meat suppliers was crucial for the argument of *de facto* discrimination, carrying the day in favour of the complainants.

2.1 *Was the US pursuing a legitimate objective through* US–COOL?

Article 2.2 TBT reads:

> Members shall ensure that technical regulations are not prepared, adopted or applied with a view to or with the effect of creating unnecessary obstacles to

6 In other words, the definitions of the two instruments are similar except that compliance is necessary only with technical regulations for market access to be guaranteed. The obligations regarding conformity assessment were not an issue in this dispute. An analysis of the legal obligation associated with conformity assessment is beyond the scope of this paper.

international trade. For this purpose, technical regulations shall not be more trade-restrictive than necessary to fulfil a legitimate objective, taking account of the risks non-fulfilment would create. Such legitimate objectives are, *inter alia:* national security requirements; the prevention of deceptive practices; protection of human health or safety, animal or plant life or health, or the environment. In assessing such risks, relevant elements of consideration are, *inter alia:* available scientific and technical information related processing technology or intended end-uses of products. (Italics in the original)

The objective sought through the COOL measure was discussed in §6.113 of the Panel report on *US–COOL*, where the Panel noted that:

the objective as identified by the United States was 'to provide consumer information on origin'. The Panel was not presented with the argument from the United States that the reduction of compliance costs for market participants also formed part of the objective pursued by the United States through the COOL measure. As Mexico points out, the United States submitted that reducing compliance costs was one of the factors that it considered in *implementing* the COOL measure to achieve the objective of providing consumer information on origin. Reducing compliance costs therefore cannot form part of the objective itself. (Emphasis in the original)

Typically, Panels have tended to adopt deferential attitudes (towards the regulating WTO Member) when it comes to reviewing the legitimacy of an objective pursued. In *US–COOL*, the Panel specified that the regulating state must define its objectives and pursue them in a coherent (e.g., not self-contradictory) manner, while underscoring that WTO Members remain exclusively responsible for defining the objectives pursued (§§7.611ff.). On appeal, in §372 the AB confirmed this approach and added:

With respect to the determination of the 'legitimacy' of the objective, we note first that a panel's finding that the objective is among those listed in Article 2.2 will end the inquiry into its legitimacy. If, however, the objective does not fall among those specifically listed, a panel must make a determination of legitimacy. It may be guided by considerations that we have set out above, including whether the identified objective is reflected in other provisions of the covered agreements.

In §410, the AB added:

Canada asserts that the fact that the COOL measure applies to some products that do not have USDA grade labelling, and does not apply to others that do, calls into question whether the measure really aims to prevent consumer confusion. Even if this were true, however, Canada has not explained why this would necessarily also vitiate the Panel's finding that the objective of the COOL measure is to provide consumers with information on origin.

The AB thus found that Panels do not violate their duty to perform an objective assessment when trying to identify the objectives sought through a national legislation, and that WTO Members aiming at challenging inconsistent, in their view, objectives, carry the associated burden of proof. Canada did not manage to persuade neither the Panel nor the AB that the US had violated Article 2.2 TBT in this respect.

Country of origin labels can provide useful information to consumers. Indeed, country of origin labels are used widely across the world and are sometimes even used by private retailers to signal the source of a particular product – for example, lamb from New Zealand. Presumably, consumers value such information because national origin can sometimes signal quality. But this is not the only reason why consumers might value information regarding national origin of products. For example, the 'local food' movement is motivated by social concerns having to do with the environmental externalities created by food that travels long distances. This is not to say, of course, that meat sold under label A under *US–COOL* would necessarily fit the criterion of being locally sourced from an environmental perspective: imported meat from cattle slaughtered in Mexico could be more 'local' for consumers in Texas than that sourced from a slaughterhouse in a mid-western US state. Nevertheless, consumers are free to make such choices only if national origin is indicated on the meat product, which was the main objective of the *US–COOL* statute.

From an economics perspective, the fact that the market had not resorted to widespread use of labels distinguishing US meat from Canadian and Mexican meat *prior* to COOL raises the legitimate question of whether consumers really wanted the information that is provided by COOL. While this is a fair concern, and one that was even acknowledged by the USDA, it does not, in of itself, imply that the stated intent behind the US regulation (i.e. of providing consumers with more information) was not legitimate and/or outright protectionist, as was charged by the complainants. A long and well-established literature in economics highlights how the presence of incomplete and/or asymmetric information can affect market outcomes in adverse ways and how the *market for information itself* is subject to various types of failures. Furthermore, individual consumers valuing such information may have neither the incentive nor the means to ensure that the market indeed provides it, particularly if the benefit to each individual consumer of such information is relatively small even though the collective benefit to all of them is large.

It is also worth clarifying that country of origin labelling requirements with respect to animal products had already been introduced in the US via the 2002 Farm Bill that obligated retailers to provide such information for a wide range of commodities including beef, pork, lamb, and fish. However, this 2002 Bill was silent on how products derived from animals originating *outside* the US were to be labelled; it simply restricted the US-origin label to those products that were derived totally from within (i.e. were born, raised, and slaughtered in the US as would be the case for those carrying label A under COOL). Thus, US COOL expanded this original 2002 scheme by specifying how to label meat products that were derived, at least in part, from outside the US.

2.2 *Was* US–COOL *Non-Discriminatory?*

Under Article 2.1 TBT:

> Members shall ensure that in respect of technical regulations, products imported from the territory of any Member shall be accorded treatment no less favourable than that accorded to like products of national origin and to like products originating in any other country.

The US never claimed that beef of foreign origin was unlike product to US beef. The only legal issue under Article 2.1 TBT was whether the US, through the challenged measure, was affording less favourable treatment to imported beef relative to domestic like goods. The complainants maintained that this had effectively been the case, since the requirements for multiple-origin beef were more onerous than those imposed on single-origin beef, and that, consequently, traders would favour US beef. The Panel found in §§7.349–7.350 that:

> Turning to the scenarios involving either exclusively domestic or exclusively imported livestock, it seems logical that the scenario of processing exclusively domestic livestock and meat is in general less costly and more viable than processing exclusively imported livestock. Livestock imports have been and remain small compared to overall US livestock production and demand, and US livestock demand cannot be fulfilled with exclusively foreign livestock. And even if it could be, in light of the evidence before us, it appears that this scenario would in all likelihood involve more than one foreign origin, and thus in general more segregation and higher compliance costs than processing exclusively domestic livestock, which by definition has one single origin. Also, in general, US livestock is often geographically closer to most if not all US domestic markets, so processing exclusively imported livestock and meat remains a relatively less competitive option.
>
> As a result, overall, the least costly way of complying with the COOL measure is to rely on exclusively domestic livestock. Thus, in general, business scenarios involving imported livestock, including the scenario involving exclusively imported products, are overall more costly than the exclusively Label A approach.

On appeal, the AB first noted:

> In assessing even-handedness, a panel must 'carefully scrutinize the particular circumstances of the case, that is, the design, architecture, revealing structure, operation, and application of the technical regulation at issue (§271).

Following a long discussion (§§287ff.), the AB applied this test to the specifics of the case underscoring that the existence of detrimental impact on imported goods does not ipso facto amount to less favourable treatment; it does only if it cannot be justified as the outcome of pursuing a legitimate objective. In this case, the AB sided with the Panel when finding that the COOL measure could not be justified on these grounds; the detrimental impact was not stemming exclusively from the pursuance of a legitimate objective but also from the arbitrary and unjustifiable regulatory distinctions that the COOL measure had introduced (§349):

> In sum, our examination of the COOL measure under Article 2.1 reveals that its recordkeeping and verification requirements impose a disproportionate burden on upstream producers and processors, because the level of information conveyed to consumers through the mandatory labelling requirements is far less detailed and accurate than the information required to be tracked and transmitted by these producers and processors. It is these same recordkeeping and verification requirements that 'necessitate' segregation, meaning that their associated compliance costs are higher for entities that process livestock of different origins. Given that the least costly way of complying with these requirements is to rely exclusively on domestic livestock, the COOL measure creates an incentive for US producers to use exclusively domestic livestock and thus has a detrimental impact on the competitive opportunities of imported livestock. Furthermore, the recordkeeping and verification requirements imposed on upstream producers and processors cannot be explained by the need to convey to consumers information regarding the countries where livestock were born, raised, and slaughtered, because the detailed information required to be tracked and transmitted by those producers is not necessarily conveyed to consumers through the labels prescribed under the COOL measure. This is either because the prescribed labels do not expressly identify specific production steps and, in particular for Labels B and C, contain confusing or inaccurate origin information, or because the meat or meat products are exempt from the labelling requirements altogether. Therefore, the detrimental impact caused by the same recordkeeping and verification requirements under the COOL measure can also not be explained by the need to provide origin information to consumers. Based on these findings, we consider that the regulatory distinctions imposed by the COOL measure amount to arbitrary and unjustifiable discrimination against imported livestock, such that they cannot be said to be applied in an even-handed manner. Accordingly, we find that the detrimental impact on imported livestock does not stem exclusively from a legitimate regulatory distinction but, instead, reflects discrimination in violation of Article 2.1 of the *TBT Agreement*. (Italics in the original).

2.3 *Was* US–COOL *Necessary?*

The Panel had found that the US measure was more restrictive than necessary to achieve its legitimate objective, but the AB reversed the Panel's finding in this respect. It did not complete the analysis, though, since in its view it lacked the necessary factual information to this effect. As a result, the AB did not make a finding regarding the necessary character (or not) of the COOL measure.

2.4 *The AB findings in a nutshell*

The AB found that the measure was discriminatory; it did not make any finding regarding the issue of whether the COOL measure was necessary to achieve its stated objective; and, finally, it did not reverse the Panel's findings that the measure was indeed pursuing a legitimate objective, namely consumer information regarding the origin of traded goods.

3. A critical evaluation of the AB report: positive analysis

3.1 Legitimate objective

On the specific issue of legitimacy of the objective, there is not much to add to the discussion by the Panel and the AB. Indeed, we share the view that WTO Members should be allowed to unilaterally define the legitimate objective they aim at pursuing, and that WTO adjudicating bodies should adopt a deferential standard of review when dealing with claims regarding the legitimacy of the objective pursued. WTO adjudicating bodies, it seems, avoid tinkering too much with national definitions in this context. This approach is consonant with the negative integration character of the TBT Agreement (and the GATT, to which the TBT Agreement is an Annex): policies will be defined unilaterally and (negative) external effects eventually stemming from policies should be internalized through the obligations to avoid unnecessary and/or discriminatory obstacles to trade.

The indicative list of legitimate objectives provided for in Article 2.2 TBT serves, in our view, two objectives:

(a) To underscore the wide discretion that WTO Members enjoy when it comes to deciding which policies to pursue: they can pursue policies that have not been included in the list.
(b) To avoid Type II errors (false negatives) by the judges who must accept as legitimate an objective featured in the indicative list.

The question arises to what extent they should also accept as legitimate any objective not mentioned in the list that has been invoked by a WTO Member, or to what extent they retain some discretion to this effect. This question, nevertheless, was not raised in this dispute.[7]

3.2 Less favourable treatment

Recall that in §349 of the report on *US–COOL* cited above, the AB had found that the treatment afforded to imported beef was less favourable than that reserved for domestic beef. The AB found that:

(a) The COOL measure was the reason for segregation which led to privileging the trade of US-origin beef; and that
(b) the disparate impact on mixed-origin beef could not be justified by the need to inform consumers, for the following reasons:

7 We believe nevertheless, that the AB got it right in *US–Clove Cigarettes*, where it stated that WTO Members cannot be inconsistent when pursuing a regulatory objective. A consistency-requirement, if properly implemented, will help adjudicators distinguish wheat from chaff in this respect.

- more information was requested from producers than was being disseminated to consumers;
- the information transmitted to consumers was inaccurate, because of the possibility of 'commingling': sometimes the three individual production stages corresponding to where traded livestock was born, raised, and slaughtered were not accurately reflected in the label, since traders could 'commingle' two different stages into one; and
- because some 'pa and ma' stores had been exonerated from the obligation to observe the COOL measure.[8]

The existence of detrimental impact on multi-origin livestock was not in the eyes of the AB, in and of itself, enough to lead to the conclusion that the US, through the COOL measure, was affording imported livestock less favourable treatment than it was affording to domestic livestock: it might have been a necessary, but not a sufficient condition. The sufficient condition would be fulfilled if the foreign origin of the good had been the reason for the detrimental impact suffered by it. This had been the case indeed, since the AB was not persuaded that the dissemination of information to consumers could have motivated the COOL measure for the reasons mentioned above (e.g. more information requested than disseminated, inaccurate information disseminated at times, exoneration of 'pa and ma' stores).

Two questions arise: first, what is the standard of review that the AB employed to reach these conclusions, and, second, on what evidentiary basis did the AB make its determination? We take each one in turn.

3.2.1 *The standard of review applied*

In §§ 127–129 of its report, the AB explained in detail its standard of review:

(a) WTO adjudicating bodies must establish a cause and effect relationship between the challenged measure and the observed effects that denote less favourable treatment;
(b) To do that, a 'but-for' test is appropriate, that is, adjudicating bodies should ask whether private operators would have adopted a particular attitude *but for* the government's intervention;
(c) There is no need to show government compulsion; it suffices that the governments provide private operators with an incentive to behave in a particular way.

8 *US–COOL* had many built-in exemptions. It applied only to muscle cuts and exempted ground beef and pork sold at the retail level. *US–COOL* also exempted retailers who sold less than $230,000 worth of fruits and vegetables per year (so that small stores and butcher shops were exempt) as well as food service establishments such as restaurants and cafeterias. Furthermore, all processed food items (such as cooked, cured, and smoked meats) also did not need to carry country of origin labels. Taken together, these exemptions implied that less than half the meat sold in the US was covered by COOL requirements at the retail level (see Jurenas and Greene, 2013).

Making repeated references to its report on *Korea–Various Measures on Beef*, the AB explained that segregation (e.g. privileging single-origin US beef) was not compelled, but the result of the incentives that traders now faced because of the enactment of the labelling measures by the US government.

In §316 of its report, the AB went so far as to state that the Panel did not need to show trade effects to reach its conclusion, a statement which is in compliance with past case law (the GATT Panel on US-Superfund providing the authority for this standard of review). Yet, it is trade effects, as we show in what immediately follows, that formed the Panel's view on this issue. To be fair, it is unclear whether the AB understands 'price effects' to be 'trade effects', or whether the latter term is confined to a narrower ambit, namely the consequence of price effects, e.g. the volume of beef sold as Label A, B etc. If this latter view were correct, then why did not the AB simply use the term 'volume'? Be it as it may, and in effort to avoid misunderstandings, we reproduce the basis of the AB's findings in what follows.

3.2.2 The evidentiary basis for the findings

As the AB did not disturb the Panel's findings in this respect, it is probably worth referring to the relevant excerpts of the Panel report. In §7.356, the Panel refers to *discounts* provided by slaughterhouses for US beef only:

> In fact, there is direct evidence of major slaughterhouses applying a considerable COOL discount of USD 40–60 per head for imported livestock. This proves that major processors are passing on at least some of the additional costs of the COOL measure upstream to suppliers of imported livestock. We have no evidence of a similar discount being applied to suppliers of domestic livestock, nor has the United States responded to the evidence submitted by Canada and Mexico in this respect.

There is no evidence that the slaughterhouses offered discounts because of the COOL labelling measures. Canada submitted a few affidavits to this effect, but this is all it submitted.[9] All we know is that discounted prices were offered to some but not for other beef, and one could imagine various reasons why this could have occurred. Based on this fact alone, we cannot even say for sure whether the government intervention was (a significant?) contributing factor.

In §§7.376–7.381, the Panel provides additional information evidencing *reduced market opportunities* for imported livestock (labels B, C, and D). The Panel refers to fewer processing plants accepting imported livestock, reduced opening hours etc., and every time it affirms that this is the result of enacting the COOL measure:

> Moreover, as a result of the COOL measure, fewer US processing plants are accepting imported livestock than before. The complainants have submitted maps

9 We return to this question infra.

and lists of US processing facilities showing how US processing plants have become less accessible for imported cattle and hog under the COOL measure. Although the United States contests the specific figures submitted by the complainants in this regard, it does not call into question the complainants' case on the overall reduction in the number of plants processing imported livestock as a result of the COOL measure.

We also have evidence before us showing that, as a result of the reduction of available processing plants, certain suppliers had to transport imported livestock longer distances than before the COOL measure. Further, several plants that continue to process imported livestock do so at specific, limited times, namely only on specific days of the week (typically at most one or two days per week), or only after specific hours of the day. Processing imported livestock only at specific times as a result of the COOL measure has created logistical problems and additional costs for certain imported livestock suppliers. Due to the congestion resulting from limited specific-time deliveries, certain imported livestock suppliers find it more difficult to obtain trucks for their deliveries or to use their trucks in an efficient way. Congestion has also increased waiting time for imported livestock crossing the border, and thus created transportation delays for certain suppliers of imported livestock. In turn, these have increased the transportation costs of certain suppliers of imported livestock, and have had a negative impact on the welfare and quality of imported livestock as a result of long waiting times in extreme temperatures and shrinkage, sometimes leading even to increased mortality. Also, transportation of imported livestock has become less efficient in that certain suppliers can make fewer deliveries due to longer distance transport and less turn-around time. Further, certain slaughterhouses accepting imported livestock only on Monday has resulted in increased costs for veterinary checks of imported livestock on Sunday.

Contractual terms for suppliers of imported livestock have also changed as a result of the COOL measure. We have evidence that several major processors introduced a COOL opt-out clause allowing them to unilaterally terminate or amend their contracts with suppliers of imported livestock. In certain other situations, supply contracts for imported livestock have been cancelled or terminated, or simply not renewed. Sometimes, the contractual relationship has survived the COOL measure, although at terms less favourable for imported livestock suppliers. For instance, in certain cases, former long-term contracts have been replaced with spot contracts at lower purchase prices. In at least one case, a former automatically renewed, 'evergreen' contract was replaced with a contract involving less favourable terms. Further, we have evidence of 14 days' advance notice being required for supplies of Mexican cattle at various US processing facilities.

Certain suppliers of imported livestock have also suffered significant financial disadvantages resulting from the COOL measure. Several suppliers reported that the price difference between imported and domestic livestock has become larger to the detriment of domestic livestock, and that discounts for imported livestock appeared or existing ones increased as a result of the COOL measure. Further, in several cases, financial institutions are reported to have refused to provide credits

> and loans to Canadian livestock producers due to the risks resulting from the COOL measure.
>
> Finally, we have evidence before us – undisputed by the United States – that imported cattle have been excluded from premium beef programmes, such as the Certified Angus Beef programme and other programmes, as a result of the COOL measure. In general, these premium programmes are particularly profitable for operators in the supply chain, including livestock suppliers.
>
> In light of the above considerations, we preliminarily conclude that the COOL measure reduces the competitive opportunities of imported livestock relative to domestic livestock. Before making a definitive finding on this matter, though, we need to address the counterarguments advanced by the United States in this regard.

The natural question to ask is how did the Panel attribute the effects discussed (reduced market opportunities, discounts etc.) to the enactment of the COOL measure? In other words, what is the intellectual process that allowed the Panel to establish a cause and effect relationship between the passage of the COOL measure and the less favourable treatment afforded to imported livestock? Econometric studies can help determine whether there existed a statistically significant relationship between the COOL measure and the competitive opportunities facing imported livestock relative to US livestock. Indeed, to reach the conclusion that a relationship between the challenged measure and disparate effects indeed existed, the Panel did base its decisions on econometric studies. The Panel noted, however, that it also took into account other evidence before it that was provided through affidavits etc. The Panel did not explain how each of the factors (econometric studies *vis-à-vis* affidavits) weighed in its evaluation, but did state that it did not base itself entirely on the econometric studies submitted. Recall, that what is of interest to us here is the intellectual process that allowed the Panel to establish that the COOL measure was associated with detrimental effects on imported livestock. The AB took the view that the Panel had not erred in its evaluation of the record before it. In §§325–326 of its report, the AB held that:

> In addition, as explained above, the Panel evaluated the Sumner Econometric Study as part of its examination of the actual trade effects of the COOL measure. The Panel made explicit that its finding of less favourable treatment was not dependent on its examination of the actual trade effects of the COOL measure and the evidence relating to such effects. Nor was the Panel required under Article 2.1 to confirm its legal conclusions based on the actual trade effects of the measure in the US market. We therefore consider that, even if the Panel were to have erred in its appreciation of the Sumner Econometric Study, such an error would not have materially affected its ultimate legal conclusion under Article 2.1 of the *TBT Agreement*.
>
> We therefore *find* that the United States has not demonstrated that the Panel acted inconsistently with Article 11 of the DSU in its assessment of the evidence relating to the price differential between domestic and imported livestock.

Footnote 622 exacerbates this finding while underlying what else the Panel observed that persuaded it that less favourable treatment had indeed been afforded to imported livestock:

> That is, the Panel found that: (i) fewer processing plants are accepting imported livestock, and those that do, do so at specific limited times; (ii) contractual terms for suppliers of imported livestock have changed as a result of the COOL measure; (iii) certain suppliers of imported livestock have suffered significant financial disadvantages resulting from the COOL measure, including an increased price differential between imported and domestic livestock and the refusal of financial institutions to provide credits and loans; and (iv) imported cattle have been excluded from profitable premium beef programmes.

(a) The econometric studies: The AB, siding with the Panel on this score, went on to suggest that the more onerous reporting requirements for B and C categories (multi-origin beef) pushed traders to segregate and favour US beef. What did the submitted econometric evidence suggest to this effect? Two studies were submitted to the Panel by Canada, referred to as the 'Informa study' and the 'Sumner report'. The focus of each study was different: the Informa study focused on the implementation costs of supply chains and the Sumner report on the willingness of operators along the supply chain to pay for mixed-origin beef. The former, because of its subject-matter, did not squarely address the issue of attribution (of detrimental effects to the COOL measure) that we care most about. Moreover, in §7.499, the Panel explicitly stated that it cannot assess if it contains reliable information due to two factors: it was silent on its methodology as well as on the sample on which its findings were based. We are thus, left with the Sumner report.

In order to assess the willingness of traders to purchase mixed-origin beef or hog, the Sumner report compared the situation before and after the enactment of the COOL measure. This report concluded that, relative to goods originating from a single country, mixed-origin goods would become costlier due to COOL but that not all of the additional costs would be passed on to consumers (especially in the hog market).[10] Consequently, the Sumner report concluded that the enactment of the COOL measure would lead to increased purchases of US hogs at the expense of those that had a mixed origin.

We should note that the Panel in §7.506 of its report had accepted that for various reasons it could not rely on the figures included in the Sumner report. This conclusion notwithstanding though, the Panel took the view that the two studies pointed to segregation costs which led traders towards privileging US-origin livestock.

10 Indeed, anytime the costs of a product increase (either due to market conditions or due to a regulation such as *US-COOL*), the extent of pass through to consumers is determined jointly by the elasticities of supply and demand. Only in a situation of perfectly inelastic demand are cost increases passed on entirely to consumers.

Let us assume that segregation did occur, that is, that segregation was the rational economic response of various market agents to the enactment of the COOL measure. Why would US beef be necessarily favoured as a result, and not Mexican, or Canadian, or any beef produced in a single country? Even if we take the most favourable view of the studies, they at best show that the measure provided an incentive for traders to move from mixed-origin to US-origin livestock in a world with no other options. However, other options are available and that is why Label D exists. From what we observe in the record, none of the studies asked whether segregation would (could) lead to increased purchases of US- over Mexican- or Canadian-origin beef/hog. Privileging US-origin beef is, at best, one plausible scenario. There exists other (equally or, probably, even more) plausible scenarios though: would, for example, traders still prefer US beef if Mexican (or Canadian) beef was significantly cheaper? We have nothing in the record that suggests that segregation would lead to preference for US beef over Mexican or Canadian beef, other than a Panel opinion that traders would prefer US beef because of the geographic proximity.[11] If geographic proximity was the decisive criterion for purchasing decisions though, there would of course be no trade at all in the majority of products. Moreover, why would geographic proximity lead traders to prefer US livestock? Traders in the Southern states of the US are certainly closer to Mexican livestock, and traders in the Northern states to Canada. In the AB's view then a substantial percentage of US traders would prefer Canadian and Mexican and not US livestock.

From a purely legal perspective, less favourable treatment invites a comparison between a domestic and an imported good. By contrast, the comparison drawn here is between a domestic and a multi-origin (including domestic-origin) good. We have no idea what the national (e.g. US, Canadian, or Mexican) value-added of each country is when dealing with multi-origin livestock. What if, for example, the US share of valued-added in multi-origin beef is consistently 90%? Would the Panel still find that less favourable treatment to imported livestock had been afforded through the COOL measure?

In our view, this is very shaky evidence to conclude that less favourable treatment has indeed been afforded. The Panel should, at the very least, have asked for additional information. As things stand, it had no basis to conclude that the US was in violation of its obligations and the AB moved too fast to condone this approach.

(b) Other evidence: The Panel, as already mentioned above, had before it affidavits submitted by Canada regarding discounts offered for US-origin beef only. Based on similar documents as well (e.g. besides the 'persuasive' power of the

11 Hence, we are not here in a 'raising the rival's cost' scenario. The AB does not believe that market analysis is warranted since it has always construed provisions regulating non-discrimination as protecting competitive conditions; to this effect, violations can occur (in the eyes of the AB) even if no data on trade effects have been provided. Moreover, why would geographic proximity lead traders to prefer US livestock?

econometric studies submitted), it concluded that the US was in violation of its obligations. These documents, however, contained absolutely no information on the question of attribution; they simply showed that price discounts were being offered. This evidence could thus at best complement evidence on attribution; it could not be regarded as substitute for attribution analysis. This evidence also suffers from the same vice as the econometric studies: the comparator is inappropriate since we have no information on whether similar discounts were also offered on Canadian, Mexican, or any other single-origin beef.

(c) Discrepancy in the amount of information requested: Both the Panel as well as the AB report concluded that there was discrepancy regarding the amount of information requested from traders, and the information eventually disclosed to the public. This cannot be an issue though when the consistency of the US measure with the obligation to not discriminate is being discussed, since more information, on the face of it, is requested from both domestic as well as imported beef. If at all, this could be an issue when the necessity of the measure is being evaluated. As we have already seen though, the AB reversed the Panel's findings with respect to the violation of the necessity-requirement, and did not complete the analysis.

How might the US eliminate the discrepancy between the amounts of information requested from producers to that supplied to consumers? There are essentially two ways. One, the US could scrap the COOL measure altogether thereby eliminating the need for both the collection and dissemination of information regarding the source of origin of meat products. Second, the US could actually make the labelling process *more elaborate rather than less*. For example, the US could require that each piece of meat being sold in the US should indicate exactly where each of three steps in the processing of livestock (i.e. born, raise, and slaughtered) took place. Under this alternative scheme, restricting attention to only the three countries involved in the dispute, the US would need to create NINE different labels since each of the three steps could potentially be carried out in any of the three countries. Perhaps this more extensive labelling practise would minimize the informational discrepancy dimension that seems to be crucial to the AB's reasoning. But what about the additional record keeping and other costs that would result from its implementation? Such costs would almost surely be higher under this more elaborate labelling scheme relative to *US–COOL*. Consequently, it would appear that this scheme would be even more susceptible to the *de facto* discrimination against imports charge that seems to have carried the day against *US–COOL*.

4. A critical evaluation of the AB report: normative analysis

4.1 The AB approach

The AB found that the measure was discriminatory, although it made no finding regarding its necessity. The AB thus, understood the two obligations to be distinct, in that, the consistency of a measure coming under the purview of the TBT Agreement can be examined under say Article 2.1 TBT irrespective of its evaluation under Article 2.2 TBT. We believe that the approach followed is correct only for a very narrow set of circumstances; namely, when it comes to cases of alleged *de jure* discrimination. When for example a national labelling scheme (like the COOL measure) adopts one set of requirements that domestic goods must in principle comply with, and another, more onerous set of requirements that imported goods must observe for market access to be guaranteed, then yes, one can review the consistency of similar measures under Article 2.1 TBT while avoiding to do so under Article 2.2 TBT.

In cases of alleged de facto discrimination, we need additional information to evaluate the functioning of the measure and this brings us squarely into the realm of Article 2.2 TBT. Recall it was the AB that suggested that a finding of less favourable treatment does not solely depend on the existence of disparate effects; the challenged measure, and no public order justification (in our case, consumer information), must be causing the observed (adverse) trade effect. Information thus, about the objectives sought and the means employed to reach the objectives sought, is necessary for deciding whether a measure de facto discriminates if we are to respect the standard of review as established by the AB, and which seems reasonable to us as well.

There should be no doubt that we are dealing with a case of alleged de facto discrimination: domestic as well as foreign beef must observe the same *labelling conditions*; it is the consequences (as opposed to conditions) of the labelling scheme that, if at all, lead to less favourable treatment.

4.2 *Our approach*

In our view, the claims made by Canada and Mexico against the COOL measure should have been addressed in a *sequential* manner:

(a) Does the COOL measure pursue a legitimate objective?
- If no, complainants prevail.
- If yes, then we move to the next question.

(b) Is the COOL measure necessary to achieve the legitimate objective pursued?
- If no, complainants prevail.
- If yes, we move to the next question.

(c) Has the COOL measure been applied in a non-discriminatory manner?
- If no, complainants prevail.
- If yes, defendant prevails.[12]

12 Mavroidis (2013) discusses all this in detail.

4.2.1 *The mechanics*

Since we are not dealing with a case of de jure discrimination here (e.g. differential regulatory requirements apply to products depending on their origin), the Panel and the AB should have first asked whether the challenged measure pursued a legitimate objective, and also respected the necessity-requirement embedded in Article 2.2 TBT in this context, the Panel could have quantified the 'external' costs of the challenged measure, that is, the costs on international trade, and could have asked the question whether the objective sought (consumer information) which it could not put into question, could have been achieved through another means that were less burdensome on international transactions; if the response was positive, following allocation of the burden of proof à la *US–Gambling*, the US should lose the argument, and in the opposite case it should have prevailed. Winning under Article 2.2 TBT though, should not be equated to winning full stop: assuming a claim to this effect, the Panel and the AB should have examined whether the necessary labelling requirements had been applied in a non-discriminatory manner to domestic and imported livestock alike.

This entails one important consequence: in our framework of analysis, the obligation to avoid discrimination (embedded in Article 2.1 TBT) is an obligation regarding the application of the challenged measure. The substantive consistency of the measure with the multilateral rules will take place within the four corners of Article 2.2 TBT: the question should be whether the US had applied the (otherwise necessary) labelling requirements in a non-discriminatory manner across livestock of different origins. If the labelling requirements were deemed necessary to achieve the stated objective (consumer information), the Panel and the AB should have asked whether the same labelling requirements were being applied to domestic and imported like goods.[13] Everything else should be an examination under Article 2.2 TBT.

4.2.2 *The rationale for our sequential approach*

The heart of the problem we perceive in the analysis by the AB is the 'lock, stock, and barrel' export of GATT solutions (inspired by case law under Article III) to the TBT Agreement; indeed, the AB did nothing other than apply its test of consistency with Article III.4 GATT (as developed in various cases) into the realm of the TBT. The GATT however was drafted without thinking too much about disciplining regulatory barriers.[14] According to Baldwin's (1970) classic account, this was the right thing to do at the time since trade barriers (e.g., high tariffs, quotas) obscured the 'bite' of regulatory barriers (e.g., domestic instruments). Under the circumstances, it was only sensible for the framers to focus on disciplining trade rather

13 Mavroidis (2013) contains a more expansive discussion of this issue and point of view.

14 Irwin *et al.* (2008) reach this conclusion after examining a very substantial percentage of the negotiating record.

than domestic instruments. Following the Kennedy round, every round (including the on-going Doha round) has mainly focused on disciplining regulatory barriers: once again, this is only sensible since import and export quotas are illegal, and tariffs have been gradually reduced to an all-time low.[15] The TBT Agreement is an integral part of this discussion and focuses on disciplining some regulatory barriers.

The TBT Agreement does not put into question the right of governments to be unhappy with market outcomes. It does not even proscribe which market outcomes governments can be unhappy with: this is the natural consequence of its negative integration character. The TBT Agreement conditions the exercise of the right of WTO Members to intervene and alter the market outcome. Consequently, the domain of the TBT Agreement is *policy* and not market *likeness*.

4.3 *What can the US do as things stand?*

As things stand, it seems there is no way out for the US other than to scrap the COOL measure altogether since the alternative of introducing more elaborate labelling schemes would be even more susceptible to the charge of de facto discrimination that seems to have carried the day in favour of the complainants. The basis of the decision is that the challenged regime leads to segregation of beef and ultimately to privileging US-origin beef by altering the conditions of market competition in its favour. There is thus, in the AB's understanding, an inherent vice in this measure which cannot be cured as long as the US insists on adopting a technical regulation. Price discounts etc. are the almost natural consequence, in the AB's reasoning, of the enactment of the COOL measure.

Note that the logic behind this charge is that since a large part of the meat is actually locally sourced (i.e. from within the US), all else equal, there is an incentive for meat processing units to shift almost entirely to US meat in order to avoid the costs of tracking and segregating meat from multiple sources. To avoid being foreclosed on, Canadian and Mexican suppliers would have to accept a lower price to make it worthwhile for downstream producers to source from all three countries as opposed to only the US. But what if the market share of foreign meat suppliers was almost 50% but still below that of the US? Would there be de facto discrimination even then? If yes, does it mean that labelling requirements such as *US–COOL* can only be used when the market share of imports is exactly equal to that of domestic suppliers?

This is not all. The AB's decision raises some other fundamental questions: Are we in the presence of a case where a legitimate objective (i.e. consumer information about the origin of birthplace, place of growth of the livestock, and place of slaughter) cannot be achieved through a labelling requirement that denotes origin? How else can it be achieved? Had it examined the measure under Article 2.2 TBT, then the AB might have been in position to point to at least one other less restrictive option.

15 Irwin (1998).

4.4 Brief recap of the major points

The AB reached its conclusions under Article 2.1 TBT inappropriately so with respect to some of them: the quantum of information requested relative to that which is disseminated is not an issue that can conceivably come under Article 2.1 TBT, unless the discrepancy is origin based. This has not been the case in this dispute. The remaining findings suffer as well: the affidavits submitted do not discuss at all the question of attribution of the detrimental (trade) impact to the COOL measure; the relevance of some of the econometric evidence submitted was reduced by the Panel itself, and, with respect to the rest, the question asked does not suffice to support a finding that discrimination has indeed been afforded.

The treatment of econometric evidence by both the Panel and the AB leaves a lot to be desired. It is quite remarkable that Panels refuse to make use of Article 13 DSU, and invite economists and econometricians to testify before it, and appraise submitted evidence. It is counter-productive to hide behind 'in house-expertise' in this area. WTO staff members that have the appropriate economics training scarcely appear before Panels and the AB, and they do not have to sign the opinions that they defend. Invited experts will have to bear the full reputational cost of their opinions, and this, on occasion, could provide them with a dis-incentive to take the whole exercise 'light-heartedly'.

5. Concluding remarks

In what preceded, we have argued that the AB should not have reached the outcome it did based on the information before it, and that, ideally, it should have applied a different methodology as well. The AB applied the wrong methodology and also reached the wrong conclusion: the AB ruled that *US–COOL* was discriminatory but made no finding regarding its necessity. Thus, *US–COOL* could have been necessary to achieve a legitimate objective.

In our view, the AB essentially threw its hands up in the air on the most critical question to emerge from this case: was the COOL measure more restrictive than necessary to meet the legitimate objective of providing consumers with more information? By choosing to not 'complete the legal analysis under Article 2.2. of the TBT' due to the 'lack of sufficient undisputed facts on the Panel record', the AB missed an opportunity to set an important precedent. If *US–COOL* was indeed more trade restrictive than necessary, what should take its place? And, as the AB correctly noted, complainants had not met the burden of proof regarding the existence of any such alternative measure.[16] For example, Canada and Mexico had

16 Three types of alternative measures were discussed: (i) a market driven voluntary labelling scheme; (ii) a mandatory labelling scheme based on substantial transformation (i.e. slaughter); and (iii) a trace back scheme under which a retailer could trace back the precise location of each processing step (farm, feedlot,

argued that market-driven 'voluntary labelling' in the US meat market would be less trade-restrictive since 'segregation costs would be borne only by those livestock producers catering to interested consumers'. But such conclusions are not straightforward in the presence of asymmetric and incomplete information in the product market.

In our view, the lack of widespread voluntary or market-based labelling prior to *US–COOL* is certainly not sufficient to conclude that *US–COOL* was more trade restrictive than necessary. After all, even if such voluntary labelling was pervasive, would regulation ensuring its accuracy not be necessary? And isn't the credibility of private labelling enhanced when it is backed by supporting government regulations that are properly enforced? Furthermore, for voluntary labelling to be less confusing to consumers than *US–COOL*, the industry would need to converge to some sort of a common standard as opposed to each retailer choosing its own approach. Of course, this brings us back full circle to the question confronting the US government: what type of labelling scheme can convey accurate information to consumers about the origin of meat products while restricting trade as little as possible? Without answering this key question, it is hard to see how the AB ruled the way that it did.

Post-scriptum

In May 2013, the US announced the specific actions it had undertaken in order to comply with the AB rulings and recommendations (Federal Register, vol. 78, No 101, Friday 24 May, 2013, pp. 31367ff.). It summarized its compliance activities in the following terms:

> Under this final rule, origin designations for muscle cut covered commodities derived from animals slaughtered in the United States are required to specify the production steps of birth, raising, and slaughter of the animal from which the meat is derived that took place in each country listed on the origin designation. In addition, this rule eliminates the allowance for commingling of muscle cut covered commodities of different origins. These changes will provide consumers with more specific information about the origin of muscle cut covered commodities.

The US estimated that the loss of the commingling flexibility would entail costs rising at \$7.16 per head for cattle, and \$1.79 per head of hogs currently commingled at the packer/processor level. Estimated costs at the retail level are \$0.050 per pound of beef, and \$0.045 per pound of pork muscle cuts currently

processing facility' for every piece of meat. The first scheme would provide highly incomplete coverage of the market (much less than under COOL); the second would simply not meet the objective of providing adequate information regarding origin; while the third would be significantly costlier to implement than the COOL measure.

commingled. Estimated total costs, because of the loss of the commingling flexibility for the beef segment, would be $21.1 million, $52.8 million, and $84.5 million at the lower, mid-point, and upper levels respectively. The corresponding figures for the pork market would be $15.0 million, $37.7 million, and $60.3 million. The inescapable conclusion is that because of the compliance activity, consumers would eventually be burdened with higher prices for beef and pork meat.

A combination of the costs for label changes as well as those resulting from the loss of the commingling flexibility would yield in the eyes of the US total adjustment costs of $123.3 million at the mid-point (the range spanning from $53.1 to $192.1 million). Note also that 'The [US] Agency believes that the incremental benefits from the labelling of production steps will be comparatively small relative to those that were discussed in the 2009 final rule.'

In the eyes of the US authorities thus, all this amounts more or less to 'much ado about nothing'. Recall that, although the AB had found that the US measure had been requesting from traders more information than what the law eventually revealed, it did not find that the US measure had failed the necessity-requirement embedded in Article 2.2 TBT.

References

Baldwin, R. E. (1970), *Non-Tariff Distortions in International Trade*, Washington, DC: Brookings Institution.

Horn, H., L. Johannesson, and P. C. Mavroidis (2011), 'The WTO Dispute Settlement System: 1995–2010, Some Descriptive Statistics', *Journal of World Trade*, **45**: 1107–1138.

Horn, H. and J. H. H. Weiler (2007), 'EC–Trade Description of Sardines: Textualism and Its Discontent', in H. Horn and P. C. Mavroidis (eds.), *The WTO Case Law of 2001–2003, the American Law Institute Reporters' Studies*, Cambridge: Cambridge University Press, pp. 551–578.

Howse, R. and P. Levy (2012), 'The TBT Panels: *US–Clove Cigarettes, US–Tuna*, and *US–COOL*', *The World Trade Review*, **12**: 327–376.

Irwin, D. A. (1998), 'Changes in US Tariffs: The Role of Import Prices and Commercial Policies', *The American Economic Review*, **88**: 1015–1026.

Irwin, D. A., P. C. Mavroidis, and A. O. Sykes (2008), *The Genesis of the GATT*, Cambridge: Cambridge University Press.

Jurenas, R. and J. L. Greene (2013), *Country of Origin Labelling for Foods and the WTO Dispute on Meat Labelling*, Congressional Research Service.

Mavroidis, P. C. (2013), 'Driftin' Too Far from Shore: Why the Test for Compliance with the TBT Agreement Developed by the WTO Appellate Body is Wrong, and what Should the Appellate Body Have Done Instead', *The World Trade Review*, **12**(3): 509–531.

CHAPTER 20

World Trade Review (2016), 15: 2, 259–286
© Kamal Saggi and Mark Wu doi:10.1017/S1474745615000750 First published online 9 February 2016

Understanding Agricultural Price Range Systems as Trade Restraints: *Peru–Agricultural Products*

KAMAL SAGGI*
Vanderbilt University
MARK WU**
Harvard Law School

Abstract: An agricultural price range system (PRS) aims to stabilize local prices in an open economy via the use of import duties that vary with international prices. The policy is inherently distortionary and welfare-reducing for a small open economy, at least according to the canonical economic model. We offer an explanation for why a government concerned with national welfare may nevertheless implement such a policy when faced with risk aversion and imperfect insurance markets. We also highlight open questions arising out of the *Peru–Agricultural Products* dispute for the WTO's Appellate Body to address in order to clarify how a PRS consistent with WTO rules could be designed. Finally, we discuss the possibility that a WTO member might resort to a free trade agreement (FTA) to preserve its flexibility to implement a PRS and how an FTA provision of this sort ought to be treated in WTO litigation.

1. Introduction

For developing economies, the question of whether to further liberalize trade often hinges on the potential impact of trade liberalization on the domestic agricultural sector. The outsized role played by this sector in employment, economic production, and social security means that governments tread rather carefully when assessing what types of agriculture-related concessions to offer in exchange for gains in other sectors. This is especially the case for small economies that lack the ability to shape world prices.

* Email: K.saggi@vanderbilt.edu
** Email: mwu@law.harvard.edu

For helpful comments and discussion, we thank Kyle Bagwell, Rick Bond, Petros Mavroidis, and participants at the 2014 WTO Case Law Conference held at the European University Institute, Florence, May 2015. In addition, we are grateful for insights provided by several individuals involved in the litigation proceedings who wish to remain anonymous.

In the course of opening up agricultural markets, governments in small economies are faced with two competing concerns. On the one hand, they fear that prices for agricultural goods may suddenly drop, leaving farmers exposed to negative income shocks. On the other hand, they also worry that prices may suddenly spike, triggering inflationary concerns and harming consumers. To guard against these concerns, some governments chose to liberalize trade while simultaneously retaining some form of a price range system (PRS) that helps insulate the domestic market from fluctuations in word prices.

By far the more common policy discussed in this context is the notion of a price band system (PBS). It may be worthwhile, at the onset, to distinguish between a PRS and a PBS, especially since the terms are sometimes used interchangeably. While both policy instruments seek to mitigate the local effects of fluctuations in global prices by keeping the price of imports within a given band/range, their exact mechanics differ slightly.

Under a PBS, the government sets a particular floor and ceiling price. Whenever the import price falls below this range, an additional tariff is imposed equal to the difference between the floor price and import price, bringing the local price of the import back up to the floor price. Similarly, whenever the import price exceeds the ceiling price, a tariff rebate equal to the difference between the import price and ceiling price is issued. This brings the local price of the import back down to the ceiling price. The additional tariff/rebate may be subject to additional adjustments, as necessary. Overall, it should serve to keep the price of the imported good within the desired price band.

A PRS operates in much the same way as a PBS, except that the adjustments are not made on a transaction-specific basis. Again, the government sets a floor and ceiling price, which may be altered over time. Instead of comparing the floor and ceiling prices against the actual import price, however, the comparison is made against a reference price. The reference price is set periodically through reliance on some external benchmark or a pre-determined formula. It may be tweaked with time, at an interval different than that of the floor and ceiling prices. Whenever the reference price falls below the floor price, an additional tariff is imposed equal to the difference between the floor price and reference price. Similarly, whenever the import price exceeds the ceiling price, a tariff rebate equal to the difference between the import price and ceiling price is issued. Again, the additional tariff/rebate may be subject to further adjustment, as necessary.

Note that unlike a price band, the additional tariff/rebate associated with the PRS does not vary with each given transaction. Instead, it is fixed for a given period of time – i.e., the period for which the reference price is constant, regardless of the actual import price. It only changes if the reference, floor, and/or ceiling prices are altered. Nevertheless, the PRS fulfills a similar objective of tweaking duties to keep the price of imported goods within a given price range. In doing so, the PRS allows a government some degree of control to guard against the unwelcome effects of agricultural trade liberalization.

Not surprisingly, such systems are not without controversy. A PRS seeks to alter price artificially and therefore distorts trade away from the market-equilibrium level. By revising duties in conjunction with the ceiling and floor price, the policy artificially limits gains for foreign producers within the given market. Some trading partners may therefore naturally view the policy as a protectionist scheme cast in the guise of a price stabilization instrument.

To date, PRS regimes have not received much attention in the academic legal literature, particularly with respect to agricultural trade and developing countries in which they are most commonly found. Much of the existing scholarship has focused on other forms of trade-related distortions in global agricultural markets, such as subsidies and export taxes, that are more commonly imposed by developed countries. Yet, as the recent *Peru–Agricultural Products* dispute[1] demonstrates, PRS policies also can give rise to trade distortions that harm farmers in other developing countries.

Why would a small developing country choose to implement a PRS? Does such a policy always represent a rent transfer to special interest group(s) that is overall welfare-reducing? Or can it be welfare-enhancing under particular conditions? We demonstrate that in the canonical model of a small open economy with risk-neutral consumers and producers that take world prices as given, a PRS is sub-optimal. This is because a PRS supported by fluctuating tariffs reduces the extent to which the local price in a country differs from its autarkic price and therefore reduces its expected gains from trade.

However, a PRS does ensure that the welfare of consumers and producers does not fall below a certain minimum threshold as a result of agricultural trade liberalization. We argue that a PRS can be welfare-enhancing in the presence of significant risk aversion on the part of either group. If some factors of production are immobile ex-post and insurance markets are incomplete, some level of trade protection can be optimal for a small open economy facing fluctuating terms of trade (Eaton and Grossman 1985). Thus, a PRS serves as an imperfect substitute for the lack of insurance and can help ensure that the welfare of consumers and producers exceeds a certain minimum threshold. Nevertheless, we note that a PRS does not constitute a first-best solution for redistributing income across domestic groups.

In light of this argument, we discuss two sets of questions related to how a PRS is treated under the laws of the World Trade Organization (WTO). First, we examine open questions in WTO jurisprudence with respect to whether a PRS could ever be designed to comply with WTO rules. Second, if a PRS is WTO-inconsistent but a country nevertheless wishes to preserve its flexibility to employ this instrument,

1 Panel Report, *Peru – Additional Duty on Imports of Certain Agricultural Products*, WT/DS457/R, 27 November 2014 [hereinafter 'Panel Report, *Peru–Agricultural Products* ']. Note that this Article is focused exclusively on the Panel Report in the dispute, as this was the scope asked of the authors for the 2014 WTO case law review analysis. The Appellate Body report was subsequently issued on 20 July 2015 and adopted on 31 July 2015.

we consider whether a WTO member can do so through a preferential trade agreement. To what extent can a free trade agreement (FTA) serve as a work-around solution to existing WTO rules? And what significance, if any, should be attached to the signing of such agreements as opposed to their ratification?

We use Peru's PRS and the resulting WTO legal dispute as the basis for the questions to be explored in this article. Section 2 discusses how a PRS operates and why it is controversial under WTO law. Section 3 assesses the economic implications of a PRS. Section 4 highlights several open questions in terms of whether the WTO affords policy flexibility to design a PRS consistent with WTO rules. Finally, Section 5 examines the question of whether a WTO member may use an FTA to preserve its ability to implement a PRS, even if it contravenes WTO law.

2. How a PRS works and why it poses a potential WTO legal controversy

Recent studies have demonstrated that the economic impact of agricultural trade liberalization varies both within and across developing countries, with outcomes dependent on the country's factor endowments and the precise contours of liberalization (Bouet *et al.*, 2005). Not all agents in developing countries necessarily gain from liberalizing trade in agriculture. As a result, some countries might choose to impose policies designed to safeguard certain groups against any potential negative impacts resulting from opening up their agricultural sector to increased foreign competition.

We examine measures taken by the Peruvian government in the early 2000s as a case study of how a developing country might utilize a PRS to advance its policy objective. We then highlight how such an instrument might give rise to trade tensions with other developing countries that are agricultural exporters.

2.1 The case study: Peru's price range system

During the 1990s, the Peruvian economy underwent a massive program of structural adjustment and economic liberalization. As part of this program, and in conjunction with Uruguay Round commitments, Peru lowered its tariffs and other trade barriers on agricultural products (Trivelli, 2003: 5). This trade liberalization exposed Peruvian farmers to increased competition from world markets.

Worried about the negative impact on its farmers, Peru established a PRS in June 2001.[2] The PRS covered 45 agricultural products, which were separated into four general categories: milk, yellow maize, rice, and sugar.[3] The PRS operated as follows:

2 Peru and its trading partners disagree as to whether the 2001 PRS was simply a modification of an earlier tariff scheme involving specific tariffs. See Panel Report, *Peru–Agricultural Products*, paras. 7.101–7.112.

3 For a complete list at the HS-10 level, see ibid., para. 7.121.

- Within each category, there was one tariff line designated as the 'marker' product and all others are designated as 'associated' products.
- A floor and ceiling price were determined for each marker product on the basis of monthly average f.o.b. (freight on board) prices for the past 60 months on the international reference market for that marker product. These prices were to be updated semi-annually and converted to a c.i.f. (cost, insurance, and freight) floor and ceiling prices.[4]
- In addition, a reference price was to be calculated every two weeks, reflecting the average international market price for the product.[5]
- The reference price was then compared to the c.i.f. floor and ceiling prices to determine whether a 'variable additional duty' should be levied or a 'tariff rebate' should be issued.

Whenever the international reference price (denoted by p^R) fell below the c.i.f. floor price $\underline{p}$, a 'variable additional duty' was levied against the imported good. Letting b denote the import costs associated with marker products, the additional variable duty AD was calculated according to the following formula:

$$AD = (1 + b)\,(\underline{p} - p^R)$$

Assuming that the additional cost associated with the variable additional duty was passed on to the consumer, this policy kept Peruvian prices for the good above world market prices. It therefore protected Peruvian farmers from negative price shocks on the global market.

In contrast, whenever the reference price rose above the c.i.f. ceiling price $\bar{p}$, a tariff rebate was issued to the importer. The tariff rebate was calculated as follows:

$$TR = (1 + b)\,(p^R - \bar{p})$$

Assuming that the tariff rebate was passed on to the consumer, this policy kept Peruvian prices for the good below world market prices. It therefore served to protect Peruvian consumers from undesired price increases on the global market.

The stated objectives of the Peruvian PRS were three-fold:[6]

> First, the PRS was designed to counter the adverse effects to domestic agricultural production on account of 'distortions ... due, in particular, to the agricultural policies implemented by the main food producing and exporting countries' and as 'reflected in the uncertainty and instability of domestic prices'.
>
> Second, the PRS was 'a stabilization and protection mechanism that makes it possible to neutralize the fluctuations of international prices and limit the negative effects of the fall in those prices'.

4 Ibid., paras. 7.127–7.135.
5 Ibid., paras. 7.136–7.139.
6 Ibid., para. 7.118.

> Third, the PRS constituted 'an appropriate means of improving the levels of competitiveness of domestic producers, by giving the market clear signals with regard to trends in prices, thereby allowing economic agents to operate efficiently and productively'.

In this sense, Peru's PRS serves as a quintessential example of a small developing country's government's employment of an instrument to safeguard against undesired price fluctuations associated with increased agricultural trade liberalization. Peru's Ministry of Economy and Finance noted that the PRS was intended to protect both domestic producers and consumers, through the establishment of a floor and ceiling prices for calculating a variable additional duty or tariff rebate, as necessary, to fulfill its various stabilization and competitiveness objectives.[7]

2.2 *Potential WTO legal controversy arising due to an agricultural PRS*

A PRS, however, encounters potential problems when examined in the context of the WTO's Agreement on Agriculture. The drafters sought to limit the types of border measures designed to restrict the volume or distort the price of imports of agricultural products.[8] To that end, they decided it would be best to require that border measures and other non-tariff barriers designed to restrict agricultural imports be converted into ordinary customs duties.

Article 4.2 of the Agreement on Agriculture states: 'Members shall not maintain, resort to, or revert to any measures of the kind which have been required to be converted into ordinary customs duties, except as otherwise provided for in Article 5 and Annex 5.' Article 4.2 includes a footnote 1 that provides an illustrative list of the types of measures that might violate this provision. These include 'quantitative import restrictions, variable import levies, minimum import prices, discretionary import licensing, non-tariff measures maintained through state-trading enterprises, voluntary export restraints, and similar border measures other than ordinary customs duties'.

To date, the bulk of WTO cases interpreting Article 4.2 have concerned quantitative import restrictions applied against agricultural imports.[9] The PRS, however, does not act as a quantitative restriction. Instead, the two types of measures that it

7 Ibid., para. 7.119.

8 Appellate Body Report, *Chile – Price Band System and Safeguard Measures Relating to Certain Agricultural Products*, WT/DS207/AB/R, 23 September 2002, adopted 23 October 2002, para. 200 [hereinafter '*Chile–Price Band System*'].

9 See Panel Report, *Turkey – Measures Affecting the Importation of Rice*, WT/DS334/R, 21 September 2007, adopted 22 October 2007, paras. 7.12–7.138; see also Panel Report, *India – Quantitative Restrictions on Imports of Agricultural, Textile and Industrial Products*, WT/DS90/R, 23 August 1999, adopted 22 September 1999, paras. 5.241–5.242; Panel Report, *Korea – Measures Affecting Imports of Fresh, Chilled and Frozen Beef*, WT/DS161/R, WT/DS169/R, 31 July 2000, adopted 10 January 2001, para. 762. Note that in the latter two cases, the Panel simply found that a measure that violated Article XI:1 of the GATT 1994 also violated Article 4.2 of the Agreement on Agriculture but did not elaborate on the provision itself.

most closely approximates are (1) variable import levy, and (2) minimum import price.[10]

Through 2013, only one WTO dispute, *Chile–Price Band System*, has opined on these issues. The Appellate Body (AB) found that Chile's PBS, which shared similarities with Peru's PRS, was inconsistent with Article 4.2 of the Agreement on Agriculture.[11]

2.3 Background on the Guatemala–Peru FTA and subsequent WTO dispute

Anticipating potential legal problems with its PRS, Peru sought guarantees from its PTA partners that they would not challenge the PRS through WTO dispute settlement. One example is the Guatemala–Peru FTA, signed on 6 December 2011. Article 9 of Annex 2.3 explicitly recognizes Peru's right to maintain its PRS.[12] The FTA also clarified that in the event of an inconsistency between the FTA and WTO agreements, the FTA 'shall prevail to the extent of the inconsistency, unless otherwise provided in this Treaty'.[13]

More than a year later, neither party had ratified the treaty. On 12 April 2013, Guatemala proceeded to file a WTO challenge, alleging that Peru's PRS violated several WTO commitments:[14] These included:

- Article 4.2 and footnote 1 of the Agreement on Agriculture, to the extent that the additional duty constitutes and encompasses elements of a variable import levy, a minimum import price, or a measure similar to the two;
- Article II:1(b) of the GATT 1994, since the measure constitutes a duty or charge other than an ordinary customs duty that was not included in Peru's schedule of concessions;
- Article X:1 and X:3(a) of the GATT 1994, regarding failures in the publication and administration of the trade regulations related to the PRS.

Should the Panel find that the duties arising from the PRS are ordinary customs duties, Guatemala argued, in the alternative, that Peru's actions would then amount to a violation of Articles 1, 2, 3, 5, 6, and 7 of the Customs Valuation Agreement.

Why did Guatemala bother to marshal resources to challenge Peru's PRS when it had previously agreed to recognize its legality in the bilateral FTA? The overall economic stakes were not large.[15] Based on our analysis of available data, bilateral

10 These are also the two cited by Guatemala in its complaint. See Request for Consultations by Guatemala, *Peru – Additional Duty on Imports of Certain Agricultural Products*, WT/DS457/1, G/AG/GEN/109, G/VAL/D/12, G/L/1024, 16 April 2013, at p. 2 [hereinafter '*Peru–Agricultural Products*'].

11 Appellate Body Report, *Chile–Price Band System*, paras. 288–289.

12 Tratado de Libre Comercio Guatemala–Perú [Guatemala–Peru Free Trade Agreement], signed 6 December 2011, art. 9 of Annex 2.3.

13 Ibid., art. 1.3 of Annex 2.3.

14 See *Peru–Agricultural Products*.

15 In 2013, only 0.07% of Peru's total imports were sourced from Guatemala while 0.30% of Guatemala's total exports went to Peru.

trade was significant in only two sugar products subject to the PRS.[16] The WTO litigation appears then to reflect the lobbying power of Guatemala's sugar producers.[17]

By the time the Panel was composed in September 2013, neither party had yet ratified the FTA, although Guatemala's Congress gave approval two months earlier. Guatemala initiated ratification procedures in December 2013, with Peru receiving a communication on 5 March 2014.[18] At that point, had Peru's President simply initiated ratification procedures and sent notice to Guatemala, the FTA would have entered into force. Peru's FTA ratification process does not require Congressional approval, only Presidential action.[19] Peru's President refused, viewing the filing of the WTO dispute as having 'created uncertainty with regard to the existence of the balance negotiated' in the FTA.[20] Thus, the bilateral FTA, as of this writing, has not yet entered into force.

On 27 November 2014, the Panel issued a report finding Peru to have violated Article 4.2 of the Agreement on Agriculture because the duties arising from the PRS constitute a variable import levy that was not permissible under the Agreement.[21] In addition, the Panel also ruled that the duties arising from the PRS violated GATT Article II:1(b) because they are not ordinary customs duties and were not declared as other duties or charges.[22] The Panel exercised judicial economy with respect to the GATT Article X:1 and X:3(a) claims.[23] Finally, the Panel did not find it necessary to rule on Peru's argument that the FTA modified the rights between the two parties with respect to the PRS, resulting in Guatemala's waiver of its WTO rights concerning the PRS; the Panel emphasized that the FTA had not yet entered into force and therefore its provisions were not legally binding.[24] Both Peru and Guatemala filed a notice of appeal. The Appellate Body ruling, issued on 20 July 2015, largely upheld the Panel's rulings except with respect to the Panel's ruling concerning the similarity of the PRS to a 'minimum import price' within the meaning of the Agreement on Agriculture.[25]

16 Authors' analysis was based on available data at the 6-digit HS level in the World Bank's WITS database. The two products are 'cane sugar' (HS 170111) and 'other cane and beet sugar' (HS 170199). We thank Chad Bown for providing us with the data and Semira Ahdiyyih for research assistance.

17 Our analysis shows that during 2007–2013, Guatemala accounted for a significant share of total Peruvian imports of both sugar products. See Tables 1A and 1B in the appendix and the discussion in the longer version of this Article, published as Vanderbilt University Working Paper No. VUECON-15-00009 and EUI Working Paper No. RSCAS 2015/58.

18 Panel Report, *Peru–Agricultural Products*, para. 7.32.

19 Ibid., para. 7.33.

20 Ibid.

21 Ibid., paras. 7.352 and 7.371–7.372.

22 Ibid., paras. 7.425–7.432.

23 Ibid., paras. 7.467 and 7.501.

24 Ibid., paras. 7.525–7.528.

25 Appellate Body Report, *Peru – Additional Duty on Imports of Certain Agricultural Products*, WT/DS457/AB/R, 20 July 2015 [hereinafter 'Appellate Body Report, *Peru–Agricultural Products*'].

3. The economic impact of a PRS on a small open economy

Why would a small economy, such as Peru, so adamantly seek to preserve its right to impose a PRS? In the Introduction above, we mentioned two reasons why a government might choose to implement the PRS: as a price stabilization policy for farmers to guard against the negative income effects of price shocks and as a price stabilization policy for consumers to guard against price increases. But what if a PRS is evaluated on the basis of aggregate economic welfare as opposed to the welfare of individual groups? Does a PRS enhance a country's overall economic welfare?

Below, we provide a formal analysis of the effects of a PRS in the standard trade model of a small importing nation. Since this analysis raises questions about the optimality of a PRS, we next discuss some modifications in the underlying assumptions of the standard model that can help explain why a small importing country might want to institute a PRS.

3.1 A stylized model of a small importing nation

Suppose Peru institutes a PRS under which it adjusts the additional duty applied to an imported commodity (call it sugar) so as to ensure that the domestic (tariff-ridden) price always lies within the interval $[\underline{p}, \bar{p}]$. Let the world price p^w of sugar fluctuate between three different states.[26] In the high state ($i = H$) $p^w = p_H$, in the medium state ($i = M$) $p^w = p_M$, and in the low state ($i = L$) $p^w = p_L$, where the following relationships hold (i) $p_H \geqslant p_M \geqslant p_L$, (ii) $p_H > \bar{p}$, (iii) $p_M \in [\underline{p}, \bar{p}]$, and (iv) $p_L < \underline{p}$. Thus, by design, the high price p_H exceeds the upper bound $\bar{p}$ of the PRS, the low price p_L lies below the lower bound $\underline{p}$ while the medium price p_M lies strictly inside the interval $[\underline{p}, \bar{p}]$.

Let θ_i denote the probability of state i so that we have:

$$p^w = \begin{cases} p_L \text{ with prob } \theta_L \\ p_M \text{ with prob } \theta_M \\ p_H \text{ with prob } \theta_H = 1 - \theta_L - \theta_M \end{cases} \tag{1}$$

Let AD_i denote the additional duty applied by Peru in state i. Then, the variable duty imposed by Peru under its PRS is given by:

$$AD = \begin{cases} AD_L = \underline{p} - p_L \textit{ if } p^w = p_L \\ 0 \textit{ if } p^w = p_M \\ AD_H = \bar{p} - p_H \textit{ if } p^w = p_H \end{cases} \tag{2}$$

Observe that $AD_H < 0 < AD_L$; i.e. the variable levy is positive when the world price is low, whereas it is negative when it is high. Finally, when the world price falls

26 In what follows, we assume that the international reference price equals the world price. This helps simplify exposition without materially affecting our main conclusions. One added benefit of this normalization is that it makes a PRS equivalent to a price band system. Furthermore, since the import cost parameter b does not affect the working of the model, we set it equal to zero.

within the price band $[\underline{p}, \bar{p}]$ established by the PRS, the additional duty imposed by Peru equals zero.[27]

Treating Peru as a small open economy (i.e. as a country that takes world prices as given), the domestic (tariff-included) price in Peru under various states of the world is simply the sum of the world price and the duty applied:

$$p = \begin{cases} p_L + AD_L = \underline{p} \; if \; p^w = p_L \\ p_M \; if \; p^{\bar{w}} = p_M \\ p_H + AD_H = \bar{p} \; if \; p^w = p_H \end{cases} \tag{3}$$

Thus, by design, the variable duty imposed ensures that the domestic price always stays within the PRS band $[\bar{p}, \underline{p}]$.

Let domestic (inverse) demand function in Peru for sugar be given by:

$$d(p) = a - p \tag{4}$$

and the domestic supply function by:

$$s(p) = p \tag{5}$$

Then, Peru's import demand curve for sugar is the difference between domestic demand and supply:

$$m(p) = d(p) - s(p) = a - 2p \tag{6}$$

In the absence of trade, we would have $m(p) = 0$ which yields $p^* = a/2$ as the autarkic equilibrium price in Peru. Given the nature of the dispute, we assume $m(p_i) > 0$; i.e. Peru imports the good under all states of the world, an outcome that is guaranteed by the inequality $p^H < p^*$, which we assume holds.

Given a domestic price p, the surplus consumers enjoy from the good equals:

$$CS = \int_p^a (a - p)dp = \frac{1}{2}(a - p)^2 \tag{7}$$

so that expected consumer welfare can be written as:

$$ECS = \sum_i \theta_i CS(p_i) \tag{8}$$

Similarly, the surplus of domestic producers equals:

$$PS = \int_0^p p dp = \frac{1}{2}p^2 \tag{9}$$

27 We should note here that in addition to the PRS, Peru also imposed a baseline tariff on the relevant commodities. However, since this fixed tariff level does not play an important role in determining the economic effects of the PRS, our model abstracts from it by setting it equal to zero.

which gives expected producer surplus as:

$$EPS = \sum_i \theta_i PS(p_i) \tag{10}$$

The tariff revenue collected by Peru under each state of the world equals:

$$TR = \begin{cases} t_L m(\underline{p}) = (\underline{p} - p_L)m(\underline{p}) \; if \; p^w = p_L \\ 0 \; if \; p^w = p_M \\ t_H m(\bar{p}) = -(p_H - \bar{p})m(\bar{p}) \; if \; p^w = p_H \end{cases} \tag{11}$$

which yields expected tariff revenue as:

$$ETR = \theta_L(\underline{p} - p_L)m(\underline{p}) - \theta_H(p_H - \bar{p})m(\bar{p}) \tag{12}$$

We can now write down Peru's expected total welfare under the PRS as a weighted sum of consumer surplus, producer surplus, and tariff revenue:

$$EW = \sum_i \theta_i[CS(p_i) + \lambda PS(p_i)] + \lambda[\theta_L(\underline{p} - p_L)m(\underline{p}) - \theta_H(p_H - \bar{p})m(\bar{p})] \tag{13}$$

where the parameter $\lambda \geqslant 1$ measures how much extra weight the government puts on producer interests and tariff revenue relative to consumer surplus. When $\lambda = 1$, the government weights all components of welfare equally, and, as λ increases, the relative weight placed on consumer welfare declines while that placed on other components increases.

Using the formulae in (6) through (13), we can directly calculate:

$$\frac{\partial EW}{\partial \underline{p}}|_{\lambda=1} = -2\theta_L\left(\underline{p} - p_L\right) < 0 \tag{14}$$

i.e. if the government weights all components of welfare equally ($\lambda = 1$), then it is optimal to reduce the lower bound of the PRS to its minimum possible value. This implies that it is optimal for Peru not to impose any minimum price on the commodity. Similarly, we have:

$$\frac{\partial EW}{\partial \bar{p}}|_{\lambda=1} = 2\theta_H(p_H - \bar{p}) > 0 \tag{15}$$

i.e. it is optimal for Peru to raise the upper bound of the PRS band. It is worth emphasizing that equations (14) and (15) imply that in the standard trade model *it is optimal for a small importing nation to allow maximum variability in its local price if its objective is to maximize expected national welfare.*

Thus, in the canonical trade model of a small open economy, the mere presence of price fluctuations does not generate a welfare-based rationale for the use of a PRS like the one employed by Peru so long as the objective of the government is to maximize expected aggregate welfare. The intuition for this result is that the

Figure 1. Effects of the PRS system on a small open economy

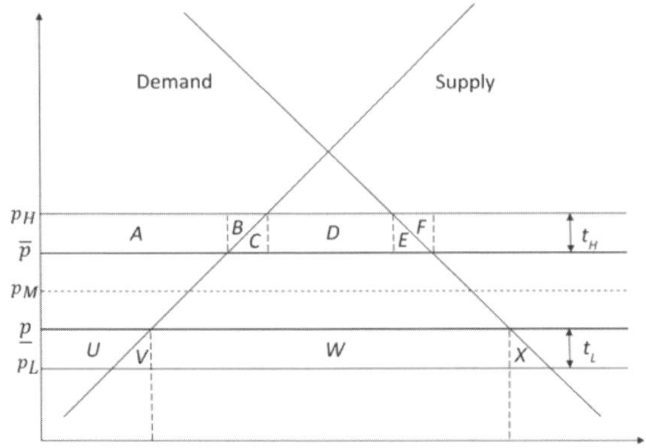

gains from trade enjoyed by an open economy depend upon whether and how much the world price of a commodity differs from its autarkic price. In our simple model above, the autarkic price equals $p^* = a/2$. Imagine the world price equals Peru's autarkic price, i.e. $p^w = p^* = a/2$. Would it gain from trade? The answer is a clear no since domestic production and consumption under free trade would exactly equal that under autarky. Now, consistent with the dispute, suppose $p^w < p^*$. Then, under free trade, Peru would import this commodity and enjoy gains from trade. While domestic producers would lose, the increase in consumer surplus would dominate their loss. Indeed, the lower the world price relative to Peru's autarkic price, the larger would be its gains from trade. A PRS band supported by fluctuating duties reduces the extent to which the domestic price in Peru differs from its autarkic price and therefore reduces its overall gains from trade.

The careful reader may observe that the above discussion seems to ignore the fact that the duties applied raise revenue. While revenue is part of domestic welfare, for the case of a small open economy, the burden of an import duty is borne entirely by local consumers – see the formula for the domestic price in equation (3). As a result, from an aggregate welfare perspective, the variable duty system instituted to support the PRS simply redistributes income within Peru. When $p^w = p_L$, the duty t_L raises the domestic price in Peru to $\underline{p}$ and redistributes income from consumers to producers and the government; whereas when $p^w = p_H$, the rebate t_H benefits local consumers at the expense of the other two groups by lowering the domestic price to $\bar{p}$.

Figure 1 in the appendix provides a graphical illustration of why the expected welfare of a small importing nation declines when it puts in place a PRS to lower domestic price variability. When $p^w = p_L$, the duty t_L raises the domestic price to the minimum acceptable price $\underline{p}$ and consumer surplus declines by the amount $U + V + W + X$. Domestic producer surplus increases by U and government collects revenue equal to area W. The net welfare loss suffered by Peru when $p^w = p_L$ then equals $U + W - (U + V + W + X) = -V - X$, which is simply the deadweight loss of the duty t_L. Now consider the case where $p^w = p_H$ so that the rebate t_H lowers the local price to $\bar{p}$. Then, when $p^w = p_H$ consumers gain the area $A + B + C + D + E$ due to the rebate that lowers the domestic price to $\underline{p}$; producers lose $A + B$; while the government loses $B + C + D + E + F$ in order to cover the subsidy payments needed to lower the local price to $\underline{p}$. Adding these gains and losses together, we find that the net welfare effect of the PRS on Peru is once again negative and it equals $-(B + F)$. Thus, regardless of whether the world price is below or above the PRS interval $[\underline{p}, \bar{p}]$, the net welfare of a small importing nation declines due to the PRS.

The above analysis has focused on the case where the government cares equally about all components of welfare (i.e. $\lambda = 1$). In the real world, it is possible that the government weighs producer interests and tariff revenue more than consumer surplus. Suppose the importing government weighs producer interests and revenue more than consumer surplus (i.e. $\lambda > 1$). Then, the first-order conditions $\frac{\partial EW}{\partial \underline{p}} = 0$ and $\frac{\partial EW}{\partial \bar{p}} = 0$ can be solved for the endpoints of the optimal PRS band. We have:

$$\underline{p}^* = \frac{2\lambda p_L - (\lambda - 1)a}{3\lambda - 1}$$

where $\underline{p}^*$ is increasing in λ and:

$$\underline{p}^* - p_L = \frac{(\lambda - 1)(a - p_L)}{3\lambda - 1}$$

from which it follows that:

$$\underline{p}^* > p_L \Leftrightarrow \lambda > 1$$

so that it is indeed optimal for the government to impose a PRS that *raises the minimum price* p_L *to* $\underline{p}^*$ if it weighs producer surplus and revenue more than consumer surplus. However, at the same time, we have:

$$\underline{p}^* - p_H = \frac{(\lambda - 1)(a - p_H)}{3\lambda - 1}$$

i.e. if $\lambda > 1$, it is optimal for the government to *also raise the maximum price* p_H *to* $\underline{p}^*$. In other words, if $\underline{p}^* > p_L$, it must also be the case that $\underline{p}^* > p_H$. Thus, the mere presence of political economy pressures that cause the government to weight producer interests (and revenue) relatively more than consumer welfare cannot yield a PRS that raises the domestic price when the world price is low *while also* lowering it when the world price is high. Allowing for $\lambda > 1$ only causes the government to raise the domestic price in all states of nature so that it cannot account for a PRS that offers a rebate to local consumers when the world price is high.

3.2 Some other relevant economic considerations

Given the results yielded by the standard model of a small importing nation, it is worth asking whether certain modifications in the assumptions of this model can make a PRS welfare-improving. The model makes two important assumptions that may be suspect in the context of agricultural trade. First, it assumes that all agents are risk neutral. In the context of agricultural commodities, consumers as well as producers might be risk averse. Second, the standard model assumes that production is completely flexible and can be adjusted up and down seamlessly depending upon the observed world price. We next investigate whether altering these assumptions can provide a rationale for why a small importing nation might want to lower fluctuations in the domestic price via import tariffs.

Consider first the role of risk aversion. In their analysis of *Chile–Price Band System*, Bagwell and Sykes (2004) note that since a PRS insulates the domestic economy from price fluctuations it would be attractive to local producers (as well as the government) if producers care not only about the average or expected price but also about its volatility.[28] The standard model of a small open economy presented above ignores the effects of price volatility since all agents (producers, consumers, as well as the government) are assumed to be risk neutral and their welfare can be evaluated in terms of their expected payoffs.

Indeed, greater price variability is *actually beneficial* in the standard model because it increases a country's expected gains from trade by causing the world price to *diverge* more from its autarkic price. If risk-averse producers are willing to sacrifice high price episodes in order to avoid low price ones, a PRS can be optimal from a domestic viewpoint. However, since a PRS suppresses the overall expected gains from trade, for a PRS to increase welfare the benefits of reduced price variability would need to be sufficiently large – i.e., a small amount of risk aversion on the part of local producers will generally not be enough to overcome the lower expected gains from trade implied by reduced price variability under a PRS.[29]

A well-established strand of the rather extensive literature on price stabilization measures argues that to identify the full impact of such measures one needs to

28 In a classic paper, Newberry and Stiglitz (1984) showed that free trade can be Pareto inferior to autarky (i.e. the absence of trade) when neither producers nor consumers can buy insurance for the risks (i.e. the variability of output and price) that are faced by them.

29 Nevertheless, it is worth emphasizing that price stabilization schemes often end up lowering not just the volatility of domestic prices but also alter the average price level, which in turn implies that such schemes invariably transfer income between domestic groups – something that is captured rather sharply by Figure 1.

examine their effect on not just the country instituting the system but also the rest of the world. The model presented above cannot capture such external effects since, by definition, a small country has no impact on the rest of the world. Bagwell and Sykes (2004) have argued that for the case of a large importing country, not only could risk-averse domestic producers be better off under a PBS relative to a fixed conventional tariff but the trading partner may also prefer a PBS if it leads to a lower average tariff. But, as Bagwell and Sykes (2004) note, while reducing price volatility in the domestic market a PBS may simultaneously amplify fluctuations in the net price received by foreign exporters. Thus, for such a system to be optimal from a joint welfare perspective, domestic producers would need to be *more* risk averse than foreign exporters so that shifting risk abroad would be efficient. Bigman (1987) considers a two-country framework in which the free trade relative price is endogenous and shows that the use of variable levies by one country causes *price instability to be exported* from its market to that of its trading partner, on the basis of which he argues that variable levies can 'destabilize thy neighbor'. In other words, reduced variability in one country's market is achieved at the *expense* of increased variability in its trading partner's market. If this spillover leads the trading partner to also institute a price stabilization measure of its own, then both countries can be worse off relative to a scenario where neither uses such measures. Indeed, price variability can even *increase* when price stabilization measures are used by both countries relative to when they are completely absent, thereby making such measures counter-productive.[30]

As Turnovsky (1974) notes, the classical argument in favor of price variability in competitive markets formalized by Oi (1961), Massell (1969), and Waugh (1966) rests on an important assumption: i.e. though producers (and consumers) face uncertainty, they make supply and demand decisions based upon actual prices whereas in the real world many critical production decisions need to be made before the resolution of price uncertainty. This is particularly true in the context of agricultural commodities where farmers make a variety of decisions well before actual prices for their crops are revealed. Thus, while the results of the simple model presented above clearly illustrate the benefits of price variability, they do not adequately capture the impact of uncertainty on production decisions. Eaton and Grossman (1985) show that free trade is not optimal for a small open economy facing uncertain terms of trade provided some factors of production are immobile ex-post and insurance markets are incomplete. In such an environment, tariff protection can serve as an incomplete substitute for the lack of insurance. In a similar vein, a PRS like the one instituted by Peru can help insure that the welfare of consumers and producers does not fall below a certain minimum

30 See Devadoss (1992). Nordström (2001) shows that it is possible to design a system of variable levies that can lower volatility in one market without necessarily exporting it to its trading partner(s). But, as the author notes, we have absolutely no evidence that real world variable duties even begin to approximate the finely calibrated system proposed in Nordström (2001).

threshold. But as Eaton and Grossman (1985) note, trade policy intervention does not constitute a first-best solution to the problem of income redistribution; for example, an income tax is preferable because it can redistribute income without distorting prices faced by domestic agents.

To summarize, although the canonical model of a small open economy suggests that a PRS is always welfare sub-optimal, this may not be the case once certain underlying assumptions of this model are altered. In particular, the economic justification for a PRS in a small open economy turns on whether producers and/or consumers are risk averse, factors of production are immobile, and insurance markets are incomplete. In the presence of such factors, a PRS may prove to be welfare-enhancing, albeit it is not necessarily the first-best option.

4. Policy flexibility for implementing a PRS under WTO law: open questions

Having explained why a small open economy might want to institute and then defend its PRS, we turn to the question of whether WTO law grants flexibility for countries to maintain such policies. In Section 2.2, we explained how WTO law forbids the use of a variable import levy and minimum import price. For a WTO member to preserve policy flexibility, it must convince the AB that its PRS is not similar to either of these.

Could a WTO member ever succeed? The ongoing dispute raises several interesting questions that we highlight below. The dispute offers the AB an opportunity to clarify if and how a PRS could be designed to be WTO-consistent.

Variable import levy

In *Chile–Price Band System*, the AB explained the nature of a 'variable import levy' which is disallowed under WTO rules. Variability alone is not determinative.[31] The AB declared that 'the presence of a formula causing automatic and continuous variability of duties is a *necessary*, but by no means a *sufficient*, condition'.[32] Instead, the AB emphasized the need for 'additional features' including 'a lack of transparency and a lack of predictability' that 'contribute to distorting the prices of imports'.[33]

A first question raised by this line of jurisprudence is the frequency with which a duty must change in order for it to be considered variable. The AB's past language refers to a formula which changes 'continuously'. The Panel found that Peru's PRS, which employed a mathematical formula that resulted in duty changes every two weeks, met this condition.[34] But suppose that the reference price employed in the

31 Appellate Body Report, *Chile–Price Band System*, para. 232.
32 Ibid., paras. 233–234 (emphases in the original) (footnotes omitted).
33 Ibid.
34 Panel Report, *Peru–Agricultural Products*, para. 7.324.

PRS formula were tweaked monthly, quarterly, or annually? At what point, if any, would the change be infrequent enough such that the PRS formula would no longer meet the 'automatic and continuous variability' requirement?

A second question is whether the introduction of some degree of discretion in the application of the formula would matter. What if the PRS formula did not result in a set duty, but instead merely set a range from which authorities could choose? Suppose the PRS formula, instead of arriving at an absolute additional duty, churned out a range, mandating that the additional duty lie between the interval $[AD_L, AD_H]$, where AD_L represents the lower bound for the additional duty and AD_H represents the upper bound. The upper and lower bound for the range are to be calculated through the use of different coefficients (c_L, c_H), to be added to the formula discussed in Section II.1, where $c_L < c_H$. In other words, $AD_L = (1 + b + c_L)(P_{floor} - P_r)$ and $AD_H = (1 + b + c_H)(P_{floor} - P_r)$. The implementing authority, whether an agency within the executive branch or the legislature itself, is free to select any duty rate within that range as the additional duty. The same notion of an upper and lower bound would exist for the tariff rebate. After selecting the duty/rebate rate, the authority would then publish the rate in a gazette for a fixed period of time to provide advance notice before it is enacted. Would such a scheme provide the necessary discretion for the PRS to not be considered an automatic formula? And, if so, would this matter in considering whether a PRS is a 'variable import levy'?

These hypotheticals suggest that the concept of a variable import levy, as elaborated upon in *Chile–Price Band System*, requires further clarification.[35] By explaining the concept further, the AB can give guidance as to how, if ever, a WTO member could design a PRS scheme that is not a 'variable import levy' deemed illegal under Article 4.2 of the Agreement on Agriculture.

Our view is that a shift toward emphasizing the design, architecture, and structure of the PRS as determinative may be the right direction in which to guide the jurisprudence.[36] This continues to allow for consideration of whether the formula results in automatic and continuous changes in which the results are predictable and transparent, but also opens the possibility for consideration of additional factors beyond what is laid out in *Chile–Price Band System*. It also falls in line with the AB's approach toward examining duty schemes under other circumstances, most notably GATT Article III:2.[37]

35 The clarification provided in the subsequent Appellate Body report notes that what is critical is the presence of the formula, along with additional features, rather than the frequency of change in the duties at issue. See Appellate Body Report, *Peru–Agricultural Products*, paras. 5.40–5.48

36 The subsequent Appellate Body Report tacks toward this approach. See ibid., para. 5.54 (emphasizing the 'structure, design, and operation of the PRS').

37 See Appellate Body Report, *Japan – Taxes on Alcoholic Beverages*, WT/DS8/AB/R, WT/DS10/AB/R, WT/DS11/AB/R, 4 October 1996, adopted 1 November 1996, p. 29.

4.2 Minimum import price

In order to stand, a PRS must also not be similar to a minimum import price. In *Chile–Price Band System*, the AB clarified that '[t]he term 'minimum import price' refers generally to the lowest price at which imports of a certain product may enter a Member's domestic market'.[38] It further noted that the Panel had clarified that '[these] schemes generally operate in relation to the actual transaction value of the imports'.[39] This notion was further reinforced during the dispute's compliance proceedings.[40]

Because a PRS operates in relation to a reference price and not the actual transaction price, it is possible, at least in theory, for imports under a PRS to enter a market below the floor price set by a PRS. For example, consider a scenario where the actual transaction price (P_t) is lower than the floor and the reference price, i.e. $P_t < P_r < P_{floor}$. This may occur if prices continue to decline in the intervening period following when the reference price was last readjusted. So long as the difference between the transaction price and floor price is larger than the sum of the original duty plus the additional duty, then the actual transaction price will fall below the floor price. Whether this proposition holds true depends, in part, on the difference between the transaction and reference price. The greater this divergence, and the lower the rate of the original duty, the more likely it is that this will hold.

Thus, the proper assessment is not whether a PRS imposes a minimum import price but whether it is *similar to* such a policy. In assessing similarity, the AB's jurisprudence suggests that one considers two factors: (1) the structure and design of the PRS, and (2) its effects.[41]

Unlike the Panel in *Chile–Price Band System*, the Panel in *Peru–Agricultural Products* found that the measure imposed by the PRS was not similar to a minimum import price.[42] Guatemala has appealed this ruling.[43]

While the Chilean and Peruvian schemes employ different names (PBS vs. PRS), a closer examination reveals that the structure and design of the two systems are largely similar. Peru also occasionally refers to its scheme as a *bando de precios* (PBS). However, three points of contrast are worth noting in the two schemes' design: First, the Peruvian reference price is updated every two weeks, as opposed to weekly for the Chilean reference price. Second, the Peruvian reference

38 Appellate Body Report, *Chile–Price Band System*, para. 236.

39 Ibid. (citing Panel Report, *Chile–Price Band System*, para. 7.36(e).

40 Panel Report, *Chile–Price Band System (Article 21.5 Argentina)*, WT/DS207/RW, 8 December 2006, adopted 22 May 2007, paras. 7.30; Appellate Body Report, *Chile–Price Band System (Article 21.5 Argentina)*, WT/DS207/AB/RW, 7 May 2007, adopted 22 May 2007, para. 195.

41 Appellate Body Report, *Chile–Price Band System (Article 21.5 Argentina)*, para. 193.

42 Panel Report, *Peru–Agricultural Products*, paras. 7.370–7.371.

43 Notification of an Other Appeal by Guatemala Under Article 16.4 and Article 17 of the Understanding of Rules and Procedures Governing the Settlement of Disputes (DSU) and Under Rule 23 (1) of the Working Procedures for Appellate Review, WT/DS457/8, 1 April 2015, at paras. 5–7.

price is based on the price in a pre-designated market, whereas the Chilean reference price is the lowest price found of several markets in relationship to one another. Third, the Peruvian scheme requires reference prices be converted to c.i.f. terms, thereby incorporating freight and insurance costs, whereas the Chilean reference price is left on lower f.o.b. terms. All three differences increase the likelihood that the actual transaction price will diverge from the reference price by a greater degree when prices fall.

The Panel, however, did not emphasize these differences in its ruling. Instead, it focused primarily on the second factor – its actual effects. Whereas Chile conceded that it was 'unlikely' for imports to enter the Chilean market at a price below the floor price,[44] Peru submitted evidence that in approximately 57% of the fortnightly periods since the PRS came into force, various transactions entered Peru at a price lower than the reference price and floor price.[45] These amounted to more than one-third of trade transactions recorded over these periods.[46] The Panel found this evidence to be decisive in illustrating that the PRS did not impose a *de facto* threshold and was therefore not similar to a minimum import price.[47]

The Panel's points to three questions for the AB to clarify:

> First, did the Panel erred in treating this analysis as primarily an effects-based test?[48] As noted above, the Panel ruling failed to elaborate upon on the design elements of the Peruvian PRS that make it more likely for actual import transactions to occur below the implicit threshold stipulated in the PRS. The AB may wish to clarify the level of analysis that a Panel must undertake if it is to find that the structure and design supports the respondent's argument that a PRS is not similar to a minimum import price.
>
> Second, when it comes to considering how the PRS affects the price of actual transactions, how ought the effect of the PRS be measured? The evidence may be expressed in terms of the percentage of total import volume (in either value or quantity), the percentage of total transactions, and/or the percentage of days/weeks/other periods in which imports priced below the threshold enter into the market. Are all of these acceptable metrics? Or should greater emphasis be placed on one over the other? Note that Peru submitted evidence only with respect to the latter two metrics, but not with respect to total imports (except for sugar).[49]

44 Panel Report, *Chile–Price Band System (Article 21.5 – Argentina)*, paras. 7.30

45 Panel Report, *Peru–Agricultural Products*, para. 7.357.

46 Ibid.

47 Ibid., paras. 7.366–7.369.

48 Note that the subsequent Appellate Body report found this to be a source of error; it reversed the Panel's ruling but was unable to complete the analysis. Appellate Body Report, *Peru–Agricultural Products*, paras. 5.139–5.142, 5.153–5.155, and 5.164–5.165.

49 Ibid., para. 7.357.

Why does the exact metric matter? At first glance, it may seem impressive that below-threshold transactions occurred in 57% of the fortnightly periods in which the PRS was in effect. But whether this is truly the case depends, in our view, on the percentage of total import volume represented by such transactions rather than the actual number of transactions themselves or the percentage of periods in which they occurred. In the one instance (sugar) where Peru submitted statistical evidence on the total volume of trade, only 3% of imports entered below the alleged threshold price.[50] We believe that the AB ought to require a respondent to demonstrate effect through data highlighting total volume of trade (rather than the other two metrics) and set forth a brighter line for the percentage of total trade exceeding the alleged threshold price.

Third, should the respondent, when seeking to prove the actual effect of a PRS, be asked to present evidence on a product-specific level? For a PRS to not amount to a measure similar to a minimum import price, the respondent ought to demonstrate that imports below the alleged *de facto* threshold entered the market with some regularity for *all* of the tariff lines. In this case, Peru appears to have focused its evidence on the four marker products rather than on the associate products.[51] The AB would do well to scrutinize the data submitted for the other products to ensure that transactions below the alleged threshold price exist for all 45 affected tariff lines.

To summarize, the *Peru–Agricultural Products* dispute raises a number of pressing questions over the evidentiary burden necessary for a WTO member to demonstrate that a PRS does not give rise to a measure similar to a variable import levy or minimum import price. In clarifying these questions, the AB will make clearer how a WTO member ought to design such a scheme and what types of statistical evidence it ought to collect, if it hopes to employ a PRS in line with Article 4.2 of the Agreement on Agriculture.

5. Circumventing WTO obligations through subsequent agreements: can a WTO-illegal PRS be preserved in a free trade agreement?

The preceding section demonstrated the difficulty of developing and maintaining a PRS in line with a country's obligations under the WTO's Agreement on Agriculture and GATT 1994. Cognizant of the possibility that a PRS might run afoul of WTO rules, Peru sought an explicit guarantee from several of its trading partners of its flexibility to maintain its PRS. Between 2005 and 2013, Peru signed a number of FTAs.[52] Our examination of the text of Peru's FTAs suggests that in at least 12 of these agreements, Peru managed to negotiate the inclusion

50 Ibid.

51 See ibid.

52 See Organization of American States, Foreign Trade Information System, Information on Peru, Trade Agreements, http://www.sice.oas.org/ctyindex/PER/PERagreements_e.asp (accessed 3 May 2015).

Table 1. Provisions in Peru's FTAs addressing the PRS

FTA partner	Date of entry into force	Provision concerning PRS
Chile	1 March 2009	Article 3.2(11)
Canada	1 August 2009	Article 218
Singapore	1 August 2009	Article 2.4(3)
China	1 March 2010	Chapter 2, Article 19
European Free Trade Association (EFTA)	1 July 2011	Article 3.3
South Korea	1 August 2011	Article 2.16
Mexico	1 February 2012	Annex to Article 3.4-A, § 3
Japan	1 March 2012	Article 28
Panama	1 May 2012	Annex 2.3, para. 9.
European Union	1 March 2013	Article 30
Costa Rica	1 June 2013	Annex 2.3, para. 9
Guatemala	(not yet entered into force)	Annex 2.3, para. 9

of a provision that explicitly recognized its right to retain the PRS. The most notable exception is the US–Peru FTA.

Table 1 provides a list of the specific provisions found within the 12 FTAs.[53] Only the Guatemala–Peru FTA has yet to enter into force.

Two questions arise from this attempt of a WTO member to utilize FTAs to safeguard a measure that may be WTO-inconsistent: First, should a provision of an FTA concluded between two countries factor into the interpretation of the WTO obligations of the two countries to each other? Second, does the answer change if the FTA is one that has not yet entered into force?

In prior case law, the AB has recognized that WTO members may modify the obligations between themselves.[54] However, the question arises as to which mechanisms employed by WTO members to modify the obligations must be recognized by WTO adjudicators. Guatemala argued that modifications of WTO rights and obligations can only be done through the procedures established in Article X of the WTO Agreement and not through a bilateral treaty.[55] Guatemala further argued that for a Panel to examine (a) whether there is an inconsistency between an FTA and the WTO Agreement and (b) if the FTA modified the WTO rights of a party would fall outside of a Panel's terms of reference, since Panels cannot

53 The precise language of each of these provisions is detailed in Annex 1 of the longer version of this Article, published as Vanderbilt University Working Paper No. VUECON-15-00009 and EUI Working Paper No. RSCAS 2015/58.

54 Appellate Body Report, *EC–Bananas III (Article 21.5 – Ecuador II) / EC–Bananas III (Article 21.5 – US)*, WT/DS27/AB/RW2/ECU, WT/DS27/AB/RW/USA, 26 November 2008, adopted 11 December 2008 and 22 December 2008, para. 217.

55 Panel Report, *Peru–Agricultural Products*, paras. 7.511–7.512.

consider matter outside of the WTO covered agreements.[56] Guatemala's views were shared by the United States as a third party.[57]

Peru, on the other hand, suggested that WTO treaty provisions are to be interpreted pursuant to the Vienna Convention on the Law of Treaties (VCLT). An FTA concluded pursuant to GATT Article XXIV serves as a form of permissible modification under VCLT Article 41.[58] Where the provisions of the FTA clash with the WTO Agreement, Peru argued the provision of the FTA should prevail as it represents a subsequent agreement.[59]

Brazil and the European Union (EU), as third parties, agreed that an FTA may modify the rights and obligations of a WTO agreement, but suggested that the scope for doing so is more limited. Brazil argued that only FTAs that have entered into force may modify the rights and obligations between two WTO members.[60] The EU argued that a modification arises in the WTO context only if the FTA includes a specific commitment that a party will refrain from initiating a WTO challenge to the other party's measure.[61]

This question of whether a ratified FTA may alter the terms of obligations between WTO members remains very much an open point of dispute. The AB, however, may opt not to address this question directly in the pending appeal.[62] Because the Peru–Guatemala FTA had not yet entered into force, it does not acquire the formal status of a modification made pursuant to VCLT Article 41. It does not acquire the status of a subsequent agreement, relevant for interpretation pursuant to VCLT Article 31(3)(a).

Pauwelyn (2014) has suggested that Peru should instead have relied on the International Law Commission (ILC)'s Articles on Responsibility of States for Internationally Wrongful Acts when making its argument. Article 20 states, 'Valid consent by a State to the commission of a given act by another State precludes the wrongfulness of that act in relation to the former State to the extent that the act remains within the limits of that consent.' Pauwelyn notes that such an argument turns the question into a factual inquiry into whether Guatemala has provided consent in allowing Peru to keep its PRS.

56 Ibid., para. 7.511.
57 Ibid., paras. 7.519–7.520.
58 Ibid., para. 7.508.
59 Ibid., para. 7.506.
60 Ibid., para. 7.518.
61 Ibid., para. 7.522.
62 The AB, in its subsequent report, simply noted that 'there appears to be ambiguity as to whether even the FTA itself, regardless of its legal status, allows Peru to maintain the PRS if it is found to be WTO-inconsistent'. See Appellate Body Report, *Peru–Agricultural Products*, para. 5.26. In light of this ambiguity, the AB rejected Peru's argument that Guatemala acted contrary to the good faith obligations of DSU Articles 3.7 and 3.10, and did not find it necessary to opine further on this question. Ibid., para. 5.28 and footnote 109.

Indeed, Peru appears to have adopted Pauwelyn's suggested tactic in its appeal. Peru's appeal contends that even if the FTA is not a subsequent agreement per VCLT Article 31(3)(a), it is nevertheless a 'relevant rule of international law' within the meaning of VCLT Article 31(3)(c).[63] This is on the basis of ILC Articles 20 and 45 of the ILC Articles on State Responsibility as rules of international law.

While this argument raises a series of interesting issues for the AB to consider in the appeal, it is still unclear to us that Peru will prevail. In *US–Line Pipe*, the AB made clear that the ILC Articles on State Responsibility 'do not constitute a binding legal instrument as such'.[64] Consequently, the AB adopted a two-part approach of analyzing whether a particular provision of the ILC Articles on State Responsibility ought to be considered when interpreting a WTO provision. First, it examined whether the particular provision of the ILC Articles is relevant to the analysis. Then, it examined whether that particular provision rose to the level of customary international law.

On both fronts, the appeal presents the AB with an opportunity to clarify when exactly the ILC Articles ought to be consulted in interpreting WTO law.[65] On the question of relevance, the AB's past jurisprudence has required a tight nexus between the particular provision of the ILC Articles and the provision of the WTO covered agreement whose interpretation is in doubt. In *US–Line Pipe*, Article 51 of the ILC Articles spoke directly to the issue concerning the proportionality of countermeasures relevant for interpreting Article 5.1 of the Safeguards Agreement.[66] Similarly, in *US–Anti-Dumping and Countervailing Measures (China)*, Article 4 of the ILC Articles spoke directly to the issue of how to consider state organs, regardless of their formal position in the organizational structure, when interpreting the term 'public body' in Article 2 of the SCM Agreement.[67] It remains to be seen whether the nexus is sufficiently tight for ILC Articles 20 and 45 to be relevant for interpreting the legal provisions at issue in this dispute.

Even if they are relevant, the AB must also find that the particular provisions amount to customary international law. The AB has made clear that the analysis

63 Notification of Appeal by Peru Under Article 16.4 and Article 17 of the Understanding on Rules and Procedures Governing the Settlement of Disputes (DSU) and Under Rule 20(1) of the Working Procedures for Appellate Review, WT/DS457/7, 26 March 2015, para. 10.

64 Appellate Body Report, *United States – Definitive Safeguard Measures on Imports of Circular Welded Carbon Quality Line Pipe from Korea*, WT/DS202/AB/R, 15 February 2002, adopted 8 March 2002, para. 259 [hereinafter '*US–Line Pipe*'].

65 For elaboration on how the Appellate Body chose to address this question in the appeal, see Appellate Body Report, *Peru–Agricultural Products*, paras. 5.100–5.105 (concluding that 'the FTA and ILC Articles 20 and 45 are not "relevant"').

66 Appellate Body Report, *US–Line Pipe*, paras. 250–260.

67 Appellate Body Report, *United States – Definitive Anti-dumping and Countervailing Duties on Certain Products from China*, WT/DS379/AB/R, 11 March 2001, adopted 25 March 2001, paras. 309–310.

is to be done on a provision-by-provision basis.[68] Because the ILC Articles are not an international agreement, the AB cannot resort to the typical approach of examining the breadth of its signatories and whether the particular parties to the dispute have ratified the agreement. Instead, the AB has relied upon consideration of two other factors to determine whether a particular provision amounts to customary international law.[69] First, has the particular provision been cited as such in another international judgment? Second, has the WTO member against whom the provision is being invoked either explicitly or tacitly acknowledged the provision as such? Again, it remains to be seen whether this can be shown for Articles 20 and 41 of the ILC Articles on State Responsibility.

Even if the AB agrees that Articles 20 and 45 are 'relevant rules of international law', it still faces interesting questions over how those provisions are to be interpreted. Article 20 speaks to 'valid consent' that 'precludes the wrongfulness of the act … to the extent that the act remains within the limits of that consent'. Article 45 speaks to the waiver of a claim by the injured party. How ought the AB consider what amounts to 'valid consent' and 'waiver' in a context where an FTA has only been ratified by one party and has not yet entered into force?

Although Guatemala did ratify the FTA during the course of the dispute, it is unclear that this ratification represents an absolute consent as opposed to a contingent consent. The ratification process does not oblige Guatemala to consent unilaterally to all that it has agreed to in the FTA, including its explicit recognition of WTO-inconsistent measures enacted by Peru, without any action on the part of Peru. Rather, Guatemala's consent is only contingent upon Peru's ratification. In the absence of such notice, Guatemala would not appear to have provided explicit consent.

A similar argument can be made with respect to the question of waiver. Again, Guatemala will likely argue that its ratification does not require it to waive claims against Peru upon the moment of ratification, but instead is contingent upon Peru's ratification. Without this reciprocal action, nothing has been waived.

Finally, there is the question of the treaty language that the FTA must employ in order for a WTO member to consent to a WTO-illegal act and/or waive its right to WTO dispute settlement. The EU has put forward the position that the language must be explicit and refer specifically to an agreement to refrain from initiating a WTO challenge. Peru, on the other hand, will likely contend that consent and waiver can be implicit, even without direct treaty language in the FTA concerning WTO challenges. The appeal also presents the AB with an opportunity to decide this question, if it desires.

Most likely, the AB will choose to confront only a subset of the questions identified above. Because the Guatemala–Peru FTA has not entered into force, the facts

68 See ibid., para. 311.
69 See footnote 222 of ibid. and Appellate Body Report, *US–Line Pipe*, footnote 256 and para. 259.

of this dispute are unusual. The appeal may not serve to definitively answer the question of how FTAs between WTO members should factor in a subsequent WTO challenge involving those parties, but it is a question that clearly lurks over the WTO. As WTO members negotiate increasing numbers of FTAs with one another, additional clarity into whether WTO members can circumvent WTO rights through FTAs – and, if so, what treaty language is necessary – will be of benefit to the system as a whole.

6. Conclusion

Because of the sensitivities associated with the agricultural sector, a PRS continues to be viewed as a potentially attractive policy instrument to complement agricultural trade liberalization. This may be particularly the case with small open economies that take world prices as given. A PRS offers it the ability to restrain prices for agricultural products in its domestic market, even after opening up its market to trade.

This article suggests that from an economic welfare standpoint, a PRS represents a sub-optimal policy intervention for a small open economy that seeks to maximize its expected welfare. However, under certain conditions, a government may nevertheless choose to implement a PRS in order to ensure that, with agricultural trade liberalization, the welfare of consumers and producers does not fall below a certain minimum threshold in light of significant risk aversion on the part of either group in the presence of incomplete or missing insurance markets.

WTO law, and in particular the obligations of Article 4.2 of the Agreement on Agriculture to convert non-tariff barriers to tariffs, present a number of significant legal constraints on the PRS. The structure and design of a PRS create an implicit minimum price threshold, and the duties generated by a PRS can operate as a variable import levy. Thus, a WTO member seeking to prove that a PRS is consistent with its WTO obligations faces a heavy burden. The Panel ruling in the *Peru–Agricultural Products* dispute gives rise to a number of unanswered legal questions as to what is required of WTO members that seek to preserve the flexibility to implement a PRS; the Appellate Body may seek to clarify some of these questions in the ongoing appeal.

Finally, the particular zeal with which Peru has sought to preserve its right to maintain the PRS through explicit recognition in preferential trade agreements raises interesting questions about the relationship between provisions in FTAs and WTO agreements. In this case, the Panel was able to avoid providing an answer outright because of the fact that the applicable FTA had not yet entered into force. But given the expanding nature of preferential trade agreements and the stalled multilateral round, it is simply a matter of time before WTO adjudicators are confronted with this question outright. We would all do well to consider carefully how we envision these multiple treaty schemes to intersect with one another in the realm of WTO dispute settlement.

References

Bagwell, K. and A. O. Sykes (2004), '*Chile – Price Band System and Safeguard Measures Relating to Certain Agricultural Products*', *World Trade Review*, **3**: 507–528.

Bigman, D. (1987), 'The Theory of Variable Levies', *Oxford Economic Papers*, **39**: 357–377.

Bouet, A., J.-C. Bureau, Y. Decreux, and S. Jean (2005), 'Multilateral Agricultural Trade Liberalisation: The Contrasting Fortunes of Developing Countries in the Doha Round', *World Economy*, **28**: 1329–1354.

Devadoss, S. (1992), 'Market Interventions, International Price Stabilization, and Welfare Implications', *American Journal of Agricultural Economics*, **74**: 281–290.

Eaton, J. and G. M. Grossman (1985), 'Tariffs as Insurance: Optimal Commercial Policy When Domestic Markets are Incomplete', *The Canadian Journal of Economics*, **18**: 258–272.

Massell, B. (1969), 'Price Stabilization and Welfare', *The Quarterly Journal of Economics*, **83**: 284–298.

Newberry, D. M. G. and J. E. Stiglitz (1984), 'Pareto Inferior Trade', *Review of Economic Studies*, **51**: 1–13.

Nordström, H. (2001), 'Do Variable Levies Beggar Thy Neighbor?', *European Journal of Political Economy*, **17**: 403–420.

Oi, W. (1961), 'The Desirability of Price Instability under Perfect Competition', *Econometrica*, **29**: 58–64.

Pauwelyn, J. (2014), 'Waiving WTO Rights in an FTA? Panel Report on Peru – Agricultural Products', International Economic Law and Policy Blog, 3 December, http://worldtradelaw.typepad.com/ielp-blog/2014/12/waiving-wto-rights-in-an-fta-panel-report-on-peru-agricultural-products.html.

Trivelli, C. *et al.* (2003), *Economic Liberalization and Evolution of Rural Agricultural Sector in Peru*, Tokyo: Institute of Developing Economies, IDE-JETRO.

Turnovsky, S. J. (1974), 'Price Expectations and the Welfare Gains from Price Stabilization', *American Journal of Agricultural Economics*, **56**: 706–716.

Waugh, F. V. (1966), 'Consumer Aspects of Price Instability', *Econometrica*, **34**: 504–508.

Appendix

Table 1A. Peru's imports of HMS 170111 (Cane Sugar), current $, thousands

1998	**Guatemala 20083.46 (71.9%)**	Bolivia 3655.23 (13.1%)	Colombia 2760.5 (9.9%)	Mexico 1411.94 (5.1%)	World 27941.05 (100%)
1999	Guatemala 0 (0%)	Colombia 267.635 (78.7%)	Brazil 68.742 (20.2%)	USA 2.212 (0.6%)	World 339.866 (100%)
2000	Guatemala 0 (0%)	Colombia 151.016 (99.0%)	USA 0.593 (0.3%)	Hong Kong 0.508 (0.3%)	World 152.584 (100%)
2001	Guatemala 0 (0%)	Colombia 2425.465 (78.3%)	Bolivia 668.27 (21.6%)	UK 1.51 (0.0%)	World 3096.469 (100%)
2002	Guatemala 0 (0%)	Colombia 557.054 (60.6%)	Bolivia 331.355 (36.0%)	USA 29.085 (3.1%)	World 918.861 (100%)
2003	Guatemala 0 (0%)	USA 3.376 (57.9%)	Italy 0.587 (10.1%)	Hong Kong 0.462 (7.9%)	World 5.828 (100%)
2004	Guatemala 0 (0%)	Bolivia 1547.17 (52.6%)	Colombia 1387.96 (47.2%)	UK 1.015 (0.0%)	World 2936.543 (100%)
2005	Guatemala 479.825 (4.6%)	Colombia 8642.85 (83.6%)	Bolivia 1207.991 (11.6%)	Belgium 17.816 (0.1%)	World 10348.812 (100%)
2006	**Guatemala 3315.398 (30.0%)**	Colombia 6551.091 (49.3%)	Nicaragua 1949.581 (14.7%)	Bolivia 645.626 (4.9%)	World 13281.523 (100%)
2007	**Guatemala 1338.976 (17.0%)**	Colombia 4501.341 (57.3%)	Nicaragua 1214.512 (15.7%)	Bolivia 767.618 (9.7%)	World 7853.985 (100%)
2008	Guatemala 0 (0%)	Colombia 813.955 (86.1%)	Bolivia 76.992 (8.1%)	Paraguay 21.075 (2.2%)	World 944.998 (100%)
2009	Guatemala 0 (0%)	Bolivia 2545.896 (72.5%)	Colombia 911.968 (26.0%)	Paraguay 33.894 (0.9%)	World 3511.172 (100%)
2010	Guatemala 0 (0%)	Brazil 4385.985 (78.6%)	Colombia 827.096 (14.9%)	Bolivia 246.82 (4.4%)	World 5577.88 (100%)
2011	Guatemala 0 (0%)	Colombia 2383.222 (87.7%)	Paraguay 215.422 (7.9%)	Chile 43.988 (1.6%)	World 2718.68 (100%)
2012	**Guatemala 8927.789 (25.5%)**	Colombia 17723.094 (50.7%)	Nicaragua 4492.297 (12.8%)	Honduras 2668.393 (7.6%)	World 34983.071 (100%)
2013	**Guatemala 441.866 (26.2%)**	Colombia 697.898 (41.3%)	Paraguay 460.101 (27.3%)	Bolivia 58.392 (3.4%)	World 1687.901 (100%)

Table 1B. Peru's imports of HMS 170199 (other cane or beet sugar), current $, thousands

1998	**Guatemala**	Brazil	Colombia	Bolivia	World
	32366.3	25313.8	23570.81	14514.83	129604.544
	(25.0%)	(19.5%)	(18.1%)	(11.2%)	(100%)
1999	Guatemala	Colombia	Brazil	Ecuador	World
	8109.546	38027.705	13336.173	9505.746	84315.545
	(9.6%)	(45.1%)	(15.8%)	(11.2%)	(100%)
2000	Guatemala	Colombia	Brazil	Mexico	World
	3656.519	24227.232	5978.214	4935.809	46074.408
	(7.9%)	(52.6%)	(13.0%)	(10.7%)	(100%)
2001	**Guatemala**	Colombia	Ecuador	Bolivia	World
	6615.852	28564.382	6603.171	4654.843	53288.648
	(12.4%)	(53.6%)	(12.4%)	(8.7%)	(100%)
2002	**Guatemala**	Colombia	Bolivia	Brazil	World
	6362.536	19895.43	3353.046	3223.715	33709.985
	(18.9%)	(59.0%)	(9.9%)	(9.8%)	(100%)
2003	Guatemala	Bolivia	France	USA	World
	0	1665.081	33.526	6.748	2963.453
	(0%)	(56.1%)	(1.1%)	(0.2%)	(100%)
2004	Guatemala	Ecuador	Bolivia	Colombia	World
	88.744	18282.151	15238.501	10953.238	47119.314
	(0.1%)	(38.8%)	(32.3%)	(23.2%)	(100%)
2005	Guatemala	Colombia	Bolivia	Ecuador	World
	892.475	33787.116	12792.212	12311.754	64000.128
	(1.4%)	(52.8%)	(20.0%)	(19.2%)	(100%)
2006	Guatemala	Colombia	Brazil	Bolivia	World
	6780.931	54332.902	13814.809	10654.803	93388.238
	(7.2%)	(58.2%)	(14.8%)	(11.4%)	(100%)
2007	**Guatemala**	Colombia	Bolivia	Brazil	World
	6077.705	54160.209	14467.328	4473.966	82860.16
	(7.3%)	(65.3%)	(17.5%)	(5.3%)	(100%)
2008	**Guatemala**	Colombia	Bolivia	Brazil	World
	9576.184	39292.018	16554.384	5683.314	78677.457
	(12.2%)	(49.9%)	(21.0%)	(7.2%)	(100%)
2009	Guatemala	Colombia	Bolivia	Brazil	World
	628.575	35222.83	18164.825	4489.098	59174.148
	(1.0%)	(59.6%)	(30.7%)	(7.6%)	(100%)
2010	**Guatemala**	Colombia	Brazil	Bolivia	World
	36476.885	59457.925	18032.946	8874.507	124713.045
	(29.2%)	(47.6%)	(14.5%)	(7.1%)	(100%)
2011	**Guatemala**	Colombia	Brazil	Honduras	World
	39082.165	66986.108	33027.344	1373.289	141246.373
	(27.7%)	(47.4%)	(23.4%)	(0.9%)	(100%)
2012	**Guatemala**	Colombia	Brazil	Bolivia	World
	32076.767	93761.102	23589.2	8351.341	164666.979
	(19.5%)	(57.0%)	(14.3%)	(0.5%)	(100%)
2013	Guatemala	Colombia	Bolivia	Brazil	World
	1100.403	67349.734	5073.969	4104.905	81209.131
	(1.3%)	(82.9%)	(6.2%)	(5.0%)	(100%)

CHAPTER 21

World Trade Review (2017), 16: 2, 279–302
 doi:10.1017/S1474745616000549

Trade and Agricultural Disease: Import Restrictions in the Wake of the *India–Agricultural Products* Dispute

KAMAL SAGGI*
Vanderbilt University
MARK WU**
Harvard Law School

Abstract: Trade in agricultural products raises sensitivities, particularly when imports originate from a trading partner experiencing an outbreak of some type of agricultural disease. In this article, we explain why despite the negative externalities associated with diseased imports, an importing country is generally not permitted to ban such imports outright under WTO law. Rather, it is allowed to do so only under specific circumstances. We also highlight how the recent *India–Agricultural Products* ruling contributes to the jurisprudence of two issues concerning the SPS Agreement: the interpretation of international standards, and the relationship between the risk assessment and scientific evidence requirements.

1. Introduction

Global exports of agricultural goods exceeded $1.7 trillion in 2014, with food accounting for over 80% of the total value (WTO, 2015). Such cross-border movement of food and agricultural goods helps ensure the sustenance and economic well-being of billions around the world. Yet, trade rules for agriculture remain an extremely sensitive issue. This is particularly the case when agricultural imports carry the threat of disease.

Not surprisingly then, under the rules of the World Trade Organization (WTO), member countries are allowed to restrict the importation of agricultural products from diseased regions. However, if governments could do so without limitation then this freedom could quickly devolve into a protectionist excuse that has the potential to seriously thwart trade liberalization in the agricultural sector. The relevant WTO rules therefore must seek to balance two competing objectives – providing sufficient flexibility for sovereign governments to regulate imports from diseased regions while simultaneously culling out protectionist measures for

* Email: k.saggi@vanderbilt.edu
** Email: mwu@law.harvard.edu

which the threat of diseased imports simply serves as an excuse for keeping imports at bay. Getting this balance right is tricky. In 1994, Uruguay Round negotiators drafted the Agreement on Sanitary and Phytosanitary Measures (SPS Agreement) to spell out in detail the requirements that a WTO member must follow when seeking to ban or restrict imports of agricultural goods.

In the intervening two decades, several high-profile and controversial WTO cases have arisen concerning imports of agricultural goods that might serve as conduits for introducing new diseases to importing nations.[1] However, until 2012, all of these disputes concerned restrictions enacted by developed countries. The *India – Agricultural Products* dispute[2] represented the first time that a developing country's restrictions on agricultural imports from a diseased region were challenged before the WTO.

Developing countries, of course, have several special considerations worth bearing in mind. Because a higher proportion of households rely upon subsistence agriculture, the introduction of a diseased product may prove more devastating than would be the case elsewhere. Furthermore, inspectors in developing countries may have fewer resources and/or less capacity to weed out diseased agricultural imports than their peers in advanced economies.

What is a developing country to do when a communicable disease has broken out in a trading partner's territory but the trading partner insists that its potentially tainted products ought to be allowed in freely? Can, and should, the developing country enact an outright import ban? Or is a more finely calibrated import quota called for? Can such a trade policy be applied to all imports of that good from the trading partner, even if the disease is confined to a particular geographic region? Or is such an act overly cautious and protectionist, especially since many of its trading partners' agricultural products may not be diseased?

These very questions surfaced in the recent *India–Agricultural Products* dispute. In that case, India sought to prohibit imports of poultry meat, eggs, and other agricultural products from trading partners afflicted with avian influenza (AI) – commonly known as 'bird flu' – in order to protect its domestic poultry stock. The WTO Appellate Body confirmed once more that a WTO Member does not have full regulatory flexibility to enact an outright ban on agricultural imports from a given trading partner afflicted with an agricultural disease. Instead, that measure must be compared against existing international standards, guidelines, and recommendations. Furthermore, a government must offer evidence that the import restriction is necessary and based on scientific principles. The Appellate Body clarified that a WTO Member need not necessarily conduct a risk assessment to

1 Such cases include *Australia – Measures Affecting Importation of Salmon* (DS18), *Japan – Measures Affecting Agricultural Products* (DS76), *Japan – Measures Affecting the Importation of Apples* (DS245), and *Australia – Measures Affecting the Importation of Apples from New Zealand* (DS367).

2 Appellate Body Report, *India – Measures Concerning the Importation of Certain Agricultural Products*, WT/DS430/AB/R (4 June 2015) (*India–Agricultural Products*).

meet this requirement. However, this does not obviate a WTO member from a separate treaty requirement to perform a risk assessment.

This Article discusses and assesses the legal and economic rationale for the Appellate Body's ruling. We explain why an outright ban on imports will generally prove to be excessive from a social welfare perspective. We develop a simple economic framework that shows how the optimal import policy is linked to the degree of damage caused by tainted imports. The SPS Agreement emphasizes the importance of international standards, risk assessment, and scientific evidence in determining the optimal policy response of an importing country when imports carry the threat of disease. We discuss how the Appellate Body ruling contributes to our jurisprudential understanding of these elements. Finally, we draw attention to the controversy concerning the appropriate scope of appellate review resulting from this ruling.

2. A short primer on the applicable law

Under international trade law, a country does not have free rein to ban or restrict imports from another country simply because its trading partner has been afflicted with an agricultural disease. The SPS Agreement establishes detailed rules concerning when countries may restrict agricultural imports to protect human, animal, or plant life or health.

Because many agricultural diseases are monitored by international agencies, the law differentiates between scenarios when an international standard, guideline, or recommendation has been issued concerning agricultural goods affected by a given disease and when it has not. If a WTO member's measure is based on an international standard, guideline, or recommendation, then it is presumed legal, pursuant to Article 3.2. Article 3.3 clarifies that a country may deviate upward so long as it meets additional requirements set forth in that provision.[3]

Additionally, Article 5.7 restricts the use of restrictions based on the precautionary principle to instances 'where relevant scientific evidence is insufficient' such as when the impact of a new pathogen remains unknown. However, a WTO Member may only apply such a restriction on a provisional basis and must 'seek to obtain additional information necessary for a more objective assessment of risk' and review the measure accordingly 'within a reasonable period of time'.

In addition, Article 5.1 requires that any restrictive measure must be based on risk assessment, keeping in mind techniques developed by relevant international organizations. Article 2.2 further requires that the restriction be based on scientific principles and is not maintained without sufficient scientific evidence.

3 This includes providing scientific justification or demonstrating that the upward departure is the appropriate level in accordance with the relevant obligations set forth in Article 5 of the SPS Agreement.

Article 6.1 requires that a WTO Member ensure that any restriction is adapted to the characteristics of the area from which the product originated and to which the product is destined. Such an area may be 'all of a country, part of a country, or all or parts of several countries'. Finally, Article 6.3 requires an exporting country claiming that part of its territory is disease-free to provide evidence and allow reasonable access to trading partners to demonstrate that this is and will remain the case.

WTO law on agriculture and food safety serves as a reminder of the trilemma confronting the global economy (Rodrik, 2011). So long as the nation-state remains the focal point for advancing globalization, deeper economic integration requires trading off some degree of direct democratic governance. Governments in WTO member-states do not possess a *carte blanche* to prohibit or otherwise restrict agricultural imports from disease-ridden trading partners. Decisions made by technocrats in international organizations affect and constrain the government's response.

3. How India's response to bird flu gave rise to a trade dispute

A government therefore finds itself in a precarious situation when an agricultural disease breaks out in a trading partner. On the one hand, it can choose to simply work through the international standard-setting organization to set the appropriate standards and guidelines and then implement the agreed-upon recommendation. As far as consistency with WTO law is concerned, this course of action is safest. However, it may prove costly domestically. Constituents may criticize the government for deferring to an international body rather than exercising its own sovereign authority.

Choosing alternatively to establish one's own policies for imports from the afflicted country carries its own risks. While WTO law allows for deviations, a government must follow a number of requirements. The *India–Agricultural Products* dispute offers a case study of how this latter approach can give rise to trade conflict.

3.1 Avian influenza and India's import restrictions

Avian influenza (AI) is an infectious viral disease that can spread quickly across birds with no apparent signs of illness. Once it hits, AI can devastate poultry stock. Incidences have been reported worldwide. AI is tracked by the World Organization for Animal Health (OIE), an international organization. The OIE establishes recommendations for different strains of AI, codified in the OIE Terrestrial Health Code. AI strains can be classified into two categories – high pathogenic (HPAI) or low pathogenic (LPAI) – with the former being much more deadly. Countries are required to report all occurrences of HPAI and of certain types of LPAI to the OIE.

Among the countries that have reported AI is the United States, the world's second-largest poultry meat exporter, which last reported a case of HPAI in 2004. In the intervening decade, the United States has reported several instances of LPAI. India, too, has notified to the OIE of 95 HPAI outbreaks in the decade between 2003 and 2013. However, India has never notified an outbreak of LPAI.

On 19 July 2011, India's Department of Animal Husbandry, Dairying, and Fisheries (DAHD), pursuant to the powers conferred to it by the Livestock Act of 1898, issued S.O. 1663(E). This regulatory measure imposed an import ban on imports of live birds, poultry, eggs, feathers, and several other poultry-related products from all countries reporting HPAI and LPAI. Restrictions could be lifted once a country demonstrated that it was AI-free. On 7 October 2011, India provided notice of S.O. 1663(E) to the WTO's SPS Committee.

India justified its restrictions on the basis of worldwide AI outbreaks. However, the government also could have been motivated by the desire to protect its poultry industry from foreign competition. India is the third-largest producer of table eggs in the world, behind China and the United States; per-capita consumption of eggs grew by 33% between 2002 and 2012 (Kotaiah, 2013). India is also the fourth-largest producer of broiler products in the world, after China, the US, and Brazil (ibid.).

Interestingly, the structure of chicken farming looks quite different in India. Only 16% of all Indian poultry is raised in intensive systems (i.e., large-scale, mechanized operations). By contrast, for developing countries as a whole, this percentage is 65%, while it exceeds 90% in China (Robinson, 2011: 57). Unlike elsewhere, Indian poultry farming involves mainly small and medium-sized farms where poultry farming is not the primary enterprise but done to supplement income and diet.

Therefore, a devastating AI outbreak affects the overall political economy differently in India. Whereas elsewhere it implicates primarily corporate interests, in India an outbreak afflicts harm on an enormous number of households. In a democratic country with over 250 million farmers and in which the majority of the workforce is dependent on agriculture-related activities to make a living,[4] this can have enormous political consequences. Not surprisingly, the Indian government was keen to keep AI outbreaks at bay.

Did India's poultry farmers face a foreign threat, necessitating government protection? Not necessarily. At present, opportunities for imported poultry products are extremely limited. Indians overwhelmingly prefer to buy their chickens and eggs fresh. Over 93% of boiler products in India are purchased live, whereas most imports are frozen (Kotaiah, 2013). Yet, consumption patterns will change

4 Salve (2014) notes that the 2011 Census reports 118.9 million cultivators, which amounts to nearly 25% of the total workforce. When agricultural laborers are included, that number rises to 263 million.

as household incomes grow and urbanization increases, and some farmers may perceive a looming threat.

What the above discussion demonstrates is that it is not always easy to discern the underlying motivation of a government imposing import restrictions on agricultural products from disease-ridden trading partners. Genuine concerns over health, political considerations, and protectionism could all be part of the equation – the exact contribution of each of these factors is difficult to know with certainty.

3.2 *Why fuss over India's import restrictions?*

Importantly, India was not alone in enacting import bans on poultry and poultry-related products from countries affected by AI. A number of other developing countries also enacted bans including Ecuador, the Philippines, and Saudi Arabia (Nedumpara *et al.*, 2016: 215–216). However, it was India's measures that the US chose to challenge. Why target India?

In their insightful analysis of the Panel Report for this series, Bown and Hillman (2016) note several useful facts about the dispute. First, the US is the largest producer of poultry in the world. Major US poultry producers have been fairly effective in getting the government to respond to its interests, leading to seven antidumping investigations, and 12 WTO disputes involving poultry between 1995 and 2014. Second, though India is a country with a large population, it is not (yet) an important market for US poultry exports. In fact, in a typical year, Indian imports of poultry from the US are estimated to be a paltry $2 million or so. Considering that the US global exports amount to roughly $5 billion a year, the Indian economy absorbs approximately 0.04% of US poultry exports.

Classical trade policy models teach us that the trade policy interventions of small markets are inconsequential for exporters since they do not affect world prices. An import ban on poultry imposed by India should simply mean that US poultry exports that would have been sold in India should find their way to alternative markets without having any real effect on world prices and therefore US exporters.

Be that as it may, there are several reasons why the US poultry industry might care about an Indian ban on poultry justified on the basis of an outbreak of avian flu in certain parts of the US. First, given the pace of economic growth in India during recent decades, the US poultry industry might rationally expect the Indian market to become significantly more important over time. As Indian consumers get richer and start to consume more animal protein, demand for poultry in India is likely to increase significantly over time. This is particularly so because roughly 80% of India's population is Hindu and most practicing Hindus do not eat beef. Furthermore, approximately 13% of Indians are Muslims and Islam forbids the consumption of pork. Poultry products are consumed by both groups and are therefore of unique relevance to India as a source of animal protein.

Since initial market penetration can play an important role in long-run market control and brand recognition, if the US expects Indian consumption to take off in the future through habit formation (enhanced by low and declining real prices of poultry), then maintaining and growing share today is critical. Losing presence in the Indian market today could result in fairly large losses in the future.

Additionally, the US might be concerned that other countries will enact a ban similar to that of India. A successful challenge at the WTO guards against this possibility.

3.3 The WTO challenge and Panel Report

On 6 March 2012, the United States requested consultations, alleging that India's restrictions violated GATT Article XI and multiple provisions of the SPS Agreement. The US asserted that India's restrictions were not based on or in conformity with international standards as set forth in the OIE Terrestrial Code (SPS Articles 3.1 and 3.2). It further alleged that the measures were discriminatory (SPS Article 2.3), not based on a risk assessment (SPS Articles 5.1 and 5.2), arbitrary or unjustifiable distinctions (SPS Article 5.5), and more trade restrictive than necessary to achieve the proper level of protection (SPS Article 5.6). The US also contended that India failed to recognize that the US had a system of certifying certain regions as AI-free and therefore its ban on imports from the entire country was unjustified (SPS Articles 6.1 and 6.2). Finally, the US argued that India violated the WTO's notification and transparency requirements (SPS Article 7 and Annex B(2) and B(5)(a), (b), and (d)).

On 14 October 2014, the Panel ruled overwhelmingly in favor of the United States. The US succeeded in all but two of its claims, for which the Panel exercised judicial economy.[5] Because Bown and Hillman (2016) have already provided an excellent analysis on the Panel Report in this series, we refer readers interested in further details to their article.

3.4 The appeal

On 26 January 2015, India appealed all of the Panel's findings of violations of the SPS Agreement, except those concerning violations of the notification and timing requirements set forth in SPS Agreement Article 7 and Annex B. For several of its claims, India alleged that the Panel violated DSU Article 11 because it failed to make an objective assessment of the matter. In addition, with respect to the Panel's ruling that India failed to conform to international standards in violation of SPS Articles 3.1 and 3.2, India argued that the Panel also violated DSU Article 13 because it had improperly consulted relevant experts when making its ruling.

On 4 June 2015, the Appellate Body circulated its ruling. In all but one instance, the Appellate Body upheld the Panel's ruling. Only on the issue of whether India violated SPS Agreement Article 2.2 did the Appellate Body find that the Panel had erred in its approach. However, the Appellate Body was not able to complete the analysis. We will focus more on the implications of this specific ruling in Section 5 of this Article.

5 The Panel exercised judicial economy on the claims concerning SPS Article 5.5 and GATT Article XI.

Although India had legitimate reasons to be concerned about AI exposure on account of the large population of farmers involved in poultry rearing, it nevertheless could not simply restrict imports of poultry products from AI-affected countries as the government saw fit. Part of the bargain of enjoying the benefits of the WTO involves agreeing to work through the international system to determine how best to regulate agricultural imports from disease-laden countries and regions.

4. An economic analysis of India's import restriction

Global pandemics know no borders. But this does not mean that the optimal policy response is simply to close off one's borders entirely to imports from disease-afflicted countries as India opted to do. Under what circumstances is such a ban justified from an economic welfare perspective? We address this question below in a simple economic model that is useful for illustrating the basic considerations at work.

4.1 A simple economic model to analyze India's import restriction

Suppose the imports of US poultry inflict a negative externality on the Indian economy that is not internalized by consumers. Let the damage caused by one unit of poultry imports be denoted by δ. The parameter δ captures all of the external costs imposed on the Indian economy by each unit of poultry imported by the US. Let p denote the local price of poultry in India. Let the domestic supply curve for poultry in India be given by

$$q_S(p) = \frac{p}{2}$$

and the domestic demand curve by

$$q_D(p) = a - \frac{p}{2}$$

Then, $m(p) = q_D(p) - q_S(p)$ measures India's imports of poultry and the Indian import demand curve for poultry is given by

$$m(p) = a - \frac{p}{2} - \frac{p}{2} = a - p$$

Assume that the US poultry industry is perfectly competitive and that India is a small buyer of poultry on world markets so that it faces a perfectly elastic export supply curve at the pricep_W. Under free trade, Indian imports of US poultry equal

$$m_F = a - p_W$$

The welfare of the Indian economy as a function of the level of imports equal the sum of the surplus enjoyed by consumers and producers net of the damage caused by imports. The net effect of trade on local producers and consumers can be measured by the area underneath the import demand curve so that the welfare of the Indian economy under free trade can be written as

$$W = \int_{p_W}^{a} (a - p_W)dp - \delta m_F$$

The above welfare function simplifies to

$$W = \frac{1}{2}(a - p_W)^2 - \delta m_F$$

which can be rewritten as

$$W(m_F; \delta) = \frac{1}{2}(m_F)^2 - \delta m_F = m_F\left(\frac{m_F}{2} - \delta\right)$$

Observe from this formula that sufficiently high damage caused by imports can make the net gains from trade enjoyed by the Indian economy negative. More specifically, we can see that given a positive level of imports, i.e. $m_F > 0$, $W(m_F; \delta) > 0$ iff $m_F > 2\delta$ which is the same as $\delta < a - p_W$. In other words, if the external damage imposed on India by each unit of poultry imported from the US is sufficiently large, then international trade in poultry with the US makes India worse off relative to no trade. This implies that the Indian trade restrictions on imported poultry could potentially be justified. But this is not to say that a complete import ban on US poultry can always be rationalized on the basis of the above analysis.

This raises the following question: what is the optimal quantity of imports from the Indian perspective? We address this question next.

4.2 The optimal import quota

Suppose the Indian government were to institute an import quota denoted by q that is less than the free trade level of imports, i.e., $q < m_F$. Since the quota creates local scarcity, the price in the Indian economy increases above the free trade price p_W. From the Indian import demand curve for poultry, the domestic price in India associated with the import quota q is given by $p = a - q$.

Since p will generally exceed the supply price of exporters p_W, those that have the right to import can derive some rent from it. Assume that this right to import is granted via licenses allocated to domestic agents via a competitive auction that allows the Indian government to collect the entire rent generated by the quota as license revenue.[6] The revenue earned by those holding quota licenses is given by

$$R = (p - p_W)q = (a - q - p_W)q$$

6 Although the economic rationale behind such auctions is fairly sound, they are rarely used in practice. Depending upon how the government allocates the quota licenses, the total rent R generated by the quota will generally be split between the government and license-holders. In the special case of a voluntary export

Total welfare in India as a function of the quota can be written as

$$W(q) = \frac{1}{2}(q)^2 - \delta q + (a - q - p_W)q$$

The optimal import quota q maximizes total welfare $W(q)$. The first order condition for this maximization problem is given by

$$\frac{dW(q)}{dq} = q - \delta + (a - q - p_W) + q(-1)$$

The above first order condition can be solved for the optimal import quota q^* from India's perspective

$$q^* = (a - p_W) - \delta$$

which can be rewritten as

$$q^* = m_F - \delta$$

The above formula for the optimal import quota for a product that inflicts a damage of δ per unit on the importing economy is quite intuitive. When $\delta = 0$, imports of poultry impose no external damage and the optimal import quota permits the free trade level of imports. Intuitively, if an economy cannot affect world prices – which in our case means that the foreign export supply price p_W facing Indian consumers is unaffected by the import quota – then free trade is the optimal policy provided imports impose no external costs on the economy. For all $\delta > 0$, however, it is optimal for India to reduce the level of its imports by an amount that is equal to the external damage imposed by each unit of the imported good. Note also that that $q^* = 0$ only when $\delta > a - p_W$, i.e., only when the external damage inflicted by imports is sufficiently high that a complete ban on imports is optimal.

Of course, instead of using an import ban, India could have restricted imports via an import tariff. Does it matter which measure is used? To answer this question, we first derive India's optimal import tariff on US poultry.

4.3 The optimal import tariff

Let t be the per-unit specific tariff imposed by India on imports of US poultry. The export supply price p_W is unaffected by the Indian tariff since India is assumed to be a small importer of poultry in world markets. Therefore, the domestic price p in India under the tariff is simply the sum of the world price and the tariff: i.e.,

restraint (which is not particularly relevant in the present dispute), the quota rent accrues to foreign exporters.

$p = p_W + t$. Indian imports with this tariff-ridden price equal

$$m(t) = a - p_W - t$$

Total tariff revenue generated by the import tariff equals

$$TR = tm(t) = t(a - p_W - t)$$

The optimal tariff from India's perspective maximizes its total welfare $W(t)$ where

$$W(t) = \frac{1}{2}(m(t))^2 - \delta m(t) + tm(t)$$

The first order condition for welfare maximization is

$$\frac{dW(t)}{dt} = m(t)\left[1 + \frac{dm(t)}{dt}\right] + [t - \delta]\frac{dm(t)}{dt} = 0$$

Using

$$m(t) = a - p_W - t$$

and

$$\frac{dm(t)}{dt} = -1$$

the above first order condition simplifies to

$$\frac{dW(t)}{dt} = -t + \delta = 0$$

from which we obtain the optimal import tariff as

$$t^* = \delta$$

The optimal Indian import tariff t^* is nothing but the Pigouvian tax that corrects for the negative externality imposed by US poultry on the Indian economy and it exactly equals the per-unit damage δ caused by imports. The level of imports under this tariff equals

$$m(t^*) = a - p_W - t^* = a - p_W - \delta = m_F - \delta$$

Observe that $m(t^*) = q^*$ i.e. the optimal import quota q^* and the optimal import tariff t^* lead to the same level of imports and are therefore equally trade restrictive and completely equivalent from a welfare perspective.[7]

7 An important hurdle in the implementation of the optimal trade policy (be it the tariff t^* or the quota q^*) is that there might be considerable uncertainty regarding the value of the damage parameter δ. Under

4.4 A Graphical illustration of the key economic tradeoffs

The general idea underlying the above analysis of import restrictions on a product imposing a negative externality on the importing country can be illustrated by a simple graph. In Figure 1, the marginal private benefit of imports to the importing economy is denoted by MPB and it is in fact the import demand curve $m = a - p$. Due to the presence of the negative externality, the marginal social benefit of a unit of imports falls short of the MPB by the amount δ, the vertical distance between the two downward sloping curves. Observe that these two lines are parallel to each other since the damage imposed by each unit of imports is assumed to be constant and equal to δ.[8]

While the socially optimal level of imports from the Indian economy's perspective equals q^*, the equilibrium level of imports under free trade equals m_F, where $m_F > q^*$. As a result, the net welfare of the Indian economy under free trade equals A + B–C, where area A measures the gain in consumer surplus net of the loss of local producers, area B measures the revenue raised by the optimal quota or tariff, and the area C captures the loss incurred by the Indian economy due to the overconsumption of imports.

For all units lying in the interval $[q^*, m_F]$, the MSB of imports is lower than the market price p_W so that these imports serve to reduce the importing country's welfare. The optimal trade policy induces the socially optimal level of imports q^* and this can be achieved via either an import quota set exactly equal to this amount or by imposing the Pigouvian import tariff $t^* = \delta$, which ensures that the MPB of imports ends up coinciding with their MSB and thereby inducing the socially optimal level of trade.

If the damage parameter δ is sufficiently large (i.e. $\delta > a - p_W$), the optimal trade measure lowers the MSB to such an extent that its vertical intercept ends up lying below the free trade price p_W. Only under such a situation is the optimal trade policy to prohibit imports altogether. This is because when $\delta > a - p_W$ the MSB of each unit of imports is lower than their price p_W.

4.5 Further discussion

While our analysis above sheds light on the incentives of an importing nation to restrict trade when imports inflict an externality on the local economy, it is worth discussing how its conclusions depend upon some of the underlying assumptions. In particular, the model assumes that imports impose a negative welfare

such a situation, in the presence of risk aversion on the part of local consumers, it could be optimal for India to impose fairly stringent restrictions on imported poultry. The economic analysis presented above assumes that the damage parameter δ is known with certainty and therefore eliminates any role for risk aversion, which can be significant in the presence of health risks.

8 If the damage imposed by imports were to increase with the level of imports, then the SMB curve would diverge away from the PMB curve with an increase in imports.

Figure 1. Optimal trade policy under an externality

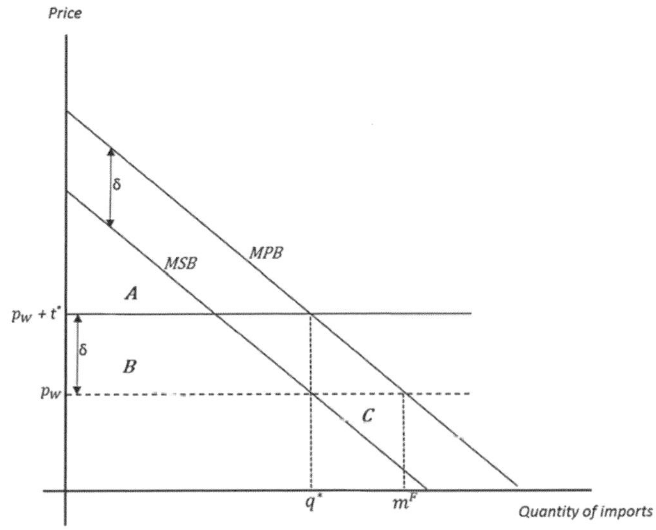

externality but is silent about the exact incidence of the externality. In the present dispute, the externality could be thought of as generating a health risk for the local population and this view is certainly consistent with our formulation above. Alternatively, one might think of imports having an adverse effect on local poultry suppliers in India due to the potential transmission of avian flu from imported to local poultry. Does it matter how one formulates this issue?

Second, our analysis above ignores the fact that restrictive trade policies were not the only available option for India. For example, India could also have subjected imports of poultry to port inspections designed at eliminating tainted birds and/or other types of mitigation measures, all of which involve significant resource costs. In what follows, we further discuss each of these issues.

Suppose each unit of imports reduces the domestic supply of poultry by δ units, where $\delta < 1$.[9] The domestic supply curve for poultry can then be written as

$$q_S(p, p_W; \delta) = \frac{p}{2} - \delta m(p_W)$$

9 Our analytical framework can be easily extended to allow the damage parameter to be uncertain. For expositional ease, we assume that it is known with certainty.

Since, by definition, $m(p_W; \delta) = q_D(p_W) - q_S(p_W; \delta)$, we have

$$m(p_W, \delta) = a - \frac{p_W}{2} - \frac{p_W}{2} + \delta m(p_W; \delta)$$

which gives[10]

$$m(p_W, \delta) = \frac{a - p_W}{1 - \delta}$$

Following our earlier analysis, we can show that local welfare under free trade declines with δ so long as the adverse impact of imports on domestic poultry is not so large that local supply is completely eliminated – in which case changes in δ have no further impact on local welfare. Thus, even under this alternative approach, the larger the negative impact of imported poultry on domestic poultry, the smaller the gains from trade. It is straightforward to show that import restrictions (in form of a tariff or a quota) once again have the potential to raise domestic welfare.[11]

While we focus on a welfare-maximizing framework, Margolis *et al.* (2005) consider a small open economy model along the lines of Grossman and Helpman (1995) in which trade policy responds to contributions made by organized lobby groups to the government and imports generate a negative local externality via the introduction of an invasive species. Their key result is that the equilibrium tariff in such a model exceeds the standard politically optimal tariff that obtains in Grossman–Helpman model (in which imports do not generate a negative externality). Thus, the point that trade restrictions can be welfare improving in the presence of trade-induced negative externalities is robust to the incorporation of political economy forces.

Motivated by the potential transmission of foot-and-mouth disease (FMD) from imported to domestic cattle, Paarlberg and Lee (1998) develop a three-country model in which imports from only one of the two exporting countries have an adverse effect on the domestic supply of beef in the importing country. They show that the optimal tariff imposed on the imports of the foreign country that is the source of the externality exceeds the standard optimal tariff (which equals the inverse of the elasticity of the export supply curve of that country) due to the risk of disease transmission. Furthermore, they show that the optimal tariff imposed on the other exporter (where there is no FMD disease) is simply the standard optimal tariff, which in our formulation is zero since we assume India to be a

10 Note that we cannot allow for $\delta = 1$ since the level of imports cannot be pinned down by the model when one unit of imports reduces local supply by exactly one unit. In other words, for $\delta = 1$, the level of imports is indeterminate.

11 Actually, one can make a stronger claim: as Bown and Hillman (2016) observe, as per the targeting principle of Bhagwati and Ramaswami (1963) trade measures are the first-best means of addressing trade-induced externalities.

small importer of poultry that it is unable to extract any terms of trade gain via restrictive trade policies. The findings of Paarlberg and Lee (1998) show that the logic underlying our economic analysis extends to a setting where the importing country has market power. Furthermore, their results also lend support to the SPS agreement's requirement that any sanitary measures imposed on imports take account of differences in regional conditions across as well as within countries.[12]

McAusland and Costello (2004) investigate how an importing country can use import tariffs in conjunction with port inspections to address the negative externality imposed on the local economy by an imported product. Their key result is that it is optimal for the importing country to use both instruments: the optimal import tariff is set at its Pigouvian level to take into account both the external damage imposed by those imports that are permitted as well as the cost of inspecting them. Intuitively, the possibility of costly inspections does not eliminate the need to reduce the level of imports in order to reduce the expected damage imposed on the local economy from infected poultry.[13]

In this context, it is also worth noting that an import ban imposed by a sizeable market could potentially help induce better regulation of poultry production in the exporting country (it could even be self-regulation by the exporting industry) where it is implicitly understood by both sides that a reduction in the probability of disease could lead to the ban being lifted. Under such an international bargain, the eventual outcome could Pareto dominate both autarky as well as a costly and imperfect inspection regime on the importing side.

What if the negative externality introduced is non-linear? An important real-world feature of disease-related negative externalities is that they can grow over time in a non-linear manner. For example, such externalities could be exponential, S-shaped, or concave. In order to keep our model relatively simple, we have abstracted from the possibility of such dynamic effects. While our approach is in line with the rest of the existing literature discussed above, it is worth noting that this is an important omission.

The work of Olson and Roy (2010) informs our understanding of optimal trade policy when the externalities induced by trade have inter-temporal consequences and the external costs imposed by imports evolve over time. They show that an efficient trade policy balances the welfare costs of any restrictive measure against the discounted stream of the future costs of control and the social damages that

12 Wilson and Anton (2006) build on Paarlberg and Lee (1998) by introducing mitigation strategies into their model. They show that provided the costs of mitigation strategies are not prohibitive, their use can generate net welfare gains and that the efficient sharing of such strategies between trading partners calls for taking account of their relative efficacy in mitigating tasks.

13 McAusland and Costello (2004) also consider a scenario where the importing country sources from multiple trade partners that are potentially heterogeneous in terms of underlying parameters (of which the extent of damage caused by imports is one). Like Paarlberg and Lee (1998), their main finding here is supportive of the idea that import measures should take into account variations in regional conditions.

are avoided due to the trade measure. They also provide conditions under which it is optimal to impose a complete ban on imports versus when non-prohibitive trade policies are efficient.

In their model, the optimal level of a SPS trade restriction varies in a non-monotonic way over time. A complete ban is optimal when the existing stock of disease is such that further entry can generate a 'big' growth or spread of the disease; if the pre-existing prevalence of disease in the importing nation is either very small or very large, the marginal growth rate of the disease is not significant and so the import of tainted birds is not as consequential – but in the middle range, it can be explosive. With regard to avian flu and poultry, it is conceivable that the rate of spread can be very large even if the existing infestation is small (i.e. the growth function maybe concave as opposed to being S-shaped). If so, relatively harsh trade restrictions may be justified from a welfare perspective.

5. Legal clarifications on key principles

As the above economic analysis demonstrates, it is not always optimal for a government to ban imports of an agricultural product from a disease-inflicted region. Under certain circumstances, other less-restrictive measures may prove preferable.

While WTO law provides countries with the freedom to determine the appropriate level of protection (ALOP) in the wake of a disease outbreak, it places constraints on the design of the policy measure to be enacted to achieve the desired ALOP. Besides emphasizing the core principles of non-discrimination and transparency, WTO law stresses: (1) the importance of international standards, and (2) the importance of risk assessment and scientific evidence. On both points, the recent *India–Agricultural Products* ruling by the Appellate Body provided additional legal clarification.

5.1 Interpretation of international standards relevant for the agricultural disease

Rather than allowing each country to set its own response to a global pandemic, WTO law provides incentives for countries to work together through an international standard-setting body to determine the appropriate response to a pandemic. Article 3.1 of the SPS Agreement requires that '[WTO] Members shall base their sanitary and phytosanitary measures on international standards, guidelines or recommendations, where they exist, except as otherwise provided for in this Agreement'.

Why privilege international standards at the expense of local governance? Why not let each country set its own response unilaterally?

As discussed, agricultural diseases carried by a pest or pathogen generate negative externalities. For example, with AI, both the production of poultry and their movement across borders can increase the prevalence of the disease. Furthermore, the negative impact of AI may spillover beyond the poultry producer itself to affect products, wild populations, producers of poultry-related commercial products, and so forth. However, neither the exporter nor the importer may concern themselves with these additional costs. In such a situation, regulation by a third party is necessary to address the negative externality involved.

At the international level, this responsibility is borne by an international organization overseeing the disease. This body serves three important functions, akin to that of the domestic regulatory agency. First, it acts as an information aggregator and disseminator. The international organization allows national authorities to pool information on the disease and serves as a clearinghouse. Second, the international body offers a forum for national actors to work out an effective policy response. Without it, countries might worry that each might engage in 'beggar-thy-neighbor' policies, leading to a harmful race-to-the-bottom. The international body provides a means for countries to agree upon a common response to be taken, including addressing the question of whether it is necessary to ban the product from the diseased region outright. Finally, the international body serves a coordination function to address free riding and inefficient resource allocation. It allows for better management of resources to fight the disease.

In this dispute, both the United States and India agreed that an international standard existed – Chapter 10.4 of the OIE Terrestrial Code. Specifically, Article 10.4.1.10 states:

> A Member shall not impose immediate bans on the trade in poultry commodities in response to a notification, according to Article 1.1.3 of the Terrestrial Code of infection with HPNAI and LPNAI virus in birds other than poultry, including wild birds.

The question presented before the Panel was whether India's ban conformed to this international standard.

India and the United States disagreed over the meaning of Article 10.4.1.10. India interpreted the language narrowly as differentiating between two scenarios – when the AI virus is introduced via poultry versus via other birds. The purpose of Article 10.4.1.10, India argued, is to clarify that a ban is impermissible in the latter scenario. According to India, Article 10.4.1.10, by logic, suggests that a ban is permissible when AI is introduced via poultry, as was the case here.[14] Thus, India asserted its response was based on the relevant international standard. The US interpreted the Terrestrial Code's meaning very differently – as endorsing trade from AI-afflicted countries with recommendations for proper safety control measures.[15]

The dispute therefore raises the question of how are WTO jurists to determine the meaning of an international standard when its meaning is unclear. The approach taken can have a direct bearing on the dispute's outcome.

14 Panel Report, *India–Agricultural Products*, paras. 7.178–7.182.
15 Ibid., paras. 7.161–7.171.

In this case, the Panel turned to consult the OIE directly over the Code's meaning. In response, the OIE clarified that '[t]he intention of Article 10.4.1.10 was to discourage Member countries from imposing bans on trade in poultry'.[16] On the basis of the OIE consultation, the Panel sided with the United States in finding that India's restriction did not conform to the applicable international standard.

On appeal, India asked that the Appellate Body overturn the Panel's ruling because the Panel had improperly consulted the OIE as to the interpretation of the Code. DSU Article 13 specifically provides Panels with the authority to seek information from experts. Additionally, in the context of the SPS Agreement, Article 11.2 states:

> In a dispute under [the SPS] Agreement involving scientific or technical issues, a panel should seek advice from experts chosen by the panel in consultation with the parties to the dispute. To this end, the panel may, when it deems appropriate, establish an advisory technical experts group or consult the relevant international organizations, at the request of either party to the dispute or on its own initiative.

India argued that a Panel is only to consult on scientific or technical issues. India asked that the Appellate Body find that the Panel had overstepped its authority in seeking input from the OIE on the actual interpretation of the OIE Terrestrial Code.[17]

As Nedumpara *et al.* (2016: 221) highlight, India's approach suggests that the matter of interpreting the text of the international standard falls to the Panel itself. Because the text is not explicit on this question, under the proposed approach, the Panel would rely upon the customary rules of interpretation as set for in Articles 31–33 of the Vienna Convention on the Law of Treaties (VCLT). In other words, the meaning of Article 10.4.1.10 of the OIE Terrestrial Convention would be a question of law for WTO adjudicators to decide.

The approach suggested by the United States, by contrast, would render this to a question of fact. As such, the US argued, it would be entirely appropriate for a Panel to consult with the OIE over the meaning of Article 10.4.1.10. After all, who better to opine on the factual meaning of an international standard than the body that issued it?

The Appellate Body has long held that WTO law does not exist in 'clinical isolation' from public international law. As the Appellate Body again highlighted in this case, 'relevant customary rules of interpretation of public international law' can be relevant to the interpretation of WTO law.[18] But these statements do not resolve the question over the nature of the relationship between WTO law and other bodies of public international law. In recent years, a sharp division has emerged over this question.

One point of view holds that WTO law is distinct. WTO covered agreements may reference other bodies of international law, but the job of a WTO jurist is

16 Ibid., para. 7.237.
17 Appellate Body Report, *India–Agricultural Products*, para. 5.82.
18 Ibid., para. 5.89.

simply to interpret the WTO covered agreements on its own terms and context. Another point of view argues that different bodies of law operate through a form of systemic integration. In certain circumstances, it may be necessary to look outside the four corners of WTO law itself and consider its context within the broader framework of international law when interpreting a treaty provision (McLachlan, 2005). Therefore, it would be entirely appropriate for WTO jurists to consider these other bodies of law, and vice versa; the system operates through a discursive dialogue. Needless to say, the two camps differ on their view of the proper role of a WTO Panel.

The approach suggested by India veers toward this latter camp. India suggested that a Panel's duty to interpret a WTO treaty provision does not stop at the boundaries of the agreements covered by the WTO. Instead, if the WTO treaty provision makes reference to an international standard promulgated by another body besides the WTO, then the duty of the WTO adjudicator is to opine on the meaning of that standard as well. By delegating this duty to outside experts instead of taking it on themselves, the Panel failed to fulfill what is required of it by the Dispute Settlement Understanding.

By siding with the US, the Appellate Body appears to be rejecting the strong version of the systemic integration narrative. At least with respect to international standards set by a non-judicial body that is relevant to the SPS Agreement, where there is textual ambiguity or uncertainty, the Appellate Body held that it is more than appropriate for a WTO Panel to consult the body that drafted and administers the standard to opine on its meaning. Because the OIE Terrestrial Code itself is not part of the WTO covered agreements, the Appellate Body suggested that the Panel was not obligated to opine on the Code's meaning by itself. Instead, it was perfectly fine for the Panel to ask the OIE, the body that administers the Code, for its interpretation instead.

Note that in so ruling, the Appellate Body is helping to prevent fragmentation of international law. Had it stated that the Panel could not consult the OIE on interpreting the Terrestrial Code, the Panel very well might have reached a different conclusion about its meaning than that of the OIE. By allowing the Panel to do so, it helps to ensure that the Code's meaning remains consistent across different bodies of international law, in line with the OIE's own interpretation.

Because international standards, recommendations, and guidelines play such an important role in trade disputes concerning agricultural diseases, the Appellate Body ruling provides important clarification over how such standards are to be interpreted. Panels can refer interpretative questions to international standard-setting organizations, just as national courts might consult regulatory agencies directly when needing to interpret a regulation. Again, this case highlights the extraordinary importance of the international standard-setting body, whose role is not simply limited to issuing standards, guidelines, and recommendations, but also weighing in on their interpretative meaning.

5.2 The relationship between the risk assessment and scientific evidence requirements

Despite the deference given to international standards, WTO law does not demand conformity. Article 3.3 of the SPS Agreement clarifies that countries retain sovereign authority to establish its ALOP. However, WTO law demands that countries wishing to set a higher level of protection meet certain requirements. Among these are the requirements of Articles 5.1 and 5.2 to perform a risk assessment and Article 2.2 to base its measure on scientific principles and evidence.

In *India– Agricultural Products*, the Appellate Body was called upon to clarify the relationship between these provisions. At issue were two questions: First, can the risk assessment requirement of Article 5.1 be circumvented simply with recourse to 'scientific evidence' pursuant to Article 2.2? Second, if not, then does failure to conduct an adequate risk assessment automatically lead to a violation of Article 2.2?

Given the resource constraints faced by many developing countries, the answers to these questions have a direct bearing on what they must do in the wake of a global agricultural pandemic. By its own admission, India did not conduct a risk assessment in line with Articles 5.1 and 5.2. Yet, India had assembled some scientific evidence concerning AI that had supposedly served as the basis for its import ban. India argued that a risk assessment is not obligatory, but simply a method to fulfill its legal obligations. An alternative, India suggested, is to base the SPS measure on Article 2.2, which India had fulfilled.

On the first question, the Appellate Body clarified that these were not distinct choices. It held that 'SPS measures adopted by Members must comply with all of the requirements of Articles 2.2, 5.1, and 5.2'.[19] Article 2.2 does not serve as a means to circumvent the risk assessment requirement of Articles 5.1 and 5.2.

On the second question, the Appellate Body clarified that a failure to perform a risk assessment does not automatically lead to a violation of the 'scientific evidence' requirement of Article 2.2. Instead, the enacting government must be given an opportunity to present arguments and evidence to rebut such a presumption.[20] Because the Panel failed to consider such arguments and evidence, the Appellate Body reversed the Panel's findings that India's measures, with respect to fresh poultry meat and eggs, were inconsistent with Article 2.2. However, the Appellate Body found that it lacked sufficient information to complete the analysis on whether the evidence submitted by India on fresh poultry meat and eggs would suffice to meet the requirement of Article 2.2.[21]

Therefore, the Appellate Body's ruling leaves unanswered the question of what information, absent a risk assessment, would suffice to meet the requirement of

19 Ibid., para. 5.32.
20 Ibid., para. 5.53.
21 Ibid., para. 5.51.

Article 2.2. The Appellate Body simply made clear that 'even though the presumption of inconsistency under Article 2.2 flowing from a violation of Articles 5.1 and 5.2 is rebuttable, establishing that there exists a rational or objective relationship between the SPS measure and scientific evidence for purposes of Article 2.2 would, in most cases, be difficult without a Member demonstrating that such a measure is based on an assessment of the risks, as appropriate to the circumstances'.[22]

What evidence might suffice? Returning to our economic model, we suggest that such evidence would have to clarify our understanding of the harm associated with the imports, as denoted by the parameter δ in the model. After all, it is the size of δ that determines whether the import restriction is justifiable or excessive. One could envision a scenario in which a government, without undertaking a full risk assessment, presents evidence concerning the expected harm associated with each unit of an import from a disease-afflicted region to justify its import restriction.

More importantly, we posit that this unanswered legal question is not a significant one. Why not? So long as the Panel finds the respondent to be in violation of Articles 5.1 and 5.2, even if the Panel further finds that scientific evidence submitted by the respondent meets the requirements of Article 2.2, the Party nevertheless will need to perform an adequate risk assessment in line with Articles 5.1 and 5.2 in order to bring its SPS measure into compliance. Thus, regardless of whether the evidence submitted is sufficient to rebut the presumption or not, the need for conducting a risk assessment remains paramount.

6. Controversy over the scope of appellate review

Finally, we draw attention to a controversy related to the Appellate Body's handling on one other legal element of this dispute. *India – Agricultural Products* represented the first time that the Appellate Body has opined on the meaning of Article 6 of the SPS Agreement concerning 'adaptation to regional conditions'. The Panel found India to have violated Articles 6.1 and 6.2 because its import ban applied across-the-board to all US exports and did not recognize the concepts of disease-free and low-disease-prevalence areas.[23] India acknowledged that it had not done so, but argued that it could not do so until the US fulfilled its obligation under Article 6.3, requiring the exporting country to provide objective evidence demonstrating that areas are, and likely to remain, disease-free or low-incidence.[24] The Panel rejected India's argument; it held that the Article 6.1 and 6.2 are independent obligations and not conditional upon an invocation of Article 6.3.[25] On appeal, India asked the Appellate Body to reverse the Panel's finding of violation of Articles 6.1 and 6.2, arguing that the Panel erred in its interpretation of the

22 Ibid., para. 5.32
23 Panel Report, *India–Agricultural Products*, paras. 7.713–7.714.
24 Ibid., para. 7.633.
25 Ibid., para. 7.680.

relationship between Articles 6.1 and 6.3 and in its application of Article 6.2.[26] The Appellate Body rejected India's arguments and upheld the Panel ruling.[27]

Having prevailed, one would not expect the Appellate Body's ruling to draw the ire of the United States. However, in its ruling, the Appellate Body chose to opine on several other elements of the Panel's analysis of Article 6, which India had not raised in its appeal. In particular, the Appellate Body 'consider[ed] it important to emphasize that what constitutes an appropriate order of analysis and approach by a Panel examining a claim under Article 6 may, at least in part, be a function of the nature of the claim and circumstances of that case'.[28] The Appellate Body explained that it was 'not persuaded that all of the statements made by the Panel would have the same resonance in every case', suggesting that the proper inquiry into Article 6 depends on the particular context surrounding the dispute.[29] The Appellate Body then proceeded to raise questions and 'concerns' over particular Panel statements.[30]

For the United States, this *obiter dictum* represented unnecessary and improper judicial activism by the Appellate Body. Neither the US nor India had challenged the particular Panel's statements and actions on appeal; thus, it was improper for the Appellate Body to opine on legal issues that had not been placed before it. In the Dispute Settlement Body meeting adopting the ruling, the United States emphasized that 'particularly at a time when workload issues were increasingly affecting the time-table for the resolution of disputes, a focus on those issues that had been appealed, and on questions that needed to be addressed in resolving the arguments raised on appeal, would facilitate the efficient functioning of the dispute settlement process'.[31]

At the time, the US protest did not register much attention. However, nearly a year later, in May 2016, the United States further underscored its displeasure by withholding its support for the reappointment of Appellate Body Member Seung Wha Chang. In explaining its action, the United States noted the actions of four Appellate Body divisions on which Professor Chang had served, of which *India–Agricultural Products* was one, to which it objected.[32] In discussing this dispute, the US again condemned the inappropriateness of the Appellate Body 'engag[ing] in a lengthy abstract discussion of a provision of the SPS Agreement without

26 Appellate Body Report, *India–Agricultural Products*, para. 5.112.

27 Ibid., paras. 5.186–5.187.

28 Ibid., para. 5.142.

29 Ibid., para. 5.143.

30 Ibid., paras. 5.143–5.144.

31 WTO Dispute Settlement Body, Minutes of the Meeting Held in the Centre William Rappard on 19 June 2015, WT/DSB/M/364, para. 7.5.

32 The other three disputes mentioned are *Argentina – Measures Relating to Trade in Goods and Services* (DS453), *United States – Countervailing Duty Measures on Certain Products from China* (DS437), and *United States – Countervailing Duty Measures on Certain Products from China* (DS449). The concerns raised in each differ from that of *India–Agricultural Products*.

ever tying that discussion to an issue on appeal and … express[ing] "concerns" in that discussion on findings of the Panel that were not raised by either party in the appeal'.[33] The US emphasized that '[i]t is not the role of the Appellate Body to engage in abstract discussions or to divert an appeal away from the issues before it in order to employ resources on matters that are not presented in, and will not help resolve, a dispute'.[34]

In blocking Professor Chang's reappointment, the United States has been roundly criticized as threatening the Appellate Body's judicial independence.[35] Nevertheless, this dispute does raise valid questions over what is the proper scope of review by the Appellate Body. Article 17.2 of the Dispute Settlement Understanding (DSU) simply states, 'The Appellate Body shall address each of the issues *raised* … during the appellate proceeding' (emphasis added). Article 3.7 also reminds us that the 'aim of the dispute settlement mechanism is to secure a positive solution to a dispute'. Nowhere in the DSU is the Appellate Body accorded the power to opine on elements of a Panel ruling with which it disagrees but which the parties have not raised. The function of the Appellate Body is not to act as a constitutional court in clarifying the law but simply to assist with resolving the dispute at hand. To the extent that the Appellate Body disagrees with elements of a Panel ruling not raised on appeal, it must wait for a future dispute raising this point to clarify – just as it would if the entire Panel ruling, and not only select parts, were not appealed.

It is unfortunate that it required as drastic a move as blocking Professor Chang's reappointment to underscore this point. To prevent further recurrences, future Appellate Body divisions ought to bear in mind the constraints placed on the scope of appellate review set forth in the DSU.

7. Conclusion

While disease outbreaks may well serve as a reason to curb trade in agricultural goods, WTO law places limits on this practice, out of fear that the response may be disproportionate and serve as an excuse for protectionism. The Appellate Body ruling in *India–Agricultural Products* reaffirms the applicability of two central tenets of the law: the importance of taking into account international standards when evaluating the legality of any restrictions and the importance of risk assessments. An underlying economic rationale underscores both tenets, related to the failure to internalize the negative externality associated with the disease and the need for information and coordination.

33 Statement of the United States at the Meeting of the WTO Dispute Settlement Body, Geneva, 23 May 2016, at 4.

34 Ibid.

35 'US Slammed at DSB For Blocking Korean Appellate Body Reappointment,' *Inside US Trade*, 34 (21), 27 May 2016.

On both issues, the Appellate Body's ruling added to the existing jurisprudence on these issues. But beyond the jurisprudential questions, the Appellate Body ruling is also historic in that it is the first ruling to challenge the SPS measure of a developing nation. While *India – Agricultural Products* is the first; more challenges are in process, including one over Russia's import restrictions on pigs. The political economy is likely to be different in the context of a developing country where an agricultural disease has the potential to ravage a large number of households dependent on agriculture for their household income. But even so, the Appellate Body makes clear that the underlying legal principles remain the same. No matter the context, an outright ban is not generally warranted. Instead, it must be justified in light of the international response and the risks at hand.

References

Bhagwati, J. and V. K. Ramaswami (1963), 'Domestic Distortions, Tariffs, and the Theory of Optimum Subsidy', *Journal of Political Economy*, **71**(1): 44–50.

Bown, C. and J. A. Hillman (2016), 'Bird Flu, the OIE, and National Regulation: The WTO's India – Agricultural Products Dispute', *World Trade Review*, **15**(2): 235–257.

Grossman, G. and E. Helpman (1995), 'Protection for Sale', *American Economic Review*, **84**(4): 833–850.

Margolis, M., J. F. Shogren, and C. Fischer (2005), 'How Trade Politics Affect Invasive Species Control', *Ecological Economics*, **52**(3): 305–313.

McAusland, C. and C. Costello (2004), 'Avoiding Invasives: Trade Related Policies for Controlling Unintentional Exotic Species Introductions', *Journal of Environmental Economics and Management*, **48**(2): 954–977.

McLachlan, C. (2005), 'The Principle of Systemic Integration and Article 31(3)(C) of the Vienna Convention', *International Comparative Law Quarterly*, **53**: 279–320.

Nedumpara, J., A. Chandra, and G. Deepak (2016), '*India – Agricultural Products*: Defending India's First SPS Dispute', in A. Das and J. Nedumpara (eds.), *WTO Dispute Settlement at Twenty: Insiders' Reflections on India's Participation*, New Delhi: Centre for WTO Studies & Springer.

Olson, L. J. and S. Roy (2010), 'Dynamic Sanitary and Phytosanitary Trade Policy', *Journal of Environmental Economics and Management*, **60**: 21–30.

Paarlberg, P. L. and J. G. Lee (1998), 'Import Restrictions in the Presence of a Health Risk: An Illustration Using FMD', *American Journal of Agricultural Economics*, **80**(1): 175–183.

Robinson, T. *et al.* (2011), *Global Livestock Production Systems*, Rome: Food and Agricultural Organization of the United Nations and International Livestock Research Institute.

Rodrik, D. (2011), *The Globalization Paradox*, New York, W. W. Norton.

Salve, P. (2014) 'How Many Farmers Does India Really Have', *Hindustan Times*, 11 August 2014.

Wilson, N. L. W. and J. Anton (2006), 'Combining Risk Assessment and Economics in Managing a Sanitary-Phytosanitary Risk', *American Journal of Agricultural Economics*, **88**(1): 194–202.

World Trade Organization (2015), *International Trade Statistics 2015*.